UNDERSTANDING HUMAN SEXUALITY

McGraw-Hill
Book Company

New York   St. Louis   San Francisco   Auckland
Bogotá   Düsseldorf   Johannesburg   London
Madrid   Mexico   Montreal   New Delhi   Panama
Paris   São Paulo   Singapore   Sydney   Tokyo   Toronto

UNDERSTANDING HUMAN SEXUALITY

Janet Shibley Hyde

Psychology Department
Bowling Green State University

This book was set in Optima by Black Dot, Inc. (ECU).
The editors were Richard R. Wright, Janis M. Yates, and Laura D. Warner;
the designer was Jo Jones;
the production supervisor was Dominick Petrellese.
The photo researcher and photo editor was Hildegard Kron.
The drawings were done by J & R Services, Inc.
Von Hoffmann Press, Inc., was printer and binder.

UNDERSTANDING HUMAN SEXUALITY

3 4 5 6 7 8 9 0 V H V H 7 8 3 2 1 0 9

Library of Congress Cataloging in Publication Data

Hyde, Janet Shibley.
    Understanding human sexuality.

    Bibliography: p.
    Includes index.
    1. Sex. 2. Sex customs. 3. Sexual hygiene. 4. Sex—
Psychology. I. Title.
HQ12.H82   613.9'5   78-18681
ISBN 0-07-031558-2

To my husband, Clark,
And my mother and father, Dorothy and Grant,
Without whom this would not have been possible.

CONTENTS

PREFACE

I suspect that my motivation for writing this text was quite similar to that of many people who write textbooks. When I began teaching an undergraduate course in human sexuality, in the fall of 1974, I was unable to find a text that suited my needs or tastes. One text treated the biological aspects of sexuality with so many forbidding Latin terms that students seemed too intimidated to study it effectively. Another had a preaching tone and a bias in favor of very traditional gender roles, neither of which seemed to be in touch with today's students. Others were far too brief and omitted important topics. As a result, I set out to write a text that would meet the needs that the others neglected.

First and foremost, I tried to keep in mind at all times that students *want* to learn about sexuality and that my job as writer was to help them learn. I covered topics completely, in as clear a presentation as possible, and made a special effort to use language that would enlighten rather than intimidate; because students so often know only slang terminology regarding sex, I have included some slang terms in parentheses following definitions of scientific sexual terms, to connect the two terminologies. Similarly, in the selection and preparation of illustrations for the book, the goal was always to convey as much information as possible, simply and clearly.

The book assumes no prior college courses in biology, psychology, or sociology. It is designed as an introduction, following the three major objectives of my own course in human sexuality:

1 To provide practical information needed for everyday living (information about sexual anatomy, contraception, and venereal disease, for example) and to deal with problems in a more psychological area (such as impotence or inability to have an orgasm).
2 To help students feel more comfortable with thinking and talking about sex, both to minimize their own personal anguish about a tension-causing topic and to help them become rational decision makers in an important aspect of their lives.
3 To familiarize students with methods used in research on sexual behavior, and particularly with problems inherent in some of

these methods, so that they can read research reports critically and intelligently.

My own course is a survey course, designed to provide students with a broad range of information about sexuality. Reflecting that approach, this book is intended to be complete and balanced in its coverage, so that students will want to save it after the course for use as a reference in future years. My own training was quite compatible with this interdisciplinary, survey approach. My original graduate training was in psychology, with specialties in behavior genetics and statistics; later my interests expanded to include psychology of women and gender roles. As a result, I feel comfortable in discussing sexuality from biological, psychological, and sociological viewpoints. I did not want to write a book just about the biology of sex, nor just about the psychology of sex, nor just about the sociology of sex. I wanted to cover all those areas with integrity.

Nonetheless, for instructors who feel they lack the time to deal with all the material or who are not prepared to cover certain topics, the chapters have been written to be fairly independent. For example, any of the following chapters could be omitted without loss of continuity: Chapter 16, Rape; Chapter 17, Love; Chapter 20, Ethics, Religion, and Sexuality; Chapter 21, Sex and the Law.

It is my belief that, in modern American culture, we are in danger of taking sex far too seriously. We may not be serious about it in the same way as were our Victorian ancestors, but we are serious nonetheless—serious about whether we are using the best and most up-to-date sexual techniques, serious about whether our partners are having as many orgasms as possible, and so on. To counteract this tendency, I have tried to use a light touch, with occasional bits of humor, in this book. I am not advocating that we treat sex in a flippant or frivolous manner, but rather that we keep it in perspective and remember that there are some very funny things about it.

Many people helped me as I wrote this book and they deserve my heartfelt thanks. I wish to express special appreciation for the efforts of Betsy Allgeier, Department of Psychology, State University of New York at Fredonia, and of Gere Fulton, Department of Health Education, University of Toledo—reviewers and good friends as well—who were painstaking in going over the entire manuscript. Valerie Pinhas, Department of Health and Physical Education, Nassau Community College, and E. W. Wickersham, Department of Biology, Pennsylvania State University, were two other reviewers who provided constructive criticism and ideas on the entire manuscript. Additional reviewers and colleagues who made helpful and careful contributions were: Gordon Bermant, Federal Judicial Center, Washington D.C.; James A. Briley, Department of Psychology, Jefferson State Junior College; Stanley Brodsky, Department of Psychology, University of Alabama; Benjamin H. Glover, Department of Psychiatry, University Hospitals, Madison, Wisconsin; Jeanne Gullahorn, Department of Psychology, Michigan State University; Cecil M. Hampton, Department of Biology, Jefferson College; Margaret Hayes, Counselor, Borough of Manhattan Community College; the Reverend Richard Hettlinger, Department of Religion, Kenyon College; Rosemary Huerter, School of Nursing, University of Minnesota; the Reverend Leo Kelty, Family Life Bureau, Diocese of Trenton; Neil Kirschner, Department of Psychology, Bowling Green State University; Susan Matusak, Head Librarian, Institute for Sex Research, Indiana University; Margaret L. May, Department of Biology, Virginia Commonwealth University; Helen McAllister, Department of Biology, Monmouth College; Charles McCaghy, Department of Sociology, Bowling Green State University; Martha Mednick, Department of Psychology, University of Connecticut; Dee Pridgen, Law School of Catholic Universities, Washington, D.C.; Ira Reiss, Department of Sociology, University of Minnesota; Charity Runden, Department of Psychology, Montclair State University; Bruce Salender, university undergraduate student; Gunter Schmidt, Department of Psychology, University of Hamburg; Robert Staples, Department of Sociology, University of California at San Francisco; Rhoda K. Unger, Department of Psychology, Montclair State University; Russell Veitch, Department of Psychology, Bowling Green State University; Ruth Westheimer, Cornell University Medical Center, New York; and Bettie Wysor, author and free-lance writer. To the people with whom I have team-taught the course—Neil Kirschner, Howard Markman, and Don Ragusa—thanks are extended for the insights they have provided me about sexuality. Don DeRosa, Hal Johnson, and John Eriksen in their role as administrators at Bowling Green, provided help and support when it was needed, offering enthusiastic encouragement of my plan to offer a sexuality course. Finally, I owe many thanks to the editors and other staff members at McGraw-Hill who worked on this book, especially Janis M. Yates; their consistent commitment to quality made it a pleasure to work with them.

I hope that students who want to learn, and teachers who want to teach them, will be able to do so with this book.

Janet Shibley Hyde

1

SEXUALITY IN PERSPECTIVE

CITED

The biologist considers sexual behavior to be of fundamental significance because it leads to perpetuation of the species and thus to the continuity of life itself. The psychologist finds in the sexual impulse wellsprings of human conduct, deep reservoirs of motivation that impel men and women to action and furnish the driving force for many of their day-to-day activities. Sociologists recognize the integrating, cohesive functioning of sex as contributing to the stability of the family unit and thus to the entire structure of the social group. For the moralist, man's perpetual attempt to reconcile his basic sexual tendencies with the ethical standards and ideal demands of his social group presents a primary problem.*

Introductory textbooks on most subjects generally begin with a section designed to motivate students to study whatever topic it is that the text is about. No such section appears in this book; the reason why people want to study sex is obvious, and your motivation for studying it is probably already quite high. Sex is an important force in many people's lives, and so there are practical reasons for wanting to learn about it. Most people are curious about sex, particularly because exchanging sexual information is somewhat taboo in our culture, and so curiosity also motivates us to study sex. Finally, most of us at various times experience problems with our sexual functioning or wish that we could function better, and we hope that learning more about sex will help us. This book is designed to meet all those needs. And so, without further ado, let us consider various perspectives on sexuality. This will give you a glimpse of the forest before you study the trees: sexual anatomy and physiology, which are discussed in the early chapters of the book (the "plumbing" part), and sexual behavior, which

is discussed in the later chapters (the "people" part).

SEX AND GENDER

We often use the word "sex" ambiguously. Sometimes it refers to being male or female, and sometimes it refers to sexual behavior or reproduction. In most cases, of course, the meaning is clear from the context. If you are filling out a job application form and one item says, "Sex: _____," you do not write, "I like it" or "As often as possible." It is clear that your prospective employer wants to know whether you are a male or a female. In other cases, though, the meaning is ambiguous. For example, when a book has the title *Sex and Temperament in Three Primitive Societies*, what is it about? Is it about the sexual practices of primitive people and whether having sex frequently gives them pleasant temperaments? Or is it about the kinds of personalities that males and females are expected to have in those societies? Not only does this use of "sex" create ambiguities, but it also clouds our thinking about some important issues.

To remove—or at least reduce—this ambi-

---

*Source: Clellan S. Ford and Frank A. Beach. *Patterns of sexual behavior*. New York: Harper & Row, 1951, p. 1.

guity, the term "sex" will be used in this book to refer specifically to sexual anatomy and sexual behavior, and the term "gender" will be used to refer to the state of being male or female. This convention will be maintained throughout the book, in the hope that it will help clarify some issues as we proceed.

This is a book about sex, not gender; it is about sexual behavior and the biological, psychological, and social forces that influence it. Of course, although it is being argued here that sex and gender are conceptually different, I would not try to argue that they are totally independent of each other. Certainly gender roles—the ways in which males and females are expected to behave—exert a powerful influence on the way people behave sexually, and so one chapter will be devoted to gender roles and their effects on sexuality.

How should we define "sex," aside from saying that it is different from "gender"? A biologist might define "sexual behavior" as "any behavior that increases the likelihood of gametic union [union of sperm and egg]" (Bermant and Davidson, 1974). This definition emphasizes the reproductive function of sex. However, particularly in the last few decades, technologies have been developed that allow us to separate reproduction from sex. Most Americans now use sex not only for procreation but also for recreation.[1]

Kinsey defined "sex" as behavior that leads to orgasm. While this definition has some merits (it does not imply that sex must be associated with reproduction), it also presents some problems. If a wife has intercourse with her husband but does not have an orgasm, was that not sexual behavior for her?

To try to avoid some of these problems, "sexual behavior" will be defined in this book as *behavior that produces arousal and increases the chance of orgasm.*[2] The term "sexual anatomy," then, refers to the parts of our bodies that are involved in sexual behavior (particularly intercourse) and reproduction.

UNDERSTANDING SEXUALITY

Religion

Throughout most of recorded history, at least until about 100 years ago, religion (and rumor) provided most of the information that people had about sexuality. Thus the ancient Greeks tolerated both heterosexuality and homosexuality in their society and explained the existence of the two in a myth in which the original humans were double creatures with twice the normal number of limbs and organs; some were double males, some were double females, and some were half male and half female. The gods, fearing the power of these creatures, split them in half, and forever after each one continued to search for its missing half. Thus heterosexuals were thought to have resulted from the splitting of the half male, half female; male homosexuals, from the splitting of the double male; and female homosexuals, from the splitting of the double female. It was through this mythology that the ancient Greek understood sexuality.

The fifteenth-century Christian believed that "wet dreams" (nocturnal emissions) resulted from intercourse with tiny spiritual creatures called *incubi* and *succubi*, a notion put forth in a papal bull of 1484 and a companion book, the *Malleus Maleficarum* ("witch's hammer");

---

[1]Actually, even in former times sex was not always associated with reproduction. For example, a man in 1850 might have fathered 10 children; using a very conservative estimate that he engaged in sexual intercourse 1500 times during his adult life (once a week for the 30 years from age 20 to age 50), only 10 in 1500 of those acts, or less than 1 percent, resulted in reproduction.

[2]This definition, though an improvement over some, still has its problems. For example, consider a woman who feels no arousal at all during intercourse. According to the definition, intercourse would not be sexual behavior for her. However, intercourse would generally be something we would want to classify as sexual behavior. It should be clear that defining "sexual behavior" is very difficult. The definition given is good, though not perfect.

(a)   (b)

FIGURE 1.1

Two important early sex researchers. (a) Sigmund Freud [*Wide World Photos*].
(b) Henry Havelock Ellis [*Culver Pictures Inc.*].

the person who had wet dreams was thus guilty of sodomy (see Chapter 21) as well as witchcraft.

The Muslim believed that sexual intercourse was one of the finest pleasures of life, reflecting the teachings of the great prophet Muhammad.

Science

It was against this background of religious understandings of sexuality that the scientific study of sex began in the late nineteenth century, although, of course, religious notions continue to influence our ideas about sexuality to the present day. In addition, the groundwork for an understanding of the biological aspects of sexuality had already been laid by the research of physicians and biologists. The Dutch microscopist Anton van Leeuwenhoek (1632–1723) and his student John Ham had discovered sperm swimming in human semen. In 1875 Oscar Hertwig first observed the actual fertilization of the egg by the sperm in sea urchins, although

the ovum in humans was not directly observed until the twentieth century.

A major advance in the scientific understanding of human sexual behavior came with the work of the Viennese physician Sigmund Freud (1856–1939), founder of psychiatry and psychoanalysis. His ideas will be discussed in detail later in this chapter.

An equally great—though not so well known—early contributor to the scientific study of sex was Henry Havelock Ellis (1859–1939). A physician in Victorian England, he compiled a vast collection of information on sexuality—including medical and anthropological findings, as well as case histories—which was published in a series of volumes entitled *Studies in the Psychology of Sex* beginning in 1896. Ellis was a remarkably objective and tolerant scholar, particularly for his era. A sexual reformer, he believed that sexual deviations from the norm were often harmless, and he urged society to accept them.

Another important figure in nineteenth-century sex research was Richard von Krafft-

4

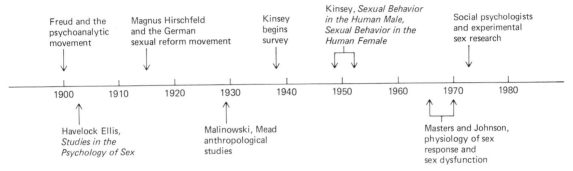

FIGURE 1.2

The history of scientific research on sex.

Ebing (1840–1902). His special interest was "pathological" sexuality, and he managed to collect over 200 case histories of pathological individuals, which appeared in his book entitled *Psychopathia Sexualis*. His work tended to be neither objective nor tolerant. One of his case histories is presented in Chapter 15.

One other early contributor to the scientific understanding of sexuality deserves mention, the German Magnus Hirschfeld (1868–1935). He founded the first sex research institute and administered the first large-scale sex survey, obtaining data from 10,000 people on a 130-item questionnaire. Unfortunately, most of the information he amassed was destroyed by Nazi hoodlums. Hirschfeld also established the first journal devoted to the study of sex, established a marriage counseling service, worked for legal reforms, and gave advice on contraception and sex problems. His special interest, however, was homosexuality. Doubtless some of his avant-garde approaches resulted from the fact that he was himself both a homosexual and a transvestite, but his contributions as a pioneer sex researcher cannot be denied (Bullough, 1976).

In the twentieth century, major breakthroughs in the scientific understanding of sex came with the massive surveys of human sexual behavior in the United States conducted by Alfred Kinsey and his colleagues in the 1940s

and with Masters and Johnson's investigations of sexual dysfunctions and the physiology of sexual response. At about the same time that the Kinsey research was being conducted, some anthropologists—most notably Margaret Mead and Bronislaw Malinowski—were beginning to collect data on sexual behavior in other cultures. Other, smaller investigations also provided important information.

The scientific study of sex has still not emerged as a separate, unified academic discipline like biology or psychology or sociology. Rather, it tends to be interdisciplinary—a joint effort by biologists, psychologists, sociologists, anthropologists, and physicians. In fact, the course you are taking in human sexuality may be taught by an interdisciplinary team of instructors. In a sense, this is a major virtue in our current approach to understanding sexuality since it gives us a better view of humans in all their sexual complexity.

Let us now consider the perspectives on sexuality provided by some major theories.

THEORETICAL PERSPECTIVES

Psychoanalytic Theory

Freud's psychoanalytic theory has been one of the most influential of all psychological theories. Since Freud saw sex as one of the key forces in human life, his theory gives full treatment to human sexuality.

Freud termed the sex drive or sex energy *libido*, and he saw it as one of the two major forces motivating human behavior (the other being *thanatos*, or the death instinct). Indeed, he felt that much apparently nonsexual behavior is actually motivated by the libido in a process of *sublimation*, whereby the libido is redirected toward higher goals. He thought, for example, that Leonardo da Vinci's interest in painting madonnas resulted from sublimation of his urge for intimacy with his mother, from whom he had been separated at a tender age.

Id, ego, and superego Freud described the human personality as being divided into three major parts: the id, the ego, and the superego. The *id* is the basic part of personality and is present at birth. It is the reservoir of psychic energy (including libido) and contains the instincts. Basically it operates on the *pleasure principle*; it cannot tolerate any increase in psychic tensions, and so it seeks to discharge these tensions.

While the id operates only on the pleasure principle and can thus be pretty irrational, the *ego* operates on the *reality principle* and tries to keep the id in line. The ego functions to make the person have realistic, rational interactions with others.

Finally, the *superego* is the conscience. It contains the values and ideals of society that we learn, and it operates on *idealism*. Thus its aim is to inhibit the impulses of the id and to persuade the ego to strive for moral goals rather than realistic ones.

To illustrate the operation of these three components of the personality in a sexual situation, consider the case of a corporate chairman of the board who is at a meeting of the board members; the meeting is also attended by his gorgeous, curvaceous secretary, Miss Luscious. He looks at Miss Luscious, and his id says, "I want to throw her on the table and make love to

her immediately. Let's do it!" The ego intervenes and says, "We can't do it now because the other members of the board are also here. Let's wait until 5 p.m., when they're all gone, and then do it." The superego says, "I shouldn't make love to Miss Luscious at all because I'm a married man." What actually happens? It depends on the relative strengths of this man's id, ego, and superego.

The id, ego, and superego develop sequentially. The id contains the set of instincts present at birth. The ego develops later, as the child learns how to interact realistically with his or her environment and the people in it. The superego develops last, as the child learns moral values.

Erogenous zones Freud saw the libido as being focused in various regions of the body known as *erogenous zones* (a term that has been used rather loosely by the general public in recent years). An erogenous zone is part of the skin or mucous membrane which is extremely sensitive to stimulation; manipulating it in certain ways produces feelings of pleasure. The lips and mouth are one such erogenous zone, the genitals are a second, and the rectum and anus are a third. Thus sucking produces oral pleasure, defecating produces anal pleasure, and rubbing of the genital area produces genital pleasure.

Stages of psychosexual development Freud believed that the child passes through a series of stages of development. In each of these stages, a different erogenous zone is the focus of the child's striving.

The first stage, lasting from birth to about 1 year of age, is the *oral stage*. The child's chief pleasure is derived from sucking and otherwise stimulating the lips and mouth. Anyone who has observed children of this age knows how they delight in putting anything they can into their mouths. The second stage, which occurs during approximately the second year of life, is the *anal stage*. During this stage, the child's interest is focused on elimination.

The third stage of development, lasting from age 3 to perhaps age 5 or 6, is the *phallic stage*. The boy's interest is focused on his phallus (penis), and he derives great pleasure from masturbating. Perhaps the most important occurrence in this stage is the development of the *Oedipus complex*, which derives its name from the Greek story of Oedipus, who killed his father and married his mother. In the Oedipus complex, the boy loves his mother and desires her sexually. He hates his father, whom he sees as a rival for the mother's affection. The boy's hostility toward his father grows, but eventually he comes to fear that his father will retaliate by cutting off his prized penis (castration). Thus the boy feels *castration anxiety*. Eventually the castration anxiety becomes so great that he stops desiring his mother and shifts to identifying with his father, taking on the father's gender role and acquiring the characteristics expected of males by society. Freud considered the Oedipus complex and its resolution to be one of the key factors in human personality development, and thus he saw the desire for incest as being extremely important.

As might be expected from the name of this stage, the girl will have a considerably different, and much more difficult, time passing through it, since she has none of what the stage is all about. For the girl, the stage begins with her traumatic realization that she has no penis, perhaps after observing that of her father or her brother. She feels envious and cheated, and she suffers from *penis envy*, wishing that she too had a wonderful wand. (Presumably she thinks her own clitoris is totally inadequate, or she is not even aware that she has it.) She believes that at one time she had a penis but that it was cut off, and she holds her mother responsible. Thus she begins to hate her mother and shifts to loving her father, forming her version of the Oedipus complex, sometimes called the *Electra complex*. In part, her incestuous desires for her

father result from a desire to be impregnated by him, to substitute for the unobtainable penis. Unlike the boy, the girl does not have a strong motive of castration anxiety for resolving the Oedipus complex; she has already lost her penis. Thus the girl's resolution of the Electra complex is not so complete as the boy's resolution of the Oedipus complex, and for the rest of her life she remains somewhat immature compared with men.

Following the resolution of the Oedipus or Electra complex, Freud said that children pass into a prolonged stage known as *latency*, which lasts until adolescence. During this stage, the sexual impulses are repressed or are in a quiescent state, and so nothing much happens sexually. The postulation of this stage is one of the weaker parts of Freudian theory, since it is clear from the data of Kinsey and others that children do continue to engage in sexual behavior during this period.

With adolescence, sexual urges reawaken, and the child passes into the *genital stage*. During this stage, sexual urges become more specifically genital, and the oral, anal, and genital urges all fuse together to promote the biological function of reproduction. Sexuality becomes less narcissistic (self-directed) than it was in childhood and is directed toward other people as appropriate sexual objects.

Of course, according to Freud, people do not always mature from one stage to the next as they should. A person might remain permanently fixated, for example, at the oral stage; symptoms of such a situation would include incessant cigarette smoking and fingernail biting, which gratify oral urges. Most adults have at least traces of earlier stages remaining in their personalities.

Freud on women In recent years a storm of criticism of Freudian theory has arisen from feminists. Let us first review what Freud had to say about women and then discuss what feminists object to in his theory.

Essentially, Freud argued that the female is biologically inferior to the male because she lacks a penis. He saw this absence as a key factor in her personality development. The penis envy she feels as a result of her biological deficiency causes her to develop the Electra complex. Yet she never adequately resolves this complex, and she is left, throughout her life, with feelings of jealousy and inferiority, all because of her lack of a penis. As Freud said, "Anatomy is destiny."

Freud believed that female sexuality is inherently passive (as opposed to the active aggressiveness of the male). He also felt that female sexuality is masochistic; in seeking intercourse, the female is trying to bring pain on herself, since childbirth, which may result, is painful and since intercourse itself may sometimes be painful. The following quotation from Marie Bonaparte, an early follower of Freud, will illustrate the psychoanalytic position:

> Throughout the whole range of living creatures, animal or vegetable, passivity is characteristic of the female cell, the ovum whose mission is to *await* the male cell, the active mobile spermatozoan to come and *penetrate* it. Such penetration, however, implies infraction of its tissue, but infraction of a living creature's tissue may entail destruction: death as much as life. Thus the fecundation of the female cell is initiated by a kind of wound; in its way, the female cell is primordially "masochistic." (1953, p. 79)

Freud also originated the distinction between *vaginal orgasm* and *clitoral orgasm* in women. During childhood little girls rub their clitoris to produce orgasm (clitoral orgasm). Freud believed, though, that as they grow to adulthood they need to shift their focus to having orgasm during heterosexual intercourse, with the penis stimulating the vagina (vaginal orgasm). Thus, not only did he postulate two kinds of orgasm for women, but he also maintained that one kind was better (more mature) than the other. The evidence that Masters and

Johnson have collected on this issue will be reviewed in Chapter 7; suffice it to say for now that there seems to be little or no physiological difference between the two kinds of orgasm. Thus the distinction between them makes little sense. Asserting that the vaginal orgasm is more mature makes even less sense, since most adult women have orgasm as a result of clitoral stimulation.

Feminists understandably object to several aspects of Freud's theory. A chief objection is to the whole notion that women are anatomically inferior to men because they lack a penis. What is so intrinsically valuable about a penis that makes it better than a clitoris, a vagina, or a pair of ovaries? Similarly, feminists find the assertion that women are inherently passive, masochistic, and narcissistic to be offensive. Is it not likelier that men simply have higher status in our culture than women do and that women's feelings of jealousy or inferiority result from these cultural status differences? Feminists argue that psychoanalytic theory is essentially a male-centered theory which may have bad effects on women, particularly when it is used on a woman who seeks psychotherapy from a therapist who uses a psychoanalytic approach.

Evaluation of psychoanalytic theory From a scientific point of view, one of the major problems with psychoanalytic theory is that most of its concepts cannot be evaluated scientifically to see whether they are accurate. Freud postulated that many of the most important forces in personality are unconscious, and thus they cannot be studied by any of the usual scientific techniques.

Another criticism is that Freud derived his data almost exclusively from his work with patients who sought therapy from him. Thus, his theory may provide a view not so much of the human personality as of the *disturbed* human personality.

Finally, many modern psychologists feel that Freud overemphasized biological determinants of behavior and instincts and that he gave insufficient recognition to the importance of the environment and learning.

Nonetheless, Freud did make some important contributions to our understanding of human behavior. He managed to rise above the Victorian era of which he was a part, and to teach that sex is an important part of personality (although he may have overestimated its importance). His notion that all behavior is motivated is also important, and his recognition that humans pass through stages in their psychological development was a great contribution. Perhaps most important from the perspective of this text, Freud took sex out of the closet; he brought it to the attention of the general public and suggested that we could talk about it and that it was an appropriate topic for scientific research.

Sexuality as Motivation

Modern psychologists, taking a view somewhat similar to Freud's, regard sex as one of the basic drives, along with hunger and thirst. A *need* is a bodily deficiency or a perceived social or psychological deficiency. A *motive* is then an internal energized state that results from the need and usually activates behavior aimed at fulfilling it. *Drives* are certain motives such as hunger that arise from physiological needs. Thus, for example, in the case of hunger, a person who is deprived of food develops a bodily deficiency or need, particularly if the deprivation lasts a long time. An internal drive state is then produced, and it energizes the person to do something, probably to eat (although if the person is on a strict diet, it might energize some other behavior, such as smoking).

A classic experiment demonstrated the existence of a sex drive and measured its intensity (Warden, 1931). Rats were placed in an apparatus consisting of a start box and an incentive box separated by an electrified grid that had to be crossed to go from one to the other. The number of times the animal crossed the grid during a 20-minute interval was used as a measure of the strength of the drive. If a male rat was placed in the start box and a female rat in estrus ("heat") was placed in the incentive box, he would cross the shock grid to get to her, demonstrating the existence of a sex drive. The longer he had been deprived of sex before being placed in the apparatus, the more times he crossed the shock grid during the 20 minutes, suggesting that the drive became stronger as deprivation was prolonged (see Bolles, 1967, for a critique of this study). The results were similar when the animal had been deprived of food and food was placed in the incentive box.

While sex is generally considered one of the basic biological drives, like hunger and thirst, it is also clear that the sex drive differs in substantial ways from hunger and thirst. If a person is deprived of food or water, a biological depletion in the body tissues results, and the person returns to the normal state after eating or drinking; hunger and thirst, then, act as drives to make up for deficits in the body. There is no known way in which the body is depleted by lack of sexual activity, though, and so the sex drive does not act like hunger and thirst to replace a biological deficit. Neither is there any evidence that a lack of sex causes a buildup in the body of substances that must be discharged through sexual activity. Similarly, eating and drinking are biological necessities if the individual is to survive, but it is quite possible to abstain completely from sex and lead a long and healthy life. On the other hand, while sex may not be necessary for the survival of the individual, it is a biological necessity if the species is to survive. Thus the sex drive has something in common with the other biological drives of hunger and thirst, but it also differs from them.

Some of these ideas having to do with motivation have come under attack since the 1950s. It is beyond the scope of our discussion here to consider them in detail. The interested reader should consult Cofer (1972) for a complete discussion. Suffice it to say here that there has been a trend toward substituting notions of rewards and punishments for some of the aspects of motivation. This brings us to a discussion of learning theory.

Learning Theory

While psychoanalytic and motivational theories are based on the notion that much of human sexual behavior is biologically controlled, it is also quite apparent that much of it is learned. Some of the best evidence for this point comes from studies of sexual behavior across different human societies; these studies will be considered in the next section. First, however, the various principles of modern learning theory will be reviewed, since they can help us understand our own sexuality.

Operant conditioning Operant conditioning, a concept that is often associated with the psychologist B. F. Skinner, refers to the following process: A person performs a particular behavior (the operant). That behavior may be followed by either a reward or a punishment. If a reward follows, the person will be likely to perform the behavior again in the future; if a punishment follows, the person will be less likely to repeat the behavior. Thus if a behavior is repeatedly rewarded, it may become very frequent, and if it is repeatedly punished, it may become very infrequent or even be eliminated.

Some rewards are considered to be primary reinforcers; that is, there is something intrinsically rewarding about them. Food is one such primary reinforcer, and sex is another. Rats, for example, can be trained to learn a maze if they find a willing sex partner at the end of it. Thus sexual behavior plays dual roles in learning theory: it can itself be a reward, but it can also be the behavior that is rewarded or punished.

Other rewards are conditioned reinforcers. For example, there is nothing inherently rewarding about receiving a $10 bill for some work you have done; only through learning or conditioning have you come to realize that such a piece of paper is valuable and to feel that it is a reward. Yet another category is social reinforcers, such as praise or a compliment from another person.

Simple principles of operant conditioning can help explain some aspects of sex (McGuire et al., 1965). For example, if a woman repeatedly experiences pain when she has intercourse (perhaps because she has a vaginal infection), she will probably want to have sex infrequently or not at all. In operant conditioning terms, sexual intercourse has repeatedly been associated with a punishment (pain), and so the behavior becomes less frequent.

What other principles of operant conditioning are useful in understanding sexual behavior? One principle is that reinforcements are most effective in shaping behavior when they occur immediately after a behavior and that the longer they are delayed after the behavior has occurred, the less effective they become. As an example of that principle, consider the male homosexual who continues to engage in homosexual behavior with his lover even though, because of this, his colleagues at work have rejected him and he is even in danger of being fired. Since he is being punished for the behavior, why does he persist in it? The delay-of-reinforcement principle might explain the situation as follows: Every time he engages in homosexual behavior, he enjoys it and finds it rewarding; this occurs immediately. These immediate rewards are effective in encouraging him to continue the behavior, and the punishments, which may not occur until a week after the behavior, are not effective in eliminating it.

Another principle that has emerged in operant conditioning studies is that, compared with rewards, punishments are not very effective in shaping behavior. Often, as in the case of the child who is punished for taking an illicit cookie, punishments do not eliminate a behavior, but rather teach the person to be sneaky and engage in it without being caught. As an example, parents, particularly in earlier times in our culture, punished children for masturbating, and yet most of those children continued to masturbate. Punishment is simply not very effective in eliminating behavior. Still using masturbation as an example, children may instead learn to do it under circumstances (such as in a bathroom with the door locked) in which they are not likely to be caught.

Behavior modification Behavior modification involves a set of techniques, based on principles of operant conditioning, that are used to change or modify human behavior. These techniques have been used to modify everything from problem behaviors of children in the classroom to the behavior of schizophrenics. In particular, these methods can be used to modify problematic sexual behaviors—sexual dysfunctions such as impotence (see Chapter 18) or deviant sexual behavior such as child molesting. Behavior modification methods differ from more traditional methods of psychotherapy such as psychoanalysis in that the behavioral therapist considers only the problem behavior and how to modify it using learning-theory principles; the therapist does not worry about a depth analysis of the person's personality to see, for example, what unconscious forces might be motivating the behavior.

One example of a behavior modification technique that has been used in modifying sexual behavior is aversion therapy (Barlow, 1973). In *aversion therapy*, the problematic sexual behavior is punished using an aversive method. For example, a child molester might be shown pictures of children; if he responds with sexual arousal, he receives an electric shock.

Trials are repeated until he no longer feels aroused when he sees a child's picture.

Social learning Social learning theory (Bandura, 1969; Bandura and Walters, 1963) is a somewhat more complex form of learning theory. It is based on principles of operant conditioning, but it also recognizes how greatly the learning process is influenced by interactions with other people. In particular, social learning theory postulates two processes at work besides conditioning: imitation and identification. Identification (the concept here is similar to the one in psychoanalytic theory) and imitation are useful in explaining the development of gender identity, or one's sense of maleness or femaleness. For example, it seems that a little girl acquires many characteristics of the female role by identifying with her mother and imitating her, as when she plays at dressing up after observing her mother getting ready to go to a party. Because most sexual behaviors in our society are kept rather private and hidden, imitation and identification have less of a chance to play a part. However, some of the more open forms of sexuality may be learned through imitation. In high school, for example, the sexiest girl in the senior class may find that other girls are imitating her behaviors and the way she dresses. Or a boy might see a movie in which the hero's technique seems to "turn women on"; then he tries to use this technique with his own dates.

Humanistic Psychology

Humanistic psychologists such as Carl Rogers and Abraham Maslow are concerned with making psychology and psychotherapy more human and with considering individuals as whole people. A key concept in humanistic psychology is *self-actualization*, a process of continually growing so as to realize one's own inherent potentialities. As Rogers says, "The organism has one basic tendency and striving—to actualize, maintain, and enhance the experiencing organism" (1951, p. 487).

Humanistic psychologists view sex and love as means of self-actualization. As Abraham Maslow put it:

> It is quite characteristic of self-actualizing people that they can enjoy themselves in love and in sex. Sex very frequently becomes a kind of game in which laughter is quite as common as panting. It is not the welfare of the species, or the task of reproduction, or the future development of mankind that attracts people to each other. The sex life of healthy people, in spite of the fact that it frequently reaches great peaks of ecstasy, is nevertheless also easily compared to the games of children and puppies. It is cheerful, humorous, and playful. (1954, pp. 251–252)

Humanistic psychologists also recognize that some forms of sex, such as impersonal sex, may not be at all self-actualizing, but rather may leave the individual feeling alienated.

Encounter groups (or *T groups* or *sensitivity training*) are one of the more visible signs of the human potential movement, which was spawned by humanistic psychology. Such groups are supposed to promote the participants' self-actualization by making them more aware of their own feelings and those of others and by enabling them to relate to others more openly. Some groups emphasize touching or nudity—which the media have capitalized on in discussing this movement—and encourage participants to explore their sexual feelings honestly. By touching, people recognize their need for touching. Adults often repress their need for touching and then confuse that need with sexuality; they think they need copulation when they really need cuddling (Forer, 1972). Thus learning to touch and to be aware of one's needs for touching is often an important part of encounter groups.

Transactional Analysis

Eric Berne (1970) has constructed a theory of human personality called *transactional analysis* (T.A.). According to Berne, an individual's personality consists of three parts or persons: a Parent part, an Adult part, and a Child part. Thus when two people interact, six persons are involved!

The Parent, according to Berne, is the part of our personality that evaluates how we or others behave, much as a parent would, and it may use words like "ridiculous," "immature," and "childish." The Adult part is our rationality; it acts much like a well-behaved computer, taking in information from the outside world and providing feedback on how best to proceed. The Child is the childlike part of our personality. It is the Child acting when we are sulky or inconsiderate or cruel, but it is also the Child at work when we are creative, spontaneous, or loving. If you admire someone, according to Berne, it is the Child in you relating to the Parent in the other person. The woman who scolds her husband for being late for dinner is playing her Parent to his Child.

Now let us consider some examples relating to sexuality. When we "turn on" to someone, it is basically the reaction of the Child in us. In the example of Mr. Executive and Miss Luscious given earlier in the chapter, Berne would say that it was the Child in Mr. Executive that wanted to make love to Miss Luscious on the spot. It was the Adult that pointed out the impracticality of doing this, and it was the Parent who said it would be wrong. Had Miss Luscious decided that she wanted to make Mr. Executive happy by letting him make love to her, that would have been the Parent (mother) in her reacting. Berne by no means considers the Child to be all bad; in fact, he feels that true intimacy is a Child-Child relationship between two people and that the Child is definitely the sexy part of us.

Although Berne's theory is not backed by much solid, scientific evidence (that is the Adult in me speaking), it remains an interesting way of looking at human sexual interactions.

Sociological Theory

While psychologists typically are concerned with the individual's sexual behavior and its biological and cultural causes, sociologists tend to think of sexual behavior as one form of social behavior or interaction between two or more people, embedded in the matrix of society.

Sociologists see numerous forces within a culture that affect sexual interactions; among these forces are norms and institutions. *Norms* are rules for behavior that are understood by the people in a culture and guide their behavior. Our society has many norms regarding sexual behavior. For example, norms forbid homosexual behavior, but they indicate that sexual behavior between married people is acceptable. Cultural *institutions*—such as law, the family, and religion—also have profound effects on sexuality. For example, if prostitution is illegal and people who engage in it are subject to arrest, the behavior of prostitutes is viewed much differently, both by others and by prostitutes themselves, from the way it would be if the behavior were legal.

Because sociologists see cultural forces as powerful determiners of sexuality, they expect that sexual behavior and attitudes may vary over various social strata. Social class is one form of social stratum, and ethnic groups are another, as are age and gender. Thus sociologists study social-class and ethnic-group variations in sexual behavior and attitudes; anthropologists extend this approach by studying variations in sexual behavior in cultures around the world.

From a sociological viewpoint, socialization is exceptionally important in determining the sexual behavior and attitudes of the individual. *Socialization* refers to the methods by which a society's norms are conveyed to the people in that society; socialization occurs particularly in childhood, but it may continue throughout the lifespan. The parents are a chief socializing agent, but television, the schools, and many other factors also contribute. Thus in our culture children are taught that they should not masturbate or that they should do so only in private, since it is a norm in our culture that one does not masturbate in public.

Sociologists also emphasize the importance of *roles* in determining how we behave sexually. Gender roles are the best example. In a given society, certain behaviors are expected of males, and certain others of females, and most people in the society conform to those roles. Thus, for example, the traditional gender roles of our culture dictate that the wife remain in the home and take care of the children when they are young and that the husband go out and be the breadwinner. Gender roles also extend to sexual behavior; for example, the male, not the female, is supposed to initiate sexual activity. There are also many other kinds of roles besides gender roles. Some roles relate to social class. Even within a gender there are numerous roles available; on a date, for example, a young woman might decide to play a "good girl" role, or she might, alternatively, decide to play a "with-it swinger" role. All of us combine numerous roles in our daily behavior, including our sexual behavior.

CROSS-CULTURAL PERSPECTIVES

We tend to be ethnocentric in our understanding of human sexual behavior. That is, most of us have had experience with sexuality in only one culture—the United States—and we tend to view it as the only pattern of sexual behavior in

(a)

(b)

FIGURE 1.3

Sexual behaviors and customs vary widely in different human cultures. (a) Among the Australian aborigines, boys undergo circumcision as part of puberty rites [*Fritz Goro*]. (b) Courtship in New Guinea [*Laurence LeGuay*]. (c) The hairstyle of this Hopi girl (*opposite page*) signifies her status as an unmarried virgin [*Arizona Historical Society*].

(c)

existence, and certainly as the only "natural" pattern. But anthropologists have discovered that there are wide variations in sexual behavior and attitudes from one culture to the next. Considering these variations should help us to put our own sexual behavior in perspective.

The data on the enormous variations in sexual behavior from one culture to the next will be reviewed below. First, however, some generalizations that emerge in cross-cultural studies will be considered. The major source of data for the conclusions that will be drawn is the classic study of anthropologist Clellan Ford and psychologist Frank Beach (1951), who surveyed sexual behavior in 190 societies around the world and also sexual behavior across various animal species.

Before proceeding, though, it is worth noting that Ford and Beach concluded that the American culture was a relatively sexually "restrictive" one; the majority of the others studied were far more permissive. This may help us put our own standards in better perspective. On the other hand, most people would agree—and scientific research supports the notion (see Chapters 9 to 11)—that sexual behavior and attitudes among Americans have undergone substantial changes in the 25 years since Ford and Beach wrote their book. It would be interesting to know whether they would now classify us as a permissive or a restrictive society.

Generalizations

The major generalization that emerges from cross-cultural studies is that all societies regulate sexual behavior in some way, though the exact regulations vary greatly from one culture to the next (Gebhard, 1971; Jensen, 1976b). Apparently no society has seen fit to leave sexuality totally unregulated, perhaps because social disruption would result. As an example, incest taboos are nearly universal: sex is regulated in that intercourse between relatives is

SEXUALITY IN TWO SOCIETIES

INIS BEAG

Inis Beag is a small island located off the coast of Ireland. It is probably one of the most naïve and sexually repressive societies in the world.

The people of Inis Beag seem to have no knowledge of a number of sexual activities such as French kissing, mouth stimulation of the breast, or hand stimulation of the partner's penis, much less cunnilingus, fellatio, or homosexuality. Sex education is virtually nonexistent; parents do not seem to be able to bring themselves to discuss such embarrassing matters with their children, and they simply trust that, after marriage, nature will take its course.

Menstruation and menopause are sources of fear for the island women because they have no idea of their physiological significance. It is commonly believed that menopause can produce insanity; in order to ward off this condition, some women have retired from life in their mid-forties, and a few have confined themselves to bed until death years later.

The men believe that intercourse is hard on one's health. They will desist from sex the night before they are to do a job that takes great energy. They do not approach women sexually during menstruation or for months after childbirth; a woman is considered dangerous to the male at these times.

The islanders abhor nudity. Only babies are allowed to bathe while nude. Adults wash only the parts of their bodies that extend beyond their clothing—face, neck, lower arms, hands, lower legs, and feet. The fear of nudity has even cost lives. Seamen who never learned to swim because it involved wearing scanty clothing have drowned when their ships have sunk.

Premarital sex is essentially unknown. In marital sex, foreplay is generally limited to kissing and rough fondling of the buttocks. The husband invariably initiates the activity. The male-superior is the only position used, and both partners keep their underwear on during the activity. The man has orgasm quickly and falls asleep almost immediately. Female orgasm is unknown, or at least it is doubted to exist or is considered deviant.

MANGAIA

In distinct contrast to Inis Beag is Mangaia, an island in the South Pacific. For the Mangaians, sex—for pleasure and for procreation—is a principal interest.

The Mangaian boy hears of masturbation when he is about 7, and he may begin to masturbate at age 8 or 9. At around age 13 he undergoes the superincision ritual (in which a slit is made on the top of the penis, along its entire length). This ritual initiates him into manhood; more important, however, the expert who performs the superincision gives him sexual instruction. He shows the boy how to perform cunnilingus, how to kiss and suck breasts, and how to bring his partner to orgasm several times before he has his own orgasm. About two weeks after the operation, the boy has intercourse with an experienced woman, which removes the scab. She provides him with practice in various acts and positions and trains him to hold back until he can have simultaneous orgasms with his partner.

After this, the Mangaian boy aggressively seeks out girls, or they seek him out; soon he has coitus every night. The girl, who has received sexual instruction from an older woman, expects demonstration of his virility as proof of his desire for her. What is valued is the ability of the male to continue vigorously the in-and-out action of coitus over long periods of time while the female moves her hips "like a washing machine." Nothing is despised more than a "dead" partner who does not move. A good man is expected to continue his actions for 15 to 30 minutes or more.

The average "nice" girl will have three or four successive boyfriends between the ages of 13 and 20; the average boy may have 10 or more girlfriends. Mangaian parents encourage their daughters to have sexual experiences with several men. They want her to find a marriage partner who is congenial.

At around age 18, the Mangaians typically have sex every night of the week, with about three orgasms per night. By about age 48, they have sex two or three times per week with one orgasm each time.

All women in Mangaia apparently learn to have orgasms. Bringing his partner to orgasm is one of the man's chief sources of sexual pleasure.

Sources: John C. Messinger. The lack of the Irish. Donald S. Marshall. Too much in Mangaia. Both in D. S. Marshall and R. C. Suggs (Eds.), *Human sexual behavior.* New York: Basic Books, 1971.

prohibited. Most societies also condemn forced sexual relations, such as rape.

Beyond this generalization, though, regulations vary greatly from one society to the next, and sexual behavior and attitudes vary correspondingly. The ways in which various societies treat some key areas of human sexual behavior will be considered below.

Sexual Techniques

Kissing is one of the most common sexual techniques in our culture. It is also very common in most other societies. There are a few societies, though, in which kissing is unknown. For example, when the Thonga of Africa first saw Europeans kissing, they laughed and said, "Look at them; they eat each other's saliva and dirt." There is also some variation in techniques of kissing. For example, among the Kwakiutl of Canada and the Trobriand Islanders, kissing consists of sucking the lips and tongue of the partner, permitting saliva to flow from one mouth to the other. Many Americans might find such a practice somewhat repulsive, but other peoples find it sexually arousing.

Grooming and delousing are widespread forms of behavior that act as a prelude to sexual relations. Describing the Siriono of South America, one observer wrote:

> Lovers also spend hours in grooming one another—extracting lice from their hair or wood ticks from their bodies, and eating them; removing worms and spines from their skin; gluing feathers into their hair; and covering their faces with utuku . . . paint. This behavior often leads up to a sexual bout, especially when conditions for intercourse are favorable. (Holmberg, 1946, p. 182)

Cunnilingus (mouth stimulation of the female genitals) is fairly common in our society, and it occurs in a few other societies as well, especially in the South Pacific. A particularly exotic variation is reported on the island of Ponape; the man places a fish in the woman's vulva and then gradually licks it out prior to coitus.

Inflicting pain on the partner is also a part of the sexual technique in some societies. The Apinaye woman of South America may bite off bits of her partner's eyebrows, noisily spitting them aside. Ponapean men usually tug at the woman's eyebrows, occasionally yanking out tufts of hair. The Trukese women of the South Pacific poke a finger into the man's ear when they are highly aroused. People of various societies bite their partners to the point of drawing blood and leaving scars, although most commonly it is the woman who inflicts the pain on the man (Ford and Beach, 1951).

The frequency of intercourse for married couples varies considerably from one culture to the next. The lowest frequency seems to be among the Keraki of the South Pacific, who copulate only about once a week. The Irish natives of Inis Beag, discussed in the Focus, may hold a record by having an even lower frequency than this, perhaps only once or twice a month; however, the anthropologists who studied them were unable to determine how often couples did have sex because so much secrecy surrounds the act. At the opposite extreme, the Aranda of Australia have intercourse as often as three to five times a night, sleeping between episodes; the Mangaians, described in the Focus, seem to have an equally high frequency, at least among the young. Our own culture, then, at least at the time of the Kinsey report, had a low frequency of intercourse compared with other societies.

Masturbation

Attitudes toward masturbation vary widely across cultures. Some societies tolerate or even encourage masturbation during childhood, while others condemn the practice at any age.

Almost all human societies express some disapproval of adult masturbation, ranging from mild ridicule to severe punishment. On the other hand, at least some adults in all societies appear to practice it.

Female masturbation certainly occurs in other societies. The African Azande woman does it with a phallus made from a wooden root; however, if her husband catches her masturbating, he may beat her severely. The following is a description of the Lesu of the South Pacific, who are one of the few societies that express no disapproval of adult female masturbation:

> A woman will masturbate if she is sexually excited and there is no man to satisfy her. A couple may be having intercourse in the same house, or near enough for her to see them, and she may thus become aroused. She then sits down and bends her right leg so that her heel presses against her genitalia. Even young girls of about six years may do this quite casually as they sit on the ground. The women and men talk about it freely, and there is no shame attached to it. It is a customary position for women to take, and they learn it in childhood. They never use their hands for manipulation. (Powdermaker, 1933, pp. 276–277)

Homosexuality

There is a wide range of attitudes toward homosexuality in various cultures. At one extreme are societies, such as our own, that strongly disapprove of homosexual behavior for people of any age. In contrast, some societies tolerate homosexual behavior for children but disapprove of it in adults. Yet other societies actively force all their male members to engage in some homosexual behavior, usually in conjunction with puberty rites. In Africa, prominent Siwan men lend their sons to one another, and they discuss their homosexual love affairs as openly as they discuss the love of women. A few societies have

a formalized role for the adult male homosexual which gives him status and dignity.

While there is wide variation in attitudes toward homosexuality and in homosexual behavior, three general rules do seem to emerge (Ford and Beach, 1951): (1) no matter how a particular society treats homosexuality, the behavior always occurs in at least some individuals; (2) males are more likely to engage in homosexual behavior than females; and (3) homosexual behavior is never the predominant form of sexual behavior for adults in any of the societies studied.

Standards of Attractiveness

In all human societies physical characteristics are important in determining whom one chooses as a sex partner. What is considered attractive varies considerably, though. In the United States, the ideal is a slim but big-bosomed blonde with a peaches-and-cream complexion and long, shapely legs. For us, physical characteristics are probably less important in determining a man's attractiveness. More important is what he *does*; he is attractive if he is a star athlete or a wealthy businessman. But his physical characteristics are also considered important; the ideal is a tall, trim man with broad shoulders, narrow hips, and a firm jaw.

The region of the body that is judged for attractiveness varies considerably from one culture to the next. For some peoples, the shape and color of the eyes are especially significant. For others, the shape of the ears is most important. Some societies go directly to the heart of the matter and judge attractiveness by the appearance of the external genitals. In a few societies, elongated labia majora (the pads of fat on either side of the vaginal opening in women) are considered sexually attractive, and it is common practice for a woman to pull on hers in order to make them longer. Elongated labia majora among the Nawa women of Africa are considered a mark of beauty and are quite prominent.

Our society's standards are in the minority in one way: in most cultures, a plump woman is considered more attractive than a thin one.

One standard does seem to be a general rule: a poor complexion is considered unattractive in the majority of human societies.

Gender Roles

Margaret Mead did some of the most important studies on gender roles in cultures other than our own, and her books, among them *Sex and Temperament in Three Primitive Societies*, are classics. Those studies will not be discussed in detail here because they are well known; the interested reader may want to consult them directly.

The point that emerges from the cross-cultural studies is that gender roles vary tremendously from one society to the next. In particular, the roles that males and females play in sexual relations may be quite different from the ones that are played in our own society. For example, there are a few societies in which the girl generally begins all love affairs (for example, the Maori and the Kwoma of the South Pacific and the Mataco of South America). While the gender roles in our society lead us to believe that rape is always committed by men against women, Malinowski described a regular process of women raping men among the Trobriand Islanders of the South Pacific:

> If they perceive a stranger, a man from any village but their own, passing within sight, they have the customary right to attack him, a right which by all accounts they exercise with zeal and energy.
>
> The man is the fair game of the women for all that sexual violence, obscene cruelty, filthy pollution, and rough handling can do to him. Thus first they pull off and tear up his pubic leaf, the protection of his modesty and, to a native,

the symbol of his manly dignity. Then by masturbatory practices and exhibitionism, they try to produce an erection in their victim and, when their manoeuvres have brought about the desired result, one of them squats over him and inserts his penis into her vagina. After the first ejaculation he may be treated in the same manner by another woman. Worse things are to follow. Some of the women will defecate and micturate all over his body. . . . Local informants from the south confirmed this account in all essentials. They were by no means ashamed of their custom, regarding it rather as a sign of the general virility of the district, and passing on any possible opprobrium to the stranger-victims. (1929)

Suffice it to say that some cultures have gender roles considerably different from our own.

Social-Class and Ethnic-Group Variations in the United States

The discussion so far may have seemed to imply that there is one uniform standard of sexual behavior in the United States and that all Americans behave alike sexually. In fact, though, there are large variations in sexual behavior within our culture. Some of these subcultural variations can be classified as social-class differences, and some as ethnic differences.

Social class and sex Kinsey found large social-class differences in sexual behavior (he generally used amount of education as a measure of social class). For example, Table 1.1 shows that males in his study who did not go beyond grade school were nearly twice as likely as males who attended college to have had premarital sex by the age of 20 (83 percent, as compared with 44 percent). Almost none of the grade school males had ever performed cunnilingus on their wives, while nearly half of the college-educated men had. Considerably more

TABLE 1.1

SOCIAL-CLASS VARIATIONS IN THE SEXUAL BEHAVIOR OF AMERICANS
AT THE TIME OF THE KINSEY STUDIES

	Educational Level		
	0-8 Years of Education, %	9-12 Years of Education, %	13 or More Years of Education, %
Males having pre-marital sex by age 20	83	75	44
Males having sex with a prostitute before marriage	80	61	35
Males having per-formed cunnilingus on their wives	4	15	45
Females who had never had an orgasm by the fifth year of marriage	28	17	15

Sources: Alfred C. Kinsey, Wardell B. Pomeroy, and Clyde E. Martin. *Sexual behavior in the human male.* Philadelphia: Saunders, 1948, pp. 352, 368, 550. Alfred C. Kinsey, Wardell B. Pomeroy, Clyde E. Martin, and Paul H. Gebhard. *Sexual behavior in the human female.* Philadelphia: Saunders, 1953, p. 401.

of the uneducated wives had never had an orgasm after five years of marriage, compared with wives who had had a high school or a college education.

Gender roles tend to be more rigid in the lower class, and this tends to extend to the realm of sexuality. As sociologist Lee Rainwater (1971) has noted, among the poor the dictum is, "Sex is a man's pleasure and a woman's duty." He found this rule to hold for lower-class people in the United States as well as those in England, Puerto Rico, and Mexico.

Thus a composite picture of social-class differences in sexuality emerged at the time the Kinsey data were collected. The lower-class married couple were more likely to have sex in the dark and with some clothing on, and the male came to orgasm quickly. The husband was also more likely to have extramarital sex with a prostitute. Middle- and upper-middle-class couples, on the other hand, were relatively more likely to sleep in the nude and to have sex in the nude with some lighting. They also used a wider variety of sexual techniques, including varied positions (such as woman-on-top) and fellatio and cunnilingus, and the husband was more likely to delay his orgasm (Kinsey et al., 1948).

More recent data, collected in the 1970s, suggest that the social-class differences found by Kinsey have diminished greatly or perhaps have even disappeared (Hunt, 1974). Social-class differences have diminished particularly among the young.

Black sexuality   The American population is composed of many ethnic groups, and there may be variations among these groups in sexual behavior. Since the data on other ethnic groups are very limited, the focus here will be on the sexuality of black Americans and the ways in which it differs from that of white Americans.

The sexuality of black Americans, of course, is influenced by many of the same factors influencing the sexuality of white Americans, such as the legacies of the Victorian era and the influence of the Judeo-Christian religious tradition. In addition, at least three other factors may act to make the sexuality of blacks somewhat different from that of whites: (1) the African heritage, (2) the forces that acted upon blacks during slavery, and (3) current economic and social conditions, particularly high unemployment among black men.

Given these forces, what are the sexual behaviors and attitudes of blacks now? There do seem to be some areas in which they differ from whites. There is more approval of premarital sex among blacks than among whites. Blacks tend to have less of a double standard concerning sex; sexual experience can be a status symbol or a sign of entering womanhood for the adolescent black girl (Ladner, 1971; Staples, 1972). Black women tend to be more open than white women about their sexual needs, both in discussion with other women and in their sexual interactions with men. Perhaps as a result, lower-class black women are more likely to have orgasms during premarital sex than lower-class white women (Staples, 1972).

There are also variations within black culture. Differences exist between the sexual behavior of black men and women that are similar to the differences between the sexual behavior of white men and women. For example, black men are more accepting of premarital sex than black women are. In addition, there are social-class variations; the sexual behavior of middle-class blacks is more similar to that of middle-class whites than it is to that of lower-class blacks (Staples, 1972).

Generally, the differences between blacks and whites in sexual behavior are not large, and they may be related more to social class than to anything else.

The Significance of the Cross-Cultural Studies

What relevance do the cross-cultural data have to an understanding of human sexuality? They are important for two basic reasons. First, they give us a notion of the enormous variation that exists in human sexual behavior, and they help us put our own society's standards and our own behavior in perspective. Second, these studies provide us with impressive evidence concerning the importance of culture and learning in the shaping of our sexual behavior; they show us that human sexual behavior is not completely determined by biology or drives or instincts. For example, the woman of Inis Beag and the woman of Mangaia presumably have vaginas that are similarly constructed and clitorises that are approximately the same size and have the same nerve supply. But the woman of Inis Beag never has an orgasm, and all Mangaian women orgasm.[3] Why? Their cultures are different, and they and their partners learned different things about sex as they were growing up. Learning is the biggest determinant of human sexual behavior, and instincts or drives play only a minor role.

CROSS-SPECIES PERSPECTIVES

Humans are one of many animal species, and all of them display sexual behavior. To put our own sexual behavior in evolutionary perspective, it is helpful to explore the similarities and differences between our own sexuality and that

---

[3] I like to use the word "orgasm" not only as a noun but also as a verb. The reason is that alternative expressions, such as "to *achieve* orgasm" and "to *reach* orgasm," reflect our tendency to make sex an achievement situation (an idea to be discussed further in Chap. 8). To avoid this, I use "to have an orgasm" or "to orgasm."

of other species. There is one other motive behind this particular discussion. In recent years some people have taken to classifying sexual behaviors as "natural" or "unnatural" depending on whether other species do or do not exhibit those behaviors. Sometimes, though, the data are twisted to suit the purposes of the person making the argument, and so there is a need for a less biased view. Let us see exactly what some other species do!

Masturbation

Humans are definitely not the only species that masturbates. Masturbation is found among many species of mammals, and it is particularly common among the primates (monkeys and apes). Male monkeys and apes in zoos can be observed masturbating, often to the horror of the proper folk who have come to see them. At one time it was thought that this behavior might be the result of the unnatural living conditions of zoos. However, observations of free-living primates indicate that they, too, masturbate (e.g., Carpenter, 1942). Techniques include hand stimulation of the genitals or rubbing the genitals against an object. In terms of technique, monkeys and apes have one advantage over humans: their bodies are so flexible that they can perform mouth-genital sex on themselves. A rather unique form of male masturbation is found among red deer; during the rutting season they move the tips of their antlers through low growing vegetation, producing erection and ejaculation (Beach, 1976).

Female masturbation is also found among many species besides our own. The prize for the most inventive technique probably should go to the female porcupine. She holds one end of a stick in her paws and walks around while straddling the stick; as the stick bumps against the ground, it vibrates against her genitals (Ford and Beach, 1951). Human females are apparently not the first to enjoy vibrators.

Mouth-Genital Stimulation

Mouth-genital stimulation is also quite natural, judging from the behavior of other species. It is quite common for the male to apply his mouth to the female's genitals, in part because the sex scents, or *pheromones*, she produces stimulate sexual behavior (see Chapter 7). The following quotation describes this practice among chimpanzees (our nearest evolutionary relatives) and points out the pleasure the female apparently receives from it:

> Wendy was turning so that her face was away from Billy and her posterior parts were turned conspicuously towards him. . . . Billy showed interest in the protruding genitalia (and) . . . gradually the manipulations of his free hand became directed more and more (toward them). . . . He picked at them with his fingers and several times took them in his lips. Shortly after this manipulation began it became apparent that Wendy was sexually stimulated. The clitoris became noticeably erect, and I could detect occasional surges as though she were voluntarily increasing the erection. (Bingham, 1928, pp. 98–99)

Observations indicate that it is less common for the female to stimulate the male's genitals with her mouth, although this does occur (Ford and Beach, 1951).

Homosexual Behavior

Homosexual behavior is found in many species besides our own (Beach, 1976). Indeed, observations of other species indicate that our basic mammalian heritage is bisexual; it is composed of both heterosexual and homosexual elements (Ford and Beach, 1951).

Males of many species will mount other males. Anal intercourse has even been observed in some male primates (Erwin amd Maple, 1976; Hamilton, 1914; Kempf, 1917). Male

(a)

(b)

(c)

FIGURE 1.4

The sexual behavior of gorillas. (a) The female "presents" to the male, soliciting
copulation. (b) Copulation in the rear-mount position. (c) Copulation in the
face-to-face position, which is rare among nonhumans. [*Ronald D. Nadler, Yerkes
Regional Primate Research Center, Atlanta.*]

porpoises have also been observed repeatedly attempting to insert their penis into the anus of an intended male partner, even though females were available (McBride and Hebb, 1948). Such attempts at anal intercourse, however, have been observed only among captive animals and may not occur among animals in the wild. Females also mount other females. I have two female dogs, and they delight in mounting each other, particularly when company is present.

In species that form long-term bonds or relationships, long homosexual bonds have been observed. For example, Konrad Lorenz (1966) has reported a long-term relationship between two male ducks.

Human Uniqueness

The general trend, as we move from lower species such as fish or rodents to higher species such as primates, is for sexual behavior to be more hormonally (instinctively) controlled among lower species and to be controlled more by the nervous system (and therefore by learning) in the higher species (Beach, 1947). Thus environmental influences are much more important in shaping primate—especially human—sexual behavior than they are in shaping the sexual behavior of other species.

An illustration of this is provided by studies of the adult sexual behavior of animals that have been raised in deprived environments. If mice are reared in isolation, their adult sexual behavior will nonetheless be normal (King, 1956, cited by Scott, 1964). But the research of the Harlows shows that if rhesus monkeys are reared in isolation, their adult sexual behavior is severely disturbed, to the point where they may be incapable of reproducing (Harlow et al., 1963). Thus environmental experiences are crucial in shaping the sexual behavior of the higher species, particularly humans; for

us, sexual behavior is a lot more than just "doin' what comes naturally."

Female sexuality provides a particularly good illustration of the shift in hormonal control from lower to higher species. Throughout most of the animal kingdom, female sexual behavior is strongly controlled by hormones. In virtually all species, females do not engage in sexual behavior at all except when they are in "heat" (estrus), which is a particular hormonal and physiological state. In contrast, human females are capable of engaging in sexual behavior— and actually do engage in it—during any phase of their hormonal (menstrual) cycle. Thus the sexual behavior of the human female is not nearly so much under hormonal control as that of females of other species.

Female orgasm is also unique to humans; it does not exist among other species. There is some recent evidence of orgasm in female rhesus monkeys, although this was obtained under very artificial laboratory conditions (Burton, 1970; Zumpe and Michael, 1968). There is no solid evidence of female orgasm among nonhumans living under natural conditions. Thus female orgasm is essentially a unique prerogative of humans.

The Nonsexual Uses of Sexual Behavior

Two male baboons are locked in combat. One begins to emerge as the victor. The other "presents" (the "female" sexual posture, in which the rump is directed toward the other and is elevated somewhat).

Two male monkeys are members of the same troop. Long ago they established which one is dominant and which one is subordinate. The dominant one mounts (the "male" sexual behavior) the subordinate one.

These are examples of the fact that animals sometimes use sexual behavior for nonsexual

FIGURE 1.5

Sexual behavior may be used for a variety of nonsexual purposes, such as to express aggression. This primitive figure is defying his opponent by sticking out his tongue and his erect penis. [*From Philip Rawson.* Primitive erotic art. *Weidenfeld and Nicolson, London, 1973. Photograph: Ferdinand Anton.*]

purposes (Ford and Beach, 1951; Jensen, 1976b). Commonly this is done to signal the end of a fight, as in the first example above. The loser indicates surrender by presenting, and the winner signals victory by mounting. Sexual behaviors can also symbolize an animal's rank in a dominance hierarchy. Dominant animals mount subordinate ones. As another example, male squirrel monkeys sometimes use an exhibitionist display of their erect penis as part of an aggressive display against another male, something that is called *phallic aggression* (Wickler, 1973).

All this is perfectly obvious when we observe it in monkeys. But do humans ever use sexual behavior for nonsexual purposes? Consider the rapist, who uses sex as an expression of aggression against, and power over, a woman (or over another man, in the case of homosexual rape in prisons). Another example is the exhibitionist, who uses the display of his erect penis to shock and frighten women, much as the male squirrel monkey uses this display to shock and frighten his opponent. Humans also use sex for economic purposes; the best examples are prostitutes and gigolos.

There are also less extreme examples. Consider the couple who have a fight and then make love to signal an end to the hostilities.[4] Or consider the woman who goes to bed with an influential—though unattractive—politician because this gives her a vicarious sense of power.

Pediatrician Michael W. Cohen and psychiatrist Stanford B. Friedman (1975) believe that adolescents may use sexual behavior for the following nonsexual purposes:

---

[4]It has been my observation that this practice does not always mean the same thing to the man and to the woman. To the man it can mean that everything is fine again, but the woman can be left feeling dissatisfied and not at all convinced that the issues are resolved. Thus this situation can be a source of miscommunication between the two.

1 *Peer approval* Sexual activity, particularly for males, can be a means of acquiring status in the peer group, getting the approval of one's peers, showing that one is part of the "in" crowd, or proving one's masculinity. "[It is] my impression that male patients feel under more pressure than ever before to prove themselves through the sex act. Many experience difficulty simply because they are more interested in the statusful than the tender aspects of lovemaking" (Halleck, 1967).

2 *Expression of hostility* Some adolescents feel real hostility toward their parents, and engaging in sexual activity may be one of the few ways they have of expressing it.

3 *Rebellion* Teenagers can also engage in sex to rebel against parents and express independence. Ironically, it is precisely because parents feel that they must enforce rules concerning sex that engaging in sexual activity becomes such an effective way for teenagers to express rebellion.

4 *Escape* For the teenage girl who finds living conditions at home intolerable, having sex and becoming pregnant is a good way to ensure getting out of her parents' house.

You can probably think of other examples of the nonsexual use of sexual behavior. Humans, just like members of other species, can use sex for a variety of nonsexual purposes (Marmor, 1969).

SUMMARY

"Sexual behavior" was defined as behavior that produces arousal and increases the chance of orgasm. A distinction was made between "sex" (sexual behavior and anatomy) and "gender" (being male or female).

Throughout most of human history, religion was the main source of information concerning sexuality. In the late 1800s and early 1900s, important contributions to the scientific understanding of sex were made by Sigmund Freud, Havelock Ellis, von Krafft-Ebing, and Magnus Hirschfeld.

Various theoretical perspectives on sexuality were reviewed. In Freud's psychoanalytic theory, the sex energy is the libido, which is part of the id, one of the three major divisions of personality. Freud introduced the concepts of erogenous zones and of psychosexual stages of development. From another theoretical perspective, sexuality is considered a form of motivation or a basic drive like hunger and thirst. Learning theory emphasizes how sexual behavior is learned and modified according to the principles of operant conditioning. Behavior modification techniques—therapies based on learning theory—are used in treating sexual variations and sexual dysfunctions. Humanistic psychologists see self-actualization as the most important process in human life; sex and love may contribute to self-actualization. Eric Berne's transactional analysis describes the personality as being composed of an Adult part, a Parent part, and a Child part; this system can be helpful in understanding sexual interactions. Finally, sociologists see cultural factors and socialization as being extremely important in shaping our sexual behavior.

Studies in various human cultures around the world provide evidence of the enormous variations in human sexual behavior. For example, in a few societies kissing is unknown. Frequency of intercourse may vary from about once a week in some cultures to three or four times a night in others. One generalization that does emerge is that all societies regulate sexual behavior in some way. The great variations provide evidence of the importance of learning in shaping our sexual behavior. Even within the United States, sexual behavior varies with social class and ethnic group.

Studies of sexual behavior in various animal species show that masturbation, mouth-genital stimulation, and homosexual behavior are by no means limited to humans. They also illustrate how sexual behavior may be used for a variety of nonsexual purposes, such as expressing dominance.

SUGGESTIONS FOR FURTHER READING

Berne, Eric. *Sex in human loving.* New York: Simon & Schuster, 1970. An entertaining explanation of Berne's transactional analysis as it applies to sexual interactions.

Freud, S. *A general introduction to psychoanalysis.* Garden City, N.Y.: Garden City Publishing, 1943. (Original in German, 1917.) Good for the reader who wants a basic introduction to Freud. For a good one-chapter summary, see Hall, C. S., and Lindzey, G. *Theories of personality.* (2nd ed.), New York: Wiley, 1970.

Mead, Margaret. *Sex and temperament in three primitive societies.* New York: Morrow, 1935. A fascinating description of Mead's investigations of sex and gender in other cultures.

2

SEXUAL
ANATOMY

CITED

All the body image problems are just heightened when you narrow your sights to your genitals. Even people who don't feel particularly sensitive about how they look to the man on the street feel shy or nervous when confronting their own or another's sexual anatomy. The endless taboos on sex in this society and the misguided romanticism of the airbrush mentality keep people from really looking at their sex organs. . . . To integrate your sex into yourself in a positive way, you have to have a clear picture of your external genitals. You also have to know what goes on inside your body sexually.*

One outgrowth of the feminist movement, the women's health movement, has emphasized that women need to know more about their bodies. Actually, that is a good principle for everyone to follow. The current trend is away from the elitist view that only a select group of people—physicians—should understand the functioning of the body and toward the view that everyone needs more information about his or her own body. The purpose of this chapter is to provide basic information about the structure and functions of the parts of the body that are involved in sexuality and reproduction. Some readers may anticipate that this will be a boring exercise. Everyone, after all, knows what a penis is and what a vagina is. But even today, we find some bright college students who think a woman's urine passes out through her vagina. And how many of you know what the epididymis and the seminiferous tubules are? If you don't know, keep reading. You may even find out a few interesting things about the penis and the vagina that you were not aware of.

*Source: Patricia Raley. Making love. New York: Dial Press, 1976, p. 84.

FEMALE SEXUAL ORGANS

The female sexual organs can be classified into two categories: the *external organs* and the *internal organs*.

External Organs

The external genitals of the female consist of the clitoris, the mons pubis, the inner lips, the outer lips, and the vaginal opening (see Figure 2.1). Collectively, they are known as the *vulva* ("crotch"; other terms such as "cunt" and "pussy" may refer either to the vulva or to the vagina—slang, alas, is not so precise as scientific language).

The clitoris   The *clitoris* (*klit'-or-is*, in slang "man in the boat") is an extremely sensitive organ which is exceptionally important in female sexual response. It is a small knob of tissue situated externally, in front of the vaginal opening. Like the male penis, the clitoris is composed of two parts: the *shaft* and the tip or *glans* (see Figure 2.2). The glans is visible, protruding like a small lump. The shaft disappears into the body beneath the *clitoral hood*, a sheath of tissue that passes around the clitoris and is an extension of the inner lips.

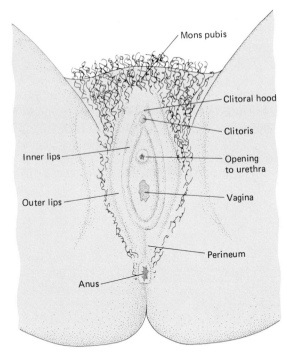

FIGURE 2.1
The external genitals of the female.

Mons pubis

Clitoral hood

Clitoris

Inner lips

Opening
to urethra

Outer lips

Vagina

Perineum

Anus

As will be discussed in Chapter 3, female sexual organs and male sexual organs develop from similar tissue; thus we can speak of the organs of one gender as being *homologous* (similar or parallel) to the organs of the other gender. The female's clitoris is homologous to the male's penis; that is, both develop from the same embryonic tissue. The clitoris has a structure similar to that of the penis in that both have a shaft and a glans. The clitoris varies in size from one woman to the next, much as the penis varies in size from man to man. Also, the clitoris, like the penis, is erectile. Its erection is possible because its internal structure contains *corpora cavernosa* that fill with blood, as the similar structures in the penis do. The corpora cavernosa and the mechanism of erection will be considered in more detail in the discussion of the male sexual organs. Like the penis, the clitoris has a rich supply of nerve endings, making it very sensitive to touch (see Figure 2.2). It is more sensitive to erotic stimulation than any other part of the female body.

The clitoris is unique in that it is the only part of the sexual anatomy with no known reproductive function. All the other sexual organs serve dual sexual-reproductive functions. For example, not only is the vagina used for sexual intercourse, but it also receives the sperm and serves as the passageway through which the baby travels during childbirth. The penis not only produces sexual arousal and pleasure but also is responsible for ejaculation and impregnation. The clitoris clearly has an important function in producing sexual arousal. Unlike the other sexual organs, however, it appears to have no direct function in reproduction.

At various times in history and in various cultures, the clitoris has been subjected to

FIGURE 2.2
The structure of the clitoris and its nerve supply.

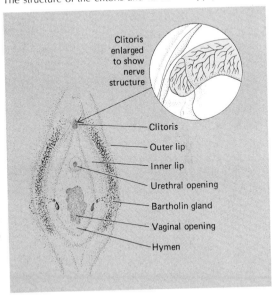

Clitoris
enlarged
to show
nerve
structure

Clitoris

Outer lip

Inner lip

Urethral opening

Bartholin gland

Vaginal opening

Hymen

mutilation. Clitoridectomy—the surgical removal of the clitoris—is rare but has been practiced in the Middle East and in some parts of Africa and Latin America. It is still done in Kenya and some parts of Egypt. It was also advocated and practiced by some physicians in the United States during the Victorian era, ostensibly to cure women who were "compulsive masturbators." The existence of the practice in this country is a commentary on the repressive attitudes of the Victorians toward sexuality and their particularly repressive attitudes toward female sexuality.

The mons In outward appearance, the more obvious parts of the vulva are the mons pubis, the inner lips, and the outer lips. The *mons pubis* (also called the *mons* or the *mons veneris,* for "mountain of Venus") is the rounded, fatty pad of tissue, covered with pubic hair, at the front of the body. It lies on top of the pubic bones (which come together in the center at a point called the *pubic symphysis*) and is the most visible part of the female sexual organs.

The labia The *outer lips* (or *labia majora,* for "major lips") are rounded pads of tissue lying along both sides of the vaginal opening; they are covered with pubic hair. The *inner lips* (or *labia minora,* for "minor lips") are two hairless folds of skin lying between the major lips and running right along the edge of the vaginal opening. Sometimes they may be folded over, concealing the vaginal opening until they are spread apart. The inner lips extend forward and come together in front, forming the clitoral hood. The inner and outer lips are well supplied with nerve endings and thus are also important in sexual stimulation and arousal.

Bartholin's glands A pair of small glands, *Bartholin's glands,* lie just inside the inner lips.

Their functioning is relatively unimportant, except that they sometimes become infected.[1] *Skene's glands* are located nearby and, similarly, attract attention only when infected.

A few more landmarks should be noted (Figure 2.1). The place where the inner lips come together behind the vaginal opening is called the *fourchette.* The area of skin between the vaginal opening and the anus is called the *perineum.* The vaginal opening itself is sometimes called the *introitus.* Notice also that the urinary opening lies about midway between the clitoris and the vaginal opening. Thus urine does not pass out through the clitoris (as might be expected from analogy with the male) or through the vagina, but instead through a separate pathway, the *urethra,* with a separate opening (see also Figure 2.5).

What you see is what you get One important difference between the male sex organs and the female sex organs—and a difference that might have some important psychological consequences—is that the female's external genitals are much less visible than the male's. A male can view his genitals directly either by looking down at them or by looking into a mirror while naked. Either of these two strategies for the female, however, will result at best in a view of the mons. The clitoris, the inner and outer lips, and the vaginal opening remain hidden. Indeed, many adult women have never taken a direct look at their own vulva. The mirror, however, makes this possible. The genitals can be viewed either by putting a mirror on

---

[1]And there is a limerick about them:

There was a young man from Calcutta
Who was heard in his beard to mutter,
  "If her Bartholin glands
  Don't respond to my hands,
I'm afraid I shall have to use butter."

Actually, there is a biological fallacy in the limerick. Can you spot it? If not, see Chap. 7.

FIGURE 2.3
Body education: the mirror exercise lets women see their own genitals. [*Anne Popkin*.]

the floor and squatting over it (see Figure 2.3) or by standing up and putting one foot on the edge of a chair, bed, or something similar and holding the mirror up near the genitals. I recommend that all women use a mirror to identify on their own bodies all the parts shown in Figure

2.1. The female genitals need not remain mysterious to their owner.

The hymen Before the internal structures are discussed, one other external structure deserves mention: the hymen. The *hymen* ("cherry," "maidenhead") is a thin membrane which, if present, is situated at the vaginal opening. The hymen may be present in a number of different conditions (see Figure 2.4), although it generally has some openings in it; otherwise the menstrual flow would not be able to pass out.[2] At the time of first intercourse, the hymen, if present, is broken or stretched as the penis moves into the vagina. This may cause bleeding and possibly some pain. Typically, though, it is an untraumatic occurrence and goes unnoticed in the excitement of the moment. For a woman who is very concerned about her hymen and what will happen to it at first coitus, there are two possible

---

[2]The rare condition in which the hymen is a tough tissue with no opening is called *imperforate hymen* and can be corrected with fairly simple surgery.

FIGURE 2.4
There are several types of hymens.

Annular hymen   Septate hymen   Cribriform hymen   Imperforate hymen

approaches. A physician can cut the hymen neatly so that it will not tear at the time of first intercourse, or the woman herself can stretch it by inserting a finger into the vagina and pressing on it (Lanson, 1975).

The hymen, and its destruction at first intercourse, has captured the interest of people of many cultures. In Europe during the Middle Ages, the lord might claim the right to deflower a peasant bride on her wedding night before passing her on to her husband (the practice is called *droit du seigneur* in French and *jus primae noctis* in Latin). The hymen has been taken as evidence of virginity. Thus bleeding on the wedding night was proof that the bride had been delivered intact to the groom; the parading of the bloody bed sheets on the wedding night, a custom of the Kurds of Arabia, is one of the more obvious rituals based on this belief. In other cultures the destruction of the mysterious hymen has been considered dangerous. In one Australian tribe, the task was accomplished by two old women a week before the wedding. If, at that time, the girl's hymen was discovered not to be in mint condition, she might be tortured or even killed.

These practices rest on the assumption that a woman without a hymen is not a virgin. However, we now know that this is not true. Some females are simply born without a hymen, and others may tear it in active sports such as horseback riding. Unfortunately, this means that some women have been humiliated unjustly for their lack of a hymen.

Internal Organs

The internal sex organs of the female consist of the vagina, the uterus, a pair of ovaries, and a pair of fallopian tubes (see Figures 2.5 and 2.6).

The vagina   The *vagina* is the organ into which the penis is inserted during intercourse, and it receives the ejaculate. It is also the passageway through which the baby travels during birth, and so it is sometimes called the *birth canal*. In the resting state, the vaginal barrel is about 8 to 10 centimeters (3 to 4 inches) long and tilts slightly backward from the bottom to the top. At the bottom it opens to the vaginal opening, or introitus. At the top it connects with the cervix (the lower part of the uterus). It is a very flexible, tube-shaped organ that works somewhat like a balloon. In the "resting" state its walls lie against each other like the sides of an uninflated balloon; during arousal it expands like an inflated balloon, allowing space to accommodate the penis.

The walls of the vagina have three layers. The inner layer, the *vaginal mucosa*, is a mucous membrane similar to the inner lining of the mouth. The middle layer is muscular, and the outer layer forms a covering. The walls of the vagina are extremely elastic and are capable of expanding to the extent necessary during intercourse and childbirth, although with age they become thinner and less flexible.

The nerve supply of the vagina is mostly to the lower one-third, near the introitus. That part is sensitive to erotic stimulation. The upper two-thirds of the vagina contains almost no nerve endings and is therefore very insensitive except to feelings of deep pressure.

The number of slang terms for the vagina (for example, "beaver," "cunt") and the frequency of their usage testify to its powers of fascination across the ages. One concern has been with size: whether some vaginas are too small or too large. As has been noted, though, the vagina is highly elastic and expandable. Thus, at least in principle, any penis can fit into any vagina. The penis is, after all, not nearly so large as a baby's head, which manages to fit through the vagina.

The part of the vagina which is most re-

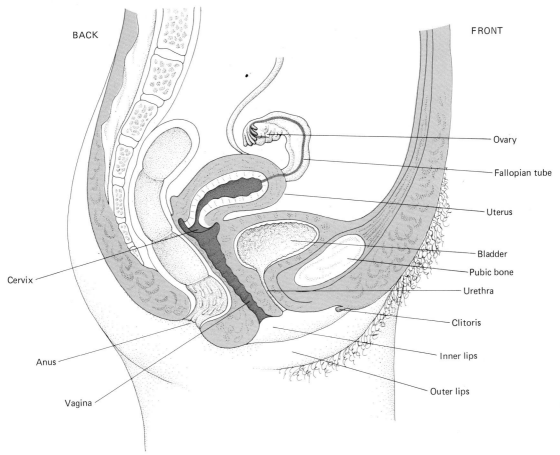

BACK   FRONT

Ovary

Fallopian tube

Uterus

Bladder

Pubic bone

Cervix

Urethra

Clitoris

Inner lips

Anus

Outer lips

Vagina

FIGURE 2.5
Internal sexual and reproductive organs of the female, side view.

sponsible for the male's sensation that it is "tight," "too tight," or "too loose" is the introitus. One of the things that can stretch the introitus is childbirth; indeed, there is a considerable difference between the appearance of the vulva of a woman who has never had a baby (*nulliparous*) and the vulva of a woman who has (*parous*) (see Figure 2.7).

Surrounding the vagina, the urethra, and the anus is a set of muscles called the *pelvic floor muscles* (see Figure 2.8). One of these muscles, the *pubococcygeal* muscle, is particularly important. It may be stretched during childbirth, or it may simply be weak. However, it can be strengthened through exercise, and this is sometimes recommended by sex therapists (see Chapter 18) as well as by many popular sex manuals and magazines.

Because the introitus is highly sensitive, both to pleasure and to pain, and because it is surrounded with muscles, it may reflect a woman's psychological response to sex. If a woman

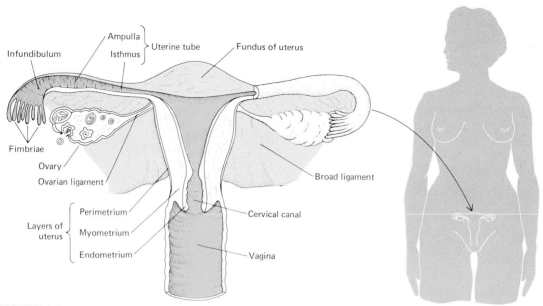

FIGURE 2.6

Internal sexual and reproductive organs of the female, front view.

responds to arousal with fear or anxiety, the muscles may tighten, making it difficult for the penis to enter the vagina. In extreme cases, the muscles become so tight that intercourse is impossible, a condition known as *vaginismus* (see Chapter 18). On the other hand, a very expansive, relaxed introitus also has some disadvantages in that it may not produce enough sensation for the male. Exercising the pubococcygeal muscle should correct this problem. One would not want to turn sex into an athletic event, but a strong pubococcygeus can result in more sensation for the male and contribute to orgasmic capacity in the female.

The vagina has also provoked some anxieties. Some people believe that the penis can be trapped inside the vagina and that the man will be unable to withdraw it. This does occur in dogs. The dog's penis expands inside the vagina, creating a "locking" effect, and separation is impossible until the erection is gone. This does not occur in humans, however. There are also many myths among primitive peoples that the vagina is lined with teeth (*vagina dentata*), thorns, or other dangerous objects that can damage the penis. For example, the Pomo Indians of California have a myth in which a young girl has thorns surrounding her vagina, which her intended husband must break off before marrying her.

The uterus The *uterus* (womb) is about the size of a fist and is shaped somewhat like an upside-down pear. It is usually tilted forward and is held in place by ligaments. The narrow lower third is called the *cervix* and opens into the vagina. The top is the *fundus*, and the main part is the *body*. The entrance to the uterus through the cervix is very narrow, about the size of a straw, and is called the *os* (or cervical canal). The major function of the uterus is to hold and nourish the developing fetus.

discharge. The middle layer, the *myometrium*, is muscular. The muscles are very strong, creating the strong contractions of labor, and are also highly elastic; they are capable of stretching to accommodate a 9-month-old fetus. The outer layer—the *perimetrium* or *serosa*—forms the external cover of the uterus.

The fallopian tubes Extending out from the sides of the upper end of the uterus are the *fallopian tubes*, also called the *oviducts* ("egg ducts") or *uterine tubes* (see Figure 2.6). It is the fallopian tubes that are tied in the tubal ligation

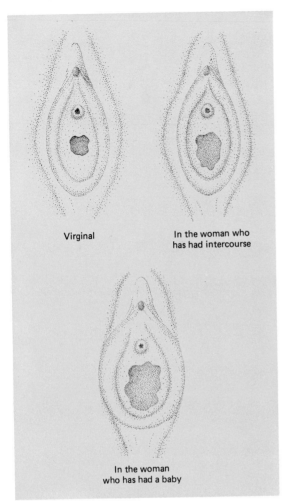

FIGURE 2.7
Appearance of the vulva of a woman who is a virgin; a woman who has had intercourse but has not had a baby (nulliparous); and a woman who has had a baby (parous).

The uterus, like the vagina, consists of three layers. The inner layer, or *endometrium*, is richly supplied with glands and blood vessels. Its state varies according to the age of the woman and the phase of the menstrual cycle. It is the endometrium which is sloughed off at menstruation and creates most of the menstrual

FIGURE 2.8
Muscles on the floor of the pelvis. Note particularly the pubococcygeal muscle, which women may want to exercise (see Chapter 18).

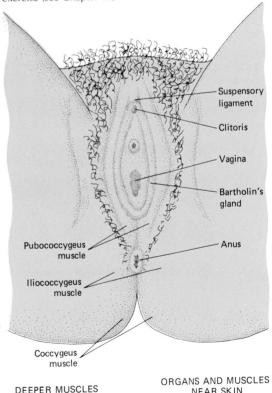

(see Chapter 6). The part of the tubes closest to the uterus is called the *isthmus*, the middle part is called the *ampulla*, and the part closest to the ovaries is called the *infundibulum*. The fallopian tubes are extremely narrow and are lined with hairlike projections called *cilia*. The fallopian tubes are the pathway by which the egg leaves the ovaries and the sperm reach the egg. Fertilization of the egg typically occurs in the infundibulum, and the fertilized egg travels the rest of the way through the tube to the uterus. The infundibulum curves around toward the ovary; at its end are numerous fingerlike projections called *fimbriae* which extend toward the ovary.

The ovaries The *ovaries* are two organs about the size and shape of an unshelled almond; they lie on either side of the uterus. The ovaries have two important functions; they produce eggs (ova), and they manufacture the female sex hormones, *estrogen* and *progesterone*.

Each ovary contains numerous follicles. A *follicle* is a capsule that surrounds an egg (not to be confused with hair follicles, which are quite different). It is estimated that a female is born with about 400,000 immature eggs. Beginning at puberty, one or several of the follicles mature during each menstrual cycle. When the egg has matured, the follicle moves to the surface of the ovary, bursts open, and releases the egg. The ovaries do not actually connect directly to the fallopian tubes. The egg is released into the body cavity and apparently reaches the tube as a result of some mysterious attraction for the fimbriae. If the egg does not reach the tube, it may be fertilized outside the tube, resulting in an abdominal pregnancy (see the section on ectopic pregnancy in Chapter 5). There have also been cases recorded of women who, although they are missing one ovary and the opposite fallopian tube, have nonetheless become pregnant. Apparently in such cases the egg migrates to the tube on the opposite side.

The Breasts

Though they are not actually sex organs, the *breasts* deserve some mention here because of their erotic and reproductive significance. The breast consists of about 15 or 20 clusters of *mammary glands*, each with a separate opening to the nipple, and of fatty and fibrous tissue which surrounds the clusters of glands (see Figure 2.9). The nipple, into which the milk ducts open, is at the tip of the breast. It is richly supplied with nerve endings and therefore very important in erotic stimulation. The nipple consists of smooth muscle fibers; when they con-

FIGURE 2.9
The internal structure of the breast.

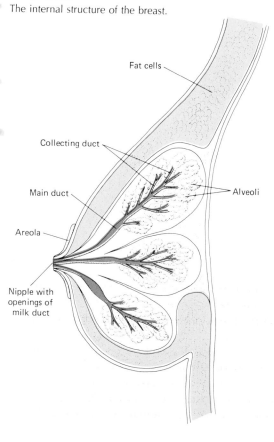

Fat cells

Collecting duct

Main duct

Alveoli

Areola

Nipple with openings of milk duct

tract, the nipple becomes erect. The area surrounding the nipple is called the *areola*.

There is wide variation among women in the size and shape of the breasts. One thing is fairly consistent, though. Few women are satisfied with the size of their breasts. Most women think they are either too small or too large, and almost no woman thinks hers are just right. It is well to remember that there are the same number of nerve endings in small breasts as in large breasts. It follows that small breasts are actually more erotically sensitive per square inch than large ones (McCary, 1973).

Breasts may take on enormous psychological meaning; they can be a symbol of femininity or a means of attracting men. Men also, particularly in the United States, may develop a nearly overpowering interest in, and attraction to, women's breasts.

The Pelvic Exam

All adult women should have an annual checkup that includes a thorough pelvic exam. Among other things, such an exam is extremely important in the detection of cervical cancer, and early detection is the key to cure (see Chapter 19). Some women neglect to have the exam because they feel anxious or embarrassed about it; however, having regular pelvic exams can be a matter of life and death. Actually, the exam is quite simple and need not cause any discomfort. The following is a description of the procedures involved in a pelvic exam (Boston Women's Health Book Collective, 1976).

First, the physician inspects the external genitals, checking for irritations, discolorations, bumps, lice, adhesions to the clitoris, skin lesions, and unusual vaginal discharge. Then there is an internal check for *cystoceles* (bulges of the bladder into the vagina) and *rectoceles* (bulges of the rectum into the vagina), for pus in the Skene glands, for cysts in the Bartholin glands, and for the strength of the pelvic floor muscles and abdominal muscles. There is also a test for stress incontinence; the physician asks the patient to cough and checks to see whether urine flows involuntarily.

Next comes the speculum exam. The *speculum* is a metal (sometimes plastic) instrument that is inserted into the vagina to hold the vaginal walls apart so as to permit examination (see Figure 2.10). Once the speculum is in place (it should be prewarmed to body temperature if it is metal), the physician looks for any unusual signs, such as lesions, inflammation, or unusual discharge from the vaginal walls, and for any signs of infections or damage to the cervix. The physician then uses a small metal spatula to scrape a tiny bit of tissue from the cervix for the Pap test for cervical cancer. If done properly, this should be painless. A smear of discharge should also be taken to check for gonorrhea.

If the woman is interested in seeing her own cervix, she can ask the doctor to hold up a mirror so that she can view it through the speculum. Indeed, some women's groups now advocate that women learn to use a speculum and give themselves regular exams with it; early detection of diseases would thus be much more likely (for a more detailed description, see Boston Women's Health Book Collective, 1976).

Next, the physician does a bimanual vaginal exam. He or she slides the index and middle fingers of one hand into the vagina and then, with the other hand, presses down from the outside on the abdominal wall (Figure 2.10). The physician then feels for the position of the uterus, tubes, and ovaries and for any signs of growths, pain, or inflammation.

Finally, the physician may also do a rectovaginal exam by inserting one finger into the vagina and one into the rectum; this provides further information on the positioning of the pelvic organs.

Once again, it is important to emphasize that these are not painful procedures and that

(a)

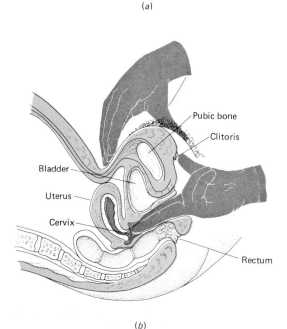

(b)

FIGURE 2.10
(a) The speculum in place for a pelvic exam. The Ayre spatula is used to get a sample of cells for the Pap test. (b) The bimanual pelvic exam.

having them performed regularly is extremely important to a woman's health.

MALE SEXUAL ORGANS

Externally, the most obvious parts of the male sexual anatomy are the penis and the scrotum, or scrotal sac, which contains the testes (see Figure 2.11).

The Penis

The *penis* (phallus, "prick," "cock," and many other slang terms too numerous to list) serves important functions in sexual pleasure, reproduction, and elimination of body wastes by urination. It is a tubular organ with an end or tip called the *glans*. The opening at the end of the glans is the *meatus*, or *urethral opening*, through which urine and semen pass. The part of the penis that attaches to the body is called the *root*, and the main part of the penis is called the *body*. The raised ridge separating the glans from the body of the penis is called the *corona*, or *coronal ridge*. While the entire penis is sensitive to sexual stimulation, the glans and corona are by far the most sexually excitable region of the male anatomy.

Internally, the penis contains three long cylinders of spongy tissue running parallel to the *urethra*, which is the pathway through which semen and urine pass (see Figure 2.12). The two spongy bodies lying on top are called the *corpora cavernosa*, and the single one lying on the bottom of the penis is called the *corpus spongiosum* (the urethra runs through the middle of it). During erection, the latter one can be seen as a raised column on the lower side of the penis. As the names suggest, these bodies are tissues filled with many spaces or cavities, much like a sponge. They are richly supplied with blood vessels and nerves. In the flaccid (unaroused) state, they contain little blood. *Erection*, or *tumescence*, occurs when they

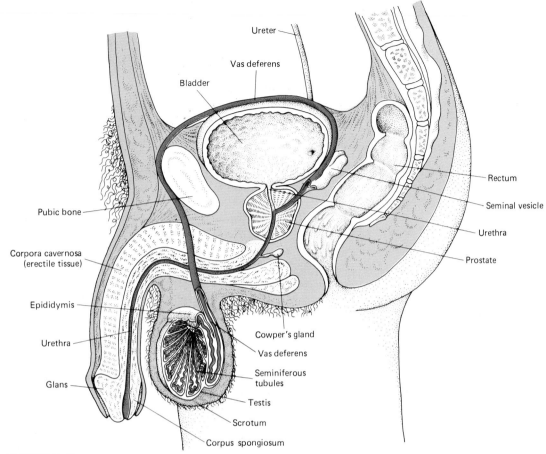

Ureter

Vas deferens

Bladder

Pubic bone

Corpora cavernosa
(erectile tissue)

Epididymis

Urethra

Glans

Cowper's gland

Vas deferens

Seminiferous
tubules

Testis

Scrotum

Corpus spongiosum

Rectum

Seminal vesicle

Urethra

Prostate

FIGURE 2.11
The male sexual and reproductive organs, side view.

become filled with blood (engorged) and expand, making the penis stiff.

Contrary to popular belief, the penis does not contain a muscle, and no muscle is involved in erection. Erection is purely a vascular phenomenon; that is, it results entirely from blood flow. It is also commonly believed that the penis of the human male contains a bone. This is not true either. In some other species—for example, dogs—the penis does contain a bone, which

aids in intromission (inserting the penis into the vagina). In human males, however, there is none, and a man must accomplish intromission purely on the strength of his own erection.

The skin of the penis is hairless and is arranged in loose folds, permitting expansion during erection. The *foreskin*, or *prepuce*, is an additional layer of skin which forms a sheath-like covering over the glans; it may be present or absent in the adult male, depending on

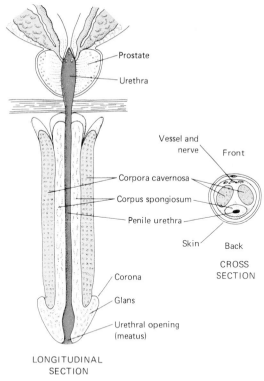

Prostate

Urethra

Vessel and
nerve   Front

Corpora cavernosa

Corpus spongiosum

Penile urethra

Skin   Back

CROSS
SECTION

Corona

Glans

Urethral opening
(meatus)

LONGITUDINAL
SECTION

FIGURE 2.12
The internal structure of the penis.

whether he has been circumcised (see Figure 2.13). Under the foreskin are small glands which produce a cheesy substance called *smegma*. The foreskin is easily retractable,[3] and its retraction is extremely important for proper hygiene. If it is not retracted and the glans washed thoroughly, the smegma may accumulate, producing a very unpleasant smell.

Circumcision refers to the surgical cutting away or removal of the foreskin. Circumcision is practiced widely throughout the world and is done routinely to most infants in the United States on the second day after birth.

---

[3]In a rare condition, the foreskin is so tight that it cannot be retracted; this is called *phimosis* and requires circumcision.

Typically, circumcision is done for hygienic reasons and ritualistic reasons. Hygienic reasons lie behind its routine practice in the United States. The hygienic argument is that removal of the foreskin permits much better cleansing of the penis; thus smegma and bacteria will not have a tendency to accumulate, as they may when the foreskin is present.

Circumcision may also be practiced for ritualistic or religious reasons. Circumcision has been a part of Jewish religious practice for thousands of years. It symbolizes the covenant between God and the Jewish people and is done on the eighth day after birth, according to scriptural teaching (Genesis 17:9–27). In some cultures circumcision may be done at puberty as an initiation ritual, or *rite de passage*. The ability of the young boy to stand the pain may be seen as a proof of manhood.

A particularly exotic mutilation of the penis occurs in a surgical ritual known as *subincision*. In this operation, which is common among primitive tribes, especially those in central Australia, a slit is made on the lower side of the penis along its entire length and to the depth of the urethra. Urine is then excreted at the base rather than at the tip.

Some proponents of circumcision extend the health arguments and say that circumcision may help reduce the risk of cancer. There is some evidence that cancer of the penis is less frequent among the circumcised than among the uncircumcised (Hand, 1970; Licklider, 1961). There is also evidence that cancer of the cervix is less frequent among wives of circumcised men than among wives of uncircumcised men (Weiner et al., 1951; but see Hand, 1970). The scientific data, however, are not nearly adequate enough to allow one to conclude that circumcision reduces the risk of cancer or that lack of circumcision increases it.

Other arguments have focused on whether the circumcised or the uncircumcised male receives more pleasure from sexual intercourse.

(a)

(b)

FIGURE 2.13

(a) A circumcised penis and (b) an uncircumcised penis, showing the foreskin. [*Albert Einstein College of Medicine.*]

One point of view has it that the circumcised male derives more pleasure because removal of the foreskin exposes the glans, the most sensitive part of the penis, thus allowing it to receive more stimulation. Another point of view is that the uncircumcised male derives more pleasure because his foreskin keeps the glans from rubbing against clothing and so being desensitized; thus when it is exposed during arousal, it is more sensitive. In fact, Masters and Johnson (1966) have found that there is no difference in excitability between the circumcised and the uncircumcised penis.

To say the least, the penis has been the focus of quite a lot of attention throughout history. In some cultures, the attention has become so pronounced that the male genitals have actually become the object of religious worship (phallic worship). Not surprisingly, the male genitals were often seen as symbols of fertility and thus were worshiped for their powers of procreativity. In ancient Greece, phallic worship centered on Priapus, the son of Aphrodite (the goddess of love) and Dionysus (the god of fertility and wine). Priapus is usually represented as a grinning man with a huge penis. The Romans apparently wore amulets which represented the male genitals.

In contemporary American society, phallic concern often focuses on the size of the penis. It is commonly believed that the man with a large penis is a better lover than the man with a small penis and can satisfy a woman more. Masters and Johnson (1966), however, have found that this is not true. While there is considerable variation in the length of the penis from one man to the next—the average penis is generally somewhere between 6.4 centimeters (2.5 inches) and 10 centimeters (4 inches) in length when flaccid (not erect)—there seems to be a tendency for the small penis to grow more in erection than the one that starts out large. As a result, there is little correlation between the length of the penis when flaccid and the length when erect. As the saying has it, "Erection is the great equalizer." The average erect penis is about 15 centimeters (6 inches) long; as indicated, there tends to be somewhat less variation in the length of the erect penis than in the length of the flaccid one, although erect penises longer than 33 centimeters (13 inches) have been measured (Dickinson, 1949). Further, as Masters and Johnson note, the vagina has relatively few nerve endings and is relatively insensitive. Hence penetration to the far reaches of the vagina by a very long penis is not essential and may not even be noticeable. Many other factors are more important than penis size in giving a woman pleasure (see Chapters 8 and 18).

Phallic concern has also included an interest in the variations in the shape of the penis when flaccid and when erect, as reflected in this famous limerick:

> There was a young man of Kent
> Whose kirp in the middle was bent.
> To save himself trouble
> He put it in double,
> And instead of coming, he went.

Phallic concern has also been expressed in psychological theory, the best example being in psychoanalytic theory. According to Freud, concern for the penis and a related castration anxiety are the key factors in male psychological development, leading to the resolution of the Oedipus complex, increased independence from parents, and increased psychological maturity. All this from such a small part of the body! (Indeed, the theory even says that the key factor in female psychological development is the *lack* of a penis.)

The Scrotum and Testes

The other major part of the external genitals in the male is the *scrotum*; this is a loose pouch of skin, lightly covered with hair, which holds the testes (the whole apparatus, scrotum plus testes, is called "balls" or "nuts" in slang[4]). The testes themselves are considered part of the internal genitals.

The *testes*[5] are the gonads, or reproductive glands, of the male, and thus they are analogous to the female's ovaries. Like the ovaries, they serve two major functions: they manufacture germ cells (sperm), and they manufacture the male sex hormone, *testosterone*. Both testes are about the same size, although the left one usually hangs lower than the right one.

In the internal structure of the testes, three parts are important: the seminiferous tubules, the interstitial cells, and the epididymis, which is really a structure adjacent to the testis (see Figure 2.14). The *seminiferous tubules* carry out the important function of manufacturing and storing sperm, a process called *spermatogenesis*. They are a long series of threadlike tubes curled and packed densely into the testes. There are about 1000 of these tubules, and it is estimated that if they were stretched out end to end they would be several hundred feet in length.

The *interstitial cells* (or *Leydig's cells*) carry out the second important function of the testes, the production of the male sex hormone, testosterone. These cells are found in the connective tissue lying between the seminiferous tubules. The cells lie close to the blood vessels in the testes and pour the hormones they manufacture directly into the blood vessels. Thus the testes are endocrine glands.

Each testis is surrounded by a tight, whitish

---

[4]That reminds me of another limerick:

There once was a pirate named Gates
Who thought he could rhumba on skates.
  He slipped on his cutlass
  And now he is nutless
And practically useless on dates.

[5]"Testes" is from the root meaning "witnesses" and comes from the same root as "testimony" does. It is derived from the ancient custom of placing the hand on the genitals when taking an oath. The singular of "testes" is "testis."

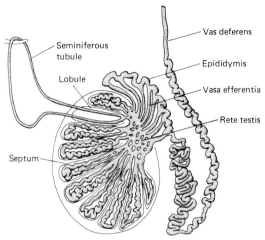

FIGURE 2.14
Schematic cross section of the internal structure of the testis.

Labels in figure:
- Seminiferous tubule
- Lobule
- Septum
- Vas deferens
- Epididymis
- Vasa efferentia
- Rete testis

fibrous sheath (the *tunica albuginea*). In addition to encapsulating the testis, the sheath also extends into it, dividing it into sections, much like a grapefruit; each section is filled with seminiferous tubules. It is this sheath which is responsible for the problem of sterility in the adult male caused by mumps. When the virus invades the testes, it causes them to swell. The tunica albuginea is tight, however, and does not permit expansion. The delicate tubules are thus crushed, which impairs their sperm-producing function. Mumps is not a problem in the female because the ovaries are not enclosed in a comparable tight sheath.

One of the clever tricks that the scrotum and testes perform, as any male will testify, is that they can move up and close to the body or down and away from the body. These changes are brought about mainly by temperature (although emotional factors may also produce them). If a man plunges into a cold lake, the scrotum will shrivel and move close to the body. If the man is working in an extremely hot place, the scrotum will hang down and away from the body. This mechanism is important because the testes should remain at a fairly constant temperature, slightly lower than normal body temperature. This constancy of temperature is necessary to protect sperm, which may be injured by extremes of temperature. Thus if the air is cold, the testes move closer to the body to maintain warmth, but if the air is too hot, they move away from the body to keep cool. The mechanics of this movement are made possible by the *dartos muscle*, which forms the middle layer of the scrotum. It contracts or relaxes reflexively, thereby moving the testes up or down.

Many people believe that taking long, hot baths, wearing tight athletic supporters, or having a high fever can cause infertility. Indeed, in some countries the men take long, hot baths as a method of contraception. Such a practice has some basis in biological fact, since sperm can be destroyed by heat. However, as a method of contraception, this practice has not been particularly effective. In one study, it was found that the use of a special jockstrap raised the temperature of the scrotum by nearly 1°C (1.7°F) and that wearing the device daily for seven weeks caused about a 25 percent reduction in the number of sperm produced (Robinson and Rock, 1967). Thus such practices might decrease a man's fertility somewhat, but they are far from 100 percent effective as contraceptives.

Sperm

Following manufacture in the seminiferous tubules, the male germ cells go through several stages of maturation. At the earliest stage, the cell is called a *spermatogonium*. Then it becomes a *spermatocyte* (first primary and then secondary) and then a *spermatid*. Finally, when fully mature, it is a *spermatozoan*, or *sperm*. *Spermatogenesis*, the manufacture of sperm, occurs continuously in the adult human male.

An average ejaculate contains about 300 million sperm.

A mature sperm is very tiny—about 60 microns, or 60/10,000 millimeter (0.0024 inch) long—and consists of a head, a neck, a midpiece, and a tail (see Figure 2.15). A normal sperm carries 23 chromosomes in the head. This 23 is half the normal number in the other cells of the human body. When the sperm unites with the egg, which also carries 23 chromosomes, the full complement of 46 for the offspring is produced.

Human cells contain two sex chromosomes: XX in the female and XY in the male (see Chapter 3). Because germ cells contain only half of the full number, they contain only one sex chromosome. Thus each egg contains one X chromosome. A sperm may contain either an X chromosome or a Y chromosome.

Landrum B. Shettles has recently provided evidence that there are noticeable differences between X-bearing sperm and Y-bearing sperm (Figure 2.15) and has argued that these differences may permit couples to control the sex of their offspring. According to Shettles, Y sperm have smaller heads and longer tails than X sperm; Y sperm are lighter and move faster, but they are also more vulnerable to destruction. X sperm have larger heads, and they are heavier, move more slowly, and survive better.

Capitalizing on these differences, Shettles recommends the following: For a couple wishing a girl, the woman should use an acidic douche (2 tablespoons of vinegar in a quart of water) before intercourse (acidity destroys sperm, and presumably the "weak" Y sperm will be destroyed, and the stronger X sperm will survive). There should be shallow penetration at the time of ejaculation, and the woman should not experience orgasm (to capitalize on the greater vulnerability of Y sperm if they have to make a long journey). The couple should have intercourse regularly and then stop two or three days before ovulation so that the weaker Y sperm will die off before the egg arrives.

FIGURE 2.15

A photomicrograph of sperm. Note the difference between the X-bearing sperm (larger, oval head) and the Y-bearing sperm (smaller head, longer tail). [*Dr. Landrum B. Shettles.*]

For a couple wishing a boy, the procedures are reversed. The woman should use an alkaline douche (2 tablespoons of baking soda in a quart of water), there should be deep penetration at the time of ejaculation, and the woman should have an orgasm. The couple should abstain from intercourse for several days before ovulation and have intercourse just after the woman ovulates. For some reason, abstinence appears to increase the proportion of Y sperm, and timing intercourse after ovulation allows the quick Y sperm an advantage in getting to the egg in time (Shettles, 1972).

Shettles has also found, interestingly, that about 160 males are conceived for every 100 females and that about 105 males are born for every 100 females. These results are peculiar if one assumes that equal numbers of X-bearing and Y-bearing sperm are produced.

After the sperm are manufactured in the seminiferous tubules, they proceed into the *rete testes*, a converging network of tubes on the surface of the testis toward the top. The sperm then pass out of the testis and into a single tube, the epididymis. The *epididymis* is a long tube (about 6 meters, or 20 feet in length) coiled into a small crescent-shaped region on the top and side of the testis. The sperm may be stored in the epididymis, in which they ripen and mature, possibly for as long as six weeks.

At the end of the epididymis, the sperm pass into another tube, the *vas deferens*, or *ductus deferens* (it is the vas which is cut in a vasectomy—see Chapter 6). The vas passes up and out of the scrotum and then follows a peculiar circular path as it loops over the pubic bone, travels across beside the urinary bladder, and then turns downward toward the prostate. As the tube passes through the prostate, it narrows, and at this point it is called the *ejaculatory duct*. The ejaculatory duct then opens into the *urethra*, which has the dual function of conveying sperm and conveying urine; sperm move, via the urethra, out through the penis.

Apparently sperm have little motility (capability of movement) of their own while in the epididymis and vas. Not until they mix with the secretions of the prostate and seminal vesicles are they capable of movement on their own. It is thought that, up to this point, they are conveyed by the cilia and by contractions of the epididymis and vas.

Other Internal Structures

The *seminal vesicles* are two saclike structures which lie above the prostate, behind the bladder, and in front of the rectum. They empty their contents into the ejaculatory duct to combine with the sperm. Their exact function has been debated. It was once assumed that they stored the sperm, but it is now thought that they secrete a fluid which activates the sperm's motility.

The *prostate* lies below the bladder and is about the size and shape of a chestnut. It is composed of both muscle and glandular tissue. The prostate secretes a milky alkaline fluid which composes the major portion of the semen, or ejaculate. It is thought that the alkalinity of the secretion provides a favorable environment for the sperm and helps prevent their destruction by the acidity of the vagina. The prostate is fairly small at birth, enlarges at puberty, and typically shrinks in old age. It may become enlarged enough so that it interferes with urination, in which case surgery is required. Its size can be determined by rectal examination.

Cowper's glands, or the *bulbourethral glands*, are located just below the prostate and empty into the urethra. During sexual arousal, these glands secrete a small amount of a clear alkaline fluid, which appears as a droplet at the tip of the penis before ejaculation occurs. It is thought that the function of this secretion is to neutralize the acidic urethra, allowing safe passage of the sperm. Generally it is not produced in sufficient quantity to serve as a lubricant in intercourse. About 20 to 25 percent of the time, the fluid contains some stray sperm (Stone, 1931). Thus a woman may become pregnant from the sperm in this fluid even though the man has not ejaculated.

SUMMARY

The important external sexual organs in the female are the clitoris, the mons, the inner lips, the outer lips, and the vaginal opening. The clitoris is an extremely sensitive organ and is very important in female sexual response. Another important external structure is the hymen, which has taken on great symbolic significance as a sign of virginity, although its absence is not a reliable indicator that a woman is not a virgin. The important internal structures are the vagina, which receives the penis during intercourse; the uterus, which houses the developing fetus; the ovaries, which produce eggs and manufacture sex hormones; and the fallopian tubes, which convey the egg to the uterus. The breasts of the female also function in sexual arousal and may have great symbolic significance.

The important external sexual organs in the male are the penis and the scrotum. The penis contains three spongy bodies which, when filled with blood, produce an erection. Circumcision, or surgical removal of the foreskin of the penis, is practiced routinely in the United States. The scrotum contains the testes, which are responsible for the manufacture of sperm (in the seminiferous tubules) and sex hormones (in the interstitial cells). The temperature of the testes is important and is regulated by the contraction and relaxation of the dartos muscle in the scrotum. Sperm pass out of the testes during ejaculation via the vas deferens, the ejaculatory duct, and the urethra. The prostate manufactures most of the fluid that mixes with the sperm to form semen. Cowper's glands and the seminal vesicles also contribute secretions.

SUGGESTIONS FOR FURTHER READING

Boston Women's Health Book Collective. *Our bodies, ourselves.* (2nd ed.) New York: Simon & Schuster, 1976. A good, easy-to-read source on female biology and sexuality.

Netter, F. H. *Reproductive system.* The Ciba Collection of Medical Illustrations. Vol. 2. Summit, N.J.: Ciba, 1965. Generally considered to be the best set of illustrations of the sexual and reproductive anatomy available. Also includes brief explanations.

Rorvik, David M., with Shettles, Landrum B. *Your baby's sex: Now you can choose.* New York: Dodd, Mead, 1970. A discussion of the history of attempts to choose the sex of offspring and a description of Shettles's research, which was mentioned in this chapter. Rorvik is a scientific writer, and he and Shettles have produced a readable and interesting book.

3

SEX HORMONES AND SEXUAL DIFFERENTIATION

The sexual anatomy of the adult male and the adult female was considered in Chapter 2. One of the marvels of human biology is that these complex and different anatomies—males with penis and scrotum; females with vagina, uterus, and breasts—arise from a single cell, the fertilized egg, which varies only in whether it carries two X chromosomes (XX) or one X and one Y (XY). Many of the structural differences between males and females arise before birth, during the *prenatal period*, in a process called *prenatal sexual differentiation.* Further differences also develop during puberty. It is this process of sexual differentiation—both prenatally and at puberty—which will be examined in this chapter. First, however, another biological system, the endocrine (hormonal) system, needs to be considered; particular attention will be given to the sex hormones, which play a major role in the differentiation process.

SEX HORMONES

Hormones are powerful chemical substances manufactured by the *endocrine glands* and secreted directly into the bloodstream. Because they go into the blood, their effects are felt fairly rapidly and at places in the body quite distant from the place in which they were manufactured. The most important sex hormones are *testosterone* (one of a group of hormones called *androgens*) in the male and *estrogen* and *progesterone* in the female. The thyroid, the adrenals, and the pituitary are examples of endocrine glands. We are interested here in the sex glands: the testes in the male and the ovaries in the female. The *pituitary gland* and a closely related region of the brain, the *hypothalamus,* are also important because the pituitary regulates the other glands, in particular the testes and ovaries. Because of its importance, the pituitary has been called the ''mastermind'' of the endocrine system. The pituitary is a small

gland, about the size of a pea, which hangs down from the lower side of the brain. It is divided into three lobes: the anterior lobe, the intermediary lobe, and the posterior lobe. The anterior lobe is the one that interacts with the gonads. The hypothalamus is a region at the base of the brain just above the pituitary (see Figure 3.1); it plays a part in regulating many vital behaviors such as eating, drinking, and sexual behavior, and it is important in regulating the pituitary.

FIGURE 3.1

The hypothalamus-pituitary-gonad feedback loop in women, which regulates production of the sex hormones.

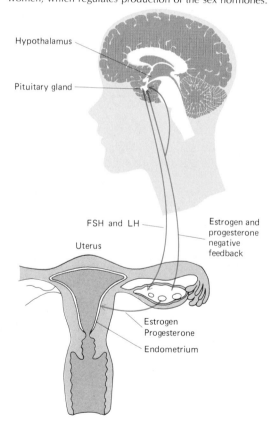

Hypothalamus

Pituitary gland

FSH and LH

Uterus

Estrogen and progesterone negative feedback

Estrogen Progesterone

Endometrium

These three structures, then—hypothalamus, pituitary, and gonads (testes and ovaries) —function together. They influence such important sexual functions as the menstrual cycle, pregnancy, the changes of puberty, and sexual behavior. Because these systems are, not surprisingly, somewhat different in males and in females, the sex hormone systems in the male and in the female will be discussed separately.

Sex Hormone Systems in the Male

The pituitary and the testes both produce hormones. The important hormone produced by the testes is *testosterone*. Testosterone, the "male" sex hormone, has important functions in stimulating and maintaining the secondary sex characteristics (such as beard growth), maintaining the genitals and their sperm-producing capability, and stimulating the growth of bone and muscle.

The pituitary produces several hormones, two of which are important in this discussion: *follicle-stimulating hormone* (FSH) and *luteinizing hormone* (LH; also called *interstitial-cell-stimulating hormone* [ICSH] in the male). These hormones affect the functioning of the testes. LH (ICSH) controls the amount of testosterone production, and FSH controls sperm production.

Testosterone levels in males are relatively constant. These constant levels are maintained because the hypothalamus, pituitary, and testes operate in a *negative feedback loop* (Figure 3.2). The levels of testosterone are regulated by LH. The output of LH is in turn regulated by a substance called *LH-releasing factor*, which is secreted by the hypothalamus (FSH levels are similarly regulated by FSH-releasing factor produced by the hypothalamus). The system comes full circle because the hypothalamus is sensitive to the levels of testosterone present, and thus

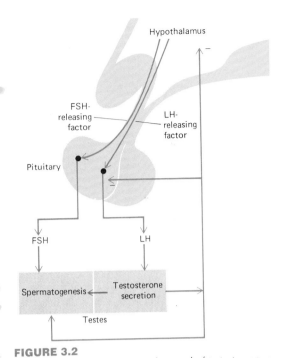

FIGURE 3.2
Schematic diagram of hormonal control of testosterone secretion and sperm production by the testes. The negative signs indicate that testosterone inhibits LH production, both in the pituitary and in the hypothalamus. [*Adapted from A. J. Vander, J. H. Sherman, and D. Luciano.* Human physiology: The mechanisms of body function. *(2nd ed.) New York: McGraw-Hill, 1975.*]

testosterone influences the output of LH-releasing factor.

This negative feedback loop operates much like a thermostat-furnace system. If a room is cold, certain changes occur in the thermostat, and it signals the furnace to turn on. The action of the furnace warms the air in the room. Eventually the air becomes so warm that another change is produced in the thermostat, and it sends a signal to the furnace to turn off. The temperature in the room then gradually falls until it produces another change in the thermostat, which then turns on the furnace, and the cycle is repeated. This is a *negative* feedback loop because *rises* in temperature turn *off* the furnace, while *decreases* in temperature turn *on* the furnace.

The hypothalamus, pituitary, and testes form a similar negative feedback loop ensuring that testosterone is maintained at a fairly constant level, just as the temperature of a room is kept fairly constant. The pituitary's production of LH stimulates the testes to produce testosterone. But when testosterone levels get high, the hypothalamus reduces its production of LH-releasing factor; the pituitary's production of LH is then reduced, and the production of testosterone by the testes consequently decreases. When it has fallen, the hypothalamus again increases production of LH-releasing factor, and the process starts again.

While the level of testosterone in men is fairly constant, there is probably some cycling, with variations according to the time of the day and possibly according to the time of the month (see Chapter 4).

Sex Hormone Systems in the Female

The ovaries produce two important hormones, *estrogen* and *progesterone*. The functions of estrogen include bringing about many of the changes of puberty (stimulating the growth of the uterus and vagina, enlarging the pelvis, and stimulating breast growth). Estrogen is also responsible for maintaining the mucous membranes of the vagina and stopping the growth of bone and muscle, which accounts for the smaller size of females as compared with males.

In adult women the levels of estrogen and progesterone fluctuate according to the various phases of the menstrual cycle (see Chapter 4) and during various other stages such as pregnancy and menopause. The levels of estrogen and progesterone are regulated by the two pituitary hormones, FSH and LH. Thus the levels of estrogen and progesterone are con-

trolled by a negative feedback loop of the hypothalamus, pituitary, and ovaries, similar to the negative feedback loop in the male (see Figure 3.3). For example, as shown in the right side of Figure 3.3, increases in the level of LH-releasing factor increase the level of LH, and the increases in LH eventually produce increases in the output of estrogen; finally, the increases in the level of estrogen inhibit (decrease) the production of LH-releasing factor and LH.

The pituitary produces a third hormone, *prolactin*, which plays a role in stimulating

FIGURE 3.3

Schematic diagram of hormonal control of estrogen secretion and ovum production by the ovaries (during the follicular phase of the menstrual cycle). Note how similar the mechanism is to the one in the male (Figure 3.2). [*Adapted from A. J. Vander, J. H. Sherman, and D. Luciano. Human physiology: The mechanisms of body function. (2nd ed.) New York: McGraw-Hill, 1975.*]

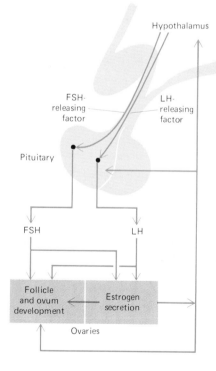

secretion of milk by the mammary glands after a woman has given birth to a child.

The female sex hormone system functions much like the male sex hormone system, except that the female system is, in two senses, somewhat more complex: the ovaries produce two major hormones (unlike the testes, which produce only one), and the levels of hormones fluctuate in females, whereas levels are fairly constant in males.

The functioning of the female sex hormone system and the menstrual cycle will be considered in more detail in Chapter 4.

PRENATAL SEXUAL DIFFERENTIATION

Sex Chromosomes

As noted above, at the time of conception the future human being consists only of a single cell, the fertilized egg. The only difference between the fertilized egg that will become a female and the fertilized egg that will become a male is the sex chromosomes carried in that fertilized egg. If there are two X chromosomes, the result will normally be a female; if there is one X and one Y, the result will normally be a male. Thus, while incredibly tiny, the sex chromosomes carry a wealth of information which they transmit to various organs of the body, giving them instructions on how to differentiate in the course of development.

Occasionally, individuals receive at conception a sex chromosome combination other than XX or XY. Such abnormal sex chromosome complements may lead to a variety of clinical syndromes.

The single cell divides repeatedly, becoming a two-celled organism, then a four-celled organism, then an eight-celled organism, and so on. By the time the embryo is 28 days of age (postconception), it is about 1 centimeter (less than $1/2$ inch) long, but the male and female embryo are still identical, save for the sex chromosomes; that is, the embryo is still in the undifferentiated state. However, by the fifth or sixth week after conception some basic structures have been formed that will eventually become either a male or a female reproductive system. At this point, the embryo has a pair of gonads (each gonad has two parts, an outer cortex and an inner medulla), two sets of ducts (the *Müllerian ducts* and the *Wolffian ducts*), and rudimentary external genitals (the *genital tubercle*, the *genital folds*, and the *genital swelling*) (see Figure 3.4).

Gonads

Around the seventh week after conception, the sex chromosomes direct the gonads to begin differentiation. In the male, the undifferentiated gonad develops into a testis at about 7 weeks. The testes develop from the part of the gonads called the medulla. In the female, the process occurs somewhat later, with the ovaries developing out of the gonadal cortex at around 11 or 12 weeks.

There has been a good deal of speculation about the exact mechanisms by which the presence of XX chromosomes causes ovaries to develop and the presence of XY chromosomes causes testes to develop. Basically, it appears that the presence or absence of a Y chromosome is critical. If no Y chromosome is present, ovaries differentiate, and female development occurs; if a Y is present, testes differentiate, and male development occurs. Apparently, the Y chromosome produces a substance which induces the differentiation of testes (Jost, 1970). Thus it seems that nature's basic plan is to make a female and that the addition of a Y chromosome produces a variation, the male.

Hormones and the Internal and External Genitals

Once the ovaries and testes have differentiated, they begin to produce different sex hormones, and these hormones then direct the differentia-

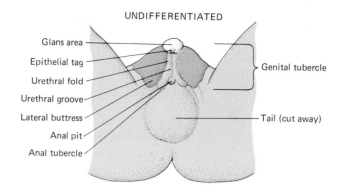

UNDIFFERENTIATED

Glans area
Epithelial tag
Urethral fold
Urethral groove
Lateral buttress
Anal pit
Anal tubercle

Genital tubercle
Tail (cut away)

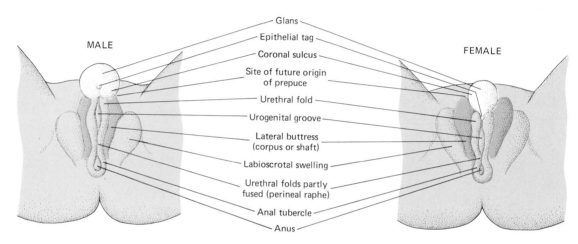

MALE   FEMALE

Glans
Epithelial tag
Coronal sulcus
Site of future origin
of prepuce
Urethral fold
Urogenital groove
Lateral buttress
(corpus or shaft)
Labioscrotal swelling
Urethral folds partly
fused (perineal raphe)
Anal tubercle
Anus

FULLY DEVELOPED

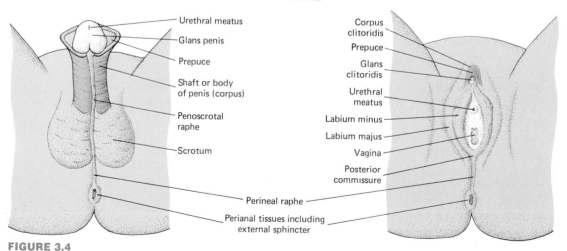

Urethral meatus
Glans penis
Prepuce
Shaft or body
of penis (corpus)
Penoscrotal
raphe
Scrotum

Corpus
clitoridis
Prepuce
Glans
clitoridis
Urethral
meatus
Labium minus
Labium majus
Vagina
Posterior
commissure

Perineal raphe
Perianal tissues including
external sphincter

FIGURE 3.4
Development of the male and female genitals from the undifferentiated stages.
This occurs during prenatal development. Note homologous organs in the female
and male.

tion of the rest of the internal and external genital system (see Figure 3.4).

In the female the Wolffian ducts degenerate, and the Müllerian ducts turn into the fallopian tubes, the uterus, and the upper part of the vagina. The tubercle becomes the clitoris, the folds become the inner lips, and the swelling develops into the outer lips.

In the male the Müllerian ducts degenerate, and the Wolffian ducts turn into the epididymis, the vas deferens, and the ejaculatory duct. The tubercle becomes the glans penis, the folds form the shaft of the penis, and the swelling develops into the scrotum.

The mechanism by which the internal and external genitals differentiate has been the subject of much research. The principle seems to be parallel to that for differentiation of gonads; it appears that the presence or absence of the testes and their hormone production is critical. The testes of the male fetus secrete androgens, which stimulate the development of male structures, and a second substance, the Müllerian inhibitor, which suppresses the development of the Müllerian ducts. Thus if the hormonal output of the testes is present, male structures develop. If it is absent, female structures develop.

By four months after conception, the gender of the fetus is clear from the appearance of the external genitals (Figure 3.4).

Descent of the Testes and Ovaries

As the developmental changes are taking place, the ovaries and testes are changing in shape and position. At first, the ovaries and testes lie near the top of the abdominal cavity. By the tenth week they have grown and have moved down to the level of the upper edge of the pelvis. The ovaries remain there until after birth; later they shift to their adult position in the pelvis.

The male testes must make a much longer journey, down into the scrotum via a passageway called the *inguinal canal*. Normally this movement occurs around the fourth month after conception. After the descent of the testes, the inguinal canal is closed off.

Two problems in this process may occur. First, one or both testes may have failed to descend into the scrotum by the time of birth, a condition known as *undescended testes*, or *cryptorchidism*. This occurs in about 2 percent of all males. In most of these cases, the testes do descend by puberty, and so only about 1 in 500 adult men has undescended testes. If the testes do not descend spontaneously by puberty, however, the condition must be corrected by surgery or hormonal therapy. Otherwise, if both testes have failed to descend, the man would be sterile because, as was discussed in Chapter 2, the high temperature of the testes inside the body would inhibit the production of sperm. Undescended testes are also more likely to develop cancer.

The second possible problem occurs when the inguinal canal does not close off completely. It may then reopen later in life, creating a passageway through which loops of the intestine may enter the scrotum. This condition is called *inguinal hernia* and can be remedied by simple surgery.

Brain Differentiation

Yes, there are differences between male and female brains. The differences are found in the hypothalamus—there are no well-documented differences in any other region of the brain—and they result from a differentiation process in prenatal development much like the differentiation process that creates reproductive-system differences (Money and Ehrhardt, 1972). Once the gonads have differentiated, if testosterone is produced, the hypothalamus differentiates in the male direction; if testosterone is absent, the differentiation is in the female direction.

Anatomically, the consequences of this differentiation are that the cells and the neural circuits of the hypothalamus differ somewhat for males and females. Physiologically, an important consequence is that, beginning in puberty, the female hypothalamus directs a cyclic secretion of sex hormones, creating the menstrual cycle; the male hypothalamus directs a relatively acyclic, or constant, production of sex hormones.

The brain differentiation probably also has some consequences in terms of behavior, most notably sexual behavior, and aggressive behavior and possibly other behaviors as well. Unfortunately, most of the research on this point has been done with animals, and so there is some debate over whether the effects also occur in humans. This research will be discussed in detail in Chapter 7.

Homologous Organs

The preceding discussion of sexual differentiation highlights the fact that, although adult men and women appear to have very different reproductive anatomies, their reproductive organs have similar origins. When an organ in the male and an organ in the female both develop from the same embryonic tissue, the organs are said to be *homologous*. When the two organs have similar functions, they are said to be *analogous*. Table 3.1 summarizes the major homologies and analogies of the male and female reproductive systems. For example, ovaries and testes are both homologous (they develop from an indifferent gonad) and analogous (they produce germ cells and sex hormones).

JOHN MONEY, HERMAPHRODITES, AND THE EIGHT VARIABLES OF GENDER

Gender is not a simple matter, a fact which is apparent from the preceding discussion. Most people, however, assume that it is. That is, people typically assume that if a person is female, she will be feminine; will think of herself as a woman; will be sexually attracted to men; will have a clitoris, vagina, uterus, and ovaries; and will have sex chromosomes XX. The parallel assumption is that all males are

TABLE 3.1

HOMOLOGOUS AND ANALOGOUS ORGANS OF THE MALE AND FEMALE REPRODUCTIVE SYSTEMS

Embryonic Source	Homologous Organs		Analogous Organs	
	In the Adult Male	In the Adult Female	In the Adult Male	In the Adult Female
Indifferent gonad (medulla plus cortex)	Testes (from medulla)	Ovaries (from cortex)	Testes (from medulla)	Ovaries (from cortex)
Genital tubercle	Glans penis	Clitoris	Glans penis	Clitoris
Genital swelling	Scrotum	Outer lips		
Müllerian duct	Degenerates, leaving only remnants	Fallopian tubes, uterus, part of vagina		
Wolffian duct	Epididymis, vas deferens, seminal vesicles	Degenerates, leaving only remnants		
Urethral primordia	Prostate, Cowper's glands	Skene's glands, Bartholin's glands	Prostate, Cowper's glands	Skene's glands, Bartholin's glands

masculine; think of themselves as male; are sexually attracted to women; have a penis, testes, and scrotum; and have sex chromosomes XY.

A major research program of the last several decades, conducted at Johns Hopkins University by the psychologist John Money and his colleagues, challenges these assumptions and provides a great deal of information about sexuality and gender and their development (for an excellent summary of this research, see Money and Ehrhardt, 1972). Before the results of this research are discussed, however, some background information is necessary.

First, it is important to understand the distinctions among the eight variables of gender:[1]

1 *Chromosomal gender* XX in the female; XY in the male
2 *Gonadal gender* Ovaries in the female; testes in the male
3 *Hormonal gender* Estrogen and progesterone in the female; testosterone in the male
4 *Internal accessory organs* Uterus and vagina in the female; prostate and seminal vesicles in the male
5 *External genital appearance* Clitoris and vaginal opening in the female; penis and scrotum in the male
6 *Assigned gender* The announcement at birth, "It's a girl" or "It's a boy," based on the appearance of the external genitals; the gender the parents and the rest of society believe the child to be; the gender in which the child is reared
7 *Gender identity* The person's private, internal sense of maleness or femaleness—which is expressed in personality and behavior—and the integration of this sense with the rest

of the personality and with the gender roles prescribed by society
8 *Choice of sexual partner* Sexual attraction to members of the same gender, members of the opposite gender, or both

These variables might be subdivided into biological variables (the first five) and psychological variables (the last three). The discussion that follows will be concerned chiefly with the first seven of these variables. Variable 8, choice of sexual partner, will be discussed in Chapter 14.

In most cases, of course, all variables 1 through 7 are in agreement in an individual. That is, in most cases the person is a "consistent" female or male. If the person is a female, she has XX chromosomes, ovaries, a uterus and vagina, and a clitoris; she is reared as a female; and she thinks of herself as a female. If the person is a male, he has the parallel set of appropriate characteristics.

However, as a result of a number of "accidents" during the course of prenatal sexual development and differentiation, the gender indicated by one or more of these variables may disagree with the gender indicated by others. When the contradictions are among several of the biological variables (1 through 5), the person is called a *pseudohermaphrodite* or a *hermaphrodite*.[2] Biologically, the gender of such a person is ambiguous; the reproductive structures may be partly male and partly female, or they may be incompletely male or incompletely female. It is these individuals upon whom Money's research is based.

A number of syndromes can cause hermaphroditism, some of the most common being the adrenogenital syndrome, progestin-induced hermaphroditism, and the testicular feminizing

---

[1]The first six variables in this list are based on Money's six variables of sex. The last two were added for completeness and clarity. The distinction between the terms "gender" and "sex," discussed in Chap. 1, is being maintained here.

[2]The term "hermaphrodite" is taken from Hermaphroditos, the name of the mythological son of Hermes and Aphrodite. The latter was the Greek goddess of love.

syndrome. In the *adrenogenital syndrome*, a genetic female develops ovaries normally as a fetus; later in the course of prenatal development, however, the adrenal gland begins to function abnormally (as a result of a recessive genetic condition unconnected with the sex chromosomes), and an excess amount of androgens is produced. Prenatal sexual differentiation then does not follow the normal female course. As a result, the external genitals are partly or completely male in appearance; the labia are partly or totally fused (and thus there is no vaginal opening), and the clitoris is enlarged to the size of a small penis. Hence at birth these genetic females are often identified as males. *Progestin-induced hermaphroditism* is a similar syndrome which resulted from a drug, progestin, which was at one time given to pregnant women to help them maintain the pregnancy if they were prone to miscarriage (the drug is no longer prescribed because of the effects described below). As the drug circulated in the mother's bloodstream, the developing fetus was essentially exposed to a high dose of androgens. (Progestin and androgens are quite similar biochemicals, and in the body the progestin acted like androgen.) In genetic females this produced an abnormal, masculinized genital development similar to that found in the adrenogenital syndrome. The reverse case occurs in *testicular feminizing syndrome*. In this syndrome a genetic male produces normal levels of testosterone; however, as a result of a genetic condition, the body tissues are insensitive to the testosterone, and prenatal development is feminized. Thus the individual is born with the external appearance of a female: a vagina (but no uterus) and undescended testes.

Several important findings have emerged from Money's studies of these individuals. First, the research provides good evidence of the great complexity of sex and gender and their development. Many variables are involved in gender and sex, and many steps are involved in gender differentiation, even before birth. Because the process is complex, it is very vulnerable to disturbances, creating conditions such as hermaphroditism. Indeed, the research serves to question our basic notions of what it means to be male or female. In the adrenogenital syndrome, is the genetic female who is born with male external genitals a male or a female? What makes a person male or female? Chromosomal gender? External genital appearance? Gender identity?[3]

A second important result from this research has to do with gender identity and how it develops. There has been a debate over whether gender identity is biologically programmed in an individual or environmentally produced through learning. Money argues a strong environmentalist position. As evidence, he cites cases of matched pairs of hermaphrodites (see Focus). If such a child is assigned to be a female and is reared as a female (with appropriate corrective surgery and hormone therapy), she adjusts well in the female role and has a female gender identity. If a child with the identical syndrome at birth is assigned to be a male and is reared accordingly (once again with surgical and hormonal treatment), he adjusts well to the male role and has a male gender identity. Since, of two individuals with initially identical biological status, one can eventually develop a female gender identity and the other can develop a male gender identity, depending on the way each was reared, Money argues that the human is "psychosexually neutral" at birth and that gender identity is produced by the environment and learning.

---

[3]This issue has recently received a great deal of attention because of the case of Dr. Renée Richards, a transsexual (see Chap. 15), who was originally a man but who now, after a sex-change operation, is a woman. She wants to compete in women's professional tennis, and the debate has concerned whether she really is a woman. The question is: Which of the eight variables of gender define gender? Dr. Richards's gender identity is female, and her genitals are now female. Are those the appropriate criteria, or should chromosomal gender (which is diagnosed by means of the buccal smear technique) be the deciding factor? Is she a male or a female?

However, there do seem to be some limitations to the arbitrariness with which gender can be assigned or reassigned by the environment. Gender reassignment can be done very successfully, as the case histories indicate, up to the age of about 18 months. After that time, reassignment is difficult (and in most cases impossible) and causes serious problems of adjustment, apparently because the child begins forming a strong concept of his or her own gender identity at around 18 months of age (Kohlberg, 1966; Money and Ehrhardt, 1972). Once this basic concept is formed, it is essentially irreversible. Attempts at reassignment are futile.

Money's research and conclusions could be criticized on two grounds. First, in all the cases given as evidence, sex reassignment was supplemented by appropriate surgical or hormonal therapy. That is, the individual's biology was modified to correspond to the assigned gender. Hence it is not reasonable to say that gender can be environmentally assigned independent of biological gender characteristics. Second, it is difficult to know how relevant the abnormal cases that Money studied are to an understanding of the normal process of acquiring a gender identity.

Nonetheless, Money's data do provide impressive evidence on abnormalities of prenatal sexual differentiation, on the complexity of sex and gender, and on the environmental determinants of gender identity.

PUBERTY

Puberty is not a point in time, but rather a process. It is the stage in life during which the body changes from that of a child into that of an adult, with secondary sexual characteristics and the ability to reproduce sexually. *Puberty* can be scientifically defined as the time during which there is sudden enlargement and maturation of the gonads, other genitalia, and secondary sex characteristics, leading to reproductive capacity (Tanner, 1967). It is the second important period—the other being the prenatal period—during which sexual differentiation takes place. Perhaps the most important single event in the process is the first ejaculation for the male and the first menstruation for the female, although the latter is not necessarily a sign of reproductive capability since girls typically do not produce mature eggs until a year or two after the first menstruation.

The physiological process which underlies puberty in both genders is a marked increase in the level of sex hormones. Thus the hypothalamus, pituitary, and gonads control the changes.

Adolescence is a socially defined period of development which bears some relationship to puberty. Adolescence represents a psychological transition from the behavior and attitudes of a child to the behavior, attitudes, and responsibilities of an adult. In the United States it corresponds roughly to the teenage years. Modern American culture has an unusually long period of adolescence. A century ago, adolescence was much shorter; the lengthening of the educational process has served to prolong adolescence. In some cultures, in fact, adolescence does not exist; the child shifts to being an adult directly, with only a *rite de passage* in between.

Before describing the changes that take place during puberty, two points should be noted. First, the timing of the pubertal process differs considerably for males and females. Girls begin the change around 8 to 12 years of age, while boys do so about two years later. Girls reach their full height by about age 16, while boys continue growing until about age 18 or later. Mother Nature's capriciousness in allowing males and females to be out of step with each other at this stage creates no small number of crises for the adolescent. Girls are interested in boys long before boys are aware that girls exist. A girl may be stuck with a date who barely reaches her armpits, while the boy may have to

TWO CASE HISTORIES FROM THE JOHNS HOPKINS CLINIC

The two individuals discussed below are interesting because both are genetic females (both with the adrenogenital syndrome), and yet one eventually became a female with a female gender identity, while the other eventually became a male with a male gender identity.

The first member of the pair was reared as a girl but was actually announced as a boy at birth because of the appearance of the genitals (Figure 3.5). The correct diagnosis was established by the age of two months, and a sex reannouncement was decided upon. The parents were counseled on how to make such an announcement within the family and the community, and they accomplished this successfully. Today it is known that the first stage of surgical feminization could have been done immediately, but at the time it was delayed until the age of two years as a precaution against surgically induced trauma. After the surgery, the child had an unremarkable childhood medically, except for the fact that she took cortisone pills daily. Breast development began at age 13; menstruation did not begin until age 20.

During childhood, she developed behaviorally as a girl, with tomboyish tendencies. In adolescence, academic and career interests had priority over dating and romance. There was no romantic inclination toward either boys or girls, but rather a projection of boyfriends and marriage into the future. Otherwise, the girl was attractive and feminine.

The second member of the pair was diagnosed at birth as a male with a hypospadiac phallus and undescended testes. Three stages of surgical masculinization ended in failure because urine backed up into the internal vagina and caused infection. At age 3½ a correct diagnosis was made, and the case was referred to Johns Hopkins. At this time, being in a hospital again terrified the child. He said that a nurse would cut off his "wee-wee" and that his baby

FIGURE 3.5
The appearance, at birth, of the genitals of a pseudo-hermaphrodite. She was a genetic female and was surgically corrected and reared as a female. The appearance of the genitals of the genetic female corrected and reared as a male was similar. [*From J. Money and A. Ehrhardt.* Man and woman, boy and girl. *Baltimore: Johns Hopkins, 1972, p. 167.*]

sister had had hers cut off. His terror abated when, with clay and water, he was shown how an imperfect penis could be repaired.

It was decided to allow him to continue living as a boy. The appropriate surgery was done, and he was given cortisone therapy during childhood. At the time of puberty, masculinization was induced by androgen therapy. Artificial testes were implanted in the empty scrotum.

Unfortunately, as he approached adolescence, the boy's family life was tortured. His parents fought. The father was incapacitated by multiple sclerosis. The mother won points by reminding him that he was not the father of this particular child, and the boy heard what she said.

In adolescence the boy was an academic underachiever, and he tended to seek the company of quasi-delinquents, with whom he could achieve status as a rebel. He was accepted by the other boys as one of them. He was not overly aggressive. Psychosexually, all his romantic feelings and approaches were directed toward girls, despite his trepidation at the prospect of attempting intercourse with a penis that was too small and with prosthetic testes that could be recognized on touching as not soft enough.

Thus, although both members of the pair were genetically and anatomically identical at birth, one eventually became a female functioning adequately in the female role, while the other became a male functioning adequately in the male role.

Source: John Money and Anke Ehrhardt. *Man and woman, boy and girl*. Baltimore: Johns Hopkins, 1972, pp. 154–156.

cope with someone who is better qualified to be on the basketball team than he is. One solution is for girls to date older boys, although this can create another set of problems (J. S. Hyde and Rosenberg, 1976).

Second, there are large individual differences (differences from one person to the next) in the age at which the processes of puberty take place. Thus there is no "normal" time to begin menstruating or growing a beard. Accordingly, age ranges are given in describing the timing of the processes.

Changes in the Female

The first sign of pubescence in the female is the beginning of breast development, which generally starts at around 8 to 13 years of age. The ducts in the nipple area swell, and there is a growth of fatty and connective tissue, causing the nipples to project forward and the small, conical buds to increase in size. These changes are produced by increases in the levels of the sex hormones by a mechanism that will be described below.

As the growth of fatty and supporting tissue

increases in the breasts, a similar increase takes place at the hips and buttocks, leading to the rounded contours that distinguish adult female bodies from adult male bodies. Individual females have unique patterns of fat deposit, and so there are also considerable individual differences in the resulting female shapes.

Another visible sign of pubescence is the growth of pubic hair, which occurs shortly after breast development begins. About two years later, axillary (underarm) hair appears.

Body growth increases sharply during pubescence, approximately during the age range of 9.5 to 14.5 years. The growth spurt for girls occurs about two years before the growth spurt for boys (Figure 3.6). This is consistent with girls' general pattern of maturing earlier than boys. Even prenatally, girls show an earlier hardening of the structures that become bones. One exception to this pattern is in fertility; boys produce mature sperm earlier than girls produce mature ova.

Estrogen eventually applies the brakes to the growth spurt in girls; the presence of estrogen also causes the growth period to end sooner in girls, thus accounting for the lesser height of adult women as compared with adult men.

At about 13 years of age, the *menarche* (first menstruation) occurs. The girl, however, is not capable of becoming pregnant until ovulation begins, typically about two years after the menarche. The first menstruation is not only an important biological event but also an important psychological one. Various cultures have ceremonies recognizing its importance. In Orthodox Jewish families, the mother slaps the girl on the face. In other families, it is a piece of news that spreads quickly to the relatives. Girls themselves display a wide range of reactions to the event, ranging from negative ones, such as fear, shame, or disgust, to positive ones, such as a sense of pride, maturity, and womanliness. Some of the most negative reactions occur

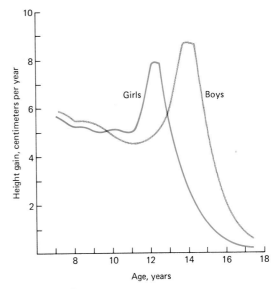

FIGURE 3.6

The adolescent spurt of growth for boys and girls. Note that girls experience their growth spurt earlier than boys do. [*From W. A. Marshall*, Sex differences at puberty. *J. Biosoc. Sci. Suppl; 1970*, **2**, 31–41.]

when the girl has not been prepared for the menarche, which is still the case in a surprisingly large number of families.

Parents who are concerned about preparing their daughters for the first menstruation should remember that there is a wide range in the age at which it occurs. It is not unusual for a girl to start menstruating in the fifth grade, and instances of the menarche during the fourth grade, while rare, do occur. The youngest mother on record was a 5-year-old Peruvian Indian girl who gave birth to a healthy baby by cesarean section in 1939. Despite her youth, she was sexually mature, and physicians confirmed that she had menstruated since she was perhaps one month old. The youngest set of parents on record was a Chinese couple who were blessed with a son in 1910. The father was 9, the mother was 8.

The age at which girls begin to menstruate has been dropping steadily for the last several centuries (Figure 3.7). For example, in Germany the average age at the menarche was 16.6 years in 1795, and 14.5 years in 1920 (Sexual maturity and climate, 1961). In the United States the average age was 13.5 in the 1930s and dropped to somewhat less than 13 in the mid-1960s. The indication now, though, is that the trend is leveling off.

Other body changes during puberty include a development of the blood supply to the clitoris, a thickening of the walls of the vagina, and a rapid growth of the uterus, which doubles in size between the tenth and the eighteenth years. The pelvic bone structure grows and widens, contributing to the rounded shape of the female and, more important, creating a passageway large enough for an infant to move through during birth. Once again, there are large individual differences in the shape of the pelvis, and it is important for the physician to identify shapes that may lead to problems in childbirth.

The dramatic changes that occur during pubescence are produced, basically, by the endocrine system and its upsurge in sex hormone production during puberty. The process begins with an increase in secretion of FSH by the pituitary gland. FSH in turn stimulates the ovaries to produce estrogen. Estrogen is responsible for many of the changes that occur; it stimulates breast growth and the growth of the uterus and vagina.

Another endocrine gland involved in pubertal changes is the adrenal gland, which is located just above the kidney. In the female, the adrenal gland is the major producer of androgens (male sex hormones), which exist at low levels in females. Adrenal androgens stimulate the growth of pubic and axillary hair and may be related to the female sex drive. They also may be related to the development of *acne*, a distressing problem of adolescence that is caused by a clogging of the sebaceous (oil-producing) glands, resulting in pustules, blackheads, and redness on the face and possibly the chest and back. Generally it is not severe enough to be a medical problem, although its psychological impact may be great. In order to

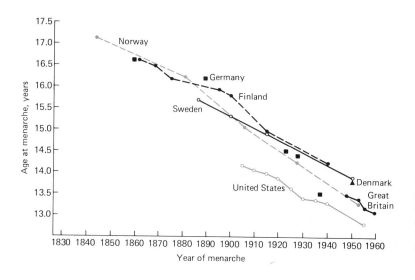

FIGURE 3.7

Girls today begin menstruating considerably earlier than girls a century ago. [*From J. M. Tanner, Growth at adolescence. (2nd ed.) Oxford: Blackwell Scientific Publications, 1962.*]

avoid scarring, severe cases should be treated by a physician, the treatment typically being ultraviolet light and/or antibiotics.

Another problem for some girls during puberty is a temporary period of overweight or obesity. If the weight gain is not excessive and lasts for only a short period, there is no cause for concern.

Changes in the Male

As noted above, puberty begins at about 10 or 11 years of age in boys, about two years later than it does in girls.

The physical causes of puberty in boys parallel those in girls. They are initiated by increased production of FSH and LH by the pituitary. Recall that LH is called ICSH (interstitial-cell-stimulating hormone) in males because it stimulates the interstitial cells of the testes to produce testosterone. At the beginning of puberty, the increase in ICSH stimulates the testes to produce testosterone, which is responsible for most of the changes of puberty in the male.

The first noticeable pubertal change in males is the growth of the testes and scrotal sac, which begins at around 10 to 13 years of age as a result of testosterone stimulation. The growth of pubic hair begins at about the same time. About a year later the penis begins to enlarge, first thickening, and then lengthening. This change also results from testosterone stimulation. Then as the testes enlarge, their production of testosterone increases even more; thus there is rapid growth of the penis, testes, and pubic hair at ages 13 and 14.

The growth of facial and axillary hair begins about two years after the beginning of pubic-hair growth. The growth of facial hair begins with the appearance of fuzz on the upper lip; adult beards do not appear until two or three years later. Indeed, by age 17, 50 percent of American males have not yet shaved. These changes also result from testosterone stimulation, which continues to produce growth of facial and chest hair beyond 20 years of age.

Erections increase in frequency. The organs that produce the fluid of semen, particularly the prostate, enlarge considerably at about the same time the other organs are growing. By age 13 or 14 the boy is capable of ejaculation. Previously, he was able to have orgasms, but they were not accompanied by ejaculation.[4] By about age 15, the ejaculate contains mature sperm, and the male is now fertile. The pituitary hormone FSH is responsible for initiating and maintaining the production of mature sperm.

Beginning about a year after the first ejaculation, the boy begins having nocturnal emissions, or "wet dreams." For the boy who has never masturbated, a wet dream may be his first ejaculation.

At about the same time penis growth occurs, the larynx ("voice box") also begins to grow in response to testosterone. As the larynx enlarges, the boy's voice drops, or "changes." Typically the transition occurs at around age 13 or 14. Because testosterone is necessary to produce the change in voice, castration before puberty results in a male with a permanently high voice. This principle was used to produce the castrati, who sang in the great choirs of Europe during the eighteenth century. They began as lovely boy sopranos, and their parents or the choirmaster, hating to see their beautiful voices destroyed in puberty, had them castrated so that they remained permanent sopranos. Female bodies are not the only ones that have been mutilated for strange reasons! Contrary to

---

[4]Note that orgasm and ejaculation are two separate processes, even though they generally occur together, at least in males after puberty. But orgasm may occur without ejaculation, and ejaculation may occur without orgasm.

popular belief, castration in adulthood will not produce a high voice because the larynx has already grown.

Like the age at which the menarche takes place, the average age at which the voice changes has declined over the last several centuries. For example, at the time of the eighteenth-century Bach Boys' Choir in Leipzig, voice change occurred, on the average, at age 18 (one assumes that castrati were excluded from the calculations). In London in 1959, it occurred on the average at age 13.3 years (Sullivan, 1971).

A great spurt of body growth begins in males at around 11 to 16 years of age (Figure 3.6). Height increases rapidly. Body contours also change. While the changes in girls involve mainly the increase in fatty tissue in the breasts

TABLE 3.2
SUMMARY OF THE CHANGES OF PUBERTY AND THEIR SEQUENCE
Note the similarities and differences between boys and girls.

	Girls			Boys		
Characteristic	Age of First Appearance (Years)	Major Hormonal Influence		Characteristic	Age of First Appearance (Years)	Major Hormonal Influence
1 Growth of breasts	8–13	Pituitary growth hormone, estrogen, progesterone, thyroxine		1 Growth of testes, scrotal sac	10–13.5	Pituitary growth hormone, testosterone
2 Growth of pubic hair	8–14	Adrenal androgen		2 Growth of pubic hair	10–15	Testosterone
3 Body growth	9.5–14.5	Pituitary growth hormone, adrenal androgen, estrogen		3 Body growth	10.5–16	Pituitary growth hormone, testosterone
4 Menarche	10–16.5	Hypothalamic releasing factors, FSH, LH, estrogen, progesterone		4 Growth of penis	11–14.5	Testosterone
				5 Change in voice (growth of larynx)	About the same time as penis growth	Testosterone
5 Underarm hair	About two years after pubic hair	Adrenal androgens		6 Facial and underarm hair	About two years after pubic hair appears	Testosterone
6 Oil- and sweat-producing glands (acne occurs when glands are clogged)	About the same time as underarm hair	Adrenal androgens		7 Oil- and sweat-producing glands, acne	About the same time as underarm hair	Testosterone

Source: After B. Goldstein. *Introduction to human sexuality.* New York: McGraw-Hill, 1976, pp. 80–81.

and hips, the changes in boys involve mainly an increase in muscle mass. Eventually testosterone brings the growth process to an end, although it permits the growth period to continue longer than it does in females.

Puberty brings changes and also problems. As noted previously, one of them is acne, which affects boys more frequently than girls. Gynecomastia (breast enlargement) may occur temporarily in boys, creating considerable embarrassment. About 80 percent of boys in puberty experience this problem, which is probably caused by small amounts of female sex hormones produced by the testes. Obesity may also be a temporary problem, although it is more frequent in girls than boys.

In various cultures around the world, puberty rites are performed to signify the boy's passage to manhood. In the United States the only remaining vestiges of such ceremonies are the Jewish bar mitzvah and, in Christian churches, confirmation. In a sense, it is probably unfortunate that we do not give more formal recognition to puberty. Puberty rites probably serve an important psychological function in that they are a formal, public announcement of the fact that the boy or girl is passing through an important and difficult period of change. In the absence of such rituals, the young person may think that his or her body is doing very strange things and may feel very much alone. This might be particularly problematic for boys, who lack an obvious sign of puberty like the first menstruation (the first ejaculation is probably the closest analogy) to help them identify the stage they are in.

SUMMARY

The sex hormone systems in males and females were discussed in the first section. The major sex hormones are testosterone, which is produced by the male's testes, and estrogen and progesterone, which are produced by the female's ovaries. Levels of the sex hormones are regulated by two hormones secreted by the pituitary: FSH (follicle-stimulating hormone) and LH (luteinizing hormone, or, in the male, interstitial-cell-stimulating hormone [ICSH]). The gonads, pituitary, and hypothalamus regulate one another's output through a negative feedback loop.

Next the process of prenatal sexual differentiation was considered. At conception males and females differ only in the sex chromosomes (XX in females and XY in males). As the fetus grows, the chromosomes direct the gonads to differentiate into the testes or ovaries. Different hormones are then produced by the gonads, and these stimulate further differentiation of the internal and external reproductive structures as well as differentiation of the hypothalamus. A male organ and a female organ which derive from the same embryonic tissue are said to be homologous to each other.

An important distinction between the eight variables of gender arises from John Money's research on hermaphrodites. Hermaphroditism is generally the result of various accidents that occur during the course of prenatal sexual differentiation. Money's work has important implications for an understanding of the development of gender identity.

Finally, the other great period of sexual differentiation, puberty, was considered. Puberty is initiated and characterized by a great increase in the production of sex hormones. Pubertal changes in both males and females include body growth, the development of pubic and axillary hair, and increased output from the oil-producing glands. Changes in the female include breast development and the beginning of menstruation. Changes in the male include the growth of the penis and testes, the beginning of ejaculation, and a deepening of the voice.

SUGGESTIONS FOR FURTHER READING

Money, John, and Ehrhardt, Anke. *Man and woman, boy and girl*. Baltimore: Johns Hopkins, 1972. An excellent, detailed summary of John Money's important research. Also contains a great deal of other information on sexuality.

Netter, F. H. *Endocrine system*. The Ciba Collection of Medical Illustrations. Vol. 4. Summit, N.J.: Ciba, 1965. The best set of medical illustrations of the endocrine system available, with some commentary as well.

Tanner, J. M. *Growth at adolescence*. (2nd ed.) Oxford: Blackwell Scientific Publications, 1962. The classic work on the changes of puberty.

Turner, C. D., and Bagnara, J. T. *General endocrinology*. (5th ed.) Philadelphia: Saunders, 1971. A good endocrinology text.

4

MENSTRUATION AND MENOPAUSE

CITED

It [menstruation] makes me very much aware of the fact that I am a woman, and that's something very important to me. . . . . It's also a link to other women. I actually enjoy having my period. I feel like I've been cleaned out inside.

—M. P. W.

Menstruation is a pain in the vagina.

—S. B. P.

Menopause, it's the best form of birth control. Face it graciously and brag about it. It's great.

—S. F.

Menopause, can I get through it without collapse? Men don't have that damned inconvenience and discomfort. God must have been a man—a woman would have done a better job on women's bodies.

—B. B. W.*

Women's sexual and reproductive lives have a rhythm of changes much like that of the seasons. And, as is true of the seasons, there are some tangible signs that mark the shifts, the two most notable being menstruation and menopause. As the women quoted above testify, these events are not only biological but psychological as well, and the psychological responses to them may range from very positive to very negative. This chapter deals with the biology and psychology of menstruation and menopause.

BIOLOGY AND
THE MENSTRUAL CYCLE

The menstrual cycle is regulated by fluctuating levels of sex hormones which produce certain changes in the ovaries and uterus. The hormone cycles are regulated by means of the negative feedback loops discussed in Chapter 3.

* *Source:* Paula Weideger. *Menstruation and menopause.* New York: Knopf, 1976, pp. 4–5.

It is important to note that humans are nearly unique among species in having a menstrual cycle. Only a few other species of apes and monkeys also have menstrual cycles. All other species of mammals (for example, horses and dogs) have *estrous* cycles. There are several differences between estrous cycles and menstrual cycles. First, in animals that have estrous cycles, there is no menstruation; there is either no bleeding or only a slight spotting (as in dogs), which is not a real menstruation. Second, the timing of ovulation in relation to bleeding (if there is any) is different in the two cycles. For estrous animals, ovulation occurs while the animal is in "heat," or estrus, which is also the time of slight spotting. That is, dogs ovulate at about the time of bleeding. In the menstrual cycle, however, ovulation occurs about midway between the periods of menstruation. A third difference is that female animals with estrous cycles engage in sexual behavior only when they are in heat, that is, during the estrous phase of the cycle. Females with menstrual cycles are capable of engaging in sexual behavior throughout the cycle. It is important to note these differences because some people mistakenly believe that women's cycles are like those of a dog or cat, when in fact the cycles are quite different.

The Phases of the Menstrual Cycle

The menstrual cycle has four phases, each characterized by a set of hormonal, ovarian, and uterine changes (see Figure 4.1). Because menstruation is the easiest phase to identify, it is tempting to call it the first phase; biologically, though, it is actually the last phase (although in numbering the days of the menstrual cycle, day 1 is counted as the first day of menstruation because it is the most identifiable day of the cycle).

Hormones and what happens in the ovaries   The first phase of the menstrual cycle is called the *follicular phase* (it is sometimes called the *proliferative phase* or the *preovulatory phase*). At the beginning of this phase, the pituitary secretes relatively high levels of FSH (follicle-stimulating hormone). As the name of this hormone implies, its function is to stimulate follicles in the ovaries. At the beginning of the follicular phase, it signals one follicle (occasionally more than one) in the ovaries to begin to ripen and bring an egg to maturity. At the same time, the follicle secretes estrogen. As the egg matures, it moves, enclosed in the follicle, toward the surface of the ovary.

The second phase of the cycle is *ovulation*, which is the phase during which the follicle ruptures open, releasing the ripened egg. By this time, estrogen has risen to a high level, which inhibits FSH production, and so FSH has fallen back to a low level. The high levels of estrogen also stimulate the hypothalamus to produce LH-releasing factor, which causes the pituitary to begin production of LH (luteinizing hormone). A surge of LH causes ovulation.

The third phase of the cycle is called the *luteal phase* (sometimes also called the *secretory phase* or the *postovulatory phase*). After releasing an egg, the follicle, under stimulation of LH, turns into a glandular mass of cells called the *corpus luteum* [1] (hence the names "luteal phase" and "luteinizing hormone"). The corpus luteum manufactures progesterone; thus progesterone levels rise during the luteal phase. But high levels of progesterone also inhibit the pituitary's secretion of LH, and as LH levels decline, the corpus luteum degenerates. Thus the corpus luteum's output leads to its own eventual destruction. And with this degeneration also comes a sharp decline in estrogen and progesterone levels at the end of the luteal phase. The falling levels of estrogen stimulate the pituitary to begin production of FSH, and the whole cycle then begins again.

The fourth and final phase of the cycle is *menstruation*. Physiologically, menstruation is a shedding of the inner lining of the uterus (the endometrium), which then passes out through the cervix and the vagina. During this phase, estrogen and progesterone levels are low, and FSH levels are rising. Menstruation is apparently triggered by the sharp decline in estrogen levels at the end of the luteal phase.

What happens in the uterus   This brings us to the changes that have been occurring in the uterus while the ovaries and endocrine system were going through the four phases described above. During the first, or follicular, phase, the high levels of estrogen stimulate the endometrium of the uterus to grow, thicken, and form glands that will eventually secrete substances to nourish the embryo; that is, the endometrium proliferates (hence the alternative name for this first phase, the "proliferative phase"). During the luteal phase, the progesterone secreted by

---

[1]"Corpus luteum" is Latin for "yellow body." The corpus luteum is so named because the mass of cells is yellowish in appearance.

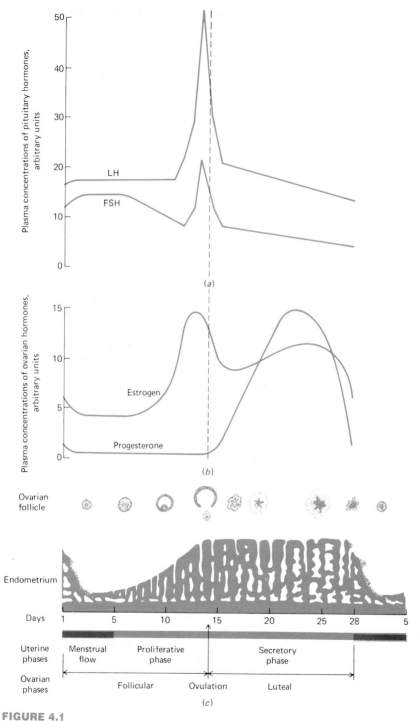

FIGURE 4.1
The biological events of the menstrual cycle. (*a*) Levels of hormones produced by the pituitary. (*b*) Hormones produced by the ovaries. (*c*) Changes in follicles in the ovary and the endometrium of the uterus. [*Adapted from A. J. Vander, J. H. Sherman, and D. Luciano. Human physiology: The mechanisms of body function. (2nd ed.) New York: McGraw-Hill, 1975.*]

the corpus luteum stimulates the glands of the endometrium to start secreting the nourishing substances (hence the name "secretory phase"). If the egg is fertilized and the timing goes properly, about six days after ovulation the fertilized egg arrives in a uterus that is well prepared to cradle and nourish it.

The corpus luteum will continue to produce estrogen and progesterone for about 12 days. If pregnancy has not occurred, its hormone output declines sharply at the end of this period. The uterine lining thus cannot be maintained, and it is shed, resulting in menstruation. Immediately afterward, a new lining starts forming in the next follicular phase.

The menstrual fluid itself is a combination of blood (from the endometrium), degenerated cells, and mucus from the cervix and vagina. Normally the discharge for an entire period is only about 2 ounces (4 tablespoons). Most commonly the fluid is absorbed with sanitary napkins, which are worn externally, or tampons, which are worn inside the vagina.

Length and timing of the cycle   How long is a normal menstrual cycle? Generally anywhere from 20 to 36 or 40 days is considered within the normal range. The average is about 28 days, but somehow this number has taken on more significance than it deserves. There is enormous variation from one woman to the next in the average length of the cycle, and for a given woman there is considerable variation in length from one cycle to the next. In one study, more than 2000 women were asked to give their cycle lengths. Fewer than 13 percent had cycles that varied in length, from the shortest to the longest cycle, by less than 6 days; the remaining 87 percent had variations of 7 days or more (Chiazze et al., 1968). Ninety-five percent of the cycles were between 15 and 45 days long. As Dr. S. Leon Israel has commented, "The absolutely regular cycle is so rare as to be either a myth or a medical curiosity" (1967).

What is the timing of the various phases of the cycle? In a perfectly regular 28-day cycle, menstruation begins on day 1 and continues until about day 4 or 5. The follicular phase extends from about day 5 to about day 13. Ovulation occurs on day 14, and the luteal phase extends from day 15 to the end of the cycle, day 28 (see Figure 4.1). But what if the cycle is not one of those perfect 28-day ones? In cycles that are shorter or longer than 28 days, the principle is that the length of the *luteal* phase is relatively constant. That is, the time from ovulation to menstruation is always 14 days, give or take only a day or two. It is the follicular phase which is of variable length. Thus, for example, if a woman has a 44-day cycle, she ovulates on about day 30. If she has a 22-day cycle, she ovulates on about day 8.

Some women report that they can actually feel themselves ovulate, a phenomenon called *Mittelschmerz* ("middle pain"). The sensation described is a cramping on one or both sides of the lower abdomen, lasting for about a day, and it is sometimes confused with appendicitis.

It is also true that ovulation does not occur in every menstrual cycle. That is, menstruation may take place without ovulation. When this happens, the woman is said to have an *anovulatory cycle.* Such cycles occur once or twice a year in women in their twenties and thirties and are fairly common among girls during puberty and among women during the menopausal period.

Other cyclic changes   Two other physiological processes that fluctuate with the menstrual cycle also deserve mention: the cervical mucus cycle and the basal body temperature cycle. The cervix contains glands that secrete mucus throughout the menstrual cycle. One function of the mucus is to protect the entrance to the cervix, helping to keep bacteria out. These glands respond to the changing levels of estrogen during the cycle. As estrogen increases at the start of a new cycle, the mucus is alkaline, thick, and viscous. When LH production begins, just before ovulation, the cervical mucus changes markedly. It becomes even more alkaline, thin, and watery. Thus the environment for sperm passage is most hospitable just at ovulation. After ovulation, the mucus returns to its former viscous, less alkaline state. If a sample of mucus is taken just before ovulation and is allowed to dry, the dried mucus takes on a fern-shaped pattern. After ovulation, during the luteal phase, that fernlike patterning will not occur. Thus the "fern test" is one method for detecting ovulation.

A woman's *basal body temperature*, taken with a thermometer either orally or rectally, also fluctuates with the phases of the menstrual cycle. Basically, the pattern is the following: The temperature is low during the follicular phase and may take a dip on the day of ovulation; on the day after ovulation it rises noticeably, generally by 0.4°F or more, and then continues at the higher level for the rest of the cycle (Figure 4.2). Progesterone raises body temperature, and the higher temperature during the luteal phase is due to the increased production of progesterone during that time. As the saying goes, "Where there's progesterone, there's heat." This change in basal body temperature is important when a couple are using the rhythm method of birth control (Chapter 6), and also when a woman is trying to determine the time of ovulation so that she may become pregnant (Chapter 5).

Menstrual Problems

The most common menstrual problem is *dysmenorrhea* (painful menstruation). Almost every woman experiences at least some menstrual discomfort at various times in her life, but the frequency and severity of the discomfort vary considerably from one woman to the next. Cramping pains in the pelvic region are the most common symptom, and other symptoms may include headaches, backaches, nausea, and a feeling of pressure and bloating in the pelvis.

Dr. Katharina Dalton, an expert in the area of menstrual-cycle research, separates painful

FIGURE 4.2

A basal body temperature graph. Note the dip in temperature, indicating ovulation on day 14. [*From R. J. Demarest and J. J. Sciarra. Conception, birth and contraception: A visual presentation. (2nd ed.) New York: McGraw-Hill, 1976.*]

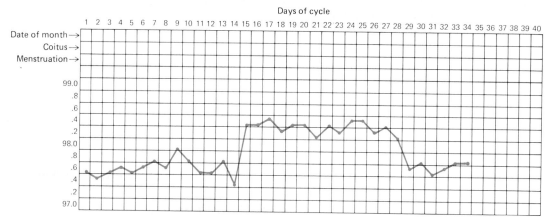

menstruation into two categories: *spasmodic dysmenorrhea* and *congestive dysmenorrhea* (1969). The symptoms of the spasmodic type are cramps, acute pain in the lower abdomen, and possibly nausea, all beginning on the first day of menstruation. It is most common between the ages of 15 and 25; usually it is not a problem for women past this age since pregnancy and childbirth generally clear it up. The symptoms of congestive dysmenorrhea are a heaviness or dull aching in the abdomen, nausea, water retention, constipation, headaches and backaches, breast pains, irritability, tension, depression, and lethargy; these problems start several days before the beginning of menstruation and are frequently over by the time of the heaviest flow of the period (for a review of the data on physical changes during the menstrual cycle, see Southam and Gonzaga, 1965). This type of painful menstruation can start at puberty and continue until menopause, and it may get worse with each pregnancy.

Although the exact causes of dysmenorrhea are unknown, there are several theories on the subject. Cramping itself is thought to result from spasms of the uterus. Dr. Katharina Dalton (1969) believes that both types are the result of hormone imbalance. She theorizes that the spasmodic type results from too much progesterone in relation to estrogen and that the congestive type (and the related "premenstrual syndrome," to be discussed later) results from too much estrogen in relation to progesterone. As a result of her analysis of the hormonal mechanisms involved in this imbalance, Dalton recommends as therapy doses of pure progesterone (as opposed to synthetic progesterone such as progestin). She herself has been treating women with pure progesterone for over 20 years, and she reports nearly 100 percent success in relieving their symptoms. Other physicians, however, have not had similar success with her treatment; it is not clear whether their inability to reproduce her results is due to their failure to

follow her methods precisely or, perhaps, whether her success is only a result of her belief in the treatment, which others do not share (Weideger, 1976).

Household remedies for painful menstruation are also available and may be helpful to some women. Aspirin appears to be the best, and cheapest, painkiller available, and it can help to relieve menstrual pain. Exercise and keeping in good shape may also help. A somewhat more provocative remedy suggested by, among others, Masters and Johnson is masturbation. This makes good physiological sense because part of the discomfort of menstruation—the pressure and bloating—results from pelvic edema (a congestion of fluids in the pelvic region). During sexual arousal and orgasm, pelvic congestion increases. After orgasm, the congestion dissipates (see Chapter 7). Thus orgasm, whether produced by masturbation or some other means, should help to relieve the pelvic edema which causes menstrual discomfort. And it's a lot more fun than taking medicine!

Another menstrual problem which may be mistaken for dysmenorrhea is *endometriosis*. As noted previously, the endometrium is the lining of the uterus; it grows during each menstrual cycle and is sloughed off in menstruation. Endometriosis occurs when the endometrium grows in a place other than the uterus. Common sites include the ovaries, fallopian tubes, rectum, bladder, vagina, vulva, cervix, and lymph glands. The symptoms vary, depending on the location of the growth, but very painful periods that last an unusually long time are the most common. Endometriosis is fairly serious and should be treated by a physician; if left untreated, it may lead to sterility. Hormones are generally used in treatment, but if the problem is severe, surgery may be required.

Another menstrual problem is *amenorrhea*, or the absence of menstruation. It is called *primary amenorrhea* if the girl has not yet menstruated by about age 18. It is called *secondary amenorrhea* if she has had at least one period. Amenorrhea has received considerable attention from physicians because, while rare, it is a symptom of infertility. Some of the causes of amenorrhea include pregnancy, congenital defects of the reproductive system, hormonal imbalance, cysts or tumors, disease, stress, and emotional factors related to puberty.

PSYCHOLOGICAL ASPECTS OF THE MENSTRUAL CYCLE

It is part of the folk wisdom of our culture that women experience fluctuations in mood over the phases of the menstrual cycle. In particular, women are supposed to be especially cranky and depressed just before and during their periods. This notion is reflected in advertisements for drugs to relieve menstrual discomforts saying that "Sally is blue" at "that time of the month." An extreme of this belief was voiced by Dr. Edgar Berman, Hubert Humphrey's personal physician, who, a few years ago, stated publicly that he believed that women were unfit to hold high public office, such as the Presidency, because of their "raging hormonal influences." In France, if a woman commits a crime during her premenstrual period, she may use the fact in her defense, claiming "temporary impairment of sanity."

What is the scientific evidence concerning the occurrence of such fluctuations in mood, and, if they do occur, what causes them?

Fluctuations in Mood: Is Sally Blue?

In 1931, R. T. Frank gave the name "premenstrual tension" to the mood changes that may occur during the three or four days immediately preceding menstruation (about days 24 to 28 of the cycle). Symptoms of premenstrual tension include depression, anxiety, irritability, fatigue, headaches, and low self-esteem. Since the time of Frank's early work, a great many data have been collected on moods during the premenstrual period and on whether moods fluctuate during the cycle.

The results seem to indicate a basic pattern. On the average, mood is positive around the time of ovulation (mid-cycle) and is negative premenstrually; the latter phenomenon is called the *premenstrual syndrome*. For example, in one study, mood was measured by means of a projective technique in which subjects told stories at regular intervals throughout the cycle; the stories were then scored for the amount of anxiety shown in them (Bardwick, 1971; Ivey and Bardwick, 1968). The results indicated that self-confidence and self-esteem are high at ovulation, while anxiety about death, mutilation, and separation are high premenstrually. The following examples illustrate these shifts.

One woman at ovulation said:

> We took our skis and packed them on top of the car and then we took off for up north. We used to go for long walks in the snow, and it was just really great, really quiet and peaceful.

The same woman showed mutilation anxiety in this story told premenstrually:

> [The car] came around a curve and did a double flip and landed upside down. I remember this car coming down on my hand and slicing it right open and all this blood was all over the place. Later they thought it was broken because every time I touched the finger, it felt like a nail was going through my hand.

Another woman expressed a positive mood at ovulation in this story:

> Talk about my trip to Europe. It was just the greatest summer of my life. We met all kinds of terrific people everywhere we went, and just the most terrific things happened.

But the same woman showed hostility premenstrually:

> Talk about my brother and his wife. I hated her. I just couldn't stand her. . . . I used to do terrible things to separate them.

Further evidence of the premenstrual syndrome comes from statistics indicating that a large proportion of the criminal acts of violence and suicides committed by women take place during the four premenstrual and four menstrual days of the cycle (Dalton, 1964). It has been found that 45 percent of the female industrial workers who call in sick do so during this period and that 46 percent of the women admitted to psychiatric care are admitted on one of these eight days; also, 52 percent of female accident-emergency admissions occur during the eight premenstrual and menstrual days. In addition, 54 percent of the children brought to a clinic with minor colds were brought during their mothers' eight premenstrual and menstrual days, perhaps indicating an increase in the mothers' anxiety at this time (Dalton, 1966).

The evidence concerning mood fluctuation and the premenstrual syndrome has not been accepted without challenge. Of the numerous criticisms that have been made (see J. S. Hyde and Rosenberg, 1976; Parlee, 1973), three deserve special mention here. First, much of the evidence depends on subjective reports of mood and symptoms, which are probably not very reliable. Second, the research has not given sufficient consideration to coping mechanisms; most women do not dissolve into tears and confine themselves to bed for the eight premenstrual and menstrual days of each month. It seems likely that women develop mechanisms for coping with the symptoms. Third, the interpretation of the direction of the differences might be questioned. The typical interpretation is that women show a psycholog-

ical "deficit" premenstrually, as compared with the "normal" state at ovulation and during the rest of the cycle. However, the opposite interpretation might also be made: that women are "normal" premenstrually and are unusually well-adjusted psychologically at mid-cycle. What defines "normal" or "average" mood, then? Men's moods? Support for a reinterpretation might come from the statistics on violent crimes committed by women. While it is true that women are somewhat more likely to commit crimes during the eight premenstrual and menstrual days, even during this period they are far less likely to commit crimes than men are. Thus women might be considered to experience "normal" or typical moods (comparable to men's moods) during the premenstrual and menstrual days and to have feelings of unusual well-being around ovulation (see also Sommer, 1975).

Taking into account the criticisms and available evidence, it might be reasonable to conclude the following:

1 Women do, on the average, experience some fluctuations in mood over the phases of the menstrual cycle.
2 Present evidence does not clearly indicate how the direction of the shifts should be interpreted—whether women are unusually "low" premenstrually or unusually "high" around the time of ovulation.
3 There is a great deal of variation from one woman to the next in the size of these shifts and the way they are expressed. Some women experience no shifts or shifts so slight that they are not noticeable, while others may experience large shifts. It would be interesting to know how many do show mood fluctuations and how many do not. Unfortunately, the studies that have tried to provide this information themselves show substantial variation in their conclusions (J. S. Hyde and Rosenberg, 1976). It appears that about 50 to

75 percent of all women show some mood fluctuation, while at least 25 percent show no fluctuation.

Fluctuations in Performance: Can Sally Be President?

So far the discussion has concentrated on fluctuations in psychological characteristics such as depression, anxiety, and low self-confidence. However, in some situations performance is of more practical importance than mood. For example, is a woman secretary's clerical work less accurate premenstrually and menstrually? Is a woman athlete's coordination or speed impaired during the premenstrual-menstrual period?

The available data do not provide evidence of fluctuations in performance with the phases of the menstrual cycle (Sommer, 1973). Thus there is no substantial evidence indicating that the kinds of performance required in a work situation fluctuate over the menstrual cycle.

Fluctuations in Sex Drive

Another psychological characteristic that has been investigated for fluctuations over the cycle is women's interest in, or desire for, intercourse—what might be called the "sex drive." Observations of female animals that have estrous cycles indicate that sexual behavior depends a great deal on cycle phase and the corresponding hormonal state. Females of these species engage in sexual behavior enthusiastically when they are in the estrous, or "heat," phase of the cycle and do not engage in sexual behavior at all during any other phase. This makes good biological sense, since the females engage in sex precisely when they are fertile.

Human females, of course, engage in sexual behavior throughout the menstrual cycle. But might there still remain some subtle cycling in drive, expressed, perhaps, in fluctuations in

frequency of intercourse? The women in Kinsey's sample (Kinsey et al., 1953) reported the greatest feelings of sexual arousal during the premenstrual period. In another study, both frequency of intercourse and frequency of orgasm showed two peaks, one at ovulation and one premenstrually (Udry and Morris, 1968). Thus there is some evidence that women's sexual behavior fluctuates in frequency across the phases of the menstrual cycle. A high frequency at ovulation is biologically functional in that it maximizes the chances for conception, but the function of the high frequency premenstrually is not known.

What Causes the Fluctuations in Mood: Why Is Sally Blue?

The answer to the question of what causes mood fluctuations during the menstrual cycle (if such fluctuations do occur) resolves down to a nature-nurture, or biology-environment, controversy. That is, some investigators argue that the mood fluctuations are caused by biological factors—in particular, fluctuations in levels of hormones—while others argue that environmental factors such as menstrual taboos and cultural expectations are the cause.

On the biology side, changes in mood appear to be related to changes in hormone levels during the cycle. The fact that depression is more frequent in women premenstrually, at menopause, and postpartum (after having a baby) and among those using birth control pills suggests that there is at least some relationship between sex hormones and depression (S. L. Smith, 1975). The exact hormone-mood relationship is not known, though. Theories of hormonal causes of premenstrual tension involving the following factors have been proposed: (1) absolute amount of estrogen; (2) absolute amount of progesterone; (3) the estrogen-progesterone ratio, or estrogen-progesterone balance; (4) hypersensitivity of some individuals to estrogen levels; and (5) withdrawal reactions to either estrogen or progesterone (during all the premenstrual, postpartum, and menopausal periods, hormone levels are dropping rapidly). Research has not determined which, if any, of these factors is the real cause, though each has some data in its favor. Neither is it known exactly what the mechanism is by which hormones influence mood. The likeliest explanation would involve the effects of estrogen and progesterone on brain neurotransmitters (substances that are involved in the transmission of nerve impulses) such as noradrenaline and dopamine.

Critics of the hormone point of view note that causality is being inferred from correlational data. That is, the data show simply a correlation between cycle phase (hormone levels) and mood. From this, it is unwarranted to infer that the hormone levels cause the mood shifts. Another equally reasonable interpretation of the data might be that moods influence hormone levels and cycle phase. For example, a bout of depression might bring on menstruation.

A study that answers this objection partially was done by psychologist Karen Paige (1971). She used a manipulation of hormone levels—birth control pills—and studied mood fluctuations resulting from the manipulation. The spoken stories of 102 married women were obtained on days 4, 10, and 16 and two days before menstruation during one cycle, and they were scored using the technique mentioned previously. The subjects fell into three groups: (1) those who were not taking oral contraceptives and never had; (2) those who were taking a combination pill (combination pills provide a steady high dose of both estrogen and progestin, a synthetic progesterone, for 20 or 21 days—see Chapter 6 for a more complete discussion); and (3) those who were taking sequential pills (which provide 15 days of estrogen followed by five days of estrogen plus progestin, which is a

fluctuation similar to the natural cycle but at higher levels). The hormone levels across the cycles of the women in these three groups are shown in Figure 4.3. Paige found that the nonpill women experienced statistically significant variation in their anxiety and hostility levels over the menstrual cycle, which was in agreement with findings from previous studies. Women taking the sequential pill showed the same mood change that nonpill women did. This agrees with the predicted outcome since their artificial hormone cycle is similar to the natural one. Most important, combination-pill women, whose hormone levels are constant over the cycle, showed *no* mood shifts over the cycle; their hostility and anxiety levels were constant. This study therefore provides evidence that fluctuations in hormone levels over

FIGURE 4.3

Hormone levels over the menstrual cycle for the three groups of women in Paige's study (see text for further explanation).

Group 1: Nonpill women

Group 2: Combination pill

Group 3: Sequential pill

the menstrual cycle cause mood fluctuations and that, when hormone levels are constant, mood is constant.

Those arguing the other side—that the fluctuations are due to cultural forces—note the widespread cultural expectations and taboos surrounding menstruation (for reviews, see Novell, 1965; Stephens, 1961; Weideger, 1976). In many nonindustrialized cultures—for example, some American Indian groups—women who are menstruating are isolated from the community and may have to stay in a menstrual hut at the edge of town for the duration of their period. Often the menstrual blood itself is thought to have supernatural, dangerous powers, and the woman's isolation is considered necessary to the safety of the community. Among the Lele of the Congo, for example:

A menstruating woman was a danger to the whole community if she entered the forest. Not only was her menstruation certain to wreck any

enterprise in the forest that she might undertake, but it was thought to produce unfavorable conditions for men. Hunting would be difficult for a long time after, and rituals based on forest plants would have no efficacy. Women found these rules extremely irksome, especially as they were regularly short-handed and later in their planting, weeding, harvesting, and fishing. (Douglas, 1970, p. 179).

Lest one think that such practices occur only among primitive people, it should be noted that they persist also in our own culture. For example, the following passage is from the Old Testament:

When a woman has a discharge of blood which is her regular discharge from her body, she shall be in her impurity for seven days, and whoever touches her shall be unclean until the evening. . . . And whoever touches her bed shall wash his clothes, and bathe himself in water, and be unclean until the evening; whether it is the bed or anything upon which she sits, when he

FIGURE 4.4
A Navaho menstrual hut. [*The Bettmann Archive, Inc.*]

touches it he shall be unclean until the evening. (Leviticus 15:19–23)

Even closer to home, the Parks Department issues the following warning:

"Special precautions apply to women. For their protection, women should refrain from wilderness travel during their menstrual periods. Bears and other large carnivores have attacked women in this physiological condition." (Weideger, 1976, p. 226)

Among the most common menstrual taboos are those prohibiting sexual intercourse with a menstruating woman. For example, the continuation of the passage from Leviticus quoted above is:

And if any man lies with her, and her impurity is on him, he shall be unclean seven days; and every bed on which he lies shall be unclean. (Leviticus 15:24)

Couples who violated the taboo could be stoned. To this day, Orthodox Jews abstain from sex during the woman's period and for seven days afterward. At the end of this time the woman goes to the mikvah (ritual bath) to be cleansed, and only after this cleansing may she resume sexual relations.

There is also evidence that these "primitive" or "archaic" practices are actually widespread in our modern culture as well. For example, a 1972 survey of 960 California families showed that half the men and women had *never* had sex during the woman's menstrual period (Paige, 1973). No wonder women get depressed around the time of menstruation!

Advocates of the cultural explanation argue, then, that women become anxious and depressed around the time of menstruation because of the many cultural forces, such as menstrual taboos, that create negative attitudes toward menstruation. Further, women's expectations may play a role. It is a well-documented phenomenon that people's expectations can influence their behavior. Our culture is filled with teachings that women are supposed to behave strangely just before and during their periods—for example, the drug company ads that explain why "Sally is blue." Thus, according to this line of reasoning, women are taught that they should be depressed around the time of menstruation, and since they expect to become depressed, they become depressed.

Surely such forces do exist in our culture. But is there any evidence that they really do have an effect on women's moods and behavior? Another study by Karen Paige (1973) does provide some evidence. She obtained information on the menstrual experiences of 298 unmarried college women and then separated the subjects into three groups depending on their religious background: Protestant, Catholic, and Jewish. The Catholics showed extreme fluctuations in anxiety level over the cycle, while the Protestants showed no fluctuation. Among the Jewish women, those who accepted the ban on sexual intercourse during menstruation were the most likely to have menstrual difficulties. Thus, while all the women presumably had similar hormone cycles, whether they experienced fluctuations in mood appeared to depend on their cultural background.

This nature-nurture argument will not be easily resolved, particularly since there is good evidence for both points of view. Perhaps the best solution is to say that some women probably do experience mood shifts caused by hormonal and possibly other physical factors and that, for many others, slight biological influences are magnified by cultural influences. Premenstrual hormonal state may act as a sort of "trigger." It may, for example, provide a state conducive to depression; and if the environment provides further stimuli to depression, the woman becomes depressed.

CYCLES IN MEN

The traditional assumption, of both lay people and scientists, has been that monthly biological and psychological cycles are the exclusive property of women. The corollary assumption has been that men experience no such monthly cycles. These assumptions are made, at least in part, because men have no obvious signs like menstruation to call attention to the fact that some kind of periodic change is occurring.

Recently there has been an interest in discovering whether men might not experience subtle monthly hormone cycles and corresponding psychological cycles. As early as 1897, it had been observed that bleeding from lung hemorrhages, hemorrhoids, and hyperemia of the liver is periodic, in both women and men (cited in Delaney et al., 1976, pp. 212–213). Epileptic attacks appear to follow a monthly cycle in men (Delaney et al., 1976, p. 213).

In one early study, male industrial workers did appear to have periodic emotional cycles, with an average cycle length of about five weeks. Individual cycle lengths varied from three to nine weeks and were remarkably consistent (Hersey, 1931). In a recent study of Harvard men, though, there was no evidence of regular emotional cycles; indeed, in that study, women students at Radcliffe did not show emotional cycles (Wessman and Ricks, 1966).

One interesting applied study did find some evidence of behavioral cycles in men (cited in Ramey, 1972). The Omi Railway Company of Japan operates more than 700 buses and taxis. In 1969 the directors became concerned about the high losses resulting from accidents. The company's efficiency experts studied each man working for the company to determine his monthly cycle pattern of mood and efficiency. Then schedules were adjusted to coincide with the best times for the drivers. Since then, the accident rate has dropped by one-third.

Finally, there is evidence that men's sex hormone levels rise and fall in a 30-day cycle (Luce, 1970, p. 111).

Since so few studies have been done on this subject, it is impossible to make any firm conclusions. There will undoubtedly be increased interest in the topic in the next few years (Ramey, 1972).

MENOPAUSE

Biological Changes

The *climacteric* is a period lasting about 15 or 20 years (from about age 45 to age 60) during which the body makes the transition from being able to reproduce to not being able to reproduce; the climacteric is marked particularly by a decline in the functioning of the ovaries. But climacteric changes occur in many other body tissues and systems as well. *Menopause* (the "change of life," the "change") refers to one specific event in this process, the cessation of menstruation; this occurs, on the average, during a two-year period beginning at around age 47 (with a normal menopause occurring anywhere between the ages of 35 and 60).

Biologically, as a woman grows older, the pituitary continues a normal output of FSH and LH; however, as the ovaries age, they become less able to respond to the pituitary hormones. Thus the major biological change during the climacteric is the aging of the ovaries with an accompanying decline in the output of their two major products: eggs and the sex hormones estrogen and progesterone. More specifically, the ovaries become less capable of responding to FSH by maturing and releasing an egg. As fewer eggs are released, the cyclic production of progesterone is interrupted, and this in turn results in a decrease in estrogen levels (which results in, among other things, decreased menstruation). The pituitary generally overreacts to the low levels of estrogen and progesterone by producing excessive amounts of FSH and LH, creating further hormonal imbalance. The hormonal changes of menopause, then, involve a decline in estrogen and progesterone levels and hormonal imbalance.

Physical symptoms of menopause include "hot flashes" or "hot flushes," headaches, dizziness, heart palpitations, and pains in the joints. Probable long-range effects of the decline in estrogen levels include *osteoporosis* (porous and brittle bones, which may lead to "dowager's hump") and increased vulnerability to heart disease and cancer. The hot flash is probably the best known of these symptoms. Typically it is described as a sudden wave of heat from the waist up. The woman may get red and perspire a lot; when the flush goes away, she may feel very chilled and sometimes may shiver. The flashes may last from a few seconds to half an hour and may occur several or many times a day. They may also occur at night, causing insomnia, and the resulting perspiration can actually soak the sheets.

Do all women experience these menopausal symptoms? In a survey of 638 women aged 45 to 55, conducted in London in 1964–1965, 30 to 50 percent of the women reported experiencing dizziness, palpitations, insomnia, depression, headache, or weight gain, and most of these women reported experiencing several of these symptoms rather than just one. About 50 percent of the women experienced hot flashes, and half of the 50 percent said the flashes were acutely uncomfortable (McKinlay and Jeffreys, 1974). It is generally estimated that only about 10 percent of all women suffer severe distress at menopause. Thus it might be concluded that at least as many as 50 percent (perhaps 80 to 90 percent) of all women suffer some of these uncomfortable menopausal symptoms, only about 10 percent are severely affected, and a sizable proportion—at least 10 percent and perhaps as many as 50 percent—display none of these symptoms.

Sexuality and Menopause

During the climacteric, physical changes also occur in the vagina. The lack of estrogen causes the vagina to become less acidic, which leaves it more vulnerable to infections. Estrogen is also responsible for maintaining the mucous membranes of the vaginal walls. With a decline in estrogen, there is a decline in vaginal lubrication during arousal, and the vaginal walls become less elastic. Either or both of these may make intercourse painful for the woman. Several remedies are available, including estrogen-replacement therapy (discussed below) and the use of artificial lubricants. Unfortunately, some women do not communicate their discomforts to their husband or physician and instead suffer quietly and develop an aversion to sex. The topic of sexuality and the elderly will be discussed in more detail in Chapter 11. Suffice it to say here that no physical changes occur during menopuase or the climacteric that prevent women from having sex or cause them to have a reduced sex drive. Indeed, some women report that sex is even better after menopause, when the fear of pregnancy no longer inhibits them.

Psychological Changes

Psychological problems of menopause include depression, irritability, anxiety, nervousness, crying spells, inability to concentrate, and feelings of suffocation. In rare cases, the depression may be extremely severe (*involutional melancholia*) in a woman who has no previous history of mental problems. It is estimated that about 10 percent of women suffer from serious depression during menopause. Less severe depression during menopause is more common.

These psychological symptoms, though, involve a subtle problem of interpretation similar to the one mentioned in conjunction with the premenstrual-tension syndrome. Women are said to have "more" problems during menopause. More than what? More than men? More

at menopause

my body is the grapevine that grows and lengthens
brown rope trained to obey the seasons
but ripening comes to an end
there will be no more fruit
no great purple triangles juices bursting the rich skins

(the seasons turn over, the harvesting ends)

my body is growing a new happiness a pungent joy
hard sinews hold up the ancient arbor
touch leaves shade the destroying sun
people shelter beneath me like birds my roots send
more roots into the kind earth, never has the earth been kinder

(the seasons turn over, the fragrances blend)

my body is the grapevine that grows and grows

Mary Winfrey, Whittier, Calif.

FIGURE 4.5

Graphic by Lyda Stock, Alachua, Fla.

than at other times in their own lives? Investigating the latter question, psychologists Bernice Neugarten and Ruth Kraines (1965) studied symptoms among women of different age groups. They found that adolescents and menopausal women reported the largest number of problematic symptoms. Postmenopausal women reported the smallest number of problematic symptoms; apparently, menopause does not permanently "wreck" a woman. Among the adolescents, psychological symptoms were the most common (for example, tension), while among the menopausal women, physical symptoms such as hot flashes were most common. Menopausal women showed an increase in only five categories of psychological symptoms: headache, irritability, nervousness, feeling blue, and feelings of suffocation (the latter being associated with hot flashes). Thus menopause may not be the worst time of a woman's life psychologically; probably it is not so bad as adolescence.

What Causes the Symptoms

The difficulties associated with menopause are attributed to biology (in particular, hormones) by some and to culture and its expectations by others.

From the biological perspective, the symptoms of menopause appear to be due to the woman's hormonal state. In particular, the symptoms appear to be related either to low estrogen levels or to hormonal imbalance. The former hypothesis, called the *estrogen-deficiency theory*, has been the subject of the most research. Proponents of this theory argue that the physical symptoms, such as hot flashes, and the psychological symptoms, such as depression, are caused by declining amounts of estrogen in the body. It is also worth noting that, hormonally, this period is similar to the premenstrual period, with its declining estrogen levels, and that the psychological symptoms are also similar: depression and irritability.

The best evidence for the estrogen-deficiency theory comes from the success of estrogen-replacement therapy. Physicians may prescribe estrogen either in its natural form, Premarin, or in a synthetic form such as Stilbestrol, Progynon, or Meprane. Estrogen-replacement therapy is very successful in relieving low-estrogen menopausal symptoms like hot flashes, sweating, cold hands and feet, osteoporosis, and vaginal discharges. It may also relieve psychological symptoms such as irritability and depression (see Bardwick, 1971, for a review). The success of this therapy suggests that low estrogen levels cause menopausal symptoms and that raising estrogen levels relieves the symptoms.

On the other hand, advocates of the environmental point of view note the cultural forces that may act to produce psychological stress in women around the time of menopause. The aging process itself may be psychologically stressful in our youth-oriented culture. The menopausal years remind a woman forcefully that she is aging. Menopause also means that the woman can no longer bear children; for women who have a great psychological investment in motherhood, this can be a difficult realization.

We also have a strong cultural bias toward expecting menopausal symptoms. Thus any quirk in a middle-aged woman's behavior is attributed to the "change." It simultaneously becomes the cause of, and explanation for, all the problems and complaints of the middle-aged woman. Given such expectations, it is not surprising that the average person perceives widespread evidence of the pervasiveness of menopausal symptoms. Ironically, idiosyncrasies in women of childbearing age are blamed on menstruation, while problems experienced by women who are past that age are blamed on the *lack* of it.

Sociologist Pauline Bart (1971) has done an important study of depression in middle-aged women and its cultural causes. Middle-aged women are likely to be afflicted with the problem of the "empty nest"; the children have left home to work or get married, leaving the woman alone with her husband in an empty house. Bart believes that the empty-nest syndrome is the major source of depression in middle-aged women. Loss of role, according to Bart, can cause depression. That is, a person's major role is a major source of identity, and if this role or identity is taken away, depression results. For many adult women, the mother role is their major role and the major definer of their identity. When their children leave home, the mother role and identity leave with them, leading to depression. Interestingly, Bart found that it is not the "rebels"—masculine women or career women—who suffer most from depression in middle age, but rather the traditional, overprotective, "supermother" or "Jewish mother" type. This finding is perfectly consistent with Bart's theory, since the supermother has the greatest investment in the mother role. Because most of her identity is defined by it, she has more to lose when the children leave home. In cross-cultural research, Bart also found that in some cultures a woman's status does not decline in middle age and may even increase at that time; in these cultures, middle-aged women have a low depression rate. This finding provides strong evidence that the "menopausal" symptom of depression is due not to the biological stress of declining hormone levels but rather to cultural factors.

As a way of resolving this biology-culture controversy, it seems reasonable to conclude that the physical symptoms of menopause, such as hot flashes, are probably due to declining estrogen levels and that the psychological symptoms, such as depression, may be due to low estrogen levels, culturally imposed stresses, or a combination of both.

The practical implications of these results are that estrogen-replacement therapy may be very helpful to many menopausal women, particularly for relief of physical discomfort. However, the therapy needs to be carefully administered by a physician, and there is considerable controversy over the correct time to begin the therapy (Weideger, 1976).[2] When depression is the main problem, estrogen replacement may also be helpful, but the woman herself, as well as those close to her, should recognize the possible cultural sources of her depression. A decision to embark on a new life and create a new identity—for example, going back to school, developing a career, or becoming seriously involved in volunteer work—can be very therapeutic.

MALE MENOPAUSE

Biological Changes

In the technical sense, men do not experience a "menopause"; never having menstruated, they can scarcely cease menstruating. However, men do experience a very gradual decline in manufacture of both testosterone and sperm by the testes, a mild version of the climacteric process in women, although viable sperm may still be produced at age 90.

One of the most common physical problems for men at this age is enlargement of the prostate gland, which is believed to be related to changes in hormone levels. Prostate enlargement occurs in 10 percent of men by age 40 and 50 percent of men who reach age 80. Enlargement of the prostate causes urination problems; there is difficulty in voluntarily initiating urination, as well as frequent nocturnal urination. These symptoms are usually remedied by surgery to remove the part of the gland pressing against the urethra. Nonsurgical treatment is not effective. Administration of female sex hor-

---

[2]Further, the benefits of estrogen-replacement therapy should be weighed against the costs, as there is recent evidence linking it to cancer of the uterus (Mack et al., 1976; Marx, 1976; N. S. Weiss et al., 1976).

mones causes shrinkage of prostate cancer but does not reduce benign (noncancerous) prostate enlargement. Contrary to a number of myths, prostate enlargement is not caused by masturbation or excessive sexual activity. The infection and inflammation resulting from venereal disease, though, can cause prostate enlargement.

Psychological Changes

As noted above, in our culture the aging process may create considerable stress. A process of reassessment and self-examination in men at around the ages of 45 to 50 may lead to a "career crisis." At this age, the man can probably look forward to no future promotions or advancements. His career will at best move sideways and may go downhill. The man who has propped up his identity with visions of future success must face the fact that if "success" has not already been achieved, it is not likely to be in the future. The man may realize that the great goals he set for himself when he was in his twenties have not been attained and probably never will be. On the job, rather than getting the respect he feels he deserves for the wisdom he has gained through experience, he may be regarded as rigid and old-fashioned.

On the home front, his wife may be having menopausal problems of her own. Not only does she have insufficient psychic resources remaining to support him in his crisis, but she also may be voicing complaints about him and their relationship. He may also come to have grave doubts about his own sexuality and virility, and these may be exaggerated by his wife's conflicting feelings about sexuality (see Chapter 11 for a more complete discussion). In extreme cases, men may rebel against these frustrations by "dropping out" and leaving their families or by having an affair (Hackett, cited in Cohn 1974).

It is important that these complaints of middle-aged men and women be recognized and that they be considered legitimate complaints. It is also important to note how many of these crises of middle age lead to satisfactory resolution, in which the person makes a positive alteration in his or her life.

SUMMARY

Biologically, the menstrual cycle is divided into four phases: the follicular phase, ovulation, the luteal phase, and menstruation. Corresponding to these phases, there are changes in the levels of pituitary hormones (FSH and LH) and in the levels of ovarian hormones (estrogen and progesterone), as well as changes in the ovaries and the uterus. A fairly common menstrual problem is dysmenorrhea, or painful menstruation.

Research indicates that some, though probably not all, women experience changes in mood over the phases of the menstrual cycle. For those who experience such changes, mood is generally positive around the middle of the cycle (that is, around ovulation), while negative moods characterized by depression and irritability are more likely just before and during menstruation. The latter phenomenon is the premenstrual-tension syndrome. On the other hand, research indicates that there are no fluctuations in performance over the cycle. There is evidence suggesting that fluctuations in mood are related to changes in hormone levels, but data are also available suggesting that mood fluctuations are related to cultural factors. Research attempting to document whether men experience monthly biological and/or psychological cycles is now in progress.

The climacteric is the period in middle age during which the functioning of the ovaries (both hormone and egg production) declines gradually. One symptom of this process is menopause, the cessation of menstruation. Physical symptoms, such as hot flashes, during this period probably result from declining levels of estrogen and may be relieved by estrogen-replacement therapy; psychological problems, such as depression, may be related either to the decline of estrogen or to cultural factors, such as the empty-nest syndrome.

Men experience a much more gradual decline in the functioning of their gonads. They may experience a psychological crisis of middle age parallel to that experienced by women.

SUGGESTIONS FOR FURTHER READING

Bart, Pauline B. Depression in middle-aged women. In V. Gornick and B. K. Moran (Eds.), *Women in sexist society.* New York: Basic Books, 1971. Chap. 6. Contains an excellent discussion of the emotional problems of middle-aged women and the cultural sources of these problems, as well as a description of Bart's own research. Also reprinted in J. Bardwick (Ed.), *Readings on the psychology of women.* New York: Harper & Row, 1972.

Dalton, Katharina. *The menstrual cycle.* New York: Pantheon, 1969. Dalton is a leading authority on the biology and psychology of menstruation. This is a very informative book.

Paige, Karen E. Women learn to sing the menstrual blues. *Psychology Today,* 1973, **7**(4), 41. A thought-provoking article on the negative attitudes in our culture toward menstruation.

Weideger, Paula. *Menstruation and menopause: The physiology and psychology, the myth and the reality.* New York: Knopf, 1976. A very detailed discussion of menstruation and menopause, and especially of the taboos and superstitions surrounding them. Weideger has some biases, but the book is basically excellent and written for the general public.

CONCEPTION, PREGNANCY, AND CHILDBIRTH

CITED

I realized I was pregnant the same night I became pregnant. I lay there all night. I'd had a very active sex life, and it was the first time I had ever felt this way. I wasn't expecting to get pregnant, but I felt different that night.

Being pregnant meant I was a woman. I was enthralled with my belly growing. I went out right away and got maternity clothes.

I was lying on my stomach and felt—something, like someone lightly touching my deep insides. Then I just sat very still and for an alive moment felt the hugeness of having something living growing in me. Then I said no, it's not possible, it's too early yet, and then I started to cry. . . . That one moment was my first body awareness of another living thing inside me.

When I was about six months pregnant, and Dick was starting school again, I was home alone, isolated for days at a time. My nightmares and daydreams started around then. Really terrible fears of the baby being deformed. All my life I've always been the good girl. I knew I wasn't really good. I knew I had bad thoughts, but I was never allowed to express them. So I thought that my baby's deformities would be the living proof of the ugliness and badness in me.

I thought it would never end. I was enormous. I couldn't bend over and wash my feet. And it was incredibly hot.*

hapter 3 described the remarkable biological process by which a single fertilized egg develops into a male or a female human being. This chapter is about some equally remarkable processes involved in creating human beings: conception, pregnancy, and childbirth.

CONCEPTION

Sperm Meets Egg: The Incredible Journey

On about day 14 of an average menstrual cycle, the woman ovulates. The egg is released from the ovary into the body cavity. Typically it is then picked up by the fimbriae (long fingerlike

structures at the end of the fallopian tube—see Figure 5.1) and enters the fallopian tube. It then begins a leisurely trip down the tube toward the uterus, reaching it in about three days. The egg, unlike the sperm, has no means of moving itself and is propelled by the cilia (hairlike structures) lining the tube. The egg has begun its part of the journey toward conception. If it is not fertilized, it disintegrates.

Meanwhile, the woman has been having intercourse. The man has an orgasm and ejaculates inside the woman's vagina. The sperm are deposited in the vagina, there to begin their journey toward the egg. Actually they have made an incredible trip even before reaching the vagina. Initially they were manufactured in the seminiferous tubules of the testes (see Chapter 2). They then collected and were stored in the epididymis. During ejaculation they moved up and over the top of the bladder in the vas

---

*Source: Boston Women's Health Book Collective. *Our bodies, ourselves*. New York: Simon & Schuster, 1973, pp. 166–167, 170–171.

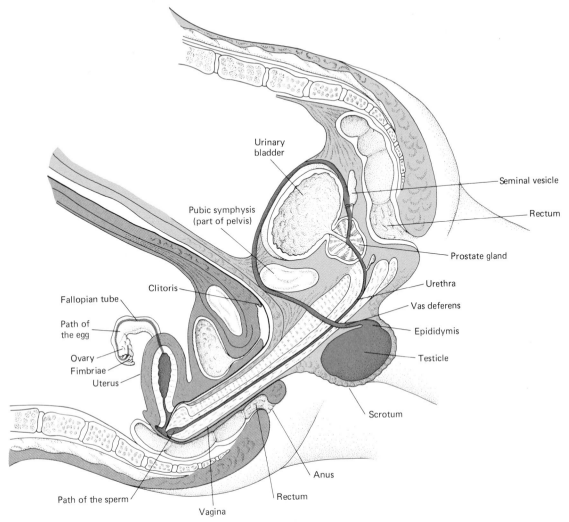

Urinary
bladder

Seminal vesicle

Rectum

Pubic symphysis
(part of pelvis)

Prostate gland

Clitoris

Urethra

Fallopian tube

Vas deferens

Path of
the egg

Epididymis

Ovary

Testicle

Fimbriae

Uterus

Scrotum

Anus

Path of the sperm

Rectum

Vagina

FIGURE 5.1

The pathway of sperm and egg from manufacture in the testes and ovary to
conception, which typically occurs in the fallopian tube.

deferens; then they traveled down through the
ejaculatory duct, mixed with seminal fluid, and
went out through the urethra.

The sperm is one of the tiniest cells in the
human body. It is composed of a *head*, a
midpiece, and a *tail* (see Figure 5.2). The head
is about 5 microns long, and the total length,
from the tip of the head to the tip of the tail, is

about 60 microns (about $^2/_{1000}$ inch, or 0.06
millimeter). The chromosomal material, which is
the sperm's most important contribution when it
unites with the egg, is contained in the nucleus,
which is in the head of the sperm. The midpiece
contains mitochondria, which are tiny structures in which chemical reactions occur that
provide energy. This energy is used when the

- Head
- Nucleus containing chromosomes
- Midpiece containing mitochondria to provide energy for swimming
- Tail

FIGURE 5.2
The structure of a mature human sperm.

sperm lashes its tail back and forth. The lashing action (called flagellation) propels the sperm forward.

A typical ejaculate has a volume of about 3 milliliters, or about a teaspoonful, and contains about 300 million sperm. While this might seem to be a wasteful amount of sperm if only one is needed for fertilization, the great majority of the sperm never get even close to the egg. Some of the ejaculate, together with the sperm in it, may flow out of the vagina as a result of gravity. Other sperm may be killed by the acidity of the vagina, to which they are very sensitive. Of those which make it safely into the uterus, half swim up the wrong fallopian tube (the one containing no egg).

But here we are, several hours later, with a hearty band of sperm swimming up the fallopian tube toward the egg, against the currents that are bringing the egg down. Sperm are capable of swimming 1 to 3 centimeters (about 1 inch) per hour, although it has been documented that sperm may arrive at the egg within 1 to 1½ hours after ejaculation, which is much sooner than would be expected, given their swimming rate. It is thought that muscular contractions in the uterus may help speed them along. By the time a sperm reaches the egg, it has swum approximately 3000 times its own length (this would be comparable to a swim of over 3 miles for a human being).

Contrary to the popular belief that conception occurs in the uterus, typically it occurs in the outer third (the part near the ovary) of the fallopian tube. Of the original 300 million sperm, only about 2000 reach the tube containing the egg. The egg is surrounded by a thin, gelatinous layer called the *zona pellucida*. While the exact mechanism that permits one and only one sperm to enter the egg is unknown, it is thought that the sperm swarm around the egg and secrete an enzyme called *hyaluronidase* (produced by the acrosome located in the head of the sperm—see Figure 5.2); this enzyme dissolves the zona pellucida, permitting one sperm to penetrate the egg.[1] Conception has occurred.

The fertilized egg, called the *zygote*, continues to travel down the fallopian tube. About 36 hours after conception, it begins the process of cell division, by which the original one cell becomes a mass of two cells, then four cells, then eight cells, and so on. About five to seven days after conception, the mass of cells implants itself in the lining of the uterus, there to be nourished and grow. For the first eight weeks of

---

[1]Thus while only one sperm is necessary to accomplish fertilization, it appears that it is important for him to have a lot of his buddies along to help him get into the egg. Therefore, maintaining a high sperm count seems to be important for conception.

gestation the *conceptus* (product of conception) is called an *embryo*; from then until birth it is called a *fetus*.

Improving the Chances of Conception: Making a Baby

While this topic may seem rather remote to the average college student, whose principal concern is probably *avoiding* conception, some couples do want to have a baby. The following are points for them to keep in mind.

The whole trick, of course, is to time intercourse so that it occurs around the time of ovulation. To do this, it is necessary to determine when the woman ovulates. If she is that idealized woman with the perfectly regular 28-day cycle, then she ovulates on around day 14. But for the vast majority of women, the time of ovulation can best be determined by keeping a *basal body temperature chart*. To do this, the woman takes her temperature every morning immediately upon waking (that means before getting up and moving around, having a cigarette, or drinking a cup of coffee). She then keeps a graph of her temperature (like the one shown in Figure 4.2). During the preovulatory phase, the temperature will be relatively constant, fluctuating by only a few tenths of a degree (the temperature is below 98.6°F because temperature is low in the early morning). On the day of ovulation the temperature drops, and on the day following ovulation it rises sharply, by 0.4°F to 1.0°F above the preovulatory level. The temperature should then stay at that high level until just before menstruation. The most reliable indicator of ovulation is the rise in temperature the day after it occurs. From this, the woman can determine the day of ovulation, and that determination should be consistent with menstruation occurring about 14 days later. After doing this for a couple of cycles, the woman should have a fairly good idea of the day in her cycle on which she ovulates.

Sperm live inside the woman's body for about 48 hours.[2] The egg is capable of being fertilized for about the first 12 to 24 hours after ovulation. Allowing the sperm some swimming time, this means that intercourse should be timed right at ovulation or one or two days before.

Assuming you have some idea of the time of ovulation, how frequent should intercourse be? While more may be merrier, more is not necessarily more effective. The reason for this is that it is important for the man's sperm count to be maintained. It takes awhile to manufacture 300 million sperm—at least 24 hours. And, as was discussed earlier, maintaining a high sperm count appears to be important in accomplishing the task of fertilizing the egg. For purposes of conceiving, then, it is probably best to have intercourse about every 24 to 48 hours, or about four times during the week in which the woman is to ovulate.

It is also important to take some steps to ensure that, once deposited in the vagina, the sperm get a decent chance to survive and to find their way into the fallopian tubes. Position during and after intercourse is important. For purposes of conceiving, the best position for intercourse is with the woman on her back (man-on-top, or "missionary," position—see Chapter 8). If the woman is on top, much of the ejaculate may run out of the vagina because of the pull of gravity. After intercourse, she should remain on her back, possibly with her legs pulled up and a pillow under her hips, preferably for about a half hour to an hour. This allows the semen to remain in a pool in the vagina, which gives the sperm a good chance to swim up into the uterus. Since sperm are very sensitive to the pH (acidity-basicity) of the vagina, this factor also requires some consideration.

---

[2]But do not assume this if you are concerned with *contraception*. A few recent reports indicate that they may survive for 5 or even 10 days.

Acidity kills sperm. Douching with commercial preparations or with acidic solutions (such as vinegar) should be avoided. If anything, the woman may want to douche before intercourse with a slightly basic solution made by adding 2 or 3 tablespoons of baking soda to a quart of water. Finally, lubricants and/or suppositories should not be used; they may kill sperm or block their entrance into the uterus.

DEVELOPMENT OF THE CONCEPTUS

For the nine months of pregnancy, two organisms—the conceptus and the pregnant woman—undergo parallel, dramatic changes. The changes that occur in the developing conceptus will be discussed in this section; following sections will be about the changes that take place in the pregnant woman.

Typically the nine months of pregnancy are divided into three equal periods of three months each called *trimesters*. Thus the first trimester is months 1 to 3, the second trimester is months 4 to 6, and the third (or last) trimester is months 7 to 9.

The Embryo and Its Support Systems

We left the conceptus, which began as a single fertilized egg cell, dividing into many cells as it passed down the fallopian tube, becoming first a *morula*, and then a *blastocyst*, and finally arriving in the uterus and implanting itself into the uterine wall.

During the embryonic period of development (the first eight weeks) most of the fetus's major organ systems are formed in processes that occur with amazing speed. The inner part of the ball of cells implanted in the uterus now differentiates into two layers, the endoderm and the ectoderm. Later a third layer, the mesoderm,

forms between them. The various organs of the body differentiate from these layers. The *ectoderm* will form the entire nervous system and the skin, as well as derivatives of it such as hair and the lens of the eye. The *endoderm* differentiates into the digestive system—from the pharynx, to the stomach and intestines, to the rectum—and the respiratory system. The muscles, skeleton, connective tissue, and reproductive and circulatory systems derive from the *mesoderm*. Fetal development generally proceeds in a cephalocaudal order. That is, the head develops first, and the lower body last. For this reason, the head of the fetus is enormous compared with the rest of the body (see Figure 5.5).

Meanwhile, another group of cells has differentiated into the *trophoblast*, which has important functions in maintaining the embryo and which will eventually become the placenta.

The *placenta* is the mass of tissues that surrounds the conceptus early in development and nurtures its growth. Later it moves to the side of the fetus. The placenta has a number of important functions, perhaps the most important of which is that it serves as a site for exchange of substances between the woman's blood and the fetus's blood. It is important to note that the woman's circulatory system and the fetus's circulatory system are completely separate; that is, with only rare exceptions, the woman's blood never circulates inside the fetus, nor does the fetus's blood circulate in the woman's blood vessels. Instead, the fetus's blood passes out of its body through the umbilical cord to the placenta. There it circulates in the numerous *villi* (tiny fingerlike projections in the placenta). The woman's blood circulates around the outside of these villi. Thus there is a membrane barrier between the two blood systems. Some substances are capable of passing through this barrier, while others are not. Oxygen and nutrients can pass through the barrier, and thus the woman's blood supplies oxygen and nutrients to the fetus, providing substitutes for breathing and eating. Carbon dioxide and waste products similarly pass back from the fetal blood to the woman's blood. Some viruses and other disease-causing organisms can pass through the barrier, including those for German measles (rubella) and syphilis. But other organisms cannot pass through the barrier; thus the woman may have a terrible cold, but the fetus will remain completely healthy. Various drugs can also cross the placental barrier, and the woman should therefore be careful about drugs taken during pregnancy (see the section on drugs during pregnancy, below).

Another major function of the placenta is that it acts as an endocrine gland; that is, it secretes hormones. The placenta produces large quantities of estrogen and does so increasingly throughout the pregnancy; thus the pregnant woman is essentially in a hyperestrogenic state. The placenta also manufactures large quantities of progesterone. Many of the physical symptoms of pregnancy may be caused by these elevated levels of hormones. The other two hormones manufactured by the placenta are *human chorionic gonadotropin* (HCG) and *chorionic somatomammotropin*. HCG is the hormone that is detected in pregnancy tests.

The *umbilical cord* is formed during the fifth week of embryonic development and is composed of several structures: the body stalk, the allantois, and the umbilical blood vessels. The fully developed cord is about 55 centimeters (20 inches) long. Normally, it contains three blood vessels: two arteries and one vein. Some people believe that the fetus's umbilical cord attaches to the woman's navel; actually, the umbilical cord attaches to the placenta, thereby providing for the interchanges of substances described above.

Two membranes surround the fetus, the *chorion* and the *amnion*, the amnion being the innermost. The amnion is filled with a watery liquid called *amniotic fluid*, in which the fetus floats and can readily move. It is the amniotic fluid that is sampled when an amniocentesis is performed (see below). The amniotic fluid maintains the fetus at a constant temperature and, most important, cushions the fetus against possible injury. Thus the woman can fall down a flight of stairs, and the fetus will remain undisturbed. Indeed, the amniotic fluid might be considered the original waterbed.

Fetal Development during the First Trimester

In a sense, the development of the fetus during the first trimester is more remarkable than its development during the second and third trimesters, for it is during the first trimester that the small mass of cells implanted in the uterus develops into a fetus with most of the major organ systems present and with recognizable human features.

By the third week of gestation, the embryo appears as a small bit of flesh and is about 0.2 centimeter ($1/12$ inch) long. During the third and fourth weeks, the head undergoes a great deal of development. The central nervous system begins to form, and the beginnings of eyes and ears are visible. The backbone is constructed by the end of the fourth week. A "tail" is noticeable early in embryonic development but has disappeared by the eighth week.

From the fourth to the eighth weeks, the external body parts—eyes, ears, arms, hands, fingers, legs, feet, and toes—develop. By the end of the tenth week they are completely formed. Indeed, by the tenth week, the embryo has not only a complete set of fingers but also fingernails.

By the end of the seventh week, the liver, lungs, pancreas, kidneys, and intestines have formed and have begun limited functioning.

FIGURE 5.3

A human embryo 38 days after conception. [*From R. Rugh and L. Shettles. From conception to birth: The drama of life's beginnings. New York: Harper & Row, 1971.*]

The gonads have also formed, but the gender of the fetus is not clearly distinguishable until the twelfth week. It is also during the twelfth week that eyebrows and eyelashes are formed.

At the end of the twelfth week (end of the first trimester) the fetus is unmistakably human and looks like a small infant. It is about 10 centimeters (4 inches) long and weighs about 19 grams (²/₃ ounce). From this point on, development consists mainly of enlargement and differentiation of structures that are already present.

FIGURE 5.4
A human embryo at 2 months of age. [*From R. Rugh and L. Shettles.
From conception to birth: The drama of life's beginnings. New York:
Harper & Row, 1971.*]

Fetal Development during the Second Trimester

Around the end of the fourteenth week, the movements of the fetus can be detected ("quickening"). This is an important event to many women. By the eighteenth week, the woman has been able to feel movement for two to four weeks, and the physician can detect the fetal heartbeat. The latter is an important point since it helps the physician determine the length of gestation. The baby should be born about 20 weeks later. If it is born at the eighteenth week, it cannot survive. If born in the twenty-third week, it weighs less than 1000 grams (2 pounds) and has about a 1 in 10,000 chance of survival, given expert care (Behrman and Rosen, 1976).

The fetus first opens its eyes around the twentieth week. By about the twenty-fourth week, it is sensitive to light and can hear sounds in utero. Arm and leg movements are vigorous at this time, and the fetus alternates between periods of wakefulness and sleep.

Fetal Development during the Third Trimester

At the end of the second trimester the fetus's skin is wrinkled and covered with downlike hair. At the beginning of the third trimester, fat deposits form under the skin; these will give the infant the characteristic chubby appearance of babyhood. The downlike hair is lost.

A baby born at the end of the seventh month has a 50 percent chance of survival. It is

CONCEPTION, PREGNANCY, AND CHILDBIRTH

FIGURE 5.5

A human fetus at 12 weeks of age. [*From R. Rugh and L. Shettles.* From conception to birth: The drama of life's beginnings. *New York: Harper & Row, 1971.*]

a misconception that babies born during the seventh month are more likely to live than those born during the eighth month. The closer to full term, the better the chance of survival. Thus a baby born at the end of the eighth month has a 90 to 95 percent chance of survival; for one born at the end of nine months, the chance of survival is 99 percent.

During the seventh month the baby turns in the uterus to assume a head-down position. If this turning does not occur by the time of delivery, there will be a *breech presentation.*

The fetus's growth during the last two months is rapid. At the end of the eighth month it weighs an average of 2500 grams (5 pounds, 4 ounces). The average full-term baby weighs 3300 grams (7.5 pounds) and is 50 centimeters (20 inches) long. According to the *Guinness*

Book of World Records, in 1961 Mrs. Saadet Cor, of Turkey, gave birth to the largest normal baby ever born; it weighed 24 pounds, 4 ounces. The smallest baby ever to survive was Marion Chapman, who was born in 1938 in England. She weighed 10 ounces. The birth took place without the help of a physician.

THE STAGES OF PREGNANCY

The First Trimester (The First 12 Weeks)

Symptoms of pregnancy For most women, the first symptom of pregnancy is a missed menstrual period. Of course, there may be a wide variety of reactions to this event. For the teenager who is not married or for the married woman who feels that she already has enough children, the reaction may be negative—depression, anger, and fear. For the woman who has been trying to conceive for several months, the reaction may be joy and eager anticipation.

In fact, there are many other reasons besides pregnancy why a woman may have a late period or miss a period; illness or emotional stress may delay a period, and women occasionally skip a period for no apparent reason.

It is also true that a woman may continue to experience some cyclic bleeding or spotting during pregnancy. It is not particularly a danger sign, except that in a few cases it is a symptom of a miscarriage.

If the woman has been keeping a basal body temperature chart, this can provide a very early sign that she is pregnant. If her temperature rises abruptly at about the time ovulation would normally occur and then stays up for more than two weeks—say, about three weeks—the chances are fairly good that she is pregnant. The increased temperature results from the high levels of progesterone manufactured by the corpus luteum and, later, the placenta.

Another early symptom of pregnancy is tenderness of the breasts—a tingling sensation and special sensitivity of the nipples—which results from hormonal stimulation of the mammary glands.

Nausea and vomiting (called "morning sickness," although these symptoms may actually happen anytime during the day) may occur during the first six to eight weeks of pregnancy and are another early sign. More frequent urination, feelings of fatigue, and a need for more sleep are other early signs of pregnancy.

Pregnancy tests A pregnancy test may be done by a physician, at a Planned Parenthood or Family Planning clinic, or at a medical laboratory.

FIGURE 5.6
A human fetus at 17 weeks of age. [*From R. Rugh and L. Shettles.* From conception to birth: The drama of life's beginnings. *New York: Harper & Row, 1971.*]

There are two main kinds of pregnancy tests—immunologic and biologic; and both are based on detecting the presence of HCG (human chorionic gonadotropin), which is secreted by the placenta. Both are urine tests. The immunologic test, which is most commonly used, can be done in a matter of minutes and is very accurate. It involves simply mixing a drop of urine with certain chemicals on a slide. If HCG is present, the mixture will not coagulate and the test for pregnancy is positive (the woman is pregnant).

FIGURE 5.7

A human fetus at 8 months of age. [*From R. Rugh and L. Shettles.* From conception to birth: The drama of life's beginnings. *New York: Harper & Row, 1971.*]

The biological test, which used to be the standard test, involves injecting the woman's urine into a laboratory animal—a mouse, rat, rabbit (hence the name "rabbit test"), or frog. If HCG is present, the animal will ovulate. The test thus takes several days. Another, similar test involves injecting a male frog with the urine; if HCG is present, the frog will ejaculate microscopically visible sperm within about two hours.

The laboratory tests for pregnancy are 95 to 98 percent accurate. A laboratory test may produce a false negative (tell the woman she is not pregnant when she really is) if it is done too early or if errors are made in processing. Also, some women simply do not show positive signs in the tests or do not do so until the second or third test. The presence of HCG can be detected as early as the third week of pregnancy (one week after the missed period), but the tests are not highly accurate until the sixth to eighth week of pregnancy.

A new test, called the *beta subunit HCG radioimmunoassay*, was developed recently in Boston. It measures HCG in a blood sample and is sensitive enough to detect a pregnancy eight days after conception or five days *before* the missed period. It is highly accurate, but it is not yet widely used.

It is important that early, accurate pregnancy tests be available and that women make use of them. This is true for several reasons. A woman needs to know that she is pregnant as early as possible so that she can see a physician and begin getting good prenatal care. She also needs to know so that she can get the nutrition she requires during pregnancy (see the section on nutrition, below). And if she does not want to carry the baby to term, she needs to know as soon as possible since abortions are much safer and simpler when performed in the first trimester than when done in the second trimester.

At around the sixth to eighth weeks, pregnancy can also be detected by a pelvic exam. The physician looks for *Hegar's sign*, which is a pronounced softening of the isthmus of the uterus (the middle part of the uterus, between the cervix and the body of the uterus). The exam is performed by placing one hand on the abdomen and two fingers of the other hand in the vagina (see Figure 5.8). A change in the color of the cervix, from pale pink to a bluish hue, is another sign of pregnancy at this time.

The signs of pregnancy may be classified as

presumptive signs, probable signs, and positive signs. Amenorrhea, breast tenderness, nausea, and so on, are presumptive signs. The pregnancy tests discussed above all provide probable signs. Three signs are interpreted as positive signs, that is, as definite indications of pregnancy: (1) beating of the fetal heart, (2) active fetal movement, and (3) detection of a fetal skeleton by x-ray (this is done only rarely because of the dangers involved). These signs cannot be detected until the fourth month.

Once the pregnancy has been confirmed, the woman generally is very interested in determining her expected delivery date (called *EDC* for a rather antiquated expression, "expected date of confinement"). The EDC is calculated using *Nägele's rule*. The rule says to take the date of the first day of the last menstrual period, subtract three months, add seven days, and finally add one year. Thus if the first day of the last menstrual period was September 10, 1978, the expected delivery date would be June 17, 1979: subtracting three months from September 10 gives June 10, adding seven days yields June 17, and adding one year gives June 17, 1979. Nägele's rule works fairly well; 39 percent of infants are born within five days of the predicted date, and 55 percent are born within 10 days of it (Burger and Korompai, 1939, cited in Hellman and Pritchard, 1971).

Physical changes The basic physical change that takes place in the woman's body during the first trimester is the large increase in the levels of hormones, especially estrogen and progesterone, which are produced by the placenta. Many of the other physical symptoms of the first trimester arise from these endocrine changes.

The breasts swell and tingle. This results from the development of the mammary glands, which is stimulated by hormones. The nipples and the area around them (areola) may darken and broaden.

FIGURE 5.8
A pelvic exam for Hegar's sign, an indicator of pregnancy. [*From N. J. Eastman and L. M. Hellman. Williams obstetrics. (13th ed.) New York: Appleton-Century-Crofts, 1966. Courtesy of Appleton-Century-Crofts, Educational Division, Meredith Corporation.*]

There is often a need to urinate more frequently. This is related to changes in pituitary hormones that affect the adrenals, which in turn change the water balance in the body so that more water is retained. The growing uterus also contributes by pressing against the bladder.

Bowel movements may become irregular because the high levels of progesterone relax the smooth muscle of the rectum and also because the growing uterus exerts pressure on the rectum. Also, if the woman reduces her activity because of feelings of fatigue, which are common during the first trimester, this may contribute to constipation.

One of the best-known symptoms is morning sickness; the woman experiences feelings of nausea, often to the point of vomiting, and of revulsion toward food or its odor. The nausea and vomiting may occur on waking or at other times during the day. The exact cause of this is

101

not known. One theory is that the high levels of estrogen irritate the stomach. The rapid expansion of the uterus may also be involved. While these symptoms are quite common, it is also true that about 25 percent of pregnant women experience no vomiting at all.[3]

Vaginal discharges may also increase at this time, partly because the increased hormone levels change the pH of the vagina and partly because the vaginal secretions are changing in their chemical composition and quantity.

The feelings of fatigue and sleepiness are probably related to the high levels of progesterone, which is known to have a sedative effect.

Psychological changes   Our culture is full of stereotypes about the psychological characteristics of pregnant women. It is supposed to be a time of happiness and calm; radiant contentment is said to emanate from the woman's face, making this a good time for her to be photographed. Pregnant women are also seen as somewhat irrational, demanding, and dependent—capable, for example, of sending their husbands to the refrigerator for dill pickles and ice cream at midnight.

Actually, the data suggest that the situation is much more complex than this (see the review by Sherman, 1971). A woman's emotional state during pregnancy appears to vary according to a number of factors: her attitude toward the pregnancy (whether she wanted to be pregnant), her social class, her general life adjustment, conflict in the marriage, and stage of pregnancy. The positive emotions noted above are probably a result of the traditional assumption in our culture that all babies are wanted and that all women want babies. However, with increased concern over population size, growing acceptance of methods of contraception, and decreased emphasis on fertility, it has be-

come increasingly recognized that pregnancy may not always be a good thing. These changes in values may make pregnant women feel freer to acknowledge their negative feelings.

Depression and fatigue are not at all uncommon during the first trimester; they may be partly the result of morning sickness. But there is great variation in pregnant women's emotional state. Happiness is more common among those who want to be pregnant, while depression is more common among those who do not. Women of lower socioeconomic status are more likely to have negative feelings (although this may be explained by the fact that there are more unwanted pregnancies among women in the lower social classes). Women who have made a generally good life adjustment tend to feel more positive at this time than women with a history of neurotic symptoms. Finally, negative emotions are commoner when there is a conflict in the marriage.

Couvade and sympathetic pregnancy   Occasionally some husbands may experience nausea and vomiting along with their pregnant wives. This reaction is called *sympathetic pregnancy*.

In some cultures this phenomenon takes a more dramatic form, known as the *couvade*. In the couvade, the husband retires to bed while his wife is in labor. He suffers all the pains of delivery, moaning and groaning as she does. Couvade is still practiced in some parts of Asia, North and South America, and Oceania (Mead and Newton, 1967).

The Second Trimester (Weeks 13 to 26)

Physical changes   During the fourth month, the woman becomes aware of the fetus's movements ("quickening"). Many women find this to be a very exciting experience.

The woman is made even more aware of the pregnancy by her rapidly expanding belly.

---

[3]About 1 woman in 200 experiences *hyperemis gravidarum*, in which the vomiting is so severe that it may have serious consequences, including malnutrition, and require hospitalization.

There are a variety of reactions to this. Some women feel that it is a magnificent symbol of womanhood, and they rush out to buy maternity clothes and wear them before they are even necessary. Other women feel awkward and resentful of their bulky shape and may begin to wonder whether they can fit through doorways and turnstiles.

Most of the physical symptoms of the first trimester, such as morning sickness, disappear, and discomforts are at a minimum. Physical problems at this time include constipation, hemorrhoids (caused by the pressure of the pelvic organs on the blood vessels of the rectum), and nosebleeds (caused by increased blood volume). *Edema*—water retention and swelling—may be a problem in the face, hands, wrists, ankles, and feet; it results from increased water retention throughout the body.

By about mid-pregnancy, the breasts, under hormonal stimulation, have essentially completed their development in preparation for nursing. Beginning about the nineteenth week, a thin amber or yellow fluid called *colostrum* may come out of the nipple, although there is no milk yet.

Psychological changes   While the first trimester can be relatively tempestuous, particularly with morning sickness, the second trimester is generally a period of relative calm and well-being. The discomforts of the first trimester are past, and the tensions associated with the close approach of delivery are not yet present. Research shows that women's emotions are more positive during this stage than during the other stages (Sherman, 1971).

The Third Trimester (Weeks 27 to 38)

Physical changes   The uterus is very large and hard now. The woman is increasingly aware of her size and of the fetus, which is becoming more and more active. In fact, some women are kept awake at night by its somersaults and hiccups.

The extreme size of the uterus puts pressure on a number of other organs, causing some discomfort. There is pressure on the lungs, which may cause shortness of breath. The stomach is also being squeezed, and indigestion is common. The navel is pushed out. The heart is being strained because of the large increase in blood volume, the strain peaking at about the thirtieth week and declining from then until labor.

The weight gain of the second trimester continues. At this point, many women have trouble restricting their weight gain to a reasonable amount. Most physicians recommend about 20 pounds of weight gain during pregnancy. The average infant at birth weighs 7.5 pounds; the rest of the weight gain is accounted for by the placenta (about 1 pound), the amniotic fluid (about 2 pounds), enlargement of the uterus (about 2 pounds), enlargement of the breasts (about 1.5 pounds), and the additional fat and water retained by the woman (about 6 pounds). Physicians restrict the amount of weight gain because the incidence of complications such as high blood pressure and strain on the heart is much higher in women who gain an excessive amount of weight. Also, excessive weight gained during pregnancy can be very hard to lose afterward, destroying a formerly trim figure.

The woman's balance is somewhat disturbed because of the large amount of weight that has been added to the front part of her body. She may compensate for this by adopting the characteristic "waddling" walk of the pregnant woman, which can result in back pains.

The uterus tightens occasionally in painless contractions called *Braxton-Hicks contractions*; these are not part of labor. It is thought that these contractions help to strengthen the uterine muscles, preparing them for labor.

In the majority of cases, around two to four

weeks before delivery the baby turns, and the head drops down into the pelvis. This is called *lightening*, *dropping*, or *engagement*.

Some women are concerned about the appropriate amount of activity during pregnancy—whether some things constitute "overdoing it." Traditionally physicians and textbooks have warned of the dangers of physical activities and have tried to discourage them. It appears now, however, that such restrictions were based more on superstition than on scientific fact. Current thinking holds that, for a healthy pregnant woman, moderate activity is not dangerous and may actually be beneficial in that it allows her to continue to participate in life, rather than being confined like a prisoner. Modern methods of childbirth encourage sensible exercise for the pregnant woman so that she will be in shape for labor (see the section on natural childbirth, below). The matter, of course, is highly individual. But one recent Olympic swimmer placed third in her event while 3½ months pregnant, and it was reported that 10 of the 25 Soviet women Olympic champions of the Sixteenth Olympiad in Melbourne, Australia, were pregnant (Bruser, 1969).

Psychological changes While the second trimester is relatively sunny, the third trimester may be somewhat stressful psychologically. The incidence of mild emotional disturbances increases, particularly during the last six weeks (Sherman, 1971). During the last month women often become very impatient, feeling as if they are in a state of suspended animation and really wanting to get on with it.

The birth of the baby becomes an ever-nearer reality. With that come some anxieties. Notable among these are worries that the baby will be deformed or defective in some way, an anxiety that may be reflected in the woman's dreams at this time and in her waking fantasies. The woman may also wonder, especially if it is a first child, whether she will be a good mother and whether anything will happen to her during delivery.

SEX DURING PREGNANCY

Many women are concerned about whether it is safe or advisable for them to have sexual intercourse while they are pregnant, particularly during the latter stages of the pregnancy. In the past, these anxieties were affirmed by the traditional attitude of physicians, who often forbade intercourse from the sixth month of pregnancy through the third month postpartum, which meant no coitus for six months. This prohibition was based on the belief that intercourse might (1) cause an infection or (2) precipitate labor prematurely or cause a miscarriage.

Masters and Johnson (1966), whose work will be considered in detail in later chapters, have investigated sexual intercourse during pregnancy. They state emphatically that, given a normal, healthy pregnancy, intercourse can continue safely at least until four weeks before the baby is due. (This is an individual matter, however, and should be decided in consultation with a physician; some women are clearly high-risk cases, for whom intercourse is inadvisable.) Masters and Johnson find that the woman is usually sufficiently recovered three weeks after birth for coitus to be safe, and the woman's sexual interest also generally returns at about that time. Thus it appears that a prohibition of no more than seven weeks is all that is necessary. Indeed, some physicians feel that intercourse is safe as long as it is comfortable for the woman and if her pregnancy is not a high-risk one; thus coitus may be permissible until delivery and again fairly soon after (Butler and Wagner, 1975).

Physicians' pronouncements aside, the available data indicate that women continue to have intercourse, and do so at a near-normal rate, until well into the third trimester. As the data in Table 5.1 indicate, intercourse contin-

TABLE 5.1

PERCENT OF WOMEN HAVING VARIOUS FREQUENCIES OF COITUS AT DIFFERENT STAGES OF PREGNANCY

Number of Acts of Coitus per Week	Baseline One Year before Conception, %	First Trimester, %	Second Trimester, %	Seventh Month, %	Eighth Month, %	Ninth Month, %
None	0	2	2	11	23	59
One	7	11	16	23	29	19
Two to five	81	78	77	63	46	23
Six or more	12	9	5	2	2	1

Source: N. Wagner and D. Solberg. Pregnancy and sexuality. *Medical Aspects of Human Sexuality,* 1974, **8**(3), 44–79.

ues through the second trimester with essentially the same frequency as before pregnancy. There is a slight decrease during the seventh and eighth months, but not until the last month do substantial numbers of women report abstaining from intercourse. Indeed, Masters and Johnson found an increased sexual interest during the second trimester, which is probably related to the passing of the nausea and fatigue of the first trimester and the positive feelings associated with the second trimester.

Of course, during the latter stages of pregnancy, the woman's shape makes intercourse increasingly awkward. The missionary position is probably best abandoned at this time. The side-to-side position (see Chapter 8) is probably the position best suited to the special problems of intercourse during the late stages of pregnancy. Couples should also remember that there are many ways of experiencing sexual pleasure and orgasm besides having intercourse—mutual masturbation or oral-genital sex[4] may be a good alternative for the very pregnant woman.

One of the best guides in this matter is the woman's own feelings. If intercourse becomes uncomfortable for her, it should be discontinued until it does feel more comfortable.

---

[4]There is, however, some risk associated with cunnilingus for the pregnant woman, as discussed in Chap. 8.

NUTRITION

During pregnancy, another living being is growing inside the woman, and she needs lots of energy, protein, vitamins, and minerals at this time. Therefore, diet during pregnancy is extremely important. If the woman's diet is good, she has a much better chance of remaining healthy during pregnancy and of bearing a healthy baby; if her diet is inadequate, she stands more of a chance of developing one of a number of diseases during pregnancy herself and of bearing a child whose weight is low at birth. Babies with low birth weights do not have as good a chance of survival as babies with normal birth weights. According to a study done in Toronto, mothers in a poor-diet group had four times as many serious health problems during pregnancy as a group of mothers whose diets were supplemented with highly nutritious foods. Those with the poor diets had seven times as many threatened miscarriages and three times as many stillbirths; their labor lasted five hours longer on the average (Newton, 1972).

The recommended diet for a pregnant woman is shown in Table 5.2. It is particularly important that she get enough protein, folic acid, iron, calcium, and vitamins A, B, C, D, E, and K. Protein is important for building new tissues. Folic acid is also important for growth; symptoms of folic acid deficiency are anemia

TABLE 5.2

RECOMMENDED DAILY DIET FOR THE PREGNANT WOMAN

Foods	Servings
Whole or skimmed milk	1 quart (1 ounce of cheddar cheese is equivalent to 8 ounces of milk)
Lean meat	One large or two small servings (4 ounces) of meat, fish, or fowl Liver once a week
Eggs	One
Fruit	Two or more servings; one serving should be citrus fruit or other good source of ascorbic acid
Vegetablés	Two or more servings, cooked or raw; should include dark green leafy or deep yellow vegetables One medium potato
Bread and cereal	Whole-grain or enriched bread, at least four slices (½ cup cereal is equivalent to one slice of bread)
Butter or margarine	1 to 2 tablespoons

Essential Nutrients	Amounts
Calories	2300
Protein	78 grams
Calcium	1.3 grams
Iron	20 milligrams
Vitamin A	6000 international units
Thiamine	1.0 milligram
Riboflavin	1.6 milligrams
Niacin equivalent	17 milligrams
Ascorbic acid	100 milligrams
Vitamin D	400 international units

Sources: Food and Nutrition Board, National Research Council. (Rev. ed.) 1963. H. S. Mitchell, H. J. Rynbergen, L. Anderson, and M. V. Dibble. *Cooper's nutrition in health and disease.* (15th ed.) Philadelphia: Lippincott, 1968.

and fatigue. Iron is important for the blood that circulates to the placenta, from which the fetus draws off additional iron for itself. Muscle cramps, nerve pains, uterine ligament pains, sleeplessness, and irritability may all be symptoms of a calcium deficiency. Sometimes even an excellent diet does not provide enough iron, calcium, or folic acid, in which case their intake should be supplemented with pills.

While most physicians agree that intake of the above nutrients is important, there is disagreement over what weight gain and what salt intake are optimal. In the 1960s, physicians advocated low-salt, low-calorie diets and little weight gain, but this approach has been questioned recently. Unfortunately, the issue has not been resolved by research.

EFFECTS OF DRUGS TAKEN DURING PREGNANCY

We are such a pill-popping culture that we seldom stop to think about whether we should take a certain drug. The pregnant woman, however, needs to know that when she takes a drug, not only does it circulate through her body, but it may also circulate through the fetus. Because the fetus develops so rapidly during pregnancy, drugs may have severe consequences, including producing serious malformations. Drugs that produce such defects are called *teratogenic*.[5] An example that attracted much attention in the early 1960s was the drug thalidomide, a tranquilizer; if taken early in pregnancy, it resulted in babies with grotesque deformities such as flipperlike appendages where there should have been arms and legs. Of course, not all drugs can cross the placental barrier, but many can. The drugs that pregnant women should be cautious in using are discussed below.

Antibiotics   Long-term use of antibiotics by the woman may cause damage to the fetus. Tetracycline may cause stained teeth and bone deformities. Gentamycin, kanamycin, neomycin, streptomycin, and vincomycin all may cause deafness. Nitrofurantoin may cause jaundice. Some drugs given in the treatment of tuberculosis can cause jaundice, and those taken by diabetics may cause various fetal anomalies.

Addictive drugs   Alcohol consumed by the woman circulates through the fetus. Alcoholic women can give birth to babies who have alcohol on their breath; the babies then have withdrawal symptoms for the first few days after they are born—scarcely a pleasant introduction to life outside the womb. Excessive amounts of alcohol lead to vitamin depletion and biochemical imbalance, and to low-birth-weight babies, premature birth, or even intrauterine death.

Heroin addiction and morphine addiction lead to similar problems. The babies undergo withdrawal symptoms after birth. Methadone can cause respiratory problems in the baby.

[5]"Teratogenic" is from the Greek words *teras*, meaning "monster," and *genic*, meaning "cause."

Steroids   Synthetic hormones such as progestin can cause masculinization of a female fetus, as discussed in Chapter 3. Corticosteroids are linked with jaundice, low birth weight, cleft palate, and stillbirth. Excessive amounts of vitamin A are associated with cleft palate. Excesses of vitamins D, B6, and K have also been associated with fetal defects. A potent estrogen, diethylstilbestrol (DES), has been shown to cause cancer of the vagina in girls whose mothers took the drug while pregnant (Herbst, 1972). (DES pops up in a number of places. It is used in the "morning-after" pill and as a diet supplement to fatten cattle, the latter use having recently been prohibited because of the possible dangers of ingesting too much DES.)

Others   According to the U.S. Public Health Service, maternal smoking during pregnancy exerts a retarding influence on fetal growth, indicated by decreased infant birth weight and increased incidence of prematurity (see Peterson et al., 1965; Ravenholt and Levinski, 1965; Yerushalmy, 1964).

Some antihistamines may produce malformations. Even plain old aspirin may cause damage.

Although not classified as a drug, x-rays deserve mention here since they can damage the fetus, particularly during the first 42 days after conception.

In a word, the pregnant woman should be very careful about all drugs that enter her body. Unfortunately, we have no information available yet on any possible effects of using marijuana during pregnancy (Leavitt, 1974). It is known, though, that the psychoactive chemical in marijuana crosses the placental barrier (Harbison and Mantilla-Plata, 1972; Idänpään-Heikkilä, 1969). There is some scanty evidence that use of LSD during pregnancy may cause chromosome damage to the infant (Dishotsky et al., 1971) and increases the risk of spontaneous abortion (McGlothlin et al., 1970).

Probably the best rule for the pregnant

woman considering using a drug is, "When in doubt, don't."

BIRTH

The Beginning of Labor

There are a few signs that labor is about to begin, although these vary considerably from one woman to the next. There may be a discharge of a small amount of bloody mucus (the "bloody show"). This is the mucus plug that was in the cervical opening during pregnancy, its purpose being to prevent germs from passing from the vagina up into the uterus. In about 10 percent of all women the membranes containing the amniotic fluid rupture (the bag of waters bursts), and there is a gush of warm fluid down the woman's legs. Labor usually begins within 24 hours after this occurs. More commonly, though, the amniotic sac does not rupture until the end of the first stage of labor.

The Braxton-Hicks contractions may increase before labor and actually may be mistaken for labor. Typically they are distinct from the contractions of labor in that they are very irregular.

The biological mechanism that initiates and maintains labor is not well understood. Hormones are clearly involved. The hormone production of the placenta drops off late in pregnancy. Prostaglandins stimulate uterine muscles and may be important in initiating labor. Oxytocin, which is released by the posterior part of the pituitary, is manufactured late in labor and stimulates the last powerful contractions necessary to push the fetus out.

The Stages of Labor

Labor is typically divided into three stages, although the length of the stages may vary considerably from one woman to the next. The whole process of childbirth is sometimes referred to as *parturition.*

First-stage labor First-stage labor begins with the regular contractions of the muscles of the uterus. These contractions are responsible for producing two changes in the cervix, both of which must occur before the baby can be delivered. These changes are called *effacement* (thinning out) and *dilation* (opening up). The cervix must dilate until it has an opening 10 centimeters (4 inches) in diameter before the baby can be born.

First-stage labor itself is divided into three stages: early, late, and transition. In *early first-stage labor,* contractions are spaced far apart, with perhaps 15 to 20 minutes between them. A contraction typically lasts 45 seconds to a minute. This stage of labor is fairly easy, and the woman is quite comfortable between contractions. Meanwhile, the cervix is effacing and dilating.

Late first-stage labor is marked by the dilation of the cervix from 5 to 8 centimeters (2 to 3 inches). It is generally shorter than the early stage, and the contractions are more frequent and more intense.

The final dilation of the cervix from 8 to 10 centimeters (3 to 4 inches) occurs during the *transition stage,* which is both the shortest and the most difficult. The contractions are very strong, and it is during this stage that women report pain and exhaustion.

The first stage of labor can last anywhere from 2 to 24 hours. It averages about 12 to 15 hours for a first pregnancy and about 8 hours for later pregnancies. (In most respects, first pregnancies are the hardest, and later ones are easier.) The woman is usually told to go to the hospital when the contractions are 4 to 5 minutes apart. Once there, she is put in the labor room for the rest of first-stage labor.

In the labor room, the hospital staff may perform a number of procedures on the woman. They "prep" her, which involves shaving off some or all of the pubic hair. The purpose of this procedure is to make the area as sanitary as possible in order to minimize the chance of infection. They may also give her an enema in order to avoid the possibility of her having an involuntary bowel movement during labor (though this procedure is controversial among feminists, who feel it is degrading and unnecessary). As she shifts to the second stage, she is moved to the delivery room.

Second-stage labor   The second stage of labor begins when the cervix is fully dilated and the baby's head (or whichever part comes first, if the baby is in some other position) begins to move into the vagina, or birth canal. It lasts from a few minutes to a few hours and is generally much shorter than the first stage.

During this stage, many women feel an urge to push or bear down, and, if done properly, this may be of great assistance in pushing the baby out. With each contraction the baby is pushed farther along.

When the baby's head has traversed the entire length of the vagina, the top of it becomes visible at the vaginal entrance; this is called *crowning*. It is at this point that many physicians perform an *episiotomy* (see Figure 5.9), in which an incision or slit is made in the perineum, the skin just behind the vagina. Most women do not feel the episiotomy being performed because the pressure of the baby against the pelvic floor provides a natural anesthetic. The incision is stitched closed after the baby is born. The reason physicians give for performing the episiotomy is that, if it is not done, the baby's head may rip the perineum; a neat incision is easier to repair than a ragged tear, and the tear may go much deeper and damage more tissue. But the use of the episiotomy has been questioned by feminists, who claim that it is unnecessary and is done merely for the doctor's convenience, while causing the woman discomfort later as it is healing. They note that episiotomies are not performed in western European countries, where delivery still takes place quite nicely.

The baby is finally eased completely out of

FIGURE 5.9
The episiotomy.

the mother's body. The physician removes any mucus that may be in the baby's mouth, and the infant has usually begun crying by this time. At this point, the baby is still connected to the mother by the umbilical cord, which runs from the baby's navel to the placenta, and the placenta is still inside the mother's uterus. As the baby takes its first breath of air, the functioning of its body changes dramatically. Blood begins to flow to the lungs, there to take on oxygen, and a flap closes between the two atria (chambers) in the heart. This process generally takes a few minutes, during which time the baby changes from a somewhat bluish color to a healthy, pink hue.

At this point, the baby no longer needs the umbilical cord, which is clamped and cut off about 7 centimeters (3 inches) from the body. The stub gradually dries up and falls off.

To avoid the possibility of gonorrhea or other eye infection, drops of silver nitrate or a similar drug are placed in the baby's eyes (see Chapter 19).

Third-stage labor   During the third stage of labor, the placenta detaches from the walls of the uterus, and the afterbirth (placenta and fetal membranes) is expelled. This stage may take from a few minutes to an hour. Several contractions may accompany the expulsion of the placenta. The episiotomy and/or any tears are sewn up.

Positions of the Fetus

As was noted earlier, in most cases the fetus rotates into a head-down position inside the uterus during the last trimester of pregnancy, and the head emerges first at birth. Such normal presentations occur most often, but the baby may also be born in a number of other positions (see Figure 5.11). Longitudinal presentations occur in 99 percent of all births. Of these, 96 percent are *cephalic*, or *head-first*, presenta-

tions, which are normal presentations. The other 4 percent of longitudinal presentations are *breech* presentations, in which the buttocks are down and appear first during birth. In 1 in 200 births, the baby is in the *transverse* position, lying crosswise in the uterus, and a shoulder, arm, or hand emerges first into the vagina. In such cases either the fetus must be turned during labor, or a cesarean section is required.

Cesarean Section (C Section)

Cesarean section is a surgical procedure for delivery; it is used when normal vaginal birth is impossible or undesirable. Cesarean section may be required for a number of different reasons: if the baby is too large, or the mother's pelvis too small, to allow the baby to move into the vagina; if the labor has been very long and hard and the cervix is not dilating or if the mother is nearing the point of total exhaustion; if the umbilical cord *prolapses* (moves into a position such that it is coming out through the cervix ahead of the baby); if there is an Rh incompatibility (see below); or if there is excessive bleeding or the mother's or the infant's condition takes a sudden turn for the worse.

In the cesarean section, an incision is made through the abdomen and through the wall of the uterus. The physician lifts out the baby and then sews up the uterine wall and the abdominal wall.

Cesarean deliveries account for about 10 percent of all deliveries in the United States, which is a rate considerably higher than that in some western European countries (*Time*, March 27, 1978). Contrary to popular opinion, though, it is not true that once a woman has had one delivery by cesarean she must have all subsequent deliveries by the same method. Normal vaginal births are possible after cesareans, although often the same conditions are present in later deliveries that necessitated the first cesare-

FIGURE 5.10
Normal delivery of a baby. [*From R. Rugh and L. Shettles.
From conception to birth: The drama of life's beginnings.
New York: Harper & Row, 1971.*]

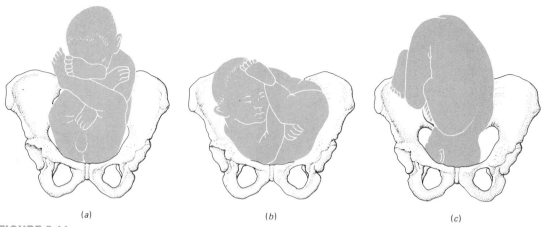

FIGURE 5.11
Possible positions of the fetus during birth. (*a*) A breech presentation. (*b*) A transverse presentation. (*c*) A normal, head-first (or cephalic) presentation.

an, making it necessary again in the later deliveries. It is also quite possible for a woman to have two or three cesarean deliveries.

With modern surgical techniques, the rate of complications from such a delivery is extremely low. The recovery period, of course, is somewhat longer than that after a vaginal birth, usually requiring 7 to 10 days.

NATURAL CHILDBIRTH

The term "natural childbirth" was coined by the English obstetrician Grantly Dick-Read in his book *Childbirth without Fear*, published in 1932. He postulated that fear causes tension and that tension causes pain. Thus to eliminate the pain of childbirth, he recommended a program consisting of education (to eliminate the woman's fears of the unknown) and the learning of relaxation techniques.

Another, similar method—more properly called *prepared childbirth* or the *Lamaze method*—has become extremely popular in the United States.

The Lamaze Method

A French obstetrician, Fernand Lamaze, developed a technique that he called a *psychoprophylactic* method of childbirth ("psycho" = "mind"; "prophylactic" = "prevention"—or a mental way of preventing pain) after observing women in Russia undergoing labor with apparently no pain. The technique became extremely popular in France and was introduced in the United States by Marjorie Karmel (who had her first baby in Paris while under the care of Dr. Lamaze) in her book *Thank You, Dr. Lamaze*, published in 1959. The method has become very popular in the last few years in the United States, and prepared childbirth classes are now offered in most areas of the country.

The two basic techniques taught in the Lamaze approach are *relaxation* and *controlled breathing*. The woman learns to relax all the muscles in her body; then she learns a related technique, dissociation, in which she tightens one muscle while keeping all the others relaxed. In labor she can use this technique, relaxing all the other muscles in her body while her uterus contracts. Knowing how to do this has a number of advantages, including conservation of energy during an event that requires considerable endurance and, more important, avoidance of the tension that increases the perception of pain. The woman also learns a series of controlled breathing exercises, which she will use to help her get through each contraction.

Some other techniques are taught as well. One, called *effleurage*, consists of a light, circular stroking of the abdomen with the fingertips. There are also exercises to strengthen specific muscles, such as the leg muscles, which undergo considerable strain during labor and delivery. Finally, because the Lamaze method is based on the idea that fear and the pain it causes are best eliminated through education, the Lamaze student learns a great deal about the processes involved in pregnancy and childbirth.

One other important component of the Lamaze method is the requirement that the woman be accompanied during the classes and during childbirth itself by her husband (or by some other person who serves as "coach" if she is unmarried or if the husband cannot participate). The husband or coach serves an important function and plays an integral role in the woman's learning of the techniques and her use of them during labor. He (we shall assume that it is the father) is present in both the labor room and the delivery room. He times contractions, checks on the woman's state of relaxation and gives her feedback if she is not relaxed, suggests breathing patterns, helps elevate her back as she pushes the baby out, and generally provides encouragement and moral support. Aside from the obvious benefits to the woman, this principle of the Lamaze method represents real progress in that it allows the man to play an active role in the birth of his own child and to experience more fully one of the most basic and moving of all human experiences, a privilege he has been denied too long.

One common misunderstanding about the Lamaze method is that it is "natural" childbirth, that is, that the use of anesthetics is prohibited. In fact, the Lamaze method is much more flexible than that. Its goal is to teach each woman the techniques she needs to control her labor so that she will not need an anesthetic; however, her right to have an anesthetic if she wants one is affirmed. This brings us to the topic of anesthetics in childbirth, which has become quite controversial in recent years.

The Use of Anesthetics in Childbirth

Throughout most of human history, childbirth has been "natural"; that is, it has taken place without anesthetics and in the woman's home or other familiar surroundings. The pattern began to change about 300 years ago, when male physicians rather than midwives started to assist during birth and when the place of delivery was moved from the home to the hospital (although home deliveries remained quite common—in fact, my mother was born at home on the kitchen table). The next major change came around the middle of the nineteenth century, with the development of anesthetics for use in surgery. When their use in childbirth was suggested, there was some opposition from physicians, who felt they interfered with "natural" processes, and some opposition from the clergy, who argued that women's pain in childbirth was prescribed in the Bible, quoting Genesis 3:16: "In sorrow thou shalt bring forth children." Opposition to the use of anesthetics virtually ceased, however, when Queen Victoria gave birth to a child under chloroform anesthesia in 1853. Since then, the use of anesthetics has become routine (too routine, according to some) and extremely effective, and women may now bear children with only minimal discomfort. Before discussing the arguments for and against the use of anesthetics, let us briefly review some of the common techniques of anesthesia used in childbirth.

Tranquilizers (such as Valium) or narcotics may be administered when labor becomes fairly intense. They relax the woman, and she may even fall asleep between contractions. Barbiturates (Nembutal or Seconal) are administered to put the woman to sleep. Scopolamine may sometimes be used for its amnesic effects; it makes the woman forget what has happened, and thus she has no memory afterward of any pain during childbirth. Some general analgesics (pain relievers), such as nitrous oxide, may be given by inhalation. General anesthetics such as ether may also be administered. Regional anesthetics, which numb only the specific region of the body that is painful, are used most commonly. An example is the pudendal block (named for the pudendum, or vulva), in which an injection numbs only the external genitals. Other examples are spinal anesthesia (a "spinal"), in which an injection near the spinal cord numbs the entire birth area, from belly to thighs, and the caudal block and epidural anesthesia, which are both administered by injections in the back and produce similar regional numbing.

Recently, the routine use of anesthetics has been questioned by some. Proponents of the use of anesthetics argue that, with modern technology, women no longer need to experience pain during childbirth and that it is therefore silly for them to suffer unnecessarily. Opponents argue that anesthetics have a number of well-documented dangerous effects, on both the mother and the infant. All anesthetics in the mother's body pass through the placenta to the infant. Thus while they have the desired effect of depressing the mother's central nervous system, they also depress the infant's nervous system. Research indicates that babies born under anesthesia have sluggish respiration, compared with that of infants born with no anesthesia (Boston Women's Health Collective, 1976). In extreme cases, infant death may result. Thus the effects on the infant are moderately to extremely harmful. There are also negative effects on the mother. They prevent her from using her body as effectively as she might to help push the baby out. If administered early in labor, they may inhibit uterine contractions and thus slow cervical dilation, and they can therefore prolong labor. They also numb a woman to experiencing one of the most fundamental events of her life.

Perhaps the best resolution of this controversy is to say that a pregnant woman should participate in prepared childbirth classes and should try to use the techniques during labor. If, when she is in labor, she discovers that she cannot control the pain and wants an anesthetic, she should feel free to request it and to do so without guilt; the anesthetic should then be administered with great caution.

AFTER THE BABY IS BORN: THE POSTPARTUM PERIOD

Physical Changes

With the birth of the baby, the woman's body undergoes a drastic physiological change. During pregnancy the placenta produces high levels of both estrogen and progesterone. When the placenta is expelled, the levels of these hormones drop sharply, and thus the postpartum period is characterized by low levels of both estrogen and progesterone. The levels of these hormones gradually return to normal over a period of a few weeks to a few months. Other endocrine changes include an increase in hormones associated with breast-feeding (discussed below).

In addition, the body undergoes considerable stress during labor and delivery, and the woman may feel exhausted, with a body that is aching almost as it would if she had undergone surgery.

Psychological Changes

For the first three or four days after parturition, the woman typically remains in the hospital. For the first two days, women often feel very elated; the long pregnancy is over, they have been successful competitors in a demanding athletic event and are pleased with their efforts, and the baby is finally there, to be cuddled and loved.

By about the third day postpartum, many women begin to experience depression and periods of crying: the "baby blues," or *postpartum depression*. Often this lasts only a day or two, but it may continue for several weeks. Estimates of the number of women experiencing postpartum depression vary from 25 to 67 percent, depending on the study (Sherman, 1971). Severe disturbance is rare; postpartum psychosis occurs in about 1 in every 400 women (R. E. Gordon and Gordon, 1967).

It appears that many factors contribute to this depression (see, for example, R. E. Gordon et al., 1965). Being in a hospital in and of itself is stressful; the woman is in an alien environment, separated from husband and friends, at a time when she is very vulnerable. Indeed, some feminist groups advocate home delivery in cases where no complications are expected so that the woman can have her baby in friendly, familiar surroundings, with her friends present for the great event. Separation from the baby, which is often required for the first 12 to 24 hours in the hospital, may also contribute to depression (Klaus et al., 1972). Once the woman returns home, another set of stresses faces her. She has probably not yet returned to her normal level of energy, and yet she must perform the exhausting task of caring for a newborn infant. For the first several weeks or months she may not get enough sleep, rising several times during the night to tend to a baby that is crying because it is hungry or sick, and she may become simply exhausted. Clearly she needs help and support from her husband and friends at this time. Some stresses vary depending on whether this is a first child or a later child. The first child is stressful because of the woman's inexperience; while she is in the hospital she may become anxious, wondering whether she will be capable of caring for the infant when she returns home. She may also worry about the long-term responsibility of rearing a child. In the case of later-born children, and some firstborns, the mother may become depressed because she did not really want the baby. In one study, 80 percent of the women were happy about their first one or two children, but only 31 percent were happy about the fourth child or later children (E. M. Gordon, 1967). It is not surprising that a woman might become depressed after the birth of a child she did not want. It is hoped that with the improvement of contraceptive technology and the increased availability and acceptability of abortions, the percentage of undesired pregnancies will decline.

Of course, physical stresses are also present during the postpartum period; hormone levels have declined sharply, and the body has been under stress. Thus it appears that postpartum depression is caused by a combination of physical and social factors.

Another view of the psychological aspects of pregnancy and the postpartum period has been proposed by psychoanalyst Grete Bibring and her colleagues (1961), who studied pregnant women over a 10-year period. Bibring and her colleagues see the pregnancy-postpartum period as a developmental stage, a time of maturational crisis, the resolution of which leads to emotional growth. Perhaps, then, we should begin to think of pregnancy and the

CONCEPTION, PREGNANCY, AND CHILDBIRTH

postpartum period as normal parts of the process of adult development.

BREAST-FEEDING

Biological Mechanisms

Two hormones, both secreted by the pituitary, are involved in lactation (milk production). One, *prolactin*, stimulates the breasts to produce milk. The initial release of prolactin is stimulated by the decline in hormones that occurs when the placenta is expelled during labor. Prolactin is then produced fairly constantly for whatever length of time the woman breast-feeds. The other hormone, *oxytocin*, stimulates the breasts to eject milk. Oxytocin is produced reflexively by the pituitary in response to the infant's sucking of the breast. Thus sucking stimulates nerve cells in the nipple; this nerve signal is transmitted to the brain, which relays the message to the pituitary, which sends out the messenger oxytocin, which stimulates the breasts to eject milk.

Actually, milk is not produced until several days after delivery. For the first few days, the breast secretes colostrum, discussed earlier, which is high in protein and is believed to give the baby a temporary immunity to infectious diseases. Two or three days after delivery, true lactation begins; this may be accompanied by pain for a day or so because the breasts are swollen and congested.

It is also important to note that, much as in pregnancy, substances ingested by the mother may be transmitted through the milk to the infant. The nursing mother thus needs to be cautious about using alcohol and other drugs.

Psychological Aspects

Although bottles for artificially feeding babies were known in Egypt and a few other places as

FIGURE 5.12
Breast-feeding. [*Mary M. Thacher, Photo Researchers, Inc.*]

early as the first century, they were used by only a small minority of very wealthy women. Thus throughout most of human history, the vast majority of babies have been breast-fed. Today in the United States, however, bottle-fed babies are in the majority. Only 33 percent of babies are initially breast-fed, and only 20 percent are still breast-fed at 2 months of age; after that the percentage drops off sharply (Mason, 1973, cited in Papalia and Olds, 1975). The decline in breast-feeding in our culture may be attributed to a number of factors, including a societal fear of nudity, the increased use of drugs during childbirth which interfere with the new baby's ability to suck, and a change in the role and life expectations of women (Papalia and Olds, 1975).

Public health officials view the decline in breast-feeding with alarm, since breast milk is the ideal food for a baby and has even been termed the "ultimate health food." It provides the baby with the right mixture of nutrients, it contains antibodies that protect the infant from some diseases; it is free from bacteria, and it is always the right temperature. Thus there is little question that it is superior to cow's milk and commercial formulas.

There is some reason to believe, however, that breast-feeding is now increasing in popularity. Recent studies indicate that it is more common among more affluent, better-educated young women than among those of lower socioeconomic status, possibly heralding a widespread return to breast-feeding.

From the mother's point of view, breast-feeding has several advantages. Breast-feeding can be a real form of sexual expression for women (Newton, 1971). It is a kind of intimate sensual contact between two humans, with the infant stimulating an erogenous zone of the mother. Some women report sexual arousal during breast-feeding, and a few even report having orgasms. Unfortunately, this sometimes produces anxiety in the mother, leading her to discontinue breast-feeding. However, there is nothing "wrong" with this arousal, and it appears to stem from activation of hormonal mechanisms. Clearly, from an adaptive point of view, if breast-feeding is important to the infant's survival, it would be wise for Nature to design the process so that it is rewarding to the mother. Further, women who breast-feed find that their sexual responsiveness returns sooner after childbirth, compared with women who do not breast-feed (Masters and Johnson, 1966).[6]

Other advantages from the mother's point of view include a quicker shrinking of the uterus to its normal size and a slightly reduced likelihood of becoming pregnant again immediately. The return of normal menstrual cycles is delayed, on the average, in women who breast-feed, compared with those who do not. This provides some period of rest between pregnancies. However, it is important to note that a woman can become pregnant again after parturition but before she has had her first menstrual period. As was discussed in Chapter 4, ovulation precedes menstruation; thus a woman may ovulate and conceive without having a period. Therefore, a woman should not count on breast-feeding as a means of contraception.

The La Leche League, an organization devoted to breast-feeding, has done much to encourage women to breast-feed their babies and has helped to spread information on breast-feeding. The organization tends to be a bit militant in its advocacy of breast-feeding, however. A few women are physically unable to breast-feed, while some others feel psychologically uncomfortable with the idea. While breast-feeding has some of the important advantages noted above, long-term studies comparing breast-fed children with bottle-fed chil-

---

[6]If you are a psychology student, you might want to note that these data are correlational. In view of this, can you infer that breast-feeding *causes* a quicker return of sexual desire? How else might one interpret the data? Why are the data correlational rather than experimental?

dren have found no significant differences between them (Schmitt, 1970). What appears to be more important than the method of feeding is the quality of the relationship between the mother and infant and the feelings that the mother communicates to the baby:

> A baby raised in a loving home can grow up to be a healthy, psychologically secure individual no matter how he receives his nourishment. While successful nursing is a beautiful, happy experience for both mother and child, the woman who nurses grudgingly because she feels she *should* will probably do more harm to her baby by communicating her feelings of resentment and unhappiness, than she would if she were a relaxed, loving, bottle-feeding mother. (S. Olds and Eiger, 1973, p. 18)

PROBLEM PREGNANCIES

Ectopic Pregnancy

Ectopic (misplaced) pregnancy occurs when the fertilized egg implants someplace other than the uterus. Most commonly, ectopic pregnancies occur when the egg implants in the fallopian tube (tubal pregnancy). In rare cases, implantation may also occur in the abdominal cavity, the ovary, or the cervix.

About 1 pregnancy in every 200 is a tubal pregnancy, and the rate is higher among women of lower socioeconomic status (Hellman and Pritchard, 1971). Tubal pregnancy may occur if, for one reason or another, the egg is prevented from moving down the tube to the uterus, as when the tubes are obstructed as a result of a gonorrheal infection, for example.

Early in tubal pregnancy, the fertilized egg implants in the tube and begins development, forming a placenta and producing the normal hormones of pregnancy. The woman may experience the early symptoms of pregnancy, such as nausea and amenorrhea, and think she is

pregnant; or she may experience some bleeding, which she mistakes for a period, and think that she is not pregnant. It is therefore quite difficult to diagnose a tubal pregnancy early.

A tubal pregnancy may end in one of two ways. The embryo may spontaneously abort and be released into the abdominal cavity, or the embryo and placenta may continue to expand, stretching the tube until it ruptures. Symptoms of a rupture include sharp abdominal pain or cramping, dull abdominal pain and possibly pain in the shoulder, and vaginal bleeding. Meanwhile, hemorrhaging is occurring, and the woman may go into shock and, in some cases, die; thus it is extremely important for a woman displaying these symptoms to see a doctor quickly.

Abdominal pregnancy, in which the fertilized egg implants in the abdominal cavity, is much rarer and occurs in less than 1 pregnancy in 4000 (Hellman and Pritchard, 1971). Often it is a secondary result of a tubal pregnancy in which the embryo was released into the abdominal cavity, where it again implanted. Occasionally abdominal pregnancies carry on to term, and the infant must be removed by cesarean section; there is a high risk of hemorrhaging in such cases, however.

Pseudocyesis (False Pregnancy)

In pseudocyesis, or *false pregnancy,* the woman believes that she is pregnant and shows the signs and symptoms of pregnancy without really being pregnant. She may stop menstruating and have morning sickness. She may begin gaining weight, and her abdomen may bulge. The condition may persist for several months before it goes away, either spontaneously or as a result of psychotherapy. In rare cases it persists until the woman goes into labor and delivers nothing but air and fluids. Readers may be familiar with the character Honey in Edward Albee's *Who's Afraid of Virginia Woolf?* (played by Sandy Dennis in the movie version), who had a false pregnancy. Pseudocyesis is an interesting example of the extent to which a psychological state (emotional factors) can have an effect on a person's physical state.

Toxemia

Metabolic toxemia of late pregnancy is a disease with several stages. The first is called *preeclampsia*, which may range from mild to severe. The symptoms of mild preeclampsia are severe edema (fluid retention and swelling), high blood pressure, and protein in the urine. Toxemia is classified as a hypertensive disease of pregnancy, meaning that it is characterized by dangerously high blood pressure. Toxemia usually does not appear until after the twentieth to twenty-fourth week of pregnancy, that is, late in pregnancy. In severe preeclampsia, the earlier symptoms persist, and the woman also experiences vision problems, abdominal pains, mental dullness, and severe headaches. In the most severe stage, *eclampsia*, the woman has convulsions, goes into a coma, and may die.

Because one of the symptoms of toxemia is too rapid weight gain and swelling from edema, in the past many physicians tried to prevent it from occurring by restricting their patients' diets and weight during pregnancy. However, it now seems more likely that toxemia results from malnutrition, although no one really knows what causes it. Toxemia seems to be related to socioeconomic factors, which probably determine whether a pregnant woman receives adequate nutrition. In one study it was found that the per capita income of a state and the rate of death due to toxemia in that state were inversely related. That is, in those states with the lowest per capita income, there was the highest rate of mortality due to toxemia (Eastman, 1968). This finding argues for the importance of proper diet during pregnancy. It also emphasizes the importance of proper medical care during pregnancy, since toxemia can be managed well during its early stages and death typically occurs only when the woman is receiving no medical care.

Illness during Pregnancy

As was discussed in a previous section, certain substances such as drugs can cross the placental barrier from the woman to the fetus, causing damage. Similarly, certain viruses may pass from the woman to the fetus and cause considerable harm, particularly if the illness occurs during the first trimester of pregnancy. The best-known example is rubella, or German measles. If a woman gets German measles during the first month of pregnancy, there is a 50 percent chance that the infant will be born deaf or mentally deficient or with cataracts or congenital heart defects. The risk then declines, and by the third month of pregnancy the chance of abnormalities is about 10 percent. While most women have an immunity to rubella because they had it when they were children, a woman who suspects that she is not immune can receive a vaccination that will give her immunity; she should do this well before she becomes pregnant.

Herpes simplex is also *teratogenic*, that is, capable of producing defects in the fetus. Symptoms of herpes simplex are usually mild: cold sores or fever blisters. Herpes genitalis (see Chapter 19) is a form of herpes simplex in which sores may appear in the genital region. Usually the infant contracts the disease by direct contact with the sore; delivery by cesarean section can prevent this. Women with herpes genitalis also have a high risk of spontaneously aborting.

Other diseases, such as influenza and the

common cold if complicated by pneumonia, may also cause complications in pregnancy. Pregnant women are thus advised to avoid situations in which they may be exposed to diseases.

Defective Conceptus

As has been noted, a number of factors, such as drugs taken during pregnancy and illness during pregnancy, may cause defects in the fetus. Other causes include genetic defects (for example, phenylketonuria [PKU], which causes retardation) and chromosomal defects (for example, Down's syndrome, or mongolism, which causes retardation).

About 250,000 babies with significant birth defects are born in the United States each year (about 7 percent of all babies born). A "significant birth defect" is one that has an adverse effect on the future mental and/or physical health and well-being of the person. The problem will affect 1 family in every 10 (Fulton, 1974).

In most cases, families have simply had to learn, as best they could, to live with a child who had a birth defect. Now, however, amniocentesis (combined with abortion) and genetic counseling are available to help prevent some of the sorrow.

The technique of *amniocentesis* involves inserting a fine tube through the pregnant woman's abdomen and removing some amniotic fluid, including cells sloughed off by the fetus, for analysis. The technique is capable of providing an early diagnosis of most chromosomal abnormalities, some genetically produced biochemical disorders, and sex-linked diseases carried by females but affecting males (hemophilia and muscular dystrophy). If a defect is discovered, the woman may then decide to terminate the pregnancy with an abortion.

Amniocentesis should be performed between the fourteenth and sixteenth weeks of pregnancy. This timing is important for two reasons. First, if a defect is discovered and an abortion is to be performed, it should be done as early as possible (see Chapter 6). Second, there is a 1 percent chance that the amniocentesis itself will cause the woman to lose her baby, and the risk becomes greater as the pregnancy progresses.

Because amniocentesis itself involves some risk, it is generally thought (although the matter is controversial) that it should be performed only on women who have a "high risk" of bearing a child with a birth defect. A woman is in that category (1) if she has already had one child with a genetic defect; (2) if she believes that she is a carrier of a genetic defect, which can usually be established through genetic counseling; and (3) if she is over 40, in which case she has a greatly increased chance of bearing a child with a chromosomal abnormality.

Of course, amniocentesis (when followed by abortion) raises a number of serious ethical questions, some of which will be discussed in later chapters. However, it is important to note the extreme psychological stress to which families of children with birth defects are often subjected.

Rh Incompatibility

The Rh factor is a substance in the blood; if it is present, the person is said to be Rh positive (Rh+); if it is absent, the person is said to be Rh negative (Rh−). The Rh factor is genetically transmitted, with Rh+ being dominant over Rh−.

The presence or absence of the Rh factor does not constitute a health problem except when an Rh− person receives a blood transfusion and when an Rh− woman is pregnant with an Rh+ fetus (which can happen only if the father is Rh+). A blood test is done routinely early in pregnancy to determine whether a woman is Rh−. Fortunately, about 85 percent of whites and 93 percent of blacks are Rh+; thus the problems associated with being Rh− are not very common.

If some Rh+ blood gets into Rh− blood, the Rh− blood forms antibodies as a reaction against the Rh factor in the invading blood. Typically, as has been noted, there is little interchange between the woman's blood and the fetus's; the placenta keeps them separate. What little interchange there is involves the woman's blood flowing into the fetus. However, during parturition there can be considerable mixing of the two. Thus during birth, the blood of an Rh+ baby causes the formation of antibodies in an Rh− woman's blood. During the next pregnancy, some of the woman's blood enters the fetus, and the antibodies attack the fetus's red cells. The baby may be stillborn, severely anemic, or retarded. Thus there is little risk for an Rh− woman with the first pregnancy because antibodies have not yet formed; however, later pregnancies can be extremely dangerous.

Fortunately, fairly adequate techniques for dealing with this situation have been developed. The fetus or newborn infant may get a transfusion. Also, an injection of a substance called *Rhogam* prevents the woman's blood from producing antibodies.

Miscarriage (Spontaneous Abortion)

Miscarriage, or *spontaneous abortion*, occurs when a pregnancy is terminated through natural causes, before the conceptus is viable (capable of surviving on its own). It is not to be confused with *induced abortion*, in which a pregnancy is terminated by mechanical or medicinal means (what is commonly called *abortion*—see Chapter 6), or with *prematurity*, in which the pregnancy terminates early, but after the infant is viable.

It is estimated that 10 percent of all pregnancies end in spontaneous abortion (Hellman and Pritchard, 1971). If anything, this is probably an underestimate, since very early spontaneous abortions may not be detected. The woman may not know that she is pregnant, and the products of the miscarriage are mistaken for a menstrual period. Thus the true incidence may be closer to 15 or 20 percent or perhaps as high as 50 percent.

Most spontaneous abortions (75 percent) occur during the first trimester of pregnancy. The first sign that a woman may miscarry is vaginal bleeding or "spotting." If the symptoms of pregnancy disappear and the woman develops abdominal cramps, the fetus is usually expelled.

Studies indicate that most spontaneous abortions occur because the conceptus was defective. That is, studies of spontaneously aborted fetuses indicate that about 50 percent showed abnormalities that were incompatible with life; for example, many had gross chromosomal abnormalities. Thus, contrary to popular belief, psychological and physical traumas are not common causes of miscarriage. In fact, spontaneous abortions seem to be functional in that they naturally eliminate many defective fetuses.

Prematurity

A major complication during the third trimester of pregnancy is premature labor and delivery of the fetus. Because the date of conception cannot always be accurately determined, prematurity is usually defined in terms of the birth weight of the infant; an infant weighing less than 2500 grams (5½ pounds) is considered premature. However, physicians have recently become concerned more with the functional development of the infant than with the weight. It is estimated that about 7 percent of the births in the United States are premature.

Prematurity is a cause for concern because the premature infant is much less likely to survive than the full-term infant. It is estimated that more than half of the deaths of newborn babies in the United States are due to prematurity. Premature infants are particularly susceptible to respiratory infections, and they must receive expert care. Prematurity may also cause damage to an infant that survives.

Maternal factors such as poor health, poor nutrition, heavy smoking, and syphilis are associated with prematurity. Young teenage mothers, whose bodies are not yet ready to bear children, are also very susceptible to premature labor and delivery. However, in over 50 percent of the cases, the cause of prematurity is unknown (Hellman and Pritchard, 1971).

INFERTILITY

It is estimated that 12 percent of all couples in the United States are involuntarily childless. When fertile couples are purposely attempting to conceive a child, about 50 percent succeed in the first month, and about 80 percent succeed in the first six months (Novak et al., 1975). Most doctors consider a couple infertile if they have not conceived after a year of "trying." The term "sterility" refers only to an individual who has an absolute factor preventing procreation.

Causes of Infertility

Contrary to popular opinion, a couple's infertility is not always caused by the woman; it is estimated that in about 40 percent of infertile couples, male factors are responsible (Speroff et al., 1973).

Causes in the female The most common causes of infertility in the female are (1) failure to ovulate, (2) blockage of the fallopian tubes, and (3) cervical mucus, called "hostile mucus," that does not permit the passage of sperm. Age may also be a factor; fertility declines in women after 35 years of age, the decline being especially sharp after age 40. Some cases of infertility in women can be successfully treated using "fertility drugs" such as Clomid.

Causes in the male The most common causes of infertility in the male are (1) low sperm count and (2) low motility of the sperm, which means that the sperm are just not good swimmers.

Combined factors In some situations a combination of factors in both the man and the woman causes the infertility. For example, there may be an immunologic response. The woman may have an allergic response to the man's sperm, causing her to produce antibodies that destroy the sperm, or the man may produce the antibodies himself. A couple may also simply lack knowledge; they may not know how to time intercourse correctly so that conception will take place, or they may lack other important information.

Psychological Aspects

It is important to recognize the psychological stress to which an infertile couple may be subjected. Their marriage may be strained. Because the male role is defined partly in our society by the ability to father children, the man may feel that his masculinity or virility is in question. Similarly, the female role is defined largely by the ability to bear children and be a mother, and the woman may feel inadequate in her role as a woman. Historically in most cultures fertility has been encouraged, and indeed demanded; hence pressures on infertile couples were high, leading to more psychological stress. For example, among Orthodox Jews, failure to conceive is grounds for a divorce. As emphasis on population control increases in our society and as childlessness[7] becomes an acceptable and more recognized option in marriage, it is hoped that some of the psychological stresses on the infertile couple will be lessened.

SUMMARY

The first section traced the journey of the sperm, which are manufactured in the testes and ejaculated out through the vas deferens and urethra into the vagina. Then they begin their swim through the cervix and uterus and up a fallopian tube to meet the egg, which has already been released from the ovary and has found its way into the end of the tube. When the sperm and egg unite in the fallopian tube, conception occurs. The single fertilized egg cell then begins dividing as it travels down the tube, and finally it implants in the uterus. Techniques for improving the chances of conception were suggested.

The development of the embryo, and then of the fetus, was traced during the nine months of prenatal development. The placenta, which is important in transmitting substances between the woman and the fetus, develops early. The fetus is connected to the placenta by the umbilical cord. The most remarkable development of the fetus occurs during the first trimester (first three months), when most of the major organ systems are formed and when human features develop.

Next, pregnancy was considered from the woman's point of view. Early signs of pregnancy include amenorrhea, tenderness of the breasts, and nausea. The most common pregnancy test is designed to detect HCG in the urine; this test is very accurate by the sixth to eighth weeks of pregnancy. Physical changes during the first trimester are mainly the result of the increasing

levels of estrogen and progesterone produced by the placenta. Despite cultural myths about the radiant contentment of the pregnant woman, some women do have negative feelings during the first trimester. During the second trimester the woman generally feels better, both physically and psychologically. During the third trimester she is very much aware that the baby will arrive soon.

Despite many people's concerns, sexual intercourse is generally quite safe during pregnancy.

Nutrition is exceptionally important during pregnancy because the woman's body has to supply the materials to create another human being. Pregnant women also must be very careful about ingesting drugs because some can penetrate the placental barrier and enter the fetus, possibly causing damage.

Labor is typically divided into three stages. During the first stage, the cervix undergoes effacement and dilation. During the second stage, the baby moves out through the vagina. The placenta is delivered during the third stage. Cesarean section is a surgical method of delivering a baby.

The Lamaze method of "natural" childbirth has become very popular; it emphasizes the use of relaxation and controlled breathing to control contractions and minimize the woman's discomfort. Anesthetics may not be necessary, which seems desirable since they are potentially dangerous to the infant.

During the postpartum period, hormone levels are very low, and postpartum depression may arise from a combination of this hormonal state and the many environmental stresses on the woman at this time.

Two hormones are involved in lactation: prolactin and oxytocin. Breast-feeding has a number of psychological as well as health advantages, although the nature of the relationship between mother and infant appears to be

---

[7]Semantics can make a big difference here. Many couples who choose not to have children prefer to call themselves "child-free" rather than "childless."

more important than whether the baby is bottle-fed or breast-fed.

Problems of pregnancy were discussed: ectopic (misplaced) pregnancy, pseudocyesis (false pregnancy), toxemia, illness (such as German measles), a defective conceptus, Rh incompatibility, spontaneous abortion, and prematurity.

Finally, the causes of infertility were discussed.

SUGGESTIONS FOR FURTHER READING

Arms, Suzanne. *Immaculate deception: A new look at women and childbirth in America.* Boston: Houghton Mifflin, 1975. A provocative, critical analysis of modern childbirth practices in the United States.

Flanagan, Geraldine, L. *The first nine months of life.* New York: Simon and Schuster, 1962. An exciting description of the baby's development in utero.

Hellman, L. M., and Pritchard, J. A. *Williams obstetrics.* (14th ed.) New York: Appleton-Century-Crofts, 1971. One of the standard obstetrics texts. Not exactly pleasant bedtime reading, but an excellent reference source on technical details.

Leboyer, F. *Birth without violence.* New York: Random House, 1975. Argues that we make the newborn's introduction to the world traumatic and suggests ways to make it more friendly.

Nilsson, A. L., et al. *A child is born.* Boston: Seymour Lawrence, 1965. Contains exceptional photographs of prenatal development.

6

BIRTH CONTROL

The average student of today grew up in the Pill era and simply assumes that highly effective methods of contraception are available. It is sometimes difficult to remember that this has been true only for about the last two decades and that previously contraception was a hit-or-miss affair at best. Contraception is also less controversial than it once was (except for the issue of side effects), and yet as recently as 1965 the use of contraceptives was illegal in Connecticut (see the Supreme Court decision in the case of *Griswold v. Connecticut,* 1965).

It is also true that before the twentieth century, motivation to use contraceptives was generally low. Having many children was considered desirable, in part because the infant mortality rate was so high. It might be necessary to have ten children in order for three to survive infancy. Further, children were expected to support their parents in old age, and thus a large family was the best form of social security. Reasons for using birth control methods were largely individual, such as possible danger to the woman if she became pregnant or simply a desire not to have any more children. In this

century, however, we have become aware that there is a world population problem and that birth control is not only desirable but also imperative.

REASONS FOR, AND ARGUMENTS AGAINST, USING CONTRACEPTIVES

Although the use of contraceptives is not so controversial as it once was, it is important to note the range of arguments for and against it.

Reasons for Using Contraceptives

Avoiding health risks to the mother While modern medicine has made pregnancy and childbirth relatively safe, it is also true that, for some women, another pregnancy and delivery may be a danger to health or may even cause death. For example, pregnancy aggravates a diabetic condition in the mother. In such cases, contraception is important in preventing pregnancy and the health risks it entails.

Spacing pregnancies If no contraceptives are used, some women will bear children at regular

---

* *Source:* Paula Weideger. *Menstruation and menopause.* New York: Knopf, 1976, p. 42.

one-year intervals or even more frequently. This is not good either for the mother's health or for the baby's. It has been claimed that when births are only one year apart, the death rate for babies is about 50 percent higher than when births are two years apart (Guttmacher, 1947). Contraception allows a couple to space pregnancies farther apart.

Avoiding having children with birth defects

As was discussed in Chapter 5, some women have a high risk of bearing a child with a serious birth defect: women over 40 (they have an increased risk of bearing children with chromosomal defects), women who are carriers of genetic diseases (for example, Huntington's chorea, muscular dystrophy, and hemophilia), and women whose husbands are carriers. Whether a couple are carriers of such diseases can be determined by genetic counseling. If they are, it would seem desirable for them to avoid conceiving a child.

Recently, the technique of amniocentesis (see Chapter 5) has modified this argument somewhat. In most cases, high-risk couples will not necessarily have a defective child; they have only a certain probability—say a 50 or a 25 percent chance—of having a defective child. Rather than avoiding conception completely, it is now feasible for them to conceive a child and then use the technique of amniocentesis to determine whether the conceptus is defective. If it is, the pregnancy can be terminated with an abortion; if it is not, they can look forward to having a healthy child. Such a strategy is reasonable, of course, only if the couple are willing to have an abortion performed in the event that the conceptus proves to be defective. Nonetheless, this provides high-risk couples with an alternative other than remaining childless.

It is also true that deciding what constitutes a birth defect can be an emotion-laden political issue. For example, some blacks in the United States carry the gene for sickle-cell anemia (a severely debilitating disease that may cause

death), while the gene is virtually unknown in the white population. Thus genetic counseling suggests that some black couples remain childless, a policy with serious racial implications.

Improving early marital adjustment

A few decades ago, many women became pregnant within the first year of their marriage, perhaps even conceiving during their honeymoon. The first year or so of a marriage is a time of psychological adjustment and a pregnancy during that time adds a set of unnecessary stresses: physical and psychological changes in the woman, a temporary cessation of sexual activity around the time of birth, possible financial strain, and the demands of rearing a child. Further, waiting a year or two before having a child allows a couple to be reasonably sure that their marriage is stable; otherwise, they might have a baby and decide two months later that they really should be divorced. Also, there are some data indicating that good methods of contraception enhance a newly married couple's sexual satisfaction (C. R. Adams, 1966).

Limiting family size

Most couples now have a definite idea of the number of children—usually two or three—that they want. A variety of personal reasons may be involved in this decision. Contraception allows a couple to limit their family to a preplanned size. (Interestingly, the burden of argument has been placed on those who have chosen to have no more children and especially on those who have chosen to have none at all. Why, instead, should an explanation not be demanded of those who want more children? That is, perhaps it would be more reasonable to ask for a rationale for having another child than for not having one.)

Avoiding pregnancy among unmarried people

Although premarital sex is now quite common and is generally accepted, particularly among those under 30 (see Chapter 10), a pregnancy resulting from premarital sex is generally considered undesirable. There are a number of reasons for the latter attitude: the couple may be young and not capable of supporting themselves or a child; their education may be interrupted, and one or both may be forced to go to work; and they may enter into a marriage for less than ideal reasons. Thus contraception is extremely important for those who engage in premarital sex but for whom pregnancy is out of the question.

Permitting more self-actualization for women
With the women's movement and the upheaval in gender roles in recent years has come a questioning of the traditional assumption that women should spend their adult lives bearing and caring for children. Many women now expect to be able to develop successful careers, and indeed this may be a kind of new norm for women. Having numerous unplanned pregnancies at intervals from age 20 to age 45 is scarcely conducive to establishing a successful career. Contraception is important in permitting women to plan how many children they will have and when they will have them, thus allowing them to integrate motherhood with an education and a career.

Avoiding having unwanted children A surprisingly large percentage of pregnancies are unplanned, and a substantial number are unwanted (as the old joke has it, most people are caused by accidents). While we have concentrated mainly on the disadvantages of an unwanted pregnancy from the parents' point of view, there are also disadvantages from the child's point of view. Being the baby who forced Mommy to drop out of college is scarcely an enviable situation, and contraception is a means of avoiding it. Unfortunately, research is lacking on the effects of being planned versus being unplanned on the child's adjustment; such research is badly needed.

Curbing population growth The size of the world population has increased dramatically—perhaps alarmingly—in the last century (see Figure 6.1). By the year 2000, it is expected that there will be twice as many people on the earth as there were in 1960. Thus there is increasing cause for concern over the size of the world population. For example, will there be enough food for all those people? Contraception thus is important not only for personal convenience but also for the welfare of society as a whole (P. A. Ehrlich and Ehrlich, 1972).

FIGURE 6.1
The growth of the world population from 6000 B.C. to 1975, with a projection to 2000. *[Ehrlich and Ehrlich.]*

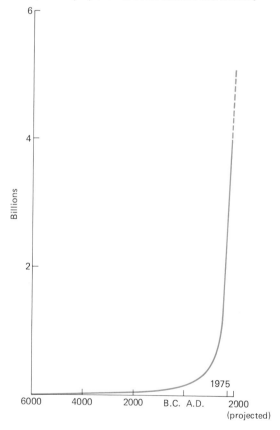

Arguments against Using Contraceptives

Ethical arguments The Roman Catholic Church has been foremost in putting forth the argument that any method of contraception other than abstinence during periods of fertility is immoral. The reason given is that contraception violates "natural law" and involves the destruction of either life or the potential for life (see Chapter 20). Research indicates, however, that this is the position mainly of the clergy and that a majority of lay people in the Roman Catholic Church now use contraceptives (Westoff and Bumpass, 1973).

Loss of spontaneity Some people, particularly those who engage in premarital sex, argue that the use of contraceptives takes the spontaneity out of sex. The argument runs something like this: If you have to stop in the middle of the preliminaries and get out a diaphragm or a condom and put it in or on, it stops the natural, spontaneous flow of things. Taking a pill every day is too calculatingly deliberate. This line of thinking is not so much an argument as it is an attitude, and a fairly common one at that.

Health risks Another argument is that contraceptives should not be used because they involve certain dangers to the user's health. The specific nature of these dangers will be reviewed as each method of birth control is discussed in the following sections. It is important to note here, though, that some methods—for example, the diaphragm and the condom—have no health risks associated with their use. And it is also true that every method is safer than a pregnancy carried to term.

Racist genocide Some black and other Third World leaders argue that their people should not use contraception because contraceptives are a form of genocide (mass extermination of a group) of Third World people. They say that white Americans have forced birth control on blacks and others so that they will decline in numbers while whites increase. Even if one does not agree with this argument, it does raise the point that birth control is, in part, a political issue.

THE PILL

With *combination birth control pills* such as Ovulen, Ortho-Novum, and Ovral, the woman takes a pill that contains estrogen and progestin (a synthetic progesterone), both at doses considerably higher than body levels, for 20 or 21 days. Then she takes no pill for seven days, after which she repeats the cycle. This discussion will concentrate on combination pills because they are by far the most widely used.

How It Works

The Pill works mainly by preventing ovulation. Recall that in a natural menstrual cycle, the low levels of estrogen during and just after the menstrual period trigger the pituitary to produce FSH, which stimulates the process of ovulation (see Chapter 4). The woman starts taking the birth control pills on about day 5 of the cycle. Thus just when estrogen levels would normally be low, they are artificially made high. This high level of estrogen inhibits FSH production, and the message to ovulate is never sent out. The high level of progesterone inhibits LH production, further preventing ovulation.

The progestin provides additional backup effects. It keeps the cervical mucus very thick, making it difficult for sperm to get through, and it changes the lining of the uterus in such a way that even if a fertilized egg arrived, implantation would be unlikely.

When the estrogen and progestin are withdrawn after day 21, the lining of the uterus disintegrates, and withdrawal bleeding or men-

FOCUS

MARGARET SANGER— BIRTH CONTROL PIONEER

Margaret Higgins Sanger (1883–1966) was a crusader for birth control in the United States; in accomplishing her goals, she had to take on a variety of opponents, including the United States government, and she served one jail term.

She was born in Corning, New York, the daughter of a tubercular mother who died young after bearing 11 children. Her father was a free spirit who fought for women's suffrage. After caring for her dying mother, she embarked on a career in nursing and married William Sanger in 1900.

She became interested in women's health and began writing articles on the subject. Later these were published as books entitled *What Every Girl Should Know* (1916) and *What Every Mother Should Know* (1917).

Perhaps her strongest motivation came from her work as a nurse. All her patients were poor maternity cases on New York's Lower East Side. Among these women, pregnancy was a "chronic condition." Margaret Sanger saw them, weary and old at 35, resorting to self-induced abortions, which were frequently the cause of their deaths. Frustrated at her inability to help them, she renounced nursing:

> I came to a sudden realization that my work as a nurse and my activities in social service were entirely palliative and consequently futile and useless to relieve the misery I saw all about me.

She determined, instead, to "seek out the root of the evil."

Impeding her work was the Comstock Act of 1873 (see Chapter 21), which classified contraceptive information as obscene and made it illegal to send it through the mail. Though she was often accused of wanting to lower the birthrate, she instead envisioned families, rich and poor alike, in which children were wanted and given every advantage.

In 1914 she founded the National Birth Control League, launching the birth control movement in the United States. Though her magazine, *Woman Rebel*, obeyed the letter of the law and did not give contraceptive information, she was nonetheless indicted on nine counts and made liable to a prison term of 45 years.

Margaret Sanger left the United States on the eve of the trial. She toured Europe, and in Holland she visited the first birth control clinics to be established anywhere. There she got the idea of

FIGURE 6.2
Margaret Sanger, a pioneer of the birth control movement. *[Culver Pictures, Inc.]*

opening birth control clinics in the United States. Meanwhile, the charges against her had been dropped.

She returned to the United States and, in 1916, opened a birth control clinic in Brooklyn. The office was closed by the police after nine days of operation, and Margaret Sanger was put in jail for 30 days. However, on appeal, her case was upheld by the courts, and in 1918 a decision was handed down allowing doctors to give contraceptive information to women for the "cure and prevention of disease."

The birth control movement was gaining followers, and the first National Birth Control Conference was held in 1921 in New York; it was attended by doctors, scientists, and lay supporters. In 1931, the Pope approved the rhythm method for use by Roman Catholics.

Margaret Sanger's role in getting birth control information to American women and in making it legal for them to use the information is unquestioned. Heywood Broun once remarked that Margaret Sanger had no sense of humor. She replied, "I am the protagonist of women who have nothing to laugh at."

Source: Current Biography, 1944.

struation occurs, although the flow is typically reduced because the progestin has inhibited development of the endometrium.

Hormonally, the action of the Pill produces a condition much like pregnancy, when hormone levels are also high, preventing further ovulation and menstrual periods. Thus it is not too surprising that many of the side effects of the Pill are similar to the symptoms of pregnancy.

Effectiveness

Before the effectiveness of the Pill is discussed, several technical terms that are used in communicating data on effectiveness need to be defined. If 100 women use a contraceptive method for one year, the number of them who become pregnant during that year is called the *failure rate* (or *pregnancy rate*). That is, if 5 women out of 100 become pregnant during a year of using contraceptive A, then A's failure rate is 5 percent. *Effectiveness* is 100 minus the failure rate; thus contraceptive A would be said to be 95 percent effective. We can also talk about two kinds of failure rate: theoretical failure rate and actual failure rate. *Theoretical failure rate* is the failure rate under hypothetical conditions in which the method is used perfectly. *Actual failure rate* is the failure rate when people actually use the method, and thus it includes not only failures due to the contraceptive itself but also failures due to improper use, as when a woman forgets to take a pill.

Combination pills are the most effective method of birth control short of sterilization. The theoretical failure rate is 0.5 percent (that is, the method is essentially 100 percent effective), and the actual failure rate is 2 to 5 percent. Failures occur primarily as a result of forgetting to take a pill for two or more days. If a woman forgets to take a pill for one day, she should simply take two the next day; this does not appear to increase the pregnancy risk appreciably. If she forgets for two days, she should take two pills on each of the next two days; however, the chances of pregnancy are now increased. If she forgets for three or more days, she should switch to some other method of birth control for the remainder of that cycle.

Side Effects

Most people have seen various reports in the media on the dangerous side effects of birth control pills. Some of these reports are no more than scare stories with little or no evidence behind them. On the other hand, there are some well-documented risks associated with the use of the Pill, and women who are using it or who are contemplating using it should be aware of them.

The most serious side effect associated with use of the Pill appears to be a slight but significant increase in problems of blood clotting (thromboembolic disorders). Women who use the Pill have a higher chance than nonusers of developing blood clots (thrombi). Often these form in the legs, and they may then move to the lungs. There may also be clotting or hemorrhaging in the brain (stroke). The clots may lead to pain, hospitalization, and (in rare cases) death. The risk of death is somewhat less than 3 per 100,000 women per year for women on the Pill, as compared with 0.4 per 100,000 women per year among nonusers. Symptoms of blood clots are severe headaches, sudden blurring of vision, severe leg or chest pains, and shortness of breath.

There have been many emotional reports in the media of the Pill causing cancer; the scientific data, however, do not provide evidence that the Pill causes cancer of the cervix, uterus, or breast. However, the Pill may aggravate already existing cancer, although there is some evidence that it may retard the growth of benign breast lumps. And, while some of the studies have looked at effects after fairly long periods of time, there is a need for studies of even longer-term effects, since it is known that cancer-causing agents (carcinogens) may not show their effects for as much as 20 years.

For some women, the Pill can cause an increase in blood pressure; thus it is important to have regular checkups so that this can be detected if it occurs. About 5 percent of women on the Pill develop bad headaches. The Pill may, like pregnancy, precipitate diabetes. It may also aggravate epilepsy and asthma. The Pill may cause chloasma (brown patches on the skin of the face and elsewhere). Although these problems are relatively rare, they underline the importance of the doctor's giving a thorough examination before prescribing birth control pills and of the woman's having regular checkups while using them.

The Pill increases the amount of vaginal discharge and the susceptibility to vaginitis (vaginal inflammations such as monilia and trichomonas—see Chapter 19) because it alters the chemical balance of the lining of the vagina. Women on the Pill have an increased suscepti-

bility to gonorrhea, probably for similar reasons. Women on the Pill are also more susceptible to gum inflammations, as pregnant women are.

The Pill may cause some nausea, although this almost always goes away after the first month or two of use. Some brands of pills can also cause weight gain, by increasing appetite or water retention, but this can often be reversed by switching to another brand. There may also be an effect on acne; some brands increase the oiliness of the skin, making the condition worse, while others tend to clear it up.

Finally, there may be some psychological effects. About 20 percent of women on the Pill report increased irritability and depression, which become worse with length of time used. These side effects are probably related to the progesterone in the Pill; switching to a different brand may be helpful. There may also be changes in sexual desire. Some women report an increase in sexual interest, mainly because they are now free of the fear of pregnancy. But

FIGURE 6.3
Birth control devices, shown from left to right: IUDs with the device for inserting them, condoms, contraceptive foam, birth control pills, and diaphragm with contraceptive cream. *[Planned Parenthood.]*

other women report a decrease in sexual desire as well as a decrease in vaginal lubrication, a loss of sensitivity of the vulva, and decreased ability to have orgasms. Once again, switching brands may be helpful.

Because of the side effects discussed above, the following women should *not* use the Pill: those with poor blood circulation or excess blood clotting; those with hepatitis or other liver diseases; those with undiagnosed abnormal genital bleeding; those with cancer of the breast or reproductive organs; those with cystic fibrosis or sickle-cell anemia (the latter because of the blood-clotting problems); nursing mothers (the Pill tends to dry up the milk supply, and the hormones may be transmitted through the milk to the baby); pregnant women (prenatal doses of hormones, as has been noted, can damage the fetus); and women over 40, particularly if they are cigarette smokers (because the risk of heart attack is considerably higher in this group). However, a woman in the last category probably should not be having a baby anyway because of the strain on her health and because of the increased incidence of birth defects in babies born to mothers over 40. A better alternative would probably be some form of sterilization, either a tubal ligation for her or a vasectomy for her husband.

Women with the following conditions can use the Pill only conditionally, under the close supervision of a physician: diabetes; migraine headaches, epilepsy, or asthma; mental retardation; high blood pressure or varicose veins; cardiac or kidney diseases or uterine fibromyomata; and a tendency to severe depression.

Well, after all this discussion, just how dangerous is the Pill? It seems that this depends on who you are and on how you look at it. If you have blood-clotting problems, the Pill is extremely dangerous to you; if you have none of the contraindications listed above, it is very safe. One's point of view and standard of comparison also matter. While a death rate of 3

per 100,000 from clotting disorders sounds high, it is important to consider that one alternative to the Pill is intercourse with no contraceptive, and that can mean pregnancy, which has a set of side effects and a death rate all its own. Thus while the death rate for the Pill is 3 per 100,000, the death rate for pregnancy and delivery is 17 per 100,000. And while the Pill may precipitate diabetes, diabetes may also be precipitated by pregnancy. Thus in many ways the Pill is no more dangerous than the alternative, pregnancy, and may even be safer. Another possible standard of comparison is drugs that are commonly taken for less serious reasons. Aspirin, for example, is routinely used for headaches. Recent reports indicate that aspirin has side effects, and thus the birth control pill may be no more dangerous than drugs we take without worrying much.

The Pill does have some serious potential dangers, particularly for high-risk individuals, but for many others it is an extremely effective method of contraception that poses little or no danger.

Advantages and Disadvantages

The Pill has a number of advantages. It is essentially 100 percent effective if used properly. It does not interfere with intercourse, as some other methods—the diaphragm, the condom, and foam—do. It is not messy. Some of its side effects are also advantages; it reduces the amount of menstrual flow and thus reduces premenstrual tension and cramps. Indeed, it is sometimes prescribed for the noncontraceptive purpose of regulating menstruation and eliminating cramps. Iron-deficiency anemia is also less likely to occur among Pill users. It can clear up acne.

The side effects of birth control pills, discussed above, are of course major disadvantages. Another disadvantage is the cost, which is about $2 a month for as long as they are used.

They also place the entire burden of contraception on the woman. In addition, taking them correctly is a little complicated; the woman must understand when they are to be taken, and she must remember when to take them and when not to take them. This would not be too taxing for the average college student, but for an illiterate peasant woman in an underdeveloped country who thinks the pills are to be worn like an amulet on a chain around the neck or for the mentally retarded (they need contraceptives too), presently available birth control pills are too complicated to use.

One other criticism of the Pill is that, for a woman who has intercourse only infrequently (say, once or twice a month or less), it represents contraceptive "overkill"; that is, the Pill makes her infertile every day of the month (with the side effects of taking it every day), and yet she needs it only a few days each month. Women in this situation might consider a method, such as the diaphragm, that is used only when needed.

Reversibility

When a woman wants to become pregnant, she simply stops taking pills after the end of one cycle. Among women who do this, 60 to 75 percent become pregnant within three months, and 90 percent become pregnant within a year (Montreal Health Press, 1975). This is essentially the same rate as for women who have never taken the Pill. Therefore, the Pill does not seem to affect the fertility of a woman after she stops taking it.

Other Kinds of Pills

To this point, the discussion has centered chiefly on the *combination pill,* so named because it contains both estrogen and progestin. This variety of pill is by far the most widely used, but there are many kinds of combination pills and several kinds of pills other than combination ones.

Combination pills vary from one brand to the next in the dosages of estrogen and progestin. The dose of estrogen is important because higher doses are more likely to induce blood-clotting problems. According to the British Committee on Safety of Drugs, only those drugs containing 50 micrograms or less of estrogen should be used; brands fulfilling that requirement are Ortho-Novum 1/50, Norinyl 1, Demulen, Norlestrin 1, Norlestrin 2.5, Ovral, and Zoran 1/50. Pills that contain more than the recommended amount of estrogen are Ortho-Novum 1/80, Ortho-Novum 2, Ovulen, Enovid-E, Enovid 5, Norinyl 2, and all sequential pills (discussed below) (Boston Women's Health Book Collective, 1976). Several "low-dose" estrogen brands have been developed recently (such as Loestrin 1.5/30), but they may have a slightly higher failure rate. High-progestin brands are related to symptoms such as vaginitis and depression. Thus, depending on what side effects the woman wants to avoid, she can choose a brand for its high or low estrogen or progesterone level (see Hatcher et al., 1976, p. 51, for a list of symptoms related to dosages of estrogen and progestin). Another variant on the combination pill is the 28-day pill. There are 28 pills in every package. The first 21 pills that the woman takes are regular combination pills, and the last seven are placebos (they contain no drugs). The purpose of this is simply to help the woman use the pills properly, the idea being that it is easier to remember to take a pill every day than to remember to take one each day for 21 days and then none for seven days; also the seven placebos eliminate confusion about when to start taking pills again.

Sequential pills are now largely of historical interest since they have been withdrawn from the market. The woman took two different kinds of pills during the 21 days (hence the name "sequential"). During the first phase she took pills that contained estrogen only; and then for the last five or six days she took pills that contained both estrogen and progestin. They were withdrawn because they had more estrogen-related side effects than combination pills and also a substantially higher failure rate.

Progestin-only pills (such as Micronor, Nor-Q-D, and Ovrette) have been developed recently. The pills contain only a low dose of progestin and no estrogen, and they were designed to avoid the estrogen-related side effects of the standard pills. The woman takes one beginning on the first day of her period and every day thereafter, at the same time each day. Although no one is exactly sure how they work, hypotheses include the following: changes in the cervical mucus such that sperm cannot get through, inhibition of the egg's ability to travel down the tube, inhibition of the sperm's ability to penetrate the egg, inhibition of implantation, and inhibition of ovulation. Progestin-only pills have a theoretical failure rate of 1 to 4 percent, which is considerably higher than that of combination pills, although much of the failure occurs during the first six months of use. They were originally developed to avoid the side effects of the estrogen in combination pills; their major side effect seems to be that they produce very irregular menstrual cycles. Some of the side effects of combination pills have also been reported. Unfortunately, the progestin-only pill has not been in use long enough (it has been marketed since January 1973) for researchers to be certain of all its side effects.

There have been several different kinds of *mini-pill,* and the meaning of the term is therefore somewhat ambiguous. It has been used to refer to the progestin-only pill, to a low-estrogen combination pill, and to another pill that was taken off the market some time ago. Typically, though, the mini-pill is a progestin-only pill.

The *morning-after pill* was approved for emergency use (for example, after a rape) by the FDA in 1973. It contains a high dose (25 milligrams) of a potent estrogen, diethylstilbes-trol (DES), and is taken twice a day for five days, beginning no more than 72 hours after the act of intercourse and preferably within 24 hours. It should be stressed that it is for emergency use only, because of its serious side effects; about 16 percent of women taking it develop severe nausea and vomiting. Possible side effects if it is taken by a pregnant woman were noted in Chapter 5. Therefore it cannot be considered a method of birth control for regular use.

THE IUD

The *intrauterine device,* or IUD (sometimes also called *intrauterine contraceptive device* [IUCD]) is a small piece of plastic; it comes in various shapes. Metal or a drug may also be part of the device. Some IUDs were named after their inventors, for example, the Lippes loop, the Grafenberg ring, and the Birnberg bow. An IUD is inserted into the uterus by a doctor or nurse practitioner (see Figure 6.4) and then remains in place until the woman wants to have it removed. One or two plastic strings hang down from the IUD through the cervix, enabling the woman to check to see whether it is in place.

The IUD actually has a rather long and illustrious history. The basic principle—that a foreign object placed in the uterus prevents pregnancy—was known in ancient Greece. For centuries, Turkish and Arab camel drivers have followed the fairly effective practice of inserting a stone into a camel's uterus to prevent pregnancy during long desert trips. The use of the IUD in humans, however, received little scientific attention until, in the 1920s, the German physician Ernst Grafenberg reported data on 2000 insertions of silk or silver wire rings. In spite of the high effectiveness he reported (98.4 percent), his work was poorly received. Not until the 1950s, with the development of plastic and stainless-steel devices, did the method gain much popularity.

How It Works

No one is really sure how the IUD works, but the data clearly show that it does. The hypothesis that is currently most favored is that the IUD prevents implantation of the egg in the uterus. Studies on humans have shown that the IUD produces no systemic effects such as changing levels of hormones. The ovaries and fallopian tubes of women with IUDs function normally. Sperm and eggs have been found in the tubes of women with IUDs, indicating that ovulation proceeds normally and that sperm are not blocked from the tubes. Thus it appears, by the process of elimination, that the action is localized in the uterus. The IUD may produce a continual slight inflammation that keeps implantation from occurring, perhaps by preventing proper development of the endometrium or perhaps by exerting a lethal influence on the fertilized egg.

The small amount of copper that is added to some of the devices (for example, the Copper "7" and the Copper "T") is thought to have an additional contraceptive effect. It seems to alter the functioning of the enzymes involved in implantation.

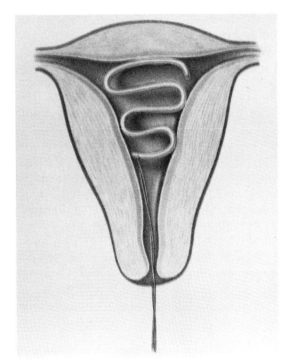

FIGURE 6.4

An IUD (Lippes loop) in place in the uterus. Note the strings hanging down through the cervix to the vagina; they enable the woman to check to make sure that the device is in place. [Ortho Pharmaceutical Corp.]

Effectiveness

The IUD is extremely effective and is second only to the Pill (and sterilization) in effectiveness. Pregnancy rates for the various types now in use range from 1 to 7 percent. The rates for the large Lippes loop and the Saf-T-Coil are about 3 percent. The copper devices seem to have a slightly lower pregnancy rate. The 3 percent failure rate is for the first year of use; after that, the failure rate is lower. Most failures occur during the first three months of use, either because the IUD is expelled or for other, unknown, reasons. Thus some physicians recommend that a backup method, such as foam, be used during the first three months. Expulsion is most likely in women who have had no children, in younger women, and in women who are menstruating. According to the FDA (1973), the expulsion rate is about 10 percent during the first year.

The IUD can be made essentially 100 percent effective when combined with another method such as a contraceptive foam or a condom.

Side Effects

The most serious possible side effect of the IUD is perforation of the uterus. This occurs in only about 1 woman in 10,000, but it can be fatal. It is caused mainly by improper insertion, and thus women should exercise care in choosing a physician or clinic when obtaining an IUD.

Uterine and tubal infection are other serious side effects that can result from careless insertion. The IUD seems to aggravate already existing pelvic infections, and so it should not be used by a woman who has such an infection or a history of such infections. One particular type of IUD, the Dalkon shield, seems to be most frequently implicated in these complications. It has had a stormy history. The FDA withdrew it from the market in 1974, but then on December 20, 1974, against the advice of its own advisory committee, it approved further use under certain specified conditions. Then the manufacturer, A. H. Robbins, decided not to return it to the market.

The most common side effects of IUDs are cramping and abdominal pain, irregular bleeding, and increased menstrual flow. These symptoms occur in 10 to 20 percent of women using IUDs and are most likely immediately after insertion. These side effects are a major reason for requests for IUD removal.

There is no evidence that the IUD causes cancer.

Because of the possible side effects, women with the following conditions should not use an IUD: pregnancy, endometriosis, venereal disease, vaginal or uterine infection, pelvic inflammatory disease, too small uterus, excessively heavy menstrual flow and/or cramping, bleeding between periods, fibroid growths, uterine deformities, disorders requiring use of anticoagulant drugs, cardiac disease, anemia, and sickle-cell disease (Boston Women's Health Book Collective, 1976).

Advantages and Disadvantages

All the side effects discussed above are disadvantages of the IUD. Another disadvantage is the cost; some private physicians in large cities charge as much as $50 for an IUD insertion. Planned Parenthood clinics generally charge much less, and some even perform the service free. Even at the high rates, though, the IUD is the cheapest method of contraception over a long period of use, since the cost is incurred once only (except in the case of devices containing copper or progesterone, which must be replaced every year or two).

Although the failure rate of the IUD is low, it is not zero, and this is another major disadvantage. In a group of 100 women using the IUD for a year, about two will become pregnant. Those women who absolutely do not want to become pregnant should use either a backup method, at least around the time of ovulation, or a different method entirely.

Once inserted, the IUD is perfectly simple to use. The woman has only to check periodically to see that the strings are in place. Thus it has an advantage over methods like the diaphragm or condom in that it does not interrupt intercourse in any way. It has an advantage over the Pill in that the woman does not have to remember to use it. For these reasons, it has been very popular in underdeveloped nations.

Contrary to what some people think, the IUD does not interfere with the use of a tampon during menstruation, nor does it have any effect on intercourse.

Reversibility

When a woman who is using an IUD wants to become pregnant, she simply has a physician remove the device. She can become pregnant immediately.

THE DIAPHRAGM

The diaphragm is a circular, dome-shaped piece of thin rubber with a rubber-covered rim of flexible metal (see Figure 6.5). It is inserted into the vagina and, when properly in place, fits snugly over the cervix. In order for it to be used properly, a contraceptive cream or jelly (such as Delfen) must be applied to the diaphragm. It may be inserted up to six hours before intercourse; it must be left in place for at least six hours afterward and may be left in for as long as 16 hours.

The diaphragm was the earliest of the highly effective methods of contraception for women. It was first described in a paper in 1882 by the German researcher Mensinga, and it was the mainstay of contraception until about 1960. Many readers may safely assume that their own parents managed to limit their number of children to two or three by careful use of the diaphragm.

How It Works

The primary action of the diaphragm itself is mechanical; it simply blocks the entrance to the uterus so that sperm cannot swim up into it. The spermicidal cream kills any sperm that manage to get past the barrier. Any sperm remaining in the vagina die after about eight hours (for this reason, the diaphragm cannot be removed until six to eight hours after intercourse).

Effectiveness

The theoretical failure rate of the diaphragm, plus cream or jelly, is about 3 percent. Thus, used properly, it is extremely effective; "used properly" means using it every time, using cream or jelly every time, and leaving it in long enough. The actual failure rate has been estimated to be between 10 and 15 percent in various studies. Most failures are due to improper use; the woman may not use it every time, or she may not use cream or jelly. Even with perfectly proper use, there is still a 2 to 3 percent failure rate. For example, Masters and Johnson have shown that the expansion of the vagina during sexual arousal (see Chapter 7) may cause the diaphragm to slip. To get closer to 100 percent effectiveness, the diaphragm can be combined with a condom around the time of ovulation.

Because the fit of the diaphragm is so important to its effectiveness, it is important that

FIGURE 6.5
A diaphragm properly inserted.
[Ortho Pharmaceutical Corp.]

the woman be individually fitted for one by her physician. She must be refitted after the birth of a child or any similar occurrence that would alter the shape and size of the vagina.

Side Effects

The diaphragm has no side effects except possibly irritation of the vagina or the penis; this is caused by the cream or jelly and can be relieved by switching to another brand.

Advantages and Disadvantages

Some people feel that the diaphragm is undesirable because it must be inserted just before intercourse and therefore ruins the "spontaneity" of sex. People with this attitude, of course, should not use the diaphragm as a method of birth control since they probably will not use it all the time, in which case it will not work. However, a student of mine told me that she and her boyfriend make the preparation and insertion of the diaphragm a ritual part of their foreplay; he inserts it, and they both have a good time! Couples who maintain this kind of attitude are much more likely to use the diaphragm effectively.

Some women dislike touching their genitals and sticking their fingers into their vagina. The diaphragm is not a good method for them.

The diaphragm requires some thought and presence of mind on the woman's part. She must remember to have it with her when she needs it and to have a supply of cream or jelly. She also needs to avoid becoming so carried away with passion that she forgets about it or decides not to use it.

Some women also dislike the fact that the cream or jelly may leak out after intercourse.

The cost of a diaphragm is about $4 to $5 plus the cost of the office visit. With proper care, a diaphragm should last about two years, and thus it is not expensive.

The major advantages of the diaphragm are that it has no side effects and, when used properly, is extremely effective. For this reason, women who are worried about the side effects of the Pill or the IUD should seriously consider the diaphragm as an alternative. The diaphragm can also be helpful to a couple wishing to have intercourse during the woman's period; the diaphragm catches the menstrual flow, which some couples consider desirable.

Reversibility

If a woman wishes to become pregnant, she simply stops using the diaphragm. Its use has no effect on her later chances of conceiving.

THE CONDOM

The condom ("rubber," "prophylactic," "safe") is a thin sheath that fits over the penis. It comes rolled up in a little packet (see Figure 6.3) and must be unrolled before use. It may be made of latex ("rubber") or of the intestinal tissue of lambs ("skin"). The widespread use of the modern condom, both for contraception and for protection against venereal disease (VD), dates from about 1843, when vulcanized rubber was developed; however, the use of a sheath to cover the penis has been known throughout most of recorded history.[1] Casanova (1725–1798) was one of the first to popularize it for its contraceptive value as well as its protective value.

To be effective, the condom must be used properly. It must be unrolled onto the erect penis before the penis ever enters the vagina— not just before ejaculation, since long before then some drops containing a few sperm may have been produced. There are two kinds of condoms: those with plain ends and those with a protruding tip that catches the semen. If a plain-ended one is used, about $1/2$ inch of air-free space should be left at the tip so that the force of the ejaculate will not burst it. Care should be taken that it does not slip during intercourse. After the man has ejaculated, he must hold the rim of the condom against the base of the penis as he withdraws. It is best to withdraw soon after ejaculation, while the man still has an erection, in order to minimize the chances of slippage.

Condoms may be either lubricated or unlubricated. Some further lubrication for intercourse may be necessary. A contraceptive foam or jelly works well and provides additional protection. A sterile lubricant such as K-Y jelly may also be used.

How It Works

The condom simply catches the semen and thus prevents it from entering the vagina.

---

[1]Condoms have also been the stimulus for humor throughout history, an example being this limerick:

There was a young man of Cape Horn
Who wished he had never been born.
   And he wouldn't have been
    If his father had seen
That the end of the rubber was torn.

Effectiveness

Condoms are actually much more effective as a contraceptive than most people think. The theoretical failure rate is only about 3 percent. The actual failure rate is about 15 percent, but many failures result from improper or inconsistent use. The FDA controls the quality of condoms carefully, and thus the chances of a failure due to a defect in the condom itself are small.

Combined with a contraceptive foam or cream or a diaphragm, the condom is close to 100 percent effective.

Side Effects

The condom has no side effects.

Advantages and Disadvantages

One disadvantage of the condom is that it must be used at the time of intercourse, raising the old "spontaneity" problem again. If the couple can make an enjoyable ritual of putting it on together, this problem can be minimized.

Some men complain that the condom reduces their sensation and thus lessens their pleasure in intercourse ("It's like taking a shower with a raincoat on"). This can be a major disadvantage. On the other hand, with condoms, as with many other things, you get what you pay for. The more expensive "skins" provide more sensation than the less expensive "rubbers." It is also true, however, that the reduction in sensation may be an advantage for some; for example, it may help the premature ejaculator.

There are several advantages to condoms. They are the only contraceptive method presently available for men except sterilization. They are cheap (around $1.25 to $1.50 for three), they are readily available without prescription at a drugstore,[2] and they are fairly easy

to use, although the man (or woman) must plan ahead so that one will be available when it is needed. Finally, it is one of the few contraceptive methods that also provides some protection against VD.

Reversibility

The method is easily and completely reversible. The man simply stops using them if conception is desired.

SPERMICIDES

Contraceptive foams (Delfen, Emko), creams, and jellies are all classified as spermicides, that is, sperm killers. They come in a tube or a can, along with a plastic applicator. The applicator is filled and inserted into the vagina; the spermicide is then pushed out into the vagina near the cervix with the plunger. Thus it is inserted much as a tampon is. It must be left in for six to eight hours after intercourse. One application provides protection for only one act of intercourse.

Spermicides are not to be confused with the various feminine hygiene products (vaginal deodorants) on the market. The latter are not effective as contraceptives.

How They Work

Spermicides consist of a spermicidal chemical in an inert base, and they work in two ways: chemical and mechanical. The chemicals in them kill sperm, while the inert base itself mechanically blocks the entrance to the cervix so that sperm cannot swim into it.

Effectiveness

Actual failure rates for spermicides are around 25 percent. Put simply, they are not very effective. Foams tend to be more effective, and creams and jellies less so. Spermicidal tablets and suppositories are also available, and they

[2]High-quality condoms can also be obtained cheaply from mail-order houses such as Population Services in Chapel Hill, N.C.

are the least effective. Spermicides are effective only when used with a diaphragm or a condom.

Side Effects
Spermicides have no side effects except that they may irritate the vagina or the penis.

Advantages and Disadvantages
The major advantage of spermicides is that they are readily available, without prescription, in any drugstore. Thus they can be used as a stopgap method until the woman can see a physician and get a more effective contraceptive. Foam and some brands of creams and jellies also help prevent venereal disease.

Their major disadvantage is that, by themselves, they are not very effective. They also interrupt the spontaneity of sex, although only very briefly. Some women dislike the sensation of the spermicide leaking out after intercourse, and some, as noted, are irritated by the chemicals. Finally, most people find that they taste terrible, and so their use interferes with oral sex.

DOUCHING
Some people believe that douching[3] with any one of a variety of solutions is an effective contraceptive technique. A popular rumor among teenagers is that douching with Coca-Cola will prevent pregnancy. Unfortunately, while it is true that acidic solutions will kill sperm, it takes only a minute for some of the sperm to reach the cervical mucus; once there, they are free to continue moving up into the uterus, and no douching solution will reach them. The woman would have to be a championship sprinter to get herself up and douched

---

[3]Flushing the vagina with a liquid.

soon enough. And the douche itself may even push some sperm up into the uterus. Douching, therefore, is just not effective as a contraceptive.

WITHDRAWAL
Withdrawal (coitus interruptus, "pulling out") is probably the most ancient form of birth control. (A reference to it is even found in Genesis 38:8–9, in the story of Onan; hence it is sometimes called *onanism,* although this term is also sometimes used for masturbation.) Withdrawal is still widely used throughout the world. The man withdraws his penis from the vagina before he has an orgasm and thus ejaculates outside the vagina.

Effectiveness
Withdrawal is not very effective as a method of birth control. The failure rate is somewhere around 20 to 30 percent. Failures occur for several reasons: The few drops of fluid that come out of the penis during arousal may carry enough sperm for conception to occur; if ejaculation occurs outside the vagina but near or on the vulva, sperm may still get into the vagina and continue up into the uterus; and sometimes the man simply does not withdraw in time.

Side Effects
Withdrawal produces no direct physical side effects. However, over long periods of time, it may contribute to producing sexual dysfunctions in the man, such as premature ejaculation, and also sexual dysfunction in the woman.

Advantages and Disadvantages
The major advantage of withdrawal is that it is the only last-minute method; it can be used when nothing else is available, although if the

situation is this desperate one might consider abstinence as an alternative. Obviously, withdrawal requires no prescription, and it is completely free.

One major disadvantage is that withdrawal is not very effective. In addition, it requires exceptional motivation on the part of the man, and it may be very psychologically stressful to him. He must constantly maintain a kind of self-conscious control. The woman may worry about whether he really will withdraw in time, and the situation is certainly less than ideal for her to have an orgasm.

THE RHYTHM METHOD

Rhythm is the only form of "natural" birth control and is therefore the only method officially approved by the Roman Catholic Church. It requires simply abstaining during the woman's fertile period (around ovulation). There are actually several rhythm methods, depending on how the woman's fertile period is determined.

The Calendar Method

The calendar method is the simplest rhythm method. It is based on the assumption that ovulation occurs about 14 days before the onset of menstruation. It works best for the woman with the perfectly regular 28-day cycle. She should ovulate on day 14, and almost surely on one of days 13 to 15. Three days are added in front of that period (previously deposited sperm may result in conception), and two days are added after it (to allow for long-lasting eggs); thus the couple must abstain from day 10 to day 17. Thus even for the woman with perfectly regular cycles, eight days of abstinence are required in the middle of each cycle.

The woman who is not perfectly regular must keep a record of her cycles for at least six months, and preferably a year. From this she determines the length of her shortest cycle and the length of her longest cycle. The preovulatory safe period is then calculated by subtracting 18 from the number of days in the shortest cycle, and the postovulatory safe period is calculated by subtracting 11 from the number of days in the longest cycle (see Table 6.1). Thus for a woman who is somewhat irregular—say, with cycles varying from 26 to 34 days in length—a period of abstinence from day 8 to day 23 (a total of 16 days) would be required.

The Basal Body Temperature Method

A somewhat more accurate method for determining ovulation is the basal body temperature (BBT) method. The principle behind this was discussed in Chapters 4 and 5. The woman takes her temperature every day immediately upon waking. During the preovulatory phase her temperature will be at a fairly constant low level. On the day of ovulation it drops (although this does not always occur), and on the day after ovulation it rises sharply, staying at that high level for the rest of the cycle. Intercourse would be safe beginning about three days after ovulation. Some of the psychological stresses involved in using this method have been noted previously. As a form of contraception, the BBT method has a major disadvantage in that it determines safe days only *after* ovulation; theoretically, according to the method, there are no safe days before ovulation. Thus the BBT method is probably best used in combination with the calendar method; the calendar method determines the preovulatory safe period, and the BBT method determines the postovulatory safe period.

The Cervical Mucus (Ovulation) Method

A recent innovation in the rhythm method has been developed by Drs. Evelyn and John Bill-

TABLE 6.1

DETERMINING THE FERTILE PERIOD USING THE CALENDAR METHOD*

Shortest Cycle (Days)	Day Fertile Period Begins	Longest Cycle (Days)	Day Fertile Period Ends
22	4	23	12
23	5	24	13
24	6	25	14
25	7	26	15
26	(8)	27	16
27	9	28	17
28	10	29	18
29	11	30	19
30	12	31	20
31	13	32	21
32	14	33	22
		34	(23)
		35	24

Example: If a woman's cycles vary in length from 26 days to 34 days, she can be fertile any time between days 8 and 23 of the cycle, and she must therefore abstain from day 8 to day 23.

*See text for further explanation.
Source: After E. Havemann. *Birth control.* New York: Time-Life, 1967, p. 23.

ings (Billings et al., 1974). Their method is based on variations over the cycle in the mucus produced by the cervix. It works in the following way:

There are generally a few days just after menstruation during which no mucus is produced and there is a general sensation of vaginal dryness. This is a relatively safe period. Then there are a number of days of mucus discharge around the middle of the cycle. On the first days, the mucus is white or cloudy and tacky. The amount increases, and the mucus becomes clearer, until there are one or two *peak days,* when the mucus is like raw egg white—clear, slippery, and stringy. There is also a sensation of vaginal lubrication. Ovulation occurs within 24 hours after the last peak day. Abstinence is required from the first day of mucus discharge until four days after the peak days. After that the mucus, if present, is cloudy or white, and intercourse is safe.

The Billingses believe that women can be taught to use this method very effectively.

Other Methods

Because of the view of some Roman Catholics that rhythm is the only acceptable method of birth control, scientists have devoted considerable effort to trying to develop more effective rhythm methods (or, essentially, better methods of determining ovulation). One such method is a litmus-type test for detecting changes in cervical secretions. Another method tests for changes in saliva. These methods are still in the experimental stages, however.

Effectiveness

The effectiveness of the rhythm method varies considerably, depending on a number of factors, but basically it is not a very effective method (giving rise to its nickname, "Vatican roulette," and a number of old jokes like, "What do they call people who use the rhythm method?" Answer: "Parents"). The failure rate is somewhere between 15 and 35 percent; there tend to be fewer failures when the woman's cycle is very regular and when the couple are highly motivated and have been well instructed in the methods.

On the other hand, the effectiveness of the rhythm method depends partly on one's purpose in using it: whether for preventing pregnancy absolutely or for spacing pregnancies. If absolute pregnancy prevention is the goal (as it would be, for example, for an unmarried teenager), the method is just not effective enough. But if the couple simply wish to space pregnancies farther apart than would occur naturally, the method will probably accomplish this. Knowing when the woman's fertile times occur can also improve the effectiveness of other methods of contraception.

Advantages and Disadvantages

For many users of the rhythm method, its main advantage is that it is considered an acceptable method of birth control by the Roman Catholic Church.

The method has no side effects except possible psychological stress, and it is cheap. It is easily reversible. It also helps the woman become more aware of her body's functioning. Finally, the method requires cooperation from both partners, which may be considered either an advantage or a disadvantage.

Its main disadvantages are its high failure rate and the psychological stress it may cause. Periods of abstinence of at least eight days, and possibly as long as two or three weeks, are necessary, which is an unacceptable requirement for many couples. Actually, the rhythm method would seem best suited to people who do not like sex very much.

Finally, a certain amount of time, usually at least six months, is required to collect the data needed to make the method work. Thus one cannot simply begin using it on the spur of the moment.

STERILIZATION

Sterilization is a surgical procedure whereby an individual is made permanently sterile, that is, unable to reproduce. Sterilization is a rather emotion-laden topic for a number of reasons. It conjures up images of government-imposed programs of *involuntary* sterilization in which groups of people—possibly the mentally retarded, criminals, or members of some minority group—are sterilized so that they cannot reproduce. (The following discussion deals only with voluntary sterilization used as a method of birth control for those who want no more children or who want no children at all.) Some people confuse sterilization with castration, though the two are quite different. This is also an emotional topic because sterilization means the end of one's capacity to reproduce, which is very basic to gender roles and gender identity. The ability to impregnate and the ability to bear a child are very important in our cultural definitions of manhood and womanhood. It is hoped that as gender roles become more flexible in our society and as concern about reproduction is replaced by a concern for limiting population size, the word "sterilization" will no longer be so frightening. However, the change will come slowly at best.

Most physicians are conservative about performing sterilizations; they want to make sure that the patient has made a firm decision on his or her own and will not be back a couple of months later wanting to have the procedure reversed. The physician has an obligation to follow the principle of "informed consent." This means explaining the procedures involved, telling the patient about the possible risks and advantages, discussing alternative methods, and answering any questions the patient has. Only after the patient has been so informed should the doctor obtain her or his written consent to have the surgery performed.

Despite this conservatism, both male sterilization and female sterilization have become increasingly popular as methods of birth control, and the number performed per year has risen phenomenally since 1969. The Association for Voluntary Sterilization estimates that 639,000 men and 674,000 women were voluntarily sterilized in 1975 (*AVS Newsletter,* September 1976). The total number of sterilized adults in the United States is now estimated to be about 7 million. Indeed, the National Fertility Survey of 1970 found that sterilization was the most common method of birth control for married couples over 30 years of age (Presser and Bumpass, 1972).

Male Sterilization

The male sterilization operation is called a *vasectomy,*[4] so named for the vas deferens, which is tied or cut (see Figure 6.6). It can be done in a physician's office under local anesthesia and requires only about 20 minutes to perform. The physician makes a small incision on one side of the upper part of the scrotum. The vas is then separated from the surrounding tissues, tied off, and cut. The procedure is then repeated on the other side, and the incisions are sewn up. For a day or two the man may have to refrain from strenuous activity and be careful not to pull the incision apart.

Typically, the man can return to having intercourse within a week. It should not be assumed that he is sterile yet, however. There may still be some stray sperm lurking in his ducts beyond the point of incision. All sperm are generally gone in two or three months, and their absence should be confirmed by semen analysis. Until this confirmation is made, an additional method of birth control should be used.

Misunderstandings about the vasectomy abound. In fact, a vasectomy creates no physical changes that interfere with erection. Neither does it interfere in any way with sex hormone production; the testes continue to manufacture testosterone and secrete it into the bloodstream. Men with vasectomies will not develop high-pitched voices! Neither does a vasectomy interfere with the process or sensation of ejaculation. As was noted earlier, virtually all the fluid of the ejaculate is produced by the prostate and seminal vesicles, and the incision is made long before that point in the duct system. Thus the ejaculate is completely normal, except that it does not contain any sperm.

How it works   The vasectomy makes it impossible for sperm to move beyond the cut in the vas; hence they cannot move out through the urethra. Thus the vasectomy prevents sperm from being in the ejaculate.

Effectiveness   The vasectomy is essentially 100 percent effective; it has a failure rate of 0.15 percent. Failures occur because stray sperm are still present during the first few months after surgery, because the physician did not successfully sever the vas, or because the ends of the vas have grown back together.

Side effects   The physical side effects of the vasectomy are minimal. In about 5 percent of cases, there is a minor complication from the surgery, such as inflammation of the vas (Gould, 1974).

Some psychologically based sexual problems such as impotence may arise. Thus the man's attitude toward having a vasectomy is extremely important.

Reversibility   Quite a bit of effort has been devoted to developing techniques for reversing

---

[4]As someone has said, "Vasectomy is never having to say you're sorry."

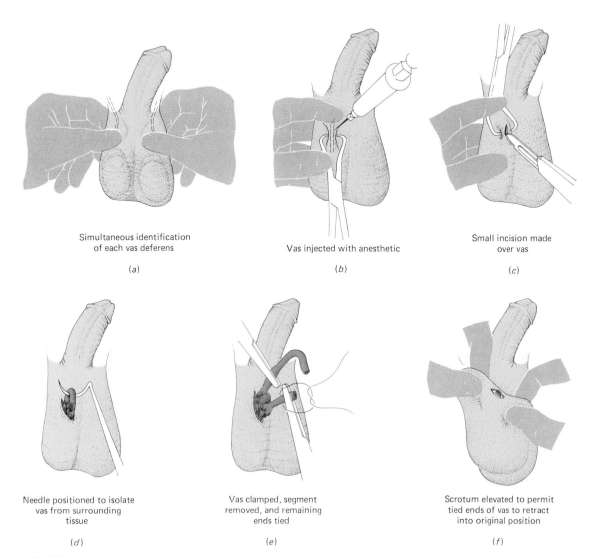

(a) Simultaneous identification of each vas deferens

(b) Vas injected with anesthetic

(c) Small incision made over vas

(d) Needle positioned to isolate vas from surrounding tissue

(e) Vas clamped, segment removed, and remaining ends tied

(f) Scrotum elevated to permit tied ends of vas to retract into original position

FIGURE 6.6
The procedure for doing a vasectomy.

vasectomies and to developing vasectomy techniques that are more reversible. At present, while some physicians have reported reversibility rates as high as 70 percent, a more reasonable estimate is 5 percent (Gillette, 1972). In making a decision about whether to have a vasectomy, it should be assumed that it is irreversible.

Currently being investigated is a plastic valve that could be implanted in the vas; if the patient desired to reverse his sterilization, the valve could be reopened in simple surgery.

It appears, however, that after a vasectomy some men begin forming antibodies to their own sperm (Katchadourian and Lunde, 1975). Because these antibodies destroy sperm, they might contribute further to the irreversibility of the vasectomy.

Advantages and disadvantages   The major advantages of the vasectomy are its effectiveness and its minimal health risks. Once performed, it requires no further thought or planning on the man's part. As a permanent, long-term method of contraception, it is very cheap. The operation itself is simple—much simpler than the female sterilization procedures—and requires no hospitalization or absence from work. Finally, it is one of the few methods that allows the man to assume contraceptive responsibility.

The permanency of the vasectomy may be either an advantage or a disadvantage. If permanent contraception is desired, the method is certainly much better than something like birth control pills, which must be used repeatedly. But if the couple change their minds and decide that they want to have another child, the permanency is a distinct disadvantage. Some men put several samples of their sperm in a frozen sperm bank so that artificial insemination can be performed if they do decide to have another child after a vasectomy.

Another major disadvantage of the vasectomy is the various psychological problems that may result if the man sees sterilization as a threat to his masculinity or virility. However, such problems are fairly rare, and the vast majority of men report satisfaction with the vasectomy and even an improved sex life (Kohli and Sobrero, 1973; Simon Population Trust, 1969; but see Wiest and Janke, 1974, for a critical review). Finally, if a married couple use the vasectomy as a permanent method of birth control, the woman is not protected if she has intercourse with someone other than her husband.

Female Sterilization

Several surgical techniques are used to sterilize a woman: laparotomy, laparoscopy, culpot-omy, and culdoscopy. These techniques differ in terms of the type of procedure used and the path of entry. All are performed under local or, more commonly, general anesthesia, and all involve blocking the fallopian tubes in some way so that sperm and egg cannot meet.

The *tubal ligation* ("having the tubes tied") is the most common method of female sterilization. A small section is cut out of each fallopian tube, and the ends of each tube are tied off at the incision. The tubes may be reached through a small incision in the abdomen, in which case the procedure is called a *laparotomy*. Another avenue is through an incision made at the end of the vagina, in which case the procedure is called a *culpotomy* (the end of the vagina, the part past the cervix, is called the *cul de sac;* hence the name "culpotomy").

A more recent procedure is the *endoscopy.* A small tube, with lights and a mirror in it, is inserted to enable the physician to locate the fallopian tubes, which are cauterized (burned) with a small instrument. If entry is through the abdomen, the procedure is called a *laparoscopy,* and if entry is through the vagina, it is called a *culdoscopy.* One other variation involves inserting the instrument through the vagina and the uterus, in which case the procedure is called a *uteroscopy* or *hysteroscopy.*

These female sterilization procedures do not interfere in any way with the body's normal functioning. The ovaries are undisturbed, and therefore the production of sex hormones continues normally; thus a tubal ligation does not bring on premature menopause or cause the woman to grow a beard. Some of the misunderstandings concerning female sterilization procedures arise from confusion of these procedures with hysterectomy (surgical removal of the uterus) or oophorectomy (surgical removal of the ovaries), which does impair hormonal functioning). These latter two operations do produce sterility, but they are generally performed for purposes other than sterilization, for example, removal of tumors.

How it works All the female sterilization procedures make it impossible for the egg to move down the fallopian tube toward the uterus. Further, they prevent sperm from reaching the egg.

Effectiveness These procedures are essentially 100 percent effective. The failure rate of 0.1 to 0.2 percent may be due to an occasional rejoining of the ends of the tubes.

Side effects The procedures have no side effects other than complications arising from the surgery, such as infections, hemorrhaging, and problems related to the anesthetic. Generally only 1 to 2 percent of women undergoing the surgery experience complications.

Reversibility The operations are essentially irreversible, although occasionally it has been possible to rejoin the ends of the tube. In deciding whether to have such an operation, it should be assumed that it is irreversible.

Advantages and disadvantages Female sterilization has some of the same advantages as male sterilization in terms of effectiveness, permanence, and cheapness when used for long-term contraception.

Compared with male sterilization methods, the methods of female sterilization currently used are somewhat more complex. A hospital stay may be required, although generally the procedures can be performed on an outpatient basis; the surgery is also somewhat more serious, and so complications are more likely.

PSYCHOLOGICAL ASPECTS: ATTITUDES TOWARD CONTRACEPTION

It is a favorite old saying among the Planned Parenthood crowd that contraceptives are only as effective as the people who use them. That is, no contraceptive method is effective if it is not used or if it is used improperly. Thus the user is at least as important as all the technology of contraception.

Each year in the United States, between 1 and 2 million unwanted pregnancies occur. Sandberg and Jacobs (1971) list the following 10 psychological factors that appear to cause ineffective use (or no use) of contraceptives and thus lead to unwanted pregnancy (although, of course, some of the unwanted pregnancies result from failures of the devices themselves, even though they were used properly):

1 *Denial* This factor is particularly common among those who engage in premarital sex, and it may take several forms. There is denial of the possibility of pregnancy ("It can't happen to me" is repeated often, even by well-informed college women); denial that contraceptives work; denial that intercourse will occur ("I didn't plan it—I was just swept off my feet"); and denial of personal responsibility for contraception

TABLE 6.2

METHODS OF CONTRACEPTION USED BY MARRIED COUPLES IN 1970 (IN PERCENTAGES)*

Method	Percentage†
Withdrawal	2.1
Douche	3.2
Other	4.6
Diaphragm	5.7
Foam	6.1
Rhythm	6.4
IUD	7.4
Husband sterilized	7.8
Wife sterilized	8.5
Condom	14.2
Pill	34.2
Total	100.00

*Based on a sample of 3810 couples. All the women were under 45.
†Percentages are of those using contraceptives. Of the total sample, 15.9 percent had never used contraceptives, and 34.9 percent were using no method at the time of the study.
Source: C. F. Westoff. The modernization of U.S. contraceptive practice. *Family Planning Perspectives,* 1972, **4,** 9–12.

(for example, the belief of some men that it is the woman's responsibility).

2 *Love* Because love is seen as self-sacrifice and willingness to take risks, it can become an excuse for having unprotected intercourse ("If you love me, you'll do it" or "I wanted to surrender totally to demonstrate my love").

3 *Guilt* While it might be expected that guilt about sex (especially premarital sex) would be a deterrent to engaging in intercourse, and particularly unprotected intercourse, in fact just the opposite often appears to be the case. For example, some young Roman Catholics view contraception as immoral, but their guilt level about premarital sex is not quite so high. Thus they engage in premarital sex without using a method of contraception, and pregnancy results. Pregnancy may even be seen as a just punishment for one's immoral acts.

4 *Shame and embarrassment* This factor is closely related to the guilt factor. The person may be ashamed of using contraceptives and may particularly fear the shame and embarrassment that would result if someone else discovered that he or she was doing so. Contraceptives, in a sense, are a too tangible symbol that one is sexually active. Some people may be too embarrassed to seek contraceptive information, to purchase contraceptives, or to use methods such as the diaphragm or condom, which must be put on or inserted at the time of intercourse.

5 *Coital gamesmanship* People engage in sex for a variety of nonsexual reasons, such as to express dominance and improve self-esteem (see Chapter 1). The decision to use or not to use a contraceptive may reflect, for example, a power struggle between the two people involved.

6 *Gender identity conflicts* Because procreation is so central to our definitions of manhood and womanhood, contraception may threaten gender identity. A woman may need to demonstrate her fertility to prove her womanhood. Men engage in ego building by impregnating women; this is particularly true of unskilled or jobless men (Rainwater and Weinstein, 1960).

7 *Hostility* Failure to use contraceptives and the resulting pregnancy may express hostility. An example is the teenage girl who becomes pregnant to "get even with" her overly strict parents.

8 *Nihilism* Some people, particularly those living in extreme poverty, feel that they have no control over their own lives and no hope for the future. Thus they have an apathetic attitude toward family planning.

9 *Opportunism* Some people simply seize the opportunity to have intercourse if it comes their way; they are unwilling to delay their gratification until a means of contraception is available.

10 *Iatrogenic (physician-caused) reactions* Some people feel anxious or ambivalent about contraception because this feeling has been conveyed to them by their physicians.

Certainly, many other factors could be added to this list (see, for example, Byrne, 1977; Groat and Neal, 1975). The point is, however, that psychological factors are extremely important in determining whether a person uses a method of contraception.

ABORTION

In the past decade, abortion (the termination of a pregnancy) has been a topic of considerable controversy in the United States. Feminist groups talk of the woman's right to control her own body, while members of Right-to-Life groups speak of the unborn fetus's rights. On January 22, 1973, the United States Supreme Court made two landmark decisions that essentially decriminalized abortion by denying the states the right to regulate early abortions. Since then, the number of abortions performed each year has risen steadily. However, abortion shows little sign of becoming a regular method of birth control; rather, it serves as a backup.

In other countries, policies on abortion vary widely. It is legal and widely practiced in the Soviet Union and Japan, parts of eastern and central Europe, and South America. The use of abortion in the undeveloped nations of Africa and Asia is limited because of the scarcity of medical facilities.

This section will be about methods of abortion and the psychological aspects of abortion; the ethical and legal aspects will be discussed in Chapters 20 and 21.

Abortion Procedures

There are several methods of abortion; which one is used depends on how far the pregnancy has progressed.

Vacuum curettage The *vacuum curettage* method (also called *dilation and evacuation* [D and E], *vacuum suction,* and *vacuum aspiration*) can be performed during the first trimester of pregnancy and up to 20 weeks from the beginning of the last menstrual period (LMP). It is done on an outpatient basis with a local anesthetic. The procedure itself takes only about 10 minutes, and the woman stays in the doctor's office, clinic, or hospital for a few hours.

The woman is prepared as she would be for a pelvic exam, and an instrument is inserted into the vagina; the instrument dilates (stretches open) the opening of the cervix. A nonflexible tube is then inserted into this opening until one end is in the uterus. The other end is attached to a suction-producing apparatus, and the contents of the uterus, including the fetal tissue, are sucked out.

FIGURE 6.7
A vacuum-suction abortion.

The vacuum curettage is becoming the most common method of early (first-trimester) abortion because it is simple and entails little risk. There are minor risks of uterine perforation, infection, hemorrhaging, and failure to remove all the fetal material.

Dilation and curettage The *dilation and curettage* (D and C), or *dilatation and curettage,* is similar to the D and E, but it must be done in a hospital under a general anesthetic. It is also done from 8 to 20 weeks LMP.

As in the D and E, the cervical opening is

dilated. Then a sharp metal loop, attached to the end of a long handle (the curette), is inserted into the uterus; it is used to scrape out the uterine contents.

The D and E is now the most common first-trimester abortion technique. The D and C used to be the method of choice, and it still is for some physicians because they are familiar with the technique, since it is also used as a nonabortion gynecological procedure. In the latter case it is used for scraping out the uterine contents in the treatment of infertility and menstrual problems. Thus if someone tells you she was in the hospital for a D and C, you cannot necessarily assume that she was having an abortion.

The D and E is considered preferable to the D and C because the latter requires hospitalization (and is therefore more expensive) and a general anesthetic. It also causes more discomfort, and the risks of complications such as uterine perforation, infection, and hemorrhaging are greater.

Induced labor During the late part of the second trimester, abortion is usually performed by inducing labor and a miscarriage. The most commonly used version of this method is the *saline-induced abortion.* A fine tube is inserted through the abdomen into the amniotic sac inside the uterus. Some amniotic fluid is removed through the tube, and an equal amount of saline solution is injected into the amniotic sac. Within several hours, the solution has caused labor to begin. The cervix dilates, and the fetus is expelled through the contractions of labor. A variation on this technique is the recently developed *prostaglandin method.* Prostaglandins (hormonelike substances that cause contractions) are injected into the amniotic sac (or intravenously or by means of a vaginal suppository) and cause labor.

Induced labor is the method used most often for abortion if pregnancy has progressed late into the second trimester. This method is both more hazardous and more costly ($350 to $750) than the previous methods. The most serious complications of the saline-induced method are shock and possibly death (if the technique is done carelessly and the saline solution gets into a blood vessel) and a bleeding disorder, although these are rare. The prostaglandin method has several advantages over the saline method: it induces labor more quickly, and the labor itself is shorter. The chances of excessive bleeding and retained placenta are higher with the prostaglandin method, however, and there is also the risk that the cervix may tear as a result of too rapid dilation. Less serious side effects such as nausea, vomiting, and diarrhea are more common.

Traditionally it was thought that abortions should not be performed during weeks 13 to 15, because the uterus was too soft and the procedure was dangerous; the recommended procedure from 16 weeks on was saline-induced abortion. However, recent data indicate that the D and E is safe through weeks 13 to 15 and is safer than saline-induced abortion through week 20 (Center for Disease Control, 1976).

Hysterotomy *Hysterotomy* is a surgical method of abortion that can be done from 16 to 24 weeks LMP. Essentially, a cesarean section is performed, and the fetus is removed. Hysterotomy is more serious and more expensive (around $1000) than the other methods, and there is a greater risk of complications. It is done only rarely, but it may be useful if the pregnancy has progressed to the late second trimester and the woman's health is such that the induction methods should not be used.

Other methods There are several other abortion methods, but they are not widely used in the United States either because they are still in the developmental stages or because they have not gained acceptance here.

Several mechanical methods of stimulating the uterus to induce abortion have been developed and are used widely in Japan (Manabe, 1969). They are simple to perform and inexpensive, but they have not become popular in the United States because they are associated with more blood loss and a greater chance of infection.

Early abortion is done as soon as a positive pregnancy test is obtained up to eight weeks LMP. It is very similar to the vacuum curettage method, described above, except that a flexible tube is inserted through the cervix without dilating it, and the uterine contents are sucked out. The procedure can be done without an anesthetic. This method is not yet widely used.

Menstrual regulation (also called *endometrial aspiration, preemptive abortion,* and *menstrual extraction*) is a similar technique. The uterine contents are sucked out before the period is due and before pregnancy has been confirmed.

Psychological Aspects

In light of the controversies surrounding abortion and the complex ethical issues it raises, it might be expected that the whole experience of becoming pregnant and having an abortion would be a traumatic one and that the stresses involved might cause some psychological disturbance in the woman.

However, according to the research that has been done on legal abortion, the experience is not traumatic (see the review by Osofsky and Osofsky, 1972). Indeed, most women feel relieved and happy after an abortion. Fewer than 10 percent of women experience psychological problems afterward, and most of these women had problems before the pregnancy and abortion.

Research in this area raises several interesting questions. Women generally appear well adjusted after having an abortion, but well

TABLE 6.3

SUMMARY OF HEALTH RISKS ASSOCIATED WITH LEGAL ABORTION

Death*	
3.2 deaths per 100,000 legal abortions:	
Suction method	1.7 per 100,000
Induced labor	16.9 per 100,000
Hysterotomy	60.8 per 100,000
Normal childbirth	14.0 per 100,000

Complications†	
All methods combined	13.1 per 100 women
Suction	7.3 per 100 women
D and C	11.1 per 100 women
Saline	26.3 per 100 women
Hysterotomy	23.1 per 100 women

*Based on 635,237 abortions, Center for Disease Control, 1977.
†Including excessive bleeding, infection, uterine perforation, retained tissue, and minor complications.
Sources: *Family Planning Digest,* 1974, **5**(3), 12. C. Tietze and S. Lewit. Early complications of abortion under medical auspices: A preliminary report. *Studies in Family Planning,* 1971, **2**(7), 137.

adjusted compared with what? That is, what is the appropriate control or comparison group? One comparison group that has been studied is women who requested an abortion but were denied it. Women in this group have a much higher rate of disturbance than women who have had abortions. Another group that has been studied is children who were born because an abortion request was denied. They, too, show a high incidence of psychiatric disturbance (Forssman and Thuwe, 1966).

NEW ADVANCES

According to some, a really good method of contraception is not yet available. The highly effective methods either are permanent (sterilization) or have associated health risks (the Pill). Other, safer methods (such as the condom and the diaphragm) have appreciable failure rates. Most of the methods are for women, not men. Because of the dissatisfaction with the currently

FOCUS

A WOMAN TELLS ABOUT HER ABORTION EXPERIENCE

Just this past summer, I learned that I was pregnant. I was never so totally unprepared for anything in my entire life. My mother was the first to notice the symptoms, and she mentioned the possibility to me—a concept that I totally and flatly rejected. Pregnancy could *never* happen to me. I was too smart; I was on the Pill. Not until it was too late did I find out that the Pill is not 100 percent effective, especially the sequential type, to which I had just switched. When I finally did go to the doctor and my mother's diagnosis was confirmed, I panicked. I drove directly to my sister's home and burst into tears as I walked through the door. It was a cold, rainy summer day, and I wanted to die. I kept asking her and myself, "What am I going to do?" I knew I was totally incapable of motherhood or marriage at that point in my life. I knew I could never carry a child and give it up. Carrying a child entailed the sacrifice of too much—college, career, independence, lifestyle. There was only one road open.

I went home to my parents and told them that I was positively pregnant. My father's reaction, after a short pause, was, "You're going to have an abortion, aren't you?" And I felt inseparably close to him at that moment. Let me say here that my parents were once very strict moralists, judging on the arbitrary basis of "right and wrong." But having raised four children before me, they had become seasoned realists. They had seen my older sister marry during her freshman year in college, give up a full scholarship, bear five children, and divorce her husband by her thirtieth birthday. They had seen my younger sister literally throw her life away in

available methods, contraception research continues. A few of the more promising possibilities for the future are discussed below.

Several possibilities for male contraception are being explored (see, for example, Sciarra et al., 1975). One is the use of hormones in a "male pill" that would stop spermatogenesis (much as the Pill inhibits ovulation in women). Both testosterone and progesterone accomplish this. Unfortunately, the hormones that have been tested so far inhibit not only sperm production, but also sex drive, and therefore they pursuit of a false sense of security that she did not find in marriage. They knew I wanted more out of life and would be able to get it, but not through marriage and motherhood, especially when it was being thrust upon me. They knew abortion was the only path to take. I, also, knew it was the only path to take. I felt the need for it to be my own decision. And my decision was a very conscious one. All I really knew was that I did not want to be pregnant any longer and that I would have given almost anything to wake up not pregnant. And I knew abortion was the only means of achieving this.

My boyfriend had returned to school in New York when I was scheduled to go to Cleveland for the abortion. The logical person to take me was my father, who was retired and available. Little did I know what a commotion it would cause among many of the other women at the clinic who did not even dare tell their parents they had ever had intercourse.

The abortion was the most moving and transitional experience I had ever had—not the actual procedure itself (which *was* slightly painful), but rather the interaction and support that abounded at the clinic. It was the warmest and most supportive atmosphere I had ever been in, other than my own home. I love the women who work in that clinic, along with all women everywhere in similar clinics, for the job they are doing. They were there when I needed them, they reached out a hand when I needed one, and they made me feel totally at peace with myself and my decision. I needed more than the love and support of my family; I needed to *talk* to a woman who once felt the way I was feeling and to other women who were in my situation.

Through this experience, I feel I have come to know myself better; I have thought about myself, my life, and what I want to do. I have made definite moves with my life; I feel in control of my life, my mind, and my body.

Source: From a student essay.

are considered unacceptable. Theoretically at least, sperm production and hormone production are separate processes, and so it should be possible to stop sperm production without affecting sex drive.

An immunologic approach might be used on either men or women. Since some cases of infertility are caused by the formation of antibodies that destroy sperm (see Chapter 5) it would seem that if antibody formation could be stimulated, it would work as a contraceptive, although this would probably be a permanent

A BRIEF SUMMARY OF THE DEVELOPMENT OF SOPHISTICATED METHODS OF CONTRACEPTION

Late 1700s	Casanova (1725–1798) popularizes and publicizes use of the sheath, or "English riding coat."
1798	Malthus urges "moral restraint."
1840s	Goodyear vulcanizes rubber. Production of rubber condoms soon follows.
1883	Mensinga invents the diaphragm.
1893	Harrison performs the first vasectomy.
1909	Richter uses the intrauterine silkworm gut.
1910–1920	Margaret Sanger pioneers in New York City; the term "birth control" is coined.
1930	Graffenberg publishes information documenting his 21 years of experience with the ring (silver and copper) and catgut.
1930–1931	Knaus and Ogino elucidate "safe and unsafe" periods of the woman's menstrual cycle: the rhythm method.
1934	Corner and Beard isolate progesterone.
1937	Makepeace demonstrates that progesterone inhibits ovulation.
1950s	Abortions are utilized extensively in Japan.
1950–1960	Hormonal contraceptive research results in FDA approval of the use of the Pill as a contraceptive in 1960.
1960s	Many Western nations liberalize abortion laws. Modern IUDs become available. Contraceptive sterilization becomes more acceptable. The laparoscopic tubal ligation technique is developed.
1973	The United States Supreme Court rules on abortion. The first "mini-pill," or low-dose progestin pill, wins FDA approval. The Shot is provided in over 50 nations.

Source: Robert A. Hatcher et al. *Contraceptive technology 1976–1977.* (8th ed.) New York: Irvington, 1976.

method. Other immunologic methods, such as immunizing the woman against placental hormones so that implantation will not occur, are also being explored (Hatcher et al., 1976).

Depo-Provera (DMPA), or the "shot," is a long-lasting progesterone that is injected only once about every three months. It works like the progestin-only pill and is about as effective as combination pills. It has the major advantage that the woman does not have to remember to take it every day. The FDA has approved it for limited use, but it has not been in use long enough for researchers to be certain of its side effects. Depo-Provera has been reported to cause various menstrual irregularities including bleeding between periods and missed periods, decreased sex drive, weight gain, headaches, and dizziness; it is not yet known whether it will produce thromboembolic problems, as combination pills do.

The use of subdermal implants of a progestin capsule is also being explored. The capsules would be surgically installed beneath the skin and would release a small amount of progestin each day. They would be effective over a long period of time, perhaps three to five years.

Variations on the Pill are being explored. Morris, at Yale, is investigating what he calls "interception," the prevention of implantation after conception has occurred (Morris, 1973).[5] Other pills might inhibit the hypothalamic releasing factors that are necessary for LH and FSH production. A once-a-month pill, using a combination of estrogen and progestin, is also being studied. It has the obvious advantage that it does not have to be taken daily, but side effects including nausea, vomiting, headaches,

dizziness, and depression have been reported (Hatcher et al., 1976).

A pill that is taken after unprotected intercourse is an attractive possibility. The use of DES in the "morning-after" pill was noted above. Unfortunately, this pill has rather serious side effects and is therefore not practical for regular use. A postcoital progestin pill is also being studied. It appears that the more frequently the couple have intercourse, the more effective it becomes, suggesting that it works essentially like the progestin-only pill.

Another use of progestins is in the progestin-coated vaginal ring. The ring containing progestins is inserted into the vagina, much as a diaphragm is, and is left there for 21 days. It slowly releases progestin into the system.

New advances in IUD design include progesterone-impregnated IUDs and hollow IUDs filled with progestins, both of which should be more effective than a regular IUD and should also reduce uterine cramping. The intrauterine membrane (IUM), which is similar to the IUD but more flexible, is also being developed (Wheeler, 1975).

SUMMARY

Table 6.4 provides a comparative summary of the various methods of birth control discussed in this chapter.

SUGGESTIONS FOR FURTHER READING

Ehrlich, Paul R., and Ehrlich, Anne H. *Population, resources, environment.* (2nd ed.) San Francisco: Freeman, 1972. A highly informative discussion of the population problem. Paul Ehrlich is one of the foremost population and ecology experts in the country.

Fleishman, N., and Dixon, P. L. *Vasectomy,*

---

[5]This would raise some interesting ethical problems for those who believe that abortion is immoral. Rather than preventing conception, this method would abort any conceptus that was produced. The same is true of the IUD, which appears to work simply by aborting the conceptus within a few days after conception. This may provide food for thought for some women using IUDs.

TABLE 6.4
SUMMARY OF INFORMATION ON METHODS OF BIRTH CONTROL

Method	Effectiveness Rating	Theoretical Failure Rate, %	Actual Failure Rate, %	Death Rate (per 100,000 Women)	Yearly Costs*	Advantages	Disadvantages
Birth control pills	Excellent	<1.0	2–3	0.3–3.0	$40	Highly effective, not aversive to use, improved menstrual cycles	Cost, possible side effects, must be taken daily
IUD	Excellent	1–5	6	0.3–2.0	$25–$50†	Requires no memory or motivation, one-time-only cost	Side effects, may be expelled
Diaphragm with cream or jelly	Very good	3	20–25	3.0‡	$15–$30	No side effects, inexpensive	Aesthetic objections
Condom	Very good	3	15–20	1.7‡	$18–$60	Easy to use, protection from VD	Interference with coitus, continual expense
Vaginal foam	Good	3	30	3.4‡	$10–$30	Easy to use, availability	Messy, continual expense
Withdrawal	Fair	15	20–25		None	No cost	Requires high motivation
Rhythm	Poor to fair	15	35		None	No cost, accepted by Roman Catholic Church	Requires high motivation, prolonged abstinence, not all women can use
Unprotected intercourse	Poor	80	80	14‡	None§		
Legal abortion	Excellent	0	0	3.2	$200–$400	Available when other methods fail	Expense, moral or psychological unacceptability
Sterilization, male	Excellent	<0.15	0.15		$150†	Is permanent and highly effective	Is permanent, psychological complications
Sterilization, female	Excellent	0.04	0.05		$200†	Is permanent and highly effective	Is permanent, expense, psychological complications

*Based on 150 acts of intercourse.
†These are one-time-only costs.
‡Based on the death rate for pregnancies resulting from the method.
§But having a baby is expensive.
Sources: Emory University Family Planning Program. *Contraceptive technology 1974–1975.* Atlanta: EUFPP, 1976. L. Hellman. Oral contraceptives: Safety and complications. In A. Rubin (Ed.), *Family planning today.* Philadelphia: Davis, 1969.

sex, and parenthood. Garden City, N. Y.: Doubleday, 1973. A thorough discussion of vasectomy from a provasectomy point of view.

Montreal Health Press. *Birth control handbook.* (12th ed.) Montreal: MHP, 1974. One of the best sources of information on birth control for the lay person, originated by a student society at McGill University. Available for 35 cents from *Birth Control Handbook,* P.O. Box 1000, Station G, Montreal, Quebec H2W 2N1, Canada.

Seaman, Barbara. *The doctors' case against the Pill.* New York: Peter H. Wyden, 1969. A classic piece of muckraking journalism on the dangers of the Pill.

7

THE PHYSIOLOGY OF SEXUAL RESPONSE

CITED

Here are some colors of different people's orgasms: champagne, all colors and white and gray afterward, red and blue, green, beige and blue, red, blue and gold. Some people never make it because they are trying for plaid.*

This chapter is about the way the body responds during sexual arousal and orgasm and also the mechanisms behind these responses. This information is very important in developing good techniques of lovemaking (see Chapter 8) and in analyzing and treating sexual dysfunctions such as premature ejaculation (see Chapter 18). Important though the topic is, it had not been investigated scientifically before the work of Masters and Johnson, beginning in the 1950s. (Actually, this absence of research is not too surprising in light of society's attitudes toward sex and especially sex research.) The Masters and Johnson results will form the foundation for this chapter.

THE FOUR STAGES OF SEXUAL RESPONSE

The Masters and Johnson research on the physiology of sexual response began in 1954 and culminated in 1966 with the publication of *Human Sexual Response*, which reported data on 382 women and 312 men observed in over

10,000 sexual cycles of arousal and orgasm. (A discussion and critique of the Masters and Johnson research techniques is presented in Chapter 9.)

According to Masters and Johnson, there are four stages of sexual response, which they call *excitement, plateau, orgasm,* and *resolution.* (This does not mean, of course, that a person makes a noticeable shift from one stage to another, as if he or she were shifting gears in a car. Rather, the stages flow together, and the differentiation into four stages is simply for convenience in describing what occurs.)

The two basic physiological processes that occur during these stages are vasocongestion and myotonia. *Vasocongestion* occurs when a great deal of blood flows into the blood vessels in a region, in this case the pelvis, as a result of dilation of the blood vessels in the region. *Myotonia* occurs when muscles contract, not only in the genitals, but also throughout the body. Let us now consider in detail what occurs in each of the stages.

Excitement

The excitement phase is the beginning of erotic arousal. The basic physiological process that

---

Source: Eric Berne. *Sex in human loving.* New York: Simon & Schuster, 1970, p. 238.

occurs during excitement is vasocongestion. This produces the obvious symptom of arousal in the male, erection. Erection results when the corpora cavernosa and the corpus spongiosum fill (becoming engorged) with blood (see Figure 7.1). Erection may be produced by direct physical stimulation of the genitals, by stimulation of other parts of the body, or by erotic thoughts. It occurs very rapidly, within a few seconds of the stimulation, although it may take place more slowly as a result of a number of factors including age, intake of alcohol, and fatigue.

The most obvious response of the woman in the excitement phase is the lubrication of the

FIGURE 7.1
The sexual response of the male genitals. *(a)* The male genitals in the unaroused state. *(b)* The male genitals in a highly aroused state. *(c)* The male genitals during orgasm. Note the contractions of the sexual organs.

(a)

(b)

(c)

vagina. While this response might seem much different from the male's, actually they both result from the same physiological process: vasocongestion. Masters and Johnson found that vaginal lubrication results when fluids seep through the semipermeable membranes of the vaginal walls, producing lubrication as a result of vasocongestion in the tissues surrounding the vagina. Lubrication is thus sometimes referred to as vaginal "sweating." This response to arousal is also rapid, though not quite so fast as the male's; lubrication begins 10 to 30 seconds after the onset of arousing stimuli.[1] Some sex manuals advise that the appearance of lubrication serves as a good indicator to the man that the woman is "ready" for intercourse; the lubrication, however, signals only the beginning of arousal. Many other changes must also occur before the woman is close to orgasm.

Several other physical changes occur in women during the excitement phase. The glans of the clitoris (the tip) swells. This results from engorgement of its corpora cavernosa and corpus spongiosum and thus is quite similar to erection in the male. The shaft of the clitoris increases in diameter.

The nipples become erect; this results from contractions of the muscle fibers (myotonia) surrounding the nipple. The breasts themselves swell and enlarge somewhat in the late part of the excitement phase (a vasocongestion response). Thus the nipples may not actually look erect but may appear somewhat flatter against the breast because the breast has swollen. Many males also have nipple erection during the excitement phase.

In the unaroused state the inner lips are generally folded over, covering the entrance to the vagina, and the outer lips lie close to each other. During excitement the inner lips swell

---

[1]Before the Masters and Johnson research, it was thought that the lubrication was due to secretions of Bartholin's glands, but it now appears that these glands contribute little if anything. At this point, you might want to go back to the limerick about Bartholin's glands in Chap. 2 and see whether you can spot the error in it.

and open up (a vasocongestion response). The outer lips move apart a bit and flatten out. In women who have had many children, particularly those who have developed varicose veins in the outer lips, the lips may swell to two or three times their normal size.

The vagina shows an important change during excitement. Think of the vagina as being divided into two parts, an upper (or inner) two-thirds and a lower (or outer) one-third. Recall that in the unaroused state the walls of the vagina lie against each other, much like the sides of an uninflated balloon. During the excitement phase, the upper two-thirds of the vagina expands dramatically (see Figure 7.2), in what is often called a "ballooning" response; that is, it becomes more like an inflated balloon. Clearly this is very functional in accommodating the entrance of the penis. The cervix and uterus also pull up during excitement, creating a "tenting effect" in the vaginal walls (Figure 7.2) and making a larger opening in the cervix, which probably allows sperm to move into the uterus more easily.

During excitement a "sex flush" may appear on the skin in both men and women, though more commonly in women. The sex flush resembles a measles rash; it often begins on the upper abdomen and spreads over the chest. It may also appear later in the sexual response cycle.

Other changes that occur in both men and women include an increase in pulse rate and in blood pressure.

In men, the skin of the scrotum thickens. The scrotal sac also tenses, and the scrotum is pulled up and closer to the body. The spermatic cords shorten, elevating the testes.

Plateau

During the plateau phase, vasocongestion reaches its peak. In men, the penis is completely erect. In addition, the coronal ridge at the edge of the glans swells. The testes are so engorged with blood that they may be 50 percent larger than in the unaroused state. They are also pulled up even higher and closer to the body. A few drops of fluid, probably secreted by Cowper's glands, appear at the tip of the penis. While they are not the ejaculate, they may contain active sperm.

In both women and men there is a further increase in the rate of breathing, in pulse rate, and in blood pressure.

In females, the most notable change during the plateau phase is the formation of the *orgasmic platform*. This is a swelling or thickening of the tissues surrounding the outer third of the vagina (Figure 7.2). Thus the size of the vaginal entrance actually becomes smaller, and there may be a noticeable increase in gripping of the penis.

Another change is the elevation of the clitoris. The clitoris essentially retracts or draws up into the body, with the shaft becoming about 50 percent shorter.

Other changes include a further swelling of the breasts and an enlargement of the uterus. Finally, the color of the inner lips changes, from bright red to a deep wine color in women who have had children and from pink to bright red in women who have not. This last change indicates that orgasm is close. If proper stimulation continues and other conditions are right, the woman will have an orgasm soon after the color change.

Essentially, then, the processes of the plateau phase are just a continuation of the basic processes—vasocongestion and myotonia—of the excitement phase. Both processes continue to build until there is sufficient tension for orgasm.

(a)

Orgasmic platform

(b)

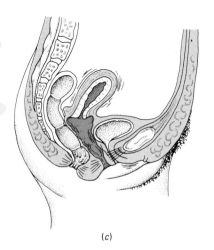

(c)

FIGURE 7.2

The sexual response of the female genitals. *(a)* The female genitals in the unaroused state. *(b)* The female genitals in a highly aroused state (plateau). *(c)* The female genitals during orgasm. Note the contractions of the the muscles surrounding the vagina.

WILLIAM MASTERS AND VIRGINIA JOHNSON

William Howell Masters was born in Cleveland in 1915. He attended Hamilton College in Clinton, New York, graduating in 1938 with a B.S. degree. At Hamilton he specialized in science courses, and yet he managed to play on the varsity football, baseball, basketball, and track teams and to participate in the Debate Club. The college yearbook called him "a strange, dark man with a future. . . . Has an easy time carrying three lab courses but a hard time catching up on lost sleep. . . . Bill is a boy with purpose and is bound to get what he is working for." His devotion to athletics persisted, and in 1966 a science writer described him as

FIGURE 7.3
William H. Masters. *[Reproductive Biology Research Foundation.]*

"a dapper, athletically trim gynecologist who starts his day at 5:30 with a two-mile jog."

He entered the University of Rochester School of Medicine and Dentistry in 1939, planning to train himself to be a researcher rather than a practicing physician. In his first year there he worked in the laboratory of the famous anatomist Dr. George Washington Corner. Corner was engaged in research on the reproductive system in animals and humans, which eventually led to important discoveries about hormones and the reproductive cycle. He had also published *Attaining Manhood: A Doctor Talks to Boys about Sex* and the companion volume, *Attaining Womanhood*.

The first-year research project that Corner assigned to Masters was a study of the changes in the lining of the uterus of the rabbit during the reproductive cycle. Thus his interest was focused early on the reproductive system.

FIGURE 7.4
Virginia Johnson. *[Reproductive Biology Research Foundation.]*

Masters was married in 1942 and received his M.D. in 1943. He and his wife had two children, born in 1950 and 1951.

After Masters received his degree, he had to make an important decision: To what research area should he devote his life? Apparently his decision to investigate the physiology of sex was based on his shrewd observation that almost no prior research had been done in the area and that he thus would have a good opportunity to make some important scientific discoveries. In arriving at the decision, he consulted with Dr. Corner and with Dr. Carl G. Hartman, an expert on comparative sexual anatomy and physiology. Both men were aware of Kinsey's progress and also of the persecution he had suffered; thus they advised Masters not to begin the study of sex until he had established himself as a respected researcher in some other area, was somewhat older, and could conduct the research at a major university or medical school.

Masters followed their advice. He completed his internship and residency and then established himself on the faculty of the Washington University School of Medicine in St. Louis. From 1948 to 1954 he published 25 papers on various medical topics, especially on hormone-replacement therapy for postmenopausal women.

In 1954 he began his research on sexual response at Washington University, supported by grants from the U.S. Public Health Service. The first paper based on that research was published in 1959, but the research received little attention until the publication, in 1966, of *Human Sexual Response* and, in 1970, of *Human Sexual Inadequacy* (to be discussed in Chapter 18), both of which received international acclaim.

Orgasm

In the male, orgasm consists of a series of rhythmic contractions of the pelvic organs at 0.8-second intervals. Actually, male orgasm occurs in two stages. In the preliminary stage, the vas, seminal vesicles, and prostate contract, forcing the ejaculate into a bulb at the base of the urethra (Figure 7.1). Masters and Johnson call the sensation in this stage one of "ejaculatory inevitability" ("coming"); that is, there is a sensation that ejaculation is just about to happen and cannot be stopped. And, indeed, it cannot be, once the man has reached this point.

In the second stage the urethral bulb and the penis itself contract rhythmically, forcing out the semen with great force. It should be noted here that orgasm and ejaculation in the male are separate, though usually related, processes, a point to be discussed in more detail below.

In both males and females, there are sharp increases in pulse rate, blood pressure, and breathing rate during orgasm. Muscles also contract throughout the body. The face may be contorted in a grimace; the muscles of the arms, legs, thighs, back, and buttocks may contract; and the muscles of the feet and hands may

In 1964 he founded the Reproductive Biology Research Foundation near the medical school, where the research continues today. Each week he spends four half-days in his gynecology practice (which supports him) and spends the rest of his time treating patients with sexual problems, doing research, and carrying out administrative duties. He works two evenings and all through one night each week; thus he has about an 80-hour workweek.

Virginia Johnson was born Virginia Eshelman in 1925 in the Missouri Ozarks. She was raised with the realistic attitude toward sex that rural children often have, as well as many of the superstitions that have grown up in that area. She began studying music at Drury College but transferred to Missouri University, where she studied psychology and sociology. She was married in 1950 and had two children, one in 1952, and the other in 1955. Shortly after that, she and her husband separated, and she went to the Washington University placement office to find a job. Just at that time, Masters had put in a request for a woman to assist him in research interviewing, preferably a married woman with children who was interested in people. Mrs. Johnson was sent over to him, and she has been a member of the male-female research team, interview team, and therapy team since 1957.

Following the divorce of Masters and his first wife, he and Virginia Johnson were married.

Source: Ruth Brecher and Edward Brecher. *An analysis of human sexual response.* New York: Signet Books, New American Library, 1966.

contract in "carpopedal spasms." Generally, of course, in the passion of the moment, one is not really aware of these occurrences, but an aching back or buttocks may serve as a reminder the next day.

The process of orgasm in females is basically similar to that in males. It is a series of rhythmic muscular contractions of the orgasmic platform. The contractions generally occur at about 0.8-second intervals; there may be three or four in a mild orgasm or as many as a dozen in a very intense, prolonged orgasm. The uterus also contracts rhythmically, with the contractions moving in waves from the top of the uterus down toward the cervix. Other muscles, such as those around the anus, may also contract rhythmically.

Female orgasm is a funny thing. As with love, you can almost never get anyone to give you a solid definition of what it is. Instead, people usually fall back on, "You'll know what it is when you have one." This evasiveness is probably related to several factors, most notably that female orgasm leaves no concrete evidence of its occurrence like ejaculation; indeed, the very existence of female orgasm has sometimes been questioned (for a clever satire on this point, see Raphael, 1973). Also, women often do not reach orgasm as quickly as men do, a point to be discussed in more detail in Chapter 13. In fact, some women, particularly young women, probably think they are having an orgasm when they are not; they have never had an orgasm, and they mistake intense arousal for orgasm.

Just what does orgasm in the female feel like? The main feeling is a spreading sensation that begins around the clitoris and then spreads outward through the whole pelvis. There may also be sensations of falling or opening up. The woman may be able to feel the contraction of the muscles around the vaginal entrance. The sensation is very intense and is more than just a warm glow or a pleasant tingling. In one study, college men and women gave written descriptions of what an orgasm felt like to them (Vance and Wagner, 1976). Interestingly, a panel of experts (medical students, obstetrician-gynecologists, and clinical psychologists) could not reliably figure out which of the descriptions were written by women, and which by men. This suggests that the sensations are quite similar for males and females.

Some of the men in my classes have asked me how they can tell whether a woman has really had an orgasm. Their question in itself is interesting. In part it reflects a cultural skepticism about female orgasm. There is obvious proof of male orgasm: ejaculation. But there is no similar proof of female orgasm. The question also reflects the fact that men know that women sometimes "fake" orgasm. Faking orgasm is a complex issue. Basically, it probably is not a very good idea, since it is dishonest. On the other hand, one needs to be sympathetic to the variety of reasons why women do it. It is often difficult for women to reach orgasm, and our culture currently places a lot of emphasis on everyone's having orgasms. Thus the woman may feel that she is expected to have an orgasm,

and, realizing that it is unlikely to happen this time, she "fakes" it in order to meet expectations. She may also do it to please her partner.[2] But back to the question: How can one tell? There really is not any very good way. From a scientific point of view, a good method would be to have the woman hooked up to an instrument that registered pulse rate; there is a sudden sharp increase in the pulse rate at orgasm, and that would be a good indicator. I doubt, though, that most men have such equipment available, and I am even more doubtful about whether most women would agree to be so wired up. Probably rather than trying to check up on each other, it would be better for partners to establish good, honest communication and avoid setting up performance goals in sex, points that will be discussed further in later chapters.

Resolution

Orgasm is not the last phase of sexual response. Following orgasm is the resolution phase, during which the body returns physiologically to the unaroused state. Orgasm triggers a massive release of muscular tension and of blood from the engorged blood vessels. These are the basic processes that occur during resolution. Resolution, then, represents a reversal of the processes that built up during the excitement and plateau stages.

The first change in women is a reduction in the swelling of the breasts, particularly of the areola. As a result, the nipples may appear to become erect, since they seem to stand out more as the surrounding flesh moves back toward the unstimulated size. This may provide the kind of sign wanted by those who are concerned about proof of female orgasm. In

[2]Indeed, many of the old sex manuals, as well as physicians' textbooks, counseled women to fake orgasm. For example: "It is good advice to recommend to the women the advantage of innocent simulation of sex responsiveness, and as a matter of fact many women in their desire to please their husbands learned the advantage of such innocent deception" (Novak and Novak, 1952, p. 572).

women who develop a sex flush during arousal, this disappears rapidly following orgasm.

In the 5 to 10 seconds after the end of the orgasm, the clitoris returns to its normal position, although it generally takes longer for it to shrink to its normal size. The orgasmic platform relaxes and begins to shrink. The ballooning of the vagina diminishes, and the uterus shrinks.

The resolution phase generally takes 15 to 30 minutes, but it may take much longer—as much as an hour—in women who have not had an orgasm. This latter fact helps to account for the chronic pelvic congestion that Masters and Johnson observed in prostitutes (see Chapter 9). The prostitutes frequently (in some cases, almost always) experienced arousal without having orgasms. Thus there were repeated buildups of vasocongestion without the discharge of it brought about by orgasm. The result was a chronic vasocongestion in the pelvis. A mild version of this occurs in some women who engage in sex but are not able to have orgasms, and it can be quite uncomfortable.

In both males and females, there is a gradual return of pulse rate, blood pressure, and breathing rate to the unaroused levels during resolution. Soon after the disappearance of the sex flush, some men and women are covered by a thin sheen of perspiration, or the perspiration may be only on the palms of the hands and the soles of the feet. This perspiration does not result from the physical exertion involved in intercourse, but rather is a distinct response of the resolution phase.

In men, the most obvious occurrence in the resolution phase is the loss of erection in the penis. This happens in two stages, the first occurring rapidly but leaving the penis still enlarged (this first loss of erection probably results from an emptying of the corpora cavernosa) and the second occurring more slowly, as a result of the slower emptying of the corpus spongiosum and the glans. The scrotum and testes return to their unstimulated size and position.

During the resolution phase, men enter into a *refractory period,* during which they are refractory to further arousal; that is, they are incapable of being aroused again, having an erection, or having an orgasm. The length of this refractory period varies considerably from one man to the next; in some it may last only a few minutes, and in others it may go on for 24 hours. The refractory period tends to become longer as men grow older.

Women do not enter into a refractory period, making possible the phenomenon of multiple orgasm in women, to be discussed below.

OTHER FINDINGS OF THE MASTERS AND JOHNSON RESEARCH

A number of other important findings on the nature of sexual response have emerged from the Masters and Johnson research, two of which will be discussed here.

Clitoral Orgasm versus Vaginal Orgasm

Some people believe that women can have two kinds of orgasm: clitoral orgasm and vaginal orgasm. The words "clitoral" and "vaginal" are not meant to imply that the clitoris has an orgasm or that the vagina has an orgasm. Rather, they refer to the locus of stimulation: an orgasm resulting from clitoral stimulation versus an orgasm resulting from vaginal stimulation. The whole notion of the distinction was originated by Sigmund Freud. Freud believed that, in childhood, little girls masturbate and thus have orgasms by means of clitoral stimulation, or clitoral orgasms. He thought that as women grow older and mature, they ought to shift from having orgasms as a result of masturbation to having them as a result of heterosexual intercourse, that is, by means of vaginal stimulation. (Freud's self-interest as a male in this matter is rather transparent!) Thus the vaginal orgasm was considered "mature," and the clitoral orgasm "immature" or "infantile," and not only did there come to be two kinds of orgasm, but also one was "better" (that is, more mature) than the other (for a review of the clitoral orgasm–vaginal orgasm controversy, see Brown, 1966).

Freud's formulation is of more than theoretical interest, since it has had an impact on the lives of many women. Many have undertaken psychoanalysis and spent countless hours agonizing over why they were not able to achieve the elusive vaginal orgasm and why they enjoyed the immature clitoral one so much. Women who could have orgasm only through clitoral stimulation were called "vaginally frigid" or "fixated" at an infantile stage.

According to the results of Masters and Johnson's research, though, the distinction between clitoral and vaginal orgasms does not make sense. This conclusion is based on two findings. First, their results indicate that all female orgasms are physiologically the same, regardless of the locus of stimulation. That is, an orgasm always consists of contractions of the orgasmic platform and the muscles around the vagina, whether the stimulation is clitoral or vaginal. Indeed, they found a few women who could have an orgasm purely through breast stimulation, and that orgasm was the same as the other two, consisting of contractions of the orgasmic platform and the muscles around the vagina. Thus physiologically there is only one kind of orgasm. (Of course, this does not mean that psychologically there are not different kinds; the experience of orgasm during intercourse may be quite different from the experience of orgasm during masturbation.) Second, Masters and Johnson found that clitoral stimula-

tion is almost always involved in producing orgasm. Because of the way in which the inner lips connect with the clitoral hood, the movement of the penis in and out of the vagina creates traction on the inner lips, which in turn pull the clitoral hood so that it moves back and forth, stimulating the clitoris. Thus even the purely "vaginal" orgasm results from quite a bit of clitoral stimulation.

It seems likely that clitoral stimulation is usually the "trigger" to orgasm and that the orgasm itself occurs in the vagina and surrounding tissues.

It is unfortunate that the distinction between clitoral and vaginal orgasms persists, since it has no scientific basis. That is, there is no physiological difference between orgasms occurring during intercourse and those occurring as a result of clitoral stimulation during masturbation.

Multiple Orgasm in Women

Traditionally it was believed that, orgasmically, women behaved like men in that they could have one orgasm and then would enter into a refractory period before they could have another. According to the Masters and Johnson research, however, this is not true; rather, women do not enter into a refractory period, and they can have multiple orgasms within a short period of time. Actually, women's capacity for multiple orgasms was originally discovered by Kinsey (Kinsey et al., 1953; see also Terman, 1938) in his interviews with women. The scientific establishment, however, dismissed these reports as another instance of Kinsey's unreliability.

Kinsey estimated that about 13 percent of all women have multiple orgasms. The Masters and Johnson research, though, suggests that many more women, perhaps most women, are capable of having multiple orgasms given the proper stimulation (though the Masters and

Johnson data are not good for estimating percentages—see Chapter 9).

The term "multiple orgasm," then, refers to having one orgasm after another within a short period of time. They do not differ physiologically from single orgasms except that there are many of them. Each is a "real" orgasm, and they are not minor experiences. One nice thing, though, is that the later ones generally require much less effort than the first one. The first one may require quite a bit of work, but subsequent ones can often be triggered by less than a minute of stimulation.

How does multiple orgasm work physiologically? Immediately following an orgasm, both males and females move into the resolution phase. In this phase, the male enters into a refractory period, during which he cannot be aroused again. But the female does not enter into a refractory period. That is, if she is stimulated again, she can immediately be aroused and move back into the excitement or plateau phase and have another orgasm.

Multiple orgasm, of course, is more likely to result from hand-genital or mouth-genital stimulation than from intercourse, since most men do not have the endurance to continue thrusting for such long periods of time. Regarding capacity, Masters and Johnson found that women in masturbation might have 5 to 20 orgasms. In some cases, they quit only when physically exhausted. When using a vibrator, less effort is required, and some women were capable of having 50 orgasms. The extent of female orgasmic capacity, then, seems to depend on the endurance of the woman's lover, not her responsiveness.

It should be noted that some women who are capable of multiple orgasm are completely satisfied with one, particularly in intercourse, and do not wish to continue. We should be careful not to set multiple orgasm as another of the many goals in sexual performance.

It is also worth noting that there is more variability in female orgasm patterns than there is in male orgasm patterns (Masters and Johnson, 1966, p. 5).

HORMONAL AND NEURAL CONTROL OF SEXUAL BEHAVIOR

Sexuality is a key behavior in which biological factors interact with the individual's environment. The previous sections were about the physiological changes that occur during sexual response. The following section will be about the biological basis of sexual response, that is, exactly what makes the sexual response possible.

The Brain, the Spinal Cord, and Sex

The brain and the spinal cord both have important, interacting functions in sexual response. First, the relatively simple spinal reflexes involved in sexual response will be discussed; then the more complex brain mechanisms will be considered.

Spinal reflexes   Several important components of sexual behavior, including erection and ejaculation, are controlled by fairly simple spinal cord reflexes (see the lower part of Figure 7.5). A reflex has three basic components: the *receptors,* which are sense organs that detect stimuli and transmit the message to the spinal cord (or brain); the *transmitters,* which are centers in the spinal cord (or brain) that receive the message, interpret it, and send out a message to produce the appropriate response; and the *effectors,* which are organs that respond to the stimulation. The reflex jerking away of the hand when it touches a very hot object is a good example.

173

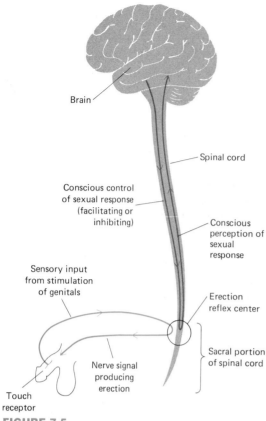

Brain

Spinal cord

Conscious control
of sexual response
(facilitating or
inhibiting)

Conscious
perception of
sexual
response

Sensory input
from stimulation
of genitals

Erection
reflex center

Sacral portion
of spinal cord

Nerve signal
producing
erection

Touch
receptor

FIGURE 7.5

Nervous system control of erection. Note both the reflex center in the spinal cord and brain control.

Mechanism of erection   Erection is produced by a spinal reflex with a similar mechanism. Tactile stimulation (stroking or rubbing) of the penis (the receptor) or nearby regions such as the scrotum or inside of the thighs produces a neural signal which is transmitted to an "erection center" in the sacral, or lowest, part of the spinal cord (there may also be another erection center higher in the cord). This center then sends out a message via the parasympathetic division of the nervous system to the muscles

(the effectors) around the walls of the arteries in the penis. In response to the message, the muscles relax; the arteries then expand, permitting a large volume of blood to flow into them, and erection results. Further, the valves in the veins and the compression of the veins, caused by the swelling in the tissue around them, prevent the blood from flowing out (H. D. Weiss, 1973).

The existence of this reflex is confirmed by the responses of men who have had their spinal cords severed, as a result of accidents, at a level above that of the reflex center. They are capable of having erections and ejaculations produced by rubbing their genitals, although it is clear that no brain effects can be operating, since signals from the brain cannot move past the point at which the spinal cord was severed (in fact, they cannot "feel" anything because neural signals cannot be transmitted up the spinal cord either). Thus it appears that erection can be produced simply by tactile stimulation of the genitals which triggers the spinal reflex.

It is clear that erection may also be produced by conditions other than tactile stimulation of the genitals; for example, fantasy or other purely psychological factors may produce erection. This points to the importance of the brain in producing erection, a topic that will be discussed in more detail below.

The major disturbance of the erection process is *impotence,* or the inability of the male to get an erection. This sexual dysfunction will be discussed in Chapter 18.

Mechanism of ejaculation   The ejaculation reflex is much like the erection reflex, except that the ejaculation center is located higher in the spinal cord, the sympathetic division of the nervous system is involved (as opposed to the parasympathetic division in the erection reflex), and the response is muscular, with no involvement of the blood vessels. In the ejaculation reflex, the penis responds to stimulation by sending a message to the "ejaculation center," which is located in the lumbar portion of the spinal cord. A message is then sent out via the nerves in the sympathetic nervous system, and this message triggers the contractions of the muscles in the internal organs involved in ejaculation.

It is clear that ejaculation can often be controlled voluntarily. This fact highlights the importance of brain influences on the ejaculation reflex, which will be discussed in detail below.

The three main problems of ejaculation are premature ejaculation, retarded ejaculation, and retrograde ejaculation. Premature ejaculation, which is by far the most common problem, and retarded ejaculation will be discussed in Chapter 18. *Retrograde ejaculation* occurs

when the ejaculate, rather than going out through the tip of the penis, empties into the bladder (Greene et al., 1970). A "dry orgasm" results, since no ejaculate is emitted. This problem can be caused by some illnesses, by tranquilizers and drugs used in the treatment of psychoses, and by prostate surgery. The mechanism that causes it is fairly simple (see Figure 7.6). Two sphincters are involved in ejaculation: an internal one, which closes off the entrance to the bladder during a normal ejaculation, and an external one, which opens during a normal ejaculation, allowing the semen to flow out through the penis. In retrograde ejaculation, the action of these two sphincters is reversed; the external one closes, and thus the ejaculate cannot flow out through the penis, and the internal one opens, permitting the ejaculate to go into the bladder. The condition

FIGURE 7.6
How a retrograde ejaculation occurs.

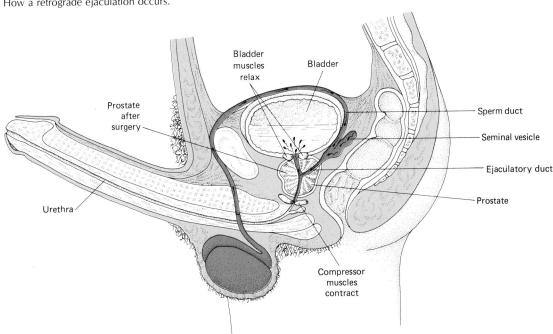

THE PHYSIOLOGY OF SEXUAL RESPONSE

itself is quite harmless, although some men are disturbed by the lack of sensation of emitting semen.

Mechanisms in women   Unfortunately, there is no comparable research on similar reflex mechanisms of arousal in women. Generally it is assumed that, since the basic processes of sexual response (vasocongestion and myotonia) are similar in males and females and since their genital organs are derived from the same embryonic tissue (and thus have similar nerve supplies), reflexive mechanisms in women are similar to those in men. That is, since the lubrication response in women results from vasocongestion, it is similar to erection in the male, and thus it might be expected to be controlled by a similar spinal reflex. This is purely speculative, though, since there is no research on the subject.

Brain control   As was noted above, it is clear that sexual responses are controlled by more than simple spinal reflexes. Sexual responses may be brought under voluntary control, and they may be initiated by purely psychological forces, such as fantasy. Environmental factors, such as having been taught as a child that sex is dirty and sinful, may also affect one's sexual response. All these phenomena point to the critical influence of the brain and its interaction with the spinal reflexes in producing sexual response (see Figure 7.5). Indeed, it has been claimed that the brain is the most important erogenous zone.

Brain control of sexual response is complex and only partly understood at the present time. It appears that the most important influences come from a set of structures called the *limbic system* (see Figure 7.7) (MacLean, 1962). The limbic system forms a border between the central part of the brain and the outer part (the cerebral cortex); it includes the amygdala, the hippocampus, the cingulate gyrus, the fornix,

and the septum. The thalamus, the hypothalamus, the pituitary, and the reticular formation are not properly part of the limbic system, but they are closely connected to it.

Several lines of evidence point to the importance of the limbic system in sexual behavior. In experiments with monkeys, an electrode was inserted into various regions of the brain to deliver electrical stimulation. It was discovered that stimulation of some areas of the brain would produce an erection. In particular, three "erection centers" were found in the limbic system, including one in the septal region. For obvious reasons, little of this research has been done with humans. But in one recent study, stimulation of the septal region of the limbic system produced orgasm in two human subjects (Heath, 1972).

The existence of a phenomenon called the *Klüver-Bucy syndrome* provides further evidence of the importance of the limbic system in sexuality. If the temporal lobes of the brain (the lobes at the side of the brain) of monkeys are destroyed, they become highly erotic and hypersexual (as well as very tame); this is the Klüver-Bucy syndrome. When the temporal lobes are destroyed, the amygdala and the hippocampus, among other things, are destroyed; since they are important structures in the limbic system, the hypersexuality that results from their destruction further implicates the limbic system in the control of sexual response.

The thalamus (see Figure 7.7), a structure closely related to the limbic system, also appears to be involved. For example, electrical stimulation of the thalamus produces ejaculation.

Structures in the central part of the brain, then, particularly the structures of the limbic system and the thalamus, are important in influencing sexual response. It is very significant that centers controlling certain other functions—most notably pleasure, olfaction (the sense of smell), and aggression—are located very close to the sex centers and are connected to them.

The important work of the physiologist James Olds (Olds, 1956; Olds and Milner, 1954) established the existence of "pleasure centers" in the brain. Electrodes were implanted in various regions of the brains of rats and were wired so that the rat could stimulate its own brain by pressing a lever. When the electrodes were placed in certain regions—in particular, the septal region and the hypothalamus—the rats would press the lever thousands of times per hour and would forgo food and sleep and endure pain in order to stimulate these regions. The location of these pleasure centers so close to the sex centers may explain why sexual experiences are so intensely pleasurable.

The study of humans noted above also points to an association between the sex centers and the pleasure centers (Heath, 1972). Electrodes were placed in the brains of two human subjects for therapeutic purposes (one male psychiatric patient and one female epileptic). When the stimulation was to certain areas, the subjects reported it as being very pleasurable; these areas were essentially the same as the pleasure centers found in the brains of animals. When the stimulation was delivered to the septal region or the amygdala (both in the limbic system), the pleasure was sexual in nature. In addition to the subjects' reports of sexual arousal and pleasurable sexual feelings, the male subject stimulated himself almost insatiably (as many as 1500 times per hour) and begged to be allowed to stimulate himself a few more times whenever the apparatus was taken away.

There are also "rage," or "aggression," centers in the brain, the stimulation of which throws the animal into a rage so that it will attack any object in the cage. These centers are located in the hypothalamus and, like the plea-

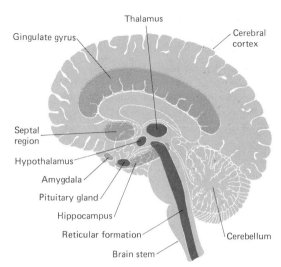

FIGURE 7.7
The limbic system of the brain, which is important in sexuality.

sure centers, are close to the sex centers; the closeness of the two may explain the association of sex and aggression in phenomena such as rape, competition over mates, and sadomasochism (MacLean, 1962).

The brain centers for sex are also close to the olfactory centers. This brings us to the topic of pheromones and their role in sexual behavior, which will be discussed later in the chapter.

Hormones and Sex
The sex hormones are another important physiological force that interacts with the nervous system to influence sexual response.

Organizing versus activating effects Endocrinologists generally make a distinction between the organizing effects of hormones and the activating effects of hormones. As was seen in Chapter 3, hormones present during prenatal development may have important influences on

THE PHYSIOLOGY OF SEXUAL RESPONSE

the hypothalamus and on the genitals (creating male or female genitals). Hormone effects such as these are called *organizing effects* because they cause a relatively permanent change in the organization of some structure, whether in the nervous system or the reproductive system. Typically there are "critical periods" during which these hormone effects may occur.

It has also been known for some time that, if an adult male mouse or rat is castrated (has the testes removed, which removes the source of testosterone), it will cease engaging in sexual behavior (and also will be less aggressive). If that animal is then given injections of testosterone, it will start engaging in sex again. Hormone effects such as these are called *activating effects* because they activate (or deactivate) certain behaviors.

The organizing effects of sex hormones on sexual behavior have been well documented. In a classic experiment, testosterone was administered to pregnant female guinea pigs. The female offspring that had been exposed to testosterone prenatally[3] were, in adulthood, incapable of displaying female sexual behavior (in particular, lordosis, which is a sexual posturing involving arching of the back and raising of the hindquarters so that the male's intromission is possible) (Phoenix et al., 1959). It is thought that this occurred because the testosterone "organized" the brain tissue (particularly the hypothalamus) in a male fashion. These female offspring were also born with masculinized genitals, and thus their reproductive systems had also been organized in the male direction. But the important point here is that the prenatal doses of testosterone had masculinized their sexual behavior. Similar results have been obtained in experiments with many other species as well.

These hormonally masculinized females in adulthood displayed mounting behavior, a male[4] sexual behavior. When they were given testosterone in adulthood, they showed about as much mounting behavior as males did. Thus the testosterone administered in adulthood *activated* male patterns of sexual behavior.

The analogous experiment on males would be castration at birth, followed by administration of ovarian hormones in adulthood. When this was done with rats, female sexual behavior resulted; these males responded to mating attempts by other males essentially in the same way females do (Harris and Levine, 1965). Apparently their brain tissue had been organized in a female direction during an early, critical period when testosterone was absent, and the female behavior patterns were activated in adulthood by administration of ovarian hormones.

It is thus supposed that males and females initially have capacities for both male and female sexual behaviors; if testosterone is present early in development, the capacity for exhibiting female behaviors is suppressed. Sex hormones in adulthood then activate the behavior patterns that were differentiated early in development.

One question that might be raised is: How relevant is this research to humans? Generally the trend is for the behavior of lower species to be more under hormonal control and for the behavior of higher species to be more under brain (neural) control. Thus human sexual behavior is probably less under hormonal control than rat sexual behavior; human sexual behavior is more controlled by the brain, and thus

---

[3]Note the similarity of these experiments to John Money's observations of human hermaphrodites (Chap. 3).

[4]The term "male sexual behavior" is being used here to refer to a sexual behavior that is displayed by normal males of the species and either is absent in females of that species or is present at a much lower frequency. Normal females do mount, but they do so less frequently than males do. "Female sexual behavior" is defined similarly.

learning and past experiences, which are stored in the brain, are more likely to have a profound effect. For example, it is estimated that only about 20 percent of cases of human sexual dysfunction (e.g., impotence) are caused by physical factors; the rest are due to psychological factors (see Chapter 18).

Let us now consider in more detail the known activating effects of sex hormones on the sexual behavior of adult humans.

Testosterone and libido   Testosterone has well-documented effects on libido in humans. If a man is deprived of his main source of testosterone by castration or if the level is sharply reduced by illness, his desire for sex (libido) and his ability to have an erection will gradually be lost. Libido and potency are rapidly lost if a man is given an antiandrogen drug. Thus testosterone seems to have an activating effect in maintaining sexual behavior in the adult male. However, in cases of castration, sexual behavior may decline very slowly and may be present for several years after the source of testosterone is gone; this points to the importance of experience and brain control of sexual behavior in humans.

Recently it has been demonstrated that androgens are a prerequisite for libido in women also. If all sources of androgen in women are removed (the adrenals and the ovaries), women lose all sexual desire and cannot be aroused. On the other hand, androgens are sometimes used in the treatment of low-libido states in women, although their use is limited by their tendency to have masculinizing side effects.[5]

_____

[5]Lest the reader be distressed by the thought that women's considerably lower levels of testosterone might mean that they have lower sex drives, it should be noted that the sensitivity of cells to hormone levels is critical. Women's cells may be more sensitive to testosterone than men's are. Thus for women, a little testosterone may go a long way.

PHEROMONES

There has been a great deal of interest recently in the role that pheromones play in sexual behavior. Pheromones are somewhat like hormones. Recall that hormones are biochemicals that are manufactured in the body and secreted into the bloodstream to be carried to the organs that they affect. Pheromones, on the other hand, are biochemicals that are secreted outside the body. Thus, through the sense of smell, they are an important means of communication between animals. Often the pheromones are contained in the animal's urine. Thus the dog that does "scent marking" is actually depositing pheromones. Some pheromones appear to be important in sexual communication, and some have even been called "sex attractants."

Much of the research on pheromones has been done with mice and demonstrates the importance of pheromones in sexual and reproductive functioning. For example, exposure to the odor of male urine induces estrus (ovulation and sexual behavior) in female mice (the *Whitten effect*). If a female mouse copulates with a male and conceives and is then exposed to the odors of a strange male mouse, the pregnancy is aborted, presumably because implantation is prevented (the *Bruce effect*).

It appears that testosterone is critical to the male pheromones' ability to have these effects on females. If a male mouse is castrated, its urine will not induce estrus or block pregnancy (Bruce, 1969).

Pheromones present in female urine also have an influence on male sexual behavior. An early study demonstrated that male rats can tell the difference between the odor of estrous females and that of females not in estrus and that the males prefer estrous females (Le-Magnen, 1952). Similar phenomena have been demonstrated in male dogs, stallions, bulls, and rams (Michael and Keverne, 1968). The ovarian hormones estrogen and progesterone are critical to the female pheromones' ability to have an effect on males (Beach and Merari, 1970).

The sense of smell (olfaction) seems to be essential in order for pheromone effects to occur. Removal of the olfactory bulbs (a part of the brain important in olfaction) severely inhibits sexual behavior both in males and females (Bronson, 1968).

Some recent research has been done on pheromones in primates. It has been found, for example, that estrogen treatment of a female rhesus monkey sexually excites the males in her cage (Herbert, 1966). If the males' sense of smell is blocked, they no longer are sexually excited.

What relevance does all this have for humans? Humans are not, by and large, "smell animals." Olfaction is not particularly important for us, especially compared with other species. We tend to rely mostly on vision and, secondarily, hearing. Compare this with a dog, which can get a wealth of information about who and what has been in a park simply by sniffing around for a few minutes. On the other hand, humans do seem to be capable of developing remarkable senses of smell; Helen Keller reportedly could recognize all people she met by their scents.

Nonetheless, humans do not depend heavily on their sense of smell. Does this mean that pheromones have no influence on our sexual behavior? Evidence is beginning to accumulate suggesting that humans produce and respond to pheromones much as other species do.

A classic study of the "exaltolide phenomenon" demonstrated the importance of hormones in the sense of smell (LeMagnen, 1952). Exaltolide is a synthetic compound with a musklike odor. The pheromones present in the urine of other species have a musky odor, and there are musklike odors in human urine. Thus, this compound may be quite similar to pheromones. Exaltolide can be perceived by adult women, but not by girls before puberty or by males. Further, the study demonstrated that the ability to perceive the smell of this compound varied according to the phase of the menstrual cycle; women were most sensitive to it around the time of ovulation. These results with exaltolide seem to be quite comparable to the findings from research on pheromones in nonhumans.

Researchers are now speculating that human pheromones exist and that they play an important role in sexual behavior (Comfort, 1971). Indeed, pheromones may be exactly the "body chemistry" that attracts people to each other. It has been speculated that human pheromones are produced by the sweat glands of the armpits and by the prepuce of the male's penis and the female's clitoris. It also should be noted that perfumes with musky scents have become quite popular and presumably increase sexual attractiveness, perhaps because they smell like pheromones.

The most exciting recent advance in this research has been the identification, in the vaginal secretions of 50 women, of chemicals known to be sex-attractant pheromones in monkeys (Michael et al., 1974). Thus it seems clear that humans do produce such pheromones.

It should be noted that the smell of pheromones would not necessarily have to be consciously perceived in order for it to have an effect. The olfactory system can respond to odors even when they are not consciously perceived. Thus, pheromones that we are not even aware of may have important influences.

If these speculations about the effects of pheromones on human sexual behavior are correct, our "hyperclean" society may be destroying the scents that attract people to each other. The normal genital secretions (assuming reasonable cleanliness to eliminate bacteria) may contain sex attractants. The feminine hygiene deodorants may destroy precisely the odors that "turn men on."

Future research on human pheromones should be interesting indeed.

SUMMARY

William Masters and Virginia Johnson have conducted an important program of research, beginning in the 1950s, on the physiology of human sexual response. They have found that two basic physiological processes occur during arousal and orgasm: vasocongestion and myotonia. They divide the sexual response cycle into four stages: excitement, plateau, orgasm, and resolution.

Their research indicates that there is no physiological distinction between clitoral and vaginal orgasms in women, which refutes an early idea of Freud's. They have also provided convincing evidence of the existence of multiple orgasm in women.

The nervous system and sex hormones are important in sexual response. The nervous system functions in sexual response by a combination of spinal reflexes (best documented for erection and ejaculation) and brain influences (particularly of the limbic system). Hormones are important to sexual behavior, both in their influences on prenatal development (organizing effects) and in their stimulating influence on adult sexual behavior (activating effects.) Testosterone seems to be important for maintaining libido in both men and women.

Pheromones are biochemicals secreted outside the body that play an important role in sexual attraction.

SUGGESTIONS FOR FURTHER READING

Bermant, G., and Davidson, J. M. *Biological bases of sexual behavior.* New York: Harper & Row, 1974. A thorough analysis of biological (neural, hormonal) influences on sexual behavior, concentrating mostly on animal research. The book was intended as a text for advanced undergraduates.

Brecher, Ruth, and Brecher, Edward. *An analysis of human sexual response.* New York: New American Library, 1966. An excellent simplified description of the original Masters and Johnson (1966) work written by two scientific writers for the general public. The original Masters and Johnson report is highly technical.

Comfort, A. Likelihood of human pheromones. *Nature,* 1971, **230,** 432–433. A provocative article exploring the possibility of human pheromones.

Raphael, Bette-Jane. The myth of the male orgasm. *Village Voice,* Oct. 25, 1973. (Reprinted in *Psychology Today,* Jan. 1974.) A marvelous satire on male scientists' skepticism about female orgasm.

TECHNIQUES
OF AROUSAL

CITED

Lust is more abstract than logic; it seeks (hope triumphing over experience) for some purely sexual, hence purely imaginary, conjunction of an impossible maleness with an impossible femaleness.*

We live in the era of sex manuals. Books like *Everything You Always Wanted to Know about Sex . . . , The Joy of Sex, The Sensuous Woman,* and *The Sensuous Man,* as well as numerous feature articles and advice columns in magazines like *Playboy,* give us information on how to produce bigger and better orgasms in ourselves and our partners. The "read-all-about-it" boom has produced not only benefits but also problems. It may turn our attention so much to mechanical techniques that we forget about love and the emotional side of sexual expression. The sex manuals may also set up impossible standards of sexual performance that none of us can meet. On the other hand, we live in a society that has a history of leaving the learning of sexual techniques to nature or to chance, in contrast to some "primitive" societies in which adolescents are given explicit instruction in methods for producing sexual pleasure. For human beings, sexual behavior is a lot more than

"doin' what comes naturally"; we all need some means for learning about sexual techniques, and the sex manuals may help to fill that need.

The purpose of this chapter is to provide information on techniques of arousal, while attempting to avoid making sex too mechanical or setting up unrealistic performance standards.

EROGENOUS ZONES

While the notion of erogenous zones originated in Freud's work, the term is now part of our general vocabulary and refers to parts of the body which are sexually sensitive; stroking them or otherwise stimulating them produces sexual arousal. The genitals and the breasts are the most obvious examples. The lips, neck, and thighs are generally also erogenous zones. But even some rather unlikely regions—such as the back, the ears, the stomach and the feet—can also be quite erogenous. One person's erogenous zones can be quite different from another person's. Thus it is impossible to give a list of sure "turn-ons." The best way to find out is to

*Source: C. S. Lewis. *The allegory of love.* New York: Oxford University Press, 1958, p. 196.

FIGURE 8.1
Erotic miniature painting from India (eighteenth century) showing the sensitive parts of the female body, which were believed to vary during each day of the lunar month. [Rapho/Photo Researchers, Inc.]

communicate with your partner, either verbally or nonverbally.

The best examples are masturbation and fantasy.

ONE-PERSON SEX

It does not necessarily take two to have sex. One can produce one's own sexual stimulation. Sexual self-stimulation is called *autoeroticism*.[1]

Masturbation

The term "masturbation" can refer either to hand stimulation of one's own genitals or to hand stimulation of another's genitals. Here the term "hand-genital stimulation" will be reserved for stimulation of another's genitals, and the term "masturbation" for self-stimulation, either with the hand or with some object, such as a pillow or a vibrator. Masturbation is a very

---

[1]For those of you who are interested in the roots of words, "autoeroticism" does not refer to sex in the back seat of a car. The prefix "auto" means "self" (as in "autobiography"); hence self-stimulation is autoeroticism.

common sexual behavior; almost all men and the majority of women masturbate to orgasm at least a few times during their lives. The techniques used by males and females in masturbation are interesting in part because they provide information to members of the other gender concerning the best techniques to use in heterosexual sex. That is, knowing how a woman masturbates gives a man an idea of how best to stimulate her, and knowing how a man masturbates gives a woman a good idea of how to stimulate him.

Techniques of female masturbation Most commonly women masturbate by manipulating the clitoris and the inner lips (Hite, 1976; Kinsey et al., 1953, pp. 158, 189). They may rub up and down or in a circular motion, sometimes lightly and sometimes applying more pressure to the clitoris. Some prefer to rub at the side of the clitoris, while a few stimulate the glans of the clitoris directly. The inner lips may also be stroked or tugged. One woman described her technique as follows:

> I use the tips of my fingers for actual stimulation, but it's better to start with patting motions or light rubbing motions over the general area. As excitement increases I begin stroking above the clitoris and finally reach a climax with a rapid, jerky circular motion over the clitoral hood. Usually my legs are apart, and occasionally I also stimulate my nipples with the other hand. (Hite, 1976, p. 20)

This finding is in distinct contrast to what many men imagine to be the techniques of female masturbation; the male pictures the woman inserting a finger, a banana, or a similar object into the depths of the vagina (Kinsey et al., 1953). In fact, this is not often done; by far the most common method is clitoral and labial manipulation. Of the women in Kinsey's sample who masturbated, 84 percent used clitoral and labial manipulation; inserting fingers or objects into the vagina was the second most commonly used technique, but it was practiced by only 20 percent of the women.

Other techniques used by women in masturbation include breast stimulation, thigh pressure exerted by crossing the legs and pressing them together rhythmically to stimulate the clitoris, and pressing the genitals against some object, such as a pillow, or massaging them with a stream of water while in the shower. A few women (about 2 percent in Kinsey's sample) are capable of using fantasy alone to produce orgasm.

Techniques of male masturbation Kinsey found that there was much less variation in male masturbation techniques than in female masturbation techniques. Almost all males reported masturbating by hand stimulation of the penis. Generally the activity is accomplished as quickly as possible, taking only a minute or two (Kinsey et al., 1948, p. 509).

Most men use the technique of circling the hand around the shaft of the penis and using an up-and-down movement to stimulate the shaft and glans. Because the penis produces no natural lubrication of its own, some men like to use a form of lubrication, such as soapsuds while showering. The tightness of the grip, the speed of movement, and the amount of glans stimulation vary from one man to the next. Most increase the speed of stimulation as they approach orgasm, slowing or stopping the stimulation at orgasm because further stimulation would be uncomfortable (Masters and Johnson, 1966). At the time of ejaculation, they often grip the shaft of the penis tightly. Immediately after orgasm, the glans and corona are hypersensitive, and the man generally avoids further stimulation of the penis at that time (Sadock and Sadock, 1976).

Fantasy

Fantasies are another form of self-stimulation, or autoeroticism. Sexual fantasies can occur by

TABLE 8.1

COMMON THEMES OF FANTASIES WHILE MASTURBATING

Theme of Fantasy	Number of People Having That Type of Fantasy	
	Males, %	Females, %
1 Having intercourse with a stranger	47	21
2 Having sex with more than one person at the same time	33	18
3 Doing sexual things one would never do in reality	19	28
4 Being forced to have sex	10	19
5 Forcing someone to have sex	13	3
6 Having sex with someone of the same gender	7	11

Source: Morton Hunt. *Sexual behavior in the 1970s.* Chicago: Playboy Press, 1974, pp. 92–93.

themselves or during masturbation or sexual intercourse with another person.

Fantasy during masturbation   In the Kinsey sample, 50 percent of the women and 72 percent of the men said they fantasized most of the time when they masturbated (Kinsey et al., 1953). Fantasies are therefore quite common, though they are reported somewhat more frequently by men than by women.

The exact content of fantasies is highly individual, but some general themes are quite common. Table 8.1 summarizes some of the themes of fantasies during masturbation that were reported by the respondents in the Hunt survey (see Chapter 9 for a discussion of this study). Common themes include having intercourse with strangers (sometimes movie stars such as Robert Redford or Brigitte Bardot), engaging in group sex, being forced to or forcing someone to have sex, or doing other things that would not actually happen in reality. Heterosexuals typically have heterosexual fantasies, and homosexuals have homosexual fantasies, but there may be some crossing over; for

example, a heterosexual may sometimes have homosexual fantasies.

As Table 8.1 indicates, the themes of fantasies differ somewhat for males and females, though there are considerable similarities. The differences might be summarized as follows: Males' fantasies tend to involve situations in which they are powerful and aggressive and are engaged in impersonal sex, while females' fantasies are more likely to involve romance or being forced to have sex (Barclay, 1973; DeLora and Warren, 1977; Shope, 1975). Here is an adolescent male's description of one of his favorite fantasies during masturbation:

> We would be riding in the back seat of the car, and I would reach over and fondle her breasts. She would reach into my pants and begin to caress my penis and finally suck me off. (Jensen, 1976a, p. 144)

This is the fantasy of a 20-year-old female:

> The bedside table light was on as I entered the room. Its dimmed light cast lavender shadows

on my soft, pink, nylon negligee, which revealed just a hint of my body beneath. He smiled as he lay in bed with his naked body half concealed by covers. With only a motion, he picked up the covers for me to join him. As I slipped beneath the covers I felt his warm body surround me. Our lips met, and our embraces grew tighter. A short time later he loosened my bow, and the nightgown fell away. Crazy, wonderful shivers went through my body, and we kissed for quite some time. Perhaps with the fear that his body weight might hurt me or perhaps with satisfaction, he moved and once again lay beside me on the bed very calmly. (Shope, 1975, pp. 215–216)

The content of male and female sexual fantasies seems to be influenced by cultural stereotypes of male and female sexuality.

Fantasy during intercourse   Fantasies are also a means of self-stimulation to heighten the experience of sex with another person. Particularly in a long-term, monogamous relationship, sexual monotony can become a problem; fantasies are one way to introduce some variety and excitement, without violating an agreement to be faithful to the other person. It is important to view such fantasies in this way, rather than as a sign of disloyalty to, or dissatisfaction with, one's sexual partner.

Fantasies during intercourse are generally quite similar to the ones people have while masturbating. In a study of married women, 65 percent said they fantasized while having sex with their husbands (Hariton, 1973; see also S. Fisher, 1973). The following were the seven most common themes of their fantasies, listed in order of frequency, beginning with the most common:

1 Thinking of an imaginary lover
2 Imagining being overpowered or forced to surrender
3 Pretending to be engaging in something that is wicked or forbidden

4 Imagining being in a different place, such as a car, a motel, a beach, or the woods
5 Reliving a previous sexual experience
6 Imagining myself delighting many men
7 Imagining observing myself or others having sex

Rather than being a sign of poor marital relations, the women who fantasized seemed to have better sexual relationships with their husbands than the women who did not fantasize. Diane is an example:

Diane is happily married. Yet she finds sexual foreplay with her husband more exciting if she imagines herself a harem slave displaying her breasts to an adoring sheik. While having intercourse, she sometimes envisions making love in the back seat of a car or in an old-fashioned house during a group orgy. She likes to imagine being forced by one man after another. In one favorite scene she goes to a drive-in movie and is raped by a masculine figure whose face is a "blur." (Hariton, 1973, p. 39)

No comparable detailed studies have been done on men's fantasies during intercourse, but the themes of these fantasies probably are about the same as the themes of their fantasies during masturbation. Men are probably even likelier than women to fantasize while having intercourse.

Vibrators, Dildos, and Such
Various sexual devices, such as vibrators and dildos, are used by some people in masturbation or by couples as they have sex together. Such devices are sold in "sex supermarkets" and through the mail.

Both male and female artificial genitals can be purchased. A *dildo* is an artificial penis; it can be inserted into the vagina or the anus. Dildos are used by women in masturbation (although, as was noted in the previous section, this is not very common), by lesbians, by male homosexuals, and by heterosexual couples. Artificial vaginas, and even inflatable replicas of the entire female body, can also be purchased.

Vibrators are generally shaped like a penis; there are models with a cord that plugs into an electric socket and also battery-operated, cordless models. Women may use them to masturbate, stimulating the clitoral and mons area, or they may insert them into the vagina. Males may use them to stimulate the genitals or the anus. They are used either in masturbation or during sex with another person. They can be purchased in "respectable" stores (where they are euphemistically called "face massagers," for example), in sex supermarkets, and by mail.

Body oils are also increasingly popular for sexual use. In fact, their use has even been encouraged by experts in the field; for example, Masters and Johnson and other sex therapists recommend them for the touching or sensate focus exercises that they prescribe for their patients in sex therapy (see Chapter 18). Oils have a sensuous quality that heightens erotic feelings. Further, if you are being stroked or massaged for an extended period of time, the oil helps ensure that the part of your body that is being stimulated will not end up feeling like a piece of wood that has been sandpapered. Oils can be used either while masturbating or while having sex with another person. The sex stores sell them in a variety of exotic scents, but plain baby oil will also do nicely.

TWO-PERSON SEX

When most of us think of techniques of two-person sex, the image that flashes across our mind generally reflects several assumptions. One assumption is that one of the people is a male and the other a female, that is, that the sex is heterosexual. This reflects a belief that heterosexual sex is normative. Further, we tend to assume that the male is supposed to do certain things during the act and that the female is supposed to do certain other things. He, for example, is supposed to take the initiative in deciding what techniques are used, while she is to follow his lead. While there is nothing particularly evil in these assumptions, they do tend to impose some limitations on our own sexual expression and to make some people think that their own sexual behavior is "not quite right." Therefore, an attempt to avoid these assumptions will be made in the sections that follow.

Kissing

Kissing (or what we might call, technically, "mouth-mouth stimulation") is an activity that virtually everyone in our culture has engaged in (Kinsey et al., 1953). In simple kissing, the partners keep their mouths closed and simply touch each other's lips. In deep kissing ("French kissing"), both people part their lips slightly and insert their tongues into each other's mouths (somehow these clinical descriptions do not make it sound like as much fun as it is). There are endless variations on these two basic approaches, such as nibbling at the partner's lips or tongue or sucking at the lips; they depend only on your imagination and personal preference. There are also plenty of other regions of the body to kiss: the nose, the forehead, the eyelids, the earlobes, the neck, the breasts, the genitals, and even the feet, to give a few examples.

Touching

Enjoying touching and being touched is essential to sexual pleasure. The hands are well designed for caressing or massaging, and such methods applied to virtually any area of the body can be exciting. The regions that are exciting vary a great deal from one person to the next and depend on how the person is feeling at the moment; thus it is important to communicate what sort of touching is most pleasurable to you. (For specific exercises on touching and being touched, see Chapter 18.)

189

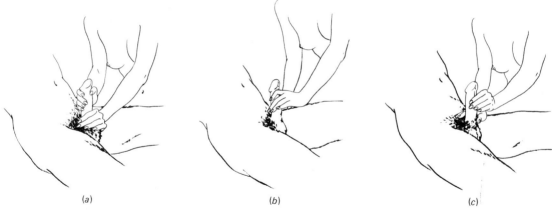

FIGURE 8.2
Techniques of hand stimulation of the penis.

As was noted earlier, one of the best ways to find out how to use your hand in stimulating the genitals of another person is to find out how that person masturbates. The common techniques of masturbation used by males and females were discussed earlier in this chapter. Since the method may vary from one person to the next, an ideal way to find out how to stimulate another person would be to watch that person masturbate.

Hand stimulation of the male genitals   As a technique of lovemaking, hand stimulation of the male genitals can be used as a pleasurable preliminary to intercourse, as a means of inducing orgasm itself, or as a means of producing an erection after the man has had one orgasm and wants to continue for another round of lovemaking (''rousing the dead'').

Alex Comfort, in *The Joy of Sex,* recommends the following technique:

> If he isn't circumcised, she will probably need to avoid rubbing the glans itself, except in pursuit of very special effects. Her best grip is just below the groove, with the skin back as far as it will go, and using two hands—one pressing hard near the root, holding the penis steady, or

fondling the scrotum, the other making a thumb-and-first-finger ring, or a whole hand grip. She should vary this, and, in prolonged masturbation, change hands often. (1972, p. 118)

As a good technique for producing an erection he also mentions rolling the penis like dough between the palms of the hands. Firm pressure with one finger midway between the base of the penis and the anus is another possibility.

One of the things that make hand stimulation most effective is for the man's partner to have a playful delight in, and appreciation of, the man's penis. Most men think their penis is pretty important. If the partner cannot honestly appreciate it and enjoy massaging it, hand stimulation might as well not be done.

Hand stimulation of the female genitals   The hand can be used to stimulate the woman's genitals as a means of producing orgasm, as a preliminary method of arousing the woman before intercourse, or simply because it is pleasurable.

Generally it is best, particularly if the woman is not already aroused, to begin with gentle, light stroking of the inside of the thighs and the inner and outer lips, moving to light stroking of the clitoris. As she becomes more aroused, the stimulation of the clitoris can become firmer. There are several rules for doing this, though. First, remember that the clitoris is very sensitive and that this sensitivity can be either exquisite or painful. Some care has to be used in stimulating it; it cannot just be manipulated like a piece of Silly Putty. Second, the clitoris should never—except, perhaps, for some light stroking—be rubbed while it is dry, for the effect can be more like sandpaper stimulation than sexual stimulation. If the woman is already somewhat aroused, lubrication can be provided by touching the fingers to the vaginal entrance and then spreading that lubrication on the clitoris. If she is not aroused or does not produce much vaginal lubrication, saliva works well too. Moisture makes the stimulation not only more comfortable but also more sensuous. Third, some women find direct stimulation of the clitoral glans to be painful in some states of arousal. These women generally prefer stimulation on either side of the clitoris instead.

With those caveats in mind, the clitoris can be stimulated with circular or back-and-forth movements of the finger. The inner and outer lips can also be stroked, rubbed, or tugged. These techniques, if done with skill and patience, can bring the woman to orgasm. Another technique that can be helpful in producing orgasm is for the partner to place the heel of the hand on the mons, exerting pressure on it while moving the middle finger in and out of the vaginal entrance. Another rule should also be clear by now: The partner needs to have close-trimmed nails that do not have any jagged edges. This is sensitive tissue we are dealing with.

The Other Senses

So far, this chapter has been focused on tactile (touch) sensations in sexual arousal. However, the other senses—vision, smell, and hearing—can also make contributions.

Sights   The things that you see while making love can contribute to arousal. Men seem, in general, to be more turned on by visual stimuli; many men have mild fetishes (see Chapter 15 for more detail on fetishes) and like to see their partners wearing certain types of clothing. If a woman's lover likes to see her in silk or in black lace, this is what she should wear. Perhaps in the next few years, as female sexuality becomes more liberated, women will become more interested in visual turn-ons.

The decor of the room can also contribute to visual stimulation. Furry rugs, placed on the floor or used as a bedspread, are sensuous both visually and tactilely. Large mirrors, hung either behind the bed or on the ceiling above it, can be a visual turn-on since they allow you to watch yourself make love. Candlelight is soft and contributes more to an erotic atmosphere than an electric light, which is harsh, or complete darkness, in which case there is no visual stimulation at all.

Perhaps the biggest visual turn-on comes simply from looking at your own body and your partner's body.

Smells   Odors can be turn-ons or turn-offs. The odors of a body that is clean, having been washed with soap and water, are themselves natural turn-ons. They do not need to be covered up with anything like "intimate deodorants."[2] In a sense, the odor of your skin, armpits, and genitals is your "aroma signature," and these natural odors can be quite arousing (Comfort, 1972).

A body that has not been washed or a mouth that has not been cleaned or has recently been used for smoking can be a real turn-off. Do

---

[2] With the increased popularity of mouth-genital sex, some women worry that the odor of their genitals might be offensive. The advertisements for feminine hygiene deodorant sprays prey upon those fears. These sprays should not be used because they may irritate the vagina (*Consumer Reports,* January 1972). And besides, there is nothing offensive about the odor of a vulva that has been washed; some people, in fact, find it arousing.

not be guilty of such offenses. Ideally, the communication between partners is honest and trusting enough so that if one offends, the other can simply request that the appropriate clean-up be done.

Burning incense is also becoming popular as an additional form of odor stimulation during lovemaking.

Sounds   Music—whether your preference is for acid rock or Brahms' Fourth—can contribute to an erotic atmosphere. Another advantage of playing music is that it helps muffle the sounds of sex, which can be important if you live in an apartment with thin walls or if you are worried about your children hearing you.

Genital-Genital Stimulation: Positions of Intercourse

One of the commonest sexual techniques involves the insertion of the penis into the vagina; this is called *coitus*[3] or *sexual intercourse*.

The couple may be in any one of a number of different positions while engaging in this basic sexual activity. Ancient love manuals and other sources illustrate many positions of intercourse (see Figure 8.3).

Some authorities state that there are only four positions of intercourse. Personally, I prefer to believe that there is an infinite number. Consider how many different angles your arms, legs, and torso may be in, in relation to those of your partner, and all the various ways in which you can intertwine your limbs—that's a lot of positions. I trust that, given sufficient creativity and time, you can discover them all for yourselves. I would agree, though, that there are a few basic positions and a few basic dimensions along which positions can vary. One basic variation depends on whether the couple face

[3]From the Latin word *coire*, meaning "to go together."

each other (face-to-face position) or whether one partner faces the other's back (rear-entry position); if you try the other obvious variation, a back-to-back position, you will quickly find that you cannot accomplish much that way. The other basic variation depends on whether one partner is on top of the other or whether the couple are side by side. Let us consider four basic positions that illustrate these variations. As Julia Child often does, I'll give you the basic recipes and let you decide on the embellishments.

Man-on-top   The face-to-face, man-on-top position ("missionary" position—see Figure 8.4) is the one used most frequently by couples in the United States. Indeed, Kinsey, commenting from his 1940s perspective, said:

> Nearly all coitus in our English-American culture occurs with the partners lying face to face, with the male above the female. There may be as much as 70 percent of the population which has never attempted to use any other position in intercourse. (Kinsey et al., 1948, p. 578)

Surveys in the 1970s, however, indicate that people are using much more of a variety of positions now (Hunt, 1974).

In the man-on-top position (which used to be called "male-superior," an unacceptable term today) the man and woman stimulate each other until they are aroused, he has an erection, and she is producing vaginal lubrication. Then he moves on top of her as she spreads her legs apart, either he or she spreads the vaginal lips apart, and he inserts his penis into her vagina. He supports himself on his knees and hands or elbows and moves his penis in and out of the vagina (pelvic thrusting). Some men worry that their heavy weight will crush the poor woman under them; however, because the weight is spread out over so great an area, most women

FIGURE 8.3
Positions of intercourse shown on modern Oriental playing cards. *[Reproduced by permission of G.P. Putnam's Sons from Philip Rawson. Erotic art of the east. New York: Putnam, 1968. Copyright © 1968 by Philip Rawson.]*

FIGURE 8.4
The man-on-top position of intercourse.

do not find this to be a problem at all, and many find the sensation of contact to be pleasurable.

The woman can have her legs in a number of positions that create variations. She may have them straight out horizontally, a position that produces a tight rub on the penis but does not permit it to go deeply into the vagina. She may bend her legs and elevate them to varying degrees, or she may hook them over the man's back or over his shoulders. The last approach permits the penis to move deeply into the vagina. The woman can also move her pelvis, either up and down or side to side, to produce further stimulation.

The man-on-top position has some advantages and some disadvantages. It is the best position for ensuring conception, if that is what you want to ensure. It leaves the woman's hands free to stroke the man's body (or her own, for that matter). The couple may feel better able to express their love or to communicate other feelings since they are facing each other. This position, however, does not work well if the woman is in the advanced stages of pregnancy or if either she or the man is extremely fat. Sex therapists have also found that it is not a very good position if the male wants to control his ejaculation; the woman-on-top position is better for this (see Chapter 18).

Woman-on-top   There are a number of ways of getting into the woman-on-top position (Figure 8.5). You can begin by inserting the penis into the vagina while in the man-on-top position and then rolling over. Another possibility is to begin with the man on his back; the woman then kneels over him, with one knee on either side of his hips. Then his hand or her hand guides the erect penis into the vagina as she lowers herself onto it. She then moves her hips to produce the stimulation. Beyond that, there are numerous variations, depending on where she puts her legs. She can remain on her knees, or she can straighten out her legs behind her, putting them outside his legs or between them. Or she can even turn around and face toward his feet.

This position has a number of advantages.

It provides a lot of clitoral stimulation, and the woman can control the kind of stimulation she gets; thus many women find it the best position for them to have an orgasm. It is also a good position for the man who wants to delay his ejaculation, and for this reason it is used in sex therapy. This position is also a good one if the man is tired and it seems advisable for the woman to supply most of the movement. Further, the couple face each other, facilitating better communication, and each has the hands free to stroke the other.

Rear-entry In the rear-entry position, the man faces the woman's back. One way to do this is for the woman to kneel with her head down; the man kneels with his legs outside hers and inserts the penis into the vagina (Figure 8.6) (This is sometimes called the "dog position" since it is

the manner in which dogs and most other animals copulate.) Another possibility is for the woman to lie on her stomach, raising her hips slightly so that the man can insert his penis while kneeling over her. Rear-entry can also be accomplished when the couple are in the side-to-side position (see below).

In this position the man's hands are free to stimulate the woman's clitoris or any other part of her body. The couple, however, do not face each other, and some couples dislike this aspect of the position. A small amount of air may enter the vagina when this position is used, producing interesting noises when it comes out.

Side-to-side In the side-to-side position, the man and woman lie beside each other, either face to face or in a rear-entry position (Figure 8.7). There are many variations beyond this,

FIGURE 8.5
The woman-on-top position of intercourse.

FIGURE 8.6
The rear-entry position of intercourse.

depending on where the arms and legs go—so many, in fact, that no attempt will be made to list them. One should be aware, though, that in this position an arm or a leg can get trapped under a heavy body and begin to feel numb, and shifting positions is sometimes necessary.

The side-to-side position is good for leisurely or prolonged intercourse or if one or both of the partners are tired. It is also good for the pregnant and the obese. At least some hands are free to stimulate the clitoris, the scrotum, or whatever.

Other variations   Aside from the variations in these basic positions that can be produced by switching the position of the legs, there are many other possibilities for variations. For example, the man-on-top position can be varied by having the woman lie on the edge of a bed with her feet on the floor while the man kneels on the floor. Or the woman can lie on the edge of a table while the man stands (don't forget to close the curtains first). Both these positions produce a somewhat tighter vagina and therefore more stimulation for the penis. Or the man can sit on a chair and insert the penis as the woman sits on his lap, using either a face-to-face or a rear-entry approach. Or, with both partners standing, the man can lift the woman onto his erect penis as she wraps her legs around his back, or she can put one leg over his shoulder (you have to be pretty athletic to manage this one, however).

Mouth-Genital Stimulation

One of the most striking features of the sexual revolution of the last few decades is the increased popularity of mouth-genital, or oral-genital, techniques (Hunt, 1974). There are two kinds of mouth-genital stimulation ("going down on" one's partner): cunnilingus and fellatio.

Cunnilingus   In cunnilingus, or "eating" (from the Latin words *cunnus,* meaning "vulva," and *lingere,* meaning "to lick"), the woman's genitals are stimulated by her partner's mouth. Generally the focus of stimulation is the clitoris, and the tongue stimulates it and the surrounding area with quick darting or thrusting movements, or the mouth can suck at the clitoris. A good prelude to cunnilingus can be kissing of the inner thighs or the belly, gradually moving to the clitoris. The mouth can also suck at the inner lips, or the tongue can stimulate the vaginal entrance or be inserted into the vagina. During cunnilingus, some women also enjoy having a finger inserted into the vagina or the anus for added stimulation. The best way to know what she wants is through communication between partners, either verbally or non-verbally.

Many women today are enthusiastic about cunnilingus and say that it is the best way, or perhaps the only way, for them to have orgasm. Such responses are well within the normal range of female sexuality. As one woman put it:

> A tongue offers gentleness and precision and wetness and is the perfect organ for contact. And, besides, it produces sensational orgasms. (Hite, 1976, p. 234)

Cunnilingus poses no health problems; in fact, some health experts say that the vagina is cleaner (has fewer bacteria) than the mouth, and few people worry about the health risks associated with kissing. One exception should be noted, though. Some women enjoy having their partner blow air forcefully into the vagina. While this technique is not dangerous under normal circumstances, when used on a pregnant woman it has been known to cause death (apparently as the result of air getting into the

FIGURE 8.7
The side-to-side position of intercourse.

uterine veins), damage to the placenta, and embolism (Sadock and Sadock, 1976). Thus it should not be used on a pregnant woman.

Cunnilingus can be performed by either heterosexual couples or lesbian couples.

Fellatio   In fellatio[4] ("sucking," "a blow job") the man's penis is stimulated by his partner's mouth. The partner licks the glans of the penis, its shaft, and perhaps the testicles. The penis is gently taken into the mouth. If it is not fully erect, an erection can generally be produced by stronger sucking combined with hand stimulation along the penis. After that, the partner can produce an in-and-out motion by moving the lips down toward the base of the penis and then back up, always being careful not to scrape the penis with the teeth. Or the tongue can be flicked back and forth around the tip of the penis or along the corona.

To bring the man to orgasm, the in-and-out motion is continued, moving the penis deeper and deeper into the mouth and perhaps also using the fingers to encircle the base of the penis and give further stimulation. Sometimes when the penis moves deeply toward the throat, it stimulates a gag reflex, which occurs anytime something comes into contact with that part of the throat. To avoid this, the partner should concentrate on relaxing the throat muscles while firming the lips to provide more stimulation to the penis.

When a couple are engaged in fellatio, the big question in their minds may concern ejaculation. The man may, of course, simply withdraw his penis from his partner's mouth and ejaculate outside it. Or he may ejaculate into it, and his partner may even enjoy swallowing the ejaculate. The ejaculate resembles partially cooked egg white in texture; it does not have a very distinctive flavor, but often leaves a salty

aftertaste. Because some people have mixed feelings about having the semen in their mouths, it is probably a good idea for the couple to discuss ahead of time (or during the activity) what they plan to do.

Most men find fellatio to be a highly stimulating experience, which no doubt accounts for the high frequency with which prostitutes are asked to do it. Enjoyment of fellatio is certainly within the normal range of male sexuality.

Fellatio can be performed by either heterosexual couples or male homosexual couples.

Sixty-nining   Fellatio and/or cunnilingus can be performed simultaneously by both partners. This is often called "sixty-nining"[5] because the numerals "69" suggest the position of the two bodies during simultaneous mouth-genital sex. Sixty-nining may be done either side to side or with one person on top of the other, each with the mouth on the other's genitals (Figure 8.8).

Simultaneous mouth-genital sex allows both people to enjoy the pleasure of that stimulation at the same time. It can give a feeling of total body involvement and total involvement between the partners. Some couples, however, feel that this technique requires doing too many things at once and is more complicated than enjoyable. For example, the woman may be distracted from enjoying the marvelous clitoral stimulation she is receiving because she has to concentrate at the same time on using her mouth to give good stimulation to the penis. If sixty-nining is done in the man-on-top position, some women also feel that they have no control over the movement and that they may be choked.

Anal Intercourse

In anal intercourse, the man inserts his penis into his partner's rectum. In legal terminology it is

---

[4]"Fellatio" is from the Latin word *fellare*, meaning "to suck." Women should not take the "sucking" part too literally. The penis, particularly at the tip, is a delicate organ and should not be treated like a straw in an extra-thick milkshake.

[5]If you want to be elegant and impress your friends, you can call it *soixante-neuf*, which is just "sixty-nine" in French.

FIGURE 8.8
Simultaneous mouth-genital stimulation in the sixty-nine position.

sometimes called *sodomy* (although this term may also refer to other things such as intercourse with animals), and it is sometimes referred to as having sex "Greek style." It may be done by either heterosexual couples or male homosexual couples.

Anal intercourse is somewhat more difficult than penis-in-vagina intercourse because the rectum has no natural lubrication and because it is surrounded by fairly tight muscles. The man should therefore begin by moistening the partner's anus, either with saliva or with a sterile surgical lubricant such as K-Y jelly (*not* Vaseline). He should also lubricate his penis. He then inserts it gently into the rectum and begins controlled pelvic thrusting. It is typically done in the rear-entry position or in the man-on-top position. The more the partner can relax, the less uncomfortable it is; if it is done properly, it need involve no pain. While some heterosexual couples find the idea repulsive, others delight in it. Some women report orgasm during anal intercourse, particularly when it is accompanied by hand stimulation of the clitoris.

Anal intercourse may be chosen if the woman is having a particularly heavy menstrual flow, if her vagina is very loose and the man wants more stimulation, or simply if more variety in sexual techniques is desired.

Another variation is *anilingus* (*feuille de rose* in French), in which the tongue and mouth stimulate the anus. The anus may also be stimulated by the hand, and some people report that having a finger inserted into the rectum near the time of orgasm provides a heightened sexual sensation.

While anal intercourse is basically perfectly safe, one health risk should be noted. The penis should never be inserted into the vagina after anal intercourse unless it has been washed thoroughly. The reason for this is that the rectum contains bacteria which do not belong in the vagina and which can cause a dandy case of vaginitis if they happen to get there.

APHRODISIACS

Is There a Good Aphrodisiac?

An *aphrodisiac* is something—such as a food, a drug, or a perfume—that excites sexual desire. Throughout history people have searched for the "surefire" aphrodisiac. Before arousing your hopes, I should note that the search has been unsuccessful; there is no known substance that works well as an aphrodisiac.

One popular idea is that oysters are an aphrodisiac. This notion appears to be an example of the "doctrine of signatures" applied to food. The idea is that foods that resemble sexual organs have sexual powers. For example, bananas resemble the penis and have been thought to be aphrodisiacs; perhaps oysters are thought to have such powers because of their resemblance to the testes (MacDougald, 1961). Another example is the Chinese belief that powdered rhinoceros horn is an aphrodisiac (perhaps this is also the origin of the term "horny"). Oysters, however, contain no substances that can in any way influence sexual functioning (Neiger, 1968).

Doubtless some substances gain a continued reputation as aphrodisiacs because simply believing that something will be arousing can itself be arousing. Thus the belief that bull's testicles ("prairie oysters") or peanuts or clams have sexual powers may produce a temporary improvement in sexual functioning, not because of the chemicals contained in them, but because of a belief in them (McCary, 1973).

Alcohol also has a reputation as an aphrodisiac. The effects of alcohol on sexual functioning will be discussed in Chapter 18. Briefly, drinking small quantities of alcohol may, for some people, decrease psychological inhibitions and therefore increase sexual desire. Moderate to large quantities, however, rapidly lead to an inability to function sexually.

Users of marijuana report that it acts as a sexual stimulant. Probably this is due, in part, to the fact that marijuana produces the sensation that time is being stretched out, thus prolonging and intensifying sensations, including sexual sensations. There is no scientific documentation of the aphrodisiac effects of marijuana except for the reports of users. Possible negative effects of marijuana on sexual functioning are discussed in Chapter 18.

Unfortunately, some of the substances that are thought to enhance sexual functioning are quite dangerous. For example, cantharides (Spanish fly) has a reputation as an aphrodisiac,

but it is poisonous (Craven and Polak, 1954; Nickolls and Teare, 1954; for further information, see Kaplan, 1974; Leavitt, 1974).

Amyl nitrate ("poppers") is popular with male homosexuals and some male heterosexuals. Users report that it produces heightened sensations during orgasms (Everett, 1975). Probably it acts by dilating the blood vessels in the genitals. It may, however, have side effects including dizziness, headaches, fainting, and, in rare cases, death; thus it can be dangerous (Louria, 1970).

Anaphrodisiacs

Just as people have searched for aphrodisiacs, so they have sought anaphrodisiacs, substances or practices that would diminish sexual desire. Cold showers are reputed to have such effects, as is potassium nitrate (saltpeter). The latter contains nothing that decreases sexual drive, but it does act as a diuretic; it makes the person want to urinate frequently, which may be distracting enough so that he or she is not much interested in sex.

There has been some medical interest in finding drugs that would decrease sex drive for use in treating aggressive sexual offenders. One such drug is cyproterone acetate. There have been some reports of its successful use in England, Germany, and Switzerland, but it is too soon to know whether it is truly effective and lacking in side effects (Associated Press, 1971; Intelligence Report, 1971).

Other drugs that may lead to a loss of sexual functioning are discussed in Chapter 18.

ARE INTERCOURSE AND ORGASM THE GOAL?

Traditionally in our culture it has been the belief that a sexual encounter should "climax" with intercourse and orgasm, at least orgasm for the man. In our modern era of multiple orgasms for women and general sexual liberation, the view that intercourse is the important part of sex and that orgasm is the goal toward which both must strive is pervasive. This belief system is reflected in the term "foreplay," which implies that activities like hand stimulation of the genitals, kissing, and mouth-genital sex are only preliminaries that take place before intercourse, the latter being "real sex." Similar beliefs are reflected in a commonly used phrase, "achieving orgasm," as if orgasm were something to be achieved like a promotion on the job.[6]

Psychologist Rollo May feels that men particularly, by concentrating on "achieving" orgasm and *satisfying* their desire, miss out on the more important part of the sexual experience: prolonging the feeling of desire and pleasure, building it higher and higher. As he puts it:

> The pleasure in sex is described by Freud and others as the reduction of tension [orgasm]; in eros, on the contrary, we wish not to be released from the excitement but rather to hang on to it, to bask in it, and even to increase it. (1974, pp. 71–72)

Marc Feigen Fasteau, a men's liberation leader, argues that, although orgasm is good, a larger part of pleasure is building up to orgasm:

> What the masculine disdain for feeling makes it hard for men to grasp is that the state of desire . . . is one of the best perhaps *the* best, part of the experience of love. (1974, p. 31)

Another one of the "goals" of sex that has emerged recently is the simultaneous orgasm. Some people consider this an event to be worked for, rather than a pleasant thing that sometimes happens.

---

[6]To avoid this whole notion, I never use the phrase "to achieve orgasm" in this book. Instead, I prefer "to have an orgasm" or simply "to orgasm." Why not turn it into a verb so that we will not have to work at achieving it?

The legacy of the Protestant ethic in our culture is that our achievement drives now seem to be channeled into our sexual behaviors (see Focus). There is nothing intrinsically wrong with expressing achievement drives in sex, except that anytime there is an achievement situation, there is also the potential for a failure. If she does not have an orgasm or if he cannot get an erection, the couple feel as if the whole experience was a disaster. The problem with setting up sexual goals, then, is that the possibility of sexual failures or sexual dysfunctions is also being set up (this idea is discussed further in Chapter 18).

The best approach is probably to enjoy all the various aspects of lovemaking for themselves, rather than as techniques for achieving something, and to concentrate on sex as a feast of the senses, rather than as an achievement competition.

FROM INEXPERIENCE TO BOREDOM

Some people, after an initial lack of experience with sex, shift rather quickly to becoming bored with it, with perhaps only a brief span of self-confident, pleasurable sexuality in between. Most of us, of course, are sexually inexperienced early in our lives, and most of us feel bored with the way we are having sex at times. How do we deal with these problems?

Sexual Inexperience

In our culture we expect men to be "worldly" about sex—to have had experience with it and to be skillful in the use of sexual techniques. A man or a boy who is sexually inexperienced (perhaps a virgin) or who has had only a few sexual experiences, with little opportunity to practice, may have a real fear about whether he will be able to "perform" (the achievement ethic again) in a sexual encounter. With the

THE PROTESTANT ETHIC: SEX AS WORK

Sociologist Philip Slater has argued that the old Protestant ethic—work hard and become successful—is alive and well in modern American sexual attitudes. According to him, we turn sex into work and then work hard to become successful at it.

Our discussions of sex tend to focus on orgasm, rather than on pleasure in general. Orgasm is the observable "product," and we are concerned with how many orgasms we can produce or have, much as a plant manager is concerned with how many cans of soup are produced on the assembly-line each day.

The emphasis on "simultaneous orgasm" may express how clock-oriented we are. It is important for us to have things running on schedule· and happening at exactly the right time, and so orgasms must also be timed perfectly.

We tend to use the term "adequacy" in relation to sex and to set standards of sexual performance, much as we would set standards of work performance on the job. Ironically, according to current definitions of "adequacy," a man is considered adequate if he can delay his orgasm, while a woman is considered adequate if she can make hers happen faster. Why does the same standard not

sexual revolution has come an increasing expectation that women also should have a bag of sexual tricks ready to use, and so they, too, are increasingly expected to be experienced.

How can one deal with this problem of inexperience? First, it is important to question society's assumption that one should be experienced (see, for example, Glassberg, 1970). Everyone has to begin sometime, and there is absolutely nothing wrong with inexperience. Second, there are many good books and articles on sexual techniques that are definitely worth reading, although it is important to be selective, since a few of these may be more harmful than helpful. This chapter should be a good intro-

duction; you also might want to consult *The Joy of Sex* or any of the self-help manuals listed at the end of Chapter 18, particularly Raley's *Making Love*. Do not become slavishly attached to the techniques you read about in books, though; they should serve basically as a stimulus to your imagination, not as a series of steps that must be followed. Third, communicate with your partner. Because individual preferences vary so much, no one, no matter how experienced, is ever a sexual expert with a new partner. The best way to please a partner is to find out what that person likes, and communication accomplishes this better than prior experience.

apply to both? The answer has to do with our concept of orgasm as a "product" and with our concern about timing.

Slater also points out that work (on the job) and sex are natural enemies. The more a person becomes dedicated to work and the more time she or he spends on it, the greater the in-roads on the sex life. This notion is substantiated in a study of successful executives, government officials, and professionals (*Sex and the Significant Americans*, by John Cuber and Peggy Harroff). For the people in the study, sex was brief and perfunctory. Their high commitment to their work left little time for, or interest in, sex.

One might even speculate that the more we see sex as work and apply performance standards to it, the more "failures"—sexual dysfunctions (see Chapter 18)—we shall have:

As Slater put it:

The preoccupation in Western sexual literature with orgasm seems to be a natural extension of the Protestant work ethic in which nothing is to be enjoyed for its own sake except striving.

The antithetical attitude would be to view orgasm as a delightful interruption in an otherwise continuous process of generating pleasurable sensations. (1973, p. 134)

Source: P. E. Slater. Sexual adequacy in America. *Intellectual Digest*, December 1973, 132–135. (See also George W. Albee. The Protestant ethic, sex, and psychotherapy. *American Psychologist*, 1977, **32**, 150–161.

Boredom

The opposite problem to inexperience is the feeling of boredom in a long-term sexual relationship. Boredom, of course, is not always a necessary consequence of having sex with the same person over a long period of time. Certainly there are couples who have been married for 40 or 50 years and who continue to find sexual expression exciting. Unfortunately, the major sex surveys have not inquired about the phenomenon of boredom, and thus it is not possible to estimate the percentage of people who eventually become bored or who experience occasional fits of boredom. However, such experiences are surely common. As some-

one once said, a rut is no place to be making love. How can we deal with the problem of boredom?

Communication can help in this situation, as it can in others. Couples sometimes evolve a routine sexual sequence that leads to boredom, and sometimes that sequence is not really what either person wants. By communicating to each other what they really would like to do and then doing it, two people can introduce some variety into their relationship. The various love manuals can also give ideas on new techniques. Finally, a couple's sexual relationship often mirrors the other aspects of their relationship, and sexual boredom may sometimes mean that they are generally bored with each other. Rejuvenating the rest of the relationship—perhaps taking up a hobby or a sport together or going on a good vacation, during which they really try to build their relationship in general—may do wonders for their sexual relationship.

One might also question the meaning of "boredom." Perhaps our expectations for sexual experience are too high. Encouraged by the media, we tend to believe that every time we have intercourse, the earth should move. We do not expect that every meal we eat will be fantastic or that we will always have a huge appetite and enjoy every bite. Yet we do tend to have such expectations with regard to sexuality. Perhaps when boredom seems to be a problem, it is not the real issue; rather, the real problem may be unrealistically high expectations.

SUMMARY

Sexual pleasure is produced by stimulation of various areas of the body; these are the erogenous zones.

Sexual self-stimulation, or autoeroticism, includes masturbation and sexual fantasies. Women most typically masturbate by rubbing the clitoris and surrounding tissue and the inner and outer lips. Men generally masturbate by circling the hand around the penis and using an up-and-down movement to stimulate the shaft. Many people have sexual fantasies while they masturbate. Common themes of these fantasies include having intercourse with a stranger and having sex with several people simultaneously. Similar sexual fantasies are also common while having intercourse with another person.

An important technique in two-person sex is hand stimulation of the partner's genitals. A good guide to technique is to find out how the partner masturbates. Touching other areas of the body and kissing are also important. The other senses—sight, smell, and hearing—can also be used in creating sexual arousal.

While there are infinite varieties in the positions in which one can have intercourse, there are four basic positions: man-on-top (the "missionary" position), woman-on-top, rear-entry, and side-to-side.

There are two kinds of mouth-genital stimulation: cunnilingus (mouth stimulation of the female genitals) and fellatio (mouth stimulation of the male genitals). Both are engaged in frequently today and are considered highly pleasurable by many people.

Anal intercourse involves inserting the penis into the rectum.

An aphrodisiac is a substance that arouses sexual desire. There is no known reliable aphrodisiac, and some of the substances that are popularly thought to act as aphrodisiacs can be dangerous to one's health.

We have a tendency in our culture, perhaps a legacy of the Protestant ethic, to view sex as work and to turn sex into an achievement situation, as witnessed by expressions such as "achieving orgasm." Such attitudes make sex less pleasurable and may set the stage for sexual failures or sexual dysfunctions.

Finally, we must all face the problem of being sexually inexperienced at some time in our lives; many people also face the problem of boredom in a long-term sexual relationship.

SUGGESTIONS FOR FURTHER READING

Comfort, Alex. *The joy of sex.* New York: Crown, 1972. (Simon and Schuster paperback.) Probably the best of the current crop of sex manuals.

Vatsyayana. *The kama sutra.* (Translated by R. F. Burton and F. F. Arbuthnot.) New York: Putnam, 1963. The classic Eastern love manual.

SEX
RESEARCH

CITED

According to the Kinsey Report,
Every average man you know,
Much prefers to play his favorite sport,
When the temperature is low,
But when the thermometer goes way up,
And the weather is sizzling hot,
 Mr. Adam
 For his madam
 Is not.
  'Cause it's too darn hot.*

In the last few decades, sex research has become increasingly common, and the names of Kinsey and of Masters and Johnson have become household words. Just exactly what do sex researchers do, and how valid are their conclusions? Those are the topics that will be discussed in this chapter.

There are many different types of sex research, but basically the techniques vary in terms of the following: (1) whether they rely on people's self-reports of their sexual behavior or whether the scientist actually observes the sexual behavior directly; (2) whether large numbers of people are studied (surveys) or whether a small number or just a single individual is studied (in laboratory studies or case studies); (3) whether the studies are conducted in the laboratory or in the field; and (4) whether sexual behavior is studied simply as it occurs naturally or whether some attempt is made to manipulate it experimentally.

Examples of studies using all these techniques will be considered and evaluated later in the chapter. First some issues in sex research—

objections frequently made to studies that have been done—will be discussed.

It is important to have some knowledge of the techniques of sex research and their limitations. This knowledge will help you evaluate the studies that are cited as evidence for various conclusions in later chapters and will also help you decide how willing you are to believe these conclusions. Perhaps more important, this knowledge will help you evaluate future sex research. The knowledge we have of sexuality at present is based on very few studies. It is hoped that many more will be done in the future. The information in this chapter should help you understand and evaluate sex research that appears 10 or 20 years from now.

ISSUES IN SEX RESEARCH

Sampling

One of the first steps in conducting sex research is to identify the *population* of people to be studied. Does the population in question consist of all adult human beings, all adults in the United States, all adolescents in the United States, all people guilty of sex crimes, or all

---

*Source: Kiss Me Kate, a musical comedy. Music and lyrics by Cole Porter; book by Sam and Bella Spewack. New York: Knopf, 1973.

married couples who engage in swinging (discussed later in this chapter)? Generally, of course, the scientist is unable to get data for all the people in the population, and so a *sample* is taken.

At this point, things begin to get sticky. If the sample is a random or representative sample of the population in question and if it is a reasonably large sample, then results obtained from it can safely be generalized to the population that was originally identified. That is, if one has really randomly selected 1 out of every 50 adolescents in the United States, then the results obtained from that sample are probably true of all adolescents in the United States. One technique that is sometimes used to get such a sample is *probability sampling*.[1] But if the sample consists only of adolescents with certain characteristics—for example, only those whose parents would agree to let them participate in sex research—then the results obtained from that sample may not be true of all adolescents. Sampling has been a real problem in sex research.

Typically, sampling proceeds in three phases: The population is identified, a method for obtaining a sample is adopted, and the people in the sample are contacted and asked to participate. The scientific techniques of the second phase—obtaining a sample—are by now fairly well developed and should not be a problem in future research, provided investigators use them. What is perhaps the thorniest problem, though, occurs in the last phase: getting the people identified for the sample to participate. If any of the people refuse to participate, then the nice probability sample is ruined. And generally in sex research, rather large numbers of people will refuse to participate;

this is called the problem of *refusal* (or *non-response*).[2] Even in Hunt's carefully designed study (to be discussed later in this chapter), the response rate was only about 20 percent. The problem of refusal in sex research is very difficult, since there is no ethical way of forcing people to participate when they do not want to.

The problem of nonresponse would not be so great if those who refused to participate were identical in their sexual behavior to those who participated. But it seems likely that those who refuse to participate differ in some ways from those who agree to, and that leads to a biased sample. Evidence suggests that volunteers who participate in sex research tend to be more liberal politically and more experienced sexually than those who do not participate (Kaats and Davis, 1971; Maslow and Sakoda, 1952; but see Barker and Perlman, 1975).

Reliability of Self-Reports of Sexual Behavior

Most sex researchers have not directly observed the sexual behavior of their subjects. Instead, most have relied on respondents' self-reports of their sexual practices. The question then becomes: How accurately do people report their own sexual behavior? There are several ways in which inaccuracies may occur. These are discussed below.

Purposeful distortion If you were an interviewer in a sex research project and a 90-year-old man said that he and his wife made love twice a day, would you believe him, or would you suspect that he might be exaggerating slightly? If a 35-year-old woman told you that she had never masturbated, would you believe

---

[1] A detailed discussion of probability sampling is beyond the scope of this book. For a good description of this method as applied to sex research, see Cochran et al. (1953). A random sample is one example of a probability sample.

[2] As a result, the researcher is essentially studying volunteers, that is, people who volunteer to be in the research. Therefore, this problem is also called *volunteer bias*.

her, or would you suspect that she had masturbated but was unwilling to admit it?

Respondents in sex research may, for one reason or another, give self-reports that are distortions of reality. These distortions may be in one of two directions. People may exaggerate their sexual activity (a tendency toward "enlargement"), or they may minimize their sexual activity or hide the fact that they have done certain things ("concealment"). Unfortunately, we do not know whether most people tend toward enlargement or concealment.

Distortion is a basic problem when using self-reports. To minimize distortion, subjects must be impressed with the fact that, since the study will be used for scientific purposes, their reports must be as accurate as possible. They must also be assured that their responses will be completely anonymous; this is necessary, for example, so that a politician would not be tempted to hide a homosexual history or an extramarital affair for fear that the information could be used to blackmail him.

But even if all respondents were very truthful and tried to give as accurate information as possible, two factors might still cause their self-reports to be inaccurate: memory and ability to estimate.

Memory   Some of the questions asked in sex surveys require respondents to recall what their sexual behavior was like many years before. For example, many of the data we have on sexual behavior in childhood come from the Kinsey study, in which adults were asked about their childhood sex behavior. This might involve asking a 50-year-old man to remember at what age he began masturbating and how frequently he masturbated when he was 16 years old. It may be difficult to remember such facts accurately. The alternative is to ask people about their current sexual behavior, although getting data like this from children raises serious ethical

and practical problems. This point is discussed further in Chapter 10.

Ability to estimate   One of the questions Kinsey asked was: How long, on the average, do you spend in precoital foreplay? If you were asked this question, how accurate a response do you think you could give? It is rather difficult to estimate time to begin with, and it is even more difficult to do so when engaged in an absorbing activity. The point is that in some sex surveys people are asked to give estimates of things that they probably cannot estimate very accurately. This may be another source of inaccuracy in self-report data.

Interviews versus questionnaires   In the large-scale sex surveys, two methods of collecting data have been used. Either interviewers question people directly about their sexual behavior, or people are given a questionnaire which they complete themselves. Each of these methods has some advantages when compared with the other.

The advantage of the personal interview is that the interviewer can establish rapport with the respondent and, it is hoped, convince that person of the research's worth and of the necessity for being honest. An interviewer can also vary the sequence of questions, depending on the person's response. For example, in the Kinsey interviewing procedure, if a person mentioned having had a homosexual experience, this would be followed by a series of questions about the experience; however, those questions would be omitted if the person reported having had no homosexual experiences. It would be hard to get this kind of flexibility in a printed questionnaire. Finally, interviews can be administered to persons who cannot read or write.

Questionnaires are much less costly, since they do not require hiring interviewers to spend the many hours necessary to interview subjects individually. Subjects will probably feel surer of their anonymity when filling out a questionnaire, and they may respond more honestly than they would in a face-to-face discussion with an interviewer. Questionnaires are less subject to the problem of responses' being influenced by extraneous factors, such as the personality of the interviewer or a grimace from the interviewer when a particular behavior is reported.

Self-Reports versus Direct Observations

As has been noted, one of the major ways of classifying techniques of sex research is according to whether the scientist relied on people's self-reports of their behavior or observed the sexual behavior directly.

The problems of self-reports have been discussed above. In a word, self-reports may be inaccurate. Direct observations—such as those done by Masters and Johnson in their work on the physiology of sexual response—have a major advantage over self-reports in that they are accurate. No purposeful distortion or poor memory can intervene. On the other hand, direct observations have their own set of problems. They are expensive and time-consuming, with the result that generally a rather small sample of subjects is studied. Further, obtaining a random or representative sample of the population is even more difficult than in survey research. While many people are reticent about completing a questionnaire concerning their sexual behavior, even more would be unwilling to come to a laboratory where their sexual behavior would be observed by a scientist or where they would be hooked up to recording instruments while they engaged in sex. Thus results obtained from the unusual group of people who would be willing to do this might

not be generalizable to the rest of the population.

Direct observations of sexual behavior in the laboratory, such as those made by Masters and Johnson, also involve one other major problem: Is sexual behavior in the laboratory the same as sexual behavior in the privacy of one's own bedroom? For example, might sexual response in the laboratory be somewhat inhibited?

Extraneous Factors

Various extraneous factors may also influence the outcomes of sex research. For example, people report more sexual feelings to an interviewer of their own gender than to an interviewer of the opposite gender (Walters et al., 1962). Generally, respondents are most open with interviewers who are of their own gender (Benney et al., 1956; J. Ehrlich and Riesman, 1961). Thus such extraneous factors as the gender or age of the interviewer may influence the outcome of sex research. Questionnaires do not get around these problems, since such simple factors as the wording of a question may influence the results. For example, if a question reads, "On the average, how many times do you have intercourse per month?", the estimates of frequency of intercourse that are obtained will not be exactly the same as if the question had read, "On the average, how many times do you have intercourse per week?" Thus sex researchers must be careful to control these extraneous factors so that they influence the results as little as possible.

Ethical Issues

In recent years, scientists as well as lay people have become more aware of the ethical problems involved in doing research. Such ethical problems are particularly difficult in sex research, since people are more likely to feel that their privacy has been invaded when you ask them about sex than when you ask them to name their favorite Presidential candidate or memorize a list of words. The ethical standards of most scientific organizations—such as the American Psychological Association and the American Sociological Association—involve two basic principles: informed consent and protection from harm (see, for example, American Psychological Association, 1973).

Informed consent According to the principle of informed consent, subjects have a right to be told, before they participate, what the purpose of the research is and what will happen to them as they participate. They may not be forced to participate or be forced to continue. Thus an investigator should, at the beginning, explain to all participants exactly what the purpose of the study is, and what will happen to them if they agree to participate, and the investigator should also tell them that they are free not to participate and that they may withdraw from the study at any time. Only then should they be asked to give their consent to participate. An investigator may not coerce people to be in a study, and it is the scientist's responsibility to see to it that all subjects understand exactly what they are agreeing to do. In the case of children who may be too young to give truly informed consent, it is usually given by the parents.

The principle of informed consent has only recently been adopted by scientific organizations, and it was violated in some of the older sex studies, as will be discussed later in this chapter.

Protection from harm Investigators should minimize the amount of physical and psychological stress to those participating in their research. Thus, for example, if an investigator must shock subjects during a study, there should be a good reason for doing this. Ques-

tioning people about their sexual behavior may be psychologically stressful to them and might conceivably harm them in some way, and thus sex researchers must be careful to minimize the stress involved in their procedures. The principle of anonymity of response is important to ensure that subjects will not suffer afterward for their participation in research.

A cost-benefit approach Considering the possible dangers involved in sex research, is it ever ethical to do such research? Officials in universities and government agencies sponsoring sex research must answer this question in every proposed sex research study. Typically they use a cost-benefit approach. That is, stress to subjects should be minimized as much as possible, but some stresses will remain; they are the cost. The question then becomes: Will the benefits that will result from the research be greater than the cost? That is, will the subjects benefit in some way from participating, and will science and society in general benefit from the knowledge resulting from the study? Do these benefits outweigh the costs? If they do, the research is justifiable; otherwise, it is not.

As an example, Masters and Johnson considered these issues carefully, and they feel that their subjects benefited from being in their research; they have collected data from former subjects that confirm this belief. Thus a cost-benefit analysis would suggest that their research is ethical, even though their subjects may be temporarily stressed by it. Even in such an ethically questionable study as Laud Humphreys's study of the tearoom trade (discussed in a Focus in Chapter 14), the potential cost to the subjects must be weighed against the benefits that accrue to society from being informed about this aspect of sexual behavior.

Having considered some of these problems with sex research—though these problems are by no means limited to sex research and are common in most research on human behavior—let us proceed to the studies that have been done.

THE MAJOR SEX SURVEYS

In the major sex surveys, the data were collected from a large sample of people by means of questionnaires or interviews. The best known of these studies are those done by Kinsey.

The Kinsey Reports

Kinsey and his colleagues Wardell Pomeroy and Clyde Martin coauthored *Sexual Behavior in the Human Male*, which appeared in 1948; *Sexual Behavior in the Human Female*, which was published in 1953, was the joint effort of these three scientists and Paul Gebhard. The two books are known as the "Kinsey reports."

Sampling A total of 5300 males were interviewed, and their responses were reported in *Sexual Behavior in the Human Male*; 5940 females contributed to *Sexual Behavior in the Human Female*. Though some blacks were interviewed, only interviews with whites were included in the publications. The interviews were conducted between 1938 and 1949, with the greatest numbers conducted from 1943 to 1946.

Initially, Kinsey was not much concerned with sampling issues. His goal was simply to collect as many sex histories from as wide a variety of people as possible. He began collecting interviews on the university campus and then moved to collecting others in large cities, such as Chicago.

Later he became more concerned with sampling issues and developed a technique called *100 percent sampling*. In this method he contacted a group, obtained its cooperation, and then got every one of its members to give a history. Once the cooperation of a group had been secured, peer pressure assured that all

members would participate. Unfortunately, while he was successful in getting a complete sample of such groups, the groups themselves were by no means chosen randomly. Thus among the groups from which 100 percent samples were obtained were 2 sororities, 9 fraternities, and 13 professional groups. About one-fourth of the sex histories came from these 100 percent samples.

In the 1953 volume, Kinsey claimed that he and his colleagues had deliberately chosen not to use probability sampling methods because of the problems of nonresponse. This is a legitimate point. But as a result, we have almost no information on how adequate the sample was.

As one scholar observed, the sampling was haphazard but not random (Kirby, 1977). For example, there were more subjects from Indiana than from any other state. Generally the following kinds of subjects were overrepresented in the sample: college students, young people, well-educated people, Protestants, people living in cities, and people living in Indiana and the Northeast. Underrepresented groups included manual laborers, less well educated people, older people, Roman Catholics, Jews, members of racial minorities, people living in rural areas, and people living west of the Mississippi. To compensate for these sampling inadequacies, Kinsey used statistical methods to correct his sample so that it would agree with the United States census. These corrected figures were called "U.S. corrections."

Interviewing While scientists generally regard Kinsey's sampling methods with some dismay, his interviewing techniques are highly regarded. The interviewers made every attempt to establish rapport with the people they spoke to, and they treated all reports matter-of-factly. They were also skillful at phrasing questions in language that was easily understood. Questions were worded so as to encourage subjects to

ALFRED C. KINSEY

Alfred C. Kinsey was born in 1894 in New Jersey, the first child of uneducated parents.

In high school he did not date or show much interest in girls. Under his picture in the yearbook was placed a quotation from *Hamlet*: "Man delights not me; no, nor woman neither." A classmate recalled that he was "the shyest guy around girls you could think of."

His father was determined that Kinsey become a mechanical engineer. From 1912 to 1914 he tried studying this at Stevens Institute, but he showed little talent for it. At one point he was close to failing physics, but a compromise was reached with the professor, who agreed to pass him if he would not attempt any advanced work in the field! In 1914 Kinsey made the break and enrolled at Bowdoin College to pursue his real love, biology. Because this went against his father's wishes, Kinsey was put on his own financially; the only financial help he received from his parents after that was a single suit costing $25.

In 1916 he began graduate work at Harvard. There he developed his interest in insects, specializing in gall wasps. Even while a graduate student he wrote a definitive book on the edible plants of eastern North America.

In 1920 he went to Bloomington, Indiana, to take a job as assistant professor of zoology at Indiana University. That fall he met Clara McMillen, whom he married six months later. They soon had four children, but the first, a boy, died in early childhood.

With his intense curiosity and driving ambition, Kinsey quickly gained academic success. He published a high school biology text in 1926, and it received enthusiastic reviews. By 1936 he had published two major books on gall wasps; they established his reputation as a leading authority in the field and contributed not only to knowledge of gall wasps but also to genetic theory.

Kinsey came to the study of human sex behavior as a biologist, not as a social reformer. His shift to the study of sex began in 1938, when Indiana University began a "marriage" course; Kinsey chaired the faculty committee teaching it. Part of the course included individual conferences between students and faculty, and these were Kinsey's first sex interviews. He quickly saw the value of extending these interviews to people beyond the university. When confronted with teaching the course, he also became aware of the incredible lack of information on human sexual behavior. Thus his

FOCUS

FIGURE 9.1
Alfred C. Kinsey. [*Culver Pictures, Inc.*]

research resulted in part from his realization of the need of people, especially young people, for sex information. In 1939 he made his first field trip to collect sex histories in Chicago. His lifetime goal was to collect 100,000 sex histories.

His work culminated with the publication of the Kinsey reports in 1948 (*Sexual Behavior in the Human Male*) and 1953 (*Sexual Behavior in the Human Female*). While the scientific community generally received them as a landmark contribution, they also provoked hate mail.

In 1947 he founded the Institute for Sex Research (known popularly as the Kinsey Institute) at Indiana University. It was financed by a grant from the Rockefeller Foundation and, later, by book royalties. But in the 1950s Senator Joseph McCarthy, the communist-baiter, dominated political attention. He made a particularly vicious attack on the Institute and its research, claiming that its effect was to weaken American morality and thus make the nation more susceptible to a communist take-over. Under his pressuring, support from the Rockefeller Foundation was terminated in 1954.

At that time, Kinsey's health began to fail, partly as a result of the incredible workload he set for himself, partly because he was so involved with the research that he took attacks personally, and partly because he saw financial support for the research collapsing. He died in 1956 at the age 62 of heart failure, while honoring a lecture engagement when his doctor had ordered him to convalesce.

Fortunately, by 1957 McCarthy had been discredited, and the grant funds returned. The Institute was headed by Dr. Paul Gebhard, an anthropologist who had been a member of the staff for many years. The Institute continues research to the present day, as well as housing a large library on sex and an archival collection including countless works of sexual art.

Sources: P. Gebhard. The Institute. In M. S. Weinberg (Ed.), Sex research: Studies from the Kinsey Institute. New York: Oxford University Press, 1976, pp. 10–22. C. V. Christensen. Kinsey: A biography. Bloomington: Indiana University Press, 1971.

---

report anything they had done. For example, rather than asking, "Have you ever masturbated?" the interviewers asked "At what age did you begin masturbating?" Thus the burden of denial was placed on the subject. They also developed a number of methods for cross-checking a subject's report so that false information would be detected. Wardell Pomeroy recounts an example:

Kinsey illustrated this point with the case of an older Negro male who at first was wary and evasive in his answers. From the fact that he listed a number of minor jobs when asked about his occupation and seemed reluctant to go into

any of them [Kinsey] deduced that he might have been active in the underworld, so he began to follow up by asking the man whether he had ever been married. He denied it, at which Kinsey resorted to the vernacular and inquired if he had ever "lived common law." The man admitted he had, and that it had first happened when he was 14.

"How old was the woman?" [Kinsey] asked.

"Thirty-five," he admitted, smiling.

Kinsey showed no surprise. "She was a hustler, wasn't she?" he said flatly.

At this the subject's eyes opened wide. Then he smiled in a friendly way for the first time, and said, "Well, sir, since you appear to know something about these things, I'll tell you straight."

> After that, [Kinsey] got an extraordinary record of this man's history as a pimp.... (1972, pp. 115–116)

Strict precautions were taken to ensure that responses were anonymous and that they would remain anonymous. The data were stored on IBM cards, but using a code that had been memorized by only a few people directly in the project, and the code was never written down. They had even made contingency plans for destroying the data in the event that the police tried to demand access to the records for the purposes of prosecuting people.[3]

Over 50 percent of the interviews were done by Kinsey himself, and the rest by his associates, whom he trained carefully.

Put simply, the interviewing techniques were probably very successful in minimizing purposeful distortion. However, other problems of self-report remained: the problems of memory and of inability to estimate some of the numbers requested.

Checking for accuracy Kinsey and his colleagues developed a number of methods for checking on the accuracy of subjects' self-reports.

They did retakes of the histories of 162 men and women, with a minimum of 18 months between the two interviews (in technical language, the correlation between the two reports estimates the test-retest reliability). Any discrepancies between the two histories would be accounted for by memory problems, purposeful distortion, and various chance factors. The re-

---

[3]From today's vantage point, Kinsey's fears were not so unrealistic. In a recent highly publicized case, police subpoenaed a psychologist who was studying heavy marijuana users and demanded that he divulge their names. The psychologist was faced with a choice between violating the anonymity of his subjects and being jailed for contempt. He chose the latter. Such actions by the police seriously jeopardize the integrity of scientific research.

sults indicated a high degree of agreement between the first and second interviews for all measures. Correlations greater than .95 between the first and second interviews were obtained for reports of incidence of masturbation, extramarital coitus, and homosexual activity. Thus these data indicate that the self-reports were highly reliable.

Another method for checking accuracy is to interview a husband and a wife independently; their reports on many items should be identical and can thus be used as a check for accuracy. Kinsey did exactly this for 231 couples and later for a total of 706 couples. The results indicated that reports of objective facts—such as the number of years they had been married, how long they were engaged, and how much time elapsed between their marriage and the birth of their first child—showed perfect or near-perfect agreement between spouses. However, as was noted earlier in this chapter, some other questions required much more subjective responses or estimates of things that might be difficult to estimate. On such items, there was less agreement between spouses. For example, the correlation between husband's and wife's estimate of the average frequency of intercourse early in marriage was only about .50 (this was the lowest correlation obtained). Even with these subjective reports, though, husbands and wives showed a fairly high degree of agreement.

Thus from the available data it appears that the self-reports varied from being fairly accurate (on the subjective items, such as reports of frequencies) to highly accurate (on items such as vital statistics and incidences of activities).

How accurate are the Kinsey statistics? When all is said and done, how accurate are the statistics presented by Kinsey?

The American Statistical Association appointed a blue-ribbon panel to evaluate the

Kinsey reports (Cochran et al., 1953; for other evaluations, see Terman, 1948; Wallin, 1949). While they generally felt that the interview techniques had been excellent, they were dismayed by Kinsey's failure to use probability sampling, and they concluded, somewhat pessimistically:

> In the absence of a probability-sample benchmark, the present results must be regarded as subject to systematic errors of unknown magnitude due to selective sampling (via volunteering and the like). (Cochran et al., 1953, p. 711)

However, they also felt that this was a nearly insoluble problem for sex research; even if a probability sample were used, refusals would create serious problems:

> In our opinion, no sex study of a broad human population can expect to present incidence data for reported behavior that are *known* to be correct to within a few percentage points. . . . If the percentage of refusals is 10 percent or more, then however large the sample, there are no statistical principles which guarantee that the results are correct to within 2 or 3 per cent. (Cochran et al., 1953, p. 675)

It is possible, then, that the Kinsey statistics are very accurate, but there is no way of proving it.

The statisticians who evaluated Kinsey's methods felt that four of his findings might have been particularly subject to error: (1) generally high levels of sexual activity, and particularly the high incidence of homosexuality; (2) little difference between older and younger generations; (3) a strong relationship between sexual activity and social class; and (4) relation between sexual activity and changes in social class. All these conclusions might have been seriously influenced by discrepancies between reported and actual behavior and by sampling problems.

Kinsey's associates felt that the most questionable statistic was the incidence of male homosexuality. Wardell Pomeroy commented: "The magic 37 percent of males who had one or more homosexual experience was, no doubt, overestimated. Probably 33 percent would have been closer to the mark" (1972, p. 466).

In sum, it is impossible to say how accurate the Kinsey statistics are; they may be very accurate, or they may contain serious errors. Probably the single most doubtful figure is the high incidence of homosexuality.

The Hunt Survey

In the early 1970s the Playboy Foundation commissioned a large-scale sex survey. Its purpose was threefold: (1) to get up-to-date data on sexual behavior, (2) to collect modern data that could be compared with Kinsey's to see whether sexual behavior has changed in the last 30 years, and (3) to collect data that would be more accurate than Kinsey's as a result of the use of better sampling procedures. The results were written up by Morton Hunt, a professional journalist who had specialized in writing popularized versions of scientific studies. The reports were initially serialized in *Playboy* magazine and were later published in a book by Hunt entitled *Sexual Behavior in the 1970s*. This study will be referred to as the "Hunt survey"; it is sometimes called the "*Playboy* survey," although that name implies a bias in the data that is probably not present.

Sampling   The Playboy Foundation commissioned the Research Guild, an independent market survey and behavioral research organization, to devise a sampling method, design a questionnaire, and collect the data.

To obtain the sample, the Research Guild chose 24 cities throughout the United States. In each city, names were chosen at random from the telephone book. The researchers called these people and asked them to participate anonymously in small, private panel discussions of present trends in American sexual behavior, for the benefit of behavioral researchers; no mention was made of filling out a questionnaire. Of those contacted, 20 percent came for the discussions. After the discussions had been held, the participants were asked to complete the questionnaire. Of those present, 100 percent cooperated. Thus 20 percent of the originally identified sample contributed data, for a total of 2026 subjects. All data were collected in 1972.

According to Hunt, the sample closely parallels the American population aged 18 and over. It consisted of 982 males and 1044 females; 90 percent were white, and 10 percent were black;[4] 71 percent were married, 25 percent had never been married, and 4 percent had previously been married but were not married at that time. In terms of other major characteristics, such as age, education, occupation, and urban-rural background, the sample was fairly similar to the American population. A number of questions on nonsexual issues, such as use of tobacco, alcohol, and other drugs and stance on women's rights, were included; the answers suggest that the sample had attitudes quite similar to those of the American population in general.

On the other hand, because the sample was done via the telephone book, certain groups of people were excluded: the very poor and those in institutions such as prisons and colleges (Kinsey, in contrast, made a special point of collecting data in such institutions). And 80 percent of the original sample refused to participate, a very high refusal rate. Although the sample's attitudes were similar to those of the American population in nonsexual areas, we do not know how similar their sexual behavior was to that of the general American popula-

tion, and we have no idea of what differences there might have been between the 20 percent who agreed to participate and the 80 percent who did not.

While Hunt's sampling techniques were probably more adequate than Kinsey's, one ethical issue should be raised. The principle of informed consent was violated because subjects were not told, at the time they were recruited, that they would be asked to fill out a questionnaire on their own sexual behavior. Often, unfortunately, there is a trade-off between ethics and sampling adequacy in sex research.

The questionnaire   There were four versions of the questionnaire used in Hunt's study; one was geared to unmarried males; one, to unmarried females; one, to married males; and one, to married females. The questionnaire asked for between 1000 and 1200 items of information covering the individual's background, sex education, sex history, and sex attitudes. It covered most of the same areas covered in Kinsey's study and also went beyond it in some areas; for example, there were questions about anal sex and about attitudes.

The relative merits of questionnaires versus the kinds of interviews Kinsey used were discussed earlier in this chapter.

The 2000 questionnaire responses were supplemented by 200 in-depth interviews that were similar to Kinsey's. Quotations from those interviews are sprinkled throughout Hunt's book; they provide a more personal view of people's sexuality than statistics do.

Comparing Kinsey and Hunt   Hunt's sample was considerably smaller than Kinsey's. However, in terms of providing estimates of the sexual behavior of Americans, the Hunt study was probably at least as accurate as the Kinsey study (and possibly more accurate), because the Hunt sample was probably better than the Kinsey sample in the sense of being closer to a

---

[4]When comparing his results with Kinsey's, Hunt dropped the blacks from his sample because the Kinsey report did not include blacks.

FIGURE 9.2
One of the visible signs of the sexual revolution of the past few decades is the more open treatment of sexuality by the media. Here Woody Allen and fellow sperm await blast-off in the film *Everything You Always Wanted to Know about Sex But Were Afraid to Ask*. [*United Artists Corporation.*]

random sample of the United States population (I say "probably" because we still do not know about the 80 percent who did not participate). Both studies have their faults, but they are still among the best sources available on the sexual behavior of Americans.

The sexual revolution It is a popular notion that there has been a "sexual revolution" (which might be called a "copulation explosion") in the United States in the last decade or so. Comparing the Hunt data and the Kinsey data can give us some idea of whether sexual behavior has changed in the approximately 30 years since Kinsey collected his data.

According to Hunt's comparison of the two sets of data, there have been major changes. In particular, premarital sex is considerably more common, gender differences are now smaller, and social-class differences have shrunk (these changes will be discussed in more detail in Chapters 10, 11, and 13).

In the chapters that follow, frequent references will be made to changes in sexual behavior in the last several decades, with the evidence for these changes coming from a comparison of the Kinsey data and the Hunt data.

The Magazine Surveys

Recently, two large-scale surveys have been conducted through magazines—*Redbook* and *Psychology Today*.

The *Redbook* survey *Redbook* included a questionnaire about female sexuality in its October 1974 issue and asked readers to complete it and mail it in. The results were published in the September and October 1975 issues of *Redbook* (Levin and Levin, 1975).

In terms of sample size, the response was incredible; questionnaires were returned by more than 100,000 women. However, in sex research, as in some other aspects of sexuality, bigger is not always better. A carefully chosen probability sample of 1000 is much better than a highly selective sample of 100,000, and the *Redbook* sample gives evidence of having been such a selective sample. First, only *Redbook* readers were surveyed, and not every woman reads *Redbook*. Among others, this omits all women who cannot or do not read. Second, only those who voluntarily returned the questionnaire were included; presumably, women who felt very uncomfortable about sex were less likely to respond.

The background data on the sample confirm the notion that it was seriously biased. For example, 90 percent of the respondents were married, while nationally the percentage is only 70. The sample tended to overrepresent young women, educated women, white women, and middle- to high-income women (one-third of the sample had family incomes between $15,000 and $25,000, and another 12 percent had incomes over $25,000, certainly much higher than the incomes of the general American population).

The sample was probably also biased in that the respondents were much more sexually experienced than women in the general American population. For example, among the married people in Hunt's sample, about 14 percent of those aged 35 to 44 and about 25 percent of those under 25 had engaged in anal intercourse at least once, whereas 50 percent of the *Redbook* women had done so.

For these reasons, the statistics from the *Redbook* survey characterize only the 100,000 women who responded; it would not be legitimate to infer that they characterize American women in general.

The *Psychology Today* survey *Psychology Today* included a 100-item sex questionnaire in its July 1969 issue. Over 20,000 readers responded, and the results were published in the July 1970 issue (Athanasiou et al., 1970).

The *Psychology Today* survey was similar to the *Redbook* survey in that the sample was large but biased. The respondents tended to be young (the majority were under 30), well educated (the median level was college graduate), and of relatively high socioeconomic status (almost two-thirds earned over $10,000 a year, and in those days $10,000 was a lot). Three-quarters of the sample rated themselves as sexually liberal, compared with the average person. These biases resulted from the sampling method; only *Psychology Today* readers were surveyed (and they are probably an even more selective group than *Redbook* readers), and only those who would voluntarily fill out a sex questionnaire were surveyed. Sexual conservatives or those who are uncomfortable about sex would presumably be less likely to do so. Indeed, a few persons wrote to say that the survey was pornographic, and one man returned a blank form, saying that as a member of the silent generation he preferred to remain silent.

As a result, it should not be inferred that statistics from this survey apply to the general American population. The authors wisely recognize this fact, saying:

We do not suggest, therefore, that findings from this survey are directly applicable to the country as a whole, but they are descriptive of a well-educated, intelligent group that just might be the wave of the future. (Athanasiou et al., 1970, pp. 39–40)

Of course, there is no more evidence that these people are the wave of the future than there is evidence that they are typical of the American population. Therefore, the results of this survey are of limited value.

Probability Samples

As has been noted, one of the biggest problems with the major sex surveys is sampling. Recently, a few investigators have conquered this problem and have actually obtained probability samples in sex surveys. Perhaps the two best examples are the studies by Westoff (1974) and by Kantner and Zelnik (1972).

The National Fertility Studies   As part of the National Fertility Studies, Charles Westoff (1974) studied a national probability sample of married women of reproductive age. In 1965, a probability sample of 4603 women were interviewed face to face. The same questions were asked in interviews in 1970, with a sample of 5432.

Most of the questions asked were not explicitly about sexual behavior. Generally, they dealt with more neutral topics, such as the number and spacing of children. Because most of the items were thus not very threatening, it was probably more feasible to get a good probability sample in this study than in a study that was just about sexual behavior. On the items that concerned sex, such as the question

about average frequency of intercourse per week, it was possible to determine the refusal rate. On that question, the refusal rate was 4.8 percent in 1965 and 7.8 percent in 1970. Thus the refusal rate was low, and statistics reported in this study should be highly accurate (assuming that those who did respond were accurate in their answers).

The median frequency of intercourse reported by the women in this sample was 7 times per 4 weeks in 1965 and 8.2 times per 4 weeks in 1970. This study provides some of the best evidence on increased frequency of some sexual behaviors, such as marital intercourse, in recent years. The evidence is good because it is based on two excellent and comparable samples taken five years apart. Nonetheless, the problems of self-report remain.

The Kantner and Zelnik survey   In 1971, John Kantner and Melvin Zelnik conducted a study in which a national probability sample of the 15- to 19-year-old female population of the United States was interviewed. A total of 4611 young women were interviewed. The study provides particularly good information on premarital sexual behavior among females and on contraceptive use among young unmarried women (Kantner and Zelnik, 1972, 1973). It provides excellent data on differences between blacks and whites in sexual behavior, since 1479 blacks were interviewed. It also provides interesting analyses of how various social factors, such as social class and religion, are related to varying patterns of sexual behavior. Kantner and Zelnik conducted a parallel survey in 1976, and comparison of the results of the two studies provides good information on increases in premarital sex and contraceptive use in the 1970s (Zelnik and Kantner, 1977).

The major virtue of these studies is that the sampling was excellent. The studies had some limitations, however. Since only young women between the ages of 15 and 19 were interviewed, it was impossible to reach any conclusions about male-female differences or about people who are older or younger. This is a particular problem for the data on premarital sex, since many young women do not begin engaging in it before their twenties.

Another limitation is that the studies relied on self-reports. In the 1976 survey, however, Kantner and Zelnik used a new research method, called the *randomized response technique*. Space does not permit a detailed explanation; suffice it to say that it enables the researcher to estimate how accurate people are being in their self-reports. Kantner and Zelnik used this method on one of the most sensitive questions—and therefore the one likeliest to yield inaccurate self-reports—namely, whether the respondent had ever had intercourse. According to self-reports, 42 percent of the women had; the estimate of the true incidence, by use of the randomized response technique, was 44 percent. This result indicates that the self-reports were highly accurate. Perhaps we can, after all, place a good deal of confidence in self-report studies.

STUDIES OF SPECIAL POPULATIONS

In addition to the large-scale studies of the American population discussed above, several studies of special populations have been done. Particularly worthy of mention are Sorensen's study of adolescents and the Weinberg and Williams study of male homosexuals.

Sorensen: Adolescents

R. C. Sorensen conducted a major survey of adolescents and their sexual behavior in 1972; the results were published in a book entitled *Adolescent Sexuality in Contemporary America,* commonly known as the "Sorensen report."

Sampling   Using randomization techniques, Sorensen obtained an initial sample of 2042 households in urban, suburban, and rural areas; 839 adolescents (ages 13 to 19) lived in those households. This initial method of sampling was excellent, and it omitted only those adolescents living in college dormitories and institutions such as reformatories.

Sorensen then required written permission to participate from all parents. He received cooperation from the parents of 60 percent of the adolescents. This left 508 adolescents eligible on the basis of parental consent. Their consent to participate was then requested, and 393 (77 percent) agreed to do so. The adolescents thus showed a high response rate.

In sum, Sorensen tried to strike a balance between getting a good sample and maintaining high ethical standards of informed consent. Nonetheless, the nonresponse rate was high— 53 percent—which limits the precision of the statistics in the study.

The questionnaire   All the adolescents filled out a self-administered questionnaire with a researcher present; this maximized rapport and the chance for researchers to explain any items that were difficult to understand. The items had been developed on the basis of 200 interviews with adolescents, the purpose being to ensure that the language used in the items was understandable to persons in this age group. In addition, items that might have proved stressful or harmful, such as questions about anal intercourse, were eliminated.

When each questionnaire was completed, it was immediately placed in an envelope and mailed, thus assuring anonymity.

Weinberg and Williams: Male Homosexuals

Under the sponsorship of the Kinsey Institute, sociologists Martin Weinberg and Colin Williams (1974) conducted a large-scale study of male homosexuals in the United States, the Netherlands, and Denmark.

Weinberg and Williams obtained their data using questionnaires. They mailed questionnaires to people on the mailing list of the Mattachine Society of New York and the Mattachine Society of San Francisco (the Mattachine Society is a gay organization). Further, questionnaires were handed out at meetings of the Society for Individual Rights in San Francisco and at private homosexual clubs in Manhattan; they were also distributed to gay bars in San Francisco and Manhattan. A total of 3667 questionnaires were handed out, and the response rate was 38.7 percent; data were obtained for 1057 male homosexuals. Similar methods of questionnaire distribution were used in Copenhagen and Amsterdam.

These techniques do not ensure a random or representative sample of male homosexuals, but it is doubtful whether such a sample could be obtained. The Weinberg and Williams sample consisted mainly of open homosexuals living in big cities with large gay communities. Male homosexuals living in smaller towns and rural areas were underrepresented, as were men who keep their homosexuality hidden. Thus if Weinberg and Williams found their sample of homosexuals to be well adjusted, this may have been simply an artifact of the sampling technique, for they may have sampled only persons who were open about their homosexuality and well adjusted to it.

Weinberg and Williams also did "ethnographies"—descriptions of the social institutions and social interactions of the gay world in San Francisco, New York, Copenhagen, and Amsterdam. They used a participant-observer method (to be discussed later in this chapter) to do this. That is, they attended gay activist meetings and frequented gay clubs and gay bars, making observations and collecting interviews. Thus they were able to provide a good view of the gay world, or at least the gay male world.

This research raises the point that studies of special populations defined by their sexual behavior—such as homosexuals or bisexuals or fetishists—are very difficult to do in any kind of representative fashion. It is almost impossible to identify all the people in the population under study, and therefore it is almost impossible to sample them properly. In contrast, samples of the general population, such as Hunt's and Kinsey's, are more feasible, though not easy.

LABORATORY STUDIES USING DIRECT OBSERVATIONS OF SEXUAL BEHAVIOR

The numerous problems associated with using self-reports of sexual behavior in scientific research have been discussed. The major alternative to using self-reports is to make direct observations of sexual behavior in the laboratory. These direct observations overcome the major problems of self-reports: purposeful distortion, inaccurate memory, and inability of subjects to estimate correctly or describe certain aspects of their behavior. The outstanding example of this approach is Masters and Johnson's work on the physiology of sexual response.

Masters and Johnson: The Physiology of Sexual Response

William Masters began his research on the physiology of sexual response in 1954 (R. Brecher and Brecher, 1966). No one had ever studied human sexual behavior in the laboratory before. Thus Masters had to develop all the necessary research techniques from scratch. He began by interviewing 118 female prostitutes (as well as 27 male prostitutes working for a homosexual clientele). They gave him important preliminary data in which they "described many methods for elevating and controlling sexual tensions and demonstrated innumerable variations in stimulative techniques," some of which were useful in the later program of therapy for sexual dysfunction.

Meanwhile, Masters began setting up his laboratory and equipping it with the necessary instruments: an electrocardiograph to measure changes in heart rate over the sexual cycle, an electromyograph to measure muscular contractions in the body during sexual response, and a pH meter to measure the acidity of the vagina during the various stages of sexual response.

The prostitutes helped with the initial "dry runs" of the apparatus. But Masters soon realized that they would not be satisfactory subjects for his research. In particular, they had a variety of pathological conditions in their pelvic organs, making them unsuitable for research on normal sexual response.

Sampling Masters made a major breakthrough when he decided that it was possible to recruit normal subjects from the general population and have them engage in sexual behavior in the laboratory, where their behavior and physiological responses could be carefully observed, measured, and recorded. This approach had never been used before, as even the daring Kinsey had settled for subjects' verbal reports of their behavior.

Most of the subjects were obtained from the local community simply by word of mouth. Masters let it be known in the medical school and university community that he needed volunteer subjects for laboratory studies of human sexual response. Some subjects volunteered because of their belief in the importance of the research, and others were referred by their own physicians. Some, of course, came simply out of curiosity or because they were exhibitionists; they were weeded out in the initial interviews. Subjects were paid for their hours in the laboratory, as is typical in medical research, and so

many young medical students and graduate students participated simply because it was a way to earn money. Some of the subjects were women who had been patients of Dr. Masters. When they heard he needed volunteers, they wanted to help, and they brought their husbands along as well.

Initially, all subjects were given detailed interviews by the Masters and Johnson team. Subjects who had histories of emotional problems or who seemed uncomfortable with the topic of sex either failed to come back after this interview or were eliminated even if they were willing to proceed. Subjects were also assured that the anonymity and confidentiality of their participation would be protected carefully.

In all, 694 people participated in the laboratory studies reported in *Human Sexual Response*. The men ranged in age from 21 to 89, while the women ranged from 18 to 78. A total of 276 married couples participated, as well as 106 women and 36 men who were unmarried when they entered the research program. The unmarried subjects were helpful mainly in the studies that did not require sexual intercourse, for example, studies of the ejaculatory mechanism in males and of the way contraceptives behave in the vagina.

Certainly the group of people Masters and Johnson studied were not a random sample of the population of the United States. In fact, one might imagine that people who would agree to participate in such research would be rather unusual. The data indicate that they were more educated than the general population, and the sample was mostly white, with only a few blacks participating. Probably paying the subjects helped, since this attracted some participants who simply needed the money. The sample omitted two notable types of people: those who are not sexually experienced or do not respond to sexual stimulation and those who are unwilling to have their sexual behavior studied in the laboratory. Strictly speaking, the results Masters and Johnson obtained might not generalize to such people.

But just exactly how critical is this sampling problem to the validity of the research? Masters and Johnson were not particularly concerned about sampling because of their assumption that the processes they were studying are normative; that is, they work in essentially the same way in all people. This assumption is commonly made in medical research. For example, a researcher who is studying the digestive process typically does not worry that the sample is composed of all medical students, since the assumption is that digestion works the same in all human beings. If this assumption is also true for the physiology of sexual response, then all people respond similarly, and it does not matter that the sample is not random. Whether this assumption is correct remains to be seen, but it does not appear to be too unreasonable. The sampling problem, however, does mean that Masters and Johnson cannot make statistical conclusions on the basis of their research; for example, they cannot say that X percent of all women have multiple orgasms. Any percentages they calculate would be specific to their subjects and might not generalize to the rest of the population.

In defense of their sampling techniques, even if they had identified an initial probability sample, they would still almost surely have had a very high refusal rate, probably higher than in survey research, and the probability sample would have been ruined. At present, this seems to be an unsolvable problem in this type of research.

Data collection techniques After they were accepted for the project, subjects then proceeded to the laboratory phase of the study. First, they had a "practice session," in which they had sex in the laboratory in complete privacy, with no data being recorded and with no re-

searchers present. The purpose of this was to allow the subjects to become comfortable with engaging in sexual behavior in a laboratory setting. Interestingly, males had a higher "failure rate" (inability to have orgasm) under these conditions than females did.

The physical responses of the subjects were then recorded during sexual intercourse, masturbation, and "artificial coition." Masters and Johnson made an important technical advance with the development of the artificial coition technique. It involves the woman stimulating herself with an artificial penis. The artificial penis is constructed of clear plastic; it is powered by an electric motor, and the woman can adjust the depth and frequency of the thrust. There is a light and a recording apparatus inside the artificial penis, and thus motion picture records can be made of the changes occurring inside the vagina. The development of this apparatus made possible observations of female sexual response that could not have been made otherwise.

Measures such as these avoid problems of distortion possible in self-reports. They also answer much different questions. That is, it would be impossible from such measures to tell whether the person had had any homosexual experiences or how frequently he or she masturbated. Instead, they measure how the body responds to sexual stimulation, with a kind of accuracy and detail that would be impossible to obtain through self-reports.

Two problems also deserve mention. One has to do with the problems of laboratory studies: Do people respond the same sexually in the laboratory as they do in the privacy of their own homes? Another problem is that the Masters and Johnson results have never been replicated, that is, independently confirmed by other investigators. Although most scientists believe that Masters and Johnson's results are correct, the scientific method nonetheless demands that they be independently confirmed. It is hoped that this will be done soon.

Ethics Masters and Johnson have been concerned with the ethical implications of their research. They were careful to use the principle of informed consent. Potential subjects were given detailed explanations of the kinds of things they would be required to do in the research, and they were given ample opportunity at all stages to withdraw from the research if they so desired. Further, Masters and Johnson eliminated from the subject pool people who appeared too anxious or distressed during the preliminary interviews.

It is also possible that participating in the research itself might have been harmful in some way to the subjects, perhaps damaging their future ability to respond sexually. Masters and Johnson have been particularly concerned with the long-term effects on their subjects of participating in the research. Accordingly, they make follow-up contacts with the subjects at five-year intervals. In no case has a subject reported developing a sexual dysfunction (for example, impotence). In fact, many of the couples report specific ways in which participating in the research has enriched their marriages. Thus the available data seem to indicate that such research does not harm the subjects and may in some ways benefit them (not to mention the benefit to society that results from gaining information in such an important area).

In sum, direct observations of sexual behavior of the type done by Masters and Johnson have some distinct advantages but also some disadvantages, compared with survey-type research. The research avoids the problems of self-reports and is capable of answering much more detailed physiological questions than self-reports could. But the research is costly and time-consuming, making large samples impossible; further, a high refusal rate is probably inevitable, and thus probability samples are impossible.

PARTICIPANT-OBSERVER STUDIES

A common research method, used by anthropologists and sociologists, is the participant-observer technique. In this type of research, the scientist actually becomes a part of the community to be studied, and she or he makes observations from inside the community. In the study of sexual behavior, the researcher may be able to get direct observations of sexual behavior combined with interview data.

Examples of this type of research are studies of sexual behavior in other cultures, such as those done in Mangaia and Inis Beag, which were discussed in Chapter 1. Two other examples are Laud Humphreys's study of the tearoom trade and Bartell's study of swinging.

Humphreys: The Tearoom Trade

Sociologist Laud Humphreys did a participant-observer study of impersonal homosexual sex in public places such as restrooms. The study is discussed in detail in a Focus in Chapter 14. Briefly, Humphreys acted as a lookout while men engaged in homosexual acts in public rest rooms; his job was to sound a warning if police or other intruders approached. This permitted Humphreys to make direct observations of the sexual behavior. He also got the license-plate numbers of the men involved, traced them, and later interviewed them in their homes under the pretext of taking a routine survey.

Humphreys got a wealth of information from the study, but in so doing he violated most of the ethical principles of behavioral research. He had no informed consent from his subjects; they were never even aware of the fact that they were subjects in research, much less of the nature of the research. Thus this study has been quite controversial.

Bartell: Swinging

Anthropologist Gilbert Bartell did a participant-observer study of swinging (a married couple having sex with another person or another couple). He and his wife contacted swinging couples by responding to ads that swingers had placed in newspapers. They took the role of "baby swingers"—a couple who is swinging for the first time—but they also state that they did not misrepresent themselves and informed all subjects that they were anthropologists interested in knowing more about swinging. In addition, they attended a large number of swingers' parties and large-scale group sexual activities and made observations in that context.

Sampling is often a problem in studies of special groups such as this one, since it is difficult to get any kind of a random sample of people who engage in a particular kind of sexual behavior. In this particular case the problem was made somewhat less difficult because many such contacts are made through newspaper ads, to which the researchers could respond. This method permitted studying only current swingers; it did not allow sampling of people who had engaged in swinging but had stopped for one reason or another (Kirby, 1977). There is also some question as to how honest the respondents were, since swingers are doing something that they take great pains to hide; in fact, Bartell cites specific examples of distortion in reports of information on such things as age and interests.

Ethically, it was easy to preserve anonymity since swingers go to great lengths to preserve their own anonymity; even with one another, they use first names only. Bartell obtained some kind of informed consent since he told his subjects that he was doing research; in other, similar studies, however, researchers have posed as swingers, have not divulged the fact that data were being collected, and therefore have seriously misled their subjects.

EXPERIMENTAL SEX RESEARCH

All the studies discussed so far had one thing in common: they all were studies of people's sexual behavior as it occurs naturally, conducted by means of either self-reports or direct observations. Data obtained from such studies are *correlational* in nature; that is, at best they can tell us that certain factors are related. They cannot tell us what *causes* various aspects of sexual behavior.

As an example, Kinsey found that women who masturbated to orgasm before marriage were more likely to have a high consistency of orgasm in marriage than women who did not. From this it would be tempting to conclude that practice in masturbating to orgasm causes women to have more orgasms in heterosexual sex. Unfortunately, this is not a legitimate conclusion to draw from the data, since many other factors might also explain the results. For example, it could be that some women have a higher sex drive than others; this high sex drive causes them to masturbate and also to have orgasms in heterosexual sex. Therefore, the most we can conclude is that masturbation experience is related to (or correlated with) orgasm consistency in marital sex.

An alternative method in behavioral research that allows us to determine the causes of various aspects of behavior is the *experiment*. According to the technical definition of "experiment," one factor must be manipulated while all other factors are held constant. Thus any differences among the groups of people who received different treatments on that one factor can be said to be caused by that factor. For obvious reasons, most experimental research is conducted in the laboratory.

One example of experimental sex research

is Julia Heiman's study of male and female responses to erotic materials, which is discussed in Chapter 13. As an example of experimental sex research here, let us consider a study of male-female differences in response to reading erotic stories, conducted by German researchers Gunter Schmidt, Volkmar Sigusch, and Siegrid Schäfer at the University of Hamburg (1973). Their subjects were 120 male and 120 female university students who volunteered to participate in an experiment involving "psychosexual stimulation." All the subjects read erotic stories that included explicit descriptions of oral-genital sex, coitus, and orgasm. Half of the subjects, however, read stories in which the characters were very affectionate with each other, while the other half read stories that were comparable except that the affection component was missing. Immediately after reading a story, subjects rated how arousing it had been on a scale from 1 to 9 (note that this was a self-report technique). Subjects also reported their physiological arousal (erection, vaginal lubrication, and so on). Thus the study could assess experimentally whether stories in which the characters were affectionate with each other were more arousing than those in which they were not. It could also assess whether males and females differed in their responses. Subjects also filled out a form 24 hours after the experiment in which they reported their actual sexual activity during those 24 hours.

The stories with the affection component were rated as being significantly more arousing than the stories without it. Thus we can conclude (at least if we believe the subjects' self-reports) that affection between characters in an erotic story *causes* it to be somewhat more arousing than it would be otherwise.

Interestingly, it was women who reported an increase in coital activity in the 24 hours after reading the story, as compared with the 24 hours before reading it. This before-and-after design is a bit weak. It would have been better if

half the subjects had read erotic stories and half had read stories with no sexual content; then we could be surer that reading the erotic story had actually caused an increase in sexual activity.

Experimental sex research permits us to make much more powerful statements about the causes of various kinds of sexual phenomena. For example, the study just discussed provides much more convincing evidence that affection in an erotic story makes it arousing than would be provided by a survey in which people were asked, "Do you find erotic stories more arousing when the characters show affection to each other or when they do not?" Laboratory studies avoid the problems of memory in much of the self-report data in survey research, but much of the experimental research, including the study described here, still does rely on self-reports. Experimental sex research is time-consuming and costly, and it can generally be done only on very restricted samples of subjects. Further, it cannot address some of the most interesting, but most complex, questions in the field of sexual behavior, such as what factors cause people to develop heterosexual or homosexual preferences.

SOME STATISTICAL CONCEPTS

It was Kinsey who pioneered the approach of using statistics to describe people's sexual behavior, and this approach is now quite common. Therefore, before you can understand the reports of sex research, you must understand some basic statistical concepts.

Average

Suppose we get data from a sample of married couples on how many times per week they have sexual intercourse. How can we summarize the data? One way to do this is to compute some average value for all the subjects; this will tell us

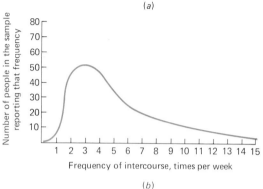

FIGURE 9.3
Two hypothetical graphs of the frequency of intercourse for married couples in a sample. In both, the average frequency is about three times per week, but in (a) there is little variability (almost everyone has a frequency between two and four times per week), while in (b) there is great variability (the frequency ranges from 0 to 15 or 20 times per week). For most sexual behavior, the graph looks like (b); there is great variability.

Variability

In addition to having an indication of the average for the sample of subjects, it is also interesting to know how much variability there was from one subject to the next in the numbers reported. That is, it is one thing to say that the average married couple in a sample had intercourse three times per week, with a range in the sample from two to four times per week, and it is quite another thing to say that the average was three times per week, with a range from 0 to 15 times per week. In both cases the mean is the same, but in the first there is little variability, and in the second there is a great deal of variability. These two alternatives are shown graphically in Figure 9.3. There is great variability in virtually all kinds of sexual behavior.

Average versus Normal

It is interesting and informative to report the average frequency of a particular sexual behavior, but this also introduces the danger that people will confuse "average" with "normal." That is, there is a tendency, when reading a statistic like "The average person has intercourse twice per week," to think of one's own sexual behavior, compare it with that average, and then conclude that one is abnormal if one differs much from the average. If you read that statistic and your frequency of intercourse is only once a week, you may begin to worry that you are undersexed or that you are not getting as much as you should. If you are having intercourse seven times per week, you might begin worrying that you are oversexed or that you are wearing out your sex organs. Such conclusions are a mistake, first because they can make you miserable, and second because there is so much variability in sexual behavior that any behavior (or frequency or length of time) within a wide range is perfectly normal.

Another version of this phenomenon is

how often, on the average, these people have intercourse. In sex research, the number that is usually calculated is either the mean or the median; both of these give us an indication of approximately where the average value for that group of subjects is. The *mean* is simply the average of the scores of all the subjects. The *median* is the score that splits the sample in half, with half of the subjects falling below that score and half falling above.

called "medical students' disease." As they read about each new disease, medical students tend to begin seeing the symptoms in themselves and to decide that they are afflicted with it. The best way to avoid such problems is not to take the statistics you read in this book too personally.

Incidence versus Frequency

In sex statistics, the terms "incidence" and "frequency" are often used. *Incidence* refers to the percentage of people who have engaged in a certain behavior. *Frequency* refers to how often people do something. Thus we might say that the incidence of masturbation among males is 95 percent (95 percent of all males masturbate at least once in their lives), while the average frequency of masturbation in males between the ages of 16 and 20 is about once per week.

A closely related concept is that of cumulative incidence (or accumulative incidence). If we consider a sexual behavior according to the age at which each person in the sample first engages in it, the *cumulative incidence* refers to the percentage of people who have engaged in that behavior before a certain age. Thus the cumulative incidence of masturbation in males might be 10 percent by age 11, 25 percent by age 12, 80 percent by age 15, and 95 percent by age 20. Graphs of cumulative incidence always begin in the lower left-hand corner and move toward the upper right-hand corner. An example of a cumulative-incidence curve is shown in Figure 9.4.

SUMMARY

This chapter reviewed the major methods that have been used in sex research and the problems and merits associated with each; the goal was to help readers better evaluate the sex

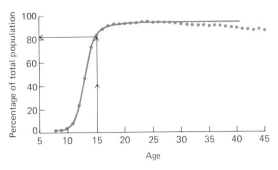

FIGURE 9.4

A cumulative-incidence curve for masturbation in males. From the graph, you can read off the percentage of males who report having masturbated by a given age. For example, about 82 percent have masturbated to orgasm by age 15. [*From Alfred C. Kinsey, Wardell B. Pomeroy, and Clyde E. Martin. Sexual behavior in the human male. Philadelphia: Saunders, 1948, p. 502. (The Institute for Sex Research.)*]

research that has been done and to aid them in developing skills for understanding and evaluating the sex research that will be done in the future.

Ideally, sex research should employ random sampling or probability sampling techniques; this is generally not possible because many persons refuse to participate in sex research.

Large-scale surveys of sexual behavior generally rely on subjects' self-reports, which may be inaccurate because of purposeful distortion, problems of memory, or inability to estimate some of the information requested. Direct observations of sexual behavior avoid these problems, but they lead to an even more restricted sample of subjects. They also answer somewhat different questions from those answered by surveys.

In all behavioral research, the ethical principles of informed consent and protection from harm must be observed, although historically some sex researchers have not done this.

Two major sex surveys are Kinsey's large-scale interview study of the sexual behavior of Americans, done during the 1940s, and a similar study done by Morton Hunt in 1972. Two other large surveys have been done, one through *Redbook* magazine and the other through *Psychology Today*; the samples in these studies, however, were so restricted that we cannot draw any general conclusions from them. Two surveys have used probability samples: the Westoff study of married women and the Kantner and Zelnik study of young unmarried women.

Studies of special populations include Sorensen's study of adolescents and the Weinberg and Williams study of male homosexuals.

In participant-observer studies, the scientist becomes a part of the community to be studied, and he or she uses a combination of direct observations and interviewing. Examples are studies of sexual behavior in other cultures, Humphreys's study of the tearoom trade, and Bartell's study of swinging.

In experimental sex research, the goal is to discover what factors cause various aspects of sexual behavior.

The following statistical terms were introduced: "average," "variability," "incidence," and "frequency."

SEXUALITY AND THE LIFE CYCLE: CHILDHOOD AND ADOLESCENCE

CITED

Adult behavior is more obviously a product of the specifically genital play which is found among children. . . . Our own interviews with children younger than five, and observations made by parents and others . . . indicate that hugging and kissing are usual in the activity of the very young child, and that self manipulation of genitalia, the exhibition of genitalia, the exploration of the genitalia of other children . . . occur in the two- to five-year olds more frequently than older persons ordinarily remember from their own histories. Much of this earliest sex play appears to be purely exploratory, animated by curiosity. . . . Nevertheless, at a very early age the child learns that there are social values attached to these activities, and his emotional excitation while engaged in such play must involve reactions to the mysterious, to the forbidden, and to the socially dangerous performance, as often as it involves true erotic response.*

top for a moment and think of the first sexual experience you ever had. Some of you will think of the first time you had sexual intercourse, while others will remember much earlier episodes, like "playing doctor" with the other kids in the neighborhood. Now think of the kind of sex life you had, or expect to have, in your early twenties. Finally, imagine yourself at 65 and think of the kinds of sexual behavior you will be engaging in then.

In recent years, scientists have begun thinking of human development as a process that occurs throughout the lifespan. This represents a departure from the Freudian heritage, in which the crucial aspects of development were all thought to occur in childhood. This chapter and Chapter 11 are based on the newer "lifespan" or "life-cycle" approach to understanding the development of our sexual behavior throughout the course of our lives. The things

you were asked to remember and imagine about your own sexual functioning at the beginning of this chapter will give you an idea of the sweep of this development.

DATA SOURCES

What kind of scientific data are available on the sexual behavior of people at various times in their lives? Two of the basic sources we have are the Kinsey reports (Kinsey et al., 1948, 1953) and the Hunt study (1974). Comparing the results of Kinsey's surveys and Hunt's survey can give us an idea of how much the sexual behavior of young people has changed in the last several decades. The scientific techniques used by Kinsey and Hunt were discussed and evaluated in Chapter 9; since there are limitations to their studies, your evaluation of them may affect how much you are willing to accept the data presented in this chapter and in Chapter 11.

In both the Kinsey studies and the Hunt study, the adult subjects were questioned about their childhood sexual behavior, and their re-

*Source: Alfred C. Kinsey, Wardell B. Pomeroy, and Clyde E. Martin. *Sexual behavior in the human male.* Philadelphia: Saunders, 1948, pp. 163–164.

sponses form some of the data to be discussed in this chapter. These responses may be even more problematic than some of the other kinds of data from those studies, though. For example, a 50 or 60-year-old man is asked to report on his sexual behavior at age 10. How accurately will he remember things that happened 40 or 50 years ago? Surely there will be some forgetting. Thus the data on childhood sexual behavior may be subject to errors that result from being asked to recall things that happened a very long time ago.

An alternative would be to interview children about their sexual behavior or perhaps even to observe their sexual behavior. Few researchers have done either. The reasons are obvious; such a study would be exceptionally difficult and would involve serious ethical problems. Might a child be harmed by being interviewed about his or her sexual behavior? Could a child truly give informed consent to participate in such a study?

In a few studies children have been questioned directly about their sexual behavior. Kinsey interviewed 432 children, aged 4 to 14, and the results of the study were published after his death by Elias and Gebhard (1969). Several studies of adolescent sexual behavior have also been done. Particularly notable is the survey done by Sorensen (1973), popularly known as the "Sorensen report," and the study by Kantner and Zelnik of young unmarried women (1972, 1973). Schoof-Tams and her colleagues (1976) administered a questionnaire to 91 percent of the students between the ages of 11 and 16 in two schools in West Germany. Questions focused particularly on sexual attitudes and morality, but a few questions on sexual behavior were also included. Broderick (1966b) administered a questionnaire dealing mainly with the romantic and social aspects of sex to "virtually every" child in the seventh through the twelfth grades in an upper-middle-class suburb in

Pennsylvania. Sociological studies of premarital sexual behavior have been done by Robert Bell (1966) and by Ira Reiss (1967).

These few studies of child and adolescent sexual behavior have all been surveys, and they have used either questionnaires or interviews. No one has made systematic, direct observations of children's sexual behavior.

INFANCY (0 to 2 YEARS)

A century ago it was thought that sexuality was something that magically appeared at puberty. Historically, we owe the whole notion that children—in fact, infants—have sexual urges and engage in sexual behavior to Sigmund Freud.

The capacity of the human body to show a sexual response seems to be present from birth. Male infants, for example, get erections. Indeed, boy babies are sometimes born with erections. In a study of nine male babies aged 3 to 20 weeks, erection was observed at least once daily in seven of the nine (Halversen, 1940). In female infants there is no such clear indicator of sexual response as erection. However, because the physiology of sexual response is so similar in males and females, it seems reasonable to assume that female infants show sexual responses similar to those of male infants.

Masturbation

Infants have been observed masturbating, that is, fondling their own genitals. There is some question as to how conscious they are of what they are doing, but at the least they seem to be engaging in some pleasurable, sexual self-stimulation. Toward the end of infancy, erotic feelings become more definitely centered in the genitals, and periods of definite sex play can be observed (Ribble, 1955, p. 26). Ford and Beach (1951), on the basis of their survey of sexual

FIGURE 10.1

Infant masturbation. *[Tana Hoban.]*

behavior in other cultures, noted that, if permitted, most boys and girls will progress from absentminded fingering of their genitals to systematic masturbation by ages 6 to 8. In fact, in some cultures adults fondle infants' genitals to keep them quiet, a remarkably effective pacifier.

Orgasms from masturbation are possible even at this early age, although before puberty boys are not capable of ejaculation. Kinsey reported that 32 percent of boys under 1 year of age were able to have orgasms. He also reported on 23 girls, 3 years old and younger, who had orgasms as a result of masturbation (Kinsey et al., 1948, 1953).

Masturbation is a normal, natural form of sexual expression in infancy. It is definitely not a sign of pathology, as some previous generations believed. Indeed, in one study comparing infants that had optimal relationships with their mothers and infants that had problematic relationships with their mothers, it was the infants with the optimal maternal relationships who were more likely to masturbate (Spitz, 1949).

Infant-Infant Sexual Encounters

Infants and young children are very self-centered (what the psychologist Jean Piaget calls *egocentric*). Even when they seem to be playing with another child, they may simply be playing alongside the other child, actually in a world all their own. Their sexual development parallels the development of their other behaviors. Thus their earliest sex is typically one-person sex—masturbation. Not until later do they develop social, two-person sex, either heterosexual or homosexual.

Nonetheless, particularly in later infancy, there may be some infant-infant encounters, either affectionate or sexual.

Nongenital Sensual Experiences

Many of the sensual experiences that infants and young children have are diffuse and not easily classified as masturbation or as heterosexual or homosexual activity. For example, as Freud noted, infants delight in putting things in their mouths. Thus sucking at the mother's breast, or even sucking on his or her own fingers, may be a sensuous experience for the infant.

Being cuddled or rocked can be a warm, sensuous experience. Indeed, the infant's experiences in such early initimate encounters might influence her or his reactions to intimacy and cuddling in adulthood. It seems that some infants are cuddlers and some are noncuddlers (Schaffer and Emerson, 1964). Cuddlers enjoy physical contact. Noncuddlers, unlike cuddlers, show displeasure and restlessness when they are handled or held. As soon as they are old enough to do so, they show resistance to such situations or crawl or walk away from them. Cuddling and noncuddling seem to be basically different personality patterns. It would be interesting to know whether these patterns remain consistent into adulthood.

The quality of the relationship with the parents at this age can be very important to the child's capacity for later sexual and emotional relationships. In psychological terms, an *attachment* forms early between the infant and the mother or other care giver. Later, attachments form to other familiar people. These are the individual's earliest experiences with love and emotional attachment.

Knowing about
Boy-Girl Differences

By age 2 or $2^1/_2$, children know what gender they are. They know that they are like the parent of the same gender and different from the parent of the opposite gender and from other children of the opposite gender. At first, infants think that the difference between girls and boys is a matter of clothes or haircuts. But by age $2^1/_2$ there may be at least some vague awareness of differences in the genital region and differences in positions during urination (Martinson, 1973).

EARLY CHILDHOOD
(3 to 7 YEARS)

Between the ages of 3 and 7, there is a marked increase in sexual interest and activity, just as there is an increase in activity and interest in general.

Masturbation

Children increasingly gain experience with masturbation during childhood, although certainly not all children masturbate during this period. On the basis of interviews with boys, one study found that 5 percent of those 6 years old or younger had masturbated, as had 10 percent of the 7-year-olds (Ramsey, 1943b, p. 224).

Children also learn during this period that masturbation is something that one does in private.

Heterosexual Behavior

By the age of 4 or 5, children's sexuality has become more social. There is some mild heterosexual play. Boys and girls may hug each other or hold hands, in imitation of adults. "Playing doctor" can be a popular game at this age. It generally involves no more than exhibiting one's own genitals, looking at those of others, and perhaps engaging in a little fondling or touching.

> When I was six years old, I consciously experienced my first erection with a neighborhood girl of the same age. My curiosity increased when I saw only a small glimpse of her genital area when we played "doctor" and my desire to know more about the female sex increased tremendously. One day after school, the girl came over to my house. We proceeded up to my bedroom where I told her, "You can see me if I can see you." After she agreed, we both pulled down our pants. She asked me what my penis was. I told her that it was my "weiner," and that she didn't have one—only boys had "weiners." I then proceeded to touch my "weiner" to her "doop" (rear). This contact lasted for only a short time, yet I noticed for the first time that my penis was stiff. I had previously seen my friend's penis become erect as we played "doctor," but my penis becoming stiff was something I had never consciously experienced before. (Martinson, 1973, p. 31)

By about the age of 5, children have formed a concept of marriage—or at least of its nongenital aspects. They know that a member

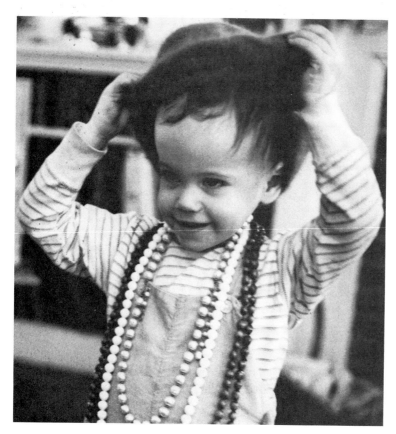

FIGURE 10.2
Children often imitate adult roles.
*[Hanna W. Schrieber/Rapho/
Photo Researchers, Inc.]*

of the opposite gender is the appropriate marriage partner, and they are committed to marrying when they get older (Broderick, 1966). They practice marriage roles as they "play house."

Homosexual Behavior

During late childhood and preadolescence, sexual play with members of one's own gender may be more common than sexual play with members of the opposite gender (Martinson, 1973). Generally the activity involves no more than handling the other's genitals (Broderick, 1966a). One girl recalled:

> I encountered a sexual experience that was confusing at kindergarten age. . . . Some afternoons we would meet and lock ourselves in a bedroom and take our pants off. We took turns lying on the bed and put pennies, marbles, etc. between our labia. . . . As the ritual became old hat, it passed out of existence. (Martinson, 1973, p. 39)

Sex Knowledge and Interests

At age 3 or 4, children begin to have some notion that there are genital differences between males and females, but their ideas are very vague. Not until they are 5 or 6 or 7 do they have a clear idea of what the true differences are (Martinson, 1973). Children generally react to their discovery of genital differences calmly, though of course there are exceptions.

At age 3, children are very interested in different postures for urinating. Girls attempt to urinate while standing. Children are also very affectionate at this age. They enjoy hugging and kissing their parents and may even propose marriage to the parent of the opposite gender (Martinson, 1973).

At age 4, children are particularly interested in bathrooms and elimination. Games of "show" are also common at this age.

Games of show become less common at age 5, as children become more modest. Generally children have well-developed principles of modesty and privacy by age 6 or 7. Children at this age are also becoming aware of the social restrictions on sexual expression. A woman recalled:

When I was six years old I climbed up on the bathroom sink and looked at myself naked in the mirror. All of a sudden I realized I had three different holes. I was very excited about my discovery and ran down to the dinner table and announced it to everyone, "I have three holes!" Silence. "What are they for?" I asked. Silence even heavier than before. I sensed how uncomfortable everyone was and answered for myself. "I guess one is for pee-pee, the other for doo-doo and the third for ca-ca." A sigh of relief; no one had to answer my question. But I got the message—I wasn't supposed to ask "such" questions, though I didn't fully realize what "such" was about at that time. (Boston Women's Health Book Collective, 1976, p. 40)

It is important to remember that children's sex play at this age is motivated largely by curiosity and is part of the general learning experiences of childhood. One man illustrated this well as he recalled:

As a child I experienced several incidents of homosexual exhibitions, many heterosexual exhibitions, and several instances of heterosexual play. This exploratory stage was experienced chiefly between the ages of four to seven. A

secluded spot would be secured for purposes of observing and touching the opposite sex's genitals. This happened repeatedly with two girls, one older and one younger. Initiation for each experience seemed to be about fifty percent my effort. . . . At the age of six or seven my friend (a boy) and I had a great curiosity for exploring the anus. It almost seemed *more like scientific research.* (Martinson, 1973, p. 40, italics added)

PREADOLESCENCE (8 to 12 YEARS)

Preadolescence is a period of transition between the years of childhood and the years of puberty and adolescence.

Freud used the term "latency" to refer to the preadolescent period following the resolution of the Oedipus complex. He believed that the sexual urges go "underground" during latency and are not expressed. The evidence indicates, however, that there is no latency stage and that children's interest in, and expression of, sexuality remain lively throughout this period, perhaps more lively than their parents are willing to believe. For many, "sexual awakening" does not occur until the teens, but for others, it is a very real and poignant part of preadolescence (Martinson, 1973).

At around age 9 or 10, the first bodily changes of puberty begin: the formation of breast buds in girls and the growth of pubic hair. An increased self-consciousness about the body develops, to the point where the child may feel uncomfortable about being seen nude by the parent of the opposite gender. All this marks the transition to adolescence.

Masturbation

During preadolescence, more and more children gain experience with masturbation. Of the women in the Kinsey study, 8 percent recalled masturbating to orgasm by age 10, and 12 percent said they had done so by age 12.[1] The comparable figures for males are 2 percent by age 10 and 21 percent by age 12 (Kinsey et al., 1948, 1953). These data, as well as those on adolescence, indicate that boys generally start masturbating earlier than girls do.

Interestingly, boys and girls learn about masturbation in different ways. Typically boys are told about it by their peers, they see their peers doing it, or they read about it; girls, on the other hand, most frequently learn about masturbation through accidental self-discovery (Kinsey et al., 1953). One man recalled:

> An older cousin of mine took two of us out to the garage and did it in front of us. I remember thinking that it seemed a very strange thing to do, and that people who were upright wouldn't do it, but it left a powerful impression on me. A couple of years later, when I began to get erections, I wanted to do it, and felt I shouldn't, but I remembered how he had looked when he was doing it, and the memory tempted me strongly. I worried, and held back, and fought it, but finally I gave in. The worry didn't stop me, and doing it didn't stop my worrying. (Hunt, 1974, p. 79)

The more recent data collected by Hunt suggest that children begin masturbating at ear-

[1]These are cumulative-incidence figures, to use the terminology introduced in Chap. 9.

lier ages now than they did in Kinsey's time and that this change is particularly marked among girls. A comparison of the Kinsey and Hunt data, as well as data from two other studies, is given in Table 10.1. Notice that about twice as many girls report having masturbated to orgasm by age 13 in the recent studies than in the Kinsey study, done a generation ago. Boys still masturbate earlier, on the average, but the gap has closed somewhat.

Heterosexual Behavior

There is generally little heterosexual behavior during the preadolescent period, mainly because of the social division of males and females into separate groups, a point to be discussed in more detail in the following section.

However, children commonly hear about sexual intercourse for the first time during this period. Their reactions to this new information are an amusing combination of shock and disbelief—particularly disbelief that their parents would do such a thing. A college woman recalled:

> One of my girlfriends told me about sexual intercourse. It was one of the biggest shocks of my life. She took me aside one day, and I could tell she was in great distress. I thought she was going to tell me about menstruation, so I said that I already knew, and she said, "No, this is

TABLE 10.1

COMPARATIVE DATA FROM DIFFERENT STUDIES ON THE AGE AT WHICH CHILDREN BEGIN TO MASTURBATE
Note that children today, especially girls, begin masturbating at an earlier age than children a generation ago.

	Number Who Had Masturbated by Age 13			
	Kinsey (1948, 1953), %	Hunt (1974), %	Arafat Cotton (1974), %*	Ramsey (1943), %†
Males	45	63	49	85
Females	15	33	32	

*Based on a sample of 300 college students in the New York area.
†Based on interviews with boys. The statistic given is the percentage of 13-year-olds who reported having masturbated. It is interesting that the percentage based on direct questioning of boys is so much higher than percentages based on adults' recall.

worse!" Her description went like this: "A guy puts his thing up a girl's hole, and she has a baby." The hole was, to us, the anus, because we did not even know about the vagina and we knew that the urethra was too small. I pictured the act as a single, violent and painful stabbing at the anus by the penis. Somehow, the idea of a baby was forgotten by me. I was horrified and repulsed, and I thought of that awful penis I had seen years ago. At first I insisted that it wasn't true, and my friend said she didn't know for sure, but that's what her cousin told her. But we looked at each other, and we knew it was true. We held each other and cried. We insisted that "my parents would never do that," and "I'll never let anyone do it to me." We were frightened, sickened, and threatened by the idea of some lusty male jabbing at us with his horrid penis. (From a student essay)

Homosexual Behavior

According to one authority, the number of females who have homosexual encounters increases steadily, from about 6 percent at age 5 to 33 percent at adolescence; approximately 60 percent of males engage in homosexual play during preadolescence (Reevy, 1967). In a sample of children aged 4 to 14, 52 percent of the boys and 35 percent of the girls said they had had some homosexual experiences (Elias and Gebhard, 1969).

It is important to understand this homosexual activity as a normal part of the sexual development of children. In preadolescence, children have a social organization that is essentially homosocial. That is, boys play separately from girls, and thus children socialize mainly with members of their own gender. This separation begins at around age 8. According to one study of children's friendship patterns, the segregation reaches a peak at around 10 to 12 years of age. At ages 12 to 13 children are simultaneously the most segregated by gender and the most interested in members of the opposite gender (Broderick, 1966b). Some of the social separation of the genders during preadolescence is actually comical; boys, for example, may have been convinced that girls have "cooties" and that they must be very careful to stay away from them. Given that children are socializing almost exclusively with other members of their own gender, sexual exploring at this age will likely be homosexual in nature.

These homosexual activities generally involve masturbation, exhibitionism, and the fondling of others' genitals. Boys, for example, may engage in a "circle jerk," in which they masturbate in a group.

Girls do not seem so likely to engage in such group homosexual activities, perhaps because the spectacle of them masturbating is not quite so impressive or perhaps because they already sense the greater cultural restrictions on their sexuality and are hesitant to discuss sexual matters with other girls. In any case, as noted above, boys seem to do their sexual exploring with a gang, while girls do it alone.

Dating

There is some anticipation of adolescent dating in the socializing patterns of preadolescents.

Group dating and heterosexual parties emerge first among preadolescents. Boys, particularly, are slow in adjusting to the behavior expected of them, and they may be more likely to roughhouse than to ask a girl to dance.

Kissing games are popular at parties, reaching their peak of popularity among children aged about 10 to 13 (Broderick, 1966b). There may also be some pairing off for "making out," which generally involves no more than kissing at this age. Genital fondling is not common (Martinson, 1973).

The first paired dating generally begins around the age of 12 or 13. It may consist simply of walking to a movie or going bowling together. At age 12, 48 percent of the boys and 57 percent of the girls in one study were dating (Broderick, 1966b). At 13, the figure was 69 percent for both. Typically, though, boys and girls at this age date only a few times a year.

Going steady also starts at this age, although often the activity centers more on symbols, such as an exchange of rings or bracelets, than it does on any real dating (Martinson, 1973).

Sexual Values

Preadolescents tend to be sexually conservative, while adolescents become increasingly liberal (Schoof-Tams et al., 1976). For example, in regard to premarital intercourse, 11-year-olds generally favor abstinence; they see intercourse as proper in marriage. Later in adolescence, the precondition for intercourse will shift to love rather than marriage.

ADOLESCENCE (13 to 19 YEARS)

Latency or no, a surge of sexual interest occurs around puberty and continues through adolescence (which is equated here roughly with the teenage years, ages 13 to 19). This heightened sexuality may be caused by a number of factors, including bodily changes and an awareness of them, rises in levels of sex hormones, and increased cultural emphasis on sex and rehearsal for adult gender roles. We can see evidence of this heightened sexuality particularly in the data on masturbation.

Masturbation

According to the Kinsey data, there is a sharp increase in the incidence of masturbation for boys between the ages of 13 and 15. This is illustrated in Figure 10.3. Note that the curve is steepest between the ages of 13 and 15, indicating that most boys begin masturbating to orgasm during that period. By age 12, 21 percent of the boys in Kinsey's study had masturbated, and by age 15, 82 percent had. Many girls also

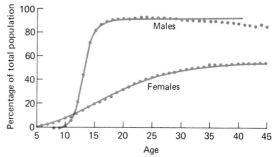

FIGURE 10.3

Cumulative incidence of males and females who have masturbated to orgasm, according to Kinsey's data. *[Adapted from Alfred C. Kinsey, Wardell B. Pomeroy, and Clyde E. Martin. Sexual behavior in the human male. Philadelphia: Saunders, 1948, p. 502, and Alfred C. Kinsey, Wardell B. Pomeroy, Clyde E. Martin, and Paul H. Gebhard. Sexual behavior in the human female. Philadelphia: Saunders, 1953, p. 141. Courtesy of the Institute for Sex Research.]*

begin masturbating at around that age, but note that the curve on the graph is flatter for them, indicating that many girls do not begin masturbating until later. Thus the increase in their masturbation behavior is much more gradual than boys' and continues past adolescence.

As was noted in a previous section, more recent data suggest that children and adolescents begin to masturbate earlier today than they did a generation ago, and thus the Kinsey data probably need to be pushed back about one or two years. However, the general shape of the curves still seems to hold.

One man recalled his adolescent experiences with masturbation and the intense feelings involved as follows:

> When I was fourteen I was like Portnoy—always rushing off to the bathroom when the urge came over me. I did it so much that my dick would get swollen and sore, but even that didn't stop me. By the time I was nineteen I was screwing, but there'd be times when I wouldn't be able to get anything, and I'd go back to jacking off—and then I felt really guilty and ashamed of myself,

like I was a failure, like I had a secret weakness. (Hunt, 1974, p. 95)

Interestingly, the frequency of masturbation among boys decreases during periods when they are having sexual intercourse; among girls, however, this situation is accompanied by an increased frequency of masturbation (Sorensen, 1973).

Attitudes toward masturbation Attitudes toward masturbation have undergone a dramatic change in this century. As a result, adolescents are now given much different information about masturbation, and this may affect both their behavior and their feelings about masturbation.

For example, a popular handbook, *What a Boy Should Know*, written in 1913 by two doctors, advised its readers:

> Whenever unnatural emissions are produced . . . the body becomes "slack." A boy will not feel so vigorous and springy; he will be more easily tired. . . . He will probably look pale and pasty, and he is lucky if he escapes indigestion and getting his bowels confined, both of which will probably give him spots and pimples on his face. . . .
> The results on the mind are the more severe and more easily recognized. . . . A boy who practices this habit can never be the best that Nature intended him to be. His wits are not so sharp. His memory is not so good. His power of fixing his attention on whatever he is doing is lessened. . . . A boy like this is a poor thing to look at. . . .
> . . . The effect of self-abuse on a boy's character always tends to weaken it, and in fact, to make him untrustworthy, unreliable, untruthful, and probably even dishonest. (Schofield and Vaughan-Jackson, 1913, pp. 30–42)

Masturbation, in short, was believed to cause everything from warts to insanity.

Attitudes toward masturbation are now considerably more positive, and few people would now subscribe to notions like those expressed above. Currently only about 15 percent of young people believe that masturbation is wrong (Hunt, 1974, p. 74). Indeed, masturbation is now recommended as a remedy in sex therapy. As psychologist Thomas Szasz said, the shift in attitudes toward masturbation has been so great that in a generation it has changed from a disease to a form of therapy.

While approval of masturbation is now explicit, people can still have mixed feelings about it. An example of a lingering negative attitude is that of the man quoted above, who likened his adolescent masturbation to Portnoy's, accompanied as it was by feelings of guilt and shame. Among the adolescents interviewed by Sorensen (1973), few felt guilty about masturbation, but many felt defensive or embarrassed about it.

Homosexual Behavior

According to the Kinsey data, 3 percent of adolescent girls and 22 percent of adolescent boys have at least one homosexual experience resulting in orgasm. In many cases the person has only one or a few homosexual experiences, partly out of curiosity, and the behavior is discontinued. Such adolescent homosexual behavior does not seem to be predictive of adult homosexual preferences.

If the definition of "homosexual behavior" is expanded to include feelings of arousal in response to a person of one's own gender, the percentages are higher. About 12 percent of females experience such arousal during adolescence (Kinsey et al., 1953, p. 493).

Currently, about 11 percent of adolescent males and 6 percent of adolescent females report having had homosexual experiences, and 25 percent say they have been approached for a homosexual experience. Of those who have had homosexual experiences, 24 percent had their first experience with a younger person, 39 percent with someone of their own age, 29 percent with an older teenager and 8 percent with an adult (Sorensen, 1973). Thus there is no evidence that adolescent homosexual experiences result from being seduced by adults; most such encounters take place between peers.

There are some discrepancies between the figures from the Sorensen report and those from the Kinsey report. These discrepancies may be due to changes in the climate of our society that took place between 1940 and the 1970s, or they may be due to memory inaccuracies among the adults in the Kinsey study who were asked to recall their adolescent behaviors. It seems safe to conclude from these studies, taken together, that about 10 percent of adolescents have homosexual experiences, with the percentages being somewhat higher for boys than for girls.

Teenagers can be quite naïve about homosexual behavior and societal attitudes toward it. In some cases, they have been taught that heterosexual sex is "bad"; having been told nothing about homosexual sex, they infer that it is permissible. In some cases, homosexual relationships naïvely develop from a same-gender friendship of late childhood and adolescence. One woman recalled:

When I was a junior and senior in high school I had an intense friendship with Jan, a girl in my school. We wrote notes and went on walks and climbed trees, sharing dreams, reciting poems that we liked, and talking about coming back to the school in later years to teach together. We vowed lifelong love and friendship, but physically we could express the energy that was between us only by clowning around, bumping into each other—and once when she was asleep I kissed her hair. The intensity of my friendship with Jan made my family uneasy—I remember comments about seeing too much of one person. Their uneasiness got to me a little, because I was a bit uncomfortable with my strong pit-of-the-stomach feelings about her anyway. I re-

member being shy about undressing with her in the room, although I undressed with other friends without thinking about it. Then during the summer after we graduated, having not seen Jan for several weeks, I was leafing through a psychology book and found a section that talked about the intense, bordering-on-homosexual friendship of young girls.

Before long I had labeled it as a silly, childishly intense friendship. I made no efforts to see her when we both went to college, for I figured we had nothing in common.

I think our feelings grew more intense as we tried to repress their sexual side. So I pulled away from Jan because I couldn't handle the natural sexual part of my feelings and affection for her. (Boston Women's Health Book Collective, 1976, p. 64)

Heterosexual Behavior

Toward the middle and end of the adolescent years, more and more young people engage in heterosexual sex, with more and more frequency. Thus heterosexual behavior rises to ascendancy and becomes the major source of sexual outlet.

PREMARITAL SEX[2]

One of the most dramatic changes to occur in sexual behavior and attitudes in recent decades is in the area of premarital sexual behavior.

How Many People Have Premarital Sex?

On the basis of his data collected in the 1940s, Kinsey concluded that about 33 percent of all

---

[2]Note that the very term "premarital sex" contains some hidden assumptions, most notably that marriage is normative and that proper sex occurs in marriage. Thus, sex among never-married (young) persons is considered premarital—something done before marrying. A more neutral term would be "nonmarital sex," although it fails to distinguish between premarital sex, extramarital sex, and postmarital sex.

FIGURE 10.4
Sexuality in early adolescence is often
playful and unsophisticated. *[Rapho/Photo
Researchers, Inc.]*

females and 71 percent of all males have premarital intercourse by the age of 25.

The Hunt data, collected in 1972, indicate
a much higher incidence of premarital sex,
particularly for females (see Table 10.2).[3] It
appears now that virtually all males and over

two-thirds of all females engage in premarital
sex.

The Hunt study, however, included adults
of all ages. To get a better idea of the behavior
of today's youth, we can look at the data on
Hunt's youngest age group, those between 18

[3]The Kantner and Zelnik study (1972), which used better scientific
techniques than the Kinsey and Hunt studies (see Chapter 9), also
found an apparent increase in the incidence of premarital sex,
compared with Kinsey's data. Kantner and Zelnik found that in
1971, 46 percent of women had had premarital sex by age 19;
Kinsey found that about 19 percent had done so by age 19. Indeed,
Kantner and Zelnik even found an increase in the incidence of
premarital intercourse from 1971 to 1976 (Zelnik and Kantner,
1977). In comparison with the 1971 finding that 46 percent of the
19-year-olds had had intercourse, 55 percent had done so in 1976.
Unfortunately, since the Kantner and Zelnik survey did not include
any women over age 19, it does not enable us to determine how
many women eventually have premarital sex.

TABLE 10.2

PERCENTAGES OF PEOPLE WHO HAD ENGAGED IN
PREMARITAL SEX, ACCORDING TO
THE KINSEY REPORTS AND THE HUNT REPORT

	Kinsey (1948, 1953)	Hunt (1974)
Males (by age 25)	71	97
Females (by age 25)	33	67

A PROFILE OF SEXUAL BEHAVIOR AND ATTITUDES AMONG STUDENTS IN A UNIVERSITY COURSE IN HUMAN SEXUALITY

Premarital Sex

90 percent of the men and 81 percent of the women approved of premarital sex when a couple are engaged; 86 percent of the men and 74 percent of the women approved of it when the couple are in love; and 51 percent of the men and 12 percent of the women approved of it when the couple are only casually acquainted.

In terms of actual behavior, 84 percent of the men and 69 percent of the women said they had engaged in premarital sexual intercourse. The men typically had had between three and five premarital partners, while the women typically had had one.

Masturbation

19 percent of the men and 21 percent of the women disapproved of masturbation.

86 percent of the men and 64 percent of the women had masturbated. Most of the men said they had begun between the ages of 13 and 15. Many women had begun somewhat later, and 10 percent had begun after age 19. Most of the students said they currently masturbated once a month or less.

Mouth-Genital Sex

Only 2 percent of the men and 14 percent of the women disapproved of mouth-genital sex.

74 percent of the men had had fellatio performed on them, and 79 percent had performed cunnilingus; 63 percent of the women had performed fellatio, and 64 percent had had cunnilingus performed on them.

Homosexuality

72 percent of the men and 45 percent of the women disapproved of homosexuality.

7 percent of the men and 4 percent of the women admitted having had a sexual experience to orgasm with someone of their own gender.

Anal Intercourse

14 percent of the men and 16 percent of the women said they had engaged in anal intercourse.

Contraception

The students reported that the last time they had intercourse the following forms of contraception were used:

	Males, %	Females, %
Birth control pills	32	26
IUD	4	2
Diaphragm	1	0
Condom	20	18
Foam or jelly	0	0
Rhythm	9	8
Nothing or do not know	18	16
Have never had intercourse	16	30

Abortion

51 percent of the men and 61 percent of the women approved of abortion on demand; an additional 42 percent of the men and 31 percent of the women approved of abortion under special circumstances, such as after rape or incest or when the mother's health is endangered; 6 percent of the men and 7 percent of the women disapproved of abortion.

5 percent of the women had had an abortion.

Note: These data were collected from students in my human sexuality class during the spring quarter of 1977. A total of 208 students provided the data (86 men and 122 women). Two percent were married, and 98 percent were single. Their ages ranged from 19 to 30, with a mean of 21. Forty-four percent were seniors, 27 percent were juniors, 29 percent were sophomores, and 1 percent were freshmen.

and 24. In that group, between 70 and 80 percent of the females and 90 to 95 percent of the males had had premarital sex. Clearly, then, it is becoming unusual for young people to remain virgins until marriage. The data from my university class in human sexuality are similar (see Focus on pages 244 and 245).

First Intercourse

The adolescents in the Sorensen report described their emotional reactions to their first act of intercourse. Contrary to what one might expect, girls generally attached less significance to it than boys did. However, positive reactions—such as feelings of maturity and joy—were about twice as common among boys as among girls. Girls more often said they felt such emotions as guilt, sorrow, and disappointment. Most typically, the immediate reaction of males was to feel excitement, while females typically felt afraid. Unfortunately, the boy usually did not realize that the girl was having a negative reaction (Sorensen, 1973).

Sex with a Prostitute

A generation ago, premarital sex with a prostitute was fairly common among males, and many young men received their sexual initiation in this manner. Among the noncollege men over 35 in the Hunt study, 20 percent had had their first intercourse with a prostitute (Hunt, 1974, p. 145). Now, however, having premarital sex with a prostitute is much less common. This can be seen by comparing the percentages of men under 35 in Hunt's study who had ever had sex with a prostitute with the percentages of men over 35 who had ever done so (see Table 10.3). From these data it appears that only about half as many men now have premarital sex with prostitutes as was the case a generation ago. Further, those who do have such contacts have far fewer of them. Sex with prostitutes is one of

TABLE 10.3

PERCENTAGES OF MARRIED MALES WHO HAD EVER HAD PREMARITAL INTERCOURSE WITH A PROSTITUTE

Education of Respondents	Age of Respondents	
	Under 35, %	35 and over, %
High school or less	30	61
Some college or more	19	52

Source: Morton Hunt. *Sexual behavior in the 1970s.* Chicago: Playboy Press, 1974, p. 144.

the few sexual behaviors to show a decline between the time of the Kinsey study and the time of the Hunt study.

Techniques in Premarital Sex

Paralleling the increase in the incidence of premarital intercourse is an increase in the variety of techniques that are used in premarital sex. One of the most dramatic changes has been the increased use of oral-genital techniques. In the Kinsey sample, 33 percent of the males had experienced fellatio premaritally, and 14 percent had engaged in cunnilingus. In the Hunt survey, 72 percent of the males had engaged in fellatio premaritally, and 69 percent had performed cunnilingus (Hunt, 1974, p. 166). In my classes, I generally find that about 5 percent of the women students have engaged in fellatio and/or cunnilingus but not in intercourse—I suspect because some have discovered that mouth-genital sex cannot cause pregnancy. Young people today also use a greater variety of positions, not just the standard man-on-top (Hunt, 1974, p. 167).

Doubtless some of this increased variety in techniques is a result of today's "performance ethic" in sexual relations, which was discussed in Chapter 8. Adolescents and young adults may feel pressured to be gold medalists in the sexual Olympics. One man said:

Sometimes I'm really good; I can make a girl have orgasms until she's about half dead. But if I don't like the girl, or if I'm not feeling confident, it can be hard work—and sometimes I can't even cut the mustard, and that bothers me a lot when that happens. (Hunt, 1974, p. 163)

Attitudes toward Premarital Sex

Attitudes toward premarital sex have also undergone marked changes, particularly among young people.

Sociologist Ira L. Reiss (1960) has distinguished between four kinds of standards for premarital sex:

1 *Abstinence* Premarital intercourse is considered wrong for both males and females, regardless of the circumstances.
2 *Permissiveness with affection* Premarital intercourse is permissible for both males and females if it occurs in the context of a stable relationship that involves love, commitment, or being engaged.
3 *Permissiveness without affection* Premarital intercourse is permissible for both males and females, regardless of emotional commitment, simply on the basis of physical attraction.
4 *Double standard* Premarital intercourse is acceptable for males but is not acceptable for females. The double standard may be either "orthodox" or "transitional." In the orthodox case, the double standard holds regardless of the couple's relationship, while in the transitional case, sex is considered acceptable for the woman if she is in love or if she is engaged.

Historically in the United States, the standard has been either abstinence or the double standard. However, in recent years, particularly among young people, the standard has shifted to one of permissiveness with affection.

We can see evidence of this new standard, and of the shift it represents from standards of previous generations, by comparing the data on current attitudes toward premarital sex among respondents in the Hunt Study (1974) with results from older surveys. These data are shown in Table 10.4. Note that in surveys conducted in both 1937 and 1959, few people approved of premarital sex, and there was some evidence of a double standard in that some people felt that premarital sex was acceptable for men only. By 1972, though, the majority of respondents felt that premarital sex was acceptable if there was strong affection between the people, and particularly if they were engaged. There is still some evidence of a double standard, in that somewhat more people approve of premarital sex for men than for women. Note also that women tend to have somewhat more conservative standards; fewer of them approve of premarital sex. The dominant view that emerges, though, is that premarital sex is acceptable if there is strong affection, and that is precisely the standard of "permissiveness with affection" that Reiss described.

Among young people, attitudes toward premarital sex vary considerably with age. The attitudes of adolescents up to 17 years of age toward premarital sex differ considerably from those of young adults over age 18 (R. R. Bell, 1966, p. 66). Many readers will recall that they disapproved of premarital sex while they were in high school but changed their minds when they entered college.

Motives for Having Premarital Sex

The adolescent respondents in the Sorensen study (1973) commonly mentioned a need to search for new experience and a desire to escape from tensions as reasons for engaging in premarital sex. Other reasons included using it as a means of communication, as a sign of

TABLE 10.4

PERCENTAGES OF PEOPLE AGREEING THAT PREMARITAL INTERCOURSE
IS ACCEPTABLE, 1937, 1959, 1972

"Do you think it is all right for either or both parties to a marriage to have had previous sexual intercourse?"

	1937, %	1959, %
All right for both	22	22
All right for men only	8	8
All right for neither	56	54
Don't know or refused to answer	14	16

Percentages Agreeing That Premarital Coitus Is Acceptable, 1972

	Male Respondents, %	Female Respondents, %
For a man:		
Where strong affection exists	75	55
Couple in love, but not engaged	82	68
Couple engaged	84	73
For a woman:		
Where strong affection exists	66	41
Couple in love, but not engaged	77	61
Couple engaged	81	68

Source: Morton Hunt. *Sexual behavior in the 1970s.* Chicago: Playboy Press, 1974, pp. 115–116.

maturity, and as a way of handing out rewards or punishments (perhaps rewarding a boyfriend or punishing parents—recall the nonsexual uses of sexual behavior). Some respondents said they engaged in premarital sex simply because it was expected by the peer group. Challenging parents or society and deriving physical pleasure were not commonly mentioned as reasons for engaging in premarital sex. As homosexuality receives more publicity and as adolescents become anxious about it, it is also possible that having premarital sex will become a means of "proving" one's heterosexuality (R. R. Bell, 1966).

Rampant Promiscuity?

Some members of our society are concerned that today's young people have no standards at all and are engaging in rampant promiscuity (undiscriminating, casual sexual relations with anyone and everyone). These concerns are encouraged by flashy newspaper and magazine articles about the sexual scene in high schools and on college campuses.

Is all this true? Not really, according to the available data. First, although the standard for acceptable sex in the previous generation was marriage, this generation has not abolished standards completely. Instead, a new standard has been substituted, and it is based on the quality (not the legality) of the relationship between the two people—its stability and the emotional commitment involved. This standard of permissiveness with affection is scarcely a license for casual or impersonal sex. Second, the number of premarital partners is generally small. Among women who engage in premarital sex, most have only one partner, whom they eventually marry. Studies indicate that 54 percent have only one partner, and for about 50 percent this partner is their fiancé (Hunt, 1974, pp. 151–152; see also Kantner and Zelnik, 1972). Typically men have about six premarital partners (Hunt, 1974), scarcely an orgy.

The present generation has probably done little more than change the time sequence of things. For their parents, the appropriate sequence was to fall in love, get married, and have sex; for young people today, the sequence is to fall in love, have sex, and get married.

Dating, Going Steady, Getting Engaged

The social forces that have produced the current changes in premarital sexual behavior and standards are complex. But among them seems to be a change in courtship stages—in the processes of dating, going steady, and getting engaged. Dating and going steady occur much earlier now than in previous generations. As psychologist Albert Ellis has commented:

[The] most significant change in American courtship procedures and its sex dance during the last ten years (from 1950 to 1960) is the enormous increase in dating, and especially in going steady, among teen-agers (twelve- to fifteen-year-olds) that has taken place. (1962, p. 84)

Dating earlier and going steady earlier create both more of a demand for premarital sex and more of a legitimacy for it. For many, sexual intimacy is made respectable by going steady (R. R. Bell, 1966). As Ira Reiss noted, "No other dating custom is quite so central to the understanding of teen-age sexual codes as going steady."

Sorensen (1973) finds the commonest premarital sexual pattern to be *serial monogamy* without marriage. In such a relationship there is

an intention of being faithful, but the relationship is of uncertain duration. Of those in the sample who had premarital sex, 40 percent were serial monogamists. Though they averaged about four partners, nearly half of them had had only one partner, and about half of them had been involved in their current relationship for a year or more.

Conflicts

We are currently in an era of transition between a restrictive sexual ethic and a permissive one. In such circumstances, conflicts are bound to arise. One is between parents and children, as parents hold fast to conservative standards while their children adopt permissive ones.

These conflicts within our society are mirrored in the messages of the mass media. As Albert Ellis describes the situation:

Premarital sex relations today are widely believed to be bad, silly and pointless; *but* thoroughly enjoyable; *but* normal and natural; *but* necessary for healthful living; *but* smart, gay, and sophisticated; *but* romantically permissible and thrilling; *but* adventurous and exciting; *but* inevitable in this all-too-fleshy world, and so on. (1962, p. 29)

Listening to such messages while growing up, it is no wonder adolescents may sometimes feel conflicts about premarital sex.

Young people may also experience conflicts between their own behaviors and their attitudes or standards. Behaviors generally change faster than attitudes do (R. R. Bell, 1966). As a result, people may engage in premarital sex while still disapproving of it. Feelings of guilt or anxiety can result. Generally with time, such conflicts are smoothed out. Among married women looking back on their premarital sexual experiences, 77 percent saw no reason to regret having had premarital coitus (Kinsey et al., 1953).

COHABITING IN COLLEGE: GOING VERY STEADY

In the stricter days of 1968, a Barnard College sophomore named Linda LeClair became an overnight celebrity after the public revelation that she was living off campus with a former Columbia University student. Linda's battle with school authorities made front-page news in *The New York Times* and other papers across the country.

Since then, a number of researchers have investigated the phenomenon of cohabitation ("living together") among college students, finding that it is an important contemporary living pattern.

Estimates of the number of students who cohabit vary from 10 percent at small liberal arts colleges that do not permit off-campus housing or overnight visits to 35 percent at large state universities that permit off-campus housing and have 24-hour visiting privileges. In a questionnaire answered by more than 1000 unmarried students at Penn State, 33 percent answered "yes" to the question: "Are you now living or have you ever lived with someone of the opposite sex?"

An intensive study of cohabitation at Cornell University indicated that there was no significant difference in academic performance between cohabitants and noncohabitants. Neither did the two groups differ in their desire to marry eventually.

The sexual aspects of cohabitation should not be overdramatized. In most cases, of course, the couple have a full sexual relationship. But in about 10 percent of the cases, the couple lived

HOW SEXUALITY AIDS IN PSYCHOSOCIAL DEVELOPMENT

Erik Erikson, a follower of Freud, has postulated a theory of psychosocial development according to which we experience crises at eight different stages of our lives (Erikson, 1950, 1968). Each one of these crises may resolve in one of two directions. Erikson notes that social influences are particularly important in determining the outcomes of these crises.

The stages postulated by Erikson are listed

in Table 10.5. Note that the outcomes of several of them may be closely linked to sexuality. For example, in early childhood there is a crisis between autonomy and shame, and later between initiative and guilt. The child who masturbates at age 5 is showing autonomy and initiative. But if the parents react to this activity by severely punishing the child, their actions may produce shame and guilt. Thus they may be encouraging the child to feel ashamed and consequently to suffer a loss of self-esteem.

together for three months or more before having intercourse. (This is a more general phenomenon in premarital sex; a couple may literally "sleep together" for some time before they begin having intercourse.) The motives for cohabitation seem to be more emotional than sexual.

In the Cornell study, the students gave a number of reasons for cohabiting: the loneliness of a large university, the superficiality of the "dating game," a search for more meaningful relations with others, the emotional satisfaction of living and sleeping with someone who cares about you, a desire to try out a relationship before marriage, and widespread doubts about the very institution of marriage. The single most important reason cited for choosing to live with someone was "emotional attachment to each other." Most of the relationships were monogamous.

For those who had not cohabited, the reason seemed to be more often lack of opportunity than ethical standards.

In most cases, though, living together was not a purposeful act based on a carefully made decision. Initially, most cohabitation relationships were drifted into, with the couple sleeping together more and more often.

The students in the Cornell study definitely did not see the relationship as a "trial marriage." They did not consider themselves married in any sense of the word, and very few of them saw marriage as a viable alternative to their present situation. Instead, they were engaged in a living out of what used to be called "going steady."

Source: Eleanor D. Macklin. Cohabitation in college: Going very steady. *Psychology Today*, 1974, *8* (6), 53–59.

In adolescence, the crisis is between identity and role confusion. Gender roles are among the most important; in later adolescence the person may emerge with a stable, self-confident sense of manhood or womanhood or, alternatively, may feel in conflict about gender roles. A choice of career is extremely important in this developing sense of identity, and gender roles influence career choice. A sexual identity also emerges—whether, for example, one is heterosexual or homosexual, popular or unpopular.

In young adulthood, the crisis is between intimacy and isolation. Sexuality, of course, can function in an important way as people develop their capacity for intimacy.

For adolescents particularly, sexuality is related to accomplishing important developmental tasks (A. P. Bell, 1974a). Among these are:

1 Becoming independent of parents. Sexuality is a way of expressing one's autonomy and

TABLE 10.5

ERIKSON'S STAGES OF PSYCHOSOCIAL DEVELOPMENT

Approximate Stage in the Life Cycle	Crisis
Infancy	Basic trust vs. mistrust
Ages 1½ to 3 years	Autonomy vs. shame and doubt
Ages 3 to 5½ years	Initiative vs. guilt
Ages 5½ to 12 years	Industry vs. inferiority
Adolescence	Identity vs. role confusion
Young adulthood	Intimacy vs. isolation
Adulthood	Generativity vs. stagnation
Maturity	Ego integrity vs. despair

one's independence from parents. The adolescent boy who masturbates, for example, may be expressing a need to cut the apron strings that tie him to his mother—as you know if you have read *Portnoy's Complaint.*

2 Establishing a viable moral system of one's own. For many adolescents, some of the most critical moral decisions of their lives made independently of parents are in the area of their own sexual conduct. A personal ethical system emerges.

3 Establishing an identity—in particular, a sexual identity.

4 Developing a capacity for establishing an intimate relationship with another person and sustaining it.

Thus we can see that sexuality is an integral part of our psychological development.

SUMMARY

A capacity for sexual response seems to be present from infancy. According to Kinsey's data, about 10 percent of children have masturbated to orgasm by age 10, although recent studies indicate that children begin masturbating at somewhat earlier ages now than a generation or so ago. Children also engage in some heterosexual play, as well as some homosexual activity.

During adolescence there is an increase in sexual activity. By age 15, nearly all boys have masturbated. Girls tend to begin masturbating somewhat later than boys, and fewer of them masturbate. Attitudes toward masturbation are considerably more permissive now than they were a century ago. About 10 percent of adolescents have homosexual experiences to orgasm, with the figure being slightly higher for boys than for girls.

Today almost all males and about two-thirds of all females have premarital sex. This is a considerable increase over the incidence reported in the Kinsey studies, done a generation ago. Adolescents today are also considerably more likely to use a variety of sexual techniques, including mouth-genital sex.

The predominant sexual standard today is one of "permissiveness with affection"; that is, sex is seen as acceptable outside marriage, provided there is an emotional commitment between the partners. The evidence does not support the notion that teenagers today are engaging in rampant promiscuity.

Following Erik Erikson's theory, experiences with sexuality can serve important functions in a person's psychosocial development. They may be important, for example, in becoming independent of parents and in establishing a viable moral system.

SUGGESTIONS FOR FURTHER READING

Reiss, Ira L. *The social context of premarital sexual permissiveness.* New York: Holt, 1967. A good discussion of premarital sex by one of the leading authorities in the field.

Simon, William, and Gagnon, John. Psychosexual development. *Transaction,* **6**(5), 1969. Reprinted in E. S. Morrison and V. Borosage (Eds.), *Human sexuality.* (2nd ed.) Palo Alto: Mayfield, 1977. A sociological approach to understanding sexual development.

11

SEXUALITY AND THE LIFE CYCLE: ADULTHOOD

Grow old along with me!
The best is yet to be.

—Robert Browning

his chapter will continue to trace the development of sexuality across the lifespan by considering sexuality in adulthood. The discussion will include sexuality in marriage and outside marriage (extramarital sex, postmarital sex, and sex among the never-married), as well as sex among the elderly.

MARITAL SEX

About 80 to 90 percent of all people in the United States marry, and of those who divorce, a high percentage remarry (Gagnon, 1977). In our society, marriage is also the context in which sexual expression has the most legitimacy. Therefore, sex in marriage is one of the commonest forms of sexual expression for adults.

Frequency of Marital Sex

It appears that the average American couple have coitus about two or three times per week when they are in their twenties, with the frequency gradually declining to about once per week for those aged 45 and over.

The precise data on this point from the Hunt, Kinsey, and Westoff studies are shown in Table 11.1. Several things can be noted from that table. First, there has been an increase in the frequency of marital sex in the last few decades. In every age group, the people in Hunt's studies reported a higher average frequency of intercourse than the people in Kinsey's study. Second, the frequency of intercourse declines with age; however, even among those over 55, the frequency is still about once per week.

It is important to note that there is wide variability in these average frequencies. For example, about 8 to 12 percent of couples in their twenties report not engaging in intercourse at all, and another 5 to 10 percent report doing so less than once per month (Wilson, 1975). The limitations of self-report data should also be remembered (see Chapter 9).

As was noted in Chapter 9, there may be serious problems with the Kinsey and Hunt data because of inadequacies in the sampling methods used. Recall that Westoff's (1974) study of married women used a probability sample and therefore probably provides better data. Note in Table 11.1 that the frequencies reported by the women in Westoff's study are generally lower than those reported by the people in Hunt's

TABLE 11.1

MARITAL COITUS: FREQUENCY PER WEEK (MALE AND FEMALE ESTIMATES COMBINED), 1938–1949 AND 1970s

1938–1949 (Kinsey)		1972 (Hunt)		1970 (Westoff)	
Age	**Median Frequency per Week**	**Age**	**Median Frequency per Week**	**Age**	**Mean Frequency per Week**
16–25	2.45	18–24	3.25	20–24	2.5
26–35	1.95	25–34	2.55	25–34	2.1
36–45	1.40	35–44	2.00	35–44	1.6
46–55	0.85	44–54	1.00		
56–60	0.50	55 and over	1.00		

Sources: Morton Hunt. *Sexual behavior in the 1970s.* Chicago: Playboy Press, 1974, table 30, p. 191. Charles Westoff. Coital frequency and contraception. *Family Planning Perspectives,* 1974, **6**(3), 136–141.

study, although the data were collected only two years apart. This suggests that Hunt's sample may indeed have been biased toward including people who were more sexually active than the general population.

The Westoff data also provide the best evidence of an increase in the frequency of marital intercourse in recent years. In that study, a national probability sample of women were interviewed in 1965, and another probability sample were interviewed in 1970. There was indeed an increase in reported frequency of coitus—even during that brief five-year period—from an average of 1.7 times per week in 1965 to 2.0 times per week in 1970. This finding confirms the general direction of the changes that occurred between the time the Kinsey report appeared and the time Hunt conducted his survey. The problems of self-report, of course, remain in the Westoff data.

Techniques in Marital Sex

Married couples now use—or at least say they use—a greater variety of sexual techniques than couples in the previous generation.

Couples today generally spend a longer time lovemaking than couples in previous generations. The women in the Kinsey sample estimated that the average duration of foreplay was about 12 minutes (Kinsey et al., 1953, p. 364). Generally the figure was somewhat higher among college-educated persons and considerably lower among those with less education. Further, about 75 percent of the men orgasmed within two minutes after inserting the penis into the vagina (Kinsey et al., 1948, p. 580). In the Hunt sample, the average duration of foreplay, among both the college-educated and the non-college-educated, was about 15 minutes (Hunt, 1974, p. 201); thus there has been a particularly substantial increase in the duration of foreplay among the non-college-educated. The reported duration of actual coitus (from insertion of the penis to the male's orgasm) increased to a median of about 10 minutes in the Hunt study.

Married couples today use a wider variety of positions during coitus than couples in past decades. For example, the female-on-top position is now used, at least occasionally, by about 75 percent of married couples, as compared with about 35 percent in Kinsey's sample (Hunt, 1974, p. 202). Experimentation with different positions is particularly common among younger couples.

The increased popularity of mouth-genital techniques is one of the most dramatic changes in marital sex to have occurred since the time of the Kinsey study. Data on this point are shown in Table 11.2. Cunnilingus and fellatio are now

TABLE 11.2

MOUTH-GENITAL TECHNIQUES IN MARITAL SEX, ACCORDING TO THE KINSEY STUDIES AND THE HUNT STUDY

Respondents	Percent of Marriages in Which Fellatio Is Used		Percent of Marriages in Which Cunnilingus Is Used	
	Kinsey (1939–1949)	Hunt (1972)	Kinsey	Hunt
Males with a high school education	15	54	15	56
Males with a college education	43	61	45	66
Females with a high school education	46	52	50	58
Females with a college education	52	72	72	72

Source: Morton Hunt. *Sexual behavior in the 1970s.* Chicago: Playboy Press, 1974, p. 198. Copyright © 1974 by Morton Hunt. Reprinted by permission of Playboy Press.

used in the majority of marriages, and they are particularly common among the college-educated.

Hunt notes that there has been a comparable change in attitudes toward various sex techniques that is particularly noticeable among the young:

> Among our older interviewees there were a number who, after a party at which they drank a great deal, or after some erotically stimulating event, might occasionally use fellatio, cunnilingus or even anal play, though ordinarily they felt squeamish about such acts or hesitant about suggesting them to their spouses. In contrast, most of the younger interviewees spoke as if they thoroughly enjoyed oral practices and took them as a matter of course, including them very frequently and naturally in their foreplay; a substantial minority, moreover, said that they also used manual-anal play anywhere from occasionally to fairly often. (1974, p. 200)

Negotiations But before these techniques themselves are executed, there is typically a "mating dance" between the man and the woman. Sexual scripts are played out in marriage as in other aspects of sex (J. H. Gagnon, 1977, pp. 208–209). Deciding to have intercourse involves some preliminary negotiations,

which are often phrased in indirect or euphemistic language, in part so that the person's feelings can be salvaged if her or his partner is not interested. For example, the husband may say, "I think I'll go take a shower" or "I think I'll go take a nap" (that means, "I want to, do you?"). The wife may respond with, "I think I'll take one too" (that means "yes") or "The kids will be home any moment" or "I have a headache" (that means "no"). Or conversely, she may put on a lot of his favorite perfume and parade around in front of him (that is *her* offer). He may respond with, "I had an exhausting day at work" (his "no") or "I'll meet you upstairs" (his "yes"). To avoid some of the risk of rejection inherent in such negotiations, some couples simply ritualize sex so that both understand when it will and when it will not occur—Thursday night may be their time, or perhaps Sunday afternoon.

Masturbation in Marriage

Many adults continue to masturbate even though they are married and have ready access to heterosexual sex. This behavior is perfectly normal, although it often evokes feelings of guilt and may be done secretly.

Recent data indicate that about 72 percent

of young husbands masturbate, with an average frequency of about twice a month. About 68 percent of young wives do so, with an average frequency of slightly less than once a month (Hunt, 1974, p. 86).

Masturbation in marriage, of course, can serve a variety of distinctly nonsexual purposes. For example, it can be used as an expression of anger or hostility toward a spouse who has not furnished the expected sexual satisfaction.

But masturbation can also serve very legitimate sexual needs in marriage. It can be a way of remaining faithful to a spouse when husband and wife are separated or cannot have sex for some reason such as illness.[1] As one man expressed it:

> Whenever I travel, it takes about a week until I can't stand it anymore. I lie there at night trying to sleep, and the damn thing won't go away, and I tell myself, "It's either do it or go out on the town." But I'm not that kind of guy, so I do it, and I feel better—and also a little worse. (Hunt, 1974, p. 96)

Masturbation can also be a pleasant adjunct to marital sex. One young man said:

> My wife and I have a great sex relationship, and always have had since before we were married. But we both still masturbate, because it seems a pleasant thing to do and because sometimes the urge comes over each one of us at times when we're alone—I'm away most of the day in the laboratory or the library, and she works at the (TV) studio until after midnight. I may suddenly have a momentary desire to ejaculate, and I run into the bathroom and do it. Or I may read something and it makes me fantasize having sex with some strange voluptuous woman—a belly dancer, maybe. Incidentally, I never have had intercourse with any woman other than my wife, so I enjoy these fantasies. There's nothing

secret about it—I tell my wife if I've done it during the day, and she tells me if she has. It doesn't diminish our lovemaking at all, although sometimes one or the other of us isn't as eager as we might be—but then, sometimes it does just the opposite, because we try out with each other some of the exotic things we've been fantasizing. (Hunt, 1974, p. 98)

Attitudes toward, and Satisfaction with, Marital Sex

The majority of married people today express satisfaction with their marital sex. Unfortunately, Kinsey did not collect data on attitudes or satisfaction, and so we have no basis for saying that attitudes or satisfaction has changed since the previous generation. But let us consider the current data.

In the Hunt sample, about two-thirds of the married men reported that marital coitus in the last year was "very pleasurable." Adding to this the group who described it as "mostly pleasurable," the percentage expressing general satisfaction with marital coitus is about 99 percent among those in the younger age groups and 94 percent among those over 45.

About 60 percent of the married women under 45 rated marital coitus as "very pleasurable"; 57 percent of those under 25 rated it this way, as did 63 percent of those aged 35 to 44. After that age the percentage dropped, to 45 percent of those in the 45- to 54-year-old group and to 38 percent of those aged 55 and over. Adding in those who rated marital sex as "mostly pleasurable," the percentages are 88 percent for those under 25, 93 percent for those aged 35 to 44, 91 percent for those aged 45 to 54, and 83 percent for those over 55. Note that the highest reported satisfaction among women is not in the youngest age group, but rather in the 35- to 44-year-old age group. Note also that women express slightly less satisfaction with marital sex than men do but that both groups are generally satisfied.

---

[1] An old Navy saying has it, "If your wife can't be at your right hand, let your right hand be your wife."

Another way of measuring satisfaction with marital sex is to ask people how satisfied they are with the frequency of marital sex. Less than 5 percent of the women in the Hunt sample said they wished it were less frequent (this is a lower percentage than in previous generations—see Chapter 13), and only 1 percent of the men did. The majority of wives and husbands at all ages felt that the frequency of marital intercourse was about right. But about 40 percent of men and 33 percent of women wished that marital sex occurred more frequently.

Sexual Patterns in Marriage

Sexual patterns can change during the course of a marriage; after 10 or 20 years of marriage they may be quite different from what they were during the first year. One stereotype is that sex becomes duller as marriage wears on, and certainly there are some marriages in which that happens. But there are also those in which the process is exactly the opposite—in which there is a gradual awakening of the sexuality of both partners over the course of the marriage. In other marriages, sexual patterns remain remarkably constant over the years. The following descriptions illustrate the diversity of patterns. First, the words of a man for whom marital sex has become less intense than it apparently once was:

> We do it maybe once a week now, or less. The underlying reason for the slowdown is that we're both pretty busy. It's not that we don't enjoy sex. We do, but I have a lot of meetings, and I get home late and she's asleep, and anyway I'm tired. I would perhaps enjoy a bit more activity, but I'm not discontented about it in any way. . . . Mostly, she does have orgasm—not that we ever discuss it, but I feel pretty sure she does. . . . Our typical sex act is about like this: I'll roll over and decide I'd like a little action. Sometimes it's very rapid—a min-

ute or so—but sometimes it goes on longer, ten minutes, say, half before I put it in, half inside. (Hunt, 1974, p. 220)

A woman described the growth of sexuality in her marriage as follows:

> After we'd been married a while, we felt there was a lot happening that we didn't understand, so I asked my husband if him and I should try to read up on it. So we went out and bought three books, and through them we found all different ways of caressing, and different positions, and it was very nice because we realized that these things weren't dirty. Like I could say to my husband, "Around the world in eighty days" and he'd laugh and we'd really go at it, relaxed and having fun. (Hunt, 1974, p. 183)

Finally, a middle-aged man described a consistent pattern of excitement in marital sex:

> I love my sex, and I've got a wife that loves it just as much as me. Our first five years of married life it was every day with us, and sometimes twice a day because my job would allow me to stop off at home at lunchtime for a quickie. Nowadays, even after twenty years of marriage, it's still about three times a week—and with the kids finally all in school, we've even started up again on the lunchtime business once in a while. Most of the time, naturally, it's in the evening, after the kids are in bed. My wife puts some of that damned perfume on and I know right away that she wants it tonight, and that really gets me going. . . . She can wiggle that ass of hers around like you wouldn't believe, and any position I want to use, she couldn't care less. . . . And sometimes I kid her about stuff I've seen in some stag movie the boys have been showing down at the garage, and would you believe she often wants me to *show* her how it went? After all these years? (Hunt, 1974, pp. 225–226)

Sociologists make a distinction between

segregated conjugal role relationships and joint conjugal role relationships (Rainwater, 1965). In the segregated relationship, each person has different interests and activities in the nonsexual area of his or her life and pursues these independently, showing little interest in the other's concerns. In the joint relationship, the husband and wife carry out their activities together, or they may take turns performing a given function. Sexual patterns tend to be different in these two types of marriage. Couples in highly segregated relationships generally report less sexual satisfaction than those in joint relationships. In the segregated relationship, moreover, the husband is considerably more likely to find sex satisfying than the wife is.

Segregated and joint role relationships vary according to social class. Joint relationships are more common among upper-middle-class couples, while segregated relationships are more common among those in the lower class. Sexual satisfaction shows a comparable social-class variation; reported satisfaction is higher among middle- and upper-class couples than among those in the lower class.

Another view of patterns of relationships in marriage and marital sex is given in the Focus.

Sex and the Two-Career Family

In our busy, achievement-oriented society, is it possible that work commitments—particularly with the increased incidence of wives holding jobs—may interfere with a couple's sex life? One couple, both of whom are professionals, commented to me that they actually have to make an appointment with each other to make love.

While there has been little scientific research on this topic, there is some evidence that patterns of marital sexuality are related to the wife's working (Westoff, 1974). As it turns out, the couple's frequency of intercourse is related not only to the fact that the woman has a job but also to her motivation for having it. Women who work for reasons other than money have a higher frequency of coitus than women who do not work or who work mainly to earn money. Career-motivated women have the highest frequency of coitus of any of the groups of women. Thus there is no evidence that a woman's commitment to a career will damage the expression of marital sexuality.

EXTRAMARITAL SEX

The term "extramarital sex" refers to sex between a married person and someone other than that person's spouse.[2] We can distinguish between three types of extramarital sex, each of which has different implications for the people involved (Clanton, 1973): (1) clandestine extramarital sex, in which the extramarital relationship is concealed from the spouse ("clandestine" means "secret"); (2) consensual extramarital sex, in which the spouse knows about the extramarital activity and may even approve of it ("consensual" means "by mutual consent"); and (3) ambiguous extramarital sex, in which the spouse knows about the extramarital relationship but chooses to pretend not to know. Consensual extramarital sex is relatively rare in our culture, as will be seen below, and most extramarital sex is either clandestine or ambiguous.

How Many People Engage in Extramarital Sex?

Nearly one-half of all married men have extramarital sex at some time in their lives, compared with about one-fifth of all married women (Kinsey et al., 1948, 1953). The relevant data

---

[2]The more traditional—and nastier—term for this is "adultery."

FOCUS

SEX IN FIVE TYPES OF MARRIAGE

Sociologist John Cuber has described the sexual patterns in five different types of "successful" marriage ("successful" in the sense that the marriage is long-lasting and is not in any immediate danger of breaking up).

In the *conflict-habituated* marriage, the couple engage in a seemingly constant verbal battle with each other. Their friends may think that they are always on the brink of divorce. However, they genuinely care for each other—although they have adopted a peculiar way of expressing it—and their sexual relationship is exciting and satisfying.

The *passive-congenial* marriage is a more common type. The relationship is stable and pleasant, and each person goes quietly about living up to his or her responsibilities. Some couples appreciate sex but believe that it should be held in close check, to avoid excess. Others are apathetic about sex or are even antisex. But the sex life can still be perceived as satisfactory if the partners have similar attitudes.

The *devitalized* marriage currently resembles the passive-congenial type, but it used to be otherwise. The couple's sex life was once exciting but has ceased to be so. The most common reason for the change was the first pregnancy or the birth of the first child. This necessitated a change in lifestyle, permitting less privacy and encouraging a preoccupation with the couple's role as parents. Some couples feel that this pattern is appropriate to their middle age, while others accept the change grudgingly.

In the *vital* marriage, the couple are deeply involved psychologically with each other, sharing each other's aspirations and interests. Sex for them is solid pleasure. Most such couples are faithful to each other; the few who are not are honest about it and do not see extramarital sex as a threat to the relationship.

Finally, there is the *total* relationship, which is rare. It is similar to the vital marriage, except that the closeness extends to all aspects of life. Infidelity—including that in nonsexual areas—is a serious breach of the relationship. Because the relationship itself is rich, the sexual relationship is also richly fulfilling.

Source: John F. Cuber. Sex in five types of marriage. In L. Gross (Ed.), *Sexual issues in marriage*. New York: Spectrum Publications, 1975.

are shown in Table 11.3. Several points should be noted from that table:

Men are more likely to report engaging in extramarital sex than women are.

About 40 to 50 percent of all males and about 20 percent of all females engage in extramarital sex at least once.

Extramarital sex does not seem to be any more common now than it was in Kinsey's time. The one possible exception is among women in the under-25 age group, who seem to be considerably more likely to engage in extramarital sex than women of this age at the time of the Kinsey study. This may be due to their rejection of the double standard; the young woman of today may believe that if extramarital sex is all right for her husband, it is all right for her as well.

As was noted above, most extramarital sex tends to be clandestine or ambiguous. Swinging, which is a form of consensual extramarital sex, was reported by only 2 percent of the males and fewer than 2 percent of the females in the Hunt study (1974, p. 271); even in the *Redbook* survey, which generally reported very high levels of sexual activity, only 4 percent of the women said they had engaged in swinging (Levin and Levin, 1975, p. 44).

For women at least, there is no indication that extramarital sex is casual or promiscuous. In the Hunt survey, of those married women who had had extramarital sex, 40 percent had done so with only one partner, and another 44 percent had had between two and five partners (Hunt, 1974, p. 269; the Kinsey figures are similar).

Attitudes toward Extramarital Sex

While attitudes toward premarital sex have changed substantially during the last several decades, attitudes toward extramarital sex have

TABLE 11.3

INCIDENCE OF EXTRAMARITAL SEX AMONG MEN AND WOMEN, ACCORDING TO THE KINSEY STUDY (1938–1949) AND THE HUNT STUDY (1972)

	Percent Who Had Had Extramarital Sex	
	Kinsey (1938-1949)	Hunt (1972)
Among Men		
Under 25	39*	32
25–34	38	41
35–44	34	47
45–54	31	38
55 and over	30	43
Among Women		
Under 25	8	24
25–34	19	21
35–44	20	18
45–54	20	12
55 and over	20	15

*Kinsey's data are difficult to summarize here because he classified extramarital sex in separate categories: sex with "companions" and sex with "prostitutes." This table shows a rough adding-together of the two, and thus these figures must be regarded as approximate and also as maximum figures.
Sources: Alfred C. Kinsey, Wardell B. Pomeroy, and Clyde E. Martin. *Sexual behavior in the human male.* Philadelphia: Saunders, 1948, tables 54, 55. Morton Hunt. *Sexual behavior in the 1970s.* Chicago: Playboy Press, 1974, pp. 258, 261.

apparently remained relatively unchanged; most people in the United States disapprove of extramarital sex. In the Hunt survey, about 75 percent of the women and over 60 percent of the men agreed with the statement, "Mate-swapping is wrong." Between 80 and 98 percent of both women and men said that they would object if their spouse engaged in sexual activity with someone else.

A 45-year-old physician described his extramarital affair and the complex emotions it involved:

She was twenty years younger than I and very seductive, and she had this fantastic, long-legged, high-breasted body. She took the initiative one afternoon when she was the last one in my office, and I couldn't stop myself; it just happened, right then and there, on the waiting-room couch—the first time for me, after fifteen years of marriage. At first I was all torn up about it, but I couldn't give it up. It made me feel totally different—younger and more attractive than I had in twenty years, completely reawakened inside. A young girl, so sexy and so marvelous to look at and touch, wanting me! It went on for months. I'd meet her and have relations with her at least once or twice a week, usually at her place, sometimes at my office after hours. And now listen to the funny part—she was *no* good at all, sexually. Despite all her sexiness, she was frigid, and she'd lie there obviously getting nothing out of it. So even though I'd enjoy the whole situation and the buildup, when it came to the actual act I'd do it in a minute or two and get it over with. And still, for months I couldn't break it off; I felt as if I were hooked on some drug. (Hunt, 1974, p. 286)

Consensual Extramarital Sex

As was noted above, most extramarital sex is kept secret. Unfortunately, there has been little research on that type of extramarital sexual activity, precisely because the participants are so careful to hide it. Therefore, this section will concentrate on consensual extramarital sex, which has been the subject of more research.

Open marriage   Nena and George O'Neill's book *Open Marriage* (1972) was a best seller, presenting the possibility for a new, open attitude toward marital and extramarital sex.

The O'Neills feel that traditional marriage—what they call "closed marriage"—is rigid and limiting to the partners and that it is no longer a realistic pattern in our society. Closed marriage is based on principles of exclusivity and possession and on a belief that the partners can control each other; it also assumes that

things will remain forever unchanged. It does not encourage the partners to grow.

"Open marriage," on the other hand, is defined as a relationship in which the partners are committed to their own and to each other's growth (N. O'Neill and O'Neill, 1976). In order for growth to take place, the partners must be able, from time to time, to rewrite their marriage "contract," the contract being a set of verbalized and nonverbalized understandings about what each person will do and will not do. In a closed marriage, the contract specifies monogamous sex, that is, that the partners will have sex with no one but each other. In open marriage, the partners may rewrite their contract to permit extramarital sex. Contracts can be completely open, or they can have varying degrees of openness. A "compartmentalized" contract, for example, may allow the marriage to be open on Thursday nights only; on Thursday night, the husband is free to play poker with the boys, the wife can play bridge with the girls, or both partners can have sex with whomever they wish.

Thus, while extramarital sex has traditionally been viewed as destructive to marriage, the O'Neills feel that it can lead to the growth of the marriage and of the spouses. One of the most useful aspects of the O'Neills' work is that it highlights the fact that we all have expectations for our own and our spouse's behavior in marriage and that these expectations can periodically be revised—the contract rewritten—in a way that is satisfactory to both partners.

Swinging   One form of such a renegotiated contract occurs in swinging. In *swinging*, married couples exchange partners with other married couples, with the knowledge and consent of all involved.[3]

---

[3]Swinging was originally called "wife-swapping." However, because of the sexist connotations of that term and the fact that women were often as eager to swap husbands as men were to swap wives, the more equitable "mate-swapping" or "swinging" was substituted.

Swingers may find their partners in several ways. Most commonly they advertise, either in one of the sensational tabloids, such as the *National Informer*, or in a swinger's magazine, such as *Swinger's Life* or *Kindred Spirits*. The following is an example:

> New Orleans, young couple, 28 and 32. She, a luscious red head, 5'7", 36-26-38. He, 5'9", 175, well built. Enjoy all cultures.[4] Attractive couple main interest, but will consider extremely attractive single girls and men. Photo required to reply. (Bartell, 1970, p. 115)

The descriptions in such advertisements are not always accurate; generally they tend to minimize age and maximize the mammary measurement of the woman (Bartell, 1970). Swingers may also meet partners at swingers' bars or "sodalities"—clubs or organizations of swingers. In some cases, couples are referred by other couples. Finally, in rare cases, a couple may try to convert a nonswinging couple.

There are three forms of swinging: simple swinging with another couple (either open or closed), swinging at parties (open or closed); and three-way swinging (Bartell, 1970; for a critique of the Bartell study, see Chapter 9). In *closed swinging*, the two couples meet and exchange partners, and each pair goes off separately to a private place to have intercourse, returning to the meeting place at an agreed-upon time. In *open swinging*, the pairs get back together for sex in the same room for at least part of the time. In 75 percent of the cases, this includes the two women having sex with each other, although male homosexual sex almost never occurs (Bartell, 1970; Gilmartin, 1975).

Swinging parties are held at the home of an organizer. At the closed party there are certain regulations concerning behavior; for example, nudity may be prohibited in the central party room, or only one couple may be permitted in a bedroom at a time. An open party is similar, but there are fewer regulations. Nudity is permitted anywhere in the house, and participants are free to form large groups for mass sex (Bartell, 1970).

Finally, a couple may sometimes swing with just one other person rather than another couple. In the majority of cases, the extra person is a female (Bartell, 1970).

Swingers may vary from those seeking purely sexual experiences to those wanting to form lasting relationships or friendships (Gilmartin, 1975). However, most swingers stress emotional noninvolvement with the other couple, and the norm is not to engage in sex with the same couple more than once (Bartell, 1970; Gilmartin, 1975). Swinging couples typically engage in swinging only about once every two weeks, and thus it is scarcely an obsession (Gilmartin, 1975).

What kind of people are swingers? In the nonsexual areas of their lives, they are quite ordinary—perhaps even dull. Although they describe themselves in their ads as exciting people with many interests, in fact they engage in few activities and have few hobbies. As one researcher observed, "These people do nothing other than swing and watch television" (Bartell, 1970, p. 122). About 90 percent of the women are housewives, a much higher percentage than in the general American population (Bartell, 1970; however, Gilmartin, 1975, found that a high percentage of the women hold jobs outside the home). Though one might expect, from their sexual behavior, that these people would be liberal, they are traditional or conservative in other areas of their lives. In one study conducted during the 1968 Presidential campaign, 60 percent of the swingers studied backed George Wallace (Bartell, 1970).

Husbands tend to initiate swinging, but wives typically become the enthusiasts (Bartell, 1970; Gilmartin, 1975). Particularly in swinging at parties, the man's biological sexual capacity may limit him, compared with a woman. He

---

[4]In this context, "cultures" refers to various sexual techniques. Mouth-genital sex, for example, would be "French culture."

goes to a party, and suddenly he is in a situation that he may have fantasized about since his youth—a roomful of naked women with whom he is permitted to have intercourse. But the pressure is on him to "perform," which may cause anxiety, and the anxiety may cause failure. Even if he "succeeds" with the first few women, he will eventually run out of steam long before the women do. Thus by the end of a swinging party, the only activity still going on may be homosexual activity between the women; 65 percent of the women in one study said they enjoyed their homosexual encounters with other women to the point where they preferred them to heterosexual encounters with males (Bartell, 1970). Thus some men can have very negative experiences at a swinging party.

SEX AND THE SINGLE PERSON

Although most adults in our society do marry, there are still many single adults—the never-married, the divorced, and the widowed—who have sexual needs and seek to express them.

The Never-Married

The person who passes age 25 without getting married gradually enters a new world (J. H. Gagnon, 1977). The social structures that supported dating—such as college—are gone, and most people of the same age are married. Dating and sex are no longer geared to mate selection, and by the time a person is 25 or 30, it no longer seems reasonable to call her or his sexual activity "premarital sex."

The attitudes of singles about their status vary widely. Some plan never to get married; they find their lifestyle exciting and enjoy its freedom. Others are desperately searching for a spouse, with the desperation increasing as the years wear on.

At one extreme, there is the *singles scene*. It is institutionalized in such forms as singles' apartment complexes and singles' bars. The

singles group, of course, is composed of the never-married as well as the divorced and the widowed. The singles' bar is a visible symbol of the singles scene. It functions in many ways like a gay bar (J. H. Gagnon, 1977). Everyone is there for a similar purpose: to meet Mr. or Ms. Right. However, most will settle for a date, and it is fairly well understood that coitus will be a part of the date. The singles' bar is somewhat like a meat market; the people there try to display themselves to their best advantage and are judged and chosen on the basis of their physical appearance—and perhaps rejected for too high a percentage of fat.

Many singles, however, do not go to singles' bars. Some are turned off by the idea; some feel that they cannot compete, that they are too old, or that they are not attractive enough; and some live in rural areas where they have no access to such places.

Unfortunately, the major studies of sexual behavior have focused primarily on premarital sexual behavior and only to a lesser extent on postmarital sexual behavior. Researchers have neglected the never-married adult, who deserves more attention in future studies.

The Divorced and the Widowed

Divorced and widowed people are in a somewhat unusual situation in that they are used to regular sexual expression and suddenly find themselves in a situation in which the socially acceptable outlet for that expression—marital sex—is no longer available. Partly recognizing this dilemma, our society places few restrictions on postmarital sexual activity, although it is not so much approved as marital sex (Gebhard, 1968).

Divorced and widowed women Most divorced women, but fewer widowed women, return to having an active sex life. Data collected between 1939 and 1956 showed that 82 percent of divorced women had postmarital coitus and that 43 percent of widowed women did (Gebhard, 1968). In the recent Hunt study, only about 10 percent of divorced women did not engage in postmarital sex.

The lower incidence of postmarital sex among widows, compared with divorcées, is due in part to the fact that widows are, on the average, older than divorcées. But even when matched for age, widows are still less likely to engage in postmarital sex. There are probably several reasons for this (Gebhard, 1968). Widows are more likely to be financially secure than divorced women and therefore have less motive for engaging in sex as a prelude to remarriage. They have the continuing social support system of in-laws and friends, and so they are less motivated to seek new friendships. There is also a belief that a widow should be loyal to her dead husband, and having a sexual relationship with another man is viewed as disloyalty. Many widows believe this or tell themselves that they will "never find another one like him."

Most widowed or divorced women who have postmarital sex begin such relationships within a year after the death or divorce. While most women who have premarital sex do so with only one partner, the fiancé, most women who have postmarital sex have multiple partners. In one study only 16 percent of widowed and 12 percent of divorced women had sex with only the fiancé (Gebhard, 1968). Divorced women average about four partners per year (Hunt, 1974).

Divorced and widowed women who return to having an active sex life generally express great satisfaction with it. Indeed, these women have a higher frequency of orgasm in posmarital sex than they did in marital sex (Gebhard, 1968; Hunt, 1974).

Divorced and widowed men   Virtually all divorced and widowed men return to an active sex life (Gebhard, 1968; Hunt, 1966). Indeed, 100 percent of the divorced men under 55 in

the Hunt study had sexual intercourse during the past year.

It is a popular stereotype that these men have a wild sex life. On the basis of his data, however, Kinsey felt that this was not true. For example, in his sample, only 2 percent of married men over 50 were not having sex at all, whereas 18 percent of divorced and widowed men were not (Kinsey et al., 1948, p. 280). However, the more recent Hunt study found that widowed and divorced men actually have sex slightly more frequently than married men of the same age. Thus the sexual liberation of recent years seems to have affected not only premarital sex but also postmarital sex. Men average eight partners per year in postmarital sex, about twice as many as women do (Hunt, 1974).

In summary, virtually all divorced women and somewhat fewer widowed women engage in postmarital sex; virtually all divorced and widowed men do so, with little distinction between the divorced and widowed.

SEX AND THE SENIOR CITIZEN

When Freud suggested that young children, even infants, have sexual thoughts and feelings, his ideas met with considerable resistance. When, 50 years later, researchers began to suggest that elderly men and women also have sexual thoughts and feelings, there was similar resistance (Pfeiffer et al., 1968). This section deals with the sexual behavior of elderly men and women, the physical changes they undergo, and the attitudes that influence them.

Sexual Behavior of the Elderly

While sexual behavior and sexual interest do decline somewhat with age, there are still substantial numbers of elderly men and women who have active sex lives, even when in their eighties.

In interviews, 40 to 65 percent of a group

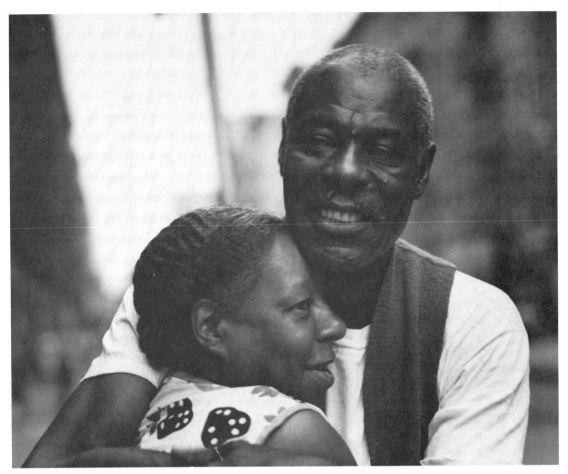

FIGURE 11.1
Affection and romance are not just for the young. [*Bruce Davidson/Magnum Photos, Inc.*]

of active, healthy people between the ages of 60 and 71 reported engaging in sexual intercourse with some frequency; about 10 to 20 percent of those aged 78 and over reported doing so (Pfeiffer et al., 1968). Yet there did not seem to be any age beyond which all people are sexually inactive. Among a group of males over 70, one-third were still potent (I. Rubin, 1966). In a study of eminent men listed in *Who's Who in America*, half of those aged 75 to 92 still had

intercourse, and about 6 percent had intercourse eight times per month or more (I. Rubin, 1966).

Some elderly people do, for various reasons, stop having intercourse after a certain age. For women, this occurs most often in the late fifties and early sixties, while it occurs somewhat later for men (Pfeiffer et al., 1968). Contrary to what one might expect, though, when a couple stop having intercourse, the husband is most frequently the cause; both wives and husbands agree that this is true. In some cases, the husband has died (and we can hardly blame him for that), but even excluding those cases, the husband is still most frequently the cause. Thus the decline in female sexual expression with age may be directly related to the male's decline (Kinsey et al., 1953). Death of the spouse is more likely to put an end to intercourse for women than it is for men, in part because women are less able to remarry (Lobsenz, 1974; Pfeiffer et al., 1968).

Physical Changes

As part of their research on the physiology of sexual response, Masters and Johnson (1966) observed the sexual behavior of elderly men and women in order to document the physical changes that take place in the later years. What follows is based mainly on their work.

Changes in the female There is a gradual decline in the functioning of the ovaries around menopause, and with this comes a gradual decline in the production of estrogen (see Figure 11.2). Because of the decline in estrogen, several changes take place in the sexual organs. The walls of the vagina, which are thick and elastic during the reproductive years, become very thin and inelastic (this condition is called, depressingly, *senile vagina*, and irritations to the vagina that may result are called *senile vaginitis*). Because the walls of the vagina are thinner, they cannot absorb the pounding of the penis as they once did, and thus nearby structures—such as the bladder and the urethra—may be irritated. As a result, elderly women may have an urgent need to urinate immediately after intercourse. Further, the vagina shrinks in both width and length, and the labia majora also shrink; thus there is a constriction at the entrance to the vagina, which may make penile insertion somewhat more difficult, and the vagina may be less

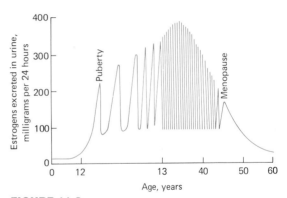

FIGURE 11.2
Levels of estrogen production in women across the lifespan.

able to accommodate the size of a fully erect penis.

Because of hormonal imbalance, the contractions of the uterus that occur during orgasm can become painful, to the point where the woman avoids intercourse. Nonetheless, the woman has the same physical capacity for orgasm at 80 that she did at 30.

By about five years after menopause, the amount of vaginal lubrication has decreased noticeably. Intercourse can then become somewhat more difficult and painful.

Lest these changes sound discouraging, it is important to realize that there are a number of ways to deal with them successfully. Many women's physicians prescribe estrogen-replacement therapy for them after menopause; with these added doses of estrogen, the changes described above are minimized or may not occur at all. A simple measure is to use a sterile surgical lubricant as a substitute for vaginal lubrication.

It also appears that these changes are related in part to sexual activity or, rather, to the lack of it. Among the women in the Masters and Johnson study, those who had intercourse infrequently (once a month or less) and who did not

masturbate regularly had difficulty accommodating the penis when they attempted intercourse. The three women over 60 in their
studies whose vaginas expanded well to accommodate the penis and who produced adequate lubrication had all maintained regular
intercourse once or twice a week. For this
reason and others, Masters and Johnson stress
the importance of regular sexual activity in
maintaining an active sex life among the elderly, a point which will be discussed in more
detail later.

Some people believe that a hysterectomy
means the end of a woman's sex life. In fact, sex
hormone production is not affected (as long as
the ovaries are not removed); orgasm, which
involves the vagina and the clitoris, is also not
affected by removal of the uterus.

Thus it appears that the continuing of sexual activity depends more on the opportunity for
such activity and on various psychological factors than it does on any physical changes, a
point that holds true for both men and women.

Changes in the male Testosterone production
declines gradually over the years (see Figure
11.3). A major change is that erections occur
more slowly. It is important for men to know
that this is a perfectly natural slowdown so that
they will not jump to the conclusion that they
are becoming impotent. It is also important for
women to know about this so that they will use
effective techniques of stimulating the man and
so that they will not mistake slowness for lack of
interest.

Morning erections also become less frequent, declining from about two per week in the
early thirties to about 0.5 per week at age 70
(Kinsey et al., 1948, p. 230).

For men, the refractory period lengthens
with age; thus for an elderly man, there may be
a period of 24 hours after an orgasm during
which he cannot get an erection. (Note that
women do not undergo a similar change;

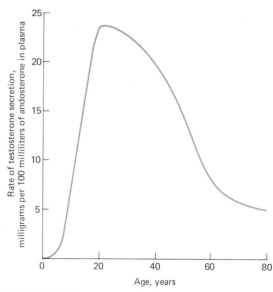

FIGURE 11.3

Levels of testosterone production in men across the
lifespan.

women do not enter into a refractory period and
are still capable of multiple orgasm at age 80.)
Other signs of sexual excitement—the sex flush
and muscle tension—also diminish with age.

The volume of the ejaculate gradually decreases, and the force of ejaculation lessens.
The testes become somewhat smaller, but viable sperm are produced by even very old men.
Ninety-year-old men have been known to father
children.

One advantage is that middle-aged and
elderly men have much better control over
ejaculation than young men; thus they can
prolong coitus and may be better sexual partners.

Despite these physical changes, though,
Masters and Johnson conclude that there need
be no time limit on sexual expression for either
men or women.

Some people erroneously believe that
prostate surgery or removal of the prostate

(prostatectomy) means the end of a man's sex life. It is true that the volume of the ejaculate will decrease, but the capacity for erection and orgasm remains—unless the man becomes the victim of a self-fulfilling prophecy, believing that he will be impotent, in which case he probably will be.

Psychological Factors

Our society has a negative attitude toward sexual expression among the elderly. Somehow it seems indecent for two 70-year-old people to have sex with each other, and even more indecent for a 70-year-old to masturbate. These negative attitudes become particularly obvious in nursing homes, where staff members frequently frown on sexual activity among the residents. Men and women are segregated into separate rooms, and even married couples may be separated; patients may have their hands tied to a wheelchair or bed in order to prevent them from masturbating. Somehow what is "virility" at 25 becomes "lechery" at 65 (I. Rubin, 1965).

A group of undergraduates at Brandeis University were asked to complete the sentence, "Sex for most old people. . . ." Almost all of them gave responses like "negligible," "unimportant," or "past" (Golde and Kogan, 1959).

Why do we have such negative attitudes toward sex among the elderly? In part, these attitudes are due to the fact that ours is a youth-oriented culture. We value youth, and the physical characteristics that are considered "sexy" are youthful ones, such as a trim, firm body and smooth skin. It is therefore hard to believe that someone with old, wrinkled skin could be sexually active. The incest taboo may also be involved in our negative attitudes. We tend to identify old people with our parents or grandparents, and we find it hard to think of them as sexual beings. Finally, our negative attitudes may be a holdover from the belief that

sex was for reproductive purposes only—those past the age of reproduction should therefore not engage in it (Pfeiffer, 1975).

These attitudes affect the way elderly people are treated, and the elderly may even hold such attitudes themselves. Various specific misunderstandings may influence sexuality. For example, a man may believe that sex will precipitate a heart attack or, if he has already had a heart attack, that it will bring on another one. Most authorities agree, though, that the benefits of sexual activity for the cardiac patient outweigh any potential dangers (Hellerstein and Friedman, 1969). Unfortunately, many physicians neglect to discuss the issue with cardiac patients, who then may simply assume that sex is dangerous or forbidden.

Some men also mistakenly believe that sexual activity saps their "vital strength." In some cases men may believe that they can have only a fixed number of orgasms during their life (as a woman has a fixed number of ova) and therefore adopt a strategy of saving them now so that they will have some left later on. One woman wrote:

> My husband has reached the age of sixty-five. He has decided that, in order to ensure a longer life and health, he will no longer engage in sex activity. He is convinced that intercourse and the emission of semen are quite debilitating, particularly in his years. (I. Rubin, 1966, p. 258)

Ideas such as this, as well as factors such as illness or hospitalization, may lead to a period of sexual inactivity. But being sexually inactive is one of the most effective ways of diminishing sexuality. In one study of elderly people, 75 percent were sexually inactive. When they were reinterviewed three to four years later, only 14 percent of the inactive group had returned to sexual activity; the rest had remained inactive (Pfeiffer et al., 1968). Thus it seems unlikely that an old person will return to sexual activity after a period of inactivity. Masters and Johnson emphasize that the most important factor in maintaining sexual capacity is regularity of sexual expression. As was noted earlier, they even have evidence that some physical changes of the sex organs in old age are related to sexual inactivity. As the saying goes, "If you don't use it, you lose it."

Various other factors that may lead to sexual problems for the elderly man include (1) the monotony of a repetitious sexual relationship (usually boredom with the wife), (2) preoccupation with his job, (3) mental or physical fatigue, (4) overindulgence in food and particularly in alcohol, (5) his own poor physical or mental health or that of his wife, and (6) fear of "failure" (I. Rubin, 1966).

Nutrition is very important in maintaining one's sexual capacity (LeWitter and Abarbanel, 1973). In one study of men with nutritional deficiencies, two-thirds had definitely impaired libido and potency (Biskind, 1947).

Women's beliefs about menopause may influence their sexuality in the later years. Some believe that menopause means the end of sex. "I was afraid we couldn't have sexual relations after the menopause," said one woman, "and my husband thought so, too" (I. Rubin, 1966, p. 256). Certainly such attitudes could lead to a diminishing, or even a cessation, of sexual activity. Probably in a few cases, women who never really enjoyed sex use menopause as an excuse to stop having intercourse. On the other hand, some women who spent their younger years worrying about getting pregnant find menopause to be a liberating experience; their sexual activity may actually increase.

Reformers urge us to change our attitudes about sex and the senior citizen. Nursing homes particularly need to revise their practices; even such simple changes as knocking before entering a patient's room would help (people masturbate, you know). Other reforms would include making provisions for spouses to stay overnight and allowing married—or unmarried—couples to share a bedroom. Indeed, some experts even advocate sex as a form of therapy for persons in nursing homes (Rice, 1974):

> Sex relations can provide a much needed and highly effective resource in the later years of life, when so often men face the loss of their customary prestige and self-confidence and begin to feel old, sometimes long before they have begun to age significantly. The premature cessation of sexual functioning may accelerate physiological and psychological aging since disuse of any function usually leads to concomitant changes in other capacities. After menopause, women may find that continuation of sexual relations provides a much needed psychological reinforcement, a feeling of being needed and of being capable of receiving love and affection and renewing the intimacy they earlier found desirable and reassuring. (L. K. Frank, 1961, pp. 177–178)

SUMMARY

Married couples today report engaging in sexual intercourse more frequently than couples several decades ago. Currently, couples in their twenties have sex about two or three times a week, on the average, with the frequency declining to about once per week for those aged 45 and over. Married couples today also tend to use a wide variety of techniques other than intercourse in the man-on-top position, including intercourse in other positions and oral-genital sex. Many people continue to masturbate even though they are married. Most people today—both women and men—express general satisfaction with their marital sex life.

Sexual patterns in marriage, however, show great variability. In part these variations are related to the husband's and the wife's relative roles in nonsexual aspects of the marriage. Sexual satisfaction tends to be greater among those with conjoint relationships than among those with highly segregated relationships.

About 40 to 50 percent of all married men and 20 percent of all married women engage in extramarital sex at some time. Extramarital sex is disapproved of in our society and is generally carried on in secrecy. In a few cases, it is agreed that both husband and wife can have extramarital sex, as in open marriage and swinging.

Single adults—whether never-married, widowed, or divorced—generally do engage in sexual activity. Virtually all widowed and divorced men return to an active sex life, as do most divorced women and about half of widowed women.

While sexual activity declines somewhat with age, it is perfectly possible to remain sexually active into one's eighties or nineties. Among healthy, active elderly people, 65 percent are sexually active in their sixties, and 10 to 20 percent are sexually active when they are over 78. When a couple stop having intercourse, most often it is the husband who is the cause. Problems with sex or the cessation of intercourse may be related to physical factors. In women, declining estrogen levels result in a thinner, less elastic vagina and less lubrication; in men, there is lowered testosterone production, combined with slower erections and longer refractory periods. Psychological factors can also be involved, such as the belief that the elderly cannot or should not have sex. Masters and Johnson emphasize that two factors are critical to maintaining sexuality in old age: good physical and mental health and regularity of sexual expression.

SUGGESTIONS FOR FURTHER READING

Kaplan, Helen S., and Sager, Clifford J. Sexual patterns at different ages. *Medical Aspects of Human Sexuality.* June 1971, **5**, 10–23. A good, readable discussion of female and male sexual patterns over the lifespan.

Rubin, Isadore. *Sexual life after sixty.* New York: Basic Books, 1965. An authoritative book on sex and the elderly.

12

GENDER ROLES

CITED

What are little girls made of?
Sugar and spice and everything nice,
and that's what little girls are made of.
What are little boys made of?
Snips and snails and puppy dog tails,
and that's what little boys are made of.

—Children's rhyme

The great mind must be androgynous.

—Samuel Taylor Coleridge

A baby is born. What is the first statement made about it? "It's a boy" or "It's a girl," of course. Sociologists tell us that gender is one of the most basic of status characteristics. That is, in terms of both our individual interactions with people and the position we hold in society, gender is exceptionally important. Consider, for example, the consternation we typically feel when we see a long-haired (or sometimes a short-haired) person in a baggy shirt and jeans whose gender is not apparent. We do not know how to interact with this person, and we feel quite flustered, not to mention curious, until we can ferret out some clue as to whether the person is a male or a female.

GENDER ROLES AND STEREOTYPES

One of the basic ways societies codify this emphasis on gender is through gender roles.[1] A *gender role* is a cluster of socially or culturally defined expectations that people of one gender are expected to fulfill.

A closely related phenomenon is *stereotyping,* in which we essentially prejudge someone, expecting the person to behave in a certain way or to have certain characteristics because that person is a male or a female. Stereotypes, like many other things, have both advantages and disadvantages. One of the basic advantages (and probably the reason why people have such a tendency to stereotype) is that stereotypes give us information in situations where we would otherwise have none. For example, if you meet a man whom you have never met before, you probably assume that he has a job, and that gives you a starter for conversation. Statistically, your chances of being right are fairly good. Similarly, you might assume that a woman whom you meet for the first time is a full-time housewife and mother.[2] Once again, you have a good chance of being correct, although not so good a chance as with the man. Somehow, it is comforting to "know" these things about people with whom we are not really acquainted. But the problem with such assumptions is that they are not always correct. The man may be unemployed, and the woman may have an

---

[1]The distinction between sex and gender will be maintained in this chapter. Male-female roles—and thus gender roles—are being discussed here.

[2]As a result of the women's movement, however, many people realize that this is not always an accurate assumption. Thus, they do not know what to assume about a woman, which can be awkward.

exciting career. One of the disadvantages of gender-role stereotypes, then, is that they lead to false assumptions about people. Another problem is that they tend to restrict people's opportunities. For example, a high school girl may have the ability to become a nuclear physicist, but she may not even consider that as a possible career because she believes that only men are nuclear physicists. Similarly, a high school boy who would make a good nurse might reject the possibility because he thinks nursing is only for women or because he fears that he would be teased and ridiculed if he decided to pursue that career.

Many adult women and men, though, do behave as gender roles say they should. Why does this happen? Psychologists and sociologists believe that it is a result of gender-role socialization. *Socialization* refers to the ways in which society conveys to the individual its expectations for his or her behavior. Socialization occurs especially in childhood, as children are taught to behave as they will be expected to in adulthood. Socialization may involve several processes. Children may be rewarded for behavior that is appropriate for their gender ("What a little man he is"), or they may be punished for behavior that is not appropriate to their gender ("Nice young ladies don't do that"). The adult models they imitate—whether these are parents of the same gender, teachers, or women and men on television—also contribute to their socialization. In some cases, simply telling children what is expected of males and females may be sufficient for role learning to take place. Socialization, of course, continues in adulthood, as society conveys its norms of appropriate behavior for adult women and men.

Who (or what) are society's agents in accomplishing this socialization? Certainly parents have an early, important influence, from dressing girl infants in pink, and boys in blue, to buying dolls for girls and footballs or baseball bats for boys. The parents' own conformity to

their roles, which children may imitate, is also important. Parents are not the only socializing agents, though. The peer group can have a big impact in socializing for gender roles, particularly in adolescence. Other teenagers can be extremely effective in enforcing gender-role standards; for example, they may ridicule or shun the boy whose behavior is effeminate. Thus peers can exert great pressure for gender-role conformity.

The media can also be important as socializing agents. For example, popular songs, despite all their counterculture pretensions, portray very stereotypical roles for males and females. In two studies of the lyrics of popular songs, it was found that males, who were the more frequent topics of the songs, were portrayed as sexually aggressive, nonconforming, rigid, egotistical, and adventurous; females were typically portrayed as sensitive, passive, insecure, and dependent. Further, in the songs, males were considerably more likely to be politically active and to use drugs (Chafetz, 1974, pp. 43–46). Preadolescents listening to these lyrics can scarcely be expected to miss the lessons the songs teach about what males are supposed to be like and what females are supposed to be like. While movies seem to be showing some trend away from portraying people only in stereotypical roles, television—both the programs and the commercials—continues to be blatant in portraying stereotyped gender roles (Chafetz, 1974; McArthur and Resko, 1976). For example, in one study of television commercials, it was found that virtually all men who did the selling used either a "factual" or an "aggressive, sales-pitch" approach, whereas women who did the selling typically used either "seductive" or "soft-spoken" approaches. Two-thirds of the commercials aimed at females took place in a domestic setting (Chafetz, 1974). Some advertisers are trying to avoid traditional stereotyping—as in the Tang commercial showing the mother who is a nuclear physicist—but traditional roles still seem to prevail.

Children's textbooks and readers are also important socializing influences, and they portray females and males in very stereotyped roles (Weitzman et al., 1972; Women on Words and Images, 1972). Women and girls are portrayed more frequently in restrictive, boring, passive, supportive, or downright stupid roles, while boys are portrayed as being unrealistically brave (for example, a small boy single-handedly wrestling an alligator).

Finally, children may themselves be the agents of their own socialization. Once children have formed concepts of gender and know whether they are boys or girls, they typically acquire a very strong motivation to adopt their gender role (Kohlberg, 1966). That is, children actively seek out information about their gender role and then try to behave as they think boys or girls are supposed to behave. Thus, not only are gender roles imposed on children by society, but children also strive to learn them.

The following sections will be more specific about the gender-role pressures that males and females experience while growing up. First, though, it should be noted that, while gender roles themselves are universal (Rosaldo, 1974)—that is, all societies have gender roles—the exact content of these roles varies from one culture to the next, from one ethnic group to another, and from one social class to another. For example, Margared Mead (1953) has studied several cultures in which gender roles are considerably different from those in the United States. One such group is the Mundugumor of New Guinea. In that cul-

ture both females and males are extremely aggressive.

Gender-role expectations may change over the lifespan. Teenagers have fairly rigid concepts of gender roles (J. F. Adams, 1973), and young married couples, particularly those with small children, may follow very stereotyped roles (the woman takes care of the home and children, and the husband is the breadwinner). However, as people reach retirement age, there may be a considerable shifting of roles. After retiring, the husband may spend all his time in the home, doing the marketing, cleaning, and cooking. Further, as people get older, they are increasingly likely to be single, because of divorce or the death of a spouse, and thus are more likely to assume both the male and the female roles (earn a living and take care of a home).

Having noted these gender-role variations, let us discuss the effect of gender roles on people as they grow up males or females. The role standards discussed will be mainly those of white middle-class America. There are several reasons for this. First, most of the research has been done on this group. Second, white middle-class culture has an overwhelming impact on our culture as a whole through its domination of the media (television and children's readers, for example). Finally, limitations of space do not permit a fuller discussion of the gender roles present in other cultures. As you read the following sections, you should keep in mind the effects that gender roles might have on sexuality.

THE RYATTS   By Cal Alley

FIGURE 12.1
Children are very interested in achieving adult gender roles. *[From J. Elrod. The Ryatts. Copyright Field Enterprises Inc. Courtesy of Field Newspaper Syndicate.]*

GROWING UP FEMALE

Stereotypes about Women

Stereotypes, by definition, are pervasive in any culture, and so we are all aware of the stereotypes about women in American society—that they are passive, unaggressive, not intellectually inclined, emotional, nurturant, and irresponsible with money, for example.

Psychologist Inge Broverman and her colleagues (1972; Rosenkrantz et al., 1968) have studied gender-role stereotypes in the United States. To do this, they simply asked people to name the characteristics on which the average man and the average woman differ. They found that there is a high degree of consensus on the ways in which men and women differ and that this consensus exists not only among adults in the general population but also among college students. The feminine traits that are considered desirable fall into a general category of "warmth" and "expressiveness." Feminine traits that are not valued include characteristics such as emotionality, illogicalness, and lack of competitiveness.

Heterosexuality is another important part of gender roles. The "feminine" woman is expected to be sexually attractive to men and, in turn, to be attracted to them. Women who violate any part of this—for example, gay women—are viewed as violators of gender roles and are considered masculine.

Keeping in mind the content of these stereotypes about women and their potential impact on developing children (and perhaps also on adults), let us look at what happens to females as they grow up.

Infancy and Early Childhood

Despite many attempts by researchers to discover differences in the behavior of girl babies and boy babies, the evidence indicates that there are not many differences (J. S. Hyde and Rosenberg, 1976). It also seems that, for the most part, parents do not treat girls and boys much differently at this early age. One difference in treatment that has been discovered is that parents are less likely to roughhouse with girls than they are with boys (Maccoby and Jacklin, 1974). Generally, it appears that parents' tendency to treat boys and girls differently accelerates as children get older (Block, 1976).

While boys and girls are quite similar in their behavior in infancy and early childhood, there are some marked differences. One is in aggression. As soon as children are old enough to behave aggressively, girls are less aggressive than boys. Another difference that appears early is in toy preference. By 2 years of age, boys and girls have different toy preferences, and by the age of 3 or 4, girls show a preference for playing at housekeeping and caring for babies (dolls), stringing beads, and sewing. It is not clear exactly why this occurs. It may be related to the different kinds of toys that adults give to children and a tendency for children to play with things they are familiar with, or it may result from the child's developing sense of gender identity and a corresponding desire to behave the way a "little woman" or a "little man" should (Maccoby and Jacklin, 1974).

One other difference that should be noted here is the developmental precocity of girls. That is, girls are developmentally ahead of boys. At birth, girls have a more mature nervous system than boys do, and it has been estimated that at the time of entrance to kindergarten, girls are on the average six months ahead of boys. The difference is also noticeable in adolescence, when girls discover boys (not to mention growing a head taller than them) long before boys are aware of their existence. This difference is thought to persist into early adulthood. In the early childhood period it may explain why girls learn to talk earlier than boys and why they adjust to school better and perform better in school (see below).

FOCUS

NONCONSCIOUS IDEOLOGIES OF GENDER ROLES

Psychologists Sandra and Daryl Bem (1970) have suggested that some of the most important—and insidious—influences in gender-role socialization come from various sources that teach *nonconscious ideologies*. While we in the United States, particularly on college campuses, are often tempted to believe that we have been totally relieved from the restraints of gender roles, the restraints do persist today, though in subtler (and sometimes not so subtle) forms.

For example, consider the following passage from St. Paul:

> Wives, submit yourselves unto your husbands, as unto the Lord. For the husband is the head of the wife, even as Christ is the head of the Church. (Ephesians 5:22–23)

Or consider this passage from the Old Testament:

> And the Lord God said unto the woman, What is this that thou has done? And the woman said, The serpent beguiled me, and I did eat. . . . Unto the woman He said, I will greatly multiply thy sorrow and thy conception; in sorrow thou shalt bring forth children; and thy desire shall be to thy husband, and he shall rule over thee. (Genesis 1–3)

What would be the effects on children of studying such passages in Sunday school? Would they not begin to absorb an ideology of gender roles?

Jokes are another source of nonconscious ideologies about gender roles. In one study, the content of over 1000 jokes published in *The Reader's Digest* over the last three decades was analyzed (Zimbardo and Meadow, 1974). In the 1940s, 37 percent of the jokes were sexist. While the percentage has declined somewhat since then, there were still six times as many antiwomen jokes as antimen jokes. Some examples of sexist humor of this type are shown in Figure 12.2. Once again, does it not seem likely that jokes like this would have an effect on people, particularly on children as they grow up?

One of the most difficult things about these nonconscious ideologies is precisely the fact that they are nonconscious. Unlike conscious ideologies such as discriminatory laws, which can be

(a)

(b)

FIGURE 12.2
Humor can be sexist. What are the sexist elements in these cartoons? [(a) London
Daily Express. (b) Copyright The News, *New York's Picture Newspaper.*
Reprinted by permission.]

argued against, nonconscious ideologies usually are not disputed.
Can you imagine a 5-year-old girl objecting to a Bible story
explaining why women experience pain in childbirth? Nonconscious ideologies, then, precisely because they are nonconscious,
are difficult to fight, even though they may have powerful effects.

As a project, you might want to try to think of other kinds of
nonconscious ideologies of gender roles that are present in our
society. You might also do a content analysis of a source of a
nonconscious ideology of gender roles—such as cartoons—to find
out something about the roles that are taught.

Childhood

In childhood, girls' school achievement is generally better than boys'. Their grades are better, and they are less frequently made to repeat a grade and are more frequently permitted to "skip" a grade. Girls' adjustment to school is also better than boys'.

In childhood, the forces of gender-role stereotyping become more prominent. Television programming and advertising messages must make girls increasingly aware that women are housewives and mothers (but rarely lawyers) and nurses (but rarely doctors) and that their chief concern—and potential source of embarrassment if they do not meet the standards—is whether they will be diligent and wise enough to avoid "ring around the collar."

While it is true that socialization exerts an increasing force, it is also true that girls, at least at this stage, actually appear to have more freedom than boys do in regard to gender roles (Hartley, 1959). It is quite permissible, especially now, for girls to play baseball and climb trees; it is still relatively taboo for boys to play with dolls. Being a tomboy is tolerated; being a sissy is not.

Adolescence

Gender-role socialization forces are much stronger in adolescence than they were at earlier ages, and they may actually be stronger during this period than at any other stage of life. The peer group exerts tremendous pressures for conformity, and most adolescents meekly obey. Interestingly, corresponding to this increased socialization pressure, some psychological gender differences (for example, spatial ability and some physical abilities, such as grip strength and speed in the 100-yard dash) appear for the first time in adolescence.

A principle that the adolescent girl becomes increasingly aware of is the *femininity-achievement incompatibility* (Horner, 1972; J.

S. Hyde and Rosenberg, 1976). The notion is that, in our culture, one cannot be both feminine and an achiever. Achievement is somehow perceived as reducing one's femininity, and the truly feminine female is not an achiever. This puts the female in a double bind; achievement is a valued human characteristic, and one that she was rewarded for in elementary school, and yet it is now incompatible with her gender role. As Margaret Mead put it, "Every step forward as a human being is a step backward as a woman." Of course, it is important to emphasize that this is simply an arbitrary rule of our culture—there is nothing intrinsically incompatible about femininity and achievement. Nonetheless, the belief has a big impact.

This situation results in *ambivalence* in women. Many areas of women's lives, including sexuality, are sources of ambivalence, and achievement is a chief source. For example, a high school girl might not admit to receiving straight A's, or she might purposely lose a game of Ping-Pong with her boyfriend. Achievement is a source of ambivalence, then, because it is both attractive and threatening. Perhaps the most relevant research on this situation is the work of psychologist Matina Horner on the *motive to avoid success* (1969, 1970, 1972). The motive to avoid success is a fear of, or anxiety about, success among high-achieving women, which Horner has documented using projective tests. The research suggests that high-achieving women pay a price for their success and, as a result, may achieve less than they would if success were not so associated with anxiety. Though this research is controversial (Shaver, 1976; Zuckerman and Wheeler, 1975), it does provide some insights into women's ambivalence about achievement.

An important psychological task of late adolescence is to begin to form an adult identity. For the male, adult identity will be defined mainly in occupational terms (see below), and so he begins preparing himself for this future identity—for example, being a doctor or a farmer—in late adolescence. For adult women, though, identity is not defined by a career, but rather by the wife-mother role. Thus in late adolescence many girls actually seek to postpone their identity formation so that they will be able to adapt their identity to that of the as-yet-unknown husband (Angrist, 1969). And rather than seeking a unique identity, the girl seeks popularity.

Adulthood

For most adult women, the wife-mother role is the major source of identity. Even today, college women tell me that they are preparing themselves to be teachers or social workers or nurses so that they will have "something to fall back on." That is, the wife-mother role, rather than the career, is expected to be the major focus of adulthood; the career will be for use in emergencies, such as widowhood or divorce.

If she defines her identity through the wife-mother role, the woman does not form a unique sense of personal identity; rather, she defines her identity in terms of others. She is Mrs. John Smith; that is, she is not Mary Smith, but rather John Smith's wife. At PTA meetings she may say that she is "Jimmy's mother," in this case defining her identity through her child.

It is true that increasing numbers of women are holding jobs outside the home. In 1976, women made up 40.5 percent of the labor force. Among women aged 20 to 24, about 65 percent held paying jobs, as did 55 percent of all women aged 25 to 55 (U.S. Bureau of the Census, 1976). However, it is important to note that most women work not for personal satisfaction, but rather because they must. That is, many women work because they are single (divorced or widowed) and have to support a family, or at least themselves, or because their husband's income is simply not adequate to support the family.

Working women may often be caught in a double bind. In adulthood the femininity-achievement incompatibility is rerun under a new format, the work-mother incompatibility. That is, it is widely believed in our society that the children of working mothers suffer and that a woman cannot both be a good mother and hold a job. Thus working mothers may be told that any problems their children have are due to their working, despite the fact that there is no evidence that the children of working mothers suffer psychological damage (Hoffman, 1974). Nonetheless, working women may feel a tension between the demands of their work and the demands of being a housewife and mother.

Middle and Old Age

A well-known phenomenon of middle age is the depression that some women suffer as a result of the "empty-nest syndrome" (Bart, 1971). When the woman is about 50, usually the last child has left home—to go to college, to go to work, or to get married—and she is left with an "empty nest." Because, as was noted above, the woman has defined her identity in terms of her children, they take her identity with them when they leave. It is not surprising that depression results.

Widowhood may contribute to further problems. Widows by far outnumber widowers in the United States; it has been estimated that the ratio of widows to widowers is 4 to 1 (Bernardo, 1968). That is, in most marriages the man dies first. Statistics indicate that the average age of widowhood is 56 and that half of the women over 65 are widows (Bernardo, 1968; U.S. Department of Commerce, 1973). The preponderance of widows is a result of two factors: the tendency of women to marry men older than themselves and the greater longevity of women. But the fact remains that many women spend the last 15 or so years of their lives as widows. This can make an empty nest even emptier and can also create financial problems and other emotional strains, as well as creating a celibate lifestyle.

Menopause may also be stressful, psychologically as well as physically, since it means that the woman can no longer have children. Because womanhood in our culture is largely defined by the ability to bear and care for children, the realization that one can no longer do this may be traumatic. On the other hand, for women who have been plagued by unwanted pregnancies, menopause may bring a sense of relief.

The loss of attractiveness that occurs in middle and old age may also be stressful. Ours is a youth-oriented culture, and women's status in adolescence and adulthood is so heavily determined by their physical attractiveness that the loss of this attractiveness may lead to a fear—and perhaps a realistic one—that they will no longer be valued or loved as much.

Evidence of the effects of these stresses and the continuing ambivalence in the lives of women can be seen in the data on male-female ratios in mental illness. Studies consistently indicate that more adult women than men are mentally ill, as measured by the number in psychotherapy (Chesler, 1972; Gove and Tudor, 1973). There are approximately twice as many women in psychotherapy as there are men.

Lest we be overwhelmed with the stresses affecting middle-aged women, it is important to note that many women successfully resolve the crisis of middle age. A woman and her husband may rediscover each other after years of being preoccupied with the children, or she may decide to get a job for the first time or to go back to school. Such changes in her life may give her a great deal of satisfaction.

Who ends up happier—women who remain in the home exclusively or career women? The answer seems to depend on when in their lives you look at them. One study of college graduates indicated that in their twenties, the full-time housewives are happier. They enjoy raising small children and may be getting creative satisfaction from the role of housewife. Career women may be enduring the stresses of building up a career and trying to mesh that with the role of wife and mother. On the other hand, in their forties, women who are employed have higher self-esteem (Birnbaum, 1976). They are now reaping the benefits of satisfaction and identity built up in their careers, while those who have not worked are suffering from the empty-nest syndrome. Indeed, research indicates that "supermothers"—those who devote themselves exclusively to their children—are most likely to suffer from the empty-nest syndrome (Bart, 1971), while working mothers have found additional sources of identity and thus have less to lose when their children leave home.

GROWING UP MALE

Stereotypes about Men

We are all aware of the stereotypes about men that are prevalent in American culture: that they are aggressive, athletic, successful, unemotional, brave, and instantly aroused by attractive women.

The Broverman research (1972) found a consensus about the traits of men in our culture. The traits that are valued in men fall into a general "competency" category, including traits like independence, objectivity, competitiveness, logicalness, and skill in business. That is, a key expectation for men in our culture is that they be competent and possess the characteristics that go along with competence.

It is important to note that sexuality itself can be important in defining gender roles. For example, in one survey, 48 percent of the women felt that a "real man" should be a skilled lover (Tavris, 1977). Even in bed, men are required to be competent.

Keeping these stereotypes in mind, let us look at what happens in the process of growing up male.

Infancy and Early Childhood

As was noted above, there appear to be few differences between the behavior of boy babies and that of girl babies, and, for the most part, parents also tend to treat them similarly.

By about age 2, however, boys are more aggressive than girls. Their toy and game preferences become gender-typed early, too. By the age of 3 or 4, boys already prefer activities such as carpentry and toys such as guns, trucks, tractors, and fire engines over "girls'" toys and activities.

Childhood

Boys do not do so well in school as girls, and they have more adjustment problems and are more often referred to psychologists (Andrews and Cappon, 1957; Dreger et al., 1964; Spivack and Spotts, 1965; Werry and Quay, 1971). This may be the result of a number of factors. First, the vast majority of elementary school teachers are women, and so the boy may not have a teacher who understands him or with whom he can identify, as the girl does. Second, since young boys are developmentally immature, compared with girls, and since entrance to kindergarten is often based on age rather than readiness, many boys may enter kindergarten or first grade before they are ready to do the work that will be demanded of them. This may lead to failure, frustration, and the formation of emotional blocks that prevent them from learning when they are mature enough. A third possible source of boys' school problems is their greater aggressiveness. Teachers generally frown on displays of aggressiveness, and thus boys may quickly become classified as "behavior problems." Further, the aggressiveness may interfere with their attention and therefore with their learning.

Boys become increasingly aware of society's expectations for them. On television they see that men frequently shoot each other or fight with each other, and they learn that men must always be brave, even in situations where anyone with any sense would be afraid. They see that, to be respected, a man must be a doctor or a lawyer or a policeman.

Boys also learn quickly that they should not show emotion and that they must not cry even if they feel terrible. While the stereotype of the unemotional man may have some advantages over the stereotype of the "hysterical" woman, many men resent the fact that their emotions were "shut off" when they were children and say that they really wish they could cry.

Adolescence

Gender roles become increasingly prominent in adolescence. While the adolescent girl must prove herself in the area of popularity and attractiveness, boys must prove themselves in athletics (Pleck and Sawyer, 1974). The message is that, to be a "big man on campus"—and get all the rewards that this entails, including the admiration of girls—the adolescent boy must be a successful athlete, especially in the glamour sports—football and basketball. As the lyrics of a popular song go, "You've got to be a football hero to get the love of a beautiful girl."

The problem with this, of course, is that not all, or even most, boys can be football heroes; in fact, only a few in any class can be. What about the boy who is uncoordinated, overweight or small for his age? The message from society is that he is less of a man because he is a "failure" at athletics. However, the benefits of the pressure toward athletics should also be recognized. The athletic training boys get at this age encourages their competitiveness, and competitiveness is probably an important factor in attaining job success in adulthood.

Late in adolescence, boys begin to realize the necessity of preparing for an occupation. Some boys may become concerned about grades for the first time and begin to realize that, to be a success, they have to go to college. Others may cultivate a hobby, such as working on cars, which they have found enjoyable and which will prepare them for an occupation.

Adulthood

The adult male's major source of identity comes from his job. Earlier it was pointed out that the female's practice of defining her identity in terms of others (her children or her husband) makes for a somewhat fragile identity whose reward may be an empty-nest depression in middle age. While the male's definition of identity in terms of occupation carries with it the potential for a great deal of satisfaction, it may also be fragile. What happens to the man who is totally wrapped up in his job and is laid off or fired? If a man must hold a job and make an income to support his family, is he less of a man when he cannot do this? And what happens when he must retire at age 70? Will he be able to handle the large amounts of time he now has on his hands, and will he feel less of a man because he no longer earns a large income?

Not only are men expected to hold jobs, but they are also expected to be very successful at them (Tavris, 1977). Yet, because in our society success is defined by comparison with others, not all men can be successes. Are they then also failures as men? Margaret Mead has said, "Women are unsexed by success, men are unsexed by failure." The pressure for success may become a great burden and a source of stress. As a slogan of men's liberation has it, "We're more than just success objects."

Middle and Old Age

Middle age is a period of reassessment for most men. At around age 50, many realize that their lives are more than half over. It is no longer realistic to suppose that they will suddenly become successful in the next few years if they have not been successful in the past. Middle-aged men must assess whether they have accomplished the goals they set for themselves when they were 20. Success is critical in the male role, and middle-aged men must assess whether they have achieved it. As noted in Chapter 4, a kind of "male menopause" may result, in which the man may become depressed or discontented as he appraises his life and accomplishments.

Until recently, most men had to retire at age 65. (New legislation has raised the age of compulsory retirement to 70.) For some, retirement may be a liberating experience; they can pursue hobbies for which they never had time before. Others, however, find the adjustment very difficult. They suddenly have vast amounts of unstructured time available, and they have no idea how to use it. Further, their ability to earn money was important to them, and they can no longer do this.

Though gender roles can be fairly rigid in adolescence and young adulthood, they may often relax and even be reversed in middle and old age. With the children grown, the woman is less restricted to the wife-mother role. And in some marriages, because the husband is older than the wife, he may retire while she is still working. Thus she becomes the breadwinner, and he spends all day at home.

This discussion has pointed out some of the forces that act upon females and males as they grow up in their respective roles. Feminists note the stresses associated with women's low status, their restriction from high achievements, and the demand that they be wives and mothers. Men's liberationists argue that, while women's low status does involve stresses, there are also stresses involved in always having to be at the top.

MALE-FEMALE PSYCHOLOGICAL DIFFERENCES

The discussion so far has centered on the gender roles and socialization forces present in our society. It is not too unreasonable to assume that these forces have some effect on people's behavior and personalities. What psychological differences between males and females result?

Personality

As has been noted, males and females differ in *aggressiveness* (Maccoby and Jacklin, 1974; this difference as well as the others discussed here are documented in detail in that volume). Males are more aggressive than females. This is true for virtually all indicators of aggression (physical aggression such as fighting, verbal aggression, and fantasy aggression). It is also true at all ages; as soon as children are old enough to perform aggressive behaviors, boys are more aggressive, and adult males dominate the statistics on violent crimes. In some situations, it is possible for women to be as aggressive as men, but it is very rare for women to be more aggressive than men (Frodi et al., 1977).

Another difference is in *self-esteem* (Block, 1976). Females tend to have lower self-esteem and less confidence in their own abilities to succeed at future tasks. For example, if a group of college students take their first examination for a course and immediately afterward they are asked to estimate how many points they will get on the test, females give lower estimates than males do (Berg and Hyde, 1976; Maccoby and Jacklin, 1974), presumably indicating that they

have less self-confidence in their own abilities. Of course, when we think of the stereotypes of women as being dumb and irrational and of men as being competent and logical, it is hardly surprising that women have less self-confidence in their own abilities.

Females' lesser aggressiveness and lower self-esteem may have far-reaching consequences; these differences might help to explain, for example, why there are relatively few women in high-prestige careers. Both aggressiveness and self-confidence are usually necessary for success in such occupations. These differences also may have important consequences for sexuality, as will be discussed below.

Abilities

While there are no gender differences in general intelligence (IQ), there are a number of gender differences in more specialized intellectual abilities. Females tend to do better than males in most tests of verbal abilities, from low-level ones, such as spelling tests, to complex ones, such as tests involving analogies and creative writing. Males, on the other hand, are superior to females in mathematical ability and spatial ability. Once again, these differences may have important consequences, both for adult occupational roles and for people's views of themselves.

With regard to achievement, girls' school achievement is better than boys', as indicated by their better grades and their relative absence in remedial classes. But in adulthood, standard measures of achievement, such as counting entries in *Who's Who in America*, indicate that males achieve far more than females do (see Figure 12.3).

Communication Styles

A number of scholars have noted that men and women differ in their styles of communicating,

(a)

(b)

FIGURE 12.3

In the United States, there are few women in positions of power and prestige.
(a) The M.I.T. faculty in 1900 *[M.I.T. Historical Collection]. (b)* President Carter
and his Cabinet in 1977 *[United Press International].*

both verbally and nonverbally (Deaux, 1976; Key, 1975; Lakoff, 1973).

Women and men tend to use language differently. For example, women enunciate more precisely; they are more likely to say "working," while men are likely to say "workin'." Men are more likely than women to use swearwords and dirty words, although this difference may have narrowed in the last few years. Many of my female students have exceptionally colorful vocabularies

In terms of total talking time, men consistently outdistance women. This is a good example of a stereotype—women as constant talkers—that turns out not to be true in reality. Men actually spend more time talking than women do. Men are also more likely to interrupt than women are (Deaux, 1976).

Social psychologists have also found gender differences in studies of self-disclosure. In these studies, people are brought into a laboratory and are asked to disclose personal information either to friends or to strangers. Women are much more willing to disclose information than men are, at least in situations like these (Cozby, 1973; Jourard and Lasakow, 1958).

In studies of nonverbal communication, or "body language," gender differences have also been found. Men are more likely to touch others, while women are more likely to be touched (Henley, 1973a, 1973b). Men and women also differ in their reactions to being touched. In one ingenious study, the effects of being touched briefly, in an accidental way, were studied (J. D. Fisher et al., 1975). The investigators arranged to have library clerks (both male and female) either touch or not touch the hands of students who were checking out books. Soon after the student left the check-out desk, he or she was approached by an experimenter with a questionnaire concerning the library and its personnel. Women who had been briefly touched by the clerk reported feeling more positive than women who had not, and they reacted more favorably toward both the clerk and the library. However, being touched seemed to have no effect on the men's feelings. This study suggests, then, that being touched may be a more positive experience for women than it is for men.

There is a related finding from studies of interpersonal space. These studies indicate that American men prefer greater distances between themselves and another person than American women do (Deaux, 1976). For example, at public exhibits women stand closer to other women than men do to other men. Women also sit closer together when they are in an experimental laboratory.

What are the implications of these gender differences in communication styles for sexuality? For example, if men are unwilling to disclose personal information about themselves, might this not hamper their ability to communicate their sexual needs to their partners (Jourard, 1971)? If women react more favorably to being touched than men do, might this suggest that women enjoy this aspect of sex and that men might be relatively hampered in their enjoyment of being touched sexually? Further research in this area should be intriguing.

Gender Similarities

Most of the research and the textbooks on gender roles, as well as most courses in the subject, tend to be based on the assumption that psychological gender differences are pervasive, that is, that men and women have quite different kinds of personalities. This notion is also quite popular among lay people; for example, in cartoons and on television, as well as in real life, we often see a man shaking his head over his inability to understand women. Their minds work so differently, after all.

Just how different are the minds of men and women? Although differences have been found to exist in personality, abilities, and communication styles, as was discussed above, for the vast majority of psychological characteristics, there are no gender differences. Therefore, *gender similarities* seem to be the rule, not gender differences (J. S. Hyde and Rosenberg, 1976). While men and women think and behave differently in some ways, for the most part they are very similar. As the British author Dorothy Sayers put it:

> The first thing that strikes the careless observer is that women are unlike men. They are "the opposite sex"—(Though why "opposite" I do not know; what is the "neighboring sex"?). But

the fundamental thing is that women are more like men than anything else in the world. (1946, p. 116)

When I bring up this notion of gender similarities, some people invariably start clucking fondly, remembering the good old days when "women were women and men were men," or they mouth phrases like "Vive la différence." That is, some people think that the more different men are from women, the better a place the world is to live in. I don't agree. I think that the real basis for understanding, communication, and enjoyment between men and women is their similarities, not their differences, particularly in the area of sexuality. If a woman and a man have totally different motives, attitudes, thoughts, desires, and goals with regard to sex, it may be very difficult for them to establish the kind of communication and understanding that is so important to a good mutual sexual experience.

Stereotypes, Real Differences, and the Nature-Nurture Issue

A conceptual distinction will be made here between gender-role stereotypes, psychological gender differences that have been determined empirically to exist ("real" differences), and the causes of gender differences, whether they be biological or environmental. Gender-role stereotypes are simply the way most people think that males and females should be psychologically. The nature of these stereotypes has been reviewed in previous sections. When data are collected on how males and females behave, the stereotypes turn out to be true for some behaviors ("real" differences) but not for others. For example, there is a stereotype that males are more aggressive than females. The data show that males are actually more aggressive than females. Therefore, this stereotype turns out also to be a real difference. But there is also a

stereotype that women are less intelligent than men, while the data show that there are no gender differences in IQ. In this case, the stereotype turns out not to be true. Finally, if a gender difference is found for some behavior, it requires one more step of analysis—and a very difficult one—to determine whether the difference is biologically caused or environmentally caused. For example, because there is a well-documented gender difference in aggression, we cannot automatically infer that it is biologically caused (e.g., by sex hormones), nor can we automatically decide that it is produced by environmental factors (e.g., socialization). Gender differences may be caused by biological factors, environmental factors, or both.

IMPACT OF GENDER ROLES ON SEXUALITY

Because gender roles and sexuality interact so closely, it seems likely that the content of gender roles has some effect on sexuality. Some of the more salient aspects of gender roles that may affect sexuality are discussed below. The reader may want to speculate about other aspects of gender roles that may affect sexuality.

Aggressive versus Passive

Certainly, one stereotype that exists in our culture is that males are aggressive (especially in the physical sense), while females are unaggressive or passive. Of course, an individual couple may not conform to these stereotypes, but if they do, what effects do these stereotypes have on them when they come together to have sex? The male may think that he has to play the aggressive role in bed just as he would on the football field. As a result, he may think that he should be strong and perhaps even rough (he may think that women want to be treated that way), that he should initiate the sexual activity, and that he should control the sequence of techniques that are used. Gentleness might seem incompatible with this masculine role. Gender role playing might even affect the positions that he thinks are appropriate in intercourse. For example, he might think that the man-on-top position is the best and that the woman-on-top position is unacceptable because a "real man" would not be on the bottom (the winner of a fight is always on top, isn't he?).

A woman who conforms strongly to the female role of passivity may feel that she should not initiate sex and that she should not take an active part in the lovemaking. Carried to an extreme, female passivity can lead to the "dead-fish" approach to experiencing sexuality.

Aroused versus Unaroused

Another stereotype is that men are easily provoked to high levels of arousal, while it is almost impossible to arouse women (as one popular but incompetent columnist of pop psychology put it, "Men are 100 percent sexual; women are 0 percent sexual"). The data on whether this is a real difference or just a stereotype will be discussed in Chapter 13. Here the emphasis will be on what conformity to this stereotype might mean for sexuality.

For a man, the "aroused" role may lead him to believe that he should always be aroused by any attractive woman and that arousal should always come easily and quickly. Failures in either respect might be interpreted as inadequacy in the masculine role. It may also lead the man or his dates to expect that he will always want sex to be part of a date, even though he may just be interested in having a good time or establishing a friendship. Some of the men in my classes tell me, "I feel like I'm expected to at least *try* to get every woman I date to go to bed with me."

For a woman, conformity to the "unaroused" stereotype may also lead to the dead-fish approach. The woman may believe that it is not appropriate for her to be easily aroused, and so she does not become aroused, or she tries to hide arousal when it occurs. But there may also be a price for lack of conformity to this role. The woman who is easily aroused and who expresses it, perhaps by initiating sex, may have her behavior interpreted as an indication that (1) she is not feminine, (2) she is a threat to men and wants to take away their prerogatives, or (3) she is an oversexed slut.

Of course, gender roles are changing and have become less rigid in the last decade. But this change may carry with it problems of its own, since expectations may not be clear. For example, a woman may honestly express her sexual interest, believing that this is now acceptable, only to have her interest interpreted as being an indication that she is "easy." Stereotypes like the saint-slut dichotomy for women die hard.

Emotional versus Unemotional

Another stereotype is that women are emotional, while men are not emotional or should not express emotion if they feel it. For example, one of the first rules of socialization enforced on boys is that they must not cry. Conformity to this stereotype might lead a man to believe that sex should be purely physical for him and that he should not express emotion (love and tenderness) or become emotionally committed (the "love 'em and leave 'em" philosophy). This stifling of emotional expression may lead him to have sexual experiences that are less fulfilling than they might be. On the other hand, a violation of the stereotype—for example, an expression of tenderness—might be interpreted by some women as an indication that the man is not masculine. Thus nonconformity may also carry a cost, although most women appreciate emotional expressiveness in a man (Tavris, 1977).

A NEW TREND: ANDROGYNY

One of the most exciting areas of recent research on gender roles is that of psychological androgyny (Bem, 1974; Heilbrun, 1973). *Androgyny*[3] refers to a combination of both feminine and masculine traits in a single individual. Thus if a person is androgynous, he or she possesses both masculine and feminine characteristics.

The traditional research on gender roles and masculinity-femininity has been based on the assumption that all (or at least most) males are masculine and that all (or most) females are feminine; it was also assumed that females are not masculine and that males are not feminine. Further, it was assumed that the more masculine a person was, the less feminine that person would be, and vice versa. That is, if a woman learned how to repair cars, for example, that would make her more masculine and therefore less feminine. Similarly, if a man took up cooking, that made him more feminine and therefore decreased his masculinity.

But human beings are not that simple. Many men have a lot of masculine qualities but also some "feminine" interests and talents as well, and many women possess both feminine traits and masculine traits. As the psychologist Walter Mischel has expressed it:

> When we observe a woman who seems hostile and fiercely independent some of the time but passive, dependent, and feminine on other occasions, our reducing value usually makes us choose between the two syndromes. We decide that one pattern is in the service of the other, or that both are in the service of a third motive. She must be a really castrating lady with a facade of passivity—or perhaps she is a warm, passive-dependent woman with a surface defense of aggressiveness. But perhaps nature is bigger than our concepts and it is possible for the lady to be a hostile, fiercely independent, passive, dependent, feminine, aggressive, warm, castrating person all-in-one. Of course which of these she is at any particular moment would not be random and capricious—it would depend on who she is with, when, how, and much, much more. But each of these aspects of her self may be a quite genuine and real aspect of her total being. (1969, p. 1015)

Once this complexity is acknowledged, we can go beyond the simple idea that people can be filed into one of two categories: the masculine category or the feminine category. We can then recognize that there are at least four kinds of individuals: those who are very masculine (and they will not necessarily all be males), those who are very feminine (and they will not necessarily all be females), those who are really neither very masculine nor very feminine, and those who are both masculine and feminine, the last group being the androgynous people.

Psychologist Sandra Bem has done some important research that provides information on androgyny and androgynous people. The first step in her work was the construction of the Bem Sex-Role Inventory, or BSRI (Bem, 1974), a paper-and-pencil test that measures a person's degree of androgyny. The BSRI contains 20 "masculine" items (for example, "aggressive," "ambitious," "willing to take risks") and 20 "feminine" items (for example, "affectionate," "loves children," "yielding"), as well as 20 "neutral" items (for example, "happy"). Items were included in the masculine list on the basis of the criterion that, in a preliminary study, subjects rated them as being significantly more desirable for males than for females in American society. A parallel criterion was used for the feminine items. To take the BSRI, subjects indicate, for each item on a seven-point scale, the extent to which the item characterizes them. Each person then gets both a masculinity score (average score on the masculine items) and a femininity score (average score on the feminine

---

[3]From the Greek roots *andro*, meaning "man" (as in "androgens"), and *gyn*, meaning "woman" (as in "gynecologist").

items). A person is considered androgynous if she or he has both a high masculinity and a high femininity score. Bem finds that about one-third of the subjects in her college samples are androgynous.

Armed with the BSRI and its ability to detect androgynous people, Bem proceeded to see how androgynous people compare with strongly gender-typed people. She began with the assumption that gender roles constrict people and keep them from enjoying and doing well at certain kinds of activities, namely, activities supposedly reserved for the other gender. She believes that androgynous people are more liberated and do not allow gender roles to stifle their behavior. She tested these assumptions in several studies. For example, in one study subjects were under pressure to conform in their judgments on how funny some jokes were (Bem, 1975). Those who refused to conform would be showing the "masculine" trait of independence. As predicted, masculine subjects and androgynous subjects of both sexes showed significantly more independence than feminine subjects, who were more likely to conform. In another study, subjects listened to a student who poured out a list of troubles in adjusting to college life (Bem et al., 1976). The subjects were scored for their responsiveness to, and sympathy toward, the talker; this was a measure of their nurturance, nurturance being a "feminine" characteristic. As predicted, feminine subjects and androgynous subjects of both sexes were significantly more nurturant to the troubled student than the masculine subjects were.

These two studies, taken together, suggest that androgynous people have the flexibility to exhibit either masculine or feminine behaviors, depending on what the situation calls for; they can be independent when pressured to conform, and they can be nurturant to an unhappy person. On the other hand, the highly masculine person may do well in a situation that requires masculine behavior but may not do so well when feminine behavior is required; similarly, feminine people do well in situations that require feminine behavior but may not be able to function when masculine behavior is necessary. The results then serve to question the traditional assumption that very masculine men and very feminine women are well adjusted; instead, the results suggest that those who are androgynous, and thus transcend gender roles, are better able to function effectively in a wider range of situations.

What implications does androgyny have for sexual behavior? The ways in which gender roles might limit our abilities to respond sexually were discussed in a previous section. Androgyny may represent a new vision not only of personality but also of sexuality. Because androgynous people have both masculine and feminine behaviors in their bag of tricks, they should be more flexible and comfortable in their sexuality.[4] For example, an androgynous person, whether male or female, should feel comfortable initiating sex but should also feel comfortable when the other person initiates sex. An androgynous person should be happy with a position in intercourse in which he or she is on top, as well as with a position in which she or he is on the bottom. An androgynous person would enjoy both the physical aspects of sex and the emotional aspects. Perhaps this androgyn, who integrates both masculinity and femininity, represents the vision of a truly liberated sexuality.

SUMMARY

One of the most basic ways we categorize people is by gender. Along with this categorization go a set of expectations for people of that

---

[4]However, the one study investigating this point found little difference between androgynous and stereotyped people in their styles of sexuality (Allgeier, 1976).

gender (gender roles) and a set of practices in the culture that teach the person to conform to that role (socialization).

Various forces act on females as they grow up. Gender-role stereotypes surely act upon them, such as the beliefs that women are talkative, emotional, and dependent. Males and females actually behave similarly in infancy and early childhood; differences become more pronounced in late childhood and adolescence. One concept learned by adolescents that helps bring about some of the differences is that of femininity-achievement incompatibility. In adulthood, most women define their identity in terms of their roles as wife and mother, although increasing numbers work outside the home. In middle and old age, women may suffer from the empty-nest syndrome.

Boys are influenced by stereotypes that say they should be aggressive, unemotional, self-confident, and so on. In childhood, boys are more aggressive than girls, and boys also have more problems in school. Athletic ability is important in adolescence. In adulthood, the assumption that all men should hold paying jobs goes without question; with it comes a corresponding demand for success. Because so much of his identity has been wrapped up in his job, a man may experience adjustment problems when he retires.

While, for the most part, males and females are quite similar, there are some differences in their behavior. Males are more aggressive and have higher self-esteem than females. While there are no gender differences in IQ, females have better verbal abilities, and males have superior mathematical and spatial abilities. Men and women also have somewhat different styles of communication.

It seems likely that gender roles influence the way people behave sexually, leading men, for example, to take an aggressive role, and women a passive role.

Recent research on androgyny (the combination of both masculine and feminine characteristics in one individual) suggests that it may provide a good alternative to being simply masculine or simply feminine. It also may permit a liberation in sexuality.

SUGGESTIONS FOR FURTHER READING

Bem, Sandra. Androgyny vs. the tight little lives of fluffy women and chesty men. *Psychology Today*, 1975, **9**(4), 58. An interesting description of Bem's research on androgyny.

Chafetz, Janet S. *Masculine/feminine or human? An overview of the sociology of sex roles.* Itasca, Ill.: F. E. Peacock, 1974. An excellent introduction to the sociological approach to gender roles.

Deaux, Kay. *The behavior of women and men.* Monterey, Calif.: Brooks/Cole, 1976. An interesting, concise discussion of the psychology of gender roles and gender differences.

Hyde, Janet S., and Rosenberg, B. G. *Half the human experience: The psychology of women.* Lexington, Mass.: Heath, 1976. I am not in a very good position to give an objective appraisal of this book, but, for what it's worth, I think it is an interesting, comprehensive summary of what is known about the psychology of women.

Pleck, J., and Sawyer, J. (Eds.) *Men and masculinity.* Englewood Cliffs, N.J.: Prentice-Hall, 1974. A good collection of articles on men's roles.

13

FEMALE SEXUALITY AND MALE SEXUALITY

CITED

Hoggity higgamous,
    men are polygamous,
Higgity hoggamous,
    women monogamous.

—Dorothy Parker

There is a widespread belief in our culture that male sexuality and female sexuality are quite different from each other. The Dorothy Parker jingle above expresses one of the ways in which they are thought to differ. In fact, some authors of textbooks on sexuality apparently believe that male sexuality and female sexuality are so different that they discuss them in entirely separate chapters.

Are these stereotypes simply outmoded cultural beliefs that do not exist in reality? Just how different are male sexuality and female sexuality? This chapter will try to answer these questions by examining the available scientific evidence.

DATA ON MALE-FEMALE DIFFERENCES IN SEXUALITY

In the sections that follow, the discussion will focus on areas of sexuality in which there is some evidence of male-female differences. As will be pointed out, there are some differences, but they are in a rather small number of areas—masturbation especially and, to a lesser extent, orgasm consistency in intercourse.

There is a danger in focusing on these differences to the point of forgetting about gender similarities. Gender similarities will be discussed later in the chapter. The reader should keep in mind that males and females are in many ways quite similar in their sexuality—for example, in the physiology of their sexual response (Chapter 7)—while considering the evidence on male-female differences that follows.

Orgasm Consistency

There is some evidence that males and females differ in the consistency with which they orgasm during heterosexual intercourse. Women, on the average, seem to be less consistent at having orgasms—at least during coitus—than men are. Investigators have repeatedly found that about 30 percent of married women never have orgasms or do so only occasionally during intercourse with their husbands (for example, Kinsey et al., 1953; Terman, 1951). Kinsey estimated that the average married female in his sample had orgasms about 75 percent of the time during intercourse with her husband (Kinsey et al., 1953, p. 375). Kinsey believed that males orgasmed 100 percent of the time, or so close to it that he did not bother to tabulate comparable statistics for them. He found, further, that about 36 percent of the women in his sample had never had an orgasm before marrying. These data generally reflect the phenomenon that it is harder for females to orgasm. In fact, one book on female sexuality contains a chapter entitled "The Struggle for Orgasm" (Kronhausen and Kronhausen, 1964), and it expresses how some women feel—as if they have to struggle to have an orgasm. One woman said:

> I don't think I've ever really experienced an orgasm. In any event, not the way I've read about them. My husband's clitoral stimulation usually leads to a climax for me but never during vaginal stimulation. I keep hoping and working at it. Sometimes I tend to think maybe I'm not supposed to experience a vaginal climax. Sometimes it bothers my husband more than it does me. He really feels badly that I don't experience the same type of pleasure he does. Sometimes I think we work at it too hard and sometimes we think we're getting closer to it, but I never experience anything physically ecstatic. (Hite, 1976, pp. 131–132)

The irony of this, of course, is that women are struggling to have their orgasms as quickly as possible, while men are struggling to delay theirs as long as possible.

More recent surveys seem to indicate a trend toward women having orgasms with greater consistency during marital sex. In the Hunt survey (1974), only about 10 to 15 percent of the women reported having orgasms seldom or never.[1] This increased consistency of orgasm might be related to a number of factors, including the increased variety of techniques—such as cunnilingus—that are used in marital sex now. The trend generally seems to be in the direction of diminishing what formerly was a large gender difference in orgasm consistency.

Desire for Sex and Motives for Having Intercourse

In a 1920 survey, two-thirds of the wives reported that they desired intercourse less frequently than their husbands did (cited by R. R. Bell, 1966, p. 137). Though Kinsey provided no direct data on the point, he noted that early in marriage many husbands desired intercourse more frequently than their wives did, although the pattern was often reversed in middle age (Kinsey et al., 1953, p. 353). Traditionally, then, there appeared to be a gender difference in desire for intercourse, with men wanting it more frequently than women did. The "I have a headache" syndrome appeared to be fairly common among women in those studies.

In the recent Hunt survey, though, fewer than 5 percent of the wives said they wished marital intercourse was less frequent (Hunt, 1974). Thus it seems that the "I have a headache" syndrome is mostly a thing of the past. In fact, in the recent *Redbook* survey, one-third of the wives said that they wished they had intercourse *more* frequently than they did.

There is a stereotype that men and women differ in their motives for having sex. Men—at least according to the stereotype—are more interested in the physical aspects of sex and have a "love 'em and leave 'em" attitude. Women, on the other hand, are thought to be most interested in love and romance and to be concerned with the interpersonal more than the physical aspects of the relationship. Unfortunately, there are not direct studies that assess whether these stereotypes are actually true. Psychologist Judith Bardwick reported the following answers from women responding to the question, "Why do you make love?":

[1] Interestingly, the Hunt survey also found some evidence of orgasm inconsistency in men. In that sample, 8 percent of the men 45 and over, 7 percent of the men between 25 and 44, and 15 percent of those under 25 failed to have orgasms a quarter of the time or more during coitus.

Because it's a means of getting closer to him.
I guess because I love him.
A very social thing to do—a way of reaching people.
Mostly to see my boyfriend's enjoyment.
Since we're getting married, it's not wrong.
(1971, pp. 55, 56)

Bardwick sees such responses as indicative of the importance that women attach to love and close relationships. What we do not know, unfortunately, is how men would respond to this same question. One study provides some evidence, though. When college males were asked to give the reason for engaging in their first act of intercourse, the commonest reason was curiosity, followed by "just wanting to"; love for the girl was the reason in only 14 percent of the cases (Shope, 1975, pp. 196–197).

Masturbation

One striking gender difference that emerged in the Kinsey studies was in masturbation. In that sample, 92 percent of the males had masturbated to orgasm at least once in their lives, as compared with 58 percent of the females. Not only did fewer women masturbate, but also, in general, those who did masturbate had begun at a later age than the males. Virtually all males said they had masturbated before age 20 (most began between ages 13 and 15), but substantial numbers of women reported masturbating for the first time at age 25, 30, or 35.

Unlike some other gender differences in behavior—which were present in the older Kinsey study but which seem to have evaporated by the time of the more recent Hunt study—gender differences in masturbation still seem to be a very real phenomenon. Hunt (1974) found that 94 percent of the males and 63 percent of the females in his sample had masturbated to orgasm at least once, percentages that are very close to those found by Kinsey a generation

before. Hunt found that both boys and girls in his study appeared to have begun masturbating earlier than those in Kinsey's study, but girls still began later than boys.

One question we must ask, though, is whether this is a real gender difference or just an inaccuracy induced by using self-reports. In our culture, particularly in previous decades, more restrictions have been placed on female sexuality than on male sexuality. It might be that these restrictions have discouraged females from ever masturbating. On the other hand, they might simply lead females not to report masturbating. That is, perhaps women do masturbate but are simply more reticent to report it than males are. Someone once said that 99 out of 100 people masturbate, and the hundredth is a liar. Are one-third of all women liars, or are they nonmasturbators?

There are, of course, no data to answer that question directly. However, a comparison of the Kinsey data and the Hunt data can provide a clue. In the time intervening between these two studies, presumably restrictions against female sexuality lessened to some extent. A likely consequence of this change is that women began to feel freer to admit that they engaged in various forms of sexual behavior; for example, many more women report that they engage in premarital sex and in oral-genital sex now than at the time of the Kinsey study. Yet the percentage of women who say they masturbate has remained relatively constant (58 percent in the Kinsey study, and 63 percent in the Hunt report). This suggests that the women in Hunt's study would have felt free to say that they masturbated if they really did; after all, they were willing to say that they engaged in premarital sex and oral-genital sex. Thus we can conclude that those who said they did not masturbate were being honest. In the absence of direct evidence, though, this reasoning is purely speculative.

The data suggest, then, that there is a substantial gender difference in the incidence of masturbation; virtually all males masturbate to orgasm, while about one-third of all women never do.

Arousal Response to Erotica

Traditionally in our society most pornographic material—sexually arousing pictures, movies, or stories—has been produced for a male audience. The corresponding assumption presumably has been that women are not interested in such things. Does the scientific evidence bear out this notion?

Kinsey found that the females in his sample were considerably less likely than the males to report responses to erotic materials. For example, about half of the males reported having been aroused at some time by erotic stories; although almost all the women had heard such stories, only 14 percent had been aroused by them. These data are often cited as evidence that women are not so easily aroused as men.[2]

Studies done in the last decade, however, have provided little evidence that males and females differ in their arousal to erotic materials. For example, in one study the responses of 128 male and 128 female university students to erotic slides and movies were studied (Schmidt and Sigusch, 1970). The slides and movies showed petting and coitus. In several tests for gender differences, either there were no differences, or the differences were small, with about 40 percent of the females reporting a stronger arousal response than the average male. All the females and almost all the males reported genital responses to the slides and movies. And women—not men—showed an increase in petting and coitus in the 24 hours after seeing the

erotic stimuli. Therefore, there seems to be little basis for saying that women are not erotically responsive to such materials.

An interesting study by psychologist Julia Heiman (1975) provides a good deal of insight into the responses of males and females to erotic materials. Her subjects were sexually experienced university students, and she studied their responses as they listened to tape recordings of erotic stories. Not only did Heiman obtain subjects' self-ratings of their arousal responses, as other investigators have done, but she also got objective measures of their physiological levels of arousal. To do this, she used two instruments: a penile strain gauge and a photoplethysmograph (Figure 13.1). The penile

FIGURE 13.1

Two devices used to measure physiological sexual response in males and females. The penile strain gauge (left) consists of a flexible band that fits around the base of the penis. The photoplethysmograph (right) is an acrylic cylinder, containing a photocell and light source, which is placed just inside the vagina. *[Photo courtesy of J. R. Heiman.]*

---

[2]Actually, though, the Kinsey data were not that simple. Kinsey noted wide variability in women's responses and speculated that perhaps one-third of all women are as erotically responsive as the average male. Further, there were no gender differences in certain behaviors; for example, about the same number of females as males reported having been aroused by erotic literary materials.

strain gauge is used to get a physiological measure of arousal in the male; it is a flexible loop that fits around the base of the penis. The photoplethysmograph measures physiological arousal in the female; it is an acrylic cylinder 4 by 1 centimeter (1³/₄ by ¹/₂ inch) that is placed just inside the entrance to the vagina. Both instruments measure vasocongestion in the genitals, which is the major physiological response during sexual arousal (see Chapter 7). These physiological measures are a great advance since they are not subject to the errors or distortions that may occur when subjects simply rate their own arousal.

Subjects heard one of four kinds of tapes. There is a stereotype that women are more turned on by romance, while men are more aroused by "raw sex." The tapes varied according to which of these kinds of content they contained. The first group of tapes was *erotic*; they included excerpts from pornographic material and popular novels giving explicit descriptions of heterosexual sex. The second group of tapes was *romantic*; a couple were heard expressing affection and tenderness for each other, but they did not actually engage in sex. The third group of tapes was *erotic-romantic*; they included erotic elements of explicit sex and also romantic elements. Finally, the fourth group of tapes served as a *control*; a couple were heard engaging in conversation but nothing else. The plots of the tapes also varied according to whether the male or the female initiated the activity and whether the description centered on the female's physical and psychological responses or on the male's. Thus the tapes were male-initiated or female-initiated and female-centered or male-centered. Three important results emerged from the study:

1 Explicit sex (the erotic and erotic-romantic tapes) was most arousing, both for women

and for men. The great majority of both males and females responded most, both physiologically and in self-ratings, to the erotic and erotic-romantic tapes. Women, in fact, rated the erotic tapes as more arousing than men did. Neither men nor women responded—either physiologically or in self-reports—to the romantic tapes or to the control tapes (except for a, couple of men who were aroused by a discussion of the relative merits of an anthropology major versus premed—ah, well).

2 Both males and females found the female-initiated, female-centered tape to be most arousing. Perhaps the female-initiated plot was most arousing because of its somewhat forbidden or taboo nature.

3 Women were sometimes not aware of their own physiological arousal. Generally there was a high correlation between self-ratings of arousal and objective physiological measures of arousal, both for men and for women. When men were physically aroused, they never made an error in reporting this in their self-ratings—it is pretty hard to miss an erection. But when the women were physically aroused, about half of them failed to report it in their self-ratings. (One might assume that women who were sophisticated enough to volunteer for an experiment of this nature and who were willing to insert a photoplethysmograph into their vagina would not suddenly become bashful about reporting their arousal; that is, it seems likely that these women honestly did not know when they were physically aroused.)

In sum, then, Heiman's study indicates that males and females are quite similar in their responses to erotic materials but that women can sometimes be unaware of their own physical arousal. This study, however, dealt only with the preliminary stages of arousal; perhaps

FIGURE 13.2
A theater that shows erotic films. Advertisers claim they have as many female patrons as male patrons. *[Bill Stanton/Magnum Photo Library.]*

women vary in the point at which they recognize arousal.

WHY THE DIFFERENCES?

The previous section reviewed the evidence on differences between male and female sexuality. Two differences—the lower percentage of females, compared with males, who masturbate and the higher percentage of females who do not have orgasms during intercourse—seem to be fairly well documented and in need of explanation.[3] Other stereotyped gender differences, such as differences in response to erotic materials, are not well documented by current data and thus are not in need of explanation. What factors, though, lead some women not to masturbate and not to orgasm during intercourse? Many different possible explanations

have been suggested by a wide variety of scholars; these will be considered below.

Biological Factors

There has been some speculation that gender differences in sexuality are created by two biological factors: anatomy and hormones (see, for example, Bardwick, 1971).

Anatomy   The male sexual anatomy is external and visible and responds with a very obvious symptom: erection. When the male is nude, he can easily see his sexual organs, either by looking down or by looking in a mirror. The female sexual organs, in contrast, are hidden. The nude female looks down and sees nothing except pubic hair (which really is not very informative); she looks in a full-length mirror and sees the same thing. Only by doing the mirror exercise described in Chapter 2 can she get a good view of her own genitals. Further, her genitals do not have an obvious arousal re-

---

[3]Unfortunately, both these differences could be interpreted as indicating that women have less of a sexual capacity than men; see, for example, the Focus.

DIFFERENT EQUALS LESS: FEMALE SEXUALITY IN RECENT SEX MANUALS

Sociologists Michael Gordon and Penelope Shankweiler have done an interesting study of the way female sexuality is discussed in marriage and sex manuals. These manuals are important both because they reflect the thoughts of the society in which they are written and because they sell widely and may influence many people's thinking.

The content of a group of old sex manuals, published in the 1800s, reflects the understanding of sex at that time; it was seen as a procreative necessity. Female sexual desire was thought to be virtually nonexistent:

> As a general rule, a modest woman seldom desires any sexual gratification for herself. She submits to her husband, but only to please him; and, but for the desire of maternity, would far rather be relieved from his attentions. The married woman has no wish to be treated on the footing of a mistress. (Hayes, 1869, p. 227)

By the early years of the twentieth century, a change in thinking had occurred. Sex was now seen, in the context of marriage, not only as right and proper but also as an important part of married life. Female sexuality was now acknowledged. But women, supposedly, did not experience sexual desires until they were married, and then only when these were brought to the surface by the husband:

> No doubt women differ greatly, but in every woman who truly loves there lies dormant the capacity to become vibrantly alive in response to her lover, and to meet him as a willing and active participant in the sacrament of marriage. (Gray, 1922, p. 145)

Indeed, sex came to be seen as such an important part of marriage

---

sponse like the male's erection. As a result, she may be less aware of her own arousal responses, a notion that is supported by Heiman's research.

The anatomical explanation, then, is that since the woman's genitals are not in plain view and since their arousal response is less obvious than that of the man's genitals, she is less likely

302
CHAPTER 13

that, by the 1930s, a "cult of mutual orgasm" had developed.

In the 1950s, the books still gave advice based on the notion that the wife entered into marriage a virgin, while the husband was furtively experienced. But by the 1960s the manuals began to acknowledge and be less critical of the fact that women did engage in premarital sex.

Extramarital sex was still overwhelmingly rejected in these books, and the major concern was with improving marital sex so as to avert this eventuality. The "gourmet" sex books, such as *Sex for Advanced Lovers*, are in this vein of rejuvenating marital sex. Hedonism within the context of marriage seems to be the current norm.

In these recent sex manuals, female sexuality is generally treated as "equal but different." Men are presented as sexually simple creatures whose desire is as easily satisfied as it is aroused. Women are seen as requiring love and slow, gentle stimulation. The Masters and Johnson evidence that women have multiple orgasms is not discussed, in terms of either technique or the possible implication that women may have greater sexual potential than men.

The assumption still remains that the man must exercise the leadership and initiative in the relationship. Even the supposedly liberated *Sensuous Woman* gives the following advice to female readers:

> In lovemaking your body is your instrument. You shouldn't settle for less than the best. An Arthur Rubenstein or Van Cliburn is not going to select a clunky, unresponsive, out-of-tune piano on which to perform his artistry. ("J," 1969, p. 28)

Thus, though the gourmet approach to sex encourages a more active role for the woman, it still has not altered the fundamental assumption that the man must take the initiative.

Source: M. Gordon and P. J. Shankweiler. Different equals less: Female sexuality in recent marriage manuals. *Journal of Marriage and the Family,* 1971, **33**, 459–466.

---

to masturbate and less likely to develop her full sexual potential. If this explanation is correct, or at least part of the answer, could anything be done to help women develop their sexuality? Perhaps parents could show their daughters the mirror exercise at an early age and encourage them to become more aware of their own sexual apparatus. It is also possible that parents should teach their daughters to masturbate, an idea that will seem more logical after you have read some of the discussion that follows.

Hormones The hormonal explanation rests on the finding that testosterone is related to sexual behavior. This evidence was reviewed in Chapter 3. Basically, the evidence comes from studies in which male animals are castrated (have their source of testosterone removed), with the result that their sexual behavior disappears, presumably reflecting a decrease in sex drive. If replacement injections of testosterone are given, the sexual behavior returns.

Females generally have lower levels of testosterone in their tissues than males do. Human females, for example, have about one-sixth the level of testosterone in their blood that human males do (Salhanick and Margulis, 1968).

The hormonal explanation, then, is that if testosterone is important in activating sexual behavior and if females have only one-sixth as much of it as males have, this might result in a lower level of sexual behavior such as masturbation in women, or a lower "sex drive."

There are several problems with this logic. First, it may be that cells in the hypothalamus or the genitals of women are more sensitive to testosterone than the comparable cells in men; thus a little testosterone may go a long way in women's bodies (Sherfey, 1966). Second, while testosterone activation of sexual behavior has been fairly well established in animals, such effects are not so well documented in humans, and they may not be nearly so strong. Thus it would be a mistake to make an inference to human males and females from studies done on animals.

Cultural Factors

Our culture has traditionally placed tighter restrictions on women's sexuality than it has on men's, and vestiges of these restrictions linger today. It seems likely that these restrictions have acted as a damper on female sexuality, and thus they may help to explain why some women do not masturbate or do not have orgasms.

One of the clearest examples of the differences in restrictions on male and female sexuality is the *double standard.* The double standard says, essentially, that the same sexual behavior is evaluated differently, depending on whether a male or a female engages in it. An example is premarital sex. Traditionally in our culture, premarital sex has been more acceptable for males than for females. Indeed, premarital sexual activity might be a status symbol for a male but a sign of cheapness for a female.

These different standards have been reflected in behavior. For example, the Kinsey data, collected in the 1940s, indicated that over twice as many males (71 percent) as females (33 percent) had premarital sex. Apparently, society's message got through to young women of that era. Most of them managed to keep themselves chaste before marriage, while their male contemporaries tended to get the experience that was expected of them.

Generally there seems to be less of a double standard today than there was in former times. For example, as the data in Chapter 10 indicate, people now approve of premarital sex for females about as much as they do for males. In Hunt's sample, 82 percent of the men felt that premarital sex was acceptable for males when the couple are in love, and 77 percent felt that it was acceptable for females under the same circumstances (Hunt, 1974). Interestingly, the females in the sample seemed to believe in a double standard more than the males did.

This change in attitudes is reflected in behavior. A much higher percentage of women report having engaged in premarital sex now than in Kinsey's time. In the Hunt sample, among respondents aged 18 to 24, 95 percent of the males and 81 percent of the females had

had premarital sex. Thus there is much less of a difference between males and females now than there was a generation ago; the vast majority of both males and females are now engaging in premarital sex. Premarital sex still remains somewhat more common among males, though.

The decline of the double standard may help to explain why some of the gender differences found in older studies of sex behavior have disappeared in more recent studies. When cultural forces do not make such a distinction between male and female, males and females become more similar in their sexual behavior.

Gender roles are another cultural force that may contribute to differences in male and female sexuality, as was discussed in Chapter 12. Gender roles dictate proper behavior for females and males in sexual interactions. For example, there is a stereotype of the male as the aggressor and the female as the passive object of his advances; surely this does not encourage the woman to take active steps to bring about her own orgasms. As a result of such stereotypes, the male has borne the whole weight of responsibility, both for his response and for the woman's response, and women have not been encouraged to take responsibility for producing their own pleasure.

Marital and family roles may play a part. When children are born, they can act as a damper on the parents' sexual relationship. The couple lose their privacy when they gain children. They may worry about their children bursting through an unlocked door and witnessing the "primal scene." Or they may be concerned that their children will hear the sounds of lovemaking. Generally, though, the woman is assigned the primary responsibility for child rearing, and so she may be more aware of the presence of the children in the house and more concerned about possible harmful effects on them of witnessing their parents engaging in sex. Once again, her worry and anxiety do not contribute to her having a satisfying sexual experience.

A related point is that a couple typically have sex in their own home or apartment; at least for the traditional homemaker, this is her place of work. Her homemaking responsibilities may then intrude into her sexual expression. For example, one hears of men complaining that their wives leap up in the middle of lovemaking to go and turn off the oven because they think the roast is overcooking. This understandably hurts a man's feelings, and it cannot be doing a thing to help the woman have an orgasm. The woman whose ear is cocked to hear whether a baby is crying or whose nose is sniffing to see whether dinner is burning is not the woman who has an orgasm.

Other Factors

A number of other factors, not easily classified as biological or cultural, may also contribute to differences between male and female sexuality.[4]

Women get pregnant and men do not. Particularly in the days before highly effective contraceptives were available, pregnancy might be a highly undesirable consequence of sexuality for a woman. Thinking that an episode of lovemaking might result in a nine-month-long pregnancy and another mouth to feed could put a damper on anyone's sexuality. Even today, pregnancy fears can be a force. For example, research in the 1970s indicated that 75 percent of sexually active single girls used contraceptives not at all or only occasionally (Teen-Age Sex, 1972). A woman who is worried about whether she will become pregnant—and, if she is not married, about whether others will find out that she has been engaging in sexual activity—is not in a state conducive to the

---

[4]Other possible causes of orgasm problems in women are discussed in Chap. 18.

enjoyment of sex, much less the experience of orgasm (although this scarcely explains why women do not masturbate).

Ineffective techniques of stimulating the woman may also be a factor. Kinsey found, for example, that women could masturbate to orgasm about as quickly as men could. This suggests that it is no harder for women to orgasm than it is for men, since they do it with about equal ease when they masturbate (and presumably they give themselves about ideal stimulation when they masturbate). The commonest techniques of intercourse, with the penis moving in and out of the vagina, may provide good stimulation for the male but not for the female, since she is not getting sufficient clitoral stimulation. As Kinsey concluded:

> Some 45 percent of all those females in the sample who had ever masturbated reported that they usually reached orgasm in three minutes or less, and another 25 percent in something between four and five minutes. . . . Many of those who took longer to reach orgasm did so deliberately in order to prolong the pleasure of the activity and not because they were incapable of responding more quickly.
>
> These data on the female's speed in reaching orgasm provide important information on her basic sexual capacities. There is a widespread opinion that the female is slower than the male in her sexual responses, but the masturbatory data do not support that opinion. The average male may take something between two and three minutes to reach orgasm unless he deliberately prolongs his activity. . . . It is true that the average female responds more slowly than the average male in coitus, but this seems to be due to the ineffectiveness of the usual coital techniques. (Kinsey et al., 1953, pp. 163–164)

Perhaps the problem, then, is that women are expected to orgasm as a result of intercourse, when that is not a very effective technique for producing orgasms in women.

There may also be a relationship between the data on women not masturbating and the data on women not orgasming. Childhood and adolescent experiences with masturbation are important early sources of learning about sexuality. Through these experiences we learn how our body responds to sexual stimulation and what the most effective techniques for stimulating our own bodies are. This learning is important to our experience of adult, two-person sex. Perhaps the women who do not masturbate, and who are thus deprived of this early learning experience, are the same ones who do not have orgasms in sexual intercourse. This is exactly what Kinsey's data suggested—that women who masturbate to orgasm before marriage are more likely to orgasm in intercourse with their husbands.[5] For example, 31 percent of the women who had never masturbated to orgasm before marriage had not had an orgasm by the end of their first year of marriage, while only 13 to 16 percent of the women who had masturbated had not had orgasms in their first year of marriage (Kinsey et al., 1953, p. 407). There seems to be a possibility, then, that women's lack of experience with masturbation in adolescence is related to their problems with having orgasms during intercourse. The following quotation illustrates how some women discover masturbation late and how this may be related to orgasm capacity in heterosexual sex:

> I thought I was frigid, even after three years of marriage, until I read this book and learned how to turn myself on. After I gave myself my first orgasm, I cried for half an hour, I was so relieved. Afterwards, I did it a lot, for many months, and I talked to my doctor and to my husband, and finally I began to make it in intercourse. (Hunt, 1974, pp. 96–97)

---

[5]Note that this is in direct contradiction to the old-fashioned advice given in manuals that suggested that "getting hooked" on masturbation might impair later marital sexuality; if anything, just the reverse is true.

Not only may women's relative inexperience with masturbation lead to a lack of sexual learning, but it also may create a kind of "erotic dependency" on men. Typically, boys' earliest sexual experiences are with masturbation, which they learn how to do from other boys. More important, they learn that they can produce their own sexual pleasure. Girls typically have their earliest sexual experiences in heterosexual petting. They therefore learn about sex from boys. Their early learning experiences are with boys, and they learn that their sexual pleasure is produced by the male. As sex researcher John Gagnon commented:

> Young women may know of masturbation, but not know *how* to masturbate—how to produce pleasure, or even what the pleasures of orgasm might be. . . . Some young women report that they learned how to masturbate after they had orgasm from intercourse and petting, and decided they could do it for themselves. (1977, p. 152)

And Betty Dodson, in her book *Liberating Masturbation,* says:

> Masturbation is the way we discover our eroticism, the way we learn to respond sexually, the way we learn to love ourselves and build self-esteem. Sex is like any other skill—it has to be learned and practiced. When a woman masturbates, she learns to like her own genitals, to enjoy sex and orgasm, and furthermore, to become proficient and independent about it. (1974, cited in Gagnon, 1977, p. 161)

Once again, these ideas might lead to a recommendation that girls be taught to masturbate. It is also possible that, as women begin having as much premarital sexual experience as men, their orgasmic response will become more consistent.

Numerous factors that may contribute to shaping male and female sexuality have been discussed. My own feeling is that a combination of several of these factors produces the differences that do exist. I think that the early differences in experiences with masturbation are very important. Although these differences may result from differences in anatomy, they could be eliminated by teaching girls to masturbate. Women may enter into adult sexual relationships with a lack of experience in the bodily sensations of arousal and orgasm, and they may also be unaware of the best techniques for stimulating their own bodies. Put this lack of experience together with various cultural forces, such as the double standard and ineffective techniques of stimulation, and it is not too surprising that some women do have problems having orgasms.

BEYOND THE YOUNG ADULTS

One of the problems with our understanding of gender differences in sexuality is that so much of the research has concentrated on college students or other groups of young adults (as is true of much behavioral research). For example, Schmidt and Sigusch used college students as subjects in their studies of male-female differences in arousal response to erotic materials, as did Heiman in her research. Using this population may provide a very narrow view of male-female differences; they are considered during only a very small part of the lifespan.

Female sexuality and male sexuality change in their nature and focus across the lifespan. For example, it is a common belief in our culture that men reach their sexual "peak" at around age 19, while women do not reach theirs until they are 35 or 40. There is some scientific evidence supporting this view. Kinsey found, for example, that women generally had orgasms more consistently at 40 than they did at 25.

Psychiatrist Helen Singer Kaplan, a specialist in therapy for sexual dysfunctions, has ad-

FEMALE SEXUALITY: THE HITE REPORT

MALE SEXUALITY: BEYOND THE MALE MYTH

The Hite Report, published in 1976, has received a great deal of publicity as providing a new view of female sexuality. The book is based on a survey of women conducted by Shere Hite, who holds an M.A. in history.

Hite's questionnaire consisted of open-ended (as opposed to multiple-choice) questions about female sexuality; respondents could make their answers as detailed as they wished. For example, one question read, "Please give a graphic description or a drawing of how your body could best be stimulated to orgasm." Hite mailed the questionnaires to women's groups, including chapters of the National Organization for Women and abortion-rights groups, and to university women's centers. Notices were also placed in *The Village Voice* and in *Mademoiselle, Bride's,* and *Ms.* magazines, as well as in church newsletters and women's newsletters, telling readers that they could write in to request copies of the questionnaire. *Oui* magazine ran a copy of the questionnaire, and an early paperback by Hite included a copy and requested that readers send replies. Beginning in 1972, Hite distributed over 100,000 copies of the questionnaire. Completed replies were received from 3019 women (a 3 percent response rate).

Hite's study has some of the same problems present in other survey-type sex research, such as the Kinsey reports and the Hunt survey; for example, only people who were willing to have their sexual behavior surveyed were included as subjects, and the data were based on people's self-reports of their sexual behavior (which may not be very accurate) rather than on actual observations of behavior. The study had an additional bias: because the questionnaires were distributed so heavily through feminist groups, the sample was probably composed of a high percentage of feminists. It was certainly not a random sample of women in the United States, and it was most probably not a representative sample of them, either. There are few Kinsey-type percentages in the book;

FIGURE 13.3
Shere Hite, author of *The Hite Report. [Bettye Lane/Nancy Palmer Photo Agency, Inc.]*

this was a wise decision on Hite's part since, because of the biased sample, the percentages would have been limited to the sample of 3019 respondents and could not have been generalized any further.

One interesting finding emerged in the report. Hite asked: "Do you regularly achieve (sic!) orgasm during intercourse without separate massaging of the clitoris?" Only 26 percent of the respondents said "yes." Unfortunately, because of the peculiarities of the sampling techniques used, one could not infer that only 26 percent of all American women would have answered "yes" to this question. The low percentage is nonetheless interesting, and the question deserves investigation in future sex research.

The Hite study is prescientific. Its main value lies in the

countless direct quotations that constitute the major part of the text of the book. Some are sad, some are happy, and some are poignant. Examples have been scattered in various chapters of the present text, and so one will suffice here:

> The Sexual Revolution tells me I am abnormal if I don't desire to make it with every Tom, Dick, or Jane that I see. I am only free to say yes. (Hite, 1976, p. 312)

In reading *The Hite Report*, some women may recognize themselves, and men may learn more about female sexuality.

Psychiatrist Anthony Pietropinto and writer Jacqueline Simenauer, apparently feeling that the Hite report was anti-male and wanting to provide a more accurate picture of male sexuality, conducted a survey of men for *Beyond the Male Myth*.

The authors commissioned an independent research organization to conduct the study. A questionnaire was developed consisting of 40 multiple-choice items and 4 open-ended questions, the latter varying in content from one respondent to the next. The sampling proceeded as follows: Field agents were sent to numerous communities; there they approached men in shopping centers, in office-building complexes, at tennis clubs, on college campuses, and at airports and bus depots, and asked them to complete the questionnaire. Responses were obtained from 4066 men; the agents "estimated" that half the men approached agreed to participate. While this method of sampling may seem better than Hite's, a probability sample of American men was not initially identified, and the nonresponse rate was still high. Therefore, the percentages given in this study may be no more true of American men than Hite's percentages are true of American women.

Some interesting findings emerged from the study:

---

vanced an interesting view of differences between male sexuality and female sexuality across the lifespan (Kaplan and Sager, 1971). According to her analysis, the teenage male's sexuality is very intense and almost exclusively genitally focused. As the male approaches age 30, he is still highly interested in sex, but not so urgently. He is also satisfied with fewer orgasms, as opposed to the adolescent male, who may have four to eight orgasms per day through

masturbation. With age, the man's refractory period becomes longer. By the age of 50, he is typically satisfied with two orgasms a week, and the focus of his sexuality is not so completely genital; sex becomes a more sensuously diffuse experience, and there is a greater emotional component.

In women, the process is often quite different. Their sexual awakening may occur much later; they may, for example, not begin mastur-

In response to the question, "How do you feel about being in love?" 38 percent of the men said that love was the most important thing in their lives.*

The majority of the men (60 percent) said they were irritated most by a woman who seemed cold or uninterested while having sex. Few of them (less than 5 percent) said they were irritated by a woman who made the first advance, by a woman who made demands, or by a woman who seemed "too easy."

About 47 percent of the men reported cheating on a wife or steady girlfriend at least once.

About 32 percent of the men said they would prefer to marry a virgin. The percentage varied with the age of the man, but even among those aged 18 to 29, it was 25 percent.

The two most frequent responses to the question, "What could your partner do to make you more excited?" were "be more active" (34 percent) and "use more oral sex" (24 percent).

The Hite Report and Beyond the Male Myth provide some interesting ideas about female and male sexuality. Unfortunately, we have no way of knowing whether they are accurate. Therefore, studies using more adequate scientific methods are still badly needed in this area.

---

*The responses may have been influenced by the alternatives listed in the multiple-choice items. For example, on this question respondents were forced to choose from among answers describing various degrees of enthusiasm about love. Their responses might have been different had they been asked to list what was most important to them, given choices of love, power, money, success, sex, etc. Many of the alternatives on the multiple-choice items in this survey seem arbitrary.

Sources: Shere Hite. The Hite report. New York: Macmillan, 1976. Anthony Pietropinto and Jacqueline Simenauer. Beyond the male myth. New York: Times Books, 1977.

---

bating until age 30 or 35. While they are in their teens and twenties, their orgasmic response is slow and inconsistent. However, by the time they reach their mid-thirties, their sexual response has become quicker and more intense, and they orgasm more consistently than they did during their teens and twenties. They initiate sex more frequently than they did in the past. Also, the greatest incidence of extramarital sex in women occurs among those in their late thirties. Vaginal lubrication takes place almost instantaneously in women in this age group.

Men, then, seem to begin with an intense, genitally focused sexuality and only later develop an appreciation for the sensuous and emotional aspects of sex. Women have an early awareness of the sensuous and emotional aspects of sex and develop the capacity for intense genital response later. To express this in another way, we might use the terminology suggested by Ira Reiss: *person-centered sex* and *body-centered-sex*. Adolescent male sexuality is body-centered, and the person-centered aspect is not added until later. Adolescent female sexuality is person-centered, and body-centered sex comes later.

It is important to remember, though, that these patterns may be culturally, rather than biologically, produced. In some other cultures—for example, Mangaia in the South Pacific (see Chapter 1)—females have orgasms 100 percent of the time during coitus, even when they are adolescents.

THE FUTURE

The data indicate that major changes in sexual behavior have occurred in the last several decades and that these changes have affected female and male sexuality. Will there be further changes in the future, and, if so, what will they be?

Gender Similarities

Comparison of the Kinsey data and the Hunt data suggests that there has been a trend toward gender similarities in sexual behavior recently; that is, male sexual behavior and female sexual behavior are becoming more similar than they were in former times. For example, premarital sex used to be much more common among males than among females, but now it is quite common among both.

It seems reasonable to expect that this trend toward gender similarities will continue. One of the best pieces of data to use for making projections into the future concerns the youngest age group (aged 18 to 24) in the Hunt (1974) survey. In that group, 95 percent of the males and 81 percent of the females had had premarital sex. This suggests that in the future nearly everyone, both males and females, will have premarital sex. Under those circumstances, there can scarcely be a double standard.

A similar trend toward gender similarities in the 18- to 24-year-old age group is also indicated by the data on extramarital sex. While that behavior traditionally was much more common among males, the data from the youngest age group suggest that women may be catching up; in that group, 32 percent of the males and 24 percent of the females had engaged in extramarital sex.

The trend toward gender similarities, though, is not limited to females' becoming more like males. Male sexuality is also changing and is showing some tendency to move in the direction of female patterns. For example, as noted earlier, some males now experience problems having orgasm in intercourse (Hunt, 1974). Men are now much less likely to have sex with prostitutes than they were a generation ago (Hunt, 1974). Males are generally less promiscuous than they were, and their premarital sexual relations tend to center on one partner (Schmidt, 1977).

The "New Impotence"?

Some magazines have been carrying articles on the "new impotence." The idea is that, with the rise of the women's liberation movement, a sexually liberated, sexually demanding woman has emerged and that some men feel so threatened by this situation that they have become impotent. As data supporting this view, some psychotherapists and sex therapists feel that they are seeing a sharp rise in the number of men seeking help for problems of impotence (Ginsberg et al., 1972).

Does the sexual liberation of women create impotence in men? There really are not any good scientific data on either side of this argument, and so I will simply offer my own opinion. I think that the apparent rise in cases of impotence is largely illusory. There have probably always been numerous cases of impotence; they appear more frequent now because of all the publicity given to sex therapy. Men probably now feel that it is more socially acceptable to admit they are having a problem with impotence and to seek therapy for it. Thus I doubt that more men are now impotent; there are simply more of them who are willing to ask for help with the problem. Masters and Johnson (1970) report that they treated many cases of impotence during the 1960s and felt that sexual dysfunctions were quite common, and this was before the women's movement was really rolling. I agree with Masters and Johnson, who feel that men stand to gain much from the women's movement (1974).

Greater Sex Drive in Women?

Masters and Johnson, among others, have speculated that women actually have an innately stronger sex drive than men have, in direct opposition to the stereotype that women's sex drive is weaker (Masters and Johnson, 1966; see also Sherfey, 1966). As evidence, they cite the insatiable sex drive of female primates in estrus. A female chimpanzee, when in estrus, "presents" herself to one male after the next, perhaps copulating with a dozen in an hour. She appears to be nearly insatiable. Could it be that human females, who are capable of having sex at any phase in their cycle, are continuously insatiable? Another piece of evidence that is cited is the capacity of women to have multiple orgasms. Unlike men, who enter into a refractory period following orgasm, women may have one orgasm after another, which might suggest a greater, not a smaller, sexual capacity than men's. The argument then goes that in prehistoric, primitive human societies, the powerful sex drive of women created havoc—not to mention making the men feel insecure—and therefore societies instituted restrictions on female sexuality to bring it more in line with male sexuality; that explains the restrictions on female sexuality that persist to the present day. Since there are really no scientific data on this point, the whole idea is purely speculative,

though intriguing. Perhaps, as restrictions on female sexuality lessen, future generations will regard women as having the greater sex drive.

One final point deserves mention. One product of the feminist movement in the last decade has been a flourishing of research on women, particularly on female sexuality, based on the notion that female sexuality had been a misunderstood and neglected topic. As a result, numerous studies of female sexuality are available now, some of them good and some of them not so good. A fairly complete understanding of female sexuality seems to be emerging. We know, for example, that coitus is not a particularly effective method for stimulating women to orgasm. In doing research for this chapter, though, I was struck by the fact that now we seem to know more about female sexuality than about male sexuality. What we need in the next decade is research on male sexuality or good studies comparing male sexuality and female sexuality. Perhaps then we will have a real understanding of both.

SUMMARY

The evidence indicates that there is a gender difference in masturbation. While virtually all men masturbate, a sizeable number—perhaps one-third—of all women never do. There is also some tendency for women to be less consistent than men in having orgasms during intercourse, although this gender difference has decreased in recent years. Gender differences in other aspects of sexuality—such as desire for sex, motives for having intercourse, and arousal response to erotic materials—are not so well documented, or else the differences that existed a generation ago have evaporated in recent years. For the most part, then, males and females are now quite similar in their sexuality.

Julia Heiman's study of arousal response to erotic stories suggests that women and men are about equally aroused by similar erotic stories but that women may sometimes not be aware of their own preliminary stages of physical arousal.

Numerous factors may contribute to creating male-female differences in orgasm consistency and masturbation. Biological factors include anatomy (the male's genitals are more observable, and his arousal response is more obvious) and hormones (males have higher testosterone levels than females). Cultural factors include the double standard and gender roles. Other factors include pregnancy fears in women, women's distraction by household and child-rearing responsibilities, and the use of ineffective techniques in stimulating the female. Because many women do not masturbate in childhood or adolescence, they miss this important sexual learning experience, which may contribute to later inconsistency in orgasm.

Patterns of gender differences in sexuality change over the lifespan. Males' sexuality is genitally focused in adolescence and early adulthood; it acquires the sensuous and emotional components later. Females' sexuality in adolescence and early adulthood is focused more on the emotional aspects of sex; the capacity for intense genital response develops later, perhaps around the ages of 35 to 40.

It seems reasonable to expect present trends toward gender similarities in sexual behavior to continue into the future.

SUGGESTIONS FOR FURTHER READING

Heiman, Julia R. The physiology of erotica: Women's sexual arousal. *Psychology Today*, 1975, **8**(11), 90–94. A report on Heiman's interesting research on women's and men's arousal response to erotic materials, discussed in this chapter.

Masters, William H., and Johnson, Virginia. What men stand to gain from women's liberation. In William H. Masters and Virginia Johnson, *The pleasure bond.* Boston: Little, Brown, 1974.

Sherfey, Mary Jane. The evolution and nature of female sexuality in relation to psychoanalytic theory. *Journal of the American Psychoanalytic Association,* 1966, **4**, 28–128. (Paperback published by Vintage Books.) An excellent discussion of female sexuality, with a refutation of some points of psychoanalytic theory that need refutation.

14

HOMOSEXUALITY
AND BISEXUALITY

CITED

The homosexual today is kind of like the invisible man. But what most people don't realize is that homosexuals are all around. They're not just somewhere "out there." They are in one's own family—they could be one's doctor, one's minister, one's friend, husband, wife, whatever. People don't like to think about this, but it is so. There are a lot of homosexuals, a group of people, in fact, numbering into the millions, and they're not going to stay invisible forever.

—Dr. Martin Hoffman*

In June 1969, in response to police harassment, homosexuals rioted in a bar in Greenwich Village, in perhaps the first open group rebellion of homosexuals in history. Gay liberation was born. Since then, the public has been forced into an awareness of a phenomenon—homosexuality—that it had previously preferred to ignore. Indeed, the September 8, 1975, issue of *Time* magazine featured a cover story on homosexuals. Gay liberationists proclaim that gay is good and that homosexuals are not "sick" and should not be treated differently from the way heterosexuals are treated. Meanwhile, the average American charitably maintains that homosexuals are sick.

Most of us want to understand homosexuality better; at the very least, we are curious about it. The purpose of this chapter is to try to provide a better understanding of homosexuality and a closely related phenomenon, bisexuality.

First, though, some terms need to be de-

fined. A *homosexual* is a person who has sexual relations with a member of the same gender (although, as will be seen later in the chapter, this is much too simple a definition). The word is derived from the Greek root *homo* meaning "same" (not the Latin word *homo,* meaning "man"). The term "homosexual" may be applied in a general way to homosexuals of both genders or specifically to male homosexuals. The term "lesbian," which is used to refer to female homosexuals, can be traced to the great Greek poetess Sappho, who lived on the island of Lesbos (hence "lesbian") around 600 B.C. She is famous for the immortal love poetry, only fragments of which remain, that she wrote to other women. Sappho was actually married, apparently happily, and had one daughter, but her homosexual feelings were the focus of her life. In her poetry one grasps the grace, beauty, and aesthetic qualities of lesbian love.

Several other terms are also used in conjunction with homosexuality. Gay liberationists prefer the term "gay" to "homosexual" because the latter emphasizes the sexual aspects of the lifestyle and can be used as a derogatory label,

*Source: Quoted in Bettie Wysor. *The lesbian myth.* New York: Random House, 1974, p. 125.

since there are so many negative connotations to homosexuality.[1] A heterosexual is then referred to as "straight."

The term "homophile" is also used to mean someone who likes people of the same gender; like the word "gay," it does not have the sexual connotations of the term "homosexual." There are, of course, a number of derogatory slang terms for homosexuals, such as "queer," "fairy," and "faggot" or "fag."

STEREOTYPES AND DISCRIMINATION

Just as there are stereotypes about other minority groups—for example, the stereotype that all blacks are stupid and lazy—so there are stereotypes about homosexuals. This section will be about some of these stereotyped ideas and attitudes in order to see whether they bear any relation to reality.

Attitudes toward Homosexuality

First, it is important to note what may be a fairly obvious point, namely, that most Americans disapprove of homosexuality. In a 1970 study conducted by the Institute for Sex Research, two-thirds of the respondents regarded homosexuality as "very obscene and vulgar." In a 1969 Harris poll, 63 percent of Americans considered homosexuals harmful to American life. The view of homosexuality held by the majority of Americans is that it is a "curable illness." Finally, few Americans are in favor of

legalizing homosexual behaviors. In a CBS poll conducted in 1966, fewer than one in five of the respondents favored legalizing private homosexual behavior between adults (M. S. Weinberg and Williams, 1974).

The intensity of these negative attitudes is illustrated in the following comments taken from letters to the editor written in response to the 1975 *Time* magazine cover story on homosexuality:

> Disgusting, repulsive, lowbrow, nauseating. I'm no Victorian, but those individuals should crawl into a hole—and take *Time* with them.

> I was revolted by Matlovich's face proclaiming "I am a homosexual." He is a disgrace to the uniform of an honorable service.

> From time immemorial we have recognized yellow fever, malaria, syphilis, leprosy, perversion, degeneracy, garbage, and homosexuality in about that order. There need be no change.

But one writer offered a rather profound thought:

> Only in the armed forces can you be highly decorated for killing thousands of your fellow men and be drummed out of the corps if you dare to love one.

It is important to recognize the psychological impact that these negative attitudes have on the gay person. Certainly they are not an institutionalized form of discrimination, like the laws that make certain behaviors illegal, but in terms of the day-to-day living of the gay person they are a much more salient form of discrimination. It is not very pleasant for gays to realize that the majority of Americans consider them vulgar and obscene. At best, this must create some alienation from society; at worst, gay persons may begin to internalize these attitudes and come to think of themselves as vulgar and obscene, an

---

[1] It is wise to have a good vocabulary on topics such as this. My husband had an aunt, a single lady, who frequently invited a pair of single young men who lived across the hall from her to her parties. The men wrote on interior decorating for a women's magazine and were fairly open about their homosexuality. Aunt Mary, while an otherwise sophisticated person, was unaware of the usage of the term "gay." Greeting them at her party, she typically complimented them on their appearance by saying, in a loud voice, "My, how gay you look." Indeed.

FIGURE 14.1
Lesbian relationships, as in Rubens's *Jupiter and Callisto,* have been shown rather frequently in art. Interestingly, though, male homosexual relationships are rarely depicted or are more carefully disguised. *[The New York Public Library.]*

insidious psychological process. Apparently, this latter process has not occurred to a large extent, though, since only about 11 percent of gays subscribe to the belief that homosexuality is an illness (M. S. Weinberg and Williams, 1974, p. 113).

In a beautiful illustration of the psychological impact of society's attitudes toward homosexuality on the gay person, the authors of a psychology text ask the reader to imagine that being anxious is as taboo as being gay:

> Imagine for a moment that you are an anxious person and that being anxious is against the law. You must try to hide your fears from others. Your own home may be a safe place to feel anxious, but a public display of apprehension can lead to arrest or at least to social ostracism. At work one day an associate looks at you suspiciously and says, "That's funny, for a crazy moment there I thought you were anxious." "Heck no," you exclaim a bit too loudly, *"not me."* You begin to wonder if your fellow worker will report his suspicions to your boss. If he does, your boss may inform the police or will at least change your job to one that requires less contact with customers, especially with those who have children. (Davison and Neale, 1974, p. 293)

Stereotypes about Gays

In addition to negative attitudes, many Americans have stereotyped ideas about homosexuals.

The swish and the dyke   One such stereotype is that all male homosexuals are effeminate; they are supposed to be limp-wristed, have a swishy walk, and talk with a lisp.[2] The corresponding stereotype about the lesbian is that she is masculine; she has short hair and wears a man-tailored suit. Because people have these stereotyped ideas, they believe that it is easy to spot homosexuals and that it is always obvious who is a gay and who is a straight. In fact, these

---

[2]In contrast to this stereotype, a recent study of male university athletes found that 40 percent of them had engaged in homosexual behavior to orgasm in the last two years (Garner and Smith, 1977).

stereotypes are far from the truth, and people's abilities to spot homosexuals are not nearly so good as they think they are. Most gay people look and behave just like everybody else. Except for a small percentage of cases, it is impossible to tell a homosexual simply by appearance and mannerisms. Kinsey estimated that only about 15 percent of male homosexuals could be identified by their appearance. This is particularly true now because recent fashions in clothing have been stolen in part from gays; women now wear pants frequently, and men wear jewelry and tight-fitting, colorful clothes. Mustaches are much in style for male gays, as they are for male straights.

The belief that male homosexuals are feminine and that lesbians are masculine represents a confusion of two important concepts: *gender identity* (masculine or feminine) and *choice of sexual partner* (heterosexual or homosexual). The gay person differs from the majority in choice of sexual partner because he or she makes the homosexual choice, but the gay person does not typically differ from the majority in gender identity. That is, the male homosexual chooses a partner of the same gender, but his identity is quite definitely masculine. He thinks of himself as male and has no desire to be a female. The same holds true for the lesbian; while she makes a homosexual choice of sexual partner, she is quite definitely a woman and typically has no desire to be a man (Wolff, 1971). (Interestingly, this confusion of the concepts of choice of sexual partner and gender identity also occurs in some of the scientific theories about homosexuality to be discussed later in this chapter.)

The role-playing stereotype   Another common stereotype is that, in their relationships, homosexuals role-play heterosexual roles: that in a pair of male homosexuals, one will assume the dominant role, and the other the submissive role, and that in a pair of lesbians, one will play the male role ("butch"), and the other the female role ("femme"). In the sexual act itself, some people believe that the inserter is playing the active (or masculine) role, while the insertee is playing the passive (or feminine) role. While such role playing does occur to some extent, in fact it is far from typical.

In regard to sexual practices, most homosexuals engage in all forms of behavior and do not restrict themselves to one or another role. One study of a group of male homosexuals (Hooker, 1965) found that 46 percent practiced all forms of sexual activity and varied their roles (insertor or insertee) depending on the preference of the partner, a wish for variety, and so on. Only 20 percent of the sample showed a distinct preference for given activities and for a particular role. Homosexual partners often switch roles during the sex act or engage in mutual oral-genital stimulation, further calling into question the notion that one plays the male role, and one the female role.

In regard to role playing outside the sexual act itself, the practice seems to be far from typical. Del Martin and Phyllis Lyon, gay activists and cofounders of the Daughters of Bilitis, observe that for lesbians such role playing occurs mainly among the young and immature. When first entering the lesbian lifestyle, women attempt to set up a relationship based on the only model they have available, that of heterosexual relations. Unfortunately, this role playing leads to all the problems inherent in heterosexual roles—dominance and submissiveness, inequality in decision making, and so on. Thus, these roles are generally discarded as the relationship progresses and matures (Martin and Lyon, 1972). With the combined influences of gay activism and a generalized questioning of gender roles in our culture, the incidence of this role playing seems to be even more on the decline; many gay young women today are also feminists and therefore reject the practice of male-female role playing.

The child-molester stereotype   Another common belief is that male homosexuals are child molesters. If an elementary school teacher or even a high school teacher is discovered to be a homosexual, there is an instant public outcry demanding that he be fired, based on the belief that he will try to seduce all the young boys in the school. Strangely, the same people who worry about this never seem to worry that heterosexual male teachers will try to seduce young girls, although that seems to be just as logical a possibility. Actually, most child molesting is done by heterosexual men to little girls; 80 percent of child molesting is in that category, and only 20 percent is homosexual (McCaghy, 1971). Further, most adolescents are initiated into homosexual activity not by an adult but rather by another teenager (Sorensen, 1973). Therefore, there is no reason to assume that a given homosexual is a child molester. Most homosexuals mind their own business and are not particularly interested in gaining converts.

Jokes about gays   Jokes are one reflection of society's negative attitudes toward homosexuals and of the fact that homosexuals have not been accepted as much by the general public as other minorities have. It is no longer considered acceptable for television comedians to make jokes about the stupidity or dishonesty of blacks or the mercenary qualities of Jews; formerly such jokes were common, but now they are extremely rare. Jokes about homosexuals are very common, though, and in a sense homosexuals have become the new minority. Recently on a single one-hour variety program, I counted five separate derogatory jokes about homosexuality—the standard routine about limp wrists and lisps.

People make jokes about things that make

them uncomfortable, and so the frequency of these jokes indicates how anxiety-provoking homosexuality is to people. (This fear of gays is called *homophobia*.) But jokes may also have an effect on the people about whom they are made. When gay people hear entertainers make jokes about their way of life, this must at least make them uncomfortable and might even encourage them to believe the stereotypes incorporated in the jokes. Jokes may represent a particularly insidious form of stereotyping because the ideas conveyed in them are not subject to rational and open debate: who would argue with the content of a joke? Thus they contribute to a kind of nonconscious ideology (Bem and Bem, 1970) that teaches that gays are limp-wristed, swishy, silly, and generally the object of public ridicule. It would be interesting to do an analysis of the content of jokes on television to see how many jokes ridicule homosexuals and to see whether the frequency of such jokes declines in the future as people come to accept homosexuality more.

Gays as a Minority Group

From the foregoing, it is clear that gay people are the subject of many stereotypes, just as other minorities are. They also have several other things in common with members of other minority groups. First, they suffer from job discrimination. Just as blacks and women have been denied access to certain jobs, so too have homosexuals. Homosexuality is grounds for a dishonorable discharge from the armed forces, and there are many cases in which this rule has been applied (Martin and Lyon, 1972; Williams and Weinberg, 1971).[3] Homosexuality has also

---

[3]The case of Leonard Matlovich, which challenges this practice, has attracted wide attention. Matlovich, an Air Force sergeant who was decorated with a Bronze Star and a Purple Heart for his service in Vietnam, has openly declared his homosexuality and is challenging the right of the Air Force to discharge him. His lawyers hope that his case will reach the Supreme Court and that the Court will make a landmark ruling on the rights of homosexuals.

been grounds for firing a person from federal employment and for denial of a security clearance. The reason commonly given for the latter two rules is that homosexuals are very susceptible to being blackmailed and therefore cannot be put in situations in which they have access to sensitive information. Actually, many heterosexuals might also be susceptible to blackmail because of their sexual activities—for example, the married man who is having an affair—although such factors are not grounds for denial of security clearance. In addition, as homosexuals become more open, they will be less subject to blackmail.

Homosexuals, like other minorities, engage in self-deprecating talk. For example, blacks, among themselves, may call each other "nigger." In part, this is a kind of joking mockery of society's view of them, but it also may represent bitterness and some of the psychological damage that results from society's view. A similar practice exists among gays; they refer to each other as "fags," or male homosexuals may call each other by female names, for the same reasons that blacks use self-deprecating language. Gay people do not do this to be obnoxious; rather, it is a kind of protest against society's stereotypes of them and against the way they are treated.

There is an important way in which homosexuals differ from other minorities, though. In the case of most other minorities, appearance is a fairly good indicator of minority-group status. It is easy to recognize a black or a woman, for example, but one cannot tell simply by looking at a person what his or her sexual practices are. Thus, homosexuals, unlike other minorities, can hide their status. There are certain advantages to this. It makes it fairly easy to get along in the heterosexual world—to "pass." However, it has the disadvantage of encouraging the person to live a lie and to deny her or his true identity; not only is this dishonest, but it may also be psychologically stressful.

Lest the picture seem overwhelmingly bleak for the homosexual, it should also be noted that there are some advantages to being a homosexual. For example, lesbians claim that other women are better lovers; many men, they say, have a shaky knowledge of female anatomy and an even shakier knowledge of how to stimulate it. The female knows her own body and how to stimulate it best. Indeed, it has been reported that lesbians have greater orgasm consistency than heterosexual women (Kinsey et al., 1953).

THE GAY LIFESTYLE
Slang
When people associate closely with one another in a subculture, they tend to share a common slang or jargon. Blacks, for example, have such a specialized language; some of the terms, like "right on" and being "into" something, have recently been picked up by whites. Homosexuals also use a jargon, and it is through this jargon that we shall get our first glimpse of the gay world.

The sexual partner is referred to as a "trick"; generally a trick is a partner in a short-term relationship, and therefore the term may have a slightly negative connotation. In a long-term relationship, the partner is called a "lover." "Cruising" means looking for a sexual partner. One can cruise, or be cruised, in a park, on the beach, in a rest room, or on a college campus. It seems that gay males generally cruise more than gay females do, although radical lesbians demand the right to appraise potential partners in the same way that males do. Of course, it is important to recognize that, in cruising, homosexuals have no intention of forcing themselves on unwilling heterosexual victims. They are very sensitive to whether they are getting positive responses when they approach someone. Like heterosexuals, they do

FOCUS

A CASE HISTORY OF PERSECUTION: THE BOYS OF BOISE

A series of events took place in Boise, Idaho, in 1955 and 1956 that provide a good illustration of the way in which homosexuals can be persecuted and homosexuality can be used as a political weapon.

Three men were arrested for allegedly having seduced two young boys (actually the boys were rough male hustlers aged 15 and 17, but this was not disclosed). The local newspaper, *The Idaho Daily Statesman*, jumped in with reports of "lewd and lascivious conduct" and "infamous crimes against nature," followed by inflammatory editorials with titles like "Crush the Monster." The police department announced that a thorough investigation was under way and that further arrests would be made soon. Meanwhile, the courts and the prosecuting attorney moved with amazing speed. One of the men was promised leniency if he pled guilty, which he did. Within nine days of his arrest he had been sentenced to life imprisonment.

Four days after the initial arrests, a prominent banker was arrested for seducing two boys, and this fed the public's belief in a homosexual "ring." Actually, the banker had never met the other three men, and the "ravaged children" were the same two hustlers. When it became necessary to obtain evidence, a sworn statement was obtained from one of them, who was now in the Army; the statement was doctored to make it sound as if the victim was an innocent child.

Later about a dozen men were arrested on similar charges,

---

not enjoy being rejected, and so they typically confine themselves to likely prospects. Most gay men express little interest in heterosexual men; thus the heterosexual man need not fear being forced into something against his will.

"Queen" is a general term for a male homosexual. It may also be used to refer to an effeminate (feminine) male homosexual, for whom the term "nellie" is also used. The term

"queen" can be paired with a variety of modifiers to describe specific kinds of male homosexuals. For example, a "closet queen" is a homosexual who pretends to be a heterosexual. He is "in the closet," or passes for a straight. After many or a few years of hiding his homosexuality, he may decide to become open or overt about it. This process is called "coming out of the closet" or simply "coming out." Some gay although the acts were between consenting adults, a fact not divulged to the public. Then *Time* magazine (December 12, 1955) reported that Boise "sheltered a widespread homosexual underworld that involved some of Boise's most prominent men and has preyed on hundreds of teenage boys for the past decade," that the "police talked with 125 youths who had been involved," and that "the usual fees given to the boys were $5 to $10 per assignation."

Hysteria now reigned in Boise. Men were embarrassed to meet in pairs or to attend their clubs without their wives. It became out of the question for a man to pause to watch football practice for fear of looking as if he were interested in boys.

The furor gradually subsided after about a year. It later became clear that the whole drama had been planned and directed by a small group of ultraconservatives and that the motives had been political. The goal appeared to have been the destruction of the power of a man who was secretly known to be a homosexual but who had such wealth and power that he could not be touched in any other way. Apparently, his power was even greater than had been supposed, since he was never touched by the scandal. Meanwhile, the careers and the lives of others had been either made or destroyed.

The Boise episode illustrates how barbarically homosexuals can be persecuted, how homosexuality can be used as a political weapon (more recently, this was an issue in the Jenkins case during Lyndon Johnson's administration, and reports of homosexual activities were also apparently part of the secret files involved in Watergate), and the extent to which an uninformed public can be aroused to hysteria over the dangers of homosexuality.

Source: J. Gerassi. *The boys of Boise.* New York: Macmillan, 1966. Gerassi, an editor of *Newsweek*, went to Boise in 1965 to uncover the facts despite many deterrents, including threats to his life.

---

liberationists express hostility toward closet queens; they believe that closet queens are betraying the gay cause and that gays will receive better treatment only when all gays become overt and band together to demand an end to discrimination against them. Other gay liberationists, however, express sympathy toward those in the closet, recognizing the difficulty of being a homosexual in our society and of leading a double life and denying what one truly is.

Other variations on the "queen" theme are the "drag queen," who is a male homosexual who dresses in women's clothing ("drag"), and the "size queen," who is a male homosexual who prefers partners with very large genitals ("well hung" or "well endowed").

Several terms are used to refer to the

masculinity or femininity of homosexuals. As has already been noted, a nellie or a swish is a feminine male homosexual. The term "butch" refers to a masculine male homosexual or a masculine female homosexual. The masculine lesbian may also be called a "bull dyke" or a "dyke." The feminine lesbian is called, logically enough, a "femme." These terms are related to the notion that in homosexual relationships there is a mimicking of heterosexual roles, with one person being the dominant partner, and the other the submissive partner. As was pointed out in the previous section, however, such role playing is not really very common.

Varieties of Homosexuality

Deprivation homosexuality   There are several other terms for various "types" of homosexuality. *Deprivation homosexuality* (sometimes also called *situational homosexuality*) is homosexual behavior that takes place when people are deprived of heterosexual outlets. This occurs most commonly in prisons, although it also appears to happen on ships that are at sea for long periods of time and in other, similar circumstances. Prison homosexuality is often associated with violence, such as rape. It also may be associated with dominant and submissive roles; one male becomes dominant and keeps a number of "girls" as a sign of his status. In other cases, prison homosexuality may simply represent a search for human contact and for an end to loneliness. The violent aspects of homosexuality in prison probably are not so much related to homosexuality per se as they are to prison life. One way of combating this situation would be to permit the wives of married prisoners to visit them, perhaps in cottages overnight or for a weekend. Such a practice is now permitted in several Scandinavian countries, in Mexico, and, in the United States, in Mississippi (California is also experimenting with the possibility). Most

men who have engaged in homosexual activities in prison return to heterosexual activity after they are released. Thus in some situations "heterosexual" men may engage in homosexual behavior. This fact has important theoretical consequences, as will be seen in a later section.

Latent homosexuality   The concept of *latent homosexuality* was originated by Freud, who argued that some people have strong homosexual tendencies that are repressed (forced into the unconscious) because they cause a great deal of anxiety. The notion, then, is that some people may think and act like heterosexuals but may actually have strong latent homosexual tendencies. In this context, the process that Freud called *reaction formation* might also occur. In a reaction formation, a person feels like doing something that is forbidden, and this leads to a great deal of anxiety; to combat the anxiety, the person frantically tries to behave in exactly the opposite fashion ("the lady doth protest too much"). According to Freud, if a person has latent homosexual tendencies, these tendencies may occasionally bubble to the surface of the conscious, producing anxiety. To combat this, the person makes dramatic efforts to be "super straight" and to prove that she or he is in no way homosexual. The person may go so far as to actively persecute homosexuals ("Let's go beat up some queers"), the goal being to prove that he or she is not one. Thus Freud raises the interesting possibility that people who persecute homosexuals may actually be expressing anxiety about their own homosexual urges.

Covert and overt homosexuality   The *covert homosexual* "passes" for a heterosexual during most of the hours of the day: on the job and perhaps in other social relationships. Other gays and perhaps close friends know about his or her homosexuality, but for the most part it is hidden. The *overt homosexual* makes no attempt to

hide her or his homosexuality and may even try
to be obvious about it. Overt homosexuals may
live and work in a gay community or choose a
career, such as acting, in which homosexuality
is not considered strange or threatening. There
are relatively few overt homosexuals, although
they are increasing in number with the advent
of gay liberation.

Varieties of Experience

Two factors are important in considering the
kind of lifestyle a homosexual leads: whether
the person is an overt or a covert homosexual
and whether the person is male or female. The
covert homosexual may be heterosexually married, have children, and be a respected professional in the community, spending only a few
hours a month engaging in secret homosexual
behavior. The overt homosexual, on the other
hand, may live almost entirely within a homosexual community, particularly if he or she lives
in a large city like New York or San Francisco
where there is a large gay subculture, and may
have relatively few contacts with heterosexuals.
The lifestyle of gay males also differs considera-

bly from that of gay females, probably as a result
of the different roles assigned to males and
females in our society and the different ways
that males and females are reared. In addition,
there is much more discrimination against male
homosexuals than there is against lesbians. For
example, it is considered quite natural for two
women to share an apartment, but if two men
do so, eyebrows are raised.

The lifestyles of homosexuals are thus far
from uniform. They vary according to whether
one is male or female and overt or covert about
the homosexuality and also according to social
class, occupation, personality, and a variety of
other factors. It is important to remember that
the personalities of gays are not all alike; they
vary as much as the personalities of heterosexuals. Some gays are highly intelligent, and some
are stupid; some are highly competent, and
some are irresponsible; some are pleasant, and
some are unpleasant. Some aspects of the gay
lifestyle are described below. The reader should
understand that there is considerable variation
from one person to the next; that is, a given
individual may engage in a particular activity
frequently, occasionally, or not at all.

FOCUS

A GAY COUPLE: TOM AND BRIAN

Tom and Brian have been living together as lovers for three years. Tom is 29, and Brian is 22; they live in a medium-sized Midwestern city.

Tom grew up in a Roman Catholic family and attended parochial schools. His father was killed in an automobile accident when Tom was 4 days old. His mother remarried when he was 8 years old; though he gets along well with his stepfather, he feels that he has never had a real father. When asked why he thought he was gay, he said he felt it was because of the absence of a father in his early years.

After graduating from high school, Tom joined the Army and served in Vietnam and Germany. His first sexual experience was with a Japanese prostitute. Though he enjoyed the physical aspects of sex with her, he felt that something was missing emotionally. When he was 23, after returning to the United States, he had his first homosexual experience with someone he met at a bar.

Tom had sex with about 20 different men before meeting Brian, including one with whom he had a long-term relationship. He is currently a student at a technical college and is working toward a career in electronics.

Brian also grew up in a Roman Catholic family and attended parochial schools. He has always gotten along well with both his parents and his four siblings, and he recalls his childhood as being uneventful. He realized he was gay when he was in his early teens, but he chose to ignore his feelings and instead tried to conform to what society expected of him. He had a girlfriend when he was in

The bars Gay bars are an important aspect of the gay social life. These are cocktail lounges that cater exclusively to gays. Drinking, perhaps dancing, socializing, and the hope of finding a sexual partner for the evening are the important elements. Some gay bars look just like any other bar from the outside, while others may have names—for example, The Open Closet—that

indicate to the alert who the clientele is. Bars are typically gender-segregated—that is, they are for either male homosexuals or lesbians—although a few are mixed. There are far more bars for gay males than for gay females. Typically, the atmosphere is different in the two, the male bars being more for picking up sexual partners, and the female bars being more for high school. After he graduated from high school, he took a job; he had his first homosexual experience when he was 18 with a man he met at work. He currently works as a salesman at Penney's. He had sex with 8 different men before meeting Tom. He has never had intercourse with a woman.

Brian and Tom have not discussed their homosexuality directly with their families. Both think their parents may have some vague suspicions, but the parents apparently prefer not to have to confront the situation directly and instead prefer to think of their sons as just being "roommates." Both Brian and Tom wish they could be more honest about their gayness with their parents. However, they also do not want to hurt them, and so they have not pressed the matter.

Their relationship with each other is exclusive; that is, they have an agreement that they will be faithful to each other and that neither will have sex with anyone else. Both of them said they would feel hurt if they found out that the other had been seeing someone else on the sly. They both consider casual sex unfulfilling and want to have a real relationship with their sexual partner.

Household chores are allocated depending on who has the time and inclination to do them. Both like to cook, and so they share that duty about equally, as they do the laundry. Tom is good at carpentry, and therefore he tends to do things of that sort.

Tom and Brian feel that the greatest problem in their relationship is lack of communication, which sometimes creates misunderstandings and arguments. Brian feels that the greatest joy in their relationship is the security of knowing that they love each other and can count on each other. Tom agrees, and he also says that it is important to him to know that there is someone who really cares about him and loves him.

Source: Based on an interview conducted by the author.

---

talking and socializing. Lest the reader be unduly shocked at the none-too-subtle nature of pick-up bars, it is well to remember that there are many bars—singles' bars—that serve precisely the same purpose for heterosexuals.

The baths For men, another feature of the gay lifestyle is the "baths" (or "steam baths" or "tubs"). The baths are clubs with many rooms in them, generally including a swimming pool or a whirlpool, as well as rooms for dancing, watching television, and socializing; most areas are dimly lit. On entering, the man rents a locker or a room, where he leaves his clothes; then he proceeds with a towel wrapped around his waist. When a sexual partner has been

FIGURE 14.3
Men dancing at the Continental Baths in New York. *[Eric Kroll.]*

found, they go to one of a number of small rooms, furnished with beds, where they can engage in sexual activity. The baths feature impersonal sex, since a partner can be found and the act completed without the two even exchanging names, much less making any form of emotional commitment. Generally there is also an "orgy room," where people can engage in group sex. Large cities generally have a number of baths, perhaps the most famous one (no longer in existence) being the Continental in New York. Interestingly, baths seem to be almost exclusively a male phenomenon. Once again, lest the reader be shocked at the blatant searches for sexual partners, it is well to remember that similar forms of impersonal sex occur among heterosexuals, for example, in massage parlors. It is also important to remember that there is great variability from one homosexual

to the next in how important the baths are to his lifestyle. I know a 42-year-old man who has been exclusively gay since he was 13 and who has never been in the baths. For others, the baths may become a focal point in their lives. Some gay males leave work at 5 P.M. on Friday, spend the entire weekend inside the baths, and do not leave again until they return to work on Monday morning. The baths can also serve as a kind of "home away from home" for the traveler; they can serve as a hotel and they provide a way to meet new people in a strange city.

Promiscuity Another feature of the gay lifestyle, or at least the gay male lifestyle, is promiscuity. Some male homosexuals, by their own admission, have large numbers of partners in short-term relationships. In perhaps the largest and most thorough study of male homosexuals available, Martin Weinberg and Colin Williams (1974) found that the modal (most common) pattern was for the male homosexual to have, during his lifetime, 1000 or more different sex partners (as compared with a control sample of heterosexual males, for whom the modal pattern was five to nine partners). Most male homosexuals, then, have had hundreds of sexual partners. The lesbian, on the other hand, appears to have much less of a tendency toward promiscuity. Lesbians are much more likely to form a long-term, exclusive relationship. Indeed, some wear wedding bands to symbolize their "marriage." Of course, some male homosexuals also enter into such marriages or long-term relationships (see the Focus on a gay couple).

The tearoom trade   A related aspect of the gay lifestyle is the "tearoom trade." This phenomenon was studied by sociologist Laud Humphreys and is reported in an important book entitled *Tearoom Trade: Impersonal Sex in Public Places* (see the Focus on the ethics of sex research). As the title of the book implies, the "tearoom trade" refers to impersonal sexual acts in places like public restrooms. Typically the man enters the rest room and conveys to another man who is already there an interest in having sex. He may do this by making certain signals while urinating or by making tapping sounds while in one of the stalls, for example. The sexual act is generally performed in a stall and may be accomplished without a single word being exchanged. The activity engaged in

FIGURE 14.4
A gay couple. *[Michael Hanulak/Photo Researchers, Inc.]*

THE ETHICS OF SEX RESEARCH: THE TEAROOM TRADE

Sociologist Laud Humphreys's study entitled *Tearoom Trade: Impersonal Sex in Public Places* (1970) is a classic in the field of sexuality. In light of recent concern on the part of both scientists and the general public about ethical standards in research, however, his methods of data collection appear somewhat questionable. Important issues are raised about the difficulty of doing good sex research within ethical bounds.

In the tearoom-trade situation, a third person generally serves as a "lookout" who watches for the police or other intruders while the other two engage in sex. To obtain his data, Humphreys became a lookout. Not only did he observe the behaviors involved in the tearoom trade, but he also wrote down the license-plate numbers of the participants. He then traced the numbers through government records, and thus was able to get the addresses of the persons involved and to obtain census information about the neighborhood in which they lived. He also went to the homes of the people and administered a questionnaire (which included questions on sexual behavior) to them under the pretense of conducting a general survey.

The research provided some important data, particularly on the extent to which these sexual practices are engaged in by "respectable" citizens. Humphreys, of course, maintained the complete anonymity of the subjects in his report of the research. However, the ethical problems are still numerous. Was there invasion of privacy, particularly when Humphreys entered someone's home and obtained personal information under false pretenses? Was there a problem of deceiving subjects, and particularly of not "debriefing" them (explaining the true purpose of the research) afterward? Would the people have consented to being involved with the research had they known its true purpose? Could Humphreys have obtained good data within the bounds of ethics? On the other hand, these clearly negative aspects of the study have to be weighed against the benefits to society from knowing more about this form of sexual behavior.

Source: Laud Humphreys. *Tearoom trade: Impersonal sex in public places.* Chicago: Aldine, 1970.

is typically fellatio, which can be done rapidly and with a minimum of encumbrance, which is important in case the police or others intrude. The police have been very concerned with eliminating this behavior. There is some justification for their attempts, since the behavior is done in public rather than in private and may therefore be a nuisance to the innocent person who happens on the scene. Police efforts to eliminate the phenomenon, though, have met with little success.

Humphreys's book provoked quite a controversy, not only because of the topic, but also because of his findings that many of the men who engaged in this behavior were heterosexually married men, some of them respected leaders in their community. Apparently, the tearoom trade served a need for quick, impersonal sex, and the behavior of choice was homosexual. But the notion that "heterosexual," respectable men could engage in homosexual behavior was shocking to many. Indeed, many gays find the tearoom trade to be shocking.

Gay liberation   Certainly in the last decade the gay liberation movement has had a tremendous impact on the gay lifestyle. In particular, it has encouraged homosexuals to be more overt and to feel less guilty about their behavior. Gay liberation meetings and activities also provide a social situation in which gay people can meet and discuss important issues rather than simply playing games as a prelude to sex, which tends to be the pattern in the bars. Gay liberation meetings also provide an opportunity to discuss common experiences, thereby producing some consciousness raising. They also provide a political organization that can attempt to bring about legal change, combat police harassment, and fight cases of job discrimination, as well as do public relations work.

Publications   Among other accomplishments, the gay liberation movement has succeeded in founding numerous gay newspapers and magazines. These have many of the same features as other newspapers: forums for political opinions, human-interest stories, and fashion news. In addition, the want-ads sections feature advertisements for sexual partners (see Figure 14.5); similar ads for homosexual and heterosexual partners can be found in underground newspapers such as the *Berkeley Barb*. Probably the best-known gay newspaper is *The Advocate*, published in Los Angeles and circulated throughout the United States. *The Ladder* is a publication of the Daughters of Bilitis, the largest organization of lesbians. There are also several publications that list all the gay bars and baths by city in the United States, which is handy for the traveler or for those newly arrived on the gay scene.

FIGURE 14.5

Advertising for sexual partners in a gay newspaper. These were found in an issue of *The Advocate*.

MEN, COME GET IT ON
Young man available for your type of massage. Call (212) nnn-nnnn.

EXPERT FR* MASSAGE
Deep throat, hunky & hung for well-endowed males exclusively. A rare man! Roy, (213) nnn-nnnn.

M.D. NEEDS LOVE IN IL.
Handsome, medium build Oriental doctor, 25, seeks thick muscular stud under 35 for permanent lover. No S & M or Gr act. Don, (312) nnn-nnnn after 5 P.M.

MODERATELY WEIRD DUDE, 35
seeks a compatible partner for serious friendship & ? Have long hair, beard, trim body, 5'11", wear glasses, average freak looks. Usually wear Levis; not clothes conscious. Am vulnerable, sensitive, responsible to a fault. Not a social creature; sometimes act like an ass, but I'm harmless. Have unusually high intelligence; ideas turn me on as much as people. Enjoy visual action fantasy adventures. Dig trains, bikes, trips, dogs, music, reading, humor, etc. If you relate to this, please call (213) nnn-nnnn.

*In slang, "French" refers to oral sex and "Greek" to anal sex. "Italian," unfortunately, just means the person is an Italian.

SEXUAL BEHAVIOR

Some people have difficulty imagining exactly what gays do in bed; after all, the important ingredients for sex are one penis and one vagina, aren't they?

The preliminaries consist, as they do for heterosexuals, of kissing, hugging, and petting. Male homosexuals engage in mutual masturbation, oral-genital sex (fellatio), and, less frequently, anal intercourse (also called *sodomy* in American legal terminology and *buggery* in England). Male homosexuals sometimes also engage in *interfemoral intercourse,* in which one man's penis moves between the thighs of the other. Lesbians engage in mutual masturbation, oral-genital sex (cunnilingus), and, more rarely, a practice called *tribadism* ("dry hump"), in which heterosexual intercourse is imitated, with one partner lying on top of the other and making thrusting movements so that both receive genital stimulation. Another rare practice is the use of an artificial penis, or dildo, by one person to stimulate the other. Of course, dildos are also used by heterosexual women in masturbation, although they probably appear much more frequently in men's fantasies than they do in women's hands.

An important point to note about these practices is that they are all behaviors in which heterosexuals also engage. That is, homosexuals do the same things sexually that heterosexuals do. The only thing that is distinctive about the homosexual act is that both partners are of the same gender.

HOW MANY PEOPLE ARE GAY?

Most people believe that homosexuality is rare. What percentage of people in the United States are gay? As it turns out, the answer to this question is complex. Basically, it depends on what is meant by "a homosexual."

One source of information we have on this question is Kinsey's research (see Chapter 9 for an evaluation of the Kinsey data). Kinsey found that about two-thirds of all males have a homosexual experience in childhood (prior to age 15); such behavior, however, did not appear to be a predictor of adult homosexual behavior. Excluding this childhood behavior, Kinsey found that 37 percent of all males have at least one homosexual experience to orgasm in adulthood. This is clearly a large percentage, and it indicates that homosexuality is not so rare as many people think. Indeed, it was this statistic, combined with some of the findings on premarital sex, that led to the furor over the Kinsey report. The comparable figure for females was 13 percent. Kinsey's collaborators later felt that the 37 percent figure for males was too high and that 25 to 33 percent might have been more accurate (e.g., Pomeroy, 1972).

After reading these statistics, though, one is still left wondering how many people are homosexuals. As Kinsey soon realized in trying to answer this question, it depends on how you count. A prevalent notion is that, like black and white, homosexual and heterosexual are two quite separate and distinct categories. This is what might be called a *typological conceptualization* (see Figure 14.6). Kinsey made an important scientific breakthrough when he decided to conceptualize homosexuality and heterosexuality not as two separate categories but rather as variations on a continuum (Figure 14.6). The black and white of heterosexuality and homosexuality have a lot of shades of gray in between: people who have had both some heterosexual and some homosexual experience, in various mixtures. To accommodate all these varying degrees of homosexual and heterosexual experience, Kinsey constructed a scale running from 0 (exclusively heterosexual) to 6 (exclusively homosexual), with the midpoint of 3 indicating equal amounts of heterosexual and homosexual experience. The percentages of people he found falling into each of these seven categories are shown in Table 14.1. Several important points emerge from the data. First, while the percentages of people who are exclu-

1 The typology

    (*Heterosexual*)   (*Homosexual*)

2 Kinsey's continuum

0	1	2	3	4	5	6
Exclusive heterosexual	Mostly heterosexual with incidental homosexual experience	Heterosexual with substantial homosexual experience	Equal heterosexual and homosexual experience	Homosexual with substantial heterosexual experience	Homosexual with incidental heterosexual experience	Exclusive homosexual

FIGURE 14.6

Two ways of conceptualizing homosexuality and heterosexuality.

sively homosexual are rather small (about 2 percent of all males and slightly less than 1 percent of all females), the number of people who have had at least some homosexual experience (ratings of 1 to 6) is large: about 37 percent of males and 13 percent of females.[4] Quite a lot of people have engaged in at least some homo-

sexual behavior. About 63 percent of the males and 87 percent of the females in Kinsey's sample claimed exclusive heterosexuality. It is also true that, although the percentages for exclusive homosexuality are small, the 2 percent of males who are exclusively homosexual represents about 2 million Americans, a substantial number. Second, it should also be noted in Table 14.1 that the incidence of homosexuality among men is considerably higher than the incidence among women. About three times as

---

[4]For females, this figure depended quite a bit on marital status. Kinsey estimated that only about 3 percent of married women, but 26 percent of single women, have overt homosexual experiences.

TABLE 14.1

PERCENTAGES OF PEOPLE IN THE KINSEY DATA WITH VARYING AMOUNTS OF HOMOSEXUAL AND HETEROSEXUAL EXPERIENCE

Rating		Females, %	Males, %
0	Entirely heterosexual experience:		
	Single	61–72*	53–78
	Married	89–90	90–92
	Previously married	75–80	
1–6	At least some homosexual experience	11–20	18–42
2–6	More than incidental homosexual experience	6–14	13–38
3–6	Homosexual as much as heterosexual experience	4–11	9–32
4–6	Mostly homosexual experience	3–8	7–26
5–6	Almost exclusively homosexual experience	2–6	5–22
6	Exclusively homosexual experience	1–3	3–16

*Ranges are given because the percentages vary depending on the age of the person, whether the person is married or single, and several other factors.

Source: Kinsey, A. C., Pomeroy, W. B., Martin, C. E., and Gebhard, P. H. *Sexual behavior in the human female.* Philadelphia: Saunders, 1953.

many males as females have a homosexual experience to orgasm in adulthood. Other studies have essentially confirmed this result; homosexuality appears to be two to three times as common among males as among females.

In light of these data on behavior, when is a person a homosexual? If you have had one homosexual experience, does that make you a homosexual, or do you have to have had substantial homosexual experience (say, a rating of 2 or 3 or higher)? Or do you have to be exclusively homosexual to be a homosexual? Kinsey dealt with this problem in part by devising the scale, but he also made another important point. He argued that we should not talk about "homosexuality" but rather about "homosexual behavior." "Homosexuality," as has been seen, is exceedingly difficult to define. "Homosexual behavior," on the other hand, can be scientifically defined as a sexual act between two people of the same gender (Kinsey collected data not only on acts culminating in orgasm but also on arousal response to members of the same gender). Therefore, we can talk more precisely about people who have engaged in varying amounts of homosexual behavior or who have had varying amounts of homosexual experience, thereby avoiding the problem of deciding exactly when a person is a homosexual, which is difficult, if not impossible, to do.

Chapter 9 included a discussion of Hunt's 1972 survey of sexual behavior comparable to Kinsey's. It indicated substantial increases in certain behaviors, most notably premarital sex. Interestingly, this survey provided no evidence that homosexuality is increasing. Hunt's statistics are similar to Kinsey's; Hunt estimated that about 20 to 25 percent of males have an overt homosexual experience in adulthood, as do about 10 percent of married women and 20 percent of single women. Studies from other countries, such as Sweden and Germany, also indicate that about 2 to 4 percent of the adult male population is exclusively homosexual.

Thus the incidence of homosexuality appears to be fairly stable both over time and across cultures.

The answer to the original question—How many people are homosexual?—is complex. Probably about 75 percent of men and 85 percent of women are exclusively heterosexual. About 2 percent of men and slightly less than 1 percent of women are exclusively homosexual. And the remaining 25 percent of men and 15 percent of women have had varying amounts of both heterosexual and homosexual experience.

HOMOSEXUALITY: NORMAL OR ABNORMAL?

As was noted earlier, most Americans consider the homosexual to be sick. Is this really true? Do psychologists and psychiatrists agree that homosexuals are poorly adjusted or deviant? Does research on homosexuality confirm the notion that the homosexual is sick?

Sin and the Medical Model

Actually, the belief that homosexuality is a sickness is something of an improvement over previous beliefs about homosexuality. Before this century, the dominant belief in Europe and the United States was that homosexuality was a sin or a heresy. During the Inquisition, those accused of being heretics were also frequently accused of being homosexuals and were burned at the stake. Indeed, in those times, all mental illness was regarded as a sin. In the twentieth century, this view has been replaced by the *medical model,* in which mental disturbance, and homosexuality in particular, is viewed as a sickness or illness. This view is widely held now by many mental health professionals as well as by the general public.

Recently, psychologist Thomas Szasz and others have become critical of the medical model. In his well-known writing on "the myth of mental illness," Szasz argues that the medical model is now obsolete and that we need to develop a more humane and realistic way of dealing with mental disorders and variations from the norm. He has argued the case particularly for homosexuality (Szasz, 1965). Gay liberationists have joined in, saying that they do not like being called "sick" and that this is just another form of persecution of homosexuals.

Research Results

Theoretical and rhetorical approaches to the question are clearly diverse. What do the scientific data say? Once again, the answers provided by the data are complex and depend on the assumptions of the particular investigator and the research design used. Basically, three kinds of research designs have been used, representing progressive sophistication and changing assumptions about the nature of homosexuality (see Rosen, 1974, for a review).

Clinical studies The first, and earliest, approach was clinical; homosexuals who were in psychotherapy were studied by the investigator (usually the therapist). He or she looked for disturbances in their current adjustment or in past experiences or homelife. The data were then reported in the form of a case history of a single individual or a report of common factors that seemed to emerge in studying a group of homosexuals (for example, Freud, 1920; see also the review by Rosen, 1974). These clinical studies provided evidence that the homosexual was sick or abnormal; she or he typically was found to be poorly adjusted and neurotic. But the reasoning behind this research was clearly circular. The homosexual was assumed to be sick, and then evidence was found supporting this view.

Studies with control groups The second group of studies made significant improvements over the previous ones by introducing control groups. The question under investigation was rephrased. Rather than: Do homosexuals have psychological disturbances? (after all, most of us have some problems) it became: Do homosexuals have more psychological disturbances than heterosexuals? The research design then involved comparing a group of homosexuals in therapy with a group of randomly chosen heterosexuals or perhaps with a group of heterosexuals matched with the homosexuals on some variables like age and education. These studies tended to agree with the earlier ones in finding more problems of adjustment among the homosexual group than among the heterosexual group (Rosen, 1974). The homosexuals tended to make more suicide attempts, to be more neurotic, and to have more disturbed family constellations. Once again, though, it became apparent that there were some problems with this research design. It compared a group of people in therapy with a group of people not in therapy and found, not surprisingly, that the people in therapy had more problems. It, too, was circular in assuming that homosexuals were abnormal (in therapy) and that heterosexuals were normal (not in therapy) and then finding exactly that. Of course, the investigator used the homosexuals in therapy as subjects at least in part because they were convenient, but this does not help to make the results any more accurate.

Nonpatient research A major breakthrough came with the third group of studies, which involved nonpatient research. In these studies, a group of homosexuals not in therapy (nonpatients) were compared with a group of heterosexuals not in therapy. The nonpatient homosexuals were generally recruited through homophile organizations, advertisements, or word of mouth. The results of these studies are mixed, but the general results seem to indicate that nonpatient homosexuals do not differ from nonpatient heterosexuals in their adjustment. For example, while one study found depression, suicide attempts, and alcohol abuse to be more common among nonpatient lesbians than among heterosexuals, these differences did not hold up in another study (see the review by Rosen, 1974). As a psychiatrist who has reviewed the literature on adjustment differences between homosexual and heterosexual women concluded, "The only difference between the lesbian and other women is the choice of love object" (Rosen, 1974, p. 65; for similar results with male homosexuals, see Evans, 1970; J. H. Gagnon and Simon, 1973; Green, 1972).

Psychologist Evelyn Hooker did an important study that sheds considerable light on the question of differences in adjustment between heterosexuals and homosexuals. The assumption that the homosexual is sick or poorly adjusted implies that there are considerable psychological differences between heterosexuals and homosexuals. If this is the case, such differences should be indicated on standard personality tests. Hooker (1957) obtained data on 30 overt, nonpatient male homosexuals and on a group of 30 male heterosexuals matched for age, education, and IQ. The homosexuals were exclusively homosexual, except for three who had had very minimal heterosexual experience. The heterosexuals, similarly, were exclusively heterosexual, except for three who had each had one homosexual experience. Hooker administered the Rorschach, a projective test, to all subjects. The Rorschach was used because it is considered a good measure of total personality and is sometimes used in the "diagnosis" of homosexuality. In the first phase of the experiment, the Rorschach responses were arranged in random order and were given to two highly skilled clinicians for interpretation. The clinicians assigned an adjustment rating from 1 (superior) to 5 (maladjusted) to each profile. According to these ratings, there were no differences in the adjustment of the homosexuals as compared with that of the heterosexuals; about two-thirds of each group were well adjusted. In the second phase, the clinicians received the profiles in the matched pairs and were asked to identify which of the pair was the heterosexual and which was the homosexual. One clinician identified 17 of the 30 pairs correctly, while the other was accurate for 18 of the 30. Since one would expect accuracy for 15 of the 30 merely by chance, the clinicians did not do better than chance in identifying the homosexuals and the heterosexuals. Apparently, even the skilled clinician cannot tell the gay from the straight without a scorecard. The notion that the homosexual has a disturbed personality receives no support in the results of this study.

While research fails to provide evidence that the homosexual is less well adjusted than the heterosexual, gay activist psychologist Mark Freedman has argued that homosexuals are *better* adjusted than heterosexuals. In the face of social pressures against them, gays may engage in "centering"—an intense developing of one's personal identity. In one study comparing lesbians with matched controls, the lesbians were higher on autonomy, spontaneity, and sensitivity to one's own needs and feelings (M. Freedman, 1975). A similar study found lesbians to be more independent, resilient, and self-sufficient (Hopkins, 1969). Freedman also believes that gays deal better with gender roles. Lesbians, for example, are better at accepting their own natural aggressiveness and assertiveness. Gay men are better at expressing tenderness. Finally, the process of coming out may encourage better self-knowledge as well as candor. According to personality tests such as the MMPI, gays tell fewer lies than straights (M. Freedman, 1975; Horstman, 1972). Thus, according to Freedman, gays are healthier than straights.

On the basis of these studies, it must be concluded that the evidence does not support the notion that the homosexual is "sick" or poorly adjusted. This position has now received official professional recognition by the American Psychiatric Association. Prior to 1973, the APA had listed homosexuality as a disorder under Section V, "Personality Disorders and Certain Other Nonpsychotic Mental Disorders," in its authoritative *Diagnostic and Statistical Manual of Mental Disorders*. In 1973, the APA voted to remove homosexuality from that listing; thus it is no longer considered a psychiatric disorder.

Therapy for Homosexuality

Related to the question of whether homosexuality is a sickness is the issue of whether the homosexual should receive psychotherapy. The psychologist's or psychiatrist's answer to this question would depend on which one of a number of theoretical models (to be discussed in the next section) he or she operated under. A psychoanalyst, for example, would probably consider homosexuality to be abnormal and would recommend psychoanalysis to "cure" it.

In recent years, behavioral therapies ("behavior modification") have become increasingly popular. These therapies do not attempt to change a person's internal psychological functioning; rather, they attempt only to change the behavior—it is the behavior, after all, that is creating the problem. Behavioral therapies involve the application of the principles of operant conditioning to modify the problem behavior. These approaches have been applied in the treatment of homosexuality. For example, a male homosexual might be shown the picture of a nude male and receive a mild electric shock if he becomes aroused. He may also be shown pictures of nude females, in which case arousal responses are followed by no shock or by a reward. Psychologists at Atascadero State Hospital, California's treatment facility for rehabilitating sex offenders, have designed a number of therapies based on behavioral principles (for an example, see Barlow and Agras, 1973).

This whole concept of therapy for homosexuality, however, conflicts with the conclusion made earlier that homosexuality is not abnormal. If there is nothing wrong with homosexuality, trying to "cure" it makes no sense. Ethical issues are raised as well: should a person be changed from a homosexual to a heterosexual against his or her will? Perhaps the best resolution to this problem is that if a person freely requests therapy to help stop being a homosexual because the homosexual behavior is causing emotional distress, then the person should receive it, particularly in light of the fact that living as a homosexual in our society is extremely difficult and that this alone might be sufficient reason for seeking therapy (but see Davison, 1976). Otherwise, there is no need for therapy.

WHY DO PEOPLE BECOME HOMOSEXUAL?

A fascinating psychological question is: Why do people become homosexual? Several theoretical answers to this question, as well as the results of empirical research on it, are discussed below.

Biological Theories

There has been some speculation that homosexuality might be caused by biological factors. The likeliest candidates for these biological causes are endocrine imbalance, prenatal doses of inappropriate hormones, and genetic factors.

Hormonal imbalance Investigating the possibility that endocrine imbalance is the cause, many researchers have tried to determine whether the testosterone ("male" hormone) levels of male homosexuals differ from those of male heterosexuals. A series of early studies failed to find any differences between the two groups in testosterone levels (Glass et al.,

337

1940), although the techniques for measuring hormone levels available at the time were not very accurate. Recently, better measurement techniques have been developed, but the studies still fail to find any hormonal differences between male homosexuals and male heterosexuals (for a review, see Rose, 1975).

Despite these results, some clinicians have attempted to cure male homosexuality by administering testosterone therapy. This therapy fails; indeed, it seems to result in even more homosexual behavior than usual. This is not an unexpected result since, as was seen in Chapter 7, androgen levels seem to be related to sexual responsiveness. As a clinician friend of mine replied to an undergraduate male who was seeking testosterone therapy for his homosexual behavior, "It won't make you heterosexual; it will only make you horny."

Virtually all these hormone studies have been done on male homosexuals. The one available study on lesbians did find higher testosterone levels and lower estrogen levels among them than among a control group of heterosexual women (Loraine et al., 1972; see also Dörner, 1969). The results have not been replicated yet, and so they should be viewed cautiously.

Prenatal hormone exposure   Another speculation about a possible biological cause is that homosexuality develops as a result of an exposure to inappropriate hormones during the prenatal period. As was seen in Chapter 3, exposure to inappropriate hormones during fetal development can lead a genetic female to have male genitals, or a genetic male to have female genitals. It has been suggested that a similar process might account for homosexuality (and also for transsexualism—see Chapter 15). Direct evidence for this hypothesis has not been produced, and so it must remain purely at the level of speculation. If homosexuality did result from prenatal hormone exposure, however, it would be reasonable to expect those hormone doses also to have some anatomical effect; this notion is not supported by available research. Contrary to the belief that the lesbian has an enlarged clitoris or other abnormal anatomical features, the available data indicate that homosexuals do not differ anatomically from heterosexuals (Perloff, 1965; Wolff, 1971).

Genetic   factors   Irving   Kallman   (1952a, 1952b) has argued that there is a genetic predisposition to homosexuality, and he has provided data to support his claim. He found perfect concordance for homosexuality among all the identical-twin pairs he studied (that is, if one was a homosexual, so was the other). Among nonidentical twins the degree of concordance was not statistically significant. Numerous criticisms of this study could be made. The identical twins were all reared together, and thus they shared not only common genes but also a common environment. Therefore, environmental factors might explain the similarities. Further, nonidentical twins are not genetically unrelated; they share, on the average, half of their genes. Hence if homosexuality were genetic, one would expect a moderate degree of concordance for them. Other investigators have failed to replicate Kallman's findings (Heston and Shields, 1968). Thus the genetic explanation for homosexuality is not generally accepted. Indeed, from a geneticist's point of view, the genetic hypothesis about homosexuality makes no sense. If homosexuality were genetically controlled, one could hardly imagine a trait against which natural selection would act more strongly. Suppose that Mr. X carries the gene or genes for homosexuality and is therefore a homosexual. Because he is a homosexual he will not have children, and therefore his genes will not be passed on to the next generation. Thus genes for homosexuality, if they existed, would quickly be removed from circulation. This does not argue against the possibility of a genetic predisposition to bisexuality, however. The bisexual would engage in homosexual behavior but would also engage in heterosexual behavior and, through the heterosexual behavior, could reproduce and pass the genes on.

In conclusion, there is little evidence supporting any of the biological hypotheses—hormonal imbalance, prenatal hormone exposure, or genetic factors—regarding the causes of homosexuality. In a sense, these biological explanations were doomed to failure from the beginning since they assume that homosexual and heterosexual are two distinct diagnostic categories and then seek to explain why a person becomes a member of the homosexual category. But as has already been noted, heterosexual and homosexual are not two separate categories, and thus the basic assumption of the biological approaches is open to question.

Psychoanalytic Theory

Freudian theory Since Freud believed sex to be the primary motivating force in human behavior, it is not surprising that he concerned himself with homosexuality and its development (his classic work on the subject is *Three Essays on the Theory of Sexuality,* published in 1910).

According to Freud, the infant is *polymorphous perverse*; that is, the infant's sexuality is totally undifferentiated and is therefore directed at all sorts of objects, both appropriate and inappropriate. As the child grows up and matures into an adult, sexuality is increasingly directed toward "appropriate" objects (members of the other gender), while the desire for "inappropriate" objects (for example, members of the same gender) is increasingly repressed. Therefore, according to Freud, the homosexual is fixated at an immature state of development.

According to Freud, homosexuality also stems from the *negative Oedipus complex*. In

the (positive) Oedipus complex, discussed in an earlier chapter, the child loves the parent of the opposite gender but eventually gives this up and comes to identify with the parent of the same gender, thereby acquiring a sense of gender identity. In the negative Oedipus complex, things are just the opposite: the child loves the parent of the same gender and identifies with the parent of the opposite gender. For example, in the negative Oedipus complex, a little boy would love his father and identify with his mother. In the process of maturation, once again, the child is supposed to repress this negative Oedipus complex. The homosexual person, however, fails to repress it and remains fixated on it. Thus according to Freud, for example, a woman becomes a homosexual because of a continuing love for her mother and identification with her father. In Freud's view, homosexuality is a continuation of love for the parent of the same gender.

Consistent with Freud's belief that the infant is polymorphous perverse was his belief that all humans are inherently bisexual; that is, he believed that all people have the capacity for both heterosexual and homosexual behavior. Thus he viewed homosexuality as very possible, if not desirable. This notion of inherent bisexuality also led to the concept of the latent homosexual, the person with a repressed homosexual component.

Freud also believed that homosexuals are narcissistic (vain and self-centered). Homosexuality then might represent making love to oneself.

Bieber's research Because Freud had such a great influence on psychiatric thought, he inspired a great deal of theorizing and research, in particular on homosexuality. Irving Bieber and his colleagues (1962) did one of the more important of these psychoanalytically inspired studies. They compared 106 male homosexuals with 100 male heterosexuals; all the subjects were in psychoanalysis, which makes the results somewhat questionable. The family pattern that Bieber and his colleagues tended to find among the homosexuals was that of a dominant mother and a weak or passive father. The mother was both overprotective and overly intimate. Bieber thus originated the concept of the "homoseductive mother" as an explanation of male homosexuality. This family pattern, according to Bieber, has a double effect: the man later fears heterosexual relations both because of his mother's jealous possessiveness and because her seductiveness produced anxiety. Bieber thus suggests that homosexuality results, in part, from fears of heterosexuality. While Bieber's findings on the homoseductive mother have received a great deal of attention, a much more striking finding in his research was of a seriously disturbed relationship between the homosexual male and his father (Bieber, 1976). The fathers were described as detached and/or openly hostile; thus the homosexual son emerged into adulthood hating and fearing his father and yet deeply wanting the father's love and affection.

Wolff's research Charlotte Wolff, a British psychiatrist, has carried out a similar program of research and theorizing about the origins of lesbianism (1971). She studied over 100 nonpatient lesbians, comparing them with a control group of heterosexual women matched for family background, profession, and social class. The family characteristics that were more frequent among the homosexual women than among the heterosexual women were a rejecting or indifferent mother and a distant or absent father. Wolff theorized that lesbianism results from the girl's receiving inadequate love from the mother; as a result, she continues, throughout her life, to seek that missing love in other women. Secondarily, because her father was distant or absent, she may not have learned to relate to men.

Psychoanalytic theories of the genesis of homosexuality clearly operate under the assumption that homosexuality is deviant or abnormal. As Irving Bieber writes:

> We consider homosexuality to be a pathologic, bio-social, psycho-sexual adaptation to pervasive fears surrounding the expression of heterosexual impulses. (Bieber et al., 1962, p. 22)

> All psychoanalytic theories assume that adult homosexuality is psycho-pathologic. (Bieber et al., 1962, p. 18)

Actually, in his later writings Freud came to consider homosexuality to be within the normal range of variation of sexual behavior; this view, however, appears not to have had much of an impact, compared with that of his earlier writings on the subject. Psychoanalytic theory could thus be criticized for the abnormality assumption since, as has been seen, there is no strong evidence for the notion that the homosexual is poorly adjusted.

The psychoanalytic approach can also be criticized for its confusion of the concepts of "gender identification" and "choice of sexual partner." As was previously noted, the homosexual differs from the heterosexual in choice of sexual partner but not in gender identification: the male homosexual has a masculine identification, and the lesbian has a feminine identification. Psychoanalytic theory, however, assumes that the homosexual not only makes an inappropriate object choice but also has an abnormal gender identification—that the male homosexual has not identified with his father and has therefore not acquired a masculine identity and that the lesbian has not identified with her mother and has therefore not acquired a feminine identity. This basic assumption of abnormal gender identification is not supported by the data and is therefore another basis for criticizing psychoanalytic theories of homosexuality.

Learning Theory

Behaviorists emphasize the importance of learning in the development of homosexuality. They note the prevalence of bisexual behavior both in other species and in young humans, and they argue that rewards and punishments must shape the individual's behavior into predominant homosexuality or predominant heterosexuality. The assumption, then, is that humans have a relatively amorphous, undifferentiated pool of sex drive which, depending on circumstances (rewards and punishments), may be channeled in any of several directions. In short, people are born sexual, not heterosexual or homosexual. Only through learning does one of these behaviors become more likely than the other. For example, a person who has early heterosexual experiences that are very unpleasant might develop toward homosexuality. Heterosexuality has essentially been punished and therefore becomes less likely. This might occur, for instance, in the case of a girl who is raped at an early age; her first experience with heterosexual sex was extremely unpleasant, and so she avoids it and turns to homosexuality. Parents who become upset about their teenagers' heterosexual activities might do well to remember this notion; punishing a young person for engaging in heterosexual behavior may not eliminate the behavior, but rather rechannel it in a homosexual direction.

Another possibility, according to a learning-theory approach, is that if early sexual experiences are homosexual and pleasant, the person may become a homosexual. Homosexual behavior has essentially been rewarded and therefore becomes more likely.

The learning-theory approach has the advantage of treating homosexuality as a normal form of behavior and recognizing that heterosexuality is not necessarily inborn but must also, like homosexuality, be learned. The learning-theory approach, however, fails to account for some phenomena. For example, it is clear that young boys receive quite considerable and repeated pleasure from masturbation. Why do they give this up (or reduce its frequency) and switch to heterosexual or homosexual sex? While human sexual behavior is no doubt determined in part by reinforcement contingencies, it probably also has much more complex determinants which are not yet understood.

Sociological Theory

Sociologists emphasize the effects of *labeling* in explaining homosexuality. The label "homosexual" has a big impact in our society. Suppose that someone said to you, "I think that you are a homosexual." How would you react? Your immediate reaction would probably be negative: anger, anxiety, and embarrassment. The label "homosexual" has very derogatory connotations and may even be used as an insult. This reflects our society's negative attitudes toward homosexuality. But the label "homosexual" may also act as a self-fulfilling prophecy. Suppose that a young boy—possibly because he is slightly effeminate, because he is poor in sports, or for no reason at all—is called a "homosexual." He reacts strongly and becomes more and more anxious and worried about his problem. He becomes painfully aware of the slightest homosexual tendency in himself. Finally he convinces himself that he is a homosexual. He begins engaging in homosexual behavior and associates with a gay group. In short, a homosexual has been created.

Sociologists also emphasize the importance of *roles* in explaining human behavior. Homosexuality might be no more than a role people play, much like the male role or the female role (McIntosh, 1968; M. S. Weinberg and Williams, 1974). As such, it is not an enduring character trait or a permanent psychiatric disorder, but rather a set of behaviors that one uses in dealing with society. This view helps explain the apparent ease with which many homosexuals pass for heterosexuals in the straight world. They simply play the heterosexual role in certain situations and the homosexual role in others.

Empirical Data

Theoretical positions on the origins of homosexuality are many and varied. Some of the various explanations that have been proposed for lesbianism alone include:

> . . . fear of growing up and assuming adult responsibilities; fear of dominance and destruction; fear of rejection; fear of the opposite sex; fear of castration and of the penis; the desire to conquer and possess the mother; neurotic dependency; heterosexual trauma (including rape); seduction in adolescence by an older female; first sexual experience with someone of the same sex and finding it pleasurable; tomboy behavior in early childhood; prolonged absence of the mother; masturbation with resulting clitoral fixation; social factors (such as heterosexual taboos and unisexual, all female, groups); and physical factors (genetic, constitutional, and endocrine abnormalities). (Rosen, 1974, p. 8)

Do any of these proposed explanations have a basis in fact? Unfortunately, most of the investigators who have collected data on the previous experiences of homosexuals have operated from a particular theoretical conviction; they then tended to obtain data supporting the theory in which they believed. Many of the early studies also have the problems of design mentioned in the discussion of whether homosexuality is abnormal. Many of the studies have been of either the first type (homosexuals in therapy, with no comparison group) or the second type (homosexuals in therapy compared with heterosexuals). Thus results of those studies should be interpreted cautiously.

Further, when studies do find differences between homosexuals and heterosexuals, the factors are generally not common enough among the homosexuals to make them the "explanation" of homosexuality. A good example is Charlotte Wolff's (1971) study of lesbians. Mothers of lesbians were more frequently indifferent or negligent, but indifference was characteristic of only 27 percent of the mothers of lesbians (as compared with 10 percent of the mothers of controls), and negligence was characteristic of only 10 percent of the mothers of lesbians (as compared with 0 percent of the mothers of controls). Hence, while maternal negligence and indifference are more common among lesbians, they certainly do not explain all cases of lesbianism.

When all the studies in this area are surveyed, no single factor emerges consistently as a cause of male homosexuality or of lesbianism (the two might have quite different causes). To be blunt, we do not know what causes homosexuality. But there may be a good theoretical lesson to be learned from this somewhat frustrating statement. It has generally been assumed not only that homosexuals form a distinct category (which, as has already been seen, is not very accurate) but also that they form a homogeneous category, that is, that all homosexuals are fairly similar. Probably this is not true. Probably there are many different kinds or "types" of homosexuals. Indeed, one psychologist, expressing this notion, has suggested that we should refer not to "homosexuality" but rather to "the homosexualities" (A. P. Bell, 1974b). If this is the case, then one would not expect a single "cause" of homosexuality, but rather many causes, each corresponding to its type. The next step in research, then, should be to identify the various types of homosexuals—not to mention the various kinds of heterosexuals—and the different kinds of development that lead to each.

BISEXUALITY

A bisexual is a person who has sex sometimes with men and sometimes with women, that is, sometimes with a member of the same gender and sometimes with a member of the opposite gender. Such a person is clearly not exclusively heterosexual or exclusively homosexual. He or she is called *bisexual* or, in slang, "ac-dc" (alternating current–direct current). Some scientists also call such a person *ambisexual.*

Bisexuality has recently become something of a fad, particularly on the East and West Coasts. In some large cities there are "bi" bars, where one can see both same-gender and opposite-gender pairs dancing together and having a good time.

Bisexuality is really not at all rare; in fact, it is far more common than exclusive homosexuality (if a "bisexual" is defined as a person who has had at least one sexual experience with a male and one with a female). For example, earlier in this chapter it was noted that about 75 percent of all males are exclusively heterosexual and that about 2 percent are exclusively homosexual. That leaves a large number, perhaps 25 percent, who are bisexual according to the definition stated above.

The proponents of bisexuality argue that it has some strong advantages. It allows more variety in one's sexual and human relationships than either exclusive heterosexuality or exclusive homosexuality. The bisexual does not rule out any possibilities and is open to the widest possible variety of experiences, characteristics which are highly valued by today's young people.

On the other hand, the bisexual may be viewed with suspicion or downright hostility by the gay community (Blumstein and Schwartz, 1975). Radical lesbians refer to bisexual women as "fence sitters," saying that they betray the lesbian cause because they can pretend to be heterosexual when it is convenient and homosexual when it is convenient. Some gays even argue that there is no such thing as a true bisexual.

A consideration of the phenomenon of bisexuality will help illuminate several theoretical points and also provide some insights into homosexuality and heterosexuality. First, though, several concepts need to be clarified. A distinction has already been made between sex (sexual behavior) and gender (being male or female) and between gender identity (the male's association with the male role and the female's association with the female role) and choice of sexual partner (heterosexual, homosexual, or bisexual). To this, the concept of *sexual identity* should be added; this refers to one's self-label or self-identification as a heterosexual, homosexual, or bisexual.[5] Sexual identity, then, is the person's concept of herself or himself as a heterosexual, homosexual, or bisexual.

Strangely, there may be contradictions between people's sexual identity (which is clearly subjective) and their actual choice of sexual partners viewed objectively. Sociologists Philip Blumstein and Pepper Schwartz (1974) have conducted perhaps the largest program of research on bisexuals, and they have provided some good examples of these contradictions. For example, one of their subjects identified herself as a lesbian, and yet occasionally she sleeps with men. Objectively, her choice of sexual partners is bisexual, but she sees herself as a lesbian. More common are persons who think of themselves as heterosexuals but who engage in both heterosexual and homosexual sex. A good example of this is the tearoom trade—the successful, heterosexually married men in gray flannel suits who occasionally stop off at a public rest room to have another male perform fellatio on them. Once again, the behavior is objectively bisexual, in contradiction with the heterosexual identity. Another example is the group of women who claim to have bisexual identities but who have experienced

---

[5]Clearly, the term "sexual identity" is not being used here the way it is generally used, which is to refer to one's sense of maleness or femaleness (for which the term "gender identity" is used in this book). However, it seems important to be able to talk about a person's sense that he or she is a heterosexual or a homosexual, and "sexual identity" seems the most likely term to use for that purpose.

CASE HISTORY OF JOAN, A BISEXUAL WOMAN

Joan, a professional woman in her middle thirties, considered herself exclusively heterosexual until about four years ago. Until that time she had never had homosexual fantasies or feelings, but she had been generally liberal about "sexual alternatives" and believed in equal rights for homosexuals. Four years ago, however, Joan became active in the women's liberation movement and developed closer friendships with some of the women with whom she worked. None of these relationships was sexualized, but her curiosity was aroused by sexual possibilities with women. Her approach to her own potential homosexual behavior was at this time still more intellectual than emotional and was not accompanied by graphic fantasies or feelings of attraction to other women whom she might meet or see in public.

During this period, Joan met another woman in her profession whom she found both intellectually and socially attractive. Vivian was also heterosexual, but she had had a few homosexual experiences. The relationship between the two women became closer, and during an exchange of confidences Joan learned that Vivian had had sexual experiences with women. At this point, Joan began

only heterosexual sex, and never homosexual sex. These women, often as a result of feminist beliefs, claim bisexuality as an ideal which they are capable of attaining at some later time. Once again, identity contradicts behavior.

The available data on bisexual development (see the Focus on the case history of a bisexual woman) suggest several important points. First, they argue for the importance of late-occurring experiences in the shaping of one's sexual behavior and identity. As has been seen, most of the research on the development of homosexuality rests on the assumption that it is somehow determined by pathological conditions in childhood. Yet many females, as the story of the woman in the Focus illustrates, have

their first homosexual encounter at age 30 or 40. It is difficult to believe that these behaviors were determined by some pathological conditions to which such women were exposed at age 5. Human behavior can be modified at any time throughout the lifespan. Situational, or deprivation, homosexuality is also a good example of this. A heterosexual man who enters prison may engage in homosexual behavior and then return to heterosexuality after his release. Once again, it seems likelier that such a man's homosexual behavior was determined by his circumstances (being in prison) than by some problem with his Oedipus complex 20 years before.

Second, a question is raised as to whether

to have sexual fantasies involving Vivian and began to be more overtly physical toward her, but she never crossed the bounds of female heterosexual friendship. The relationship intensified, and intimate discussions about sexuality turned to the possibility of sex between the two women. After about six months of such discussions, they slept together, first having overcome their initial worries concerning the effect that any guilt feelings about their "experimentation" might have on their friendship.

After the first successful sexual experience, Joan and Vivian repeated it approximately once every month for over a year. Vivian, however, continued to think of herself as a heterosexual, while Joan began to feel that she was in love with her friend and to want a more committed relationship. Joan stopped sleeping with Vivian when she realized that Vivian did not agree with her terms for the relationship. The two remained close friends, but Joan looked for someone else who might wish to share a committed relationship. She eventually fell in love with another woman, and an intense romantic and sexual relationship continued for two years. At the present, Joan is unsure of what sexual label to apply to herself, but she prefers "bisexual." At the time of her interview, she had both a male and a female lover.

Source: Philip W. Blumstein and Pepper Schwartz. Bisexual women. In J. P. Wiseman (Ed.), *The social psychology of sex.* New York: Harper & Row, 1976, pp. 154–162.

---

heterosexuality is really the "natural" state. The pattern in some theories has been to try to discover those pathological conditions which cause homosexuality (for example, a father who is an inadequate role model or a homoseductive mother)—all on the basis of the assumption that heterosexuality is the natural state and that homosexuality must be explained as a deviation from it. As has been seen, this approach has failed; there appear to be multiple causes of homosexuality, just as there are multiple causes of heterosexuality. The important alternative to consider is that bisexuality is the natural state, a point acknowledged both by Freud and by the behaviorists. This chapter will close, then, with some questions. Psychologically, the real ques-

tion should not concern the pathological conditions that lead to homosexuality, but rather the causes of exclusive homosexuality and exclusive heterosexuality. Why do we eliminate some people as potential sex partners simply on the basis of their gender? Why is everyone not bisexual?

SUMMARY

Homosexual behavior is sexual behavior with a member of the same gender; it is considerably more complex to define what a "homosexual" is.

Homosexuals suffer from discrimination and from a number of derogatory stereotypes.

The majority of Americans consider homosexuality to be obscene and vulgar; homosexuals are thought to be suffering from a curable illness. Although one stereotype is that male homosexuals are effeminate and lesbians are mannish, this is not true; in most cases one cannot tell a homosexual from a heterosexual on the basis of appearance. The belief that male homosexuals tend to be child molesters is also not true. Discrimination against homosexuals can take many forms; gay people may lose their jobs when their sexual practices become known, and derogatory jokes about homosexuals are common.

The gay lifestyle includes gay bars and the baths. It is important to remember, however, that homosexuals are not all identical and that they differ as much among themselves as heterosexuals do.

Homosexuals engage in mutual masturbation, oral-genital sex, and anal intercourse, all practices engaged in by heterosexuals.

In order to describe the homosexual behavior of the people in his sample, Kinsey devised a seven-point scale ranging from 0 (exclusively heterosexual) through 6 (exclusively homosexual), with the midpoint of 3 representing equal amounts of heterosexual and homosexual experience. Probably about 25 percent of males have had a homosexual experience to orgasm (not counting childhood experiences). About 2 percent of males are exclusively homosexual. Among females, about 15 percent have had a homosexual experience to orgasm, and slightly fewer than 1 percent are exclusively homosexual.

Available data do not support the notion that homosexuals are poorly adjusted or "sick." Psychologically they do not appear to differ substantially from heterosexuals except for their choice of sexual partner. The American Psychiatric Association no longer classifies homosexuality as a mental disorder.

In regard to the causes of homosexuality, biological explanations (endocrine imbalance, prenatal hormone exposure, and genetic factors) are not supported by the data. According to the psychoanalytic view, homosexuality results from a fixation at an immature stage of development and a persisting negative Oedipus complex. Learning theorists stress that the sex drive is undifferentiated and is channeled, through experience, into heterosexuality or homosexuality. Sociologists emphasize the importance of roles and labeling in understanding homosexuality. Available data do not point to any single factor as a cause of homosexuality, but rather suggest that there may be many types of homosexuality with corresponding multiple causes.

Bisexuality is much more common than exclusive homosexuality. A person's sexual identity may be discordant with his or her actual behavior. Bisexuality may be more "natural" than either exclusive heterosexuality or exclusive homosexuality.

SUGGESTIONS FOR FURTHER READING

Martin, Del, and Lyon, Phyllis. *Lesbian/woman.* San Francisco: Glide Publications, 1972. Two lesbian activists discuss the lesbian lifestyle.

Warren, Patricia. *The front runner.* New York: Morrow, 1974. A novel about a gay male track star and his lover, this has been called the gay *Love Story.* It is really much better than that, however.

Weinberg, G. H. *Society and the healthy homosexual.* New York: St. Martin's Press, 1972.

15

VARIATIONS IN SEXUAL BEHAVIOR

ost lay people, as well as most scientists, have a tendency to classify behavior as normal or abnormal. There seems to be a particular tendency to do this with regard to sexual behavior. Many terms are used for abnormal sexual behavior, including "sexual deviance," "perversion," "sexual variance," and "paraphilias." The term "sexual variations" will be used in this chapter because it is currently favored in scientific circles and because defining exactly what is "deviant" or what is a "perversion" is rather difficult.

In Chapter 14 it was argued that homosexuality per se is not an abnormal form of sexual behavior. This chapter will deal with some behaviors that might more justifiably be considered abnormal, and so it seems advisable at this point to consider exactly when a sexual behavior is abnormal. That is, what is a reasonable set of criteria for deciding what kinds of sexual behavior are abnormal?

*Source: Wayland Young. *Eros denied.* New York: Grove Press, 1964.

WHEN IS SEXUAL BEHAVIOR ABNORMAL?
Definitions and Criteria

As was seen in Chapter 1, sexual behavior varies a great deal from one culture to the next. There is a corresponding variation across cultures in what is considered to be "deviant" sexual behavior. Given this great variability, how can one come up with a reasonable set of criteria for what is deviant? Perhaps it is best to begin by considering the way others have defined "deviant" or "abnormal" sexual behavior.

First, what does the average American classify as deviant sexual behavior? According to psychiatrist Judd Marmor (1971), there is a consensus in our culture that the following are deviant: practices that involve the habitual and preferential use of nongenital outlets for sexual release; activity that is homosexual; and sexual activity with immature partners of either sex (pedophilia), animals (bestiality), dead people (necrophilia), or inanimate objects (fetishism). Marmor further argues that, in any society, sexual behavior that causes serious injury to one of the participants should be considered deviant because such behavior could ultimately jeopardize the survival of that society.

The American Psychiatric Association, in its authoritative *Diagnostic and Statistical Manual of Mental Disorders,* defines sexual deviations as follows:

> This category is for individuals whose sexual interests are directed primarily toward objects other than people of the opposite sex, toward sexual acts not usually associated with coitus or toward coitus performed under bizarre circumstances as in necrophilia, pedophilia, sexual sadism, and fetishism. Even though many find their practices distasteful they remain unable to substitute normal sexual behavior for them. This diagnosis is not appropriate for individuals who perform deviant sexual acts because normal sexual objects are not available to them.

As was noted in Chapter 14, though, in 1974 this official list was changed to exclude homosexuality as a sexual deviation and to create a new category called "sexual orientation disturbance," which includes people whose sexual interest is directed toward persons of the same gender and who are disturbed by, or in conflict with, that orientation or who wish to change it. Homosexuality per se is thus not included as deviant behavior and is considered abnormal only if the person feels in conflict about it.

Another approach is to use a *statistical definition* (Pomeroy, 1966). According to this approach, a deviant sexual behavior is one that is rare, that is, one that is not practiced by many people. Following this definition, then, standing on one's hands while having intercourse would be considered deviant because it is rarely done, although it does not seem very "sick" in any absolute sense. This definition, unfortunately, does not give us much insight into the deviant person's psychological or social functioning.

In the *sociological approach,* the problem of culture dependence is explicitly acknowledged. A sociologist might define a deviant sexual behavior as a sexual behavior that violates the norms of society. Thus if a society says that a particular sexual behavior is deviant, it is—at least in that society. This approach recognizes the importance of the individual's interaction with society and of the problems that people must face if their behavior is labeled "deviant" in the culture in which they live.

A modern *psychological approach* was stated by Arnold Buss in his text entitled *Psychopathology* (1966). He says: "The three criteria of abnormality are discomfort, inefficiency, and bizarreness." The last of these criteria, bizarreness, has the problem of being culturally defined; what seems bizarre in one culture may seem normal in another. However, the first two criteria are good in that they focus on the discomfort and unhappiness felt by the person with a truly abnormal pattern of sexual behavior and also on inefficiency; for example, if a man has such a fetish for women's undies that he steals them, gets himself arrested, and cannot hold a job, that is inefficient functioning, and the behavior can reasonably be considered deviant.

Buss's definition is the one that will be used in this chapter: A sexual behavior is deviant or abnormal when it is uncomfortable for the person, inefficient, and/or bizarre. A fourth criterion should also be added, that of doing harm, either physically or psychologically, to oneself or others (although this might implicitly be included under the category of inefficient or bizarre). But it is clearly a complex matter to define "deviant" or "abnormal," and for this reason the term "sexual variations" is used in this chapter.

Categories of Sexual Variations

Several schemes for categorizing the various kinds of variant sexual behavior have been developed. One of the first was Freud's distinction between variations of sexual *object* and variations of sexual *aim.* Variations of sexual object are those in which the object of one's sexual attraction is abnormal (a "normal" object being a member of the opposite gender, but of the same species, and of approximately the same age). Thus Freud would consider homosexuality a variation in the choice of sexual object, since he viewed a member of the same gender as an abnormal sexual partner. Other examples of variations in the choice of sexual object would be pedophilia (sex with a child), incest (sex with a relative), bestiality (sex with an animal), fetishism (sex with an object), and necrophilia (sex with a dead person). The other category, variations of sexual aim, includes sexual behaviors with an abnormal goal (the "normal" goal being coitus). Thus if the goal is to watch others have sex (voyeurism), this would be a variation in sexual aim. Other examples are exhibitionism, sadism, and masochism.

John H. Gagnon and William Simon (1967), using a sociological approach, have defined three types of deviance: "normal" deviance, pathological deviance, and community-producing deviance. They recognize that laws, mores (internalized norms of a group of people), and the actual behavior of a group all influence and reflect what is considered deviant in that society. Certain behaviors, though, are deviant according to one of these criteria but not according to another; for example, a behavior might be illegal but quite common in the actual behavior of the society. Normal deviant behaviors, then, are those that are considered deviant according to laws or mores but are actually quite commonly practiced. Examples in our culture are masturbation, premarital sex, and oral-genital sex. Such behaviors are disapproved of (mores) but are practiced by many people. Normal deviant behaviors often carry a mixed message: "It's wrong only if you get caught." The next category, pathological deviance, includes those behaviors that are deviant according to laws and mores and also are not practiced widely. That is, such behaviors are

illegal, disapproved of, and very rare in the society. Examples in our society include necrophilia and pedophilia. Finally, the third category, community-producing deviance, includes those behaviors that generate a community or subculture. Examples are homosexuality and prostitution. Individuals in such a subculture may lose the sense of being deviant because the subculture defines new norms for itself (Bancroft, 1974).

The above discussion should provide some conceptual scheme for understanding the various sexual variations that will be considered in this chapter.

FETISHISM

In *fetishism,* a person becomes sexually fixated on some object other than another human being and attaches great erotic significance to that object. In extreme cases the person is incapable of becoming aroused and having an orgasm unless the fetish object is present.

There are two major forms of fetishism: fetishism in which the fetish object is a part of the body and fetishism in which it is an inanimate object. When the fetish object is a part of the body, it may be a sexual part such as the breasts or buttocks, or it may be a nonsexual part such as the feet or hair. This sort of fetish, of course, is difficult to detect, since the person simply finds a particular part of the body to be erotically appealing.

The more obvious form of fetishism occurs when the fetish item is an inanimate object. Typically, the fetish item is something closely associated with the body, such as clothing. Inanimate-object fetishes can be roughly divided into two subcategories: media fetishes and form fetishes.

Media Fetishes

In the media fetish, it is the material out of which an object is made that is important in its erotic value. An example would be a leather fetish, in which any leather item is arousing to the person. Media fetishes can be further subdivided into hard media fetishes and soft media fetishes. In the hard media fetish, the fetish is for a hard substance, such as leather or rubber. Hard media fetishes may often be associated with sadomasochism (see below). In the soft media fetish, the substance is soft, such as fur or silk.

Form Fetishes

In the form fetish, it is the object and its shape that are important. An example would be a shoe fetish, in which shoes are highly arousing (see Focus). Often shoe fetishists require that the shoes be high-heeled; this fetish may be associated with sadomasochism, in which the fetishist derives sexual satisfaction from being walked on by a woman in high heels. Other examples of form fetishes are fetishes for boots (which also may be associated with sadomasochism), garters, and lingerie (almost all fetishists are men).

The Normal-Abnormal Continuum

Perhaps reading that being aroused by lingerie is deviant has made you rather uncomfortable because you yourself find lingerie arousing. Fetishes are discussed first in this chapter because they provide an excellent example of the continuum from normal to abnormal sexual behavior. That is, normal and abnormal sexual behavior (like other normal and abnormal behavior) are not two separate categories, but rather gradations on a continuum. Many people have mild fetishes—they find things such as silk underwear arousing—and that is well within the range of normal behavior; only when the fetish becomes extreme is it abnormal.

This continuum from normal to deviant behavior might be conceptualized using the scheme shown in Figure 15.1. A mild prefer-

FIGURE 15.1
The continuum from normal to abnormal behavior in the case of fetishes.

ence, or even a strong preference, for the fetish object (say, silk panties) is within the normal range of sexual behavior. When the silk panties have become an absolute necessity—when the man cannot become aroused and have intercourse unless they are present—then we have probably crossed the boundary into abnormal behavior. In extreme forms, the silk panties may become a substitute for a female sexual partner, and the man's sexual behavior consists of masturbating with the silk panties present. In these extreme forms, the man may commit burglary or even assault to get the desired fetish object (Karpman, 1954), and this would certainly fit our definition of abnormal sexual behavior.

The continuum from normal to abnormal behavior holds for many of the sexual variations discussed in this chapter, such as voyeurism, exhibitionism, and sadism. This point should be kept in mind when reading the following sections.

Why Do People Become Fetishists?

Psychologists are not completely sure what causes fetishes to develop. A likely explanation is based on learning theory (see, for example, McGuire et al., 1965). This approach would say that fetishes result from a learned association between the fetish object and sexual arousal and orgasm. In some cases a single learning trial might serve to cement the association. For example, a 12-year-old boy might masturbate to orgasm for the first time while standing on a

FOCUS

A CASE HISTORY OF A SHOE FETISHIST

The following case history is taken directly from *Psychopathia Sexualis*, by von Krafft-Ebing, the great early investigator of sexual deviance. It should give you the flavor of his work.

Case 11. X., aged twenty-four, from a badly tainted family (mother's brother and grandfather insane, one sister epileptic, another sister subject to migraine, parents of excitable temperament). During dentition he had convulsions. At the age of seven he was taught to masturbate by a servant girl. X. first experienced pleasure in these manipulations when the girl happened to touch his member with her shoe-clad foot. Thus, in the predisposed boy, an association was established, as a result of which, from that time on, merely the sight of a woman's shoe, and finally, merely the idea of them, sufficed to induce sexual excitement and erection. He now masturbated while looking at women's shoes or while calling them up in imagination. The shoes of the school mistress excited him intensely, and in general he was affected by shoes that were partly concealed by female garments. One day he could not keep from grasping the teacher's shoes—an act that caused him great sexual excitement. In spite of punishment he could not keep from performing this act repeatedly. Finally, it was recognized that there must be an abnormal motive in play, and he was sent to a male teacher. He then revelled in the memory of the shoe-scenes with his former school-mistress and thus had erections, orgasms, and, after his fourteenth year, ejaculation. At the same time, he masturbated while thinking of a woman's shoe. One day the

---

fuzzy bathroom rug and ever after require fuzzy objects to become aroused. Another example appears to be the shoe fetishist described in the Focus. In this case, shoes were associated with sexual arousal as the result of an early learning experience.

TRANSSEXUALISM

A *transsexual* is a person who believes that he or she is trapped in the body of the wrong gender. Transsexuals are the candidates for the

sex-change operations that have received so much publicity, beginning with the case of Christine Jorgenson. The term "transsexual" is used to refer to the person both before and after the operation. There are, of course, two kinds of transsexuals: those with male bodies who think they are females (called *male-to-female transsexuals*) and those with female bodies who think they are males (called *female-to-male transsexuals*). The former outnumber the latter by about 3 to 1 (Green, 1975); that is, the majority of transsexuals are people with male

CHAPTER 15

thought came to him to increase his pleasure by using such a shoe for masturbation. Thereafter he frequently took shoes secretly and used them for that purpose.

Nothing else in a woman could excite him; the thought of coitus filled him with horror. Men did not interest him in any way. At the age of eighteen he opened a shop and, among other things, dealt in ladies' shoes. He was excited sexually by fitting shoes for his female patrons or by manipulating shoes that came for mending. One day while doing this he had an epileptic attack, and, soon after, another while practicing onanism in his customary way. Then he recognized for the first time the injury to health caused by his sexual practices. He tried to overcome his onanism, sold no more shoes, and strove to free himself from the abnormal association between women's shoes and the sexual function. Then frequent pollutions, with erotic dreams about shoes occurred, and the epileptic attacks continued. Though devoid of the slightest feeling for the female sex, he determined on marriage, which seemed to him to be the only remedy.

He married a pretty young lady. In spite of lively erections when he thought of his wife's shoes, in attempts at cohabitation he was absolutely impotent because his distaste for coitus and for close intercourse in general was far more powerful than the influence of the shoe-idea, which induced sexual excitement. On account of his impotence the patient applied to Dr. Hammond, who treated his epilepsy with bromides and advised him to hang a shoe up over his bed and look at it fixedly during coitus, at the same time imagining his wife to be a shoe. The patient became free from epileptic attacks and potent so that he could have coitus about once a week. His sexual excitation by women's shoes also grew less and less.

Source: R. Von Krafft-Ebing. *Psychopathia sexualis*, 1886. (Reprinted by Putnam, New York, 1965.)

---

bodies who think of themselves as women and want to have the appropriate surgery. Because this kind of transsexual is more common, and also because the surgery required in such cases is easier, most of the discussion that follows will focus on male-to-female transsexuals.[1]

Keeping in mind the distinction between sex and gender, it is important to note that transsexualism is a problem not of sexual behavior but of gender and gender identity. That is, the transsexual is preoccupied not with some specific kind of sexual behavior, but rather with wanting to be a female when her body is male. Sex, of course, is involved insofar as being sexually attracted to a member of the opposite gender (which is expected in our society) is concerned. But I also know of one transsexual who has never engaged in any sexual activity beyond kissing since she had surgery to make her a female. She is delighted with the results of

---

[1]Because this kind of transsexual thinks of himself as a female, he prefers to be called "she," and to simplify matters in this discussion, "she" will be used to refer to the transsexual. Otherwise, figuring out which pronoun to use would be extremely difficult.

the surgery and loves being a woman, but she is not particularly interested in sex. One male-to-female transsexual expressed her motivation for having a sex-change operation as follows:

> I did it for the psychological thing. . . . I need the reassurance that I am a woman. I don't have a man to make love to me and I don't care. . . . I wanted to be a woman, whether the sex part was successful or not. I wanted to be of one sex, dress like one, act like one. . . . Well, mentally I always thought of myself as a woman. I don't even remember thinking of myself as a man. (Kando, 1973, p. 96)

References to transsexuals are found in much of recorded history, although of course they are not referred to by that modern, scientific term (Green, 1966). Philo, the Jewish philosopher of Alexandria, described them as follows: "Expending every possible care on their outward adornment, they are not ashamed even to employ every device to change artificially their nature as men into women. . . . Some of them . . . craving a complete transformation into women . . . have amputated their generative members." The American Indians had an institutionalized role for men who dressed as women and performed the functions assigned to women. Transsexualism is therefore by no means a phenomenon of modern, industrialized cultures.

Psychologically the transsexual is, to put it mildly, in an extreme conflict situation (Levine et al., 1976). The body says, "I'm a man," but the mind says, "I'm a woman." The person may understandably react with fright and confusion. Believing herself truly to be a female, she may try desperate means to change her body accordingly. Particularly in the days before the sex-change operation was performed, or among people who were unaware of it, self-castrations have been reported. The woman I mentioned above ate large quantities of women's face cream containing estrogens to try to bring about the desired changes in her body.

The Sex-Change Operation

Gender reassignment is rather complex and proceeds in several stages. In this country, the surgery was first performed at the Johns Hopkins Hospital in Baltimore. The Stanford University School of Medicine also pioneered. More recently, the procedure has been performed at several other hospitals.

The first step in the process is very careful counseling and psychiatric evaluation. It is important to establish that the person is a true transsexual, that is, someone whose gender identity does not match her body type. Some people mistakenly seek gender reassignment; for example, a man who is simply poorly adjusted, unhappy, and not very successful might think that things would go better for him if he were a woman. It is important to establish that the person truly has a problem of gender identity before going ahead with a procedure that is fairly drastic.

The next step is hormone therapy. The male-to-female transsexual is given estrogen and must remain on this for the rest of her life. The estrogen gradually produces some feminization. The breasts enlarge. The pattern of fat deposits becomes feminine; in particular, the hips become rounded. Balding, if it has begun, stops. Secretions by the prostate diminish, and eventually there is no ejaculate. Erections become less and less frequent, a phenomenon with which the transsexual is pleased since they were an unpleasant reminder of the unwanted penis. The female-to-male transsexual is given androgens, which bring about a gradual masculinization. A beard may develop, to varying degrees. The voice deepens. The pattern of fat deposits becomes more masculine. The clitoris enlarges, although not nearly to the size of a penis, and becomes more erectile. The pelvic bone structure, of course, cannot be reshaped, and breasts do not disappear except with surgery.

Many experts now also require, often at the same time that the hormone therapy is being administered, that the person live as a member of the new gender for a period of six months or so. This is done to ensure that the person will be able to adjust to the role of the new gender; once again, the idea is to be as certain as possible that the person will not regret having had the operation. Some transsexuals, even before consulting a physician, spontaneously enter this "transvestite" stage in their efforts to become women. Problems may arise, though. Cross-dressing is illegal in many cities, and they may be arrested.

The final step is the surgery itself (transsexuals refer to it simply as "the operation"). In the male-to-female transsexual, the penis and testes are removed. The external genitalia are then reconstructed to look as much as possible like a woman's (see Figure 15.2). Next, an artificial vagina—a pouch 15 to 20 centimeters (6 to 8 inches) deep—is constructed. It is lined with the skin of the amputated penis so that it will have sensory nerve endings that can respond to sexual stimulation. For about six months afterward, the vagina must be dilated with a plastic device so that it does not reclose. Other cosmetic surgery may also be done, such as reducing the size of the Adam's apple.

The female-to-male change is more complex and generally less successful. A penis and scrotum are constructed from tissues in the genital area (see Figure 15.2). The penis, unfortunately, does not have erectile capacity; in some cases a rigid silicone tube is implanted in the penis so that it can be inserted into a vagina, making coitus possible. Some female-to-male transsexuals choose not to have genital surgery and just go through breast removal and possibly hysterectomy.

Adjustment following gender reassignment

(a)

(b)

FIGURE 15.2
The genitals following transsexual surgery. (a) A female-to-male transsexual. (b) A male-to-female transsexual. [Courtesy of Dr. D. Laub, Gender Dysphoria Program, Department of Plastic and Reconstructive Surgery, Stanford University.]

is generally excellent, providing, of course, that the person is not someone who should have been screened out in the initial counseling process. Most transsexuals are very happy in their new gender.

What Causes Transsexualism?

Scientists have not found a definite cause of transsexualism. One speculation is that it might be due to some prenatal exposure to hormones of the wrong gender, causing improper brain differentiation. There is no direct evidence supporting this idea, though, and so it must remain speculative at present.

Two studies have investigated hormone levels in transsexuals before gender reassignment, one in male-to-female transsexuals and the other in female-to-male transsexuals (J. R. Jones, 1972; Migeon et al., 1968). In both studies the hormone levels were found to be within the normal range for the individuals' "original" gender (not the gender to which they wanted to be reassigned), suggesting that transsexualism does not result from a hormonal imbalance.

One idea for which there is some supporting evidence is that transsexualism results from early learning experiences. In one sample of 17 male-to-female transsexuals, all had had their gender treated inappropriately or ambiguously from infancy to puberty by their parent or parents (J. P. Driscoll, 1971; see also Green, 1975). Though they had the bodies of boys, they had been given girls' toys or had been dressed in girls' clothing. Feminine behavior, such as putting on the mother's high heels when guests were present, had been rewarded as "cute." When the interviewer asked whether they had been reared as boys or girls, one responded, "I was raised as a girl by my mother and aunts. My sex was discovered by a school nurse when I was six." It seems likely that such early learning experiences would be critical in giving the child

a gender identity that is incongruent with her body. On the other hand, there are transsexuals who had no such learning experiences; thus learning theory does not seem adequate to explain every case.

By the time these transsexuals were of school age, they hated gym class and were labeled "freaks" by their peers. Not surprisingly, problems of adjustment arose. In adulthood, transsexuals often have trouble holding steady jobs, at least in part because they are so preoccupied with their gender problem. With a history of problems of this sort, the good adjustment of transsexuals following gender reassignment is even more impressive.

One interesting phenomenon that requires explanation is the greatly disproportionate ratio of men to women requesting gender reassignment. Several explanations have been advanced (Green, 1975). A psychodynamic explanation is that all children initially identify with the mother, who is the most important person in their lives. Girls have the simple task of continuing this identification, but boys have the difficult chore of giving it up and identifying with the father. Some boys fail to make this shift and continue with a female gender identity. A sociological explanation holds that females have more gender-role freedom in our society than males do; it is acceptable, for example, for women to wear slacks, while it is not at all acceptable for men to wear dresses. The female-to-male transsexual, therefore, can live quite comfortably with masculine characteristics, does not need to go to the extreme of having a sex-change operation, and so may never come to the attention of physicians or scientists. The male-to-female transsexual, on the other hand, needs to receive some definite sanction—a sex-change operation—to be allowed to behave as a female. Finally, prenatal hormone effects have also been used as an explanation. As was seen in Chapter 3, during the process of prenatal sexual differentiation,

Nature's basic plan is to make a female; a specific ingredient, testosterone, must be added to make a male. Male development is therefore somewhat more fragile and more subject to errors caused by prenatal "accidents." The result of such an accident may be a person with a male body but a female gender identity.

Other Issues

The phenomenon of transsexualism raises a number of interesting psychological, legal, and ethical questions for our contemporary society.

One case that has attracted attention is that of Dr. Renée Richards, formerly Richard Raskind, a physician who has had her gender reassigned to that of a woman. When she was a man, she was a successful tennis player. In 1976 she attempted to enter a women's tennis tournament. The women players protested that she was not a woman, and she protested that she was. Officials subsequently decided to use the bucchal smear test for gender, which is also the one used in the Olympics. In this test a sample of cells is scraped from the inside of the mouth and is stained. If the sex chromosomes are XX, a Barr body should be present and will show up under the stain; if the chromosomes are XY the Barr body should be absent. The test is therefore one of genetic gender. Dr. Richards protested that this was not the appropriate test to be used on her. Psychologically she is a female, she has female genitals, and she functions socially as a female, and she feels that these are the appropriate criteria. She does, though, have a male pelvic bone structure and other bone structures that are masculine, and these may have important consequences for athletic performance. The issue will require some time to settle. But the important question

FIGURE 15.3
Transsexual Renée Richards before the sex-change operation (left) as tennis player Richard Raskind and following transsexual surgery (right) as a female tennis player. *[New Times Magazine and World Wide Photos.]*

it raises is: What should the criteria be for determining a person's gender? Should it be chromosomal gender (XX or XY) as tested by the bucchal smear? Should it be the gender indicated by the external genitals? Should it be psychological gender identity?

Another question that might be raised concerns religious groups that do not permit women to become members of the clergy. Is a male-to-female transsexual, for example, qualified to be a priest before "the operation" but not after? Is the female-to-male transsexual qualified to be a priest by virtue of having had a sex-change operation?

Another problem arises in classifying the sexual behavior of the transsexual. For example, many male-to-female transsexuals prefer to engage in sex with men, even before gender reassignment. Is that sexual behavior homosexual (it is between two men), or is it heterosexual (because one of them thinks she is a woman)? Or is the behavior homosexual before surgery and heterosexual after surgery?

The transsexual also encounters a number of practical problems following gender reassignment. Official records, such as the social security card, must be changed to show not only the new name but also the new gender. Sometimes a new birth certificate is issued, and the old one is sealed away. However, when the person reaches retirement age, it is not clear whether she should receive social security benefits beginning at age 62, the proper age for females, or age 65, the age for males. If the person was married before the sex change, often—though not always—the spouse must be divorced. Changing one's gender is, to say the least, a complicated process.

In the next decade, as more transsexuals are discovered and studied scientifically, they should be able to give us, through their own personal accounts, new insights into the nature of sex and gender. For example, most of us have wondered, at some time, how members of the opposite gender feel during sexual intercourse. The transsexual is in a unique position for giving us information on this question.

TRANSVESTISM

Transvestism ("trans" = "cross"; "vest" = "dressing") refers to dressing as a member of the opposite gender. Cross-dressing may be done by a variety of people for a variety of reasons. As has been noted, transsexuals may go through a stage of cross-dressing in the process of becoming women. Some male homosexuals—the drag queens—dress up as women, and some lesbians dress in masculine clothes ("butch"); these practices, though, are basically caricatures of masculinity and femininity. Female impersonators are men who dress as women, often as part of their jobs as entertainers. For example, comedian Flip Wilson is a female impersonator when he plays the character Geraldine. Finally, some—perhaps many—adolescent boys cross-dress, usually only once or a few times (Green, 1975). This behavior does not necessarily doom them to a life of transvestism; it may simply reflect the sexual drives, confusions, and frustrations of adolescence.

In contrast to people who engage in the kinds of cross-dressing discussed above, the true transvestite[2] is a person who derives sexual gratification from cross-dressing. Thus transvestism is probably basically a fetish (Pomeroy, 1975) and seems to be quite similar to a clothing fetish. The cross-dressing may often be done in private, perhaps even by a married man without his wife's knowledge.

As a result, no one has accurate data on the incidence of transvestism. One authority,

---

[2]A common abbreviation for transvestism, used both by scientists and by members of the transvestite subculture, is TV. Therefore, if you see an ad in an underground newspaper placed by a person who is a TV, this is *not* someone who has delusions of broadcasting the six-o'clock news, but rather a transvestite.

(a)

(b)

FIGURE 15.4

Two examples of cross-dressing. *(a)* A modern female impersonator *[Eric Kroll]. (b)* Edward Hyde (1661–1723), governor of the colonies of New York and New Jersey from 1702 to 1708, who apparently chose to be painted this way while he was governor *[The New York Historical Society].*

though, estimates that more than a million males in the United States are involved in it, if all instances of men getting at least a temporary erotic reward from wearing female clothing are counted (Pomeroy, 1975). The vast majority of transvestites are heterosexuals (Prince and Butler, 1972); most are married and have children.

Transvestism is almost exclusively a male sexual variation; it is essentially unknown among women. There may be a number of reasons for this phenomenon, including our culture's tolerance of women who wear masculine clothing and intolerance of men who wear feminine clothing. The phenomenon illustrates a more general point, namely, that many sexual variations are defined for, or practiced almost exclusively by, members of one gender; the parallel practice by members of the other gender is often not considered deviant. Most sexual variations, with the exception of prostitution, are practiced mainly by males.

Transvestism is one of the harmless, victimless sexual variations, particularly when it is done in private. Like other forms of fetishism, it is a problem only when it becomes so extreme that it is the person's only source of erotic gratification. For the person who is severely disturbed by the problem and wants to be cured of it, aversion therapy appears to be highly effective (Marks and Gelder, 1967). Electrodes are applied to the person's wrists, and mild shocks are delivered as the person fantasizes cross-dressing or actually cross-dresses. Such aversion therapies have also been used in treating other sexual variations.

SADISM AND MASOCHISM

A *sadist* is a person who derives sexual satisfaction from inflicting pain on another person. The term "sadism" derives from the name of the

historical character the Marquis de Sade, who lived around the time of the French Revolution. Not only did he practice sadism—several women apparently died from his attentions (Bullough, 1976)—but he also wrote novels about these practices (the best known is *Justine*), thus assuring his place in history.

A *masochist* is a person who is sexually aroused by experiencing pain. This variation is named after Leopold von Sacher-Masoch (1836–1895), who was himself a masochist and who wrote novels expressing masochistic fantasies. Notice that the definitions of these variations make specific their *sexual* nature; the terms are often loosely used to refer to people who are cruel or to people who seem to bring misfortune on themselves, but these are not the meanings used here.

Though many sadists and masochists trade on physical pain, another version of sadomasochism, *bondage,* depends on the person's feeling restricted; this is usually done by tying him or her up with ropes. In yet another psychological version, the sadist adopts a "master" role, and the masochist a "slave" role. The master then exerts psychic dominance over the slave, who submits.

Sadomasochism is often accompanied by elaborate rituals and gadgetry, such as tight black leather clothing, pins and needles, ropes, whips, and hot wax (Figure 15.6). In the case of the psychological forms, the slave may actually wear a dog's collar and be led around on a leash by the master.

Sadism and masochism are, of course, complementary to each other. The sadist needs a masochist for a partner, and vice versa. It appears, though, that the numbers do not work out quite right, since there are more masochists than sadists.

Interestingly, sadists and masochists do not consistently find experiencing pain and giving pain to be sexually satisfying. For example, the masochist who smashes a finger in a car door will yell and be unhappy just like anyone else. Pain is arousing for such people only when it is part of a carefully scripted ritual.

Sadomasochism (S-M) is a rare form of sexual behavior, although in its milder forms it is probably more common than many people think. Kinsey found that about 10 percent of males and 3 percent of females reported definite or frequent arousal responses to sadomasochistic stories. He also found that 26 percent of females and the same percentage of males had experienced definite or frequent erotic responses as a result of being bitten during sexual activity (Kinsey et al., 1953, pp. 677–678). In the Hunt survey (1974), about 4 to 5 percent of all respondents said they had at some time obtained sexual pleasure from inflicting or receiving pain. Sadistic or masochistic fantasies appear to be considerably more common than real-life sadomasochistic behavior.

The causes of sadism and masochism are not precisely known. Conditioning seems to be one of the likelier explanations. For example, a little boy is being spanked over his mother's knee; in the process, his penis rubs against her knee, and he gets an erection. Or a little girl is caught masturbating and is spanked. In both cases, the child has learned to associate pain or spanking with sexual arousal, possibly setting up a lifelong career as a masochist.

FIGURE 15.6
Some of the paraphernalia used by sadists and masochists and those who enjoy bondage. [Sepp Seitz/Magnum Photo Library.]

VOYEURISM

The term "voyeur" ("Peeping Tom")[3] generally refers to a person who derives sexual pleasure from watching nudes or from watching others have sex. Actually, there are some variations within this category. In *scoptophilia*, sexual pleasure is derived from observing sexual acts

and the genitals; in *voyeurism,* technically, the sexual pleasure comes from viewing nudes, often while the voyeur is masturbating.

Voyeurism appears to be much more common among males than among females, a fact that is reflected in the common name for it, "Peeping Tom." According to FBI reports, nine men to one woman are arrested on charges of "peeping."

Voyeurism provides another good illustration of the continuum from normal to abnormal behavior. For example, many men find it arousing to watch a nude woman—otherwise there

---

[3]"Voyeur" comes from the French word *voir,* meaning "to see." "Peeping Tom" comes from the story of Lady Godiva; when she rode through town nude to protest the fact that her husband was raising his tenants' taxes, none of the townspeople looked except one, Tom of Coventry.

would be no burlesque houses—and this is certainly well within the normal range of behavior. Some women are "crotch watchers," much as men are breast watchers (Friday, 1973, 1975). The voyeurism is abnormal when it replaces sexual intercourse or when the person commits a crime such as breaking and entering to observe others, thereby risking arrest.

Peepers typically want the woman they view to be a stranger and do not want her to know what they are doing (Yalom, 1960). The element of risk is also important; while one might think that a nudist camp would be heaven to a peeper, it is not because the elements of risk and forbiddenness are missing (Sagarin, 1973).

Voyeurs generally are not dangerous. Potentially dangerous voyeurs can be identified by the following characteristics: (1) they enter the confines of a building or other structure in order to view their subject, and (2) they draw the attention of their subject to the fact that they are watching (Yalom, 1960).

The voyeur is generally young and a "late bloomer" (R. S. Smith, 1976). He is typically a shy, sexually inadequate person who has difficulty establishing romantic relationships with others. It is rare to find a peeper who has a good sex life (Gebhard et al., 1965; Yalom, 1960).

In one study of arrested peepers, it was found that they were likely to be the youngest child in their family and to have good relationships with their parents but poor relationships with their peers (Gebhard et al., 1965). They had few sisters and few female friends. Few were married. This study, however, points up one of the major problems with the research on sexual variations: much of it has been done only on people who have been arrested for their behavior. The "respectable deviant" who has the behavior under somewhat better control or who is skillful enough or can pull enough strings not to get caught is not studied in such research. Thus the picture that research provides us of these variations may be very biased.

EXHIBITIONISM

The complement to voyeurism is *exhibitionism* ("flashing"), in which the person derives sexual pleasure from exposing his genitals to others in situations where this is clearly inappropriate.[4] The pronoun "his" is used advisedly, since exhibitionism is defined almost exclusively for men. The woman who wears a dress that reveals most of her bosom is likely to be thought of as attractive rather than deviant. When the male exposes himself, it is considered offensive. Once again, whether a sexual behavior is considered deviant depends greatly on whether the person doing it is a male or a female. Homosexual exhibitionism is also quite rare, and so the prototype we have for exhibitionism is a man exposing himself to a woman.

About 35 percent of all arrests for sexual offenses are for exhibitionism (Ellis and Brancale, 1956). In one study of arrested exhibitionists, the subjects seemed to fall into three categories (Gebhard et al., 1965). The commonest category, accounting for about 50 percent of the offenders, was that of the repetitive, compulsive exhibitionist. The behavior is repeated again and again, compulsively, even though the man has a wife to provide a sexual outlet. Some of these men seemed to be trying to prove their masculinity ("Look, I'm a man, and here's the proof!"). Others seemed to be expressing hostility or sadism. While most exhibitionists are quite harmless, about 1 in 10 has attempted or seriously contemplated rape; typically the one who stays at a distance is harmless, while the one who comes close (within arm's length) is more likely to be dangerous. The second category of exhibitionists described by Gebhard and his colleagues was that of the mental deficient who mistakenly believes that such a gesture will

---

[4]Here is a classic limerick on exhibitionism:

There was a young lady of Exeter
So pretty, men craned their necks at her.
   One was even so brave
   As to take out and wave
The distinguishing mark of his sex at her.

arouse or attract a woman. The third category was drunks. Like the voyeur, the exhibitionist emerges as a person who has difficulty establishing social and sexual relationships.

Many women, understandably, are quite alarmed by the exhibitionist. But since the exhibitionist's goal is to produce shock or some other strong emotional response, the woman who becomes extremely upset is gratifying him. Probably the best strategy for a woman to use in this situation is to remain calm and make some remark indicating her coolness, such as suggesting that he should seek professional help for his problem.

PEDOPHILIA

The *pedophiliac*[5] ("child molester") engages in or desires sexual contact with a child. Pedophilia is typically regarded as one of the most despicable of sex offenses because of the naïve trust of children and because the pedophiliac uses his power and authority as an adult over the child.

How common is child molesting? Kinsey found that 24 percent of the women in his sample had been approached, between the ages of 4 and 13, by males at least 5 years older than they were who made or tried to make sexual contacts. John Gagnon reanalyzed the Kinsey data and estimated that 20 to 25 percent of middle-class and 33 to 40 percent of lower-class female children have experienced some kind of molesting. In a survey of 1800 university students, 30 percent of the men and 35 percent of the women reported having had childhood experiences with sexual deviants (Landis, cited by McCaghy, 1971).

What kind of a person is a child molester? The common stereotype is that he is a dangerous stranger who lurks in the shadows, wait-

ing to pounce on the unsuspecting child. A number of facts contradict this notion, however. In at least one-half to two-thirds of the cases, the molester is a friend, acquaintance, or relative of the child; when he is a relative, a form of incest is involved. In most cases, then, the offender is not a stranger. It is also true that force is rarely used; violence is involved in probably no more than 3 percent of all cases (McCaghy, 1971). Intercourse is rarely attempted; the activity is generally limited to genital fondling (Gebhard et al., 1965). Finally, in some cases the child may collaborate in or even initiate the contact; this is probably true in about 8 percent of offenses, the percentage being higher for homosexual contacts.

As is true for many other kinds of sexual variation, there is no typical child molester (McCaghy, 1971). Several general categories have been found to exist, though. One is that of the *incestuous molester,* who will be discussed further below. Another category is that of *molesters who work with children,* such as teachers or choirmasters. Though these people apparently do not enter their profession with the intent of molesting, they do have a keen interest in children; they have their contacts with children for whom they have high regard, seeing the contact as part of a love relationship. Homosexual molesting is quite common in this category, but many such contacts are collaborative or are initiated by the child. For the *asocial molester,* a third type, the sexual offense is simply one of many crimes he has committed. There are also *aged offenders;* for example, they may be retired men who molest children in their neighborhood. The *career molester* has a history of repeated, deliberate, systematic molesting of children, typically children he does not know. He generally does not use force, but he may have a puppy or monkey with him to lure the child. Finally, the *spontaneous-aggressive molester* uses violence against his victims, who are usually not known to him. Fortunately, this last type is rare.

---

[5]Those of you who are interested in the roots of words might mistakenly guess that a pedophiliac is a foot fetishist. The root "ped-," however, refers to "child," as in "pediatrician."

Generally, child molesters do tend to be from the lower class. In one study, most were between 30 and 40, with an average age of 37 (McCaghy, 1971). Only about 20 percent of child molesters are homosexual offenders (sexual activity between a man and a boy is called *pederasty*).

What effects does the molesting have on the child? Some authorities believe that the molesting itself is not traumatic for the child (J. H. Gagnon, 1965a; McCaghy, 1971). Often the trauma arises from the highly emotional reaction of the parents or from the police and judicial procedures. While the experience itself is often not traumatic, there are two exceptions to this general rule. The experience may be psychologically damaging to the child if violence or extreme coercion is used. Repeated, serious sexual contacts, particularly if they are with a close relative, may also be very damaging.

It is important for parents to encourage open communication with their children so that the children will confide in them if molesting occurs. If a child does bring such a report to a parent, the parent should not overreact, but rather should encourage the child to talk about the incident, while calmly reassuring the child.

NECROPHILIA

Necrophilia is sexual contact with a dead person. It is a very rare form of behavior and is considered by experts to be psychotic and extremely deviant. Necrophilia involves deriving sexual gratification from viewing a corpse or actually having intercourse with it; the corpse may be mutilated afterward (Thorpe et al., 1961).

INCEST

Incest is defined as sexual relations between blood relatives, although the definition is typically extended to include sex between non-blood relatives (for example, between stepfather and stepdaughter) (Maisch, 1972; Sagarin, 1977).

Incest is generally thought to be very rare. For example, in one study it was found that the incidence of prosecuted incest in the United States was about one or two people per million per year (S. K. Weinberg, 1955). However, all one has to do is read the Ann Landers column to know that incest is considerably more common than that. The vast majority of cases probably go unreported. In a survey of people in the United States, it was found that about 4 percent of the average population had experienced incest and that 13 percent of the prison population had (Gebhard et al., 1965). Most of these cases, of course, had not been reported to the police. Comparison of these two studies shows how biased much of the research on incest is; it has been done almost exclusively on people arrested and/or convicted for the offense, while the unreported cases—which are the vast majority—have been ignored.

Father-daughter incest has generally been regarded as the commonest form. In a study of 159 cases of reported incest, father-daughter cases did indeed constitute 78 percent of the sample; 18 percent were brother-sister cases, 1 percent were mother-son cases, and the remaining 3 percent were multiple incestuous relationships (S. K. Weinberg, 1955). However, in the survey of the United States population mentioned above, which doubtless included many cases of unreported incest, brother-sister incest was by far the most common form, outnumbering father-daughter incest by about 5 to 1 (Gebhard et al., 1965). Therefore, it seems that brother-sister incest is actually the most common form (Lester, 1972); probably it is simply less likely to be reported or discovered than father-daughter incest.

The results of the recent Hunt survey (1974) confirm those of Gebhard and his associates. Most people reporting incest experiences said that the incest was with siblings or cousins, and rarely with parents. In many cases, the activity went no further than petting. Excluding this and counting only actual coital activity, about 7 percent of the sample had had sexual contact with a relative (Hunt, 1974).

What kind of people commit incest? Since most researchers have believed that father-daughter incest is most common, virtually all the research has been on this form. Therefore, we have the most data on the kind of man who commits incest with his daughter or daughters. In a study of men arrested for this offense, they typically had had a poor relationship with their parents and came from unhappy, unstable homes (Gebhard et al., 1965). They had engaged in much premarital sex, chiefly with girls. They were typically ineffectual, nonaggressive, and dependent, and most of them drank heavi-ly, worked sporadically, and were preoccupied with sex; 84 percent had engaged in extramarital sex.

The activity generally occurs repeatedly over a substantial period of time. Often it occurs in collusion with another member of the family. For example, the mother may terminate her sexual relationship with her husband, at which point he turns to the daughter; when the mother discovers the incest, she typically does not report it, or she may even deny that it exists. She may construct a psychological defense to avoid the cold reality; her husband is, in effect, being unfaithful to her, and she would prefer not to believe that this is happening. Further, if she reports it, her husband may be arrested, and the family might be exposed to embarrassing publicity.

The effects of the incest experience on the daughter—or on anyone involved in incest, for

FIGURE 15.7
Incest in art: Lot and his daughter. [The Bettman Archive, Inc.]

that matter—have not been well documented (Lester, 1972), and so no statement concerning the effects will be made here. Probably they vary depending on the age at which the daughter experiences the incest, the extent to which coercion is used (it rarely is), and the extent to which the family is disrupted by the activity, disruption being more likely when it is reported to the police. It may be that incestuous sexual activity is not so damaging as seductive behavior by a parent that never results in actual sexual activity.

Taboos against incest have been found in virtually all human societies, although some exceptions have been documented, including the Incan society and the societies of ancient Iran and ancient Egypt (Middleton, 1962; Murdock, 1949; Slotkin, 1947). It is possible that these taboos arose because people noted the harmful effects, either physical or social, of incest.

Genetically, incest may have bad consequences because it leads to inbreeding. In a study done in Japan in which marriages between cousins were compared with marriages of unrelated persons, it was found that the offspring of the cousin marriages were significantly worse in school performance and did worse on tests of physical performance, tests of intelligence, and some measures of health, although on some other measures there were no differences (Schull and Neel, 1965). Incest may also have bad social consequences; it can cause conflict and rivalry within the family, and it may also cause role strain ("Should I behave like a father or a boyfriend to her?" "How can I discipline her when I just had sex with her?").

BESTIALITY

Bestiality is sexual contact with animals; this behavior is also called *zoophilia* and *sodomy,* although the latter term is also used to refer to anal intercourse or even mouth-genital sex.

About 8 percent of the males in Kinsey's sample reported sexual experiences with animals. Most of this activity was concentrated in adolescence and probably reflected the experimentation and diffuse sexual urges of that period. Not too surprisingly, the percentage was considerably higher among boys on farms; 17 percent of boys raised on farms had had animal contacts resulting in orgasm. Kinsey found that about 3 to 4 percent of all females have some sexual contact with animals, and thus females appear to be less likely to engage in this behavior than males.

NYMPHOMANIA AND SATYRIASIS

Nymphomania and satyriasis are both conditions in which there is an extraordinarily high level of sexual activity and sex drive, to the point where the person is apparently insatiable and where sexuality overshadows all other concerns and interests. When this occurs in women, it is called *nymphomania;* in men it is called *satyriasis.*[6] While this definition seems fairly simple, in practice it is difficult to say when a person has an abnormally high sex drive. As was seen in Chapters 10 and 11, there is a wide range in the frequencies with which people engage in coitus; therefore, the range we define as "normal" should also be broad. In real life, the "nymphomania" or "satyriasis" is often defined by the spouse. Some men, for example, might think that it was unreasonable for a wife to want intercourse once a day or even twice a week, and they would consider such a woman a nymphomaniac.[7] Other men might think it would be wonderful to be married to a woman

---

[6]Satyriasis is named for the satyrs, who were part-human, part-animal beasts in Greek mythology. A part of the entourage of Dionysus, the god of wine and fertility, they were jovial and lusty and have become a symbol of the sexually active male.

[7]Someone once defined a nymphomaniac as a woman that a man can't keep up with.

who wanted to make love every day. Labels like "nymphomaniac" can be used as weapons in marital squabbles. Because such terms are so loaded, some scholars think the term "hypersexuality" is preferable.

The term "nymphomaniac" is used particularly loosely by lay people. A nymphomaniac is more than just a woman who likes sex. True nymphomania is very rare, a point that should be kept in mind when reading the Focus. What defines the true nymphomaniac, then? Probably it is her insatiability and the compulsiveness of her behavior. It is compulsive in the sense that she feels driven to it, even when there may be very negative consequences. She is also never satisfied by the activity. Similar criteria could be used to define satyriasis. Such cases would meet the criteria for abnormal behavior discussed at the beginning of this chapter: the compulsiveness of the behavior leads it to become extremely inefficient, with the result that it impairs functioning in other areas of the person's life.

Once again, these variations illustrate the extent to which the person's gender is important in defining abnormality. Since the stereotype is that women have a very low sex drive, a woman with a high sex drive is classified as a "nympho," a term that is commonly used. Men, according to the stereotype, have a high sex drive; thus it is scarcely even recognized that a few men might have problems with an abnormally high sex drive, and the term "satyriasis" is rarely used.

CELIBACY

At the opposite end of the continuum of sexual behavior from nymphomania and satyriasis is *celibacy*, in which the person abstains totally from sexual activity.

Some religious groups require celibacy of their clergy, as the Roman Catholic Church does for priests. Some religions even demand celibacy from all members (for example, the Shakers), although such groups have a tendency to die out, not surprisingly. Some radical feminists also advocate celibacy, both as a form of separatism from men and as a way to free their emotional energies so that they can work even more devotedly for women's rights.

One woman expressed her feelings about being celibate:

> I have been celibate for over a year, since the beginning of my involvement with the women's movement, which gave me a lot of support. I work very hard and feel good about working. I have created my own physical environment, building a house, and have provided my own psychological space—a good combination. I masturbate a lot and enjoy it. I feel happy, independent and free to figure out my own expectations of me. (Boston Women's Health Book Collective, 1976, p. 78)

Other people become celibate simply as a result of circumstance; an example would be a widow who chooses not to remarry and not to engage in sexual activity. Yet another pattern is experimental celibacy, in which people experiment with being celibate for a period, just as they may experiment with premarital or homosexual sex.

We commonly speak of the sex "drive," as if it, like hunger, must be satisfied, or a person will die. Yet there is no evidence that celibacy is in any way damaging to one's health, and it is clear that many celibates lead long, happy lives. Celibacy should be recognized as a valid alternative sexual lifestyle, although probably not everyone is suited to it.

PROSTITUTION

Prostitutes ("hookers," "whores") engage in sexual acts in return for money. As some social critics have pointed out, though, some marriages and dating arrangements would also fall into this category. Thus one should probably

A CASE HISTORY OF NYMPHOMANIA

Mrs. M. was a lower-middle-class, attractive, slightly overweight young woman. She was 19 years old and the mother of an 8-month-old child. She was referred to a neurosurgeon by her family physician because she had persistent headaches and lower back pain. No physical causes of these symptoms could be found, and so she was referred to a psychologist for evaluation and psychotherapy. Testing revealed that she was preoccupied with sexual matters, loneliness, suicide, and hostility.

In an initial interview Mrs. M talked readily about her insatiable sexual appetite and her early sexual experiences. She said that she and her husband, aged 20, had sexual relations every night for several hours, or for as long as he could sustain the pace. He was a kind and cooperative man who believed it was his duty to provide his wife with as much sex as she wanted, but he was bewildered by her overwhelming sexual demands and could not understand why she was as sexually hungry after hours of coitus and dozens of orgasms as she had been at the beginning of the activity. On rare occasions, Mrs. M reported, she was relatively sexually satisfied, and following such occurrences her headache would disappear for a day or so.

The dynamics of the case were fairly easy to establish. Mrs. M had begun having sexual intercourse with her stepfather when she was 9 years old, and she had enjoyed it from the beginning. Since her father had left the home when she was 5, she had been deprived of male attention, and that was what she enjoyed about the intercourse with her stepfather. Further, her mother gave her little attention. She continued having coitus with the stepfather two or three times a week for the next seven years. She also discovered that she could win the affection and attention of other older men, and she became sexually involved with two uncles and several quite old

---

add the conditions that prostitutes are promiscuous and fairly nondiscriminate in their choice of partners. Female prostitution will be discussed first.

Kinds of Prostitutes

There are many kinds of prostitutes; they vary in terms of social class, status, and the kind of lifestyle they lead.

men in her neighborhood. Sometimes they initiated the behavior, and sometimes she did.

When Mrs. M was about 14, she began to feel guilty about the sexual involvement with her stepfather and confessed all to her mother. Her mother refused to believe the story and made heated accusations against her, saying that she was a seductress and a generally worthless person. The sexual relationship with the step-father continued for about two more years. Then she felt so guilty that she broke it off. Not coincidentally, the stepfather left Mrs. M's mother at this time and was never heard from again. It was at this point that Mrs. M developed the headaches, and she was subsequently unsatisfied in all her episodes of intercourse except on rare occasions with her husband.

Her mother became even more rejecting after the departure of the stepfather. Mrs. M managed to seduce or be seduced by most of her mother's suitors. Her headaches continued to worsen. Her mother, jealous over the attention the suitors paid to her daughter, pressured her into moving into her grandparents' home. They, however, were critical of her behavior, and the grandmother was suspicious of the girl's interaction with the grandfather. At this time Mrs. M met her future husband and they were married two months later. For the first time in her life, she was in a warm, affectionate relationship, although she managed to create some friction with her in-laws by being seductive toward her father-in-law.

Over the course of 10 months of psychotherapy, attempts were made to help Mrs. M create a positive self-image and accept her husband's love as sincere and valuable. She made an initial sexual advance to the therapist, but he helped her to see that her seductive behavior with an older man—the therapist—was merely an attempt to prove her worth as a human being. As the therapy progressed and Mrs. M came to understand the causes of her behavior, her frequency of sexual intercourse and the satisfaction she found in it gradually became quite normal.

Source: J. L. McCary. Nymphomania: A case history. *Medical Aspects of Human Sexuality,* November 1972, **6,** 192–202.

The *call girl* is the Cadillac of prostitutes. She is expensively dressed, lives in an attractive apartment in a good section of town, and probably charges a minimum of $50 for an hour's worth of her services (more if she is classier or is asked to engage in more exotic sexual acts, such as anal intercourse). She can thus earn over $50,000 a year, tax-free. But she does have high business expenses: an expensive wardrobe and apartment, high medical bills for VD prevention, expenses for makeup and hairdressers, high tips for doormen and landlords, and the cost of an answering service.

She obtains her clients through personal referrals and may have many regular customers; thus she maintains close control over whom she services. She may also provide other than sexual services; for example, she may be an attractive companion for a party, or she may be part of a "reward" that businesses provide for executives. The contact is often made over the phone, or perhaps in an expensive bar; the sexual activity may then take place in either her apartment or his.

The call girl is typically from a middle-class background, has more self-discipline than other prostitutes, and is better educated; some are college graduates. The movie *Klute,* starring Jane Fonda, provides a good look into the life of a call girl.

Other prostitutes work out of *brothels.* In the 1800s and early 1900s there were many successful brothels in the United States. They varied from clip joints, where the customer's money was stolen by an accomplice while he was sexually occupied, to the sporting houses and mansions. There the women were beautifully dressed, and fine food and liquor were served. The customer could choose his partner in an attractive living room downstairs; the bedrooms were upstairs, and no time limits were imposed on the customer (Bess and Janus, 1976). Brothels have declined in numbers and success since World War II. In the last decade, though, a replacement seems to have cropped up: the *massage parlor.*

Some women sell their sexual services in massage parlors (Velarde and Warlick, 1973). Massage parlors—and massages, of course—are perfectly legal, and so this setup has some advantages over more standard forms of prostitution, which are illegal. Once the customer is inside the private massage room, though, it is understood that he can get whatever services he pays for. Intercourse is not always possible, since massage parlors are not legally permitted to have beds, but fellatio and hand stimulation of the penis (a "local") are quite practical.

At the lower end of the status hierarchy is the *streetwalker,* which is the style of the majority of prostitutes. She sells her wares on the streets of cities. She is generally less attractive and less fashionably dressed than the call girl, and she charges correspondingly less for her services, perhaps as little as $5 for a "quickie." She is more likely to impose strict time constraints on the customer. Because her mode of operation is obvious, she is likely to be arrested, and she is also more likely to be exposed to dangerous clients.

Bar girls are similar to streetwalkers, except that they operate out of working-class bars. A *fleabag* is an old bar girl, perhaps 60 or 70 years old, who caters mostly to skid-row alcoholics and bums.

A *baby pro* is generally younger than 16 years old and works conventions, resorts, and hotels. There has been an increasing demand in recent years for this kind of prostitute.

Psychological Functioning of Prostitutes

Contrary to common belief, most prostitutes are not lesbians; in their private, noncommercial sex lives, most are heterosexual (Gallo and Alzate, 1976; Gebhard, 1969).

Although most prostitutes are of average intelligence, the majority—with the exception of call girls—are not well educated (Bess and Janus, 1976). Given that they are not simply a group of retardates, they must surely perceive the low esteem in which society holds them. How do they cope with this degrading image of themselves?

According to one study, several rationalizing strategies may be adopted (Jackman et al., 1963). One group of prostitutes become a part of a criminal subculture and adopt its set of values. The prostitute then has a set of counterculture values and is critical of conventional values. She might say that middle-class, conventional mores are hypocritical and boring. A second group of women shift their lives between two worlds. They are middle-class, are often married and have children, and use prostitution as a means of supporting themselves and their families. These women have very conventional values and maintain a strict dissociation between their two worlds. One said:

> I think that I am a good mother who takes care of her children. I love my family very much. I have a normal family life other than being a prostitute. I hope that my husband can find a job and gets to working steadily again so I can be an ordinary housewife. (Jackman et al., 1963, p. 157)

Finally, Jackman and his colleagues described a third group as totally alienated. Their lives have no orientation and seem meaningless, and they have no well-defined set of values.

Pimps and Madams

The *pimp* is the companion-master of the prostitute. She supports him with her earnings, and in return he gives her companionship and sex, gets her out of jail, and provides her with food, clothing, shelter, and drugs, especially cocaine. He also provides protection against theft and other crimes, since the prostitute is scarcely in a position to go to the police if she is robbed by a customer. The *procurer,* or *panderer,* helps the prostitute and client find each other. Pimps sometimes, though not always, function as panderers.

The prostitutes working for a pimp are called his "stable," and each is called a "wife." An "outlaw" is a prostitute who has no pimp.

Typically, the pimp returns only 5 percent of the prostitute's earnings to her (Sheehy, 1973).

A *madam* is a woman who manages a brothel. Typically, she is quite intelligent and has excellent financial and social skills. The best-known madam of the 1970s was Xaviera Hollander, who managed a brothel in New York and wrote *The Happy Hooker.*

The Career of a Prostitute

The first step in a prostitute's career is entry. There appear to be many reasons why a woman enters prostitution (Bess and Janus, 1976). One is sheer economics. This factor is particularly likely during war, when prostitution may be the only means of survival. But even in times of peace, prostitution can be economically appealing, particularly for the woman who has no job skills. Why take a boring, restrictive job as a secretary for $150 a week when you can make that much in a day, or even a few hours, as a call girl? A related factor is a dislike of routine and regimen and an attraction for the glamour and excitement of the world of the prostitute. For some women—for example, a poor but very attractive black woman—prostitution is a means of attaining upward economic mobility. Some women become prostitutes in order to support a drug addiction. Another category of reasons involves gaining power. For example, a woman who serves as a call girl to famous politicians may think of herself as having access to real political power. As a woman who was involved in one of the Capitol Hill sex scandals uncovered in the 1970s said, "I was only a pillowcase away from the Presidency." Still other women gradually drift into prostitution, perhaps because they have a friend who is a prostitute who encourages them to do it. Rumors that there is a large "white slave" market in the United States are untrue, however; only about 4 percent of prostitutes were actually forced into the profession (Gebhard, 1969).

On entering prostitution, some women—particularly if they want to be call girls—go through an apprenticeship in which they pay an experienced call girl to teach them the skills of the profession (Bryan, 1965). The apprentice learns not only sexual techniques but also how to manage finances, how to control customers, how to avoid being robbed, and how to make contacts.

One problem with prostitution is that it is a short-lived career, in this respect bearing a resemblance to the career of a professional basketball or football player. Even a woman who starts as a high-priced call girl may find herself drifting down in status, either as she ages and begins to show wrinkles or if she gets hooked on alcohol or other drugs. In prostitution, seniority is not rewarded.

"Squaring up" or "leaving the life" refers to giving up prostitution. Financially it is a difficult thing to do, particularly for the woman with no job skills; recognizing this, some rehabilitation programs provide job training, as well as a halfway house to integrate the woman back into society (Winick and Kinsie, 1971).

The married prostitute may simply go back to being a housewife. The unmarried woman may escape through marriage, since she may get proposals from her regular customers (Benjamin and Masters, 1964; Young, 1970).

Other reasons for leaving include arrest and the threat of a long-term jail sentence, government agencies' insistence that she give up her children, and the knowledge that a friend was the victim of violence while she worked as a prostitute (Bess and Janus, 1976).

Customers

At the time of the Kinsey research, about 69 percent of all white males had had some experience with prostitutes (Kinsey et al., 1948). The recent Hunt survey, however, found that the use of prostitutes is becoming less common in the under-35 age group, particularly among middle-class males; only 19 percent of the men under 35 with some college education had had premarital intercourse with a prostitute (Hunt, 1974). Thus the use of prostitutes seems to be declining.

Prostitutes refer to their customers as "johns." About 60 percent of the clients are occasional johns; they may be respectable businessmen who seek only occasional contacts with prostitutes, perhaps while on business trips. Others are habitual johns who seek a regular relationship with a prostitute. Some are compulsive johns, who use prostitutes for their major sexual outlet. They are driven to them and cannot stay away. Some of these men are potent only with prostitutes (Bess and Janus, 1976).

Men use the services of prostitutes for a variety of reasons. Some are married but want sex more frequently than their wives do or want to engage in practices—such as fellatio—that they feel their wives would not be willing to do. Some use prostitutes to satisfy their exotic sexual needs, such as being whipped or having sex with a woman who pretends to be a corpse. The motivation for the unmarried man or the one who is away from home for a long period of time (for example, during a war) may simply be release of sexual tension. Others, particularly adolescents, may have sex with prostitutes to prove their manhood or to get sexual experience. Finally, some men enjoy sex with prostitutes because it is "forbidden."

Male Prostitutes

Some male prostitutes serve a heterosexual clientele, selling their services to women; they are called *gigolos*. They often cater to wealthy, middle-aged women and provide them with escort as well as sexual services. Their approach is generally subtle and romantically flattering to their clients. The character played by Jon Voight

FOCUS

ADVERTISING FOR SEXUAL PARTNERS

Many underground newspapers now carry advertisements placed by people seeking sexual partners, particularly those with unusual tastes. The following examples were all found in a single issue of the *Berkeley Barb:*

SPANKINGS
W/M, 30 seeks female who digs sharing erotic discipline. I can give or take spankings. Let's explore fantasies. Box xxxx, San Francisco.

Beautiful black bitch would love to step on you. Call F_____, xxx-xxxx

IMPOTENT MATURE WM discreet clean thoughtful will go down on woman any age no reciprocation required can bring friend, husband may watch. No $ involved call xxx-xxxx anytime. Sincere only.

CLOTHING FETISHISTS! Black silk stockings and high heels, garter belts, etc. . . . worn by exquisite nude model, 10 am to 10 pm, xxx-xxxx.

MUSCULAR YOUNG GYMNAST. Model, masseur. xxx-xxxx

---

in *Midnight Cowboy* made an attempt to support himself in this way.

Hustlers are male prostitutes who cater to a homosexual clientele. Interestingly, some of them consider themselves to be heterosexual, not homosexual. They may have strict rules for their customers to follow, such as only permitting the customer to perform fellatio on them. To indicate their masculinity, they may wear leather jackets and tight jeans. Other hustlers are open homosexuals who earn money by selling their services. Some brothels, called "peg houses," specialized in a homosexual clientele. Now, however, hustlers must work on the streets, in gay bars, or both. Some work through "massage parlors" or "modeling agencies," that advertise in gay newspapers. There is

also some market for "chickens" (young boys) as prostitutes.

MISCELLANY

The sexual variations discussed below are too rare to have had much research devoted to them; they are nonetheless interesting because of their bizarreness.

Troilism, or *triolism,* refers to having sex with another person while a third person looks on. It combines elements of exhibitionism and voyeurism.

Saliromania is a disorder found mainly in men; there is a desire to damage or soil a woman or her clothes or the image of a woman, such as a painting or statue. The man becomes sexually excited and may ejaculate during the act.

Coprophilia and *urophilia* are both variations having to do with excretion. In coprophilia the feces are important to sexual satisfaction. In urophilia it is the urine that is important. The urophiliac may want to be urinated on as part of the sexual act.

SUMMARY

It seems reasonable to define "abnormal sexual behavior" as behavior that is uncomfortable for the person, inefficient, bizarre, and/or physically or psychologically harmful to the person or others.

A fetishist is a person who becomes erotically attached to some object other than another human being. Most likely, fetishism arises from conditioning, and it provides a good example of the continuum from normal to abnormal behavior.

The transsexual has a gender identity problem. He or she feels trapped in a body of the wrong gender and hence is a candidate for a sex-change operation.

The transvestite derives sexual satisfaction from dressing as a member of the opposite gender. Like many other sexual variations, transvestism is more common among men than among women.

The sadist derives sexual pleasure from inflicting pain, while the masochist is sexually excited by experiencing pain.

The voyeur is sexually aroused by looking at nudes or by watching others have sex, while the exhibitionist displays his sexual organs to others. Both are generally harmless.

The pedophiliac, or child molester, desires sex with children. Though this behavior is fairly common, violence is rarely associated with it. Necrophilia is sex with a dead person. Bestiality is sex with an animal.

Incest is sex between relatives; brother-sister incest is the most common form, and father-daughter incest is the second most common form.

Nymphomania in women and satyriasis in men are conditions in which there is an extraordinarily high, insatiable sex drive. Both syndromes are very rare. Celibacy, or complete abstinence from sex, is a requirement in some religious communities; there is no evidence that it is damaging to one's health.

There are several kinds of prostitutes, ranging from call girls to streetwalkers to male prostitutes.

SUGGESTIONS FOR FURTHER READING

Morris, Jan. *Conundrum.* New York: New American Library, 1974. James Morris, a successful journalist and World War II veteran, was also a transsexual. In this fascinating autobiography, she gives an inside view of her earlier life, her sex-change operation, and her new life as a woman, Jan Morris.

Shafer, Peter. *Equus.* A gripping play about a sadistic act performed by a boy. It focuses on the interaction between the boy and his psychiatrist as they unravel the causes of the act in sexuality and religion.

Sheehy, Gail. *Hustling: Prostitution in our wide-open society.* New York: Delacorte Press, 1971. An inside look at prostitution, written by a well-known journalist.

RAPE

CITED

Rape Poem

There is no difference between being raped
and being pushed down a flight of cement steps
except that the wounds also bleed inside.

There is no difference between being raped
and being run over by a truck
except that afterward men ask if you enjoyed it.

There is no difference between being raped
and going head first through a windshield
except that afterward you are afraid
not of cars
but half the human race.

—Marge Piercy*

In 1975 there were 56,090 cases of reported rape in the United States; that means there were 51 reported rapes for every 100,000 women (FBI, 1975). However, according to the FBI, forcible rape is "one of the most underreported crimes." It is generally estimated that only about one rape in every five is reported; that is, about 80 percent go unreported (Amir, 1971, pp. 27–28; FBI, 1973, p. 15). Why do rape victims not report the crime?

This chapter will examine what is known about the rape victim, about the rapist, and about what can be done to prevent rape. First, however, some terms need definition. Though the legal definition of rape varies from state to state, the following is typical of the definitions used in the United States (Snelling, 1975):

. . . the perpetration of an act of sexual intercourse with a female, not one's wife, against her will and consent, whether her will is overcome by force or fear resulting from the threat of force, or by drugs or intoxicants; or when, because of

mental deficiency, she is incapable of exercising rational judgment; or when she is below an arbitrary "age of consent." (Brownmiller, 1975, p. 368)

The last phrase refers to a specific kind of rape, *statutory rape*, which is intercourse with a girl who is below the legal age of consent. The idea is that, in this particular offense, resistance or will is irrelevant since the girl is simply too young to make a judgment; therefore, the man is automatically considered to have taken advantage of her. The legal age of consent varies from state to state, ranging from a low of 7 years in Delaware (changed in 1973 to 16 years) to a high of 21 years, under certain conditions, in Tennessee; in most states, it ranges between 12 and 16 years.

THE RAPE VICTIM

Psychological Responses of the Rape Victim

One of the largest programs of research on rape victims has been carried out at Boston City Hospital by Ann Wolbert Burgess, a nurse, and

---

Lynda Holmstrom, a sociologist (Burgess and Holmstrom, 1974a, 1974b). They have found that rape is a time of real crisis for a woman and that the effects on her adjustment may persist for six months or more. On the basis of their analysis of the responses of 92 victims of forcible rape, they documented the existence of a *rape trauma syndrome*, which refers to the emotional changes that a woman undergoes following a rape or an attempted rape.

The rape trauma syndrome progresses in two phases: an acute phase and a long-term reorganization phase. The *acute phase* begins immediately after the rape and may last for several weeks. During the first few hours following the rape, women have a wide variety of emotional reactions that may be classified into two basic types: an expressive reaction, in which the woman cries and expresses feelings of fear, anger, anxiety, and tension, and a controlled reaction, in which the woman apparently masks or subdues her feelings and appears calm and composed or subdued. The women studied by Burgess and Holmstrom reported many physical reactions during the acute phase. Some of these were direct results of the bruises and cuts they had received during the scuffle. Some women who were forced to have oral sex suffered irritation or damage to the throat. Rectal bleeding and pain were reported by the women who had been forced to have anal intercourse. Various irritations of the genitals were also common,[1] as were symptoms of tension such as headaches, sleeplessness, and a feeling of jumpiness. Women also reported stomach pains and nausea. Emotional reactions varied widely, from fear, humiliation, and embarrassment to anger and a desire for revenge. Two feelings were especially prominent:

fear and self-blame. Many women reported an overwhelming fear of physical violence, and said that they had believed they would be murdered during the attack; these feelings of fear sometimes persisted long after the rape had taken place. Self-blame also occurred, with the woman spending hours agonizing over what she had done to bring on the rape or what she might have done to prevent it: "If I hadn't worn that tight sweater, . . ." "If I hadn't worn that short skirt, . . ." "If I hadn't been stupid enough to walk on that dark street, . . ." "If I hadn't been dumb enough to trust that guy, . . ." This is an example of a tendency on the part of both the victim and others to "blame the victim."

The acute phase is followed by a *long-term reorganization phase*. The rape creates a major disruption in the woman's life. For example, some women are unable to return to work after being raped, particularly if the rape occurred at work (Brodsky, 1976). They may quit their jobs and remain unemployed for some time. The seriousness of these lasting effects is illustrated in the Focus. Many of the women studied by Burgess and Holmstrom moved during the long-term reorganization phase, sometimes several times; many also changed their telephone number, and some got an unlisted number. These actions seemed to result from a fear that the rapist would find them and attack them again. Some women who had been raped indoors developed fears of being indoors, and some who had been raped outdoors developed fears of being outdoors. Sexual phobias were also common. The women's normal sexual lifestyles were often severely disrupted for long periods. For example, one woman reported, five months after being raped, "There are times I get hysterical with my boyfriend. I don't want him near me; I get panicked" (Burgess and Holmstrom, 1974a, p. 984). In some cases, it may be years before the victim returns to a normal lifestyle and is able to cope with the crisis she experienced.

If a woman reports the rape and decides to

[1]Tests for venereal disease should routinely be done as part of the hospital treatment of rape victims. Pregnancy tests can be done four to six weeks afterward if the woman's period is late. Another alternative, if pregnancy seems likely, is to administer the morning-after pill immediately, although it has some serious side effects (see Chap. 19).

THE STORY OF A
RAPE VICTIM: DENISE

FOCUS

Denise, a 25-year-old woman, had moved to southern California shortly before she was attacked. She had had four years of teaching experience and had found a job soon after arriving in the Los Angeles area.

One morning Denise arrived at her classroom. She found no one else there. One student came to the door, and because it was raining, Denise let him inside. Suddenly a young man entered the classroom and told the one child who was in the classroom to stand facing the wall. He then took a gun from his pocket and threatened Denise. The man told her that if she did not let him do what he wanted, he would kill her. He then raped her.

When the man left, Denise called the school authorities. She was taken to the hospital and examined. Then she was sent home. Denise stayed home for three weeks in a state of shock. She was especially upset when the police asked her to look at pictures of males who had been involved in sexual offenses, in an effort to identify her attacker. Denise recalled the procedure as being as traumatic as the initial attack.

After a month Denise returned to her job. She was able to work for only three days. She could not drive to work herself because she was too nervous; she would jump whenever she heard a loud noise. Even in her own apartment, she would hide if she heard someone walking up or down the stairs. One evening when her husband

press charges, the police investigation and the trial itself may be further crises for her. She must recall the traumatic experience in detail. The police and the courts have a history of callous or even abusive treatment of rape victims. The woman may be offered little sympathy, and the police may adopt a cynical attitude, suggesting that she agreed to have sex but then changed her mind afterward. The attitudes of the police are not too surprising, growing up as they did in a culture that abounds with stereotypes about women, including the one that says that rape is

only a situation in which a woman changed her mind. Of course, not all police officers have been guilty of such cynicism, but too many victims report treatment like this:

> They finally told me they thought I was lying. They said I'd probably been having sex with my boyfriend and probably was afraid I was pregnant. They also theorized that my boyfriend had set me up for it. They wanted to know if he'd ever asked me to have relations with his friends. (Brownmiller, 1975, p. 366)

378

CHAPTER 16

returned home, Denise met him at the door with a gun they owned. She herself was frightened by this, and they decided to get rid of the gun.

Denise had nightmares repeatedly. She would awaken in terror, perspiring profusely. The nightmares were not of rape but of other fears—fears of mutilation and fears of falling. She would wake up in the morning feeling sick and would begin vomiting. She was given tranquilizers, but they did not seem to help. Prior to the rape incident, Denise and her husband had what they considered an excellent sexual relationship. After the rape, she could not tolerate the thought of sexual intercourse. She feared being alone.

Denise was referred to a psychiatrist. Slowly, over a period of several months, her startle reactions lessened. Her nightmares diminished in intensity and frequency. After two months, she was able to drive alone. Denise returned to teaching but continued to be insecure and anxious. Whenever she saw a man who reminded her of the attacker, she jumped. She had problems in relating to her husband sexually and emotionally.

Fourteen months after the attack, Denise's psychiatrist thought she had overcome the "traumatic neurosis" which had resulted from the rape. She continued to have marital problems and started having gynecologic problems. Denise was assigned to a new school and received high ratings there. Eighteen months later her therapist noted that there were times when she was symptom-free. However, Denise was still afraid of being alone.

Source: Carroll M. Brodsky. Rape at work. In M. J. Walker and S. L. Brodsky (Eds.), *Sexual assault: The victim and the rapist.* Lexington, Mass.: Lexington Books, 1976, pp. 40–42. Copyright 1975, D. C. Heath and Company. Reprinted by permission of the publisher.

Or this:

> I went to the police station and said, "I want to report a rape." They said, "Whose?" and I said, "Mine." The cop looked at me and said, "Aw, who'd want to rape you?" (Brownmiller, 1975, p. 364)

The defense lawyer, in attempting to defend the rapist, may try to make it look as if the victim was actually the criminal—that she seduced him and later decided to call it rape, that she is a slut and therefore cannot be raped, and so on. She may be questioned about her prior sexual experiences, the idea being that if she has had premarital or extramarital sex, she is promiscuous and cannot be raped. As one woman expressed it:

> They trotted out my whole past life, made me go through all these changes, while he just sat at the defendant's table, mute, surrounded by his lawyers. Of course that was his right by law, but it looked like I was the one who was on trial. (Brownmiller, 1975, p. 372)

Recently some states have passed "reform" evidence laws, which do not permit the woman's previous sexual experience (except with the alleged rapist) to be a topic during a trial for rape.

In one study, judges were interviewed about their attitudes toward rape (Bohmer, 1974). They appeared to divide rape cases into three types. First, there were clear cases of "genuine victims," in which there was no question that a forcible rape had occurred; the attack had been brutal, carried out by a total stranger on an unsuspecting victim. Second, the judges saw some rapes as being "consensual intercourse," in which the woman had "asked for it," for example, by allowing herself to be picked up in a bar. They had a variety of cute expressions for this, including "friendly rape," "felonious gallantry," and "assault with failure to please." Finally, the judges felt that there was a third category, "female vindictiveness," in which the woman was trying to get even with a former husband or boyfriend by accusing him of rape.

Recently, perhaps partly as a result of several excellent television programs dramatizing the plight of the woman who has been raped, many police departments have tried to change their handling of rape victims. Some even have special "rape squads" composed of women police officers who record the woman's story and investigate the case; this spares the woman the embarrassment of describing the incident to a man.

It also appears that the victim's sense of guilt over the crime contributes to the trauma she experiences. According to a specialist in criminal psychiatry, "The victim who is beaten into almost senselessness may suffer far less emotional trauma than the woman who submits to rape when her life is threatened" (Brussel, 1971, p. 30). That is, emotional noninvolvement between the victim and the criminal helps the victim adjust better afterward. The woman who is beaten unconscious is much less likely than the woman who escapes with only minor scratches to have others imply (or to think in her own mind) that she brought on the attack or that she cooperated or enjoyed it.

To say the least, then, rape is an extremely traumatic experience for many women, and it may have effects lasting six months or more after the attack. In view of this, Burgess and Holmstrom emphasize the need for counseling for rape victims. The counselor provides support and encourages the victim to vent her feelings. The counselor should be with the victim during the hospital procedures and while the police are questioning her and then should provide follow-up counseling; the counselor should also be with the woman during the court procedures since, as has been noted, they can be extremely traumatic.

Silent Rape Reaction

Burgess and Holmstrom (1974a) have also documented the existence of a phenomenon they call the "silent rape reaction." As was noted, probably the majority of rapes are not reported. However, not only do some women fail to report the rape to the police, but they also tell no one about it. They, of course, experience the same problems of adjustment that other rape victims do, but they have no way of expressing or venting these feelings. People who do counseling or psychotherapy should be aware of this syndrome. For example, a woman may come for counseling complaining of quite different problems—perhaps inability to have orgasms or anxiety and depression—when her real problem is that she has been raped but is unable to talk about it. Symptoms of this silent rape reaction are similar to those associated with the rape trauma syndrome, described above. Such women should be helped gently to begin to talk about the experience so that they can start to deal with it.

FIGURE 16.1
In a simulation demonstration program a professional model (left) gives a "rape report" in a new police training program at Brandeis University designed to increase police sensitivity and improve rape investigations. The man and woman at the right are both students in the course. *[Wide World Photos.]*

Female Socialization: Creating Rape Victims

How do women become victims of rape? This section will discuss the notion that many of the qualities for which females are socialized make them vulnerable to rape (Russell, 1975; Weis and Borges, 1973).

For example, according to gender-role stereotypes, weakness is feminine, while strength is masculine. The stereotype of weakness is compounded by the lack of athletic training that females generally receive, compared with males. As a result, many women think of them-

selves as being physically weak, and, because they lack training and do not exercise, they may actually be weak. This weakness is symbolized in many ways, as when men open doors for women or carry heavy bundles for them. To expect a person who needs such assistance to fight off a 220-pound attacker would be silly, Thus, the weakness and passivity for which females are socialized contribute to making them rape victims.

Females are also socialized for nurturance (taking care of others) and altruism (paying attention to the needs of others rather than one's own needs). The woman who has been socialized to be nurturant and who spends her days expressing her gentleness toward her children can scarcely be expected to attempt to gouge out a man's eyes with her fingernails, as some self-defense experts advise. Female altruism has an ironic effect in the rape situation. Some women report the rape but then choose not to press charges because they say they are afraid that the rapist might have to go to jail for a long time[2] or that his reputation will be ruined. Thus, the victim may adopt a nurturant, altruistic attitude toward her attacker, considering his needs and feelings first.

The feelings of altruism that lead to nonreporting are magnified by the fact that, in nearly half the cases, the victim knows her attacker at least casually. Statistics indicate that in 53 percent of all cases, the attacker is a total stranger. However, in 30 percent of all cases, the woman and the rapist are slightly acquainted; in 7 percent, they are relatives (father and daughter, brother and sister, uncle and niece, etc.); and in 3 percent, they are not related but have had a previous close association (Mulvihill et al., 1969).

Females are also socialized for a group of qualities that might be called collectively "being ladylike." Ladies, for example, do not make scenes. To fight off a rapist, of course, one needs to make a scene, but many women may be inhibited from screaming or engaging in a rough scuffle because that is not ladylike behavior. Ladies are also neat and clean and pretty. Some women, immediately after a rape, go home to shower, wash their hair, and change their clothes; then they proceed to the police station. While their emotional need to get themselves clean is understandable, they have destroyed most of the evidence of the crime, and the

skeptical reaction of the police is not surprising. If you look neat and clean and pretty, it is hard to believe that you have just been raped.

Children, and girls especially, are taught to fear sex crimes. They are told never to accept rides with strange men or to take candy from them. Yet the exact nature of the potential danger remains unknown, and so the girl may build up an exceedingly great dread of a mysterious crime, perhaps thinking that it would be the worst thing that could ever happen to her. Thus, when she is attacked, she may be absolutely immobilized with fear. She freezes and is unable to wage an effective counterattack.

The reader can probably think of other examples of qualities that females are socialized for that contribute to making them rape victims. However, the important point is that conformity to traditional standards of femininity makes women more vulnerable to rape, at least when they are in a situation in which a man intends to rape them (Russell, 1975).

RAPISTS

The Typical Rapist

What is the profile of the typical rapist? The basic answer to that question is that there is no typical rapist. Rapists vary tremendously from one to the next in occupation, education, marital status, previous criminal record, and motivation for committing the rape. To deal with this diversity, some scientists have attempted to develop typologies of rapists (ways of classifying them). These will be discussed in the next section.

A few generalizations can be made about rapists. Most are young. According to the FBI *Uniform Crime Reports*, 61 percent are under 25. Many have a tendency to repeat their offense (M. L. Cohen et al., 1971). It is also true that most rapists are not murderers (Selkin, 1975). Probably only about 1 rape in 500 is

---

[2]Those who worry about condemning a man to a long jail sentence may be interested to know that the average convicted rapist spends less than four years in jail for the offense (Brownmiller, 1975).

accompanied by a murder (Brownmiller, 1975).[3] This statistic is important for women who wonder how best to react in a rape situation. Statistically, although the rapist may threaten the woman with violence or murder, he is unlikely to carry through on this and is only using the threat to get her to submit. This may encourage women to resist the attacker rather than submitting.

A Typology of Rapists

In an attempt to deal with the diversity in the personalities and approaches of rapists, psychiatrist Murray Cohen and his colleagues (1971) have developed a typology or scheme for categorizing rapists. The typology is based on the motivation of the rapist for committing the crime, in particular whether he was motivated by sex or by aggression. According to this typology, there are four kinds of rapists: the aggressive-aim rapist, the sexual-aim rapist, the sex-aggression-fusion rapist, and the impulse rapist.

The *aggressive-aim* rapist is motivated by a desire to hurt his victim. Sex has little to do with the act for him, except insofar as he uses sex to hurt his victim. Aggressive-aim rapists may try to damage the victim's breasts or genitals, or they may painfully insert objects into the woman's vagina.[4] Their emotional state during the rape is anger, and their victims are typically strangers. They often have a stable work history, with the work being in a very "masculine" occupation such as that of truck driver or machinist. Rapists in this category are often married, but they have a history of irritating or even violent relationships with women. A case

history of an aggressive-aim rapist is given in the Focus. Rapes of this type are an excellent example of the nonsexual use of sexual behavior.

The *sexual-aim* rapist is quite different. For him the motivation for the rape is clearly sexual. Generally he uses a minimal amount of violence and aggression—only what is needed to accomplish his sexual aim. During the act, he is highly sexually aroused and is fully aware of what he is doing. The act is not impulsive. He has lived through it many times in a fantasy in which the woman first protests but then submits; he shows great skill in his sexual performance, and she is so pleased that she falls in love with him. He has a history of poor sexual adjustment. As a child and early adolescent he may have shown signs of voyeurism, exhibitionism, and fetishism; adequate heterosexuality was present only in fantasy. In adolescence he became increasingly shy, lonely, and passive. He is characterized by low self-esteem and is simply incapable of forming mature relationships. He often commits the rape outdoors and releases his victim if she resists. Fighting back against such a rapist may thus be quite effective and probably involves little danger.[5]

The *sex-aggression-fusion* rapist appears to be motivated by sadism. For him, violence is necessary in order to experience sexual excitement. Indeed, he may be unable to get an erection unless the woman resists. Rapist-murderers are an extreme version of this type; most sex-aggression-fusion rapists use violence only to become aroused, and they employ no further aggression once the act is over. This type

---

[3]If anything, this is probably an *over*estimate of the number of rapes that end in murder, since rape-murders are almost invariably discovered, whereas the rape in which the woman escapes with minor scratches is likely to go unreported.

[4]It is clear from the statistics that intercourse is not always the goal of the rapist. In one study, vaginal intercourse occurred in less than half the rape cases investigated (Selkin, 1975).

[5]Applying the results of scientific research in one's own life can be fraught with difficulties, however. Whether resistance will be effective and how much danger it entails depend a lot on the type of rapist. With a sexual-aim rapist there is little danger, while resistance may spur a sex-aggression-fusion rapist (to be discussed next) on to further violence. But when a woman is in a rape situation, how can she tell which type is attacking her? She can scarcely interrupt the struggle to inquire, "Are you a sex-aim rapist or a sex-aggression-fusion rapist?"

CASE HISTORY OF A RAPIST: PHILLIP

Phillip is 25. He is tall and well built, and although his walk, voice, and manner are assertive, he has a boyish smile enhanced by a cowlick and deep blue, guileless eyes.

He was committed to the center four years ago following a sexual assault on a young girl. He was driving along a city road when he saw a girl, whom he did not know. He stopped his car beside her, stepped out, and asked her where she was going. He did not hear her answer and asked again in an angry manner. She turned to walk away, and Phillip felt she was trying to make a fool of him. He believed that she had been interested in him at first but had rejected him when he showed his interest in her. He punched her in the stomach, pulled her into his car, and drove away to a secluded area. After he had parked, he climbed into the back and dragged her over the seat beside him. He undressed her and violently penetrated her. He states that he then withdrew, without having an orgasm, and let her out of the car, threatening to kill her if she made mention of the attack. When he was arrested shortly thereafter, he immediately admitted his guilt.

During the diagnostic interviews he discussed the incident, describing himself as enraged at the time, not sexually excited. He had gone to visit his girlfriend, a "good" girl whom he had been seeing off and on since early adolescence; there had been no sexual activity throughout the courtship. He found her necking on the porch with a black man, and he drove away from her house in a blind rage. He was partially aware as he drove away that he was going to look for someone to attack sexually.

Phillip has had an active sexual life, but only with girls whom he considered "bad." These relationships were short-lived, ending

of rapist may also project his own confusion of sex and aggression onto his victim, saying that women like to be roughed up. While he may be married, there is often a history of marriages and divorces, and he appears uncommitted to any of the marriages. His personality is similar to that of the psychopath; he has a history of antisocial behavior, an inability to form stable relation-ships, a noncaring attitude toward others, little control over his impulses, and no feelings of guilt over his behavior. He may have had a history of aggressive behavior toward younger children, peers, and animals even before he reached puberty. This type of rapist is clearly the most dangerous, but fortunately he is also the rarest.

when he was directly confronted with the girls' promiscuity. The relationships were always terminated violently, with Phillip assaulting either the girl or the boyfriend who had replaced him.

Although Phillip has had no history of homosexual experiences, his behavior toward homosexuals indicates the presence of homosexual desires and the tenuousness of their repression. Within the center, he reacted with exaggerated, explosive anger toward homosexual invitations.

Phillip began to have sexual intercourse at age 15 with the girls described above. He remembers his first heterosexual experience as being somewhat traumatic. When he was 9 or 10 years old, he was approached by a girl who engaged him in sexual play, telling him that girls liked this kind of play. Shortly thereafter a neighborhood girl asked him to play with her, and he began to fondle her, believing that this was what she desired. She ran home and told her parents, who in turn called Phillip's father. According to Phillip, his father felt so disgraced that they moved to a different part of town.

Phillip's father was a strict man, the disciplinarian of the family. His mother was a somewhat passive, quiet woman. Their family life was quite stable, with the father working as a machinist for the same company for 25 years. There were two other children in the family, an older sister and a younger brother, both of whom appear to be living normal lives.

Phillip is a very likable young man; he is well thought of by the officers and his fellow patients. His anger appears to be very specific to threats to his sense of independence or challenges to his sense of masculinity.

Phillip dealt at some length in therapy with his self-destructive behavior, showing some awareness of the self-inflicted pain in his relationships.

Source: M. L. Cohen, R. Garofalo, R. Boucher, and T. Seghorn. The psychology of rapists. *Seminars in Psychiatry*, 1971, **3,** pp. 315–317. According to the authors' typology, Phillip is an example of an aggressive-aim rapist.

Finally, the *impulse* rapist has neither a sexual nor an aggressive motive. Rather, he commits the rape on impulse. For example, he may be involved in robbing an apartment when he notices that it is unoccupied except for one woman who is asleep in her bed. He sees the opportunity for rape, and he seizes it. He does it simply because it gives him satisfaction. This type has also been called the *predatory* rapist (Selkin, 1975).

The Date Rape
Though often not categorized as rape, some acts of coitus on dates involve a great deal of force and could at least be called *sex aggression*.

Incidents of this type were investigated by Eugene J. Kanin (1969). He began by contacting a random sample of unmarried male university students; 95 percent cooperated. Of those who responded, 25 percent reported having performed at least one act of sex aggression, defined as making a forceful attempt at coitus to the point of being disagreeable and offensive to the woman, with the woman responding by fighting or crying, for example. The 87 males who had engaged in such acts reported 181 episodes with 142 females.

The incidents of sex aggression were not confined to cases of casual bar pick-ups. They occurred in every degree of involvement, from pick-ups and first dates to couples who dated regularly or were pinned.

In some cases, the sex aggression appears to result from female-male miscommunication. There is a saying among males that "When she says 'no,' she really means 'yes.'" How, then, is a woman supposed to say "no" when she really means it? Such confused communication patterns between men and women can contribute to the date rape, as described in the following example:

> I picked up M and she suggests we go and park and "talk." Talk shifts to "old times." I move over and kiss her. One thing leads to another and I am petting her breasts. M begins to complain about her girdle and removes it. The pace increases to the point where I try to lay her down on the front seat of the car. She resists and I keep going until she suddenly starts fighting and screaming at me. I finally told her to shut up and took her home. She was really sore. (Kanin, 1969)

In this case, the man doubtless interpreted the woman's taking off her girdle as an invitation to intercourse, while she probably in fact took it off because it felt very uncomfortable.

In some cases, miscommunication and misunderstanding are so great as to be nearly unbelieveable. For example, some rapists have been reported to ask, after the rape, whether the victim had an orgasm (see, for example, the case reported by Anonymous, 1975).

In other cases, the rape appears to be a way for the man to exert social control over the woman. For example, sex aggression was apparently used by some men to punish women whom they perceived as being "teases" or "gold diggers."

Other factors also appeared to contribute to cases of date rape; however, the more important point is that such incidents were not found to be rare.

Male Socialization: Creating Rapists

Broadly speaking, there are two theoretical views about the nature of rapists and what causes them to commit rape. According to the psychopathology view, the rapist has an extremely pathological personality, probably resulting from such factors as a disturbed family life in childhood. Psychotherapy would be necessary to cure him. The work of Murray Cohen and his colleagues on the typology of rapists, discussed above, is an example of this type of thinking. In contrast, feminists view rapists as being the result of standard gender-role socialization practices in our culture. Feminist theorists deemphasize the sexual aspects of rape and instead view rape as an expression of power and dominance by men over women (Albin, 1977). To remedy the situation, radical changes in gender-role socialization practices would be necessary. The ideas in this section reflect this second theoretical view.

A previous section reviewed the argument that many of the characteristics for which we socialize females contribute to making them rape victims. The parallel argument is also informative, namely, that males are socialized for characteristics that contribute to making them rapists (Russell, 1975; Weis and Borges, 1973).

Aggression, dominance, power, and strength are manly. In the study of gender-role stereotypes discussed in Chapter 12, it was found that Americans consider aggression to be a desirable characteristic of males. Having been socialized to be aggressive, it is not surprising that men commit the aggressive crime of rape. Further, rapists may themselves be victims of our culture's confusion of sex and aggression. For example, we often refer to the male as playing the "aggressive" role in sex, suggesting that sex is supposed to have an aggressive component. Sex and aggression are also combined in the sadomasochistic pornography that is so common. The rapist's confusion of sex and aggression reflects a confusion existing in our society.

It may be, then, that rape is a means of proving masculinity for the male who is insecure in his role. For this reason, the statistics on the youthfulness of rapists make sense; youthful rapists may simply be young men who are trying to adopt the adult male role, who feel insecure about doing this, and who commit a rape as proof of their manhood. Further, heterosexuality is an important part of manliness. Raping a woman is a flagrant way to prove that one is a heterosexual. Interestingly, some rapists have a history of passivity, heterosexual inadequacy, and being called "queers" or "pansies" by their peers in adolescence. Rape for them may establish their heterosexual manliness.

The view that pressures of male socialization and a desire to prove masculinity contribute to rape is illustrated well by cases of gang rape. A psychologist studied two sets of adolescent gang rapists (Blanchard, 1959). One group of five boys had been out drinking and decided to "scare" some lovers who were parked. With one boy as their leader, they assaulted the couple, raping the girl. When the psychologist studied them individually, they were relatively tame, but when they came together as a group, they immediately began to compete for dominance to see who could find the most sexual symbols in a group of Rorschach cards. The leader, Pete, appeared to be "a very sadistic youngster with a strong need to prove his masculinity." And rape was the way to do it.

Prison Rape

In most states, rape is legally defined as a crime that has a male offender and a female victim. However, this definition ignores a whole set of "homosexual" rapes of men by other men, many of which, in the United States, occur in prisons (Brownmiller, 1975).

Indeed, it is becoming increasingly apparent that, for a male, one of the worst things about going to prison today is the danger of being the object of sexual violence. One case history will suffice as an illustration. In 1973, a 28-year-old Quaker pacifist named Robert A. Martin held a press conference in which he told the story of his experience of prison rape (Aiken, 1973; Stout, 1973). Arrested during a peace demonstration, Martin had chosen to go to jail rather than post a $10 bond. His first week in the District of Columbia jail was uneventful. But then he was transferred to another cellblock. During the first evening recreation period, he was invited into a cell by some other inmates. Then, "My exit was blocked and my pants were forcibly taken off me, and I was raped. Then I was dragged from cell to cell all evening." He was promised protection from further assaults by two of the men. The next night his "protectors" initiated a second round of oral and anal rape, collecting cigarettes from prisoners wanting a turn. When he was given a brief rest to overcome gagging and nausea, he escaped, alerted a guard, and was taken to a hospital; bond was posted for him the next day by a Quaker friend. Where were the guards when all this was going on? No one knows. Martin called the press conference to help prevent others from being subjected to this experience.

Prison rapes are the most tangible symbol of the dominance hierarchy among prisoners. Those at the bottom of the dominance hierarchy are the objects of this sexual violence, and, interestingly, they are called "girls." Prison rape is a particularly clear example of the way in which rape is an expression of power and aggression.

THE WIDER IMPACT OF RAPE

To this point, the discussion has centered on rapists and the impact of rape on the victim. But rape has much broader ramifications in our society, and it affects many people besides the victim. Most women perform a number of behaviors that stem basically from rape fears. For example, a single woman is not supposed to list her full first name in the telephone book, since that is a giveaway that she is alone; rather, she should list a first initial or a man's name. Many women, when getting into their car at night, almost reflexively check the back seat to make sure that no one is hiding there. Most college women avoid walking alone through dark parts of the campus at night. At least once in their lives, most women have been afraid of spending the night alone. If you are a woman, you can probably extend the list from your own experience; however, the point is that most women experience the fear of rape, if not rape itself.[6] Further, this fear restricts their activities.

There is also reason to be concerned about the effects of rape on relationships between men and women. If women see men as potential rapists, how can trusting relationships be built? One authority, advising women on how to avoid being raped, said:

> A woman's first act of resistance should be to refuse to help or be helped by strange men. It is unwise to stop on the street to give a man a light or explain street directions. . . . The safest stance for a woman alone, either on the street or in her home, is to be aloof and unfriendly. (Selkin, 1975, pp. 72, 74)

This may be good advice for avoiding rape, but what does it do to human relationships?

PREVENTING RAPE

Rape is clearly an important problem in our society. What can be done to prevent it? The first answer is self-defense training for women. Many universities, YWCAs, and other organizations now offer self-defense classes for women, and I believe that every woman should take at least one such course. Many techniques are available. Judo (and aikido, which is similar) emphasizes throwing and wrestling. Tae kwon do (Korean karate) emphasizes kicking. Jujitsu uses combinations of these strategies. The exact method the woman chooses is probably not too important, as long as she does know some techniques. Related to this is the importance of getting exercise and keeping in shape; this gives a woman the strength to fight back and the speed to run fast.

Self-defense, though, is useful to the woman only in defending herself once an attack has been made. Feminists argue that it would be far better if rape could be rooted out at an earlier stage so that attacks never occurred. To do this, our society would need to make a radical change in the way it socializes males and females. If little boys were not so pressed to

---

[6]Actually, statistics indicate that the chances of being raped are higher than you might think. *Psychology Today* (January 1975) did a sample calculation of the chances that a female resident of Los Angeles would be the victim of a rape attempt at some time in her life. Using the number of reported rapes and rape attempts in 1972 (2205) and the conservative estimate that 50 percent of all rapes go unreported, it was estimated that the chances that a woman in Los Angeles would be the victim of a rape attempt at some time during a 30-year period were about 1 in 10. The rape rate in Los Angeles, of course, is higher than rape rates in some other areas of the country, but the statistic is nonetheless disturbing.

Turn head into
the crook of his arm

Try to pry his little
finger back and break it

Jab elbow into
his solar plexus

Drive heel down
over his kneecap
and onto his instep

Hop backward if he tries
to pull you off balance

FIGURE 16.2
Self-defense suggestions for a woman.

be aggressive and tough, perhaps rapists would never develop. If adolescent boys did not have to demonstrate that they are hypersexual, perhaps there would be no rapists. As anthropologist Margaret Mead has noted, rape is unheard of in some societies where males are socialized to be nurturant rather than aggressive (Mead, 1935).

Changes would also need to be made in the way females are socialized, particularly if

389

If he leans forward,
grab his hair and
double him over

Claw at eyes; use Mace

Slam heel of hand up
under chin or nose

Blow to ear or
temple

Poke to hollow
of throat

Jab to solar
plexus

Snap knee into
groin (do not try
a kick unless
it is very fast)

Wrench little
finger; try to
break it

Kick to kneecap

If grabbed from
rear, bring heel
down over
kneecap

Keep kicks
aimed low

FIGURE 16.3
Vulnerable spots of a rapist.

women are to become good at self-defense. Weakness is not considered a desirable human characteristic, and so it should not be considered a desirable feminine characteristic, especially because it makes women vulnerable to rape. Mothers particularly need to think of the kind of role models they are providing for their daughters and should consider whether they are providing models of weakness. The stereotype of female weakness and passivity is so pervasive in our society that a complex set of strategies will be required to change it. Girls also need increased experience with athletics as they grow up. This change might have a number of beneficial effects: building strength, speed, and agility in women; building up their confidence in their ability to use their own bodies; and decreasing their fear of rough body contact, all of which should help them defend themselves against rape. While some people think that it is silly for the federal government to rule that girls must have athletic teams equal to boys' teams, it seems quite possible that the absence of athletic training for girls has contributed to making them rape victims.

Some authors, though, have argued that just changing the way we socialize girls and boys is not enough (Russell, 1975). These socialization practices exist precisely to prepare children for their adult roles and as long as women and men have substantially different roles, the problem will not be solved.

Finally, for both males and females, we need a radical restructuring of ideas about sexuality. As long as females are expected to pretend to be uninterested in sex and as long as males and females play games on dates, rape will persist.

SUMMARY

Rape victims often do not report the crime. Common psychological responses to being raped are fear, guilt, and shame. The psychological aftermath of being raped has been documented in studies of the rape trauma syndrome, which includes responses such as anxiety and phobias, persisting perhaps six months after the rape. Women who keep the incident a complete secret may experience a silent rape reaction. The treatment of rape victims by the police and the courts has further increased their suffering. Many people in our society hold a cynical view of rape victims. It is commonly believed that women who are raped were "asking for it."

While rapists vary tremendously, most are young, many repeat the offense, and most are not murderers. Rapists have been classified, according to their motivations, into the following four categories: aggressive-aim rapists, sexual-aim rapists, sex-aggression-fusion rapists, and impulse rapists. The "date rape" is not at all uncommon.

Rape may be an exaggerated expression of many of the traits, such as aggression, for which males are socialized.

Most women are affected by the fear of rape. Further, such fears may have damaging effects on male-female relationships.

Self-defense instruction is important for women in avoiding rape. A radical change in gender-role socialization practices is also necessary before rape can be eliminated.

SUGGESTIONS FOR FURTHER READING

Brownmiller, Susan. *Against our will: Men, women, and rape*. New York: Simon & Schuster, 1975. An award-winning, scholarly book on rape.

Horos, Carol V. *Rape*. New Canaan, Conn.: Tobey Publishing Co., 1974. A comprehensive coverage of rape, including the psychological aspects of rape, advice on how to avoid being raped, and techniques of self-defense.

Weis, Kurt, and Borges, Sandra A. Victimology and rape: The case of the legitimate victim. *Issues in Criminology*, **8**(2), 1973, 71–115. An interesting sociological perspective on rape, particularly on how society turns the victim into the criminal.

LOVE

CITED

To be in love is merely to be in a state of perceptual anesthesia—to mistake an ordinary young man for a Greek god or an ordinary young woman for a goddess.*

The lyrics to the old song, "Love and marriage, love and marriage, go together like a horse and carriage," might today be rewritten, "Love and sex, love and sex, go together. . . ." The standard of today is that sex is appropriate if one loves the other person (see Chapter 10), and sex seems to be the logical outcome of a loving relationship. Therefore, it seems important in a text on sexuality to spend some time considering that emotion that we link so closely to sex, love.

Love is one of those things that people seem to feel uncomfortable about defining. Perhaps when you were an adolescent, you were curious about love and asked an adult, "What is love?" or "How can you tell when you're in love?" Adults in this situation have a tendency to give answers like, "It's not something you can define, but you'll know when you're in it." Such a response is not very scientific, nor even very informative. This chapter will provide a little deeper understanding of what love really is. First, various theoretical views of the nature and meaning of love will be

discussed; then the research that has been done on love and attraction will be reviewed.

THEORETICAL VIEWS

The Greeks

Our language is rather limited in that we have only one word, "love," to express a wide variety of feelings and relationships. "Love" can mean everything from a mother's love for her child to the kind of love that leads quickly to an intense affair that burns itself out after a week. Sometimes we seek to express these various kinds of love by adding modifiers, such as "brotherly" love, or "platonic" love, or "passionate" love.

The ancient Greeks had a much richer vocabulary that allowed them to express more precisely the different kinds of love that exist. They had four different words, all of which translate to "love"; eros (*air'-ohs*), agape (*ah'-gah-pay*), philia (*fil'-ee-ah*), and storge (*store'-gay*).

Eros refers to passionate love or erotic love; it is the kind of love we refer to when we say that we are "in love." *Storge* means affection, particularly the kind of affection that parents

---

*Source: H. L. Mencken, *Prejudices*. (First Series.) New York: Knopf, 1919, p. 16.

feel toward their children or that children feel toward their parents. *Philia* means solid friendship. *Agape* refers to a kind of selfless, giving love that it has become popular to celebrate in love feasts (or agapes) in Christian churches.

C. S. Lewis

The British writer C. S. Lewis (author of *The Screwtape Letters*), writing from a Christian perspective, has expanded on the Greeks' concepts of different kinds of love in his book entitled *The Four Loves* (1960).

Lewis uses the term "affection" for what the Greeks would have called "storge." Affection is the kind of warm feeling that a parent has when cuddling a baby. Lewis says that we see this affection in:

> . . . the mere ease and ordinariness of the relationship (free as solitude, yet neither is alone) as it wraps us round. No need to talk. No need to make love. No needs at all except perhaps to stir the fire. (1960, p. 57)

Affection is a nondiscriminating love; indeed, it may even fail to discriminate among species, since it is probably the way you feel about your dog or cat. It is also a humble love and is rather like the feeling one has about soft slippers or some favorite old clothes; they do not give one much status, but they are loved affectionately nonetheless. According to Lewis, affection does not expect too much, turns a blind eye to faults, and revives easily after quarrels.

Philia, or friendship, is, in a sense, the least physical of the loves. It does not raise your pulse rate or make you blush or turn pale. Indeed, some people probably never experience true friendship. Lewis contrasts friendship with eros: lovers are face to face, absorbed in each other; friends stand shoulder to shoulder, absorbed in some common interest. Because of this aspect of friendship, Lewis argues that, in a strictly gender-role-stereotyped society, friendship can rarely exist between a man and a woman. They have none of the things in common that make for friendship. Lewis sees as the critical definer of friendship the following question: "Do you see the same truth?" (As will be seen in a later section, the social psychologist rephrases this to ask, "Do you have similar attitudes?")

Eros is "being in love," or the kind of love that lovers are "in." Lewis uses the term "Venus" to refer to the specifically sexual aspect of eros. But eros is more than Venus or lust. In lust, the person wants only another body to have sex with. In eros, one wants a specific person, the beloved. One of the characteristics of eros is preoccupation; the person is scarcely able to think of anything other than the beloved and longs to be with the beloved when they are separated. However, eros does not always produce happiness:

> For it is the very mark of Eros that when he is in us we had rather share unhappiness with the Beloved than be happy on other terms. (Lewis, 1960, p. 150)

Finally, Lewis uses the word "charity" as a translation of "agape." In doing this, he means charity in its older sense, not in its modern sense, which has a connotation of condescension. Charity is a basic feeling of goodness and decency toward the other. As he says, "charity suffers long and is kind and forgives."

Lewis also distinguishes between Gift-love and Need-love. In Gift-love, we enjoy giving to the other person; this kind of love is expressed, for example, when a father takes out a life insurance policy, knowing that it will provide for his family, whom he loves, though he would not himself benefit from it. In Need-love, we need or depend upon the person whom we love, and that dependency forms the basis for the love. Need-love clearly has a potential for being neurotic. But it can also be very natural and healthy; for example, a little boy who hurts himself and runs to his mother for help does so because he loves her.

Whether or not one agrees with the categorizations of love proposed by Lewis, the important point is that there are many different kinds of love.

Maslow: B-love and D-love

The psychologist Abraham Maslow, founder of humanistic psychology, distinguishes between B-love and D-love (1968). B-love (short for Being love) is an unneeding, unselfish love for another. In contrast, D-love (short for Deficiency love) is a need for love, a selfish love. Maslow clearly believes that B-love is better than D-love. As he says, "B-love is, beyond the shadow of a doubt, a richer, 'higher,' more valuable subjective experience than D-love." (1968, p. 43).

Maslow believes that some people are B-lovers and some are D-lovers. He views B-lovers as far more healthy and self-actualizing:

> B-lovers are more independent of each other, more autonomous, less jealous or threatened, less needful, more individual, more disinterested, but also simultaneously more eager to help the other toward self-actualization, more proud of his triumphs, more altruistic, generous and fostering. (1968, p. 43)

Thus D-love is the kind of love that arises between two people because of their psychological needs; each seems to satisfy some needs that the other has. B-love occurs between two self-actualized people who are independent and yet appreciative of each other.

Fromm: *The Art of Loving*

Psychoanalyst Erich Fromm developed his ideas about love in his book *The Art of Loving* (1956).

As the title of the book implies, Fromm believes that loving is an art, something that one must learn about and practice. He also emphasizes that love is something one *does*, not a state one is *in*.

Fromm believes that a central problem of human existence is a sense of separateness or isolation from others. This sense of separateness causes anxiety. We therefore have a basic need to overcome the sense of separateness, and loving—establishing a union with another person—is one of the best ways of doing this. Sexual experiences themselves help to conquer the sense of separateness, but Fromm believes that they do so only temporarily unless there is love too.

Fromm distinguishes between immature love, which is characterized by a symbiotic[1] union between two people, and mature love, which he believes to be one of the most important human emotions:

> In contrast to symbiotic union, mature *love* is *union under the condition of preserving one's integrity*, one's individuality. *Love is an active power in man*: a power which breaks through the walls which separate man from his fellow men, which unites him with others; love makes him overcome the sense of isolation and separateness, yet it permits him to be himself, to retain his integrity. In love the paradox occurs that two beings become one and yet remain two. (1956, p. 17)

Fromm says that mature love is characterized by care, responsibility, respect, and knowledge of the loved person.

Fromm disagrees with Freud, who saw sexual desire as being a drive to discharge energy. Fromm instead views sexual desire as a basic need for love and union, a desire to

---

[1]"Symbiotic" is a term with origins in biology; it refers to a relationship between two organisms in which each essentially lives off the other. They are highly dependent on each other, and neither could survive without the other.

overcome the sense of separateness. One of the basic kinds of separateness that exist among humans is the separateness between men and women, and Fromm believes that heterosexual lovemaking is a means of overcoming it.

Fromm distinguishes between brotherly love, motherly love, erotic love, and self-love. Most relevant for this discussion are his ideas about erotic love.

Fromm says that erotic love is:

> . . . the craving for complete fusion, for union with one other person. It is by its very nature exclusive and not universal; it is also perhaps the most deceptive form of love there is. . . . Erotic love, if it is love, has one premise. That I love from the essence of my being—and experience the other person in the essence of his or her being. (1956, pp. 44, 47)

Thus Fromm sees erotic love as exclusive—something one can do with only one other person at a time—because it is a total fusion with the other person. He also believes that erotic love is fairly permanent; this idea is tied up with his notion that it is something one does, not a state one is in:

> To love somebody is not just a strong feeling—it is a decision, it is a judgment, it is a promise. If love were only a feeling there would be no basis for the promise to love each other forever. A feeling comes and it may go. How can I judge that it will stay forever, when my act does not involve judgment and decision? (1956, p. 56)

Thus Fromm views erotic love as a craving for total union with the other, which is exclusive and enduring.

John Alan Lee: Lovestyles

On the basis of his research, sociologist John Alan Lee (1974, 1977) believes that there are three basic types of love, and he uses Greek and

FIGURE 17.1

One view of the nature of love. [© Washington Star Syndicate, Inc., 1976. Permission granted by King Feature Syndicate Division.]

Latin words to distinguish them: eros, storge, and ludus.

Eros, according to his view, is a powerful attraction to the physical appearance of the loved person. The erotic lover often has an ideal partner in mind, and it may be "love at first sight" when he or she meets that person. Erotic lovers cultivate a variety of sexual techniques so that they will continually delight in each other's bodies.

Ludus refers to playful love. For ludic lovers, love is a pleasant pastime; however, they refuse to get too involved, to become dependent on the beloved, or to let the beloved become too attached to them. Because of their low commitment, ludic lovers may have more than one lover at a time. They also show little interest in improving sexual techniques, since they find it easier to get a new partner than to work out problems in an old relationship.

Storge is "love without fever, tumult or folly, a peaceful and enchanting affection." It is the kind of love that sneaks up unnoticed in a relationship; storgic lovers remember no special point in the relationship when they "fell" in love. Because the relationship develops gradually, sex typically does not occur for some time. Storge is the kind of quiet affection expressed by the lyrics to the song "I've Grown Accustomed to Her Face." Storge also tends to be a very stable love that can last through crises in the relationship and even through long separations.

Lee sees these three basic types of love as being analogous to the three primary colors: red, yellow, and blue. Just as new colors are produced by combining primary colors— orange is a mixture of red and yellow, for example—so other types of love result from blendings of the three basic types. For example, in *mania*, which may be viewed as a combination of eros and ludus, love is an obsession. In mania, the person is consumed with thoughts of the beloved, may feel furious jealousy, and may suffer from symptoms such as agitation, sleeplessness, and loss of appetite. The manic lover alternates between feelings of ecstasy and despair. Manic lovers have the passion of eros but play the games of ludus. Needless to say, this is the sort of stuff that makes for great novels and plays.

Pragma is a kind of practical love; it combines the compatibility of storge with the game playing of ludus. The pragmatic lover consciously tries to find a lover who has a certain set of characteristics that are thought desirable. Once a good match is found, pragmatic love may grow over the years. It is the kind of love that existed for centuries when marriages were arranged by persons other than the lovers themselves.

Agape, the classic Christian view of love, is altruistic, undemanding, never jealous, and always kind and patient. It seems to represent a combination of storge and eros.

Of what practical significance are these ideas? Lee believes that many conflicts arise when two different types of lovers are paired with each other. People often think that it is the quantity of love that is the problem—the old complaint is "you don't love me enough"—but instead there may be a mismatch of the types of lovers. For example, suppose we have a ludic man and a storgic woman. He feels that she is trying to trap him into a commitment when he just wants to have some fun. She wants to develop a slow, lasting relationship and accuses him of playing games just to get her to go to bed

with him. According to Lee, two lovers of the same type are most compatible.

RESEARCH ON LOVE

Measuring Love

So far the discussion has focused on theoretical definitions of various kinds of love. As has been noted, different people may mean different things when they use the word "love." One of the ways that psychologists define terms is by using an operational definition. In an *operational definition* a concept is defined by the way it is measured. Thus, for example, "IQ" is sometimes defined as the sort of abilities that are measured by IQ tests. "Job satisfaction" can be defined as a score on a questionnaire that measures one's attitudes toward one's job. Operational definitions are very useful because they are precise and because they help clarify exactly what a scientist means by a complex term such as "love" or "aggression."

Psychologist Zick Rubin (1970) has used the operational-definition approach to study love. That is, he has constructed a paper-and-pencil test to measure romantic love (he has also constructed another test to measure "liking"). Basically, Rubin sees love as an attitude one has toward another person. Thus the items on the scale involve reporting feelings about a specific person. Some items from Rubin's love scale and liking scale are shown in the Focus. Subjects rate each item on a scale from 1 to 9 to indicate how much they agree with it. If you feel that you are in love with someone, you might want to think of how you would answer the questions, keeping that person in mind.

The content of the love items seems to imply that there are three major components of romantic love:

1 *Affiliative and dependency needs* For example, "If I could never be with_____, I would feel miserable."

(a)

(b)

(c)

FIGURE 17.2
Various kinds of love.
(a) Companionship in an egalitarian
love relationship, or storge, to use
Lee's terminology *[Ken Heyman].*
(b) Romantic love, or eros, to use
Lee's terminology *[Richard
Frieman/Photo Researchers, Inc.].*
(c) Playful love, or ludus, to use
Lee's terminology *[Ken Heyman].*

SOME ITEMS FROM A LOVE SCALE AND A LIKING SCALE

LOVE-SCALE ITEMS

These items measure how much you love a person.
1 I would do almost anything for _____.
2 If I could never be with _____, I would feel miserable.
3 If I were lonely, my first thought would be to seek_____ out.

LIKING-SCALE ITEMS

These items measure how much you like a person.
1 I would highly recommend _____ for a responsible job.
2 In my opinion, _____ is an exceptionally mature person.
3 _____ is the sort of person whom I myself would like to be.

Source: Zick Rubin. Measurement of romantic love. *Journal of Personality and Social Psychology,* 1970, **16**, p. 267. Each item is ranked on a scale from 1 (not at all true; disagree completely) to 9 (definitely true; agree completely).

---

2 *A predisposition to help* For example, "I would do almost anything for_____."
3 *Exclusiveness and absorption* For example, "I feel very possessive toward_____."

In contrast, liking seems to involve respect and admiration.

Rubin administered the questionnaire to a group of dating couples at the University of Michigan. He found that loving and liking were only moderately correlated. That is, we seem to have some tendency to like the person we love, but not a very strong tendency. Love scores did, however, tend to be highly correlated with subjects' estimates of the likelihood that they would eventually marry this dating partner. Rubin also found that the love scores of men (for

their girlfriends) were almost identical to the love scores of women (for their boyfriends). That is, there was no evidence that either men or women had a stronger tendency to feel more loving toward their partners. There was, however, a tendency for women to like their boyfriends more than men liked their girlfriends.

Using this instrument, Rubin was able to do further investigations of love relationships. For example, he found that couples who were strongly in love (both had high scores on the love scale) spent more time gazing into each other's eyes than couples who were only weakly in love (both had low scores on the love scale).

Rubin (1973) found some evidence that interfaith couples loved each other more strongly than same-faith couples. This may be an example of the "Romeo and Juliet effect" (R. Driscoll et al., 1972): the more parents object to a relationship, the stronger the love becomes.

Rubin's research is a good example of the way psychologists study an important but complex topic—such as love—scientifically.

Love and Adrenalin

Social psychologists Ellen Berscheid and Elaine Walster (1974) have proposed a two-component theory of love. According to their theory, passionate love occurs when two conditions exist simultaneously: (1) the person is in a state of intense physiological arousal, and (2) the situation is such that the person applies a particular label—"love"—to the sensations being experienced. Their theory is derived from an important experiment conducted by psychologist Stanley Schachter (1964); it will be necessary to explain that work first.

The Schachter and Singer study Suppose that your heart is pounding and your palms are sweating. What emotion are you experiencing? Love? Anger? Fear? Embarrassment? Sexual arousal? As it turns out, it may be any of these. Psychologists have discovered that a wide variety of strong emotions produce similar physiological states (pounding heart and sweating palms) and that what differentiates these emo-

tions is the way we interpret or label what we are experiencing. Schachter's (1964) two-component theory of emotion says just this: that an emotion consists of a physiological state of arousal plus a mental labeling of it as a particular emotion.

Schachter and Singer (1962) demonstrated this phenomenon in a classic experiment in which they manipulated both the physiological arousal of subjects and the labeling of emotions. Male college-student volunteers were the subjects. When they arrived at the laboratory, they were told that they were participating in a study designed to measure the effects of a new vitamin, Suproxin, on vision. Physiological arousal was manipulated using the drug epinephrine (adrenalin). Epinephrine stimulates the sympathetic nervous system, producing an arousal state including increased heart rate and increased rate of breathing. Subjects were in one of four groups (see Table 17.1). Subjects in the *informed group* received an injection of Suproxin (really adrenalin) and were told to expect the exact effects of adrenalin: pounding heart, flushed face, and so on. Subjects in the *misinformed group* also received the adrenalin injection, but they were told to expect a wrong set of side effects: numbness, itching, and a slight headache. Subjects in the *ignorant group* received the injection of adrenalin but were given no information about side effects. Finally, subjects in the *placebo group* were given an injec-

TABLE 17.1
THE SCHACHTER-SINGER EXPERIMENT

Group	Injection	Expectations	Resulting State	Model	Effects
Informed	Adrenalin	Told precise side effects of adrenalin	Not bewildered	Euphoric	No effect
			Aroused	Angry	No effect
Ignorant	Adrenalin	Told nothing about side effects	Bewildered	Euphoric	Euphoric
			Aroused	Angry	Angry
Misinformed	Adrenalin	Misled about side effects	Bewildered Aroused	Euphoric	Euphoric
Placebo	Neutral solution	Told nothing about side effects	Not bewildered	Euphoric	No effect
			Not aroused	Angry	No effect

tion that contained no drug and were told nothing about side effects.

After receiving the injections, subjects were put in a waiting room for 20 minutes. An accomplice of the experimenter was also in the waiting room. It was his job to create a situation that would lead the subjects to apply a certain label to their feelings of arousal. Half of the subjects were in the *euphoria* condition. The accomplice behaved in a deliriously happy way; among other things, he shot paper airplanes and danced wildly with a hula hoop. The other half of the subjects were in the *anger* condition. The accomplice and the subjects were asked to fill out forms. The questions began innocuously but gradually became insulting. The accomplice became increasingly angry; finally he threw the questionnaire on the floor and stomped out shouting, "I'm not wasting any more time. I'm getting my books and leaving."

The experimenters watched the interaction from behind a one-way mirror and rated the kind of emotion the subjects expressed. The subjects also rated themselves as to the kind of emotions they felt.

Schachter and Singer made the following predictions for the outcomes of the study: Subjects in the informed group are aroused, but they can easily explain it, and so they should not be susceptible to the accomplice's suggestions of emotion. Subjects in the misinformed and ignorant groups, however, are aroused, but they have no easy way to explain it. These subjects should seek a label for their emotional state and will use the one provided by the accomplice. Finally, subjects in the placebo group are not aroused, and so they are not likely to think they are experiencing strong emotions, regardless of the accomplice's behavior.

The results turned out exactly as predicted (Table 17.1). Subjects in the misinformed and ignorant groups felt either euphoric or angry, depending on the accomplice's behavior. Sub-

jects in the informed and placebo groups were unaffected by the accomplice.

On the basis of these results, Schachter (1964) proposed his two-component theory of emotion: that an emotion consists of a physiological arousal state plus the labeling of it as a particular emotion. Berscheid and Walster have applied this to the emotion of "love." What they suggest is that we feel passionate love when we are aroused and when conditions are such that we believe it is love that we are feeling.

Evidence on Berscheid and Walster's theory
While Berscheid and Walster's theory has not been tested directly, several experiments designed for other purposes provide indirect evidence for it. For example, one study suggests that fear can increase a man's attraction to a woman (Dutton and Aron, 1974; see also Brehm et al., cited in Berscheid and Walster, 1974). An attractive female interviewer contacted male passersby either on a fear-arousing suspension bridge or on a non-fear-arousing bridge. The fear-arousing bridge was constructed of boards attached to cables and had a tendency to tilt, sway, and wobble; the handrails were low, and there was a 230-foot drop to rocks and shallow rapids below. The "control" bridge was made of solid cedar; it was firm, and there was only a 10-foot drop to a shallow rivulet below. The interviewer asked subjects to fill out questionnaires that included projective test items. These items were then scored for sexual imagery.

The men in the suspension-bridge group should have been in a state of physiological arousal, while those in the control-bridge group should not have been. In fact, there was more sexual imagery in the questionnaires filled out by the men in the suspension-bridge group, and these men made more attempts to contact the attractive interviewer after the experiment than the subjects on the control bridge. Intuitively this might seem to be a peculiar result: that men who are in a state of fear are more attracted to a woman than men who are relaxed. But in terms of the Berscheid and Walster two-component theory, it makes perfect sense. The fearful men were physiologically aroused, while the men in the control group were not. And according to this theory, arousal is an important component of love or attraction.[2]

Now, of course, if the men had been approached by an 80-year-old woman or a crippled woman or a child, probably their responses would have been different. In fact, when the interviewer in the experiment was male, the effects discussed above did not occur. Society tells us what the appropriate objects of our love, attraction, or liking are. That is, we know for what kinds of people it is appropriate to have feelings of love or liking. For these men, feelings toward an attractive woman could reasonably be labeled "love" or "liking," while such labels would probably not be attached to feelings for an 80-year-old woman. Thus in this experiment subjects were provided with a situation in which "love" or "liking" was a reasonable label for their feelings; however, only the suspension-bridge group also had the physiological arousal that is necessary to create the emotion. Our society generally encourages people to attach the label "love" to a wide variety of confused feelings (Walster and Berscheid, 1974).

Of course, the physical arousal that is important for love need not always be produced by unpleasant or frightening situations. Pleasant stimuli, such as sexual arousal or praise from the other person, may produce arousal and feelings of love. Indeed, Berscheid and Walster's theory does an excellent job of explaining why we seem to have such a strong tendency to

associate love and sex. Sexual arousal is one method of producing a state of physiological arousal, and it is one that our culture has taught us to label as "love." Thus both components necessary to feel love are present: arousal and a label (see, for example, Stephan et al., 1971).

Berscheid and Walster's two-component theory is an interesting explanation of the emotion of love. It is hoped that experiments testing their hypotheses will be done in the next decade.

INTERPERSONAL ATTRACTION

What causes you to be attracted to another person? While psychologists have done relatively little research on love, social psychologists have done extensive research on interpersonal attraction. The major results of this research are discussed below.

Birds of a Feather

We tend to like people who are similar to us. We are attracted to people who are approximately the same as we are in terms of economic and social status, ethnicity, intelligence, and attitudes (Byrne, 1971; Laumann, 1969; Vandenberg, 1972).

Social psychologist Donn Byrne (1971) has done numerous experiments demonstrating that we are attracted to people whose attitudes and opinions are similar to ours. In these experiments, Byrne typically has subjects fill out an opinion questionnaire. They are then shown a questionnaire that was supposedly filled out by another person and are asked to rate how much they think they would like that person. In fact, the questionnaire was filled out to show either high or low agreement with the subject's responses. Subjects report more liking for a person whose responses are similar to theirs than for one whose responses are quite different.

Folk sayings are sometimes wise and some-

[2]According to the terminology of Chap. 9, note that the Schachter and Singer study and the Dutton and Aron study are both examples of *experimental* research.

times foolish. The interpersonal-attraction research seems to indicate that the saying "Birds of a feather flock together" contains some truth.

"Hey, Good-Lookin'"

We also tend to be attracted to people who are physically attractive, that is, "good-looking." For example, in one study snapshots were taken of college men and women (Berscheid et al., 1971). A dating history of each subject was also obtained. Judges then rated the attractiveness of the men and women in the photographs. For the women there was a fairly strong relationship between attractiveness and popularity; the women judged attractive had had more dates in the last year than the less attractive women. There was some relationship between appearance and popularity for men, but it was not so marked as it was for women. In general, then, we are most attracted to good-looking people. However, this phenomenon is somewhat modified by our own feelings of personal worth, as will be seen in the section on the interpersonal marketplace, below.

From the Laboratory to Real Life

The phenomena discussed so far—feelings of attraction to people who are similar to us and who are good-looking—have been demonstrated mainly in psychologists' laboratories. Do these phenomena occur in the real world?

Donn Byrne and his colleagues (1970) did a study to find out whether these results would be obtained in a real-life situation. They administered an attitude and personality questionnaire to 420 college students. Then they formed 44 "couples." For half of the couples, both people had made very similar responses on the questionnaire; for the other half of the couples, the two people had made very different responses. The two people were then introduced and sent to the student union on a "Coke date." When they returned from the date, an unobtrusive

measure of attraction was taken—how close they stood to each other in front of the experimenter's desk. The subjects also evaluated their dates on several scales.

The results of the study confirmed those from previous experimental work. The couples who had been matched for similar attitudes were most attracted to each other, and those with dissimilar attitudes were not so attracted to each other. The students had also been rated as to their physical attractiveness both by the experimenter and by their dates, and greater attraction to the better-looking dates was reported. In a follow-up at the end of the semester, those whose dates were similar to them and were physically attractive were more likely to remember the date's name and to express a desire to date the person again in the future. Thus in an experiment that was closer to real life and real dating situations, the importance of similarity and of physical appearance was again demonstrated.

The Interpersonal Marketplace

Although this may sound somewhat callous, whom we are attracted to and pair off with depends a lot on how much we think we have to offer and how much we think we can "buy" with it (see, for example, Rubin, 1973, pp. 67ff.). Generally, the principle seems to be that women's worth is based on their physical beauty, whereas men's worth is based on how successful they are. There is a tendency, then, for beautiful women to be paired with wealthy, successful men.

Data from many studies document this. For example, in one study, high school girls were rated on their physical attractiveness. Years later they were followed up to see whom they had married. The girls who had been rated as better looking were more likely than their less attractive classmates to have married higher-status men (Elder, 1969).

In another study, women students were

rated on their physical attractiveness (Rubin, 1973, p. 68). They were then asked to complete a questionnaire about what kind of men they would consider desirable dates. A man's occupation had a big effect on his desirability as a date. Men in high-status occupations—physician, lawyer, chemist—were considered highly desirable dates by virtually all the women. Men in low-status occupations—janitor, bartender—were judged hardly acceptable by most of the women. A difference emerged between attractive and unattractive women, however, when rating men in middle-status occupations—electrician, bookkeeper, plumber. The attractive women did not feel that these men would be acceptable dates, whereas the unattractive women felt that they would be at least moderately acceptable. Here we see the interpersonal marketplace in action. Men with more status are more desirable. But how desirable the man is judged to be depends on the woman's sense of her own worth. Attractive women are not much interested in middle-status men because they apparently think they are "worth more." Unattractive women find middle-status men more attractive, presumably because they think such men are reasonably within their "price range."

The Girl Next Door

There is also evidence that we tend to be more attracted to people with whom we have had contact many times than we are to people with whom we have had little contact (Rubin, 1973). This has been demonstrated in laboratory studies in which the amount of contact between subjects was varied. At the end of the session, subjects gave higher "liking" ratings to those with whom they had had much contact and lower ratings to those with whom they had had little contact (Saegert et al., 1973). Mere repeated exposure to someone seems to make us like that person. Thus, there does seem to be a "girl-next door" or a "boy-next-door"

phenomenon; we tend to be attracted to people with whom we have had much contact, to whom we have been exposed, and who are familiar to us.

Playing Hard-to-Get

The traditional advice that has been given to girls—by Ann Landers and others—is that boys will be more attracted to them if they play hard-to-get. Is there any scientific evidence that this is true?

In fact, two experiments provide no support for this kind of strategy; according to these experiments, playing hard-to-get does not work (Walster et al., 1973). In one of these experiments, college men were recruited for a computer-dating program. They were given the phone number of their assigned date and were told to phone her and arrange a date from the experimenter's laboratory; after they phoned her, they assessed their initial impressions of her. In fact, all the men were given the same telephone number—that of an accomplice of the experimenter. For half of the men, she played easy-to-get; she was delighted to receive the phone call and to be asked out. With the other half of the men, she played hard-to-get; she accepted the date with reluctance and obviously had many other dates. The results failed to support the hard-to-get strategy: the men had equally high opinions of the hard-to-get and easy-to-get woman.

The same experimenters reported an ingenious field experiment in which a prostitute played either hard-to-get or easy-to-get with her clients and then recorded the clients' responses, such as how much they paid her. Once again, the hard-to-get hypothesis was not supported; the men seemed to like the easy-to-get and the hard-to-get prostitute equally well.

The experimenters were faced with the bald fact that a piece of folk wisdom just did not seem to be true. They decided that they needed a somewhat more complex hypothesis. They

FOCUS

JEALOUSY

Jealousy is a negative emotion that is often associated with love and with sexual relationships. Traditionally in the United States, jealousy has been considered a normal, even necessary, emotion; it has been viewed as strengthening monogamy and marriage. Recently, though, young people interested in radical lifestyles have expressed the view that jealousy is a threat to a relationship and reflects the insecurity of the two people and the weakness of their partnership.

Psychologists Gordon Clanton and Lynn G. Smith have studied jealousy and have provided some insights into its nature and how we can cope with it. They believe that there are two basic types of jealousy. The mild and relatively harmless form is a feeling of being left out. Suppose you are at a party and you see your date talking animatedly with someone else. You feel a twinge of jealousy mainly because you feel excluded and wish you were a part of the interaction. This kind of jealousy is relatively harmless and passes quickly. The more serious form of jealousy is related to a fear of loss, and it becomes a persistent fear. What do you fear losing? You may fear loss of face; what will all the other women think when they see your husband flirting openly with someone else? Perhaps you fear loss of control—not being in command of the relationship or your own future or perhaps facing the prospect of no dates for some time. Finally, you may fear the loss of your partner and the love and affection that person provides. Basically, Clanton and Smith see jealousy as a sort of instinctive reaction to a threat to oneself or to a relationship.

Clanton and Smith believe that jealousy is an emotion we begin experiencing early in life and that our experiences with it as we grow up shape the way we react in jealousy-provoking situations when we are adults. From earliest infancy, we are dependent on our mother and feel jealous when we have to share her with someone else—our father or siblings. Later, we feel sibling rivalry and have another experience of jealousy. How our parents handle these situations may have a great deal to do with our later tendencies toward jealousy. For example, if your parents tried to make you feel loved and wanted when you cried because your mother was sharing her attentions with a sibling, you may develop a low propensity to jealousy. If they punished you severely for behaving that way, you may develop tendencies to repress jealousy. And if they reacted by depriving you of your mother's attentions even more, you may develop a deep sense of insecurity and jealousy in adulthood.

Clanton and Smith believe that we have a choice in dealing with our own jealousy: we can react in an insecure, defensive manner, or we can react in a secure, constructive way. The following two reactions illustrate the difference. The first one is defensive:

> His interest in her confirms my suspicion that he is on the make. I never did trust him. Her interest in him shows she is dissatisfied with me. He's quite attractive. I guess she's grown tired of me. And he's so attentive to her, so appreciative. I guess I've come to take her for granted. No wonder she's so turned on by his courtesies. They want to go to the opera together, and I feel left out. I wonder what other excuses they'll find to spend time together. Maybe she'll take time away from me to be with him. Maybe I'll have to cook dinner and take care of the kids while she's off at the "opera." If I can't count on my own wife, what the hell can I count on?

This is a constructive reaction:

> His interest in her confirms her attractiveness. I'm proud of her. Her interest in him shows she is alert and alive. I'm glad for that. An inert partner, no matter how secure the relationship, is a bad deal. He's like me in some ways, so I am affirmed by her choice of him. He's different from me in some ways, which suggests she has some needs that I don't meet. I must consider these needs carefully and try to find out if I could do a better job of meeting them. But I realize I cannot meet all of her needs without violating my own autonomy, so I must work to become glad she has other friends who can fulfill her in ways I do not and would rather not. Thank God, she's found someone who wants to go to the opera with her. I want to be reassured that our relationship means as much to her as it does to me, but I won't demand that she renounce all others in order to demonstrate that to me.

Source: Gordon Clanton and Lynn G. Smith. The self-inflicted pain of jealousy. *Psychology Today,* 1977, **10**(10), p. 44.

hypothesized that it is not the woman who is generally hard-to-get or generally easy-to-get who is attractive to men, but rather the one who is *selectively hard-to-get*. That is, she is easy-to-get for you, but she is hard-to-get for other men or unavailable to them. A computer-dating experiment supported this notion; the selectively hard-to-get woman was the most popular with men.

In practical terms, this means that if a woman is going to use hard-to-get strategies, she had better use them in a skillful way. It seems that the optimal strategy would be to give the impression that she has many offers for dates with others but refuses them, while being delighted to date the young man in question.

Interestingly, in all the research discussed, it is always the woman who is playing hard-to-get and the man who is rating her. This reflects cultural gender-role stereotypes, in which it is the woman's role to do things like play hard-to-get. What we do not know is how men's use of hard-to-get strategies would affect the way women perceive them.

Evaluating the Interpersonal-Attraction Research

Much of the research discussed in this section is an investigation not so much of love as of first impressions, or of attraction in the early stages of a relationship. Thus many of the results might not be true of long-term, deeply committed relationships. On the other hand, first impressions have a lot to do with casual dating, and casual dating is the usual prelude to serious relationships. In this way, first impressions may influence whom we eventually come to love.

AN AFTERTHOUGHT

Senator William Proxmire, watchdogging the spending of federal funds for research, has been very critical of research on sex and love. Ac-cording to him, the last thing we need to do is understand love (Shaffer, 1977).

Personally, I think that it is one of the first things we should try to understand, and I hope that much more research will be done in this area. As Abraham Maslow put it, "We *must* understand love; we must be able to teach it, to create it, to predict it, or else the world is lost to hostility and to suspicion" (1970, p. 181).

SUMMARY

The Greeks had a richer vocabulary than we do for describing the various kinds of love. Their terms included eros (erotic or passionate love), storge (affection), philia (friendship), and agape (selfless love). C. S. Lewis has expanded on these four different kinds of love.

Abraham Maslow distinguishes between B-love, or Being-love (a high, unselfish form of love), and D-love, or Deficiency-love (a kind of love based on dependency or needs). Erich Fromm sees loving as an art; it is something we must learn and practice and something we do rather than a state we are in. Sociologist John Alan Lee believes that there are three basic kinds of love: eros (passionate physical attraction), ludus (playful love), and storge (long-lasting affection). According to him, mania, pragma, and agape are other types of love that result from the blending of the three basic types.

Zick Rubin has constructed a scale to measure romantic love and another scale to measure liking. This makes it possible to do further scientific research on love.

Berscheid and Walster have hypothesized that there are two basic components of romantic love: being in a state of physiological arousal and attaching the label "love" to the feeling.

Research on interpersonal attraction suggests that we tend to be attracted to people who are similar to us (in terms of attitudes, intelligence, and social status) and to people who are physically attractive. We also tend to be attracted to people whom we believe to be "within reach" of us, depending on our sense of our own attractiveness or desirability. Mere exposure to another person also seems to facilitate attraction. Playing hard-to-get seems to work only if the person is able to convey the sense of being selectively hard-to-get.

SUGGESTIONS FOR FURTHER READING

Peele, Stanton, and Brodsky, Archie. *Love and addiction*. New York: New American Library, 1975. A provocative book in which the authors argue that love is much like a physical addiction to heroin or a similar drug.

Rubin, Zick. *Liking and loving: An invitation to social psychology*. New York: Holt, 1973. A beautifully written book that explains social psychologists' research on interpersonal attraction and love.

Walster, Elaine, and Berscheid, Ellen. Adrenalin makes the heart grow fonder. *Psychology Today*, 1971, **5**(1), 46. Presents Walster and Berscheid's two-component theory of romantic love.

18

SEXUAL DYSFUNCTION AND SEX THERAPY

We have nothing to fear but fear itself.

—Franklin Delano Roosevelt

Sexual dysfunctions such as premature ejaculation in men and inability to have orgasms in women have been the cause of a great deal of mental anguish, not to mention marital discord. Psychoanalysts, psychiatrists, and psychologists have for years used long-term therapy to treat sexual dysfunctions; however, a new era in understanding and treatment was ushered in with the publication, in 1970, of *Human Sexual Inadequacy*, by Masters and Johnson. This book reported not only their research on sexual dysfunctions and the causes of these dysfunctions but also their rapid-treatment program of therapy for such disorders. The work of Masters and Johnson, as well as that of others currently working in the field, will be discussed in this chapter.

First, though, it is necessary to define the term "sexual dysfunction." A *sexual dysfunction* (the prefix "dys-" means "impaired") is any one of various disturbances or impairments of sexual functioning. A synonym might be "sexual malfunctioning." Examples are inability to get an erection (erectile dysfunction) in the male and inability to have an orgasm (orgasmic dysfunction, or anorgasmia) in the female. This

definition seems fairly simple; as will be seen in the following sections, however, in practice it can be difficult to determine exactly when something is a sexual dysfunction.

No one knows exactly how many people have sexual dysfunctions. We know only about those who seek some kind of treatment for the problem, and they may be few in number compared with those who have a dysfunction but suffer quietly and never seek therapy, as a result of either ignorance or embarrassment. According to Masters and Johnson (1970), "A conservative estimate would indicate half the marriages [in this country] as either presently sexually dysfunctional or imminently so in the future." While this may be a slight overestimate, it seems safe to say that many Americans either have a sexual dysfunction or are affected by one in their partner and that perhaps an even more sizable number of people are affected by occasional instances of sexual dysfunction; many men, for example, occasionally experience problems in getting an erection.

In this section, the various kinds of sexual dysfunctions will be discussed: erectile dysfunction (impotence), premature ejaculation, and retarded ejaculation in men; orgasmic dysfunction and vaginismus in women; and painful intercourse and sexual apathy which may occur in men or women.

KINDS OF SEXUAL DYSFUNCTION

Erectile Dysfunction (Impotence)

Erectile dysfunction (also called *impotence*) is the inability to have an erection or to maintain one. As a result, the man is not able to engage in penis-inside-vagina intercourse (or anal intercourse, for that matter), since an erection, at least a moderate one, is necessary for the penis to be inserted into the vagina. Masters and Johnson further classify cases of erectile dysfunction into primary erectile dysfunction and secondary erectile dysfunction. *Primary erectile dysfunction* refers to cases where the man has never been able to have intercourse; *secondary erectile dysfunction* refers to cases where the man has difficulty getting or maintaining an erection but he has been able to have vaginal or anal intercourse at least once. Masters and Johnson classify a man as secondarily dysfunctional if he has erection problems 25 percent or more of the time in sexual encounters.

In the initial 790 cases of sexual dysfunction that Masters and Johnson treated and reported on in *Human Sexual Inadequacy*, erectile dysfunction was the most frequent dysfunction in men, accounting for 245 of the cases of dysfunction reported. Secondary erectile dysfunction is apparently much more common than primary erectile dysfunction. In the 245 cases of erectile dysfunction reported by Masters and Johnson, 32 were primary, and 213 were secondary. In fact, it has been estimated that half of the general male population has experienced occasional episodes of erectile dysfunction, and this is certainly well within the range of normal sexual response (Kaplan, 1974).

Erectile difficulties affect men of all ages,

from teenagers to the elderly. The incidence rate does not seem to be affected by race or socioeconomic factors.

One problem of terminology is present. The word "impotence," which is often used, certainly carries many negative connotations (the word means "lack of power"). A man who has erection problems has enough trouble without having people call him "impotent" besides. Further, the term is often confused with others, such as "sterility." There are many sterile men who do not have erectile dysfunction; they get fine, hard, lasting erections, but they just do not produce enough viable sperm to cause pregnancy. Conversely, many men with erectile dysfunction produce fine sperm and will be able to impregnate a woman as soon as they are able to have erections. The term "erectile dysfunction" is preferable to "impotence," since it gives a precise description of the problem but does not have the negative connotations.

Psychological reactions to erectile dysfunction may be severe. It is undoubtedly one of the most embarrassing things that can happen to a man. Depression may follow from repeated episodes. The situation is also embarrassing to the man's partner. Women in this situation should try to put aside their own feelings of disappointment or embarrassment and instead try to be understanding and supportive.

The causes of erectile dysfunction and its treatment will be discussed later in the chapter.

Premature Ejaculation

Premature ejaculation (*ejaculatio praecox*, in medical terminology, or "PE", if you want to be on familiar terms with it) occurs when the man ejaculates too soon or is not able to postpone ejaculation long enough. In extreme cases, ejaculation may take place so soon after erection that it occurs before the penis can even be inserted into the vagina. In other cases, the man is able to delay the ejaculation to some extent, but not as long as he would like or not long enough for his partner to have an orgasm.

While the definition given above—ejaculating prematurely or too soon—seems simple enough, in practice it is much more difficult to define when a man is a premature ejaculator. What should the precise criterion for "too soon" be? Should the man be required to last for 30 seconds after erection? For 12 minutes? The definitions used by authorities in the field vary widely. One source defines "prematurity" as the occurrence of orgasm less than 30 seconds after the penis has been inserted into the vagina. Another group has extended this to $1^1/_2$ minutes; a third uses the criterion of ejaculation before there have been 10 pelvic thrusts. Masters and Johnson define premature ejaculation as inability to delay ejaculation long enough for the woman to have an orgasm at least 50 percent of the time. This last definition is interesting in that it stresses the importance of the interaction between the two partners; however, it carries with it the problem of how easily the woman is stimulated to orgasm. Psychiatrist Helen Singer Kaplan (1974) believes that the key to defining the premature ejaculator is the absence of voluntary control of ejaculation; that is, the premature ejaculator has little or no control over when he ejaculates, and this is what causes the problem. One of the best definitions, though, is self-definition; if a man finds that he has become greatly concerned about his ejaculatory control or that it is interfering with his ability to form intimate relationships, or if a couple agree that it is a problem in their relationship, then a dysfunction is present.

Masters and Johnson found premature ejaculation to be the second most common sexual dysfunction among the men who sought therapy from them, accounting for 186 of the cases reported in their book. In fact, though, these statistics may be somewhat misleading because they include only people who have requested therapy; it is quite possible that premature ejaculation is the most common dysfunction in the general male population but that men are not quite so likely to seek therapy for it as they are for erectile dysfunction. Premature ejaculation is particularly common among young men who have a very high sex drive and have simply not yet learned to control ejaculation.

Like erectile dysfunction, premature ejaculation may create a host of related psychological problems. Because the ability to postpone ejaculation and the ability to "satisfy" a woman are so important in our concept of a man who is a competent lover, premature ejaculation can cause a man to become anxious about his masculinity and sexual competence. Further, the condition may affect his partner and create friction in the relationship. The woman may be frustrated because she is not having a satisfying sexual experience either.

The negative psychological effects of premature ejaculation are illustrated by a young man in one of my sexuality classes who handed in an anonymous question. He described himself as a premature ejaculator and said that, after several humiliating experiences in intercourse with dates, he was now convinced that no woman would want him in that condition. He now did not have the courage to ask for dates, and so he had stopped dating. Basically, he wanted to know how the women in the class would react to a man with such a problem. The question was discussed in class, and most of the women agreed that their reaction to his problem would depend a great deal on the quality of the relationship they had with him. If they cared deeply for him, they would be sympathetic and patient and help him overcome the difficulty. The point is, though, that the premature ejaculation had created problems so severe that the young man not only had stopped having sex but also had stopped dating.

Retarded Ejaculation

Retarded ejaculation (*ejaculatio retardata*) is the opposite of premature ejaculation. The man is unable to ejaculate, even though he has a solid erection and has had more than adequate stimulation. Masters and Johnson call this syndrome "ejaculatory incompetence," although this term has the disadvantage of the negative connotations of the word "incompetence." The severity of the problem may range from only occasional problems ejaculating to a history of never having experienced an orgasm. In the most common version, the man is incapable of ejaculating into the woman's vagina but may be able to ejaculate as a result of hand or mouth stimulation.

In the original Masters and Johnson report, retarded ejaculation appeared to be a fairly rare condition, accounting for only 17 of the 448 cases of male sexual dysfunction. However, other authorities now believe that, in its mild forms, retarded ejaculation may be fairly common, at least as judged by the number of people seeking therapy for it (Kaplan, 1974).

Retarded ejaculation, to say the least, is a frustrating experience for the man. One would think that his partner, though, would be in an enviable position, being made love to by a man with a long-lasting erection that is not terminated by orgasm. In fact, though, some women react negatively to this condition in their partners, seeing the man's failure to ejaculate as a personal rejection. Some men, anticipating these negative reactions, have adopted the practice of "faking" orgasm.

Let us now turn to some of the sexual dysfunctions in women.

Orgasmic Dysfunction

Orgasmic dysfunction (or *anorgasmia*) in women is the condition of being unable to have an orgasm. The more commonly used term for this situation is "frigidity," but Masters and Johnson reject this term because of its derogatory connotations, substituting the more neutral term "orgasmic dysfunction."[1] Like some other sexual dysfunctions, cases of orgasmic dysfunction may be classified as primary or secondary. *Primary orgasmic dysfunction* refers to cases where the woman has never in her life experienced an orgasm; *secondary orgasmic dysfunction* (or *situational orgasmic dysfunction*) refers to cases where the woman has orgasms in some situations but not in others, or had orgasms at some time in her life but no longer does so.

Once again, though, these definitions become more complicated in practice than they are in theory. Consider the case of the woman who has orgasms as a result of masturbation or of manual or oral stimulation by a partner but who does not have orgasms in vaginal intercourse (what might be called "coital orgasmic inadequacy"). Is this really a sexual dysfunction? The notion that it is a dysfunction can be traced back to Freud's distinction between clitoral orgasms and vaginal orgasms and his belief that "mature" women should be able to have vaginal orgasms (see Chapter 1), both of which ideas have been debunked by Masters and Johnson. It can also probably be traced to beliefs that there is a "right" way to have sex—with the penis inside the vagina—and a corresponding "right" way to have orgasms. However, survey data indicate that this condition is quite common among women and may even characterize the majority of women (see Chapter 13). Some authorities (for example, Kaplan, 1974) consider such a condition to be well within the normal range of female sexual response. Perhaps the woman who orgasms as a

---

[1]The term "frigidity" is ambiguous since it is used to refer to women who are unable to have orgasms and also to refer to women who show a total lack of sexual responsiveness and do not even become sexually aroused. The scientific term for this latter condition is "general sexual dysfunction."

result of manual or oral stimulation, but not penile thrusting, is simply having orgasms when she is adequately stimulated and is not having them when she is inadequately stimulated. Thus there is some doubt as to whether "coital orgasmic inadequacy" is a dysfunction or an inadequacy at all and a corresponding doubt about whether it requires therapy.

On the other hand, there should be room for self-definition of dysfunctions. If a woman has this coital orgasmic inadequacy, is truly distressed that she is not able to have orgasms during vaginal intercourse, and wants therapy, then it might be appropriate to classify her condition as a dysfunction and provide therapy for it, simply because she herself sees it as a problem (Zeiss et al., 1977). The therapist, however, should be careful to explain to her the issues and problems of definition raised above, in order to be sure that her request for therapy stems from her own dissatisfaction with her sexual responding rather than from a casual reading of Freud. Therapy in such cases probably is best viewed as an "enrichment experience" rather than "fixing a problem."

Orgasmic dysfunctions in women are quite common. They accounted for the vast majority—342 out of 371—of cases of female sexual dysfunction reported by Masters and Johnson. In their work, the cases of primary orgasmic dysfunction (193 cases) outnumbered the cases of situational orgasmic dysfunction (149 cases). This, however, might have been due to the fact that women with primary orgasmic dysfunction are more likely to seek therapy than those with secondary orgasmic dysfunction. Surveys such as those of Kinsey and Hunt (see Chapter 9) indicate that orgasmic dysfunction is quite common among women but that secondary orgasmic dysfunctions are probably more common than primary ones. These surveys indicate that probably about 10 percent of all women have never had an orgasm and that an additional 20 percent have them only irregularly.

In recent years, particularly with the advent of the "*Playboy* ethic," female orgasm has come to be highly prized, and multiple orgasm may even be expected. In view of these cultural pressures, it is not surprising that the woman who has difficulty having orgasms feels inadequate. Further, her partner may feel guilty if he cannot stimulate her to orgasm. Thus orgasmic dysfunctions in women are a cause for concern.

Vaginismus

Vaginismus[2] is a spastic contraction of the outer third of the vagina; in some cases it is so severe that the entrance to the vagina is closed, and the woman cannot have intercourse (see Figure 18.1). Vaginismus and dyspareunia (see below) may be associated. That is, if intercourse is painful, one result may be spasms that close off the entrance to the vagina.

Vaginismus does not appear to be a very common sexual dysfunction. It accounted for only 29 (9 percent) of the 371 cases of sexual dysfunction reported by Masters and Johnson. Unfortunately, because the problem is rare and because it is often not discussed in the medical literature, physicians may fail to diagnose it or may misdiagnose it as something else, such as a small hymen.

Painful Intercourse

Painful intercourse, or *dyspareunia*, is often thought to be only a female problem, but it may affect males too. In women, the pain may be felt in the vagina, around the vaginal entrance and clitoris, or deep in the pelvis. In men, the pain is felt in the penis. To put it mildly, dyspareunia decreases one's enjoyment of the sexual experi-

---

[2]The suffix "-ismus" means "spasm."

ence and may even lead one to abstain from sexual activity.

While complaints of occasional pain during intercourse are fairly common among women, persistent dyspareunia was not very common among the cases reported by Masters and Johnson. Painful intercourse may be related to a variety of physical causes, to be discussed below.

Sexual Apathy

Sex therapists encounter the problem of sexual apathy with some frequency, in both men and women. In this dysfunction, the individual reports a lack of desire for, or interest in, sex. It may be caused by such factors as boring, routine sexual interactions with the partner; interpersonal conflict with the partner; and, in some cases, biological factors, such as hormonal imbalance.

WHAT CAUSES SEXUAL DYSFUNCTION?

There are many causes of sexual dysfunction, varying from person to person and from one dysfunction to the next. Three general categories of factors may be related to sexual dysfunctions: organic causes, drugs, and psychological causes.

Organic Causes

About 10 to 20 percent of cases of sexual dysfunction result directly from organic (physical) factors. Because of this, any responsible sex therapist requires the patient to undergo a thorough physical examination at the beginning of treatment. It is useless to apply behavioral therapy such as that developed by Masters and Johnson if the dysfunction is a result of a physical condition, such as infection. Some

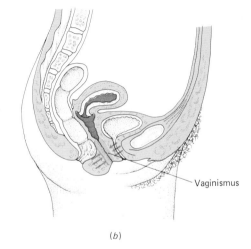

FIGURE 18.1

Vaginismus. (a) A normal vagina and other pelvic organs, viewed from the side, and (b) vaginismus, or involuntary constriction of the outer third of the vagina.

specific organic factors that are known to cause sexual dysfunctions are discussed below.

Erectile dysfunction Most cases of erectile dysfunction appear to be due to psychological rather than physical factors. For example, only 7

A CASE OF ORGASMIC DYSFUNCTION IN A WOMAN

Mr. and Mrs. F were referred for treatment six years after they were married. He was 29, and she was 24. They had one child, a girl, 3 years old.

Mrs. F came from a family of 7 children; she remembers growing up in a warm, loving environment, with harried but happy parents.

Mr. F had a much different background. He was an only child who had been overindulged by his devoted parents. He began masturbating in his early teens, and he had a number of heterosexual experiences, including one relationship in which he had intercourse with his fiancée for six months before he broke the engagement.

The school years were uneventful for both Mr. and Mrs. F. They met and married almost by accident. When they first began dating, each was interested in someone else, but their mutual interest increased rapidly, and a courtship developed. They had intercourse regularly during the three-month period before their marriage.

During the courtship, Mr. F made every social decision, and he continued to exercise total control in the marriage. He insisted on making all decisions and was consistently concerned only with his

---

of the 213 cases of secondary erectile dysfunction reported by Masters and Johnson (3.2 percent) were found to have a physiological cause. Nonetheless, a number of physical conditions can cause erectile dysfunction.

Any severe illness may cause erectile dysfunction as well as loss of libido. Diseases associated with the heart and the circulatory system are particularly likely to be associated with the condition, since erection itself depends on the circulatory system. Heart attacks may be indirectly associated with erectile dysfunction if

the man comes to fear that sexual activity or orgasm will trigger another attack.

One of the best-documented associations of erectile dysfunction with a disease is with diabetes mellitus. Either diabetes or a prediabetic condition may cause erectile dysfunction, although the exact mechanism by which this happens is not known. In fact, erectile dysfunction may in some cases be the earliest symptom of a developing case of diabetes. The incidence of erectile dysfunction among diabetic men is about two to five times higher than the inciown demands, paying little or no attention to his wife's needs. As a result, constant friction developed between the two.

Mrs. F did not have an orgasm before she was married. Afterward, she did have an orgasm on several occasions as a result of manual stimulation by her husband, but never during coitus. As the personal friction between the two increased, she found herself less and less responsive during coitus, although she occasionally had orgasms through manual stimulation. Pregnancy intervened at this time, distracting her for a year, but after that the problem became distressing to her and most embarrassing to her husband. He seemed to worry as much about his image as a sexually effective male as he did about his wife's frustration. Mrs. F's lack of sexual response was considered a personal affront by her uninformed husband.

Mr. F sent her to authorities to do something for "her" sexual inadequacy several times. The thought that the situation might have been in any way his responsibility was utterly foreign to him. When they were referred to Masters and Johnson for therapy, he at first refused to join her in treatment on the grounds that it was "her" problem. When he was told that the problem would not be accepted for treatment unless both partners cooperated, Mr. F grudgingly consented to participate.

According to Masters and Johnson's analysis, this was a case of secondary orgasmic dysfunction resulting from the woman's lack of identification with, or rejection of, her partner.

Source: William H. Masters and Virginia E. Johnson. *Human sexual inadequacy.* Boston: Little, Brown, 1970, pp. 243–344.

---

dence in the general population (Marmor, 1976b). Of course, this by no means suggests that all diabetic men have erectile dysfunction; indeed, the majority do not.

Any disease or accident that damages the lower part of the spinal cord may cause erectile dysfunction, since that is the location of the erection reflex center (see Chapter 7).

Erectile dysfunction may also result from severe stress or fatigue. Some diseases of, or defects in, the genitals or reproductive tract may also create erectile dysfunction. Finally, some—though not all—kinds of prostate surgery may cause the condition.

One of the easiest ways to separate cases that are physically caused from cases that are psychologically caused is by noting the presence or absence of morning erections. If a man sometimes wakes with an erection, it is clear that there is no physical impairment.

Premature ejaculation Premature ejaculation is almost always caused by psychological, rather than physical, factors (Kaplan, 1974). Particularly in the man who has never been able to control his ejaculating, the causes are almost invariably psychological. In a case of secondary dysfunction, though, in which the man at one time had ejaculatory control but later lost it, physical factors may occasionally be involved. A local infection such as prostatitis may be the cause, as may a degeneration in the related parts of the nervous system, which may occur in degenerative neural disorders such as multiple sclerosis.

Retarded ejaculation Retarded ejaculation may be caused by various diseases attacking the nervous system and by Parkinson's disease. It is most commonly caused, though, by psychological factors.

Orgasmic dysfunction in women Orgasmic dysfunction in women may be caused by an extremely severe illness, by general ill health, or by extreme fatigue. Most cases of orgasmic dysfunction, though, are caused by psychological factors. They may also be a result of the loss of libido that occurs in severe depressions.

Hormonal factors are usually *not* the cause of orgasmic dysfunction in women, and treatment with estrogen is generally not effective (Marmor, 1976a).

Painful intercourse Dyspareunia in women is often caused by organic factors (Marmor, 1976a; Wabrek and Wabrek, 1975). These include:

1 *Disorders of the vaginal entrance* Intact hymen or irritated remnants of the hymen; painful scars, perhaps from an episiotomy; or infection of the Bartholin glands
2 *Irritation or damage to the clitoris*
3 *Disorders of the vagina* Vaginal infections; allergic reactions to douches, creams, jellies, or the latex in condoms and diaphragms; a thinning of the vaginal walls (senile vaginitis),

which occurs naturally with age; or scarring of the roof of the vagina, which may occur after hysterectomy
4 *Pelvic disorders* Pelvic infection, endometriosis, tumors, cysts, or a tearing of the broad ligaments supporting the uterus

Masters and Johnson found 11 patients suffering from dyspareunia due to torn ligaments. Five of the cases had resulted from childbirth, three from illegal abortion, and three from gang rape.

Painful intercourse in men can also be caused by a variety of organic factors. In an uncircumcised man, poor hygiene may be a cause; if the penis is not washed thoroughly, material may collect under the foreskin, causing infection. Proper hygiene practices require that the man frequently retract the foreskin completely and wash the penis thoroughly with soap and water. Phimosis, a condition in which the foreskin cannot be retracted, can also cause painful intercourse. An allergic reaction to vaginal douches, creams, jellies, and foams may also be involved. Vaginal infections may cause irritation, as may gonorrhea. Finally, various prostate problems may cause pain on ejaculation.

Vaginismus Vaginismus generally results when a woman has learned to associate pain or fear with intercourse (Kaplan, 1974). In some cases vaginismus is a result of prior episodes of painful intercourse, which may itself be caused by organic factors; in such cases, vaginismus may be considered to be caused indirectly by the same physical factors that cause dyspareunia.

Drugs

Some drugs may have side effects causing sexual dysfunctions (A. M. Freedman, 1976; Kaplan, 1974). For example, the drugs used in treating peptic ulcers may cause erectile dysfunction, and those used to treat allergies may in some cases decrease libido in women and erection capacity in men. A list of drugs that may decrease libido or impair sexual response is provided in Table 18.1.

The effects of illicit (illegal) drugs on sexual response vary widely. For example, some stimulants taken intravenously are powerful sexual stimulants (Rylander, 1969). One addict was quoted as saying that a shot of phenmetrazine "goes straight from the head to the scrotum." The opiates, on the other hand, can severely depress sexual behavior (Hollister, 1975; Isbell, 1965). In one report, nearly half of the 100 heroin addicts studied had erectile dysfunction (Chein et al., 1964, p. 166; see also Cushman, 1972; H. Jones and Jones, 1977). Because of their tendency to sharpen experiences, hallucinogens, such as LSD and marijuana, may increase the enjoyment of sexual activity. In a survey of 200 marijuana users, 44 percent said that their sexual desires were increased, and frequent users agreed that enjoyment was also enhanced (Good, 1970; Halikas et al., 1971; see also Tart, 1970).

A recent study of the potential effects of marijuana on sexual responding, conducted at the Reproductive Biology Research Foundation, which is headed by William Masters, received a great deal of publicity (Kolodny et al., 1974). The study compared the levels of testosterone in the blood of 20 men, aged 18 to 28, who smoked marijuana frequently (they smoked at least four days per week for a minimum of six months before the study) with the testosterone levels in the blood of 20 other men, matched for age, who had never smoked marijuana. All subjects used no other drugs at the time of the study, and none had ever used "hard" drugs. The investigators found that the smokers had significantly lower testosterone levels than nonsmokers. Further, testosterone levels were related to frequency of usage. Heavy smokers (10 or more joints per week) had significantly lower testosterone levels than light smokers (9 or fewer joints per week). Heavy smokers also had significantly lower sperm counts than light smokers. Two of the smokers (as compared with none of the nonsmokers) had erection problems. Finally, three of the smokers stopped smoking for two weeks; their testosterone levels rose considerably during that time (by 57 and 141 percent). This study raises serious questions about the effects of marijuana use on sexual and reproductive functioning, since testosterone is so important to both. On the other hand, the study suggests that the results are quickly reversible when use is discontinued. We should also be cautious about sounding an alarm before the results have been replicated by other investigators; at least one other study failed to find the same results (Mendelsohn et al., 1974; see also E. M. Brecher, 1975). But another study found a 66 percent reduction in sperm count after one month of marijuana use (Hembree et al., 1976). At the very least, these studies indicate a need for more research in this area.

The effects of alcohol vary considerably. A small amount of alcohol may reduce anxiety and inhibitions, thereby improving sexual responsiveness. A large amount of alcohol, however, acts as a depressant and may therefore prevent sexual arousal, thereby causing sexual dysfunction. Alcoholics, who are exposed to repeated high doses of alcohol, frequently have sexual dysfunctions, particularly erectile dysfunction (H. Jones and Jones, 1977). As one alcoholic put it, "I started out Early Times, but quickly wound up as Old Grandad" (Lemere and Smith, 1973).

Some of the drugs used in treating psychiatric disorders may also affect sexual functioning. For example, "dry orgasm," an orgasm in which the man produces no ejaculate, may be a side effect of some of the drugs used in the treatment of schizophrenia. Tranquilizers and antidepressants, while producing occasional cases of sexual dysfunction, often help improve

TABLE 18.1

DRUGS THAT MAY DECREASE LIBIDO OR IMPAIR SEXUAL RESPONSE

Drug	How It Is Thought to Affect Sexual Functioning	Some Common Medical Indications*
Drugs That Act on the Brain†		
1 Sedatives		
Alcohol and barbiturates	Depress CNS activity in a single large dose; long-term heavy use leads to neural damage	Sedatives and hypnotics (sleep inducers)
Narcotics Heroin Morphine	General depression of the CNS plus depression of the sex centers	Analgesics (pain relievers); Methadone used in treatment of narcotic addiction
2 Antiandrogens	Oppose the stimulating action of androgen on the brain and sexual organs	
Estrogen	May decrease libido in women and decrease erections in men	Replacement therapy in postmenopausal women; birth control; men with prostatic cancer; after urinary-tract surgery, used to prevent erection
Cyproteroneacetate		Experimental—used in treatment of compulsive sexual disorders
Adrenal steroids Cortisone ACTH		Allergies and inflammatory disorders
Drugs That Act on The Genitals‡		
1 Anticholinergic drugs Banthine Probanthine Atropine Quaternary ammonium compounds	Inhibit the parasympathetic nerves and so may cause erectile dysfunction	Peptic ulcers, dyskinesias, glaucoma and other eye problems
2 Antiadrenergic drugs Phentolamine Ergo alkaloids Halp-alkylamines Guanethidine (Ismelin) Rauwolfia alkaloids Methyldopa (aldomet)	Inhibit the sympathetic nerves and so may cause ejaculatory problems; may also diminish libido and erection Erectile dysfunction is a frequent complication	Hypertension (high blood pressure) and other vascular disorders Psychosis
Miscellaneous		
Disulfiram (Antabuse)	Occasional erectile dysfunction reported	Alcohol abuse
Chlorphentermine (presate)	Occasional erectile dysfunction reported	Weight reduction
Antihistamines	Continuous use may interfere with sexual activity	Colds and allergies

*"Medically indicated" means that a physician may prescribe it for the condition.
†These primarily decrease libido and the sexual responses.
‡These block the nerves controlling the smooth muscles and blood vessels of the genital organs.
Sources: Helen S. Kaplan. *The new sex therapy.* New York: Brunner/Mazel, 1974. John Money and R. Yankowitz. The sympathetic-inhibiting effects of the drug Ismelin on human male eroticism with a note on Melloril. *Journal of Sex Research,* 1967, *3,* 69–82. James S. Woods. Drug effects on human sexual behavior. In N. F. Woods (Ed.), *Human Sexuality in Health and Illness.* St. Louis: Mosby, 1975.

sexual responding as a result of their improvement in the person's mental state. (For a more complete discussion, see Kaplan, 1974; Leavitt, 1974.)

Psychological Causes

The psychological sources of sexual dysfunction have been categorized into immediate causes and prior learning (Kaplan, 1974). *Prior learning* is the things that people learned earlier—for example, in childhood—which now inhibit their sexual response. *Immediate causes* are various things that happen in the act of lovemaking itself that inhibit the sexual response.

Immediate causes The following four factors have been identified as immediate causes of dysfunction: (1) anxieties such as fear of failure, (2) the constructing of barriers to the experience of erotic pleasure, (3) failure of the partners to communicate, and (4) failure to engage in effective, sexually stimulating behavior.

Anxiety during intercourse can be a source of sexual dysfunction. Anxiety may be caused by fear of failure, that is, fear of being unable to perform. But anxiety itself can block sexual response. Often anxiety can create a vicious circle of self-fulfilling prophecy in which fear of failure produces a failure, which produces more fear, which produces another failure, and so on. For example, a man may have one episode of erectile dysfunction, perhaps after drinking too much at a party. The next time he has sex, he anxiously wonders whether he will "fail" again. His anxiety is so great that he cannot get an erection. At this point he is convinced that the condition is permanent, and all future sexual activity is marked by such intense fear of failure that erectile dysfunction results. The prophecy is fulfilled.

Similarly, anxiety in a woman may block arousal. If she is not aroused, she does not produce vaginal lubrication, and the result can be painful intercourse.

Fears of failure can also be created by a demand for performance by the partner. For example, some cases of erectile dysfunction apparently began when the woman demanded intercourse but the man did not feel aroused and therefore did not get an erection. Following that failure, anxiety built up in anticipation of future failures. Such a process is illustrated by the case history presented in the Focus later in this chapter. Demands for performance, of course, are generally harder on men than they are on women; to engage in intercourse, the man must be aroused and have an erection, and it is painfully obvious when this does not occur. Arousal is not an absolute necessity for a woman to have intercourse, though. The parallel demand for performance in women is the demand that they have orgasms. Once again, if the woman is unable to meet this demand, the result is anxiety and fear of failure, which further inhibit her response.

While a desire to please one's partner is generally a good thing in lovemaking, it can create anxiety if carried to an extreme. For example, a man may obsessively wonder whether he is using the right techniques to stimulate his partner; a woman may anxiously worry that her breasts are not large enough to please her partner. Such compulsive desires to please are often rooted in insecurity and fears of rejection. While many people in sex therapy need to be taught to be more sensitive to their partner's needs, people in the desire-to-please category need the opposite training; they need to learn the value of temporary selfishness and of enjoying of one's own sexual experience.

Constructing barriers to the experience of erotic feelings is another way to produce sexual dysfunction. *Spectatoring*, a term coined by Masters and Johnson, is one of the most common of these barriers. The person behaves like a spectator or judge of his or her own sexual "performance." People who do this are constantly (mentally) stepping outside the sexual act in which they are engaged to evaluate how they are doing, mentally commenting, "Good job," or "Lousy," or "Could stand improvement." Since a full sexual response requires abandonment to the experiencing of erotic feelings, this compulsive evaluation inhibits sexual response.

Failure to communicate is one of the most important causes of sexual dysfunction. Many people expect their partners to have ESP concerning their own sexual needs. You are the leading expert in the field of what feels good to you, and your partner will never know what turns you on unless you make this known, either verbally or nonverbally. But many people do not communicate their sexual desires. For example, a woman who needs a great deal of clitoral stimulation to have an orgasm may never tell her partner this; as a result, she does not get the stimulation she needs and consequently does not have an orgasm.

One final immediate cause of sexual dysfunction is a *failure to engage in effective, sexually stimulating behavior*. Often this is a result of simple ignorance. For example, some couples seek sex therapy because of the wife's failure to have orgasms; the therapist soon discovers that neither the husband nor wife is aware of the location of the clitoris, much less of its fantastic erotic potential. Often such cases can be cleared up by simple educational techniques.

Prior learning The other major category of psychological sources of sexual dysfunction is prior learning and experience. This includes various things that were learned or experienced in childhood, adolescence, or even adulthood.

In some cases of sexual dysfunction, the person's first sexual act was a very traumatic experience. An example would be a young man who could not get an erection the first time he attempted intercourse and was laughed at by his partner. Such an experience sets the stage for future erectile dysfunction. Rape is another traumatic experience that may lead to sexual dysfunction.

Seductive parents may contribute to early traumatic sexual experiences. A parent may be seductive or may even force the child to engage in intercourse; the child is in no position to refuse, but she or he feels terribly guilty. Once again, sex becomes associated with psychic pain, laying the groundwork for a lack of sexual responsiveness later.

In other cases of sexual dysfunction, the person grew up in a very strict, religious family and was taught that sex was dirty and sinful. Such a person may grow up thinking that sex is not pleasurable, that it should be gotten over as quickly as possible, and that it is for purposes of procreation only. To say the least, such learning inhibits the enjoyment of a full sexual response.

Another source of dysfunction originating in the family occurs when parents punish children severely for sexual activity such as masturbation. An example is the little girl who is caught masturbating, is punished severely, and is told never to "touch herself" again; she obeys, and in adulthood she finds that she cannot have an orgasm through masturbation or as a result of manual stimulation by her partner.

Parents who teach their children the double standard may also contribute to sexual dysfunction, particularly in their daughters. Women whose sexual response is inhibited in adulthood often have a history of being taught, when they were children, that no nice lady is interested in sex or enjoys it.

We should, though, note one major problem with the evidence of Masters and Johnson and others on these factors as causes of sexual dysfunction: the evidence comes from clinical data. This means that a group of people seeking therapy for their sexual problems were studied, certain factors emerged as common in their life histories, and it was therefore concluded that those factors must cause sexual dysfunction. The problem is that no data were collected on a comparison group of people who were functioning adequately in their sex lives to see whether those "causes" were also common in their histories. A classic example of this problem in logic is the following: A psychiatrist studies a group of schizophrenic patients and finds that every single one of them had a mother. The psychiatrist concludes that having a mother must cause schizophrenia. Had the psychiatrist also studied a comparison group of normal people, she or he would have discovered that they all had mothers too and that having a mother is therefore not a very likely cause of schizophrenia. We might apply this same critique to the statement that sexual dysfunction is caused by strong religious teachings. While strong religious teachings were common in the backgrounds of many of the patients with sexual dysfunctions, it might be that such a factor is also very common among those who function quite well sexually; religious homes were, after all, quite common 30 or 40 years ago.

One study on female orgasm capacity provides some information that is relevant here. A large sample of adult women filled out a questionnaire about their own sexual behavior, as well as providing other background information on such things as how religious they were (S. Fisher, 1973). The results indicated that the extent to which a woman was religiously devout had no relationship to her orgasm capacity. Similar results have been obtained in other studies (e.g., Kinsey et al., 1953). In fact, in a recent survey done by *Redbook* magazine (see Chapter 9), the results indicated that the most religious women were actually happier with their sex lives than those who were less religious or not at all religious. These findings seem to contradict Masters and Johnson.

The point is that the conclusions made by Masters and Johnson and other sex therapists concerning the causes of sexual dysfunction are not based on very good evidence. Our knowledge of exactly what factors in a person's past experience contribute to making that person sexually dysfunctional is highly speculative at the present time, and further research is needed.

Marital conflict Although Masters and Johnson and others using similar forms of sex therapy concentrate on treating the immediate and prior learning causes of dysfunction, there are some other, more complex causes that are also worth considering. One of these is disturbances in the relationship between the two partners. If there is severe discord in the marriage, sexual dysfunction may develop. Hating one's sexual partner does not create an optimal environment for sexual enjoyment. Sex can also be used as a weapon to hurt a partner; for example, a woman can hurt her husband by refusing to engage in a sexual behavior that he enjoys. Sexual dysfunction, then, may be one of many symptoms of marital discord.

Intrapsychic conflict In contrast to Masters and Johnson and other behavior therapists who view sexual dysfunction as a simple result of learning, Freudian analysts view sexual dysfunction as a result of unconscious *intrapsychic conflict*. The idea is that while humans have a strong craving for sexual expression, they also have unconscious anxieties about it and are afraid that they will be punished for engaging in sex. Put the two together, and you have conflict.

According to Freud, much of this conflict originates in childhood, specifically in the Oedipus complex. Resolving the Oedipus complex—identifying with the same-gender parent and repressing the incestuous sexual desires for the parent of the opposite gender—is essential for attaining mature, good adjustment. Sexual problems in adulthood result when an unresolved Oedipus complex, which has lain dormant for years, is reactivated. For example, an adult man is about to make love to a woman; suddenly, however, old castration anxieties are evoked, and he loses his erection. According to Freud, all sexual problems are caused by an unresolved Oedipus complex.

It follows from this theoretical model that sexual dysfunctions could be cured only by intensive, long-term psychoanalysis designed to uncover these unconscious, unresolved conflicts.

The high success rate of the Masters and Johnson rapid-treatment program using behavior therapy provides evidence against the psychoanalytic model; according to Freud, their therapy techniques should not be successful. On the other hand, they do have a failure rate—about 20 percent, and higher for certain dysfunctions—and it is possible that those who fail in their treatment program are precisely the people whose dysfunction is caused by intrapsychic conflict. Accordingly, some therapists, such as Helen Singer Kaplan (1974), use a joint approach, combining the Masters and Johnson behavior therapy with psychotherapy for intrapsychic conflicts.

Sexuality and the Handicapped

It is commonly believed that the person in a wheelchair is sexless. The physically handicapped are thought not to be interested in sex, much less to be capable of engaging in sexual activity. Such ideas are perpetuated by novels such as *Lady Chatterley's Lover,* in which a woman who is sexually frustrated because of her husband's paralysis turns to another man.

About 10 percent of adults in the United States have a physical handicap that imposes a substantial limitation on their activities. Given a chance to express themselves, these people emphasize the importance of their sexuality and sex drive, which may be unaltered by their disability (Richardson, 1972).

Just what can physically handicapped people do sexually? Space does not permit a complete enumeration of all types of physical disabilities and their consequences for sexuality. Instead, the discussion will concentrate on one illustrative example: spinal-cord injury. The reader who is interested in further information may consult an excellent review by Dr. Theodore M. Cole (1975). It forms the basis for the following discussion.

Sexuality and the spinal-cord-injured Spinal-cord-injured people are becoming increasingly common, with the rising numbers of high-speed car crashes and motorcycle accidents, surfboard accidents, civilian gunshot wounds, and injuries sustained during war.

Paraplegia (paralysis of the lower half of the body on both sides) and quadriplegia (paralysis of the body from the neck down) are both caused by injuries to the spinal cord. Many ablebodied people find it difficult to understand what it feels like to be paralyzed. Imagine that your genitals and the region around them have lost all sensation. You would not know they were being touched unless you saw it happen. Physical orgasm is impossible. For the male, no matter how erotic his thoughts, no erection occurs. Further, there is loss of bladder and bowel control, which may produce embarrassing problems if sexual activity is attempted.

However, these limitations do not rule out sexual activity completely, and many people with spinal-cord injuries have satisfying sex lives. Exactly what the person can and cannot do depends on the location and extent of the damage to the spinal cord. As the discussion in Chapter 7 indicated, there are erection and ejaculation reflex centers located in the lower part of the spinal cord. If these have been destroyed, of course, neither erection nor ejaculation is possible. But more commonly, the cord has been severed at some level above these centers. This makes it impossible for nerve stimulation from the brain to reach the erection center, and so erotic thoughts can no longer produce erection. However, reflex erection as a result of stimulation of the genitals is still quite possible. Thus many spinal-cord-injured men experience the same sexual responses as able-bodied men—including erection, elevation of the testes, and increases in heart rate—except that they generally cannot ejaculate, nor can they feel the physical stimulation. In one study of 655 spinal-cord-injured men, 54 percent were able to have erections, the number rising to 80 percent one year after injury (Tsuji et al., 1961).

Spinal-cord-injured women generally experience the same sexual responses as able-bodied women, including engorgement of the clitoris and labia, erection of the nipples, and increases in heart rate. However, vaginal lubrication and orgasm generally do not occur. Amenorrhea may occur after injury, but there is generally a return to normal menstrual cycling. Further, such women ovulate and are quite capable of becoming pregnant and carrying a baby to term.

Because sexuality in our culture is currently so orgasm-oriented (see Chapter 8), the orgasm problems common among spinal-cord-injured people may appear to be devastating. But many of these handicapped people report that they have been able to cultivate a kind of "psychological orgasm" that is as satisfying as the physical one. Fantasy is a perfectly legitimate form of sexual expression that has not been ruled out by their injury.

There are three general points to be made about sexuality and the handicapped: (1) They generally do have sexual needs and desires; (2) they are often capable of sexual response quite similar to that of ablebodied people; and (3)

there is a real need for more information—and communication—about what people with various handicaps can and cannot do sexually.

THE MASTERS AND JOHNSON SEX THERAPY PROGRAM

The Format and Basic Principles

Masters and Johnson operate out of a behavior therapy model because they believe that sexual dysfunction has been learned. As they put it:

> Sociocultural deprivation and ignorance of sexual physiology, rather than psychiatric or mental illness, constitute the etiologic background for most sexual dysfunction. (1970, p. 21)

They see sexual dysfunction, then, as a learned behavior rather than a psychiatric illness. If sexual dysfunction is learned, it can be unlearned. Thus Masters and Johnson use a two-week, rapid-treatment program of intensive therapy. The therapy consists mainly of discussions and specific behavioral exercises, or "homework assignments." The sequence of events in the two-week therapy program is outlined in the Focus.

One of the most basic goals of Masters and Johnson's therapy is to eliminate goal-oriented sexual performance. Many patients believe that in sex they must perform and achieve certain things. If sex is an achievement situation, it also can become the scene of failure, and it is these perceived failures that lead people to believe they have a sexual problem. Spectatoring contributes to the problem.

In part, Masters and Johnson eliminate the couple's goal-oriented attitude toward sex by forbidding, from the beginning of therapy, any sexual activity not explicitly ordered by the therapists. Then they assign exercises, such as the sensate focus exercise, that make no demands on the patients whatever. As the patients

THE SCHEDULE OF TREATMENT IN THE MASTERS AND JOHNSON THERAPY PROGRAM

Day 1

1 *The initial interview* Both therapists meet with the couple to explain their commitments to the program and the procedure for the first few days. The rule that both partners must participate in the therapy is explained. Patients are told that they should not have intercourse or engage in any other sexual activity until told to do so by the therapists.

2 *The first history-taking interview* The female therapist interviews the woman, and the male therapist interviews the man. They collect information on the sexual problem and on the patients' sexual functioning. Life history data are also collected: the patient's childhood and family relationships, sexual experiences, marital relationships, and what is sensuous to the patient.

Day 2

The second history-taking interview The female therapist interviews the husband, and the male therapist interviews the wife. Sensitive areas are probed. The motivation of the patients for seeking therapy is discussed; for example, did one partner drag the other one there?

Day 3

1 *Medical examination* In order to rule out physical causes of the dysfunction, a complete medical history is taken of each patient,

successfully complete these, they are given assignments in which the sexual components are gradually increased. The couple continue to chalk up successes until eventually they are having intercourse and the dysfunction has disappeared. Masters and Johnson operate on the notion that adequate sexual functioning is quite natural and that all they must do in therapy is remove unnatural impediments to sexual functioning. For example, as they put it, a man is born with the capacity to have an erection. His first erection did not happen because he tried to make it happen; he simply found himself with it. Sexual response is natur-

and a physical examination and diagnostic laboratory tests are performed.

2 *Roundtable discussion*   Both therapists and both patients participate in a roundtable discussion. The therapists summarize the findings of the history-taking interviews, and the patients correct any errors. The therapists present the probable causes of the dysfunction. Spectatoring is discussed.

3 *Homework assignment: sensate focus*   The patients are instructed to complete two periods of sensate focusing before the therapy session the next day. The genitals and breasts, though, are "out of bounds" for stroking at this stage. The "getting" partner tells the "giving" partner when any stimulation is unpleasant.

Day 4

1 *Discussion of actions and reactions to the homework assignment.*

2 *Discussion of the anatomy of the genital organs.*

3 *Homework assignment: sensate focus*   The couple are again instructed to complete two sensate focus sessions, this time extending stimulation to the breasts and genitals. Also, this time the "getting" partner guides the hand of the "giving" partner to show personal preferences concerning how and where she or he likes to be touched.

Days 5 to 14

Homework assignments are given to treat the specific dysfunction. The exercises vary, depending on the dysfunction (see text for further discussion).

Source: Fred Belliveau and Lin Richter. *Understanding Human Sexual Inadequacy.* New York: Bantam, 1970.

---

al, and after impediments to it have been removed, the couple should begin to enjoy satisfying sexual responses.

One distinctive feature of the Masters and Johnson therapy program is the use of *cotherapists.* That is, two people, one male and one female, always function together as therapists.

There are several advantages to this practice. First, each member of the couple in therapy has a "friend in court," that is, a therapist of the same gender who can understand his or her problems and help express them to the other spouse and the other therapist. Having cotherapists also ensures that neither member of the couple in therapy has the feeling of being "ganged up against"; for example, if there were only one therapist, a male, the female patient would be outnumbered 2 to 1. With a male-female therapy team, no one is outnumbered. Having cotherapists also reduces the possibility of getting biased information from the patients, particularly since it permits interviewing the two people at the same time, but separately. Finally, the male-female cotherapy team minimizes the possibility that "transference" will occur. Transference is a well-known phenomenon in psychotherapy in which the patient becomes emotionally attached to, and has sexual desires for, the therapist. Masters and Johnson feel that any kind of sexual or intense emotional relationship between the patient and the therapist should never be allowed to develop because it would destroy the very marital relationship that is being treated. Having two therapists minimizes the chances that transference will take place.

Another distinctive feature of the Masters and Johnson therapy format is that both members of the couple must participate in therapy. For example, a man cannot simply come to them with a problem of erectile dysfunction and be treated. His wife must participate also. There are two basic reasons behind this requirement. First, many of the therapy techniques, such as the "homework" exercises, require the cooperation of the other partner as well as some training of the partner. For example, the "squeeze technique" is used in treating premature ejaculation, but it must be performed by the man's partner, and thus she must be trained to do it. The second reason for the requirement that both people participate in therapy is that each is almost invariably affected by the other's dysfunction and thus needs therapy as well. For example, the wife of a man with erection problems is probably having some difficulties with orgasm herself and thus will benefit from therapy. The husband of a woman who has orgasmic dysfunction may be feeling that he is

inadequate as a lover, and thus the therapy will help him also. As Masters and Johnson put it, "There is no such thing as an uninvolved partner in any marriage in which there is some form of sexual inadequacy" (1970, p. 2). They believe that it is the couple and their relationship that are the real patient in therapy.

The requirement that both people participate in the therapy raises one problematic issue, however. Should therapy be denied to the married person who has a sexual dysfunction but whose spouse absolutely refuses to participate? Or should a single person who has no steady relationship but who nonetheless has a sexual dysfunction and wants to be treated for it also be denied therapy? One strategy that Masters and Johnson developed for dealing with such people was the use of a surrogate, or a third member of the therapy team who served as a sexual partner for the patient during the two-week therapy program. The surrogates were a group of volunteers carefully chosen by Masters and Johnson. They were not prostitutes; rather, they were people who were sincerely concerned with helping those with sexual dysfunctions. In fact, one of the female surrogates was a physician. The use of surrogates proved to be effective, judged by the success rate for people in this type of therapy, which was the same as the success rate for married couples in therapy. The use of surrogates did attract considerable publicity, though, and it remains a controversial practice to the present day, as well as opening up a confused mass of legal difficulties, such as the possibility of being charged with prostitution. Nonetheless, the use of surrogates does seem to be a reasonable solution to the problem of treating certain people who otherwise would be denied sex therapy.

Basic Therapy Techniques

Masters and Johnson use several basic techniques in therapy. The sequence of these techniques is outlined in the Focus. Notice that the therapy begins with a set of standard exercises for the first four or five days and then proceeds to a special set of exercises for the specific dysfunction and the set of conditions that produced it.

One of the basic techniques used is simple education. Masters and Johnson give the couple thorough instruction in the anatomy and physiology of the male and female sexual organs. Some couples, for example, have no idea of what or where the clitoris is. There is also an opportunity to clear up some of the misunderstandings that either the man or the woman may have had since childhood. For example, a man with problems of erectile dysfunction may have learned as a child that men can have only a fixed number of orgasms in their lifetime. As he approaches middle age, he starts to worry about whether he may have used up almost all his orgasms, and this inhibits his sexual response. It is important for such men to learn that nature has imposed no such quota on them.

The *sensate focus* exercises are perhaps the most important of the Masters and Johnson therapy techniques. They are based on the notion that touching and being touched are important forms of sexual expression and that touching is also an important form of communication; for example, a touch can express affection, desire, understanding, or lack of caring. In the exercises, one member of the couple plays the "giving" role (touches the other), while the other person plays the "getting" role (is touched by the other). The giving partner is instructed to massage or fondle the other, while the getting partner is instructed to communicate to the giver what is most pleasurable. Thus the exercise fosters communication between the two. The couple then switch roles after a certain period of time. At the beginning, the giver is not to stroke the genitals or breasts, but may touch any other area. As the couple progress through the exercises, they are instructed to begin touching the genitals and breasts. These exercises also encourage the people to focus their

attention or concentrate on the sensuous pleasures they are receiving. Many people's sexual response is dulled because they are distracted; for example, they are thinking about what to cook for dinner, or they are spectatoring on their own performance. The sensate focus exercises train people to focus on their sexual experience, thereby increasing their pleasure.

Masters and Johnson combine these basic therapy techniques with specific treatments for specific dysfunctions. These specific treatments will be discussed later in the chapter.

Even with the use of these exercises, though, the Masters and Johnson therapy program still requires quite a bit of clinical skill and insight on the part of the therapists. In addition to prescribing exercises, they must, for example, be able to understand the feelings of the patients and to get the partners to understand each other's feelings. These are not simple or mechanical procedures.

The Success Rate

Masters and Johnson have been quite careful to collect data on the success and failure rates of their therapy. In *Human Sexual Inadequacy* they reported on the treatment of 790 individuals. Of these, 142 were still dysfunctional at the end of the two-week therapy program. This yields a failure rate of 18 percent, or *a success rate of 82 percent*. While the failure rate ran around 18 percent for most dysfunctions, there were two exceptions: premature ejaculation had a very low failure rate (2.2 percent), and primary erectile dysfunction had a very high failure rate (40.6 percent). That is, premature ejaculation seems to be quite easy to cure, while primary erectile dysfunction is rather difficult. Masters and Johnson's success rate is very impressive and is considerably higher than the success rate in many forms of traditional psychotherapy. Further, others using their method have approximately the same success rate.

Masters and Johnson have also been able

to follow up 226 people five years after therapy. The former patients were interviewed about their current sexual functioning. After the five years, the failure rate had risen to only about 25.5 percent; that is, the therapy seems to have lasting effects, and few people seem to develop their old problems again afterward.

OTHER THERAPIES

While Masters and Johnson have dominated the field of sex therapy, they are by no means the only sex therapists, nor is their method of treatment the only one available. Other kinds of therapeutic approaches are discussed below.

Variations on the Masters and Johnson Method

One of the problems with the Masters and Johnson treatment program is that it is extremely expensive. In 1977, the two-week treatment program cost $2500. Thus a number of people have developed variations on their program with the goal of making treatment available more cheaply to more people. Having two therapists essentially doubles the price of the therapy, and so some people use a single therapist, apparently with good results. Others have explored group therapy, in which five or ten people, all with the same dysfunction, are treated together in a group (see, for example, Schneidman and McGuire, 1976; Zilbergeld, 1975). Therapy for a group with a mixture of dysfunctions has also been explored (Leiblum et al., 1976). The Masters and Johnson program is also expensive because it requires taking off two weeks from work, traveling to St. Louis, and staying in a motel for two weeks. Many therapists have therefore changed from the two-week, rapid-treatment program to a format of one or two sessions per week for 10 or 15 weeks. Many major-medical health insurance programs now cover psychiatric treatment and

therefore sex therapy, which makes cost somewhat less of a problem for many people.

Two other books provide comprehensive approaches to sex therapy: Helen Singer Kaplan's *The New Sex Therapy* (1974) and Hartman and Fithian's *Treatment of Sexual Dysfunction* (1974). The approaches are in many respects similar to that of Masters and Johnson. They differ chiefly in three ways: treatment is provided once or twice a week for 10 weeks or so, only one therapist is used, and treatment tends to combine psychotherapy or marital therapy with the Masters and Johnson type of behavior therapy.

Specific Treatments for Specific Problems

Kegel exercises One technique that is used with women is the *Kegel exercises*, named for the physician who devised them (Kegel, 1952). They are designed to exercise and strengthen the *pubococcygeal muscle*, or PC muscle, which runs along the sides of the entrance of the vagina (see Figure 2.8, in Chapter 2). This exercise is particularly helpful for women who have had this muscle stretched in childbirth and for those who simply have poor tone in the muscle. The woman is instructed first to find her PC muscle by sitting on a toilet with her legs spread apart, urinating, and stopping the flow of urine voluntarily. The muscle that stops the flow is the PC muscle. After that, the woman is told to contract the muscle 10 times during each of six sessions per day. Gradually she can work up to more.[3] The most important effect of this exercise is that it seems to increase women's sexual pleasure by increasing the sensitivity of the vaginal area. It also permits the woman to stimulate her partner more, and it is a cure for

---

[3]Students should recognize the exciting possibilities for doing this exercise. For example, it is a good way to amuse yourself in the middle of a boring lecture, and no one will ever know you are doing it.

women who have problems with involuntarily urinating as they orgasm.

Squeeze technique   A method that Masters and Johnson and others use to treat premature ejaculators is the *squeeze technique*. The woman sits on the bed with her back against the backboard, propped up by pillows. The man lies on his back, facing her, with his feet outside her thighs (Figure 18.2). The woman caresses his genitals until he gets an erection. When he has a full erection, she holds his penis between the thumb and first two fingers of her hand. The thumb is placed on the lower surface of the penis, just below the corona, and the two fingers are placed on the opposite side of the penis, one above the coronal ridge and the other below it. When he feels that ejaculation is about to

happen, he tells her, and she then squeezes the penis fairly hard for 3 to 4 seconds. This causes the man to lose his urge to ejaculate. He may also lose some of his erection. After waiting 15 to 30 seconds, the woman again stimulates him to a full erection, squeezes, and so on. The couple may thus engage in 15 to 20 minutes of continuous sex play, and the man gradually gains some control over his ejaculation. Lest this technique sound like cruel and unusual punishment, it should be noted that the squeeze, when done properly, does not hurt.

After the man has gained some control with this method, the couple assume the woman-on-top position (see Figure 18.3), and he inserts his penis into the vagina; however, no pelvic thrusting is permitted. If the man feels that he is about to ejaculate, the woman simply raises her

FIGURE 18.2
Techniques for treating premature ejaculation. (*a*) The squeeze technique and (*b*) the position the couple use while doing the squeeze technique.

Urethral meatus

Penile glans

Coronal ridge

Penile shaft

(*a*)

(*b*)

FIGURE 18.3

The woman-on-top position is used in treating sexual dysfunctions in both women and men.

body and uses the squeeze technique. After there is control in this situation, the man is instructed to begin some pelvic thrusting. As he gradually gains more control, they may proceed to the side-to-side position for intercourse (Figure 18.5) and finally to the man-on-top position.

The squeeze technique is actually a variant on the *stop-start technique*, which was originally devised by Dr. James Semans (1956) and is used by Dr. Helen Singer Kaplan and others. The woman uses her hand to stimulate the man to erection. Then she stops the stimulation. Gradually he loses his erection. She then starts stimulation again, he gets another erection, she stops, and so on. Dr. Kaplan finds that this procedure is less uncomfortable than the

squeeze technique and that couples respond better to it in the treatment of premature ejaculation.

Masturbation One interesting form of behavior therapy for women with orgasmic dysfunction has been developed: masturbation (LoPiccolo and Lobitz, 1972). The data indicate that masturbation is the technique most likely to produce orgasm in women. Kinsey found that the average woman reaches orgasm 95 percent of the time when masturbating, as opposed to 73 percent of the time in intercourse. Masters and Johnson found that masturbation produces the most intense orgasm in women. Masturbation therefore seems to be a likely treatment for women with primary orgasmic dysfunction. The therapists, of course, must first deal with the patient's negative attitude toward masturbation. Following this, they use a nine-step (one per week) program to treat the dysfunction:

1 The woman is instructed to do the mirror exercises (see Chapter 2) and to begin a program of Kegel exercises.
2 The woman is instructed to explore her genitals by touch.
3 The woman again explores her genitals by touch, this time trying to find the most pleasurable, sensitive area (this is almost invariably the clitoris).
4 The woman stimulates the area she found to be pleasurably sensitive.
5 If the woman has not yet had an orgasm, she is instructed to increase the intensity and duration of her self-stimulation and to use fantasy in addition.
6 If the woman still has not had an orgasm, she stimulates herself with a vibrator.
7 Once the woman is having orgasms, her husband is integrated into her sexual experience. The first step in this process is for her to masturbate in his presence.
8 He then stimulates her manually.
9 They have intercourse while he stimulates her manually.

Marital Therapy

While the above approaches are essentially all forms of behavior therapy, based on a learning-

FIGURE 18.4
A position used in treating female sexual dysfunction.

435

A CASE OF ERECTILE DYSFUNCTION IN A MAN

FOCUS

Mr. X was a handsome and successful 30-year-old businessman who had been divorced two years earlier. He and his fiancée, who was 26 years old, were planning to be married shortly.

The chief complaint was erectile dysfunction. The man was easily aroused and had an erection quickly upon commencing sex play. Almost invariably, though, his erection diminished when he was about to begin coitus. His fiancée had no sexual difficulty; she was easily aroused and orgastic on clitoral stimulation.

Neither had a history of psychiatric problems. In fact, they seemed to be very well-adjusted individuals. Their relationship also seemed to be excellent.

In his prior marriage, which had lasted five years and produced two children, Mr. X had experienced no sexual difficulty. He and his wife had intercourse two or three times per week, and he invariably functioned well. His wife left him because she was in love with and wished to marry a close friend of the family.

The divorce was very traumatic for Mr. X. He became depressed and was left with deep feelings of insecurity. He kept wondering why his wife had left him and whether he was inferior to the other man.

Eight months after the separation he went to a party and met a woman who wanted to have sex with him right there. On her urging, they went to an upstairs room (which did not have a lock) and attempted to have intercourse on the floor. He became excited and erect, but for the first time in his life, he lost his erection. He tried to regain it to no avail.

Mr. X reacted to this experience with alarm. He felt depressed and extremely humiliated and embarrassed. He never saw this

---

theory model, another approach is marital therapy. Marital therapy rests on the assumption that sexual dysfunction is caused by a problem in the marital relationship, that is, that the dysfunction is a symptom of interpersonal conflict between the husband and wife. In marital therapy, the relationship between them is treated, with the goal of reducing the antagonisms and tensions in the marriage. The idea is that as the marital relationship improves, the sexual dysfunction should disappear.

Individual Psychotherapy

If one believes that sexual dysfunction is caused by intrapsychic conflict, the appropriate form of woman again. One month later he tried to make love to another woman, but again he lost his erection when the memory of his previous failure intruded into his mind. From then on the problem escalated. He met his fiancée shortly thereafter, but initially he avoided making love to her because he anticipated failure. Later, when they became more intimate, he confessed his problem to her. They attempted to have sex, but in most instances Mr. X was unable to function. Questioning revealed that he was preoccupied with thoughts about whether he would fail during lovemaking. He continued to feel humiliated and feared rejection, despite his fiancée's reassurance and sensitivity.

According to psychiatrist Helen Singer Kaplan's analysis, this was a case in which performance anxiety (an immediate cause) caused secondary erectile dysfunction.

In therapy Mr. X responded very readily to methods designed to dispel his performance anxiety. Initially, intercourse was forbidden. During this time he and his fiancée engaged in mutual caressing. This proved most pleasurable to both. They then proceeded to gentle, teasing genital stimulation. Specifically, the woman stimulated the penis until it was erect. Then she stopped. When the erection abated, she resumed stimulation. This was repeated several times, still without orgasm for him.

Meanwhile, in the sessions with the therapist, Mr. X was told to stop watching the process of his erection and worrying about his "performance." He was confronted with the destructive effects of his spectatoring and his performance anxiety. In addition, the therapist was able to work through the dynamics of his reactions to his former wife's rejection of him, which seemed to be related to his current problems. The therapy thus combined elements of behavior therapy and psychotherapy.

Treatment proceeded to a successful conclusion.

Source: Helen S. Kaplan. *The new sex therapy.* New York: Brunner/Mazel, 1974, pp. 128–129.

---

therapy is psychotherapy or psychoanalysis. The idea is that the sexual dysfunction is a symptom of poor adjustment or a disordered personality. The therapy would then treat the person's individual adjustment, with the goal of trying to resolve conflicts. The idea is that sexual functioning should improve as adjustment improves.

David Reuben, in his popular *Everything You Always Wanted to Know about Sex,* voices this viewpoint when he says: "The only effective treatment for total orgasmic impairment is psychotherapy, because the condition is a psychiatric one. The sexual difficulty is simply a manifestation of a deeper emotional dysfunction" (1969, p. 129).

Which Therapy Is Best?

At the present time we have no definitive evidence on which of the three basic therapy approaches—behavior therapy (the Masters and Johnson program being an example), marital therapy, or individual psychotherapy—is the "right" one for treating sexual dysfunction. (For a critical review, see Sotile and Kilmann, 1977.) The high success rate of the Masters and Johnson program argues strongly for the assumptions and methods of behavior therapy. But probably there is no "right" method. Marital therapy or psychotherapy may be just what is needed by people who are not helped in the Masters and Johnson program. Indeed, many therapists who use techniques like those of Masters and Johnson refuse to treat people with severe adjustment problems or those whose marital relationships are severely disturbed; such people may be referred for marital therapy or psychotherapy. It may also be feasible to combine behavior therapy with marital therapy or psychotherapy when this seems appropriate, a practice that is illustrated in the Focus.

SOME PRACTICAL ADVICE

Avoiding Sexual Dysfunction

Since I was raised by a father who worked for the National Safety Council, I learned well their motto, "Prevention Is Better than Cure." It seems to me that this principle could be applied not only to accidents but also to sexual dysfunction. That is, it seems to me that people could use some of the principles that emerge from Masters and Johnson's work to avoid having sexual dysfunctions in the first place. I think the following are some principles of good sexual mental health:

1 Communicate with your partner. Don't expect him or her to be a mind reader concerning what is pleasurable to you. One way to do this is to make it a habit to talk to your partner while you are having sex; verbal communication then does not come as a shock. Some people, though, feel uncomfortable talking at such times; nonverbal communication, such as placing your hand on

FIGURE 18.5

The side-to-side position is used in treating premature ejaculation.

top of your partner's and moving it where you want it, works well too.

2 Don't be a spectator. Don't feel as if you are putting on a sexual performance that you constantly need to evaluate. Concentrate on the giving and receiving of sensual pleasures, not on how well you are doing.

3 Don't set up goals of sexual performance. If you have a goal, you can fail, and failure produces dysfunctions. Don't set your heart on having simultaneous orgasms or, if you are a woman, on having five orgasms before your partner has one. Just relax and enjoy yourself.

4 Be choosy about the situations in which you have sex. Don't have sex when you are in a terrific hurry or are afraid you will be disturbed. This produces anxiety, and anxiety produces dysfunction, as in the case of a man whose first sexual experiences were "quickies" in the back seats of cars and who becomes a premature ejaculator as a result. Also be choosy about who your partner is. Trusting your partner is essential to good sexual functioning; similarly, a partner who really cares for you will be understanding if things don't go well and will not laugh or be sarcastic.

Picking a Sex Therapist

Unfortunately, most states do not have licensing requirements for sex therapists (most states do have requirements for marriage counselors and psychologists). Particularly with the popularizing of Masters and Johnson's work, quite a few quacks have hung out shingles saying "Sex Therapist," and many states make no attempt to regulate this. Some of these "therapists" have no more qualifications than having had a few orgasms themselves.

On the other hand, Masters and Johnson are not the only sex therapists in the land; even if they were, they could not possibly treat everyone with dysfunctions. So how do you go about finding a good, qualified sex therapist? Your local medical association or psychological association can provide a list of psychiatrists or psychologists and may be able to tell you which have special training in sex therapy. There are also professional organizations of sex therapists. The American Association of Sex Educators, Counselors, and Therapists (Washington, D.C.) certifies sex therapists.

SUMMARY

In men, the major kinds of sexual dysfunction are erectile dysfunction, premature ejaculation, and retarded ejaculation; in women, the major dysfunctions are orgasmic dysfunction, dyspareunia, vaginismus, and sexual apathy (dyspareunia and sexual apathy may also occur in men). Masters and Johnson reported on these dysfunctions and the way they treat them in their important book *Human Sexual Inadequacy* (1970).

Sexual dysfunction may be caused by a variety of organic (physical) factors such as some illnesses, infections, and damage to the spinal cord. Certain drugs may also create problems of sexual functioning. Most cases, though, are caused by various psychological factors. Some of these are immediate causes—anxieties about failure, spectatoring, and failure to communicate. Others may result from prior experiences such as an early traumatic sexual experience. Other theorists believe that marital discord or intrapsychic conflict may cause dysfunctions. There has been an increased interest in what the handicapped can and cannot do sexually.

Masters and Johnson's program is a kind of behavior therapy based on the assumption that sexual dysfunction is learned and can therefore be unlearned. One of their major goals in therapy is the elimination of goal-directed sexual performance. They use a male-female team of therapists and require that both husband and wife participate in therapy.

Some of the therapy techniques they use are education, sensate focus exercises, Kegel exercises, and the squeeze technique. Their overall success rate in therapy is about 80 percent.

Others have developed variations on the basic Masters and Johnson techniques, often in an effort to reduce the cost of the therapy. Marital therapy and psychotherapy, which are based on different theoretical models, are two other approaches to treating sexual dysfunction.

SUGGESTIONS FOR FURTHER READING

Barbach, Lonnie G. *For yourself: The fulfillment of female sexuality.* Garden City, N.Y.: Doubleday, 1975. Provides good information for women with orgasmic dysfunction, based on the author's program of group therapy for sexually dysfunctional women.

Belliveau, Fred, and Richter, Lin. *Understanding Human Sexual Inadequacy.* New York: Bantam, 1970. An easy-to-read, accurate condensation of the Masters and Johnson (1970) book on sexual dysfunction. The authors are professional writers, and the book is intended for a general audience (the original work by Masters and Johnson is written in highly technical language).

McCarthy, B. W., Ryan, W., and Johnson, F. A. *Sexual awareness.* San Francisco: Boyd & Fraser, 1975. Provides practical advice on sexual functioning for both men and women.

SEXUAL DISEASES

As long as you and your partner have never had sex with anyone else and have sex only with each other, there is no risk of VD (venereal disease). But if you or your partner starts to have sex with someone else or if your partner has had previous partners, the risk of VD is introduced. Your health is very important, and a good way to ruin it or cause yourself a lot of suffering is to have an untreated case of VD (some of the possible results are sterility and blindness). Consequently, it is very important to know the symptoms of the various kinds of VD so that you will seek treatment if you develop any of them. Also, there are some ways to prevent VD or at least reduce your chances of getting it, and these are certainly worth knowing about. Finally, after you have read some of the statistics on how many people contract VD every year and on your chances of getting it, you may want to modify your sexual behavior somewhat. If you love, love wisely.

VD in women is typically treated by gynecologists, whose specialty is the female reproductive system. VD in men is generally treated by urologists, whose specialty is the urinary system, which happens to coincide at least partially with the sexual system in men. Finally, since many of the symptoms of VD are skin problems, dermatologists (skin specialists) may also be consulted.

This chapter will be about not only venereal diseases (diseases spread primarily through sexual intercourse) but also other diseases of the sexual apparatus.

GONORRHEA

Historical records indicate that gonorrhea ("the clap," "the drip") is the oldest of the sexual diseases. Its symptoms are described in the Old Testament, Leviticus 15 (about 1500 B.C.). The Greek physician Hippocrates (400 B.C.) believed that gonorrhea resulted from "excessive indulgence in the pleasures of Venus," the goddess of love (hence the name "venereal" disease). Albert Neisser identified the bacterium that causes it, the gonococcus (*Neisseria gonorrhoeae*), in 1879.

Gonorrhea has always been a particular problem during wars, when it spreads rapidly among the soldiers and the prostitutes they patronize. In this century, a gonorrhea epidemic occurred during World War I, and gonorrhea

FIGURE 19.1
Reported cases of gonorrhea in the United States, 1950 to 1976. Note how sharply the number has risen during the 1960s and 1970s.

442
CHAPTER 19

was also a real problem during World War II. Then, with the discovery of penicillin and its use in treating gonorrhea, the disease became much less prevalent in the 1950s; indeed, public health officials thought that it had been virtually eliminated.

Gonorrhea is now once again at epidemic proportions. Of the communicable diseases, it is second only to the common cold in prevalence (running ahead of measles and mumps). In 1971 there were 620,000 *reported* cases of gonorrhea in the United States; however, since public health officials believe that only about 25 percent of the cases are reported, it is estimated that there were about 2.5 million cases (Millar, 1972).[1] In 1976 there were 1 million reported cases (U.S. Public Health Service, 1976b). Most cases occur in the 15- to 29-year-old age group, and it is currently estimated that 50 percent of American young people today will contract either gonorrhea or syphilis by the time they are 25. Thus to say that there is an "epidemic" does not seem to be an exaggeration.

The current epidemic seems to be due to a number of factors. One is the Vietnam war, which produced the old story of the soldiers and the prostitutes, with the soldiers then bringing the disease back to the States. Another factor contributing to the epidemic is the shift in contraceptive practices from 1950 to 1970. The condom, which provides some protection against gonorrhea, has been replaced by the Pill, which not only provides no protection but

actually increases susceptibility. Finally, increased sexual permissiveness has probably contributed. If everyone were completely monogamous, there would be no VD; it is spread only when a person has intercourse with an infected person and then has intercourse with someone else.

Symptoms

Most cases of gonorrhea result from penis-in-vagina intercourse. In the male, the gonococcus invades the urethra, producing gonococcal urethritis (inflammation of the urethra). White blood cells rush to the area and attempt to destroy the bacteria, but the bacteria soon win the battle. In most cases, symptoms appear three to five days after infection, although they may appear as early as the first day or as late as two weeks after infection. Initially a thin, clear mucous discharge seeps out of the meatus (the opening at the tip of the penis). Within a day or so it becomes thick and creamy and may be white, yellowish, or yellow-green. This is often referred to as a "purulent" (puslike) discharge. The area around the meatus may become swollen. There is a burning sensation when urinating, and the urine may contain pus or blood. In some cases, the lymph glands of the groin become enlarged and tender.

Because the early symptoms of gonorrhea in the male are painful and obvious, most men seek treatment immediately and are cured. If the disease is not treated, however, the urethritis spreads up the urethra, causing inflammations in the prostate (prostatitis), seminal vesicles (seminal vesiculitis), urinary bladder (cystitis), and epididymis (epididymitis). Pain on urination becomes worse and is felt in the whole penis. Then these early symptoms may disappear as the disease spreads to the other organs. If the epididymitis is left untreated, it may spread to both testicles, and the resulting scar tissue may cause sterility.

---

[1] These statistics are even more remarkable when one realizes that gonorrhea is not all that contagious. The chances of catching it from one act of intercourse with an infected partner are only about 1 in 20 (Fulton, 1974); that is, you do not always get it. Thus an even greater number of people were exposed to it, but some were lucky and did not contract it. (I debated for a long time over whether to mention that statistic. I fear it will create an "it can't happen to me" attitude. But don't count on it. And remember that the more times you have intercourse with an infected partner, the greater your chances of getting the disease on one of those occasions. Also remember that certain conditions, like taking birth control pills, increase your susceptibility.)

Asymptomatic gonorrhea (gonorrhea with no symptoms) does occur in males, but it is fairly rare (Hansfield et al., 1974).

About 80 percent of women infected with gonorrhea are asymptomatic during the early stages of the disease (this is one of Nature's little sexisms, since it means that women are less likely to get treatment). Many women have no way of knowing that they are infected unless they are told by a male partner. Therefore, it is extremely important for any male who is infected to inform all his contacts.

The gonorrheal infection in the woman invades the cervix. Pus is discharged, but the amount may be so slight that it is not noticed. When present, it is yellow-green and irritating to the vulva, but it is generally not heavy (it is not to be confused with normal cervical mucus, which is clear or white and nonirritating, or with discharges resulting from the various kinds of vaginitis—see below—which are irritating but white). Although the cervix is the primary site of infection, the inflammation may also spread to the urethra, causing burning pain on urination (not to be confused with cystitis—see below).

If the infection is not treated, the Bartholin glands may become infected and, in rare cases, swell and produce pus. The infection may also be spread to the anus and rectum, either by a heavy cervical discharge or by the menstrual discharge.

Because so many women are asymptomatic in the early stages of gonorrhea, many receive no treatment, and thus there is a high risk of serious complications. In about 50 percent of women who go untreated for 8 to 10 weeks, the gonococcus moves up into the uterus, often during the menstrual period. From there it infects the fallopian tubes, causing *salpingitis*.[2] The tissues become swollen and inflamed, and thus the condition is also called *pelvic inflammatory disease* (PID—although PID can be caused by diseases other than gonorrhea). The major symptom is pelvic pain and, in some cases, irregular or painful menstruation. If the salpingitis is not treated, scar tissue may form, blocking the tubes and leaving the woman sterile. Indeed, untreated gonorrhea is one of the commonest causes of sterility in women. If the tubes are partially blocked, so that sperm can get up them but eggs cannot move down, ectopic pregnancy can result, since the fertilized egg is trapped in the tube.

Rarely, in both males and females, the gonococcus may enter the bloodstream and travel to the joints, causing *gonococcal arthritis*, or to the heart valve.

There are three other major sites for non-genital gonorrhea infection: the mouth and throat, the anus and rectum, and the eyes. If fellatio is performed on an infected person, the gonococcus may invade the throat, causing gonococcal pharyngitis and tonsillitis (cunnilingus is unlikely to spread gonorrhea, and mouth-to-mouth kissing never does). Such an infection is often asymptomatic; the typical symptom, if there is one, is a sore throat. Rectal gonorrhea is contracted through anal intercourse, and thus affects both women in heterosexual relations and, more commonly, men in homosexual relations. Symptoms include some discharge from the rectum and itching, but many cases are asymptomatic. Gonorrhea may also invade the eyes. This occurs only rarely in adults, when they touch the genitals and then transfer the bacteria-containing pus to their eyes by touching them. This eye infection is much more common in newborn infants (*gonococcal ophthalmia neonatorum*). The infection is transferred from the mother's cervix to the infant's eyes during birth. For this reason, most states require that silver nitrate, or penicillin or some other antibiotic, be put in every newborn's eyes to prevent any such infection. If left untreated, the eyes become swollen and painful within a few days, there is a discharge of pus, and the eyes are destroyed within a few more days.

---

[2] "Salpinx" is another name for the fallopian tubes.

Diagnosis

In males, the physician can generally make a "clinical diagnosis" by inspecting the genitals and the discharge; absolute confirmation, however, must be based on a laboratory analysis of the discharge. A sample is obtained by inserting a cotton-tipped swab about $1/2$ inch up the urethra (this causes some pain, but it is not severe).

The simplest laboratory test of the discharge is performed by wiping the coated swab across a microscope slide. The slide is then treated with Gram stain, and the gonococcus should show up, stained by the dye. Unfortunately, this test is somewhat inaccurate in men and highly inaccurate in women. The alternative is a somewhat more complex, time-consuming test, in which the bacteria are grown ("cultured") by wiping the swab onto a medium on a culture plate. After 24 to 48 hours, under appropriate conditions, the bacteria have multiplied so that the colonies are visible to the naked eye as grayish dots. These bacteria are then given the Gram stain and subjected to two other chemical tests to determine whether they are the gonococcus.

If gonorrhea is suspected in the throat, a swab should be taken and cultured using the same technique. Male homosexuals who suspect that they may have rectal gonorrhea should request that a swab be taken from the rectum, since most physicians will not automatically think to do this.

The penis and testes should also be examined for signs of swelling and soreness.

In females, the vulva is first inspected for inflammations. Then a speculum is inserted into the vagina, and a sample of the cervical discharge is obtained by inserting a cotton-tipped swab about 1 inch into the cervix, a procedure that may be uncomfortable but is usually painless. This discharge is then cultured as described above. A pelvic examination should also be performed. Pain during this exam may indicate salpingitis. Women who suspect throat or rectal infection should request that samples be taken from those sites as well.

Treatment for gonorrhea should not be started until these tests have been performed.

At the present time there is no good blood test for gonorrhea available, as there is for syphilis. This is unfortunate since a blood test would permit routine diagnosis, especially in asymptomatic cases and in pregnant women.

Treatment

The treatment of choice is a large dose of penicillin (procaine penicillin G) administered by a shot in the buttocks. In the early stages, a large dose consists of two doses of 2.4 million units each.[3] This large dose is essential to ensure that all the bacteria are killed so that penicillin-resistant strains will not develop. This treatment is extremely effective. If complications are present, penicillin is still the treatment of choice, although the dose may have to be larger. The recommended dose will also cure syphilis if it is present.

For people who are allergic to penicillin, the treatment of choice is tetracycline taken orally; however, tetracycline should not be given to pregnant women.

Routine dosing with penicillin in the absence of a diagnosis of gonorrhea is unwise since it may contribute to the development of resistant strains and to allergic reactions in the individual.

SYPHILIS

There has been considerable debate over the exact origins of syphilis. The traditional theory has been the "Columbian theory," which states that syphilis was brought back to Europe by Columbus and his crew after their first voyage to

---

[3]This dose is 8 to 10 times larger than the dose required 20 years ago. Some physicians are expressing concern that the buttocks may not be able to accept the dosages required in the future.

FIGURE 19.2

Treponema pallidum, the spiral-shaped organism that causes syphilis. *[Center for Disease Control, Atlanta.]*

way home, spread the disease throughout Europe. The disease, called "The Great Pox," became a pandemic by 1500. It was further spread to India, China, and Japan by sailors.

An alternative theory concerning the origin of syphilis is the "pre-Columbian" or "evolutionary" theory (Hackett, 1963; Rosebury, 1971). According to this theory, syphilis is not a disease itself, but one form of the disease treponematosis, the other forms being yaws, endemic syphilis, and pinta. All are caused by the same organism (see below), but the disease takes on different forms as it evolves with humans in different environments and societies. According to this theory, yaws was present from the time of the evolution of the first humans in tropical Africa. Indeed, a disease resembling yaws can still be found in African monkeys and apes. Yaws is a childhood disease affecting the skin, and it is spread by skin contact. It is still common in some tropical areas.

As humans migrated to the cooler, drier parts of North Africa and Asia, the skin became less cozily moist. Then the treponemata organism, which is actually rather delicate, retreated to the remaining moist areas of the body—the underarms, mouth, nostrils, crotch, and anus—and endemic syphilis developed. Later, the organism retreated again, this time to the safe, moist areas of the genitals and rectum. Transmission then was by sexual intercourse.

There is some evidence in support of each of these theories (Catterall, 1974). In support of the Columbian theory, syphilis damage has been found in the bones of Indians from the pre-Columbian period in the Americas, while no similar damage has been found in the bones of Egyptians before that time (although this point has been disputed—Rosebury, 1971). Further, the disease is not described in the writings of Europeans before the time of Columbus. Supporters of the evolutionary theory point to the fact that the organisms causing yaws and syphilis are indistinguishable.

Whatever the precise origin of the disease,

the West Indies in 1493. In 1495, King Charles VIII of France besieged the city of Naples, which was defended by mercenaries, many of them from the port cities of Spain. The armies were struck by a strange new disease, which soon ended the fighting. The French army, on its

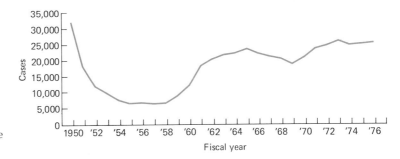

FIGURE 19.3

Reported cases of syphilis in the United States, 1950 to 1976.

its naming seems to have been a good example of "it wasn't my fault." The French called it "the Naples disease." In Naples it was called "the French disease." And in England it was called "the Spanish disease." (Although one person commented profoundly that it was really "the disease of him who has it.") It received the name we use today in 1530, when an Italian physician, Fracastoro, wrote a poem about a shepherd boy named Syphilis who was afflicted with the French disease as punishment for violating the will of the sun god. The poem was widely read, and the name stuck.

For the next few centuries there was considerable confusion about venereal diseases. It was thought that gonorrhea and syphilis were a single disease. In a famous bit of experimentation, John Hunter (1728–1793) attempted to differentiate between the two by inoculating himself with some pus from a patient suffering from gonorrhea. Unfortunately, the patient also had syphilis, and so Hunter developed symptoms of both diseases. Thus the experiment caused further confusion, not to mention Hunter's death.

In 1837 the two diseases were finally distinguished by Philip Ricord.

The organism causing syphilis was identified by the German scientists Shauddin and Hoffman in 1905. The bacterium they identified is called *Treponema pallidum* (*T. pallidum*, if you want to be on cozy terms with it). It is spiral-shaped and is thus often called a *spirochete* (see Figure 19.2). In 1906, Wasserman,

Neisser, and Bruck described the test for diagnosing syphilis; this is now known as the *Wassermann test* or *Wassermann reaction*. This test has been replaced by more modern blood tests, but the "Wasserman" label hangs on.

The incidence of syphilis, unlike that of gonorrhea, has not increased dramatically in the last decades. Thus statements about the "VD epidemic" refer to gonorrhea, not syphilis. There were about 25,000 reported cases in 1971; allowing for failure to report, that might mean 100,000 actual cases (as compared with an estimated 2,500,000 cases of gonorrhea).[4] Nonetheless, syphilis ranks fourth among the commonest communicable diseases. And, while the disease is not nearly so common as gonorrhea, nor is it increasing in frequency, the effects of syphilis are much more serious than those of gonorrhea. In most cases, gonorrhea causes only discomfort and, sometimes, sterility; syphilis can kill.

Symptoms

The major early symptom of syphilis is the *chancre* (pronounced *shank'-er*). It is a round, ulcerlike lesion with a hard, raised edge, resembling a crater (Figures 19.4 and 19.5). One of the distinctive things about it is that, although it looks terrible, it is painless. The chancre ap-

---

[4]Syphilis is considerably more contagious than gonorrhea. The chances of catching it from a single act of intercourse with an affected partner are 1 in 2 (Fulton, 1974).

FIGURE 19.4

A chancre on the female labia, a symptom of primary-stage syphilis. *[Department of Public Health, The Commonwealth of Massachusetts.]*

pears about three to four weeks (as early as ten days or as late as three months) after intercourse with the infected person. The chancre appears at the point where the bacteria entered the body. Typically, the bacteria enter through the mucous membranes of the genitals as a result of intercourse with an infected person. Thus in men the chancre often appears on the glans or corona of the penis (Figure 19.5), or it may appear anywhere on the penis or scrotum. In women, the chancre often appears on the cervix, and thus the woman does not notice it and is unaware that she is infected (Nature's sexism

again; this may be a good reason for a woman to do the pelvic self-exam with a speculum described in Chapter 2). The chancre may also appear on the vaginal walls or, externally, on the vulva.

If oral intercourse or anal intercourse with an infected person occurred, the bacteria can also invade the mucous membranes of the mouth or rectum. Thus the chancre may appear on the lips, tongue, or tonsils or around the anus.

Finally, the bacteria may enter through a cut in the skin anywhere on the body. Thus it is possible (though this happens rarely) to get syphilis by touching the chancre of an infected person. The chancre would then appear on the hand at the point where the bacteria entered through the break in the skin.

The progress of the disease once the person has been infected is generally divided into four stages: primary-stage syphilis, secondary-stage syphilis, latent syphilis, and late (tertiary) syphilis. The phase described above, in which the chancre forms, is *primary-stage syphilis*. If left untreated, the chancre goes away by itself within one to five weeks after it appears. This marks the end of the primary stage. The important thing to remember is that the disease has not gone away just because the chancre has healed. The disease has only gone underground.

A week or two after the chancre has disappeared, the bacteria are well into the bloodstream and have circulated throughout the body. Beginning one to six months after the original appearance of the chancre, a generalized body rash develops, marking the beginning of *secondary-stage syphilis*. The rash is very variable in its appearance, the most distinctive feature being that it does not itch or hurt. It generally appears as raised bumps on various parts of the body. When the rash appears on the palms of the hands or the soles of the feet, it is a particularly distinctive symptom of syphilis. On white skin the bumps are first cherry- or ham-colored and then become coppery or brown. On black skin the bumps are grayish blue. In the crotch area, the bumps may form large growths called *condylomata lata*. When these break, a thick fluid oozes out; this fluid is highly infectious because it contains many of the bacteria.

Hair loss may also occur during the secondary stage (a slang expression for syphilis is "haircut"). Other symptoms of secondary syphilis are a sore throat; headaches; loss of appetite; nausea; constipation; pain in the bones, muscles, or joints; and a low, persistent fever. For this reason, syphilis is sometimes called "the great imitator" since its symptoms in the secondary and later stages look like those of so many other diseases.

Usually the symptoms are troublesome enough that the person seeks medical help. With appropriate treatment in this stage, the disease can still be cured, and there will be no permanent effects.

Even without treatment, the secondary-stage symptoms go away in two to six weeks, leading people to believe mistakenly that the disease has gone away. Instead, it has entered a more dangerous stage.

After the symptoms of the secondary stage have disappeared, the disease is in the *latent stage*, which may last for years. While there are no symptoms in this stage, *T. pallidum* is busily burrowing into the tissues of the body, especially the blood vessels, central nervous system (brain and spinal cord), and bones. After the first year or so of the latent stage, the disease is no longer infectious, except that a pregnant woman can still pass it on to the fetus (see the section on congenital syphilis, below).

About half of the people who enter the latent stage remain in it permanently, living out the rest of their lives without further complications. The remaining half, however, move into the dangerous *late (tertiary-stage) syphilis*. There are three major kinds of late syphilis. In *benign late syphilis*, the skin, muscles, digestive

FIGURE 19.5

A chancre on the penis, a symptom of primary-stage syphilis. *[Department of Public Health, The Commonwealth of Massachusetts.]*

organs, liver, lungs, eyes, or endocrine glands may be affected. The characteristic effect is the formation of a *gumma*—a large, destructive ulcer—on the affected organ. With prompt treatment, the gumma can heal and the patient recovers completely. In *cardiovascular late syphilis* the heart and major blood vessels are attacked; this occurs 10 to 40 years after the initial infection. Cardiovascular syphilis can lead to death. In *neurosyphilis* the brain and spinal cord are attacked, leading to insanity and paralysis, which appear 10 to 20 years after infection. Neurosyphilis is usually fatal.

If a pregnant woman has syphilis, the fetus may be infected when the bacteria cross the placental barrier, and the child gets *congenital*

449

FIGURE 19.6
The famous artist Albrecht Durer did a self-portrait in which symptoms of syphilis seem to appear on the scrotum. *[The Bettman Archive, Inc.]*

(from birth) *syphilis*. If the woman is in the primary or secondary stage, the child is likely to die before or shortly after birth. If the woman is in the latent stage, the fetus either may not be infected or may develop syphilis, which is not immediately dangerous to its life. If the disease is diagnosed and treated before the fourth month of pregnancy, the fetus will not develop the disease. For this reason, a syphilis test is done as a routine part of the blood analysis in a pregnancy test.

Diagnosis

Syphilis is somewhat difficult to diagnose because, as noted above, its symptoms look like those of many other diseases.

The physical exam should include inspection not only of the genitals but also of the entire body surface. Women should have a pelvic exam so that the vagina and the cervix can be checked for sores. If the patient has had anal intercourse, a rectal exam should also be performed.

If a chancre is present, some of its fluid is taken and placed on a slide for inspection under a dark-field microscope. If the person has syphilis, *T. pallidum* should be present, with its characteristic shape (Figure 19.2).

The commonest tests for syphilis are the blood tests, which can be used either for individual diagnosis or for mass screening (as with everyone who obtains a marriage license). The VDRL (named for the Venereal Disease Research Laboratory of the U.S. Public Health Service, where the test was developed) is the most frequently used of these blood tests, all of which are based on antibody reactions. The VDRL is fairly accurate, cheap, and easy to perform. However, it has some limitations. It does not give accurate results until at least four to six weeks after the person has been infected. Even then, it correctly diagnoses only about 75 percent of the cases of primary syphilis; in the other 25 percent it gives a "false negative." It is completely accurate in detecting secondary syphilis. The VDRL also gives a "false positive" in the case of people who have recently had diseases like measles or chicken pox and in the case of drug addicts.

Treatment

The treatment of choice for syphilis is penicillin. *T. pallidum* is actually rather fragile, and so the large doses used in the treatment of gonorrhea are not necessary in the treatment of syphilis; however, the bacteria may survive for several days, and therefore a long-acting penicillin is used. The recommended dose is two shots of benzathine penicillin, of 1.2 million units each, one in each of the buttocks. Latent, late, and congenital syphilis require larger doses.

For those allergic to penicillin, tetracycline is the recommended treatment, but it should not be given to pregnant women.

Follow-up exams should be performed to make sure that the patient is completely cured.

OTHER DISEASES OF SEXUAL TRANSMISSION

Nonspecific Urethritis

Nonspecific urethritis (*NSU*; also called *nongonococcal urethritis,* or *NGU*) is any inflammation of the male's urethra that is not caused by a gonorrhea infection. The exact causes of nonspecific urethritis are not always known, and, indeed, it may not always be transmitted by sexual intercourse. It may be that the NSU is actually a group of infections caused by various organisms, the leading contenders being *Chlamydia* and T-strain mycoplasma. Allergic reactions may also be involved.

Although nonspecific urethritis is not yet widely diagnosed in the United States, it is clear from data from other countries, such as Great Britain, that its incidence is increasing even faster than that of gonorrhea. In England in 1971 there were about as many cases of NSU as of gonorrhea (Catterall, 1974). Thus when a man consults a physician because of a urethral discharge, his chances of having NSU are about as good as his chances of having gonorrhea. It is important that the correct diagnosis be made since NSU does not respond to penicillin treatment.

The main symptom is a thin, usually clear discharge. The other symptoms are generally similar to those of gonorrhea. Several differences make it possible to distinguish between the two. The NSU discharge is thin and clear or slightly white, while the gonorrhea discharge is thick and white. Pain on urination with NSU is mild, but it is severe with gonorrhea. Among the sexual partners of someone with gonorrhea, there should be at least one with gonorrhea, while partners of the person with NSU generally have no infection. If gonorrhea is present, of course, microscopic examination of the discharge should reveal the gonococcus.

The treatment of choice for nonspecific urethritis is tetracycline since, as noted above, the disease does not respond to penicillin. In some cases, the disease simply goes away by itself.

Chancroid

Chancroid (also called *soft chancre* or *ulcus molle*) is common in the tropics but is rare in the United States. It is caused by the bacterium *Hemophilus ducreyi.*

The major symptom is the appearance, one to five days after intercourse with an affected person, of small bumps in the genital region. They come to resemble a syphilis chancre, except that they are quite painful, and the surrounding rim is soft, not hard, as in syphilis. The symptoms appear more frequently in men, while women are likely to be "carriers."

Chancroid is somewhat difficult to diagnose because it may be confused with syphilis or lymphogranuloma venereum (discussed below). Laboratory examination is done of the pus from the sore.

Lymphogranuloma venereum

Lymphogranuloma venereum (LGV) is rare in the United States, but it is becoming more common as a result of being brought here by American soldiers returning from Vietnam. The organism that causes it is not well known, but it appears to be a virus that has some of the characteristics of bacteria.

LGV is a disease of the lymphatic system. The first symptom is the formation of a small, painless sore at the point of entry of the bacteria, which generally goes unnoticed. The obvious symptom is swelling and pain in the lymph glands of the groin. A painful swelling, the *bubo*, is formed. In women this may not occur, since the bacteria invade lymph glands deeper in the pelvis. Other symptoms include fever, chills, abdominal pains, loss of appetite, and joint pains; backache may be present in women.

If the disease is left untreated, complications may result, including damage to the rectum and swelling of genital organs called *elephantiasis*.

In diagnosis, LGV may be confused with syphilis, chancroid, and granuloma inguinale (see below). Positive diagnosis is made by means of a skin test and a blood test.

The treatment of choice is tetracycline; sulfa drugs are used when tetracycline cannot safely be administered. However, the disease is somewhat difficult to cure.

Granuloma Inguinale

Granuloma inguinale is also a disease found mainly in the tropics. It is caused by an organism called the *Donovan body*, which is thought to be a bacterium.

The symptom is a bump in the genital-groin-thigh region; it ulcerates and becomes larger.

Diagnosis is made by looking at a small piece of skin from the edge of the sore under a microscope. The presence of the Donovan body indicates granuloma inguinale.

The treatment of choice is tetracycline.

Venereal Warts

Venereal warts (*condylomata acuminata*) are warts that appear on the genitals. They are caused by a virus of the papillomavirus group, which is similar to the virus that causes common skin warts. The disease is believed to be transmitted by sexual intercourse.

Diagnosis can generally be made simply by inspecting the warts, since their appearance is distinctive. Treatment consists of painting on a solution of podophyllin in alcohol. The warts then dry up and fall off within a few days. If the warts are large, they must be removed surgically.

Herpes Genitalis

Herpes genitalis has received quite a bit of publicity recently because of its apparent link with cervical cancer in women. Herpes genitalis is a disease of the genital organs caused by the herpes simplex virus Type II. Herpes simplex Type I causes symptoms on other parts of the body: cold sores and fever blisters, for instance. It is thought that herpes genitalis is transmitted by sexual intercourse, although there are cases of people who have it but whose only sexual partner does not.

The symptoms are small, painful bumps or blisters on the genitals. In women, they are usually found on the vaginal lips; in men, they usually occur on the penis. They may be found around the anus if the person has had anal intercourse. The blisters burst and are extremely painful. Gradually they heal on their own. The virus continues to live in the body, however. It may remain dormant for the rest of the person's life, or the symptoms may recur unpredictably. The disease may also be transmitted from a pregnant woman to the fetus. Some children recover, but others develop a brain infection that rapidly leads to death.

Because it is fairly rare, herpes genitalis is often misdiagnosed as syphilis or chancroid. Actually, it has been estimated that 6 percent of the women and 3 percent of the men coming to VD clinics have herpes genitalis (Montreal Health Press, 1972). Another estimate is that there are 350,000 cases per year in the United States, making it more common than syphilis.

Unfortunately, there is not yet any known antibiotic that kills the virus. Treatments used now are mostly for the purposes of preventing infection in the open sores and minimizing their pain.

The major long-term risk associated with the disease is cervical cancer. Women who have been exposed to herpes genitalis should have a Pap smear every six months.

Pubic Lice

Pubic lice ("crabs") are tiny lice that attach themselves to the base of pubic hairs and there feed on blood from their human host. They are about the size of a pinhead and, under magnification, resemble a crab (see Figure 19.7). They live for about 30 days, but they die within 24 hours if they are taken off a human host. They lay eggs frequently, the eggs hatching in seven to nine days. Crabs are transmitted by sexual contact, but they may also be picked up from sheets, towels, sleeping bags, or toilet seats. (Yes, Virginia, there are some things you can get from toilet seats.)

The major symptom of pubic lice is an itching in the region of the pubic hair, although some people do not experience the itching.

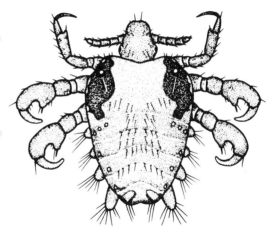

FIGURE 19.7
A pubic louse, enlarged.

Diagnosis is made by finding the lice or the eggs attached to the hairs.

Pubic lice are treated with the drug gamma benzene hexachloride, which is available as a cream, lotion, or shampoo under the brand name Kwell (Kwellada in Canada); it kills the lice. After treatment, the person should put on clean clothing. Since the lice die within 24 hours, it is not necessary to disinfect clothing that has not been used for over 24 hours.

PREVENTING VD

While most of the literature one reads concentrates on the rapid diagnosis and treatment of VD, prevention would be much better than cure, and there are some ways in which one can avoid getting VD, or at least reduce one's chances of getting it. The most obvious, of course, is abstaining from sexual activity. This would not be an acceptable strategy to many of you, but some of the following may be.

The condom, in addition to being a decent contraceptive, gives good protection against gonorrhea and some protection against syphilis. With increasing disillusionment over birth control pills and the rise of the VD epidemic, the condom may again become popular. Contraceptive foams, creams, and jellies (for example, Delfen foam, Emko foam, and Ortho cream) help to kill VD bacteria.

Some simple health precautions are also helpful. Successful prostitutes, who need to be careful about VD, take such precautions. Washing the genitals before intercourse helps remove bacteria. This may not sound like a romantic prelude to lovemaking, but prostitutes make a sensuous game out of soaping the man's genitals. You can do this as part of taking a shower or bath with your partner. The other important technique is inspecting your partner's genitals. If you see a chancre or a discharge, put on your clothes and leave (do not fall for the "it's only a pimple" routine). This technique may sound a little crude or embarrassing, but it seems to me that if you are intimate enough with someone to make love with that person, you ought to be intimate enough to look at her or his genitals. Once again, if you are cool about it, you can make this an erotic part of foreplay.

Urinating both before and after intercourse helps to keep bacteria out of the urethra.

Finally, each person needs to recognize that it is his or her social responsibility to get early diagnosis and treatment and not to have sex until the disease is cured. Probably the most important responsibility is that of informing prospective partners if one has VD and of informing past partners if one discovers that one has it. Because so many women are asymptomatic for gonorrhea, it is particularly important for men to take the responsibility for informing their female partners if they find that they have the disease.

OTHER INFLAMMATIONS

Vaginitis (vaginal inflammation or irritation) is very common among women and is endemic in college populations. Three kinds of vaginitis, as well as cystitis (inflammation of the urinary bladder), will be considered here. Strictly speaking, vaginitis is not a venereal disease because it is generally not transmitted by sexual contact; it is, however, a common inflammation of the sex organs.

Monilia

Monilia (also called *candida, yeast infection, fungus,* and *moniliasis*) is a form of vaginitis caused by the yeast fungus *Candida albicans. Candida* is normally present in the vagina, but if the delicate environmental balance there is disturbed (for example, if the pH is changed), the growth of *Candida* can get out of hand. Conditions that encourage the growth of *Candida albicans* include long-term use of birth control pills, menstruation, diabetes or a prediabetic condition, pregnancy, and long-term doses of antibiotics such as tetracycline. It is not a sexually transmitted disease, although intercourse may aggravate it.

The major symptom is a thick, white, curdlike vaginal discharge, found on the vaginal lips and the walls of the vagina. The discharge can cause extreme itching, to the point where the woman is not interested in having intercourse. Because monilia can be very uncomfortable, physicians need to take their patients' complaints about it seriously.

Treatment is by the drug nystatin (Mycostatin) in vaginal suppositories. The problem sometimes resists treatment, though. Women, especially those who have frequent bouts of monilia, may want to take some steps to prevent it (see Focus).

If a woman has monilia while she is pregnant, she can transmit it to her baby during birth. The baby gets the yeast in its digestive system, a condition known as *thrush.* Thrush can also result from oral-genital sex.

PREVENTING VAGINITIS

The following steps help to prevent vaginitis:

1 Wash the vulva carefully and dry it thoroughly.
2 Do *not* use feminine hygiene deodorant sprays. They are not necessary, and they can irritate the vagina (*Consumer Reports*, January 1972).
3 Wear cotton underpants. Nylon and other synthetics retain moisture, and vaginitis-producing organisms thrive on moisture.
4 Avoid wearing pants that are too tight in the crotch; they increase moisture and may irritate the vulva. Loose-fitting clothes are best since they permit air to circulate.
5 Keep down the amount of sugar and carbohydrates in your diet.
6 Wipe the anus from front to back so that bacteria from the anus do not get into the vagina. For the same reason, never go immediately from anal intercourse to vaginal intercourse. After anal intercourse, the penis must be washed before it is put into the vagina.
7 Douching with a mildly acidic solution (1 or 2 tablespoons of vinegar in a quart of water) can help to prevent vaginitis.

Trichomoniasis

Trichomoniasis ("trich") is caused by a single-celled organism, *Trichomonas vaginalis*; it has four strands protruding from it that whip back and forth, propelling it (see Figure 19.8).

Trichomoniasis can be passed back and forth from the man to the woman, and so it is technically a venereal disease (for this reason, it is important for the man as well as the woman to be treated), but it can also be transmitted by such means as toilet seats and washcloths.

The symptom is an abundant, frothy, white or yellow vaginal discharge which irritates the vulva and also has an unpleasant smell. There are usually no symptoms in the male.

It is extremely important that accurate diagnoses of the different forms of vaginitis be made, since the drugs used to treat them are

FIGURE 19.8

Trichomonas vaginalis, one of the organisms that causes vaginal inflammations.

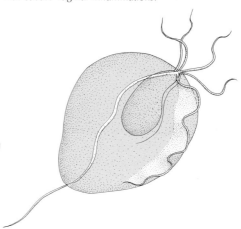

different and since the long-term effects of untreated trichomoniasis can be bad (see below). A drop of the vaginal discharge should be put on a slide and examined under a microscope. If the infection is trichomoniasis, then *Trichomonas vaginalis* should clearly be present. Cultures can also be grown.

The treatment of choice is metronidazole (Flagyl) taken orally, although Nader's health research group has raised some questions about its safety (see also *Medical Letter*, June 20, 1975). Vaginal suppositories such as Floraquin may also be helpful.

If left untreated for long periods of time, trichomoniasis may cause damage to the cells of the cervix, making them more susceptible to cancer.

Nonspecific Vaginitis

Nonspecific vaginitis occurs when there is a vaginal infection, with accompanying discharge, but no cause can be found. This diagnosis can be made only when microscopic examination of the discharge, as well as other laboratory tests, has eliminated all the other common causes of vaginitis (trichomoniasis, monilia, gonorrhea) as possibilities. Treatment is by sulfa creams or suppositories.

Cystitis

Cystitis is an infection of the urinary bladder that occurs almost exclusively in women. In most cases it is caused by the bacterium *Escherichia coli*. These bacteria are normally present in the body (in the intestine), and in some cases, for unknown reasons, they get into the urethra and the bladder. Sometimes frequent, vigorous sexual intercourse will irritate the urethral opening, permitting the bacteria to get in. For this reason, it used to be called "honeymoon cystitis," since many women got it on their honeymoons. But with the demise of the virgin bride and the "wedding night," the name no longer seems appropriate.

The symptoms are a desire to urinate every few minutes, with a burning pain on urination. The urine may be hazy or even tinged with red; this is caused by pus and blood from the infected bladder. There may also be backache. Diagnosis can usually be made simply on the basis of these symptoms. A urine sample should be taken and analyzed, though, to confirm that *E. coli* is the culprit.

Treatment is usually with a sulfa drug (such as Gantrisin) taken orally.[5] The drug may include a dye that helps relieve the burning sensation on urination, and the dye turns the urine bright orange-red. If the cause is a bacterium other than *E. coli*, ampicillin is typically prescribed.

If cystitis is left untreated (which it seldom is, since the symptoms are so unpleasant), the bacteria may get up to the kidneys, causing a kidney infection, which is dangerous.

To prevent cystitis or prevent recurring bouts of it, drink lots of water and urinate frequently. This will help flush any bacteria out of the bladder and urethra.

CANCER OF THE SEX ORGANS

Cancer, of course, is not a sexually transmitted disease, but it is a disease that can affect the sex organs.

Breast Cancer

Cancer of the breast is the most common form of cancer in women. It is rare, though not

---

[5]Sulfa drugs can be dangerous to black people. About 10 to 14 percent of American blacks have an inherited enzyme deficiency called *glucose-6-phosphate-dehydrogenase* (G6PD). Sulfa administered to such people can cause hemolytic anemia, which can cause death. A simple test can detect G6PD, and blacks should refuse to take sulfa drugs unless they have been tested and are sure that they do not have G6PD.

unheard of, in women under 25, and a woman's chances of developing breast cancer increase every year after that age. About 1 out of every 15 American women (7 percent) has breast cancer at some time in her life (Lanson, 1975). Every year, 32,000 women in this country die of breast cancer.

Diagnosis Because of the statistics cited above, it is extremely important for women to do a breast self-exam regularly (see Figure 19.9). The exam should be done once a month. For purposes of remembering to do it, one strategy might be to do it on the first day of the menstrual period. Unfortunately, the exam should not be done at that time because there tend to be natural lumps in the breast during the premenstrual and menstrual phases. Ideally, the exam should be done at about mid-cycle, around the time of ovulation. It is extremely important to do the self-exam once a month because the earlier breast cancer is detected, the better the chances of a complete recovery with proper treatment. Physicians say that the woman is the best detector of a lump in her breast because she can do the exam frequently and can become familiar with the feel of her own breasts, which makes her better able to detect lumps.

Unfortunately, psychological factors can interfere with this process. Many women do not do the self-exam because they are afraid they will find a lump; thus one can go undetected for a long time, making recovery less likely. Some other women do the self-exam but, when they discover a lump, become so frightened that they do nothing about it. First Lady Betty Ford did a great service to the women of the nation when, in 1974, she announced that a lump had been detected in her breast and that she would have surgery for it. In doing so, she brought the subject "out of the closet" so that it could be discussed. She also alerted millions of women (among them Happy Rockefeller) to the impor-

tance of doing the self-exam, probably saving many lives.

Perhaps knowing a bit more about the realities of breast lumps and the surgery that is performed when they are discovered will help dispel some of the fears surrounding the subject of breast cancer. There are three kinds of breast lumps: *cysts* (fluid-filled sacs, also called *fibrocystic disease* or *cystic mastitis*), *fibroadenomas*, and *malignant tumors*. The important thing to realize is that 80 percent of breast lumps are cysts or fibroadenomas and are benign, that is, not dangerous. Therefore, if you find a lump in your breast, the chances are fairly good that it is not malignant; of course, you cannot be sure of this until a doctor has made a diagnosis.

Once you have discovered a lump, you should see a doctor immediately. One of several diagnostic procedures may then be carried out. Until recently, surgery was routinely done to remove any lump. However, several preliminary diagnostic techniques are now in use that reduce the need for surgery. One is *needle aspiration*, in which a fine needle is inserted into the breast; if the lump is a cyst, the fluid in the cyst will be drained out. If the lump disappears after this procedure, then it was a cyst; the cyst is gone, and there is no need for further concern. If the lump remains, it must be either a fibroadenoma or a malignant tumor. Several other procedures can then be used to determine whether it is malignant: thermography, mammography, and xeroradiography. *Thermography* detects heat variations over the body. Because malignant cells multiply rapidly, they produce heat, which should show up on the thermograph. The advantage of this method is that it does not involve x-rays and the dangers they entail, but it also has a very high rate of "false positives" (telling a woman that a benign tumor is malignant or spotting lumps that do not exist). Basically, *mammography* involves taking an x-ray of the breast. *Xeroradiography* is a

THE BREAST SELF-EXAM

First stand in front of a mirror with your arms at your sides and inspect your breasts. Then inspect them with your arms raised above your head. Look for any difference in the size of the breasts, for any flattening or bulging, for a puckering of the skin, for a discharge from the nipple, or for a reddening or scaliness on the nipple.

Then lie down. As you examine each breast, have the arm on that side up and crooked around your head. Feel the breast gently with the flat part of the fingers on the opposite hand. Move your fingers in small circles, systematically covering the whole breast. Pay particular attention to the part between the nipple and the armpit, which is where most tumors occur.

Source: Boston Women's Health Book Collective. *Our bodies, ourselves.* New York: Simon & Schuster, 1976, p. 127.

refinement of this technique; there is less exposure to x-rays, the test is processed more efficiently, and there is a higher degree of accuracy. Both these x-ray techniques are highly accurate, although some errors are still made. Their major advantage, though, is that they are capable of detecting tumors that are so small that they cannot yet be felt; thus they can detect cancer in very early stages, making recovery more likely. For this reason, some experimental mass-screening programs, in which women were given yearly mammograms routinely, were begun a few years ago. In 1976, Dr. Lester Breslow of U.C.L.A. provided data suggesting that mammograms themselves may cause breast cancer (see also Breast Cancer, 1976). The question is: Which is more dangerous—having yearly mammography or not detecting breast cancer until a later stage? The National Cancer Institute has issued guidelines saying that routine mammography should not be performed on women aged 35 to 50 unless they are high-risk cases.

Most physicians feel that the only definitive way to differentiate between a fibroadenoma and a malignant tumor is to do an *excisional biopsy.* A small slit is made in the breast, and the lump is removed. A pathologist then examines it to determine whether it is cancerous. If it is simply a fibroadenoma, it has been removed, and there is no further need for concern.

Mastectomy Several forms of surgery may be performed when the lump is malignant (radiation therapy, chemotherapy, and hormone therapy may also be used). The most serious is *radical mastectomy,* in which the entire breast as well as the underlying muscle (pectoral muscle) and the lymph nodes are removed. Advocates of this procedure argue that, if the cancer has spread to the adjoining lymph nodes, the procedure ensures that all the affected tissue is removed. The disadvantage of the procedure is that there is difficulty in arm movement following the removal of the pectoral muscles. In *modified radical mastectomy* the

(a)

(b)

(c)

FIGURE 19.9

The breast self-exam. (a) *In the shower*: Examine your breasts during bath or shower; hands glide more easily over wet skin. Fingers flat, move gently over every part of each breast. Use right hand to examine left breast, left hand for right breast. Check for any lump, hard knot, or thickening. (b) *Before a mirror*: Inspect your breasts with arms at your sides. Next, raise your arms high overhead. Look for any changes in contour of each breast, a swelling, dimpling of skin, or changes in the nipple. Then rest palms on hips and press down firmly to flex your chest muscles. Left and right breasts will not exactly match—few women's breasts do. Regular inspection shows what is normal for you and will give you confidence in your examination. (c) *Lying down*: To examine your right breast, put a pillow or folded towel under your right shoulder. Place right hand behind your head—this distributes breast tissue more evenly on the chest. With left hand, fingers flat, press gently in small circular motions around an imaginary clock face. Begin at outermost top of your right breast for 12 o'clock, then move to 1 o'clock, and so on around the circle back to 12. A ridge of firm tissue in the lower curve of each breast is normal. Then move in an inch, toward the nipple. Keep circling to examine *every part of your breast* including nipple. This requires at least three more circles. Now slowly repeat the procedure on your left breast, with a pillow under your left shoulder and left hand behind your head. Notice how your breast structure feels. Finally squeeze the nipple of each breast gently between thumb and index finger. Any discharge, clear or bloody, should be reported to your doctor immediately. [*American Cancer Society, Inc.*]

FIGURE 19.10
Appearance of a breast reconstructed after mastectomy. [Randolph H. Guthrie, Jr., M.D.P.C.]

breast and lymph nodes, but not the muscles, are removed. In *simple mastectomy* only the breast (and possibly a few lymph nodes) is removed. In *partial mastectomy*, or *lumpectomy*, only the lump itself and a small bit of surrounding tissues are removed. The breast is thus preserved, and silicone-envelope implants can restore it to its original shape. Unfortunately, the available data do not provide definite evidence of whether the more radical procedures lead to a higher survival rate (Lanson, 1975). Further, surgeons disagree among themselves as to which procedure is best. Thus it is not possible at this time to provide definitive advice to women making a decision on their own surgery.

A lot more is involved in the subject of breast cancer and mastectomy than technical details about diagnosis and surgery, though. The psychological impact of a mastectomy can be enormous (Asken, 1975). Any surgery, of course, and especially an amputation, is a psychologically stressful experience. But mastectomy seems to be unusually stressful. Our culture is very breast-oriented. For a woman whose identity has been defined in terms of her beauty and voluptuous figure, mastectomy can

be perceived as a destruction of her womanhood and a blow to her sense of personal identity. Severe depressions as well as suicides following mastectomy have been reported (Ervin, 1973). The woman's sexuality may be affected; she may feel that no man would want her with such a disfigurement. She may begin to avoid sexual encounters. Further, her husband, if she is married, may not know how to deal with the situation, particularly if she is giving out forbidding signals; thus he may deal with her poorly, and she concludes that he is rejecting her, just as she knew he would. Thus it is extremely important for a mastectomy patient and her husband to have some form of counseling available to them. In many towns the American Cancer Society has organized support groups for mastectomy patients; these are composed of women who have themselves had mastectomies and who are willing to share their experiences and provide emotional support to mastectomy patients.

Unfortunately, no one yet knows what causes breast cancer. The likeliest candidate currently seems to be a particular virus. It is not clear, if a virus is the cause, how it is transmitted, but there is some evidence that it is transmitted from mother to infant during breast feeding (Lanson, 1975). This would help explain the fact that women whose mothers had breast cancer are themselves more likely to develop it than women whose mothers did not. A great deal of research is currently being focused on this problem.

Cancer of the Cervix

Cancer of the cervix is the second most common form of cancer in women; about 2 to 3 percent of all women develop it at some time in their lives. In the next 12 months, 9000 American women will die of cervical cancer, and another 25,000 new cases will be detected.

The exact causes of cervical cancer are unknown, but, as in the case of breast cancer, a virus is suspected. A number of pieces of data lead to this conclusion. First, there is the apparent connection between cervical cancer and the herpes simplex virus, noted earlier in this chapter. There also seems to be an association between heterosexual intercourse and cervical cancer; the greater the number of partners, the greater the chances of developing cervical cancer. Teenagers who start having intercourse very early seem especially susceptible (Rotkin, 1962, 1973), suggesting that the virus may be spread by intercourse. Cervical cancer is unknown among nuns, and it is rare among other celibate women and among lesbians (F. Gagnon, 1950; Towne, 1955).

If detected in the early stages, cervical cancer is quite curable. Fortunately, there is a good, routine test to detect it, the *Pap test*, which is highly accurate and can detect the cancer long before the woman feels any pain from it. Every woman over the age of 20 should have one done annually. The procedure itself is simple and painless. The woman lies on the examining table with her feet in metal "stirrups." A speculum is inserted into her vagina, and then a sample of the cervical mucus is obtained on a cotton swab. It is smeared on a

slide, stained, and inspected under a microscope for signs of any abnormal cells. The results of the test may be either negative (Class 1—normal) or positive (Classes 2 through 5—some sign of abnormality). It is important to know that a positive result does not necessarily mean cancer. Class 2 results generally indicate some sort of infection. Class 3 and 4 results indicate the need for further testing, and Class 5 results indicate a malignancy. Given Class 3, 4, or 5 results, positive confirmation of malignancy should be done by taking a biopsy (surgical removal of a small piece of cervical tissue, which is then examined under a microscope).

If cervical cancer is confirmed, the treatment is usually a complete *hysterectomy*, which involves the surgical removal of the entire uterus and cervix (although in some cases, less radical procedures may be possible). The side effects of hysterectomy are minimal, except, of course, for the risks associated with any major surgery. A hysterectomy does not leave the woman "masculinized," with a beard growing and a deep voice developing, because hormone production is not affected; recall that it is the ovaries that manufacture hormones, and they are not removed (except in rare cases where there is evidence that the cancer has spread to them).

Other cancers of the female sexual-reproductive organs include uterine (endometrial) cancer, ovarian cancer, and cancer of the vulva, vagina, and fallopian tubes, but these are all rare in comparison with cervical cancer.

Cancer of the Prostate

Cancer of the prostate is the most common form of cancer in men. It is not, however, a major cause of death because it generally affects old men (25 percent of men over 90 have prostate cancer) and because most of the tumors are small and spread only very slowly.

Early symptoms of prostate cancer are frequent urination (especially at night), difficulty in urination, and difficulty emptying the bladder (these are also symptoms of benign prostate enlargement). These symptoms result from the pressure of the prostate growth on the urethra. In the early stages, there may be frequent erections and an increase in sex drive; however, as the disease progresses, there are often problems with sexual functioning.

Preliminary diagnosis of prostate cancer is by a rectal examination, which is simple and causes no more than minimal discomfort. The physician (wearing a lubricated glove) simply inserts one finger into the rectum and palpates (feels) the prostate. All men over 50 should have a rectal exam at least once a year. If the rectal exam provides evidence of a tumor, further laboratory tests can be made as confirmation.

Treatment is generally by hormone therapy. Surgical castration (surgical removal of the testes, which also removes the source of testosterone) is often part of the treatment and appears to halt the disease. Administration of estrogen also seems to be helpful, although it may induce feminine breast development, erectile dysfunction, and loss of sex drive. The prostate itself may also be removed surgically (*prostatectomy*). Because the pituitary controls hormone output, another treatment involves surgical removal of the pituitary (*hypophysectomy*).

Cancer of the penis is another cancer of the male sexual-reproductive system, but it is rare compared with prostate cancer. It seems to be much more common among uncircumcised than among circumcised men, suggesting that the accumulation of smegma under the foreskin may be related to its cause. Treatment may consist of surgery or radiation therapy.

SUMMARY

VD is at epidemic levels in the United States, and it is estimated that 50 percent of young people today will contract gonorrhea or syphilis by the time they are 25.

Gonorrhea is by far the commonest of the sexually transmitted diseases. The primary symptoms in the male, appearing three to five days after infection, are a white or yellow discharge from the penis and a burning pain on urination. About 80 percent of all women with gonorrhea are asymptomatic. Gonorrhea is caused by a bacterium, the gonococcus; it is treated quite successfully with a large injection of penicillin. If left untreated, it may lead to sterility.

Syphilis is caused by the bacterium *Treponema pallidum*. The first symptom is a chancre, which appears three to four weeks after infection, generally on the sexual organs. The chancre is painless and ulcerlike, with a round, hard rim. Many women do not notice this symptom since the chancre often appears on the cervix. Diagnosis is made through a blood test. Treatment with penicillin is very successful. If left untreated, the disease progresses past this primary stage to the secondary stage, the main symptom of which is a generalized rash of bumps all over the body. Left untreated, the disease enters the latent stage; however, it may reappear as late-stage syphilis, in which various body organs—including the heart, blood vessels, and nervous system—are attacked, leading to death. Congenital syphilis results when the disease is transmitted to the fetus by an infected mother.

Other "minor" venereal diseases include nonspecific (nongonococcal) urethritis in the male, chancroid, lymphogranuloma venereum, granuloma inguinale, and venereal warts. There is some evidence that herpes genitalis is spread through sexual contact. Pubic lice are tiny lice that infect the pubic hair; they are spread through sexual contact.

Techniques for preventing VD include thorough washing of both partners' genitals before intercourse, urination both before and after intercourse, inspecting the partner's genitals for symptoms like a chancre or urethral discharge, and the use of a condom or contraceptive foam or cream.

Three types of vaginitis (vaginal inflammation), all of which lead to irritating vaginal discharges, are monilia, trichomoniasis, and nonspecific vaginitis. Cystitis is an infection of the urinary bladder in women, leading to frequent, burning urination.

Breast cancer is the commonest form of cancer in women. Most breast lumps are not cancerous, but are instead either cysts or fibroadenomas. The usual treatment for those that are cancerous is some form of mastectomy.

Cancer of the cervix is also fairly common in women. It is extremely important for all adult women to have yearly Pap tests; early detection is the key to cure. If a malignancy is found, the usual treatment is hysterectomy.

Cancer of the prostate is the commonest form of cancer in men, although it spreads very slowly. Symptoms are a frequent need to urinate and difficulty in urination. Hormone therapy is the usual treatment.

SUGGESTIONS FOR FURTHER READING

Boston Women's Health Book Collective. *Our bodies, ourselves.* New York: Simon & Schuster, 1976. Mentioned in previous chapters, this book contains a much more detailed discussion of breast cancer and cervical cancer than space permitted here. One of the things I noted while doing my research, though, is that while there are many excellent books like this for women (a result of the feminist movement), there are no comparable books for men dealing with their health problems. We need some.

Kushner, Rose. *Breast cancer: A personal history and an investigative report.* New York: Harcourt Brace Jovanovich, 1975. The author tells of her own experiences with breast cancer and surgery and reviews the important issues surrounding breast cancer and its treatment.

Montreal Health Press. *VD handbook.* Montreal: MHP, 1972. One of the best and most thorough discussions of VD available for the lay person. It is available from the same address listed for *Birth Control Handbook* at the end of Chapter 6.

Rosebury, T. *Microbes and morals.* New York: Viking Press, 1971. A fascinating (really!) discussion of VD. The author is a physician who also happens to be an excellent writer.

ETHICS,
RELIGION,
AND SEXUALITY

CITED

Let us say with all possible emphasis that human sexuality is a very good thing. It is part of man's nature, very central to his personality in the making. It is part of God's creation, a creation which the myth in Genesis tells us God found to be "very good." It is tied in with and expressive of the urgent desire to love, which is deepest and highest in the universe.*

† A college student is very much in love with her boyfriend and wonders whether they ought to begin sleeping together. A corporation executive hears rumors that one of his employees is a homosexual, and he tries to decide what to do about it. A clergyman is asked to counsel a man and wife, one of whom is involved in an affair. A Presidential candidate is confronted by a Right-to-Life group demanding that he support a constitutional amendment to ban abortion. All these people are facing the need to make decisions which involve sexuality, and they find that issues of values and principles make the decisions difficult. The two principal conceptual frameworks for dealing with questions of value are religion and ethics, which are therefore the topics of this chapter.

There are two concerns that give force to our consideration of the religious and ethical aspects of human sexuality. First, there is the scientific concern to describe observable sexual phenomena. Since religion and ethics are important influences on people's behaviors, espe-

cially in matters of sex, one cannot fully appreciate why people do what they do without looking at these influences. Second, there is also a personal side to this coin. We are all ethical decision makers; we all have a personal system of values. Each of us must make decisions with respect to our own sexuality. Therefore, we would do well to consider how such decisions are made.

An ethical system is a priority of values, a way of deciding what is most important to us, particularly when there is a conflict between things we value or desire highly. Sexual gratification may be an important value for one person, and something to be avoided for another. However, regardless of the importance we attach to sex, we need a way of integrating our sexuality into our patterns of decision making. To do this we use such categories as "right or wrong," "good or bad," "appropriate or inappropriate," and "moral or immoral." These are the kinds of distinctions made in the field of ethics; since we use them every day, we are all practical ethicists.

Religion enters the picture as a source and creator of values, attitudes, and ethics. For believers, religion sets forth an ethical code and provides sanctions (rewards and punishments)

Source: Norman Pittenger. *Making sexuality human*. Philadelphia: Pilgrim Press, 1970, pp. 76–77.
†This chapter was contributed by Clark Hyde, M.A., M. Div., an Episcopal priest.

that motivate them to obey the rules. When a particular religion is practiced by many people in a society, it helps create culture, which then influences even those who do not accept the religion. Therefore, it is important to study the relationship of religion to sexuality for two reasons. First, it is a powerful influence on the sexual attitudes of many individuals. And second, as a creator of culture, it often forms a whole society's orientation toward human sexuality.

Let us begin by defining some terms that will be useful in discussing ethics, religion, and sexuality. *Hedonism* and *asceticism* have to do with one's approach to the physical and material aspects of life in general and to sexuality in particular. The word "hedonism" comes from the Greek word meaning "pleasure" and may be used to refer to the belief that the ultimate goal of human life is the pursuit of pleasure, the avoidance of pain, and the fulfillment of physical needs and desires: "Eat, drink, and be merry, for tomorrow we die." Asceticism, in contrast, holds that there is more to life than its material aspects, which must be transcended to achieve true humanity. Ascetics are likely to view sexuality as neutral at best and evil at worst; they will prize self-discipline, the avoidance of physical gratification, and the cultivation of spiritual values. Orders of monks, found in Eastern religions as well as Christianity, are good examples of institutionalized asceticism, with their affirmation of celibacy, virginity, poverty, and so on.

Two other terms, *legalism* and *situationism*, refer to methods of ethical decision making. As an approach to ethics, legalism concentrates on following some sort of law which comes from a source outside the individual, such as nature or religion. Legalistic ethics sets forth a series of rules and regulations—"Do this" and "Don't do that"—and calls for persons to behave according to them. In today's ethical theory, the term "situationism" is usual-

ly used to refer to the opposite tendency (the word derives from the title of Joseph Fletcher's book *Situation Ethics*—see Focus). Situationists would contend that although there may be broad general guidelines for ethical behavior, essentially each ethical decision should be made according to the individual persons and situations involved. Whereas legalism deals in universal laws, situationism decides matters on a case-by-case basis, informed by certain guiding principles, such as love. Classical religious ethical systems—Old Testament Judaism, Roman Catholicism, and Protestant fundamentalism—have tended to be quite legalistic. However, today situationism has become more popular, and this factor has helped create a real ferment in religious ethics, which will be examined later.

Of course, few ethical systems are purely hedonistic or ascetic or entirely legalistic or situationist; most lie between these extremes. However, the terms are useful in pointing to tendencies and will be used for that purpose in this chapter. The concluding section will try to put them into perspective and offer some critique of their strengths and weaknesses as approaches to sexual ethics.

SEXUALITY IN GREAT ETHICAL TRADITIONS

With these ways of looking at ethics, especially sexual ethics, as background, let us examine certain great ethical traditions to see how they deal with norms for sexual behavior. Although some attention will be given to non-Western sexual ethics, the thrust of this section will be on ethical traditions of Western culture, primarily because this is a text for American undergraduates, who are part of that culture. We are understandably interested in *our* story, in the world of ideals and practice in which *we* live. That culture can, at the risk of oversimplification, be seen as originating in the confrontation

JOSEPH FLETCHER AND SITUATION ETHICS

Any discussion of situation ethics, which is sometimes called the "New Morality," must deal with the figure of Joseph Fletcher, not because he invented the approach, but because he articulated it with great style and clarity. In this sense, Fletcher has become a symbol of an approach and has received much undeserved criticism from those who have not read him but who think they know what he stands for.

When he was professor of Christian ethics at the Episcopal Theological School in Cambridge, Massachusetts, Fletcher wrote *Situation Ethics*, published in 1966. Describing his approach and proposing some cases for thought and discussion, he wrote:

> In this moral strategy the governing consideration is the situation, with all of its contingencies and exigencies. The situationist enters into every decision-making situation armed with principles, just as the legalist does. But the all-important difference is that his moral principles are *maxims* of general or frequent validity; their validity always depends upon the situation. The situationist is prepared in any concrete case to suspend, ignore, or violate any principle if by doing so he can effect more good than by following it. (pp. 31–34)

Since Fletcher consciously writes against legalism as a valid approach to ethics, his concepts help define a continuum with legalism. Writing in a Christian context, Fletcher makes his guiding imperative love, that is, a firm intent to do good to others. This can be seen in the Six Ethical Propositions of his 1967 work, *Moral Responsibility*:

1 Only one thing is intrinsically good, namely, love: nothing else.
2 The ultimate norm of Christian decisions is love: nothing else.
3 Love and justice are the same thing, for justice is love distributed.
4 Love wills the neighbor's good whether we like him or not.
5 Only the end justifies the means; nothing else.
6 Decisions ought to be made situationally, not prescriptively. (pp. 14–25)

Although Fletcher's principles are explicitly Christian, it would be possible to formulate a nonreligious situational ethics. Joseph Fletcher, his critics, and his supporters have carried on a vigorous debate for the last decade which makes the field of ethics extremely interesting, if a bit confusing.

of Greek culture, preserved and developed by the Romans, and Jewish tradition, extended by Christianity in the first three centuries. From that point on, until rather recently, Western culture was Christian, at least officially. Even self-conscious revolts against Christian culture in the West are part of that tradition because of their roots.

Classical Greek Philosophy

During the Golden Age of Greek culture, covering roughly the fifth and fourth centuries B.C., philosophers such as Socrates, Plato, and Aristotle pondered most of the great ethical questions that have continued to interest Western intellectuals. These Athenians regarded the beautiful-and-good as the chief goal of life, and they admired the figure of the warrior-intellectual, who embodied the virtues of wisdom, courage, temperance, justice, and piety.

While nothing in Greek culture rejected sex as evil—the gods and goddesses of Greek mythology are often pictured enjoying it—the great philosophers did develop a kind of asceticism that assumed an important place in Western thought. They thought that virtue resulted from wisdom, and they believed that people would do right if they could, failing to live morally only through ignorance. To achieve wisdom and cultivate virtue, violent passions must be avoided, and these might well include sex. Plato believed that love (eros) led toward immortality and was therefore a good thing. However, since this kind of love was rather intellectual and more like friendship than vigorous sexuality, the term "platonic love" has come to mean sexless affection. There was also, among the warrior class, a certain approval of pederasty, that is, a sexual relationship between an older man and a younger one. However, the practice was far from universal and was frequently ridiculed (Brinton, 1959).

Later, Greek philosophy became even more ascetic than in the Golden Age. Epicurus

(341–270 B.C.) taught that the goal of life was *ataraxia*, a tranquil state between pleasure and pain in which the mind is unaffected by emotion. The Stoics of the same period valued detachment from worldly anxieties and pleasures and, indeed, a total indifference to either life or death. Sex was seen not necessarily as evil but as less important than wisdom and virtue, something to be transcended to achieve the beautiful-and-good.

Judaism and the Old Testament

The basic source for the Judeo-Christian tradition, which is the religious foundation of Western culture, is the Old Testament of the Bible, which is the basis for Judaism and a major source for Christianity as well. Written between approximately 800 and 200 B.C., the Old Testament is the national literature of the Jewish people and has a great deal to say about the place of sexuality in human life and society. However, sexuality and all aspects of life are always seen in religious terms.

To begin, the Old Testament view of sexuality is fundamentally positive. In the Genesis myth of creation we read, "So God created man in his own image, in the image of God he created him; male and female he created them" (Genesis 1:27). Human sexual differentiation is not an afterthought or an aberration; it is part and parcel of creation, which God calls "good." Judaism sees sexuality as a gift to be used responsibly and in obedience to God's will, never as something evil in itself. Looking at the Old Testament as a whole, we can find three themes in this view of sexuality.

First, sex is seen not as just another biological function but as a deep and intimate part of a *relationship* between two people. The very ancient story of Adam and Eve states that "a man leaves his father and cleaves to his wife and the two become one flesh" (Genesis 2:24). Frequently, biblical Hebrew uses the verb "to know" to mean sexual intercourse (as in "Adam

ETHICS, RELIGION, AND SEXUALITY

knew Eve and she conceived a child"). It also uses the word "knowledge," with this suggestion of deep intimacy, to describe the relationship between God and his people.[1] The use of sexual imagery in describing both marital and divine-human relationships testifies to the positive view of the Old Testament toward sex.

Second, in the Old Testament, sexuality could never be separated from its *social consequences*. Historically, Israel began as a small group of nomadic tribes fighting to stay alive in the near-desert of the Arabian peninsula. Sheer survival demanded that there be enough children, especially males, so that there would be enough herdsmen and warriors.[2] Thus, nonprocreative sex could not be allowed. Further, since the tribes were small and close-knit, sex had to be regulated to prevent jealousy over sexual partners, which could have divided and destroyed the group. It is not surprising, then, that so much of the Old Testament is concerned with laws for people living together in society and that these laws often include the regulation of sexual practices.

Finally, the Old Testament sees sexual behavior as an aspect of *national and religious loyalty*. Individual sexual morality significantly affected the moral and religious health of the whole people. This health was threatened when the Israelites settled in what is now the state of Israel, about 1200 to 1000 B.C.. Here, they came into contact with the Canaanites, the original inhabitants, and with their culture and religion. The Canaanites were farmers whose chief concern was the fertility of the land. Like the religions of many other ancient Near Eastern peoples, theirs was based on fertility and was acted out in sexual terms. They believed that Baal, the Sky Father, must mate with Asherah (Astarte or Ishtar), the Earth Mother, in order for the crops to grow. They sought to encourage this mating by ritual performance of the sexual act; thus temple prostitutes were very much a part of the Canaanite religion.

Pure Judaism was always under the threat of either apostasy (abandonment for the attractions of the fertility cult) or syncretism (the introduction of elements from other religions). Because of this threat, sexual misconduct was seen not only as an ethical lapse but also as a betrayal of one's nation and religion. Many sexual practices are forbidden by the Old Testament because they were found in Canaanite religion, which meant that they might lead to infidelity to the God of Israel.

It is my contention that the sexual regulations of the Old Testament need to be seen against this historical background. From the struggle for survival of Israel during the nomadic period, we see laws against illegitimacy and nonprocreative sex, as well as institutions such as polygamy (many wives) and concubinage (slaves kept for child-bearing purposes) designed to produce many children. From the confrontation with the fertility cult, Israel derived prohibitions against sexual laxity, nakedness, cultic prostitution, and other such typically Canaanite practices. Both themes are present in this passage from Leviticus 20:10–19:

> If a man commits adultery with his neighbor's wife, both adulterer and adulteress shall be put to death. The man who has intercourse with his father's wife has brought shame on his father. They shall both be put to death; their blood shall be on their own heads. . . . A man who has intercourse with any beast shall be put to death, and you shall kill the beast. . . . If a man takes his sister, his father's daughter or his mother's daughter, and they see one another naked, it is a scandalous disgrace. They shall be cut off in the presence of their people. . . . If a man lies with a woman during her monthly period and brings shame upon her, he has

---

[1]See, for example, Hosea, The Song of Solomon, and, in the New Testament, Revelation.

[2]Note that the heart of God's promise to the patriarch Abraham was descendants as numberless as the sand or the stars in the sky (Genesis 13:14–17, among many other places).

exposed her discharge and she has uncovered the source of her discharge; they shall both be cut off from their people.

Adultery and incest are threats to the peaceful life of the group. Not only is bestiality "unnatural," but it is also nonprocreative and may have been a feature of Canaanite religion. The menstral taboo is typical of many societies (see Chapter 4).

It should be noted that all societies have had laws regulating sex (Chapter 1) and that these laws, however exotic they may seem to us, made sense in their historical context and were, for the most part, remarkably humane for the time. The Old Testament is also marked by a great regard for married love, affection, and sexuality; this is in marked contrast to, for example, the Greek view of marriage as an institution for breeding and housekeeping. Old Testament Judaism is highly legalistic but not particularly ascetic in its high regard for responsible sexuality as a good and integral part of human life.

The New Testament and Christianity

As the discussion turns to Christianity, which grew in three centuries from an obscure Jewish sect to the dominant religion in the West, the complex conditions of the Mediterranean world between 100 B.C. and 100 A.D. must be noted. The world in which Christianity developed was one of tremendous ferment in the spheres of philosophy, religion, and morals. Although Stoicism remained popular among intellectuals, ordinary folk preferred various blends of mythology, superstition, and religion. Few people were much concerned with the pursuit of wisdom and virtue. There were many strange cults, often characterized by some sort of *dualism*. This was the notion that body and spirit were unalterably opposed to each other and that the goal of life was to become purely spiritual by

FIGURE 20.1

According to Jewish law, menstruation makes a woman unclean. The period of uncleanness must be ended by a ritual bath, or mikvah, as shown in this medieval woodcut. [Ploss and Bartles.]

transcending the physical and material side of life. Public morals were notably decadent, and even ethical pagans were shocked by a society in which people prized pleasure above all things, at least those who could afford it (Brinton, 1959).

Revulsion at the excesses of Roman life affected even Judaism, which became markedly

471

more dualistic and antisex by the time of Jesus' birth and the growth of his Church. That Church's ethical tradition is rooted in Old Testament Judaism and was given its direction by the teachings of Jesus, the writings of St. Paul, and the theology of the Fathers of early Christianity. From these beginnings, Christian ethics has evolved and developed over 2000 years in many and various ways. This makes oversimplification a real danger, and yet it is possible to speak in general terms of a Christian tradition of sexual ethics and morality.

Jesus   It would be very difficult to elaborate a sexual ethic from the teachings of Jesus, since he said almost nothing on the subject. Jesus urged his followers to strive for ethical perfection, and he spoke strongly against pride, hypocrisy, and self-righteousness. Toward humble and penitent sinners, including those whose sins were sexual, the Gospels show him to have been compassionate and understanding (see, for example, his dealings with "fallen women" in John 4:1–30, John 8:53–9:11, and Luke 7:36–50). His ethical teaching is strongly based in the tradition of the Old Testament prophets and includes sexual conduct as a part of a whole moral life of loving God and neighbor.

St. Paul   The task of applying the principles of Jesus in concrete situations fell to St. Paul, the first Christian theologian, whose letters form the earliest part of the New Testament. A complex personality, Paul was very much a child of his time and quite ambivalent in his attitude toward sexuality. Above all, he, along with the whole early Church, expected the *parousia* (Second Coming) of Christ and the end of the world to occur at any time. He therefore advocated celibacy, not necessarily because he was opposed to sex, but because, in a world that was about to end, the demands of marriage might prove a distraction from prayer, worship, and the proclamation of the Gospel. Like Jesus, Paul opposed all sexual expression outside marriage, and he had a number of harsh things to say about sexual immorality. However, he saw these in the larger context of humanity's total revolt against the will of God. He wrote a good deal, for example, about the "sins of the flesh," but by this he meant all aspects of fallen humanity, such as "immorality, impurity, sorcery, enmity, strife, jealousy, anger, selfishness, paltry spirit, envy, drunkenness, carousing, and the like" (Galatians 5:19–21). Later Christian theologians tended to understand the "sins of the flesh" primarily in sexual terms; thus, from Paul's writings, Christianity acquired a bias against sexuality which goes well beyond what Paul probably intended. Indeed, the New Testament, like the Old Testament, is ambivalent about sexuality.

The early Christian church   The "Fathers of the Church," who wrote roughly between 150 and 600 A.D., completed the basic theological shape of the Christian faith. During this time, Christian ethics became increasingly ascetic, partly as a result of its natural tendencies, partly as it assimilated dualistic tendencies from Greek philosophy, partly as a response to the decadence of Roman society, and partly because of the conversion of the Roman Emperor Constantine in 325. This last event ended nearly three centuries of persecution and moved most of the Mediterranean world into the Christian Church by 400. Suddenly part of the "establishment," the Church began to grow corrupt and worldly, and, for the first time, the lip-service believer entered the picture.

Serious Christians revolted against this situation by moving to the desert to become monks and hermits, to fast, to pray, and to practice all sorts of self-denial, including, of course, celibacy. From this point on, monasticism and the religious orders become a permanent reform movement within the Church, a vanguard of ascetics calling Christians to greater rigor. Their success can be seen in the twelfth-century requirement that all clergy in the West be celibate, a departure from early church practice.[3] The Fathers of the Church, almost all of whom were celibates, allowed that marriage was good and honorable but thought virginity to be a much superior state. The message could not have been lost on the laity: sexuality, even in marriage, was incompatible with true holiness.

St. Augustine The most notable of the Western Fathers was St. Augustine (354–430 A.D.), who had had a promiscuous youth and overreacted after his conversion to Christianity.[4] For Augustine, sexuality was a consequence of the Fall, and every sexual act was tainted by concupiscence (from the Latin word *concupisencia*, meaning "lust" or "evil desire of the flesh"). Even sex in marriage was sinful, and in *The City of God* he wrote that "children could not have been begotten in any other way than they know them to be begotten now, i.e. by lust, at which even honorable marriage blushes" (1950 ed., Article 21). The stature of Augustine meant that this negative view of sexuality was perpetuated in subsequent Catholic theology.

St. Thomas Aquinas During the Middle Ages, these basic principles continued to be elaborated and extended. The most important figure of the period, and even today the basic source of Catholic moral theology, was St. Thomas Aquinas (1225–1274). His great achievement was to synthesize Christian theology with Aristotelian philosophy in such a way as to answer virtually

FIGURE 20.2

The Virgin Mary. During the Middle Ages, a great devotion to the mother of Jesus developed, emphasizing her perpetual virginity, purity, and freedom from all sin. Thus the great female figure of Christianity was perceived as almost entirely sexless. [*Allinari/Scala.*]

any question a Christian might ask on any topic. Thomas combined reason with divine revelation to arrive at the moral law of the universe, which, as God's intention for creation, is to be obeyed as His will. For example, Thomas believed that sex was obviously intended for procreation and that nonprocreative sex therefore violated the natural law and was sinful, being opposed to both human nature and the will of God.

In the *Summa Theologica*, Thomas devoted a chapter to various sorts of lust and their

---

[3]The First Epistle of Timothy, chap. 3, shows the clear expectation that clergy will be married and fathers.
[4]Byron once remarked that Augustine's youthful escapades, as reported in the *Confessions*, "make the reader envy his transgressions."

gravity, treating premarital intercourse (fornication), nocturnal emissions, seduction, rape, adultery, incest, and "unnatural vice," which included masturbation, bestiality, and homosexuality. He asked, "Is simple fornication a grave sin?"

> Beyond all doubt we should hold that simple fornication is a mortal sin. . . . To explain, a sin which directly attacks a requirement for human life is deadly. Now simple fornication is an inordinate act of a sort to injure life that may be formed from the intercourse. . . . Now it is evident that the bringing up of a human child requires the care of the mother who nurses him and much more the care of a father, under whose guidance and guardianship his earthly needs are supplied and his character developed. . . . Accordingly, since fornication or intercourse between people who are not committed to one another is outside marriage, which is for the good of the children, it is a mortal sin. (1968 ed., Second Part of the Second Part, Question 154, Article 2)

Thomas's theological supremacy ensured the triumph of natural law in Western Catholic ethics and has great consequences even today.

The Protestants   The Protestant Reformation in the sixteenth century destroyed the Christian unity of Europe and shook the theological foundations of the Catholic Church. However, in matters of sexual ethics there were only rather modest changes. The Protestant churches abandoned clerical celibacy, regarding it as unnatural and the source of many abuses, and placed a higher value on marriage and family life. However, Reformers feared illegitimacy and saw sexuality only in the confines of matrimony. Even then, they were often ambivalent. For example, Martin Luther, who was the founder of the Reformation and was happily married to a former nun, called marriage "a hospital for the sick" and saw its purpose as being to "aid human infirmity and prevent unchastity" (quoted in Thielicke, 1964, p. 136)—scarcely an enthusiastic approach.

A significant contribution of Reformation Protestantism to Christianity was a renewed emphasis on the individual conscience in matters such as the interpretation of the Bible and in ethical decision making. Such an emphasis on freedom and individual responsibility has led to the serious questioning of legalistic ethics and, in part, to today's ethical ferment.

The Reformation also gave rise to Puritanism, an English movement inspired by the French Reformer John Calvin (1509–1564). Calvin and the Puritans followed Augustine in emphasizing the doctrine of "original sin" and the "total depravity" of fallen humanity. This led them to use civil law to regulate human behavior in an attempt to suppress frivolity and immorality. As will be seen in the next chapter, this urge to make people good by law has many sexual applications, although the Puritans were probably no more sexually repressive than other Christians of the time. What we often think of as "Puritan" sexual rigidity is probably more properly referred to as "Victorian." During the reign of Queen Victoria (1819–1901), English society held sexual expression in exaggerated disgust and probably exaggerated its importance. While strict public standards of decency and purity were enforced, many Victorians indulged in the private vices of pornography, prostitution, and the rest. It is against this typically Victorian combination of repressiveness and hypocrisy that many in the twentieth century have revolted, wrongly thinking the Victorian period to be representative of the whole Christian ethical tradition.

It should be noted that across Western history there has been a great deal of consensus in sexual ethics. Sex has been seen as part of God's creation, but a source of temptation which needs to be controlled. Although at various times chastity has been exalted, marriage and the family have always been held in esteem, and sex outside marriage has been condemned in theory, if not in practice. Finally, it is only within this century that sex has been seen as having any "official" purpose beyond procreation.

Current trends Today, however, even within the Christian Church the old consensus is breaking down, and sexual ethics is a subject for renewed discussion and argument. The Reformation emphasis on individual conscience calls natural law into question, even within Roman Catholicism. Among Jews, while the Orthodox still live by the rabbinic interpretation of Old Testament law, Conservative and Reform Judaism are in the same flux. Several factors have contributed to this ferment, both within the religious community and outside it.

Modern biblical scholars hold that many of the prohibitions against various sexual practices in the Bible must be seen in historical and cultural context and may not be applicable today. Modern post-Freudian psychology suggests that sexuality is not simply a matter of will and that sexual "misconduct" may not be sin so much as neurosis. Behavioral scientists are likely to stress the importance of sexuality to all human life and to question whether it is a lesser or evil aspect of personality. Technology has made it possible, for the first time in human history, to prevent conception reliably and to terminate pregnancy safely. Theologians and ethicists are still wrestling with this problem, which, for example, blunts the force of natural law arguments against premarital intercourse, since illegitimate children need not be the result.

However, the "Old Morality" is not dead, and the "New Morality" is still in the process of formulation. The controversy can be quite heated, as will be seen in the discussions of specific topics, and a new consensus has not yet been achieved.

Nontheistic Western Ethics

It would be misleading to suggest that within Western culture, at least since the Renaissance, all ethical thinking has been religious in origin. Many ethicists have quite consciously tried to find a framework for moral behavior that does not rely on divine revelation or any direction from a source outside or beyond human intellect and personality. Nonreligious ethics covers the whole spectrum; however, we can look at a fairly broad mainstream called *humanism*.

Humanistic ethics accepts no supernatural source for direction and insists that values can be found only in human experience in this world, as observed by the philosopher or social scientist. Most humanists would hold that the basic goals of human life are happiness, self-awareness, the avoidance of pain and suffering, and the fulfillment of human needs. Of course, the individual pursuit of these ends must be tempered by the fact that no one lives in the world alone and that some limitation of individual happiness may be required by the common good. Another important humanistic principle is that the individual must make his or her own decisions and accept responsibility for them and their consequences, without appeal to some higher authority, such as God.

In the area of human sexuality, humanism demands a realistic approach to human behavior that does not create arbitrary or unreasonable standards and expectations; it is very distrustful of the legalistic approach. It seeks real intimacy between persons and condemns impersonal and exploitative relationships, though probably not with the vigor that marks religious ethics. It tends to be tolerant, compassionate, and skeptical of claims of absolute value.

Sexuality in Other Religions

While the discussion so far has been most concerned with Western culture and the Judeo-Christian tradition, this tradition and this

(a)

(b)

FIGURE 20.3

(a) Arab man and his harem. The Moslem religion permits polygamy, and the practice is common today in Arab countries [Diane Rawson/Photo Researchers, Inc.]. (b) Polygamy, American style. Until forbidden to do so by the U.S. Supreme Court, members of the Church of Jesus Christ of Latter-Day Saints (Mormons) were allowed to have several wives. The Mormons took the practice from the Old Testament patriarchs [The Bettmann Archive, Inc.].

culture certainly do not contain the only possible approaches to sexual ethics. Therefore, it may broaden our outlook if we briefly consider human sexuality in religious traditions outside our own experience. Obviously, this could be the topic for a very large book itself, and the reader will have to be content with a rather brief look at the three non-Western religions with the largest number of adherents: Islam, Hinduism, and Buddhism.

Islam Geographically, and in terms of its roots, Islam is the closest faith to the Judeo-Christian heritage. It was founded by the Prophet Muhammad, who lived from 570 to 632, in what is now Saudi Arabia. Its followers are called *Moslems* (or *Muslims*), and its sacred scripture is the Koran. Islam shares some of its basic precepts with a neighboring faith, Judaism, but it has a flavor all its own. Classical Islam values sexuality very positively, and Muhammad saw intercourse, especially in marriage, as the highest good of human life. Islam sanctions both polygamy and concubinage, and the Prophet had several wives. In legend, great sexual prowess is attributed to him, although it may be exaggerated. He opposed celibacy, and Islam has very little ascetic tradition. A male-dominated faith, Islam has a strong double standard but recognizes a number of rights and prerogatives for women as well. Although sex outside either marriage or concubinage is viewed as a sin, Islam is ethically quite moderate and is rather tolerant of sexual sin, including homosexuality. All these aspects combine to create a "sex-positive" religion (Bullough, 1976, p. 205).

Hinduism "Hinduism" is a rather inclusive term which refers to a highly varied complex of mythology and religious practice founded on the Indian subcontinent. Here can be found virtually every approach to sexuality the human species has yet invented. However, certain themes are worth mentioning. In Hinduism, four possible approaches to life are acceptable:

Kama, the pursuit of pleasure; Artha, the pursuit of power and material wealth; Dharma, the pursuit of the moral life; and Moksha, the pursuit of liberation through the negation of the self in Nirvana. Kama is notable because it has produced an extensive literature on the achievement of sexual pleasure, notably the *Kama Sutra* of Vatsyayana, a masterpiece of erotic hedonism. This testifies to the highly positive view of sexuality to be found in Hinduism.

However, in contrast, the ways of Dharma

FIGURE 20.4
A yoga master's view of sex: "Sexual life is not unnatural nor condemned by God. Those who are interested in it should get into matrimonial life and experience it in moderation. Overindulgence in anything will be detrimental to both physical and mental health. Others whose interest is in serving God and his creation full-time should stay away from matrimony to avoid personal obligations and to conserve and redirect their sexual, physical and mental energies toward their service." In this statement, Sri Swami Satchidananda summarizes much Hindu teaching on sexuality. *[Office of Sri Guradev, International Headquarters, Integral Yoga Institutes.]*

and Moksha can be as rigorously ascetic as anything in Christianity. By avoiding all passions, including sex, the follower of these ways of renunciation seeks to pass out of the cycle of continual rebirth to absorption into the Godhead. Part of this is *brahmacarya*, or celibacy, which is to be cultivated at the beginning of life (for the purposes of education and discipline) and at the end of life (for the purpose of finding peace). It is interesting to note that in between it is permissible to marry and raise a family, and thus this form of Hinduism makes active sexuality and asceticism possible in the same lifetime.

Buddhism   Buddhism was a development of Hinduism; it originated in the life and thought of Guatama (560–480 B.C.) and has been elaborated in many forms since then. There is little discussion of sex in the teachings of the Buddha; his way is generally ascetic and concentrates on the achievement of enlightenment and on escape from the suffering of the world. Two main traditions, Therevada and Mahayana, are found in contemporary Buddhism, and they differ greatly. The ethics of Therevada includes the strict nonindulgence of the desires which bring joy; understanding, morals, and discipline are emphasized. The ethics of Mahayana is more active and directed toward love of others. Both encourage men to live celibate lives as monks. Originally, Buddha sought a "middle way" between extreme asceticism and extreme hedonism, but today the situation is rather like that of medieval Christianity: the masses live ordinary and usually married lives, and the monks cultivate ascetic wisdom.

Tantric Buddhism, found particularly in Tibet, is a form of Buddhism which is of particular interest. There is a devotion to natural energy (*shakti*), and followers are taught that passion can be exhausted by passion. For example, sexual desire can be overcome while satisfying it according to occult knowledge. Sexuality can therefore be used as a means of transcending the limitations of human life. This sexual mysticism is by no means common, but it is one of the various forms which Eastern religion may take.

Only the surface has been scratched here. The interested reader is referred to Noss (1963) for a general discussion and to Bullough (1976) for the more exotic and erotic aspects.

CONTEMPORARY ISSUES IN SEXUAL ETHICS

Premarital Intercourse

About once a quarter, I find myself addressing an undergraduate class in human sexuality on sexual ethics, and invariably the liveliest discussion concerns premarital sexual behavior. The general direction of comments from the class is usually along the lines of, "What is so wrong with it after all, if nobody gets hurt?" The implicit assumption, supported by statistics, is that "everybody (or almost everybody) is doing it," and this has led contemporary ethicists to do a good deal of rethinking. This is a typical process in ethics; pastoral considerations—that is, dealing with people as they are—often lead to developments in theology.

The traditional position of the Christian Church is, of course, that sex before marriage is wrong. This is the position of conservative Protestantism and also of Roman Catholicism. In January 1976, the Congregation for the Doctrine of the Faith, with the support of Pope Paul VI, issued a "Declaration on Certain Questions concerning Sexual Ethics," which stated:

> Today there are many who vindicate the right to sexual union before marriage, at least in those cases where a firm intention to marry and an affection which is already in some way conjugal

in the psychology of the subjects require this completion which they judge to be connatural. . . . This option is contrary to Christian doctrine which states that every genital act must be within the framework of marriage. (Sacred Congregation for the Doctrine of the Faith, 1976, p. 11)

This statement reiterates the basic papal encyclical on the subject, Pope Pius XI's *Casti Connubi* of 1930, which forbade premarital intercourse, adultery, birth control, sterilization, abortion, and divorce—in short, all sexual activity outside marriage or not for the purpose of procreation (Pope Pius XI, 1930).

On the other hand, proponents of situation ethics would allow for sexual expression in precisely the situation mentioned in the Vatican Declaration, that is, where there is commitment and affection. Many ethicists would say that it is the quality of the relationship, not its legal status, that determines whether intercourse is appropriate. Further, there is a concern for helping people form good relationships, and this may allow a certain amount of "experimentation" to be, if not endorsed, at least not vigorously condemned.

Related to this is a concern for personhood, a concern which is broader than simply sexual. Liberal ethicists often argue that the gravest sin consists not in the violation of certain rules but in the violation of persons, that is, the exploitation of other human beings for one's own gratification. Premarital sex may thus be all right if it does not involve the exploitation of one individual by another. Such exploitation can occur within marriage, as well as outside it, as, for example, when a man uses his wife simply for his own pleasure or when a woman "withholds her favors" until her husband promises to give her something she wants. Again, it is the quality of the relationship, and not the legality, which matters most.

In summary, the conservative or legalistic answer to the question of whether premarital intercourse is permissible is a resounding "no." The more liberal answer may be said to be "maybe" or "yes, but." Few ethical thinkers today take the position that either promiscuity or impersonal sex is a good thing, and most would pose fairly hard questions about commitment and intent to an unmarried couple contemplating a sexual relationship.

Extramarital Sex

The Judeo-Christian tradition has always taken a very dim view of extramarital sex (or adultery, to use the biblical term). In the Old Testament, the penalty for adultery was being stoned to death; in the New Testament, we find that it is the only grounds for divorce which Jesus allows (Matthew 6:21–22). In subsequent Christian theology, adultery is seen in the context of unfaithfulness to God, since marriage is seen as a sacramental—that is, symbolic—sign of God's relationship to his people. Therefore, adultery is regarded as one of the gravest sins possible.

This view has changed little even in today's ethical ferment. Contemporary ethicists regard extramarital sex as the breaking of a trust and the violation of a relationship which must be based on commitment. However, many ethicists would avoid absolute condemnation, in favor of a more understanding approach when extramarital relationships occur. For them, the problem is to help a couple establish a more satisfying relationship, sexually and otherwise, that will eliminate the need for sex outside marriage. Such an approach also recognizes that it often takes two to create such a situation and that an extramarital relationship may be a symptom of problems shared by both persons. Such an approach seeks reconciliation based on forgiveness and love, rather than punishment based on law, and takes seriously the individuality of the persons involved and their circumstances.

Contraception

The situation today with respect to birth control is clearer than the situation with respect to some of the other topics dealt with here. Roman Catholics and Orthodox Jews oppose any "artificial" means of contraception; other Jews and most Protestants favor responsible family planning by married couples. Moreover, most ethicists would suggest that unmarried persons who are sexually active ought to be using some means to prevent pregnancy.

Those who oppose birth control for religious reasons see it as being contrary to the will of God, against the natural law, or both. Orthodox Judaism cites the biblical injunction to "be fruitful and multiply" (Genesis 1:26) as God's command to his people, not to be disobeyed in any way. Further, some members of other Jewish communities warn that limiting family size threatens the future existence of the Jewish people, and they call for a return to the traditionally large Jewish family.

The Roman Catholic position is best articulated in Pope Paul VI's 1968 encyclical, *Humanae Vitae*:

> Marriage and conjugal love are by their nature ordained toward the begetting and educating of children. . . . In the task of transmitting life, therefore, they are not free to proceed completely at will, as if they could determine in a wholly autonomous way the honest path to follow, but they must conform their activity to the creative intention of God, expressed in the very nature of marriage and by its acts, and manifested by the constant teaching of the Church. (Pope Paul VI, 1968, p. 20)

The encyclical continued the Church's approval of abstinence or "rhythm" as legitimate methods of family planning. *Humanae Vitae* was not enthusiastically accepted by all Catholics, and, as noted in Chapter 6, there is evidence to suggest that many Catholic couples, often with the encouragement or tacit approval of their priest, ignore the encyclical and use contraceptives anyway.

Those in the religious community who favor the use of contraceptives do so for a variety of reasons. Many express a concern that all children who are born should be "wanted," and they see family planning as a means to this end. Others, emphasizing the dangers that the population explosion poses to the quality and future of human life, the need for a more equitable distribution of natural resources, and the needs of the emerging nations, call for family planning as a matter of justice. Another point of view regards the use of contraceptives as part of the responsible use of freedom required of the believer. In this view, any couple who are unwilling or unready to assume the responsibility of children have an actual duty to use contraceptives. For these groups, the decision to use contraceptives is a highly individual one, and the government must allow each individual the free exercise of his or her conscience.

Abortion

Related to the issue of contraception is the thorny question of abortion, the center of one of the most vigorous ethical debates of our time. Indeed, just how related abortion and contraception are is an issue itself. For the Roman Catholic Church, abortion and contraception are, in intent, the same thing, and for Joseph Fletcher and other liberals, abortion is also seen as a variety of contraception—less desirable, perhaps, but better than unwanted pregnancy. For many other ethicists, abortion and contraception are clearly distinguished, and while advocating contraception, they may question the morality of abortion.

A distinction is often made between therapeutic abortion and abortion on demand. Therapeutic abortion is a termination of pregnancy when the life or mental health of the woman is threatened or in cases of trauma such as rape and incest. Many ethicists are willing to endorse therapeutic abortion as the lesser of two evils but do not sanction abortion on demand, that is, abortion whenever requested by a woman for whatever reason (see, for example, Thielicke, 1964, pp. 226–244).

The leadership of the antiabortion movement clearly comes from the Roman Catholic Church, which sees it as one of the most crucial ethical issues confronting modern society. Catholic theology regards human life as beginning at the moment of conception; therefore, the termination of any pregnancy is murder. Interestingly, for most of its history, the Roman Catholic Church accepted Aristotle's teaching that "ensoulment," that is, the entry into the fetus of its distinctively human soul, took place at 40 days after conception for a male and at 80 or 90 days after conception for a female. Theoretically, this permitted abortions at least until the fortieth day. In 1869, Pope Pius IX eliminated the concept of ensoulment, holding that human life begins at conception and that all abortion is therefore murder (Fulton, 1974). From this, the Catholic political position, as seen in the Right-to-Life movement, is clear; if you regard abortion as murder, you cannot in good conscience permit your government to allow it.

The Roman Catholic position is shared by Orthodox Jews, the Eastern Orthodox, and many conservative Protestants, although some of the latter will allow therapeutic abortions in some cases. Antiabortionists also fear that legal abortion might lead to a general decline in respect for human life and open the door to euthanasia (mercy killing), genocide (the killing of "undesirable" groups), and other threats to life and civilization.

For those who favor at least some form of abortion under certain circumstances, and this includes most liberal Protestants and Conservative and Reformed Jews, the problem is one of balancing several goods against one another. Human life is good and ought to be preserved, but the *quality* of life is also important. An unborn child may have a right to life, but does it not also have a right to be wanted and cared for? Might not the danger to the well-being of a woman already alive take precedence over the well-being of an unborn fetus? Does not a woman have the right to determine what happens to her own body? Since until quite recently all ethicists were male, ought women to follow rules made by men, who can never be in their situation?

One position, which might be called the "civil liberties" position, emerges from the "liberal" camp. This holds that since the issue is so complex and since no practical consensus has been reached in society, the government ought to keep out and let the individual woman make up her own mind. Many church people who might themselves have severe ethical qualms about abortion still oppose state laws prohibiting abortion in the first and second trimesters. One thing is sure: until a consensus is reached, this debate is likely to go with unabated force (see Callahan, 1970).

Homosexuality

If the abortion debate has been lively in the recent past, homosexuality may be the great ethical issue of the future. Gay liberation has made its mark on the Church, despite the overwhelming Judeo-Christian tradition of condemning any and all homosexual acts. This change has occurred in part because modern biblical scholarship suggests that scriptural prohibitions of homosexuality may derive from a context that is questionable today and in part because the impact of social science has led some ethicists to question whether homosexuality is truly abnormal and unnatural and therefore against the will of God.

Nonetheless, both the Bible and tradition are uniformly against it. In addition to the story of the destruction of Sodom (see Focus), homosexual practices are included in lists of cultic offenses against God in the Old Testament. In the New Testament, although Jesus made no comment on the subject, St. Paul was unambiguous. He apparently believed that homosexual acts were committed by fundamentally heterosexual people for sheer perverse pleasure. Thus he included them in lists of sexual sins, such as adultery and fornication, which are in opposition to the will of God and symptomatic of human depravity. However, Paul does not seem to have found homosexuality any more dreadful than other sexual sins (Thielicke, 1964).

All the Fathers of the early Church strongly condemned homosexuality, partly because of the dreadful morals of the pagan world at that time. They saw it as a crime against nature which might bring down the wrath of God upon the whole community. Aquinas stated that "unnatural vice . . . flouts nature by transgressing its basic principles of sexuality and is in this matter the gravest of sin" (1968 ed., Second Part of the Second Part, Question 154, Article 12). Thielicke notes a similar attitude among Reformation theologians and quotes a seventeenth-century Lutheran, Benedict Carpzov, as listing the following results of homosexuality: "earthquakes, famine, pestilence, Saracens, floods, and very fat voracious field mice" (1964, p. 276).

A strong condemnation of homosexuality is found in most quarters of the Christian community today. However, there are various shadings of this essentially negative approach. Biblical fundamentalists, for example, would be likely to condemn all homosexual activity and see the homosexual person as a sinner needing radical cure. The Roman Catholic Church takes a somewhat different position. It maintains that while, as a matter of natural law, homosexual *acts* are not permissible, it is not necessarily sinful to *be* homosexual. Catholic homosexuals are therefore not to be rejected, but they must accept celibacy as the only way to deal with their sexual nature. As stated in the recent Vatican document:

> In the pastoral field these homosexuals must certainly be treated with understanding and sustained in the hope of overcoming their personal difficulties and their inability to fit into society. . . . But no pastoral method can be employed which would give moral justification to these acts on the grounds that they would be consonant with such people. . . . [The] judgment of scripture does not, of course, permit us to conclude that all who suffer from this anomaly are personally responsible for it, but it does attest to the fact that homosexual acts are intrinsically disordered and can in no way be approved. (Congregation for the Sacred Doctrine of the Faith, 1976, p. 11)

Various Protestant groups have taken roughly the same stance—that is, being gay per se may not be sinful, but homosexual acts are—and a statement by the 1976 General Conference of the United Methodist Church is typical: "We do not condone the practice of homosexuality and consider this practice incompatible with Christian teaching" (*The Christian Century*, 1976, **93**, p. 557).

Those holding this position are often willing to concede civil rights and liberties to homosexuals, although there are differences in the willingness to press for them. When the Wolfenden Report was published (see Chapter 21), the Roman Catholic hierarchy in England endorsed decriminalization of homosexual acts between consenting adults, stating that they were matters for the confessional and not for the courts (Griffin, 1956). While condemning the seduction of minors, prostitution, and force in

THE SIN OF SODOM

FOCUS

The most important passage of Scripture in the traditional Christian understanding of homosexuality is probably the biblical account of the visit of two angels (in disguise) to Lot, Abraham's nephew, in the city of Sodom. According to the sacred laws of hospitality, Lot invited them into his home for the night.

> But before they lay down, the men of the city, the men of Sodom, both young and old, all the people to the last man, surrounded the house; and they called to Lot, "Where are the men who came to you tonight? Bring them out to us that we may know them." Lot went out of the door to the men, shut the door after him, and said, "I beg you, my brothers, do not act so wickedly. Behold I have two daughters who have not known man; let me bring them out to you, and do to them as you please; only do nothing to these men, for they have come under the shelter of my roof." But they said, "Stand back!" And they said to him, "This fellow came to sojourn, and he would play the judge! Now we will deal worse with you than with them." Then they pressed hard against the man Lot, and drew near to break the door. But the men [the angels] put forth their hands and brought Lot into the house to them, and shut the door. And they struck with blindness the men who were at the door of the house, both small and great, so that they wearied themselves with groping for the door. (Genesis 19:4–11)

The next day Sodom and its sister city Gomorrah were destroyed by fire and brimstone because of their great wickedness.

Much of the interior evidence of the Bible suggests that the "sin of Sodom" was inhospitality or general sexual excess. However, at the start of the Christian era, when Jews were beginning to encounter Greek and Roman practices, the desire of the men of Sodom "to know" the angels was understood to indicate homosexual interest. This is the origin of the terms "sodomy" and "sodomite." The relatively few other biblical references to homosexuality were interpreted in the light of the great and terrible sin of Sodom, and therefore homosexual acts were punished with great severity by the Church and in Western law. Many modern scholars doubt the traditional interpretation of the sin of Sodom and indeed question whether the Bible deals at all with homosexuality as an aspect of human personality (McNeill, 1976).

ETHICS, RELIGION, AND SEXUALITY

sexual relations, a number of Protestant groups have arrived at the same conclusion.

A real point of conflict seems to be the ordination of avowed homosexuals to the ministry. While many groups will, at least unofficially, admit that there may be ministers who are "in the closet," only two major American churches have, to date, ordained openly gay people, and in both cases the action has resulted in a great deal of controversy. In 1973 William Johnson was ordained to the ministry in the United Church of Christ, after vigorous debate over his homosexuality. In 1976, the Episcopal Bishop of New York ordained Ellen Moore, a lesbian, as a deacon and then, in 1977, as a priest (Figure 20.5).

These ordinations are expressive of some movement toward a greater acceptance of the homosexual person within the religious community. The first significant step took place in 1963 when a group of English Friends challenged traditional Christian thinking about sexuality, including homosexuality, in *Toward a Quaker View of Sex*. Since that time, Quakers and Unitarians have been notable for their acceptance not only of the homosexual but also of his or her sexual behavior, as long as it is conscientious. Similarly, the 1976 General Convention of the Episcopal Church declared:

> Homosexual persons are children of God who have a full and equal claim with all other persons upon love, acceptance, and pastoral concern and care of the Church. (Daily of the General Convention, Sept. 15, 1976, p. 1)

With the establishment of organizations like Dignity (Roman Catholic), Integrity (Episcopalian), and gay caucuses in many denominations, it seems likely that the ferment will continue, despite any potential backlash.

Several serious theologians—most notably John McNeill (Roman Catholic) and Norman Pittenger (Anglican)—have laid the groundwork for a positive view of homosexual relationships. They argue that a relationship of mutual respect, concern, and commitment, of love in its fullest sense, is to be valued and supported, whatever the sex of the partners. Related to this is the observation that a person's sexual orientation is an integral part of his or her personhood and can be affirmed as part of God's creation. The homosexual may then, in Thielicke's words, "accept this predisposition as a divine dispensation and . . . see it as a task to be wrestled with, indeed, to think of it as a talent to be invested" (1964, p. 284).

The ethical problem of homosexuality is not likely to be solved easily, for it raises the question of the very purpose of sexuality itself. How the religious community comes to grips with it may prove indicative of the future treatment of all questions regarding sexuality, the New Morality, and the relationship of theology to the social sciences.

TOWARD AN ETHICS OF *HUMAN* SEXUALITY

The combined forces of the sexual revolution and the New Morality have strongly attacked the traditional Judeo-Christian sexual ethic as narrow and repressive. This may be true, but it has not yet been proved to everyone's satisfaction that the alternatives proposed are a real improvement upon the Old Morality. Whether the debate will be resolved, and how, remains to be seen. Some of the arguments and possibilities are considered below.

The Old Morality tends to be ascetic and legalistic and, at its worst, reduces ethical behavior to following a series of rules. Its asceticism may downgrade the goodness of human sexuality and negate the very real joys of physical pleasure. A healthy personality needs to integrate the physical side of life and affirm it, and this kind of self-acceptance may be made more difficult by the Old Morality. Further, if morality is simply a matter of applying universal rules, there is no real choice, and human freedom is seriously undermined. In short, opponents of the Old Morality might argue, this approach diminishes the full nature of humanity and impoverishes human life. On the other hand, the traditional approach deserves a few kind words as well. For one thing, with the traditional morality people almost always know where they stand. Right and wrong, good and bad, are clearly, if somewhat inflexibly, spelled out. Moreover, asceticism does witness to the fact that human personality is more than merely the body and that physical urges often need to be controlled in order for higher, more human ends to be achieved.

The New Morality, with its situational approach and tendencies toward hedonism, has its own share of pluses and minuses. It does affirm quite positively the physical and sexual side of human nature as an integral part of the individual. This is helpful, but if it is pushed too far, it can also leave people under the control of their impulses and thus less than fully human. Situation ethics quite properly calls for an evaluation of every ethical decision on the basis of the concrete aspects of the personalities involved and the context of the decision. Its broad principles of love, respect, and interpersonal responsibility are sound, but it can be argued that situationism does not take sufficiently into account the problem of human selfishness. Dishonesty about our real motives may blind us to the actual effects of our actions, however sincere we profess to be. Further, situationism is a much less certain guide than the older approach, since so many situations are ambiguous.

There is a middle way between these two extremes, one which may yet prove to be the synthesis that sexual ethics seems to be searching for. This approach would use the traditional

FIGURE 20.5
The first lesbian priest. Changing attitudes toward homosexuality in some Christian churches are reflected in the ordination of Ellen Barrett as a priest of the Episcopal Church, shown here with The Right Reverend Paul Moore, Bishop of New York, who ordained her. *[Bettye Lane/Nancy Palmer Photo Agency.]*

principles (laws) as guidelines for actions, while insisting that they must be applied in concrete situations and occasionally reworked to conform to changes in the human situation. This approach differs from the Old Morality by stating that ethical principles must be flexible, and it differs from the New Morality by holding that departures from tradition must be based on very strong evidence that the old rules do not apply. For those adopting this position, healthy decision making functions in the tensions between the rigid "thou shalt not" of the legalist and the "do your own thing" of the situationist.

In the specific case of sexual ethics, such a middle-of-the-road approach would affirm the goodness of human sexuality, but insist that sexual impulses need to be brought under the control of reason, experience, and conscience. It would accept sexuality as a vital part of human personality, but not the sum total of who we are. Such an approach to sexual ethics would, indeed, be consistent with what was shown earlier in this chapter to be the heart of the Judeo-Christian tradition, shorn of some of its unnecessary rigidity and distrust of sexuality.

SUMMARY

It is important to study religion and ethics in conjunction with human sexuality because they frequently provide the framework within which people judge the rightness or wrongness of sexual activity. They give rise to attitudes and approaches which influence the way members of a society regard sexuality, and they are therefore powerful influences on behavior. Religion and ethics may be hedonistic (pleasure-oriented) or ascetic (emphasizing self-discipline). They may be legalistic (operating by rules) or situational (making decisions in concrete situations, with few rules).

In the great ethical traditions, the Greeks tended toward a philosophical asceticism, while the Old Testament had a positive, though legalistic, view of sexuality. Christian New Testament sources are ambivalent about sexuality, with Jesus saying little on the subject and with St. Paul, influenced by the immorality of Roman culture and his expectation of the end of the world, being somewhat negative. Later, Chris-

tianity became much more ascetic; this is reflected in the writings of Augustine and Thomas Aquinas, who also confirmed Catholic moral theology in the natural-law mold. The Protestant Reformation abolished clerical celibacy and opened the door to greater individual freedom in ethics. Today, technological development and new forms of biblical scholarship have led to a wide variety of positions on issues of sexual ethics.

Humanistic ethics rejects external authority, replacing it with a person-centered approach to ethics. A variety of approaches to sexuality can be found in Islam, Hinduism, and Buddhism.

Five ethical issues involving human sexuality have provoked lively debate recently. Among liberals, there is a greater acceptance of premarital intercourse, although the legalistic tradition is firmly against it. Extramarital sex is opposed by virtually all ethicists, but a more compassionate approach is often urged. Contraception is opposed by Roman Catholicism and Orthodox Judaism on scriptural and natural-law grounds, but it is positively valued by many other groups. Abortion is a very emotional argument on which there are many positions, ranging from adamant opposition on the grounds that it is murder to a view that urges each woman to make her own decision on the matter. Another very vigorous debate is going on today over homosexuality, with some movement away from the traditional view that condemns it absolutely and toward either a qualified approval at least of civil rights and liberties for gay people or a warmhearted acceptance of their sexuality.

A possible resolution of the conflict between the Old Morality and the New Morality is an ethics of *human* sexuality, neither hedonistic nor rigidly ascetic, which takes seriously the historical tradition of ethical thinking, while making decisions on the basis of the concrete situation.

SUGGESTIONS FOR FURTHER READING

Barnhouse, R. T., and Holmes, U. T. *Male and female: Christian approaches to sexuality.* New York: Seabury Press, 1976. A collection of readings from many points of view on the issues discussed in this chapter, and more.

Brinton, Crane. *A history of Western morals.* New York: Harcourt, Brace, & World, 1959. With remarkable scholarship and great wit, this eminent historian traces Western ethics from the time of the Greeks to the present.

Cox, Harvey (Ed.) *The situation ethics debate.* Philadelphia: Westminster Press, 1968. This book, together with the two books by Joseph Fletcher cited below, give the outline of the great debate over the New Morality. All three are very readable.

Fletcher, Joseph. *Situation ethics.* Philadelphia: Westminster Press, 1966. Fletcher, Joseph. *Moral responsibility: Situation ethics at work.* Philadelphia: Westminster Press, 1967.

Heron, Alastair (Ed.) *Toward a Quaker view of sex.* (Rev. ed.) London: Friends Service Committee, 1964. A classic in the contemporary understanding of sexuality. It is especially good on the issue of homosexuality.

Pittenger, W. Norman. *Making sexuality human.* Philadelphia: Pilgrim Press, 1970. A short but well-thought-out work which grounds the New Morality in good theology.

21

SEX AND
THE LAW

CITED

What the consenting adult does in private has become everybody's
business to the precise extent that debate waxes hot over whether it
is nobody's business.*

†One day I stood chatting on a
Berkeley street corner with David
and Ken, who are gay. David
leered at his companion and announced in mock conspiratorial
tones, "We're going to commit an illegal act."
And they were. And so, that day, were a great
many other people—gay and straight, male and
female, single and married. All would be violating one or another of various state laws telling
them, in effect, what they might do, how,
where, and with whom. The average citizen
might be very surprised by what the law has,
over the years and even today, seen fit to
regulate in this most private act. In a massive
work on the subject, legal scholar Ralph Slovenko concluded that "Americans commonly
and regularly engage in sexual practices which
are technically forbidden by law" (1965, p. 5).
Kinsey estimated that about 95 percent of the
males in his sample had engaged in illegal
sexual acts (Kinsey et al., 1948, p. 392). It will
be the purpose of this chapter to consider why

there are laws that attempt to regulate sexual
behavior, what sorts of behaviors are affected,
how these laws are enforced, how they are
changing, and what the future prospects for
sex-law reform might be.

WHY ARE THERE SEX LAWS?

To begin, we might well ask why there are laws
regulating sexual conduct in the first place. This
actually is a very modern question, for throughout most of Western history such laws were
taken for granted. Sexual legislation is quite
ancient, dating back certainly to the time of the
Old Testament (see Chapter 20). Since then, in
countries where the Judeo-Christian tradition is
influential, attempts to regulate public morals
have been the rule. Today we are likely to
regard sex as a private matter, of concern only
to those involved. However, historically it has
been seen as a matter which very much affects
society and therefore as a fit subject for law.

Even today, certain kinds of sex laws are
probably legitimate and necessary. Stanford law
professor Herbert Packer argues that the following might be rationally included in law: protection "against force and equivalent means of
coercion to secure sexual gratification," "pro-

*Source: Herbert Packer. The limits of the criminal sanction.
Stanford, Calif.: Stanford University Press, 1968, p. 301.
†This chapter was contributed by Clark Hyde, M.A., M. Div.

tection of the immature against sexual exploitation," and, although this is somewhat problematic, "the prevention of conduct that gives offense or is likely to give offense to innocent bystanders" (1968, p. 306). It seems obvious that people ought to be free from sexual assault and coercion and that children should not be sexually exploited; individual rights and the interests of society are here in agreement.

However, sex laws have been designed for purposes which may be more open to question. Historically, the rationale was to preserve the family as the principal unit of the social order by protecting its integrity from, for example, adultery or desertion of a spouse. Sex laws also seek to assure children of a supportive family by prohibiting conduct such as fornication, which is likely to result in out-of-wedlock births. Changing social conditions may call for revision of these statutes, but the principles behind them are understandable.

There is yet another realm of motivation behind sex laws which is highly problematic, and that is the protection of public morals. However, this tends to become a matter of religion, and the constitutional separation of church and state is designed to prevent one religious group from enforcing its tenets on others. The concern for public morality results in laws against any form of nonprocreative sex, for reasons outlined in Chapter 20. Thus there have been laws against homosexual acts, bestiality, and contraception. Religious beliefs as to what is "unnatural," "immoral," or "sinful" have found expression in law, as it was often held that the state had a duty to uphold religion as a pillar of civilized society, using the law to make people good. The example of England is instructive since American law derives so extensively from English law. Both before and after the Reformation, church and state in England were seen as identical, and the state had an obligation to protect the interests of the Church. A secular state, such as we have in our country,

was unthinkable, and morals were a matter of public concern.

This tradition, the prudery of the Victorian period (during which much of the American legal system came into being), and the zealousness of such individuals as Anthony Comstock (see Focus) combined to provide the United States with an enormous amount of sexual legislation. This legislation reflects a great deal of ambiguity in our attitudes toward sex, which is perhaps unsurprising in such a varied population. It also contrasts with other societies in which the trend since 1800 has been away from such laws. According to one authority, "The United States apparently has more laws on the subject than all of the European countries combined" (Slovenko, 1965, p. 9). The American legal tradition assumes both the right of the state to enforce morals and a consensus in society as to which morals are to be enforced. However, contemporary citizens have come to question the legitimacy of government interference in what they regard as their private affairs. This tension has led to a widespread demand for a radical overhaul of laws that regulate sexual conduct. It all makes for a fascinating, if frustrating, field of study, for law has a way of reflecting the ambiguities and conflicts of society.

WHAT KINDS OF SEX LAWS ARE THERE?

Cataloging the laws pertaining to sexual conduct would be a difficult project. It is possible that no one really knows how many such laws there are, given the huge number of jurisdictions in the American legal system. When one considers federal law, the Uniform Code of Military Justice, state laws, municipal codes, county ordinances, and so on, the magnitude of the problem becomes clear. In addition to *criminal* law, portions of civil law that may penalize certain sexual behaviors—such as licensing for professions, personnel rules for pub-

ANTHONY COMSTOCK: CRUSADER AGAINST VICE

In any discussion of laws regulating sexual behavior, the name of Anthony Comstock looms large. His zeal for moral reform is reflected in the use of the term "Comstock laws" for the sort of statutes considered here.

Comstock was born in Connecticut in 1844 and was reared as a strict Puritan Congregationalist; he had a well-developed sense of his own sinfulness—and of others' as well. He served in the Union Army during the Civil War and worked as a dry-goods salesman. While still a young man, he became very active in the Young Men's Christian Association, seeking the arrest and conviction of dealers in pornography. He helped found the Committee for the Suppression of Vice within the YMCA. This later became an independent society, as his efforts gained him national attention.

Comstock's most noteworthy success was probably a comprehensive antiobscenity bill which passed the United States Congress in 1873. The law prohibited the mailing of obscene matter within the United States, as well as advertisements for obscenity, which included matter "for the prevention of conception." Comstock initiated the passage of a similar law in New York, making it illegal to give contraceptive information verbally, and many other states followed suit. At the same time, Comstock received an appointment as a special agent of the U.S. Post Office, and this gave him the authority personally to enforce the Comstock Law. He did, with a

---

lic servants, and immigration regulations—must also be considered. Further, these laws are changing all the time, and any list would be obsolete before it went to press. Therefore, what is offered here is not so much a statistical summary of specific sex laws as a look at the *kinds* of laws that are, or have been, on the statute books.[1] The subheadings, all of which contain the word "crime," have been chosen with care, as a reminder that we are discussing

legal offenses which can carry with them the loss of freedom, reputation, property, or all these. However quaint and amusing some of these laws may seem, they are a serious matter.

Crimes of Exploitation and Force

Recalling Packer's suggestions about the kinds of laws that seem to make sense in a pluralistic society, let us begin with those which seek to prevent the use of force or exploitation in sexual relations—chiefly laws against rape and sexual relations with the young.

---

[1]State-by-state listings may be found in Boggan, Haft, Lister, and Rupp, 1975; Rhodes, 1972; and Rosenbleet and Pariente, 1973.

vengeance, claiming at the end of his career to have been personally responsible for the jailing of over 3600 offenders against public decency.

Comstock's energies were directed not only against pornography but also against abortionists, fraudulent advertisers and sellers of quack medicines, lotteries, saloonkeepers, artists who painted nude subjects, and advocates of free love. Among the object of his wrath were many of the most famous advocates of unpopular opinions of his day. He carried on a crusade against women's movement pioneers Vjctoria Woodhull and her sister Tennessee Claflin; he helped jail William Sanger, husband of Margaret Sanger, the birth control crusader; he attacked Robert Ingersoll, the atheist; and he tried to prevent the New York production of George Bernard Shaw's play about a prostitute, *Mrs. Warren's Profession*. For the last of these efforts, Shaw rewarded him by coining the word "comstockery."

Anthony Comstock was a controversial figure during his own lifetime and has often been blamed for all legislation reflecting his views. However, it is important to understand that he had a great deal of support from the public, without which he could not have jailed his 3600 miscreants. He will probably go down in history as a symbol of the effort to make people moral by legislation. He died in 1915 shortly after representing the United States at an International Purity Congress.

Source: Heywood Broun and Margaret Leech. *Anthony Comstock: Roundsman of the Lord.* New York: Boni, 1927.

For a fuller discussion of rape, the reader is referred to Chapter 16. The standard legal definition of rape is:

> The act of sexual intercourse with a female person not the wife of, or judicially separated from bed and board from, the offender, committed without her lawful consent. Emission is not necessary; and any sexual penetration, however slight, is sufficient to accomplish the crime. (Slovenko, 1965, p. 48)

Notice that, according to this definition, only a woman can be a rape victim and that a husband cannot be tried for raping his wife, however unwilling she may be. In a rape trial, the principal issue is the consent of the victim. Many states allow the victim's prior sexual activities to be considered as evidence of her consent, thus, in effect, putting the *victim* on trial. The women's movement has argued that reform of rape laws is needed in order to protect victims from unjust treatment, but every state has rape laws and no one would argue for their complete abolition.

Laws that seek to prevent the sexual exploitation of children are a bit more problematic.

493

FIGURE 21.1

Wisconsin judge Archie Simonson attracted national attention in 1977 for a remark he made in sentencing a 15-year-old boy for the rape of a high school girl. Criticizing the sexual permissiveness of the times, Judge Simonson commented on the provocative clothing worn by women and asked, "Are we supposed to take an impressionable person 15 or 16 years of age, who can respond to something like that, and punish that person severely because he reacts to it normally?" Although it was never argued that the victim was scantily clad, or that she consented, Judge Simonson seemed to imply that the rapist was not entirely responsible for his act. The light sentence and Judge Simonson's remarks created a public outcry which led to a recall election in which he was defeated by Moria Krueger, a female attorney. [Wide World Photos.]

Most states have laws against what is called either *carnal knowledge of a juvenile* or *statutory rape*. These laws prohibit a male over 17 or 18 from having intercourse with a female under the age of consent. The age of consent may be as young as 12 or as old as 17. The law applies regardless of consent or of the "victim's" previous sexual history (Slovenko, 1965, p. 56). Under this arrangement, it is quite possible, in a state where 17 is the age of consent, for an 18-year-old male to be charged with statutory rape because he had intercourse with his 16-year-old girlfriend. Such an act is probably different from the same girl's seduction by a man in his thirties or forties, and the law may need to find a way to differentiate between them.

Child-molestation laws forbid certain acts (other than intercourse) with the "immature." Such laws tend to be vague and may be found under many different headings. They may include physical or genital contact, use of sexual language, exhibitionism, or showing a child pornography (Slovenko, 1965, p. 74). Such laws may permit arrest for rather innocuous acts. It is reasonable to try to prevent pedophilia, but many of the laws which attempt to do so are suspect because of their vagueness.

Finally, every state includes laws against incest in its penal codes. This is a nearly universal taboo whose purpose seems to be to provide children with a place—namely, the home—where they will be free from sexual pressure. Incest laws also seek to prevent the genetic problems of inbreeding. Laws against incest assign penalties in proportion to the closeness of the relationship; for example, a cousin would be punished less severely than a parent (Slovenko, 1965, p. 36).

The problem with laws against sexual force and exploitation is the vagueness or unreasonableness of their definitions of key concepts, such as "coercion" and "immaturity." Packer suggests that the following situations be included in laws against coercion:

> . . . where the actor knows that the other person is unconscious; where he has surreptitiously administered drugs or other intoxicants in order to impair the other person's ability to control his or her conduct; where he knows that the other person is mentally ill and incapable of controlling his or her conduct; and where he uses a threat other than one of force that would nonetheless be likely to be yielded to by an ordinarily resolute person, such as a threat of discharge from employment. (1968, p. 308)

The same author suggests that definitions of immaturity be more carefully drawn to distinguish between a child who can be seriously harmed by sexual exploitation and an adolescent whose judgment is deficient and who needs protection, though, perhaps, to a lesser degree. Beyond that, the differential in ages between the victim and the aggressor is likely to be more helpful than a line drawn at an arbitrary age of consent (Packer, 1968). Such definitions will require careful thought as to what values ought to be supported by statute, and changes are likely only when a state revises its entire criminal code.

Criminal Consensual Acts

While it is not hard to see the logic of laws against force and exploitation of the young, many people are amazed to discover the number of sexual acts forbidden to consenting adults. These laws, as has been noted, were designed to protect marriage and the family, but a quick look at the divorce statistics will suggest that they are not doing a very good job.

With respect to heterosexuals, there are a number of laws against fornication (intercourse between unmarried parties), cohabitation (unmarried persons living together), and adultery (intercourse between unmarried persons, at least one of whom is married to someone else). Although these laws have been revised in many states recently, it is remarkable how many were still on the books in 1972, when *Playboy* magazine summarized them (Rhodes, 1972). Twenty-three states forbade fornication, with fines ranging from $10 to $1000 and with jail terms up to a year. Cohabitation was illegal in 26 states and punishable by fines of up to $500 and jail sentences of up to five years. Adultery, in addition to being grounds for divorce in all jurisdictions, was a crime in 41 states; adulterers could be fined as little as $10 and as much as $200 and could be incarcerated for as long as five years.

It is also rather disconcerting to realize that as recently as 1965 there were laws in 25 states against miscegenation, that is, against sex between members of different races, married or not (Slovenko, 1965, p. 41). The number of states indicates that such laws were not confined to the Deep South alone. Antimiscegenation laws did not make any distinction between married and unmarried parties; rather, they sought to prevent any sexual contact between whites and blacks. All such laws were invalidated by the United States Supreme Court in the 1967 case of *Loving v. Virginia.*

Besides specifying with whom one might have sex, laws have also attempted to regulate what acts are permissible, even in the case of a legally married couple. Until quite recently, virtually all states had laws prohibiting sodomy, or "crimes against nature."[2] These laws attempt to prohibit "unnatural" sex acts, even among consenting adults. Sodomy laws are many and varied, and they differ in terms of specificity, acts prohibited, and severity of the penalties.

---

[2]As of 1976, 18 states had repealed their sodomy laws, most within the last five years (*Sexual Law Reporter,* 1976, pp. 45, 57). For a complete list of such laws, with their penalties, see Boggan et al., 1975.

Sodomy laws are notoriously vague, as if the state legislatures did not wish to turn the statute books into pornography by describing the behaviors they wanted to prevent. The Louisiana law, which is clearer than most, describes sodomy as follows:

> The crime against nature is the unnatural carnal copulation by a human being with another of the same or opposite sex or with an animal. Emission is not necessary, and, when committed by a human being with another, the use of the genital organ of one of the offenders of whatever sex is sufficient to constitute the crime. (Quoted by Slovenko, 1965, p. 82)

From this, the reader is meant to understand that oral-genital and anal-genital acts, as well as bestiality, are forbidden. In some jurisdictions, the statute also includes necrophilia, or sex with a dead person.

The severity of the penalties against "unnatural acts" is remarkable. While in five states consensual sodomy is a misdemeanor with minor penalties, in 25 states it is a felony. In New Jersey, for example, it is punishable by a fine of $5000 and/or up to 20 years in jail (Boggan et al., 1975). Although these laws are theoretically enforceable against heterosexuals, in practice most people prosecuted for sodomy are gay. This may indicate that the severity of

FIGURE 21.2

Anita Bryant versus the gay of Miami. In 1977, a Dade County, Florida, ordinance forbidding discrimination against homosexuals was contested at the polls and defeated by a 2 to 1 margin. (a) The leader of the antiordinance forces was singer Anita Bryant, a fundamentalist Christian and spokeswoman for Florida orange juice. Relying on the traditional Christian view of homosexuality for support, Ms. Bryant argued that the ordinance would allow gays to seduce children. Asked why she thought God hates homosexuality, she argued, "Sperm is the most concentrated form of blood. The homosexual [engaging in fellatio] is eating life. That's why God calls homosexuality an abomination" [Photo: David Vance; quotation: Bill Hutchinson and James Kukar, Miami Magazine]. (b) Gay Miamians responded in kind to Ms. Bryant in a campaign that drew gay activists from all over the country [Bettye Lane/Nancy Palmer Photo Agency].

(a)

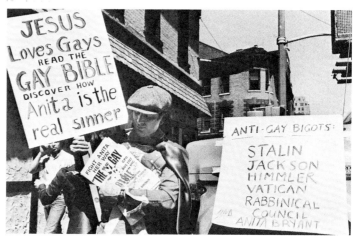
(b)

the penalties reflects the attitude of legislators toward homosexuality. Such an attitude is peculiarly American. Consensual sodomy has been legal in France since the time of Napoleon and is presently legal in most of Europe, being outlawed only in Ireland, Rumania, Bulgaria, Yugoslavia, and the Soviet Union (Barnett, 1973).

Crimes Against Taste

Another broad category of sex offenses can be viewed as crimes against community standards of taste and delicacy. In this company we find laws against exhibitionism, voyeurism, solicitation, disorderly conduct, being a public nuisance, and "general lewdness." These statutes are by and large quite vague and punish acts which are offensive, or *likely* to be offensive, to someone. There are also laws criminalizing the *status* of certain classes of persons—prostitutes, gays, or "sexual psychopaths"—who do not conform to approved patterns of behavior. Over half the states have such laws, and they carry penalties of from 30 days to 5 years in jail, with fines of $5 to $5000 (Boggan et al., 1975; Rosenbleet and Pariente, 1973). As will be seen below, unequal enforcement of these laws, their vagueness, and the difference between what is offensive and what is actually criminal make these statutes suspect.

Crimes Against Procreation

As was noted in the Focus on their instigator, the Comstock laws included a ban on the giving of information concerning the prevention of conception. Comstock apparently regarded contraception and abortion as identical, and so, until recently, did many laws. These issues will be discussed more fully in the section on the right to privacy, below; here it will be mentioned only that, until recently, abortion was absolutely prohibited in all jurisdictions, and contraception was prohibited in many. These laws are clear examples of the values of another day enshrined in statute books. They arise from an understanding of procreation as the only legitimate purpose of sex and a belief in the necessity of vigorous propagation of the species. Such laws have been overturned by Supreme Court action, but continuing agitation, at least in the case of abortion, ensures that public debate will continue for some time.

Criminal Commercial Sex

The law has also deemed it illegal to make money from sex, at least in certain circumstances. It is not illegal to sell products with subtle promises of sexual fulfillment, but it is illegal actually to provide such fulfillment, either in direct form (that is, prostitution) or on paper, as in pornography. Since attitudes toward sex are changing, it is not surprising that there are attacks against these last limitations on sexual free enterprise. Both will be treated in greater detail below; first, however, the kinds of laws made on these subjects should be noted.

Prostitution is the exchange of sex for money. Except for Nevada, where counties may allow it, prostitution is illegal in every jurisdiction in the United States, though not in many other countries. The law also forbids activities related to it, such as solicitation, pandering (pimping, procuring), renting premises for prostitution, and enticing minors into prostitution (Slovenko, 1965). Laws against vagrancy and loitering are also used against prostitutes. However, the prostitute's client is almost never charged or chargeable with a crime. These laws have proved very difficult to enforce, and so the "oldest profession" goes on unabated.

Obscenity will be discussed in more detail in a later section. Suffice it to say here that in most jurisdictions it is a crime to sell material or

(a)

FIGURE 21.3

The oldest profession. (a) Modern prostitute "working the street" [Bob Adelman/Magnum Photos, Inc.]. (b) Fifteenth-century prostitutes "in the women's house" [The New York Public Library].

(b)

to present a play, film, or other live performance which is "obscene." That much is fairly simple, although many civil libertarians attack censorship as an infringement on freedom of the press. The real problem comes in deciding *what* exactly is obscene and how that will be determined without doing violence to the First Amendment. So far, no satisfactory answer has been found. Obscenity laws seem to have a twofold basis. First, they attempt to prevent the corruption of morals by materials that incite sexual thoughts and desires. Second, they attempt to ensure that no one will profit by the production and distribution of such materials. Whether either can be done, or is worth doing, is a question that will be taken up in a later section.

SEX-LAW ENFORCEMENT

From the foregoing, it is clear that the law has intruded into areas which the reader may well have thought were his or her own business. We can now ask: How are sex laws enforced? The answer is simple: With *great* inconsistency. Packer estimates that "the enforcement rate of private consensual sex offenders must show incredibly heavy odds against arrest—perhaps one in ten million" (1968, p. 304). The contrast between the number and severity of the laws themselves and the infrequency and capriciousness of their enforcement reflects the ambiguity of society's attitude toward the whole subject.

However, this contrast leads to serious abuses and demands for radical reform of sex laws. A summary of the arguments for reform will be presented later in this chapter. First, however, it should be noted that as long as the laws are on the books, the *threat* of prosecution, or even of arrest, can exact a great penalty from the "offender." Loss of job, reputation, friendship, family, and so on, can result from the sporadic enforcement of sex laws. For persons engaging in the prohibited acts, especially ho-

mosexuals, the threat of blackmail is ever present. Of course, for those actually convicted on "morals charges," the situation is even worse (see Focus). That individuals should be subjected to such liabilities for private acts is questionable.

Second, the uneven enforcement of sex laws may have a very bad effect on law enforcement generally. It invites arbitrary and unfair behavior and abuse of discretionary authority by police and prosecutors, and it may even lead them to corruption and extortion. One serious abuse is entrapment, in which an undercover police agent, posing, for example, as a homosexual or a prostitute's potential client, actually solicits the commission of a crime. Since a sexual act between consenting parties means that there is no one to report the act to the authorities, undercover agents must create the crime in order to achieve an arrest for it. Such entrapment hardly leads to respect for the law. Moreover, the knowledge that sex laws are violated with impunity creates a general disrespect for the law, particularly among those who know that they are, strictly speaking, "criminals" under it. If nothing else, the failure of Prohibition ought to demonstrate that outlawing activities of which a substantial proportion of the population approves is bad public policy. It may well be said that more violations of the public good result from the enforcement of sex laws than from the acts they seek to prevent.[3] Keeping this in mind, let us turn to the prospects for the future.

TRENDS IN SEX-LAW REFORM

It has been difficult to specify the number and details of certain types of sex laws because change is very rapid in this area. My distaste for these attempts to regulate human behavior

---

[3]For a good exposition of these and other arguments, see Packer, 1968, pp. 301–306.

THE TRIAL OF OSCAR WILDE

One of the more famous examples of the criminal prosecution of sexual behavior is the 1895 conviction of Oscar Wilde (1854–1900), the Irish author of *The Picture of Dorian Gray, The Importance of Being Earnest*, and other plays, stories, and poems. Wilde was a major figure in the "aesthetic movement" and was known for his flamboyant dress, witty conversation, and eccentric behavior. He was also an active member of the Victorian homosexual underground. He favored one-night stands with lower-class boys, many of whom he paid. His downfall was a long-running affair with Lord Alfred Douglas (known as "Bosie"), son of the Marquis of Queensberry, the codifier of the rules of boxing. Queensberry objected to the relationship and sought to "save" Bosie from the older man's influence. He precipitated a crisis by leaving his card at Wilde's club with the misspelled accusation, "To Oscar Wilde, posing as a Somdomite."

Egged on by Bosie, Wilde rashly sued the Marquis for criminal libel, which required that he prove Queensberry's charge to be false. In preparing his defense, Queensberry's lawyers found a number of Wilde's partners who were willing to testify against him, or who could be bribed or coerced into doing so. In the face of this evidence, Wilde dropped the prosecution. The result of this was to ensure his own arrest for "gross indecency with another male person."

Wilde's first trial ended in a hung jury, but at the second he was found guilty and sentenced in these words:

---

leads me to call this "reform," although many in our society would contend that the change is for the worse. Since sex is a topic heavily laden with values, such reform is not likely to be accomplished without a good deal of conflict. This makes it difficult to predict either the precise directions of change or its speed. However, some important legal principles are used to bring about changes in sex laws; these trends in reform are discussed below.

Early Efforts at Sex-Law Reform

In recent years, there have been two landmark efforts to get oppressive sexual legislation off the statute books—one English and one American. In 1954, largely at the instigation of the Moral Welfare Council of the Church of England, a blue-ribbon Committee on Homosexual Offenses and Prostitution was appointed to advise Parliament on possible reform of the laws in

Oscar Wilde . . . the crime of which you have been convicted is so bad that one has to put stern restraint upon oneself for describing, in language which I would rather not use, the sentiments which must rise in the breast of every man of honour who has heard the details of these two terrible trials. That the jury have arrived at a correct verdict in this case I cannot persuade myself to entertain the shadow of a doubt; and I hope, at all events, that those who sometimes imagine that a judge is half-hearted in the cause of decency and morality, because he takes care no prejudice shall enter into the case, may see that it is consistent at least with the utmost sense of indignation at the horrible charges brought home to . . . you.

It is no use for me to address you. People who can do these things must be dead of all sense of shame, and one cannot hope to produce any effect upon them. It is the worst case I have ever tried . . . That you, Wilde have been the center of a circle of extensive corruption of the most hideous kind among young men, it is equally impossible to doubt. I shall, under such circumstances, be expected to pass the severest sentence that the law allows. In my judgment it is totally inadequate for such a case as this. The sentence of the Court is that . . . you be imprisoned and kept at hard labour for two years. (Hyde, 1975, p. 293)

Wilde's imprisonment was unpleasant, although not as severe as he indicated in some of his writings, the most notable of which was the poem "The Ballad of Reading Gaol." Upon his release, Wilde left England. He died three years later in France at the age of 46, broken in health and spirit.

Source: H. Montgomery Hyde. *Oscar Wilde.* New York: Farrar, Straus & Giroux, 1975, pp. 191–322. Rupert Croft-Cooke. *The unrecorded life of Oscar Wilde.* New York: McKay, 1972, pp. 197–237.

these two areas. After much careful research and deliberation, in 1957 the committee issued its report, commonly known by the name of its chairman, J. F. Wolfenden. The recommendations were rather startling, most notably that "homosexual behavior between consenting adults in private be no longer a criminal offense" and that prostitution be decriminalized, leaving laws only against public nuisance (Great Britain Committee on Homosexual Offenses and Prostitution, 1963, p. 187). Essentially, the Wolfenden report concluded that private sex ought to be a private matter, and the British Parliament gradually came to agree with it.

On this side of the Atlantic, the American Law Institute's Model Penal Code recommended decriminalization of many kinds of sexual behavior previously outlawed. Under the section dealing with sexual offenses, it includes only rape, deviate sexual intercourse by force or imposition, corruption and seduction of minors, sexual assault, and indecent exposure (American Law Institute, 1962, Article 213). With the notable exception of prostitution, which it still makes illegal, the American Law Institute follows the principle that private sexual behavior between consenting adults is not really the law's business. The recommendation of the Model Penal Code has been followed by a few states.

While there are exceptions, a state is more likely to reform its sex laws as part of a complete overhaul of its criminal code than it is to make specific repeal of such laws. The reason for this is political and is grounded in the distinction between legalization and decriminalization.[4] If legislators "legalize" unconventional sexual practices, people are likely to become upset and accuse the state of "condoning" them. It is therefore important to note that what is advocated is decriminalization, that is, ceasing to define certain acts as criminal or removing the penalties attached to them. Decriminalization is morally neutral; it neither approves nor disapproves, and it simply revises the definitions. Recent trends do seem to indicate some movement toward increased decriminalization of private consensual acts.

Right to Privacy

A legal principle which has been very important in sex-law reform is the constitutional right to privacy. This has come into play chiefly in attacks on such laws through the courts. Interestingly enough, although the right to privacy is invoked in connection with an amazing variety of matters—criminal records, credit bureaus and banks, school records, medical information, government files, wiretapping, and the

---

[4]One exception is California, where laws prohibiting adulterous cohabitation, sodomy, and oral copulation were specifically rescinded by the narrowest possible margin in the state senate (*Sexual Law Reporter*, 1975, p. 18).

1974 amendment to the Freedom of Information Act, known as the Privacy Act, to name a few—the definitive articulation of the constitutional principle came in a sex-related case (Brent, 1976).

In 1965 the Supreme Court decided the case of *Griswold v. Connecticut* and invalidated a state law under which a physician was prosecuted for providing information, instruction, and medical advice concerning contraception to a married couple. Mr. Justice Douglas stated flatly that "we deal with a right of privacy older than the Bill of Rights, older than our political parties, older than our school system" (*Griswold v. Connecticut*, 1965, p. 486). The problem that Douglas, and the six justices who voted with him, faced was finding the specific provisions of the Constitution which guaranteed this right. Douglas found it not in any actual article of the Bill of Rights but in "penumbras, formed by emanations from those guarantees that help give them life and substance" (*Griswold v. Connecticut*, 1965, p. 484). Critics have found this a splendid example of constitutional double-talk, and the debate over the origin of the right to privacy continues. Nonetheless, in invalidating the Connecticut law, the Court defined a constitutional right to privacy which was, in this instance, abridged when a married couple was denied access to information on contraception.

While the decision in the Griswold case declared the marriage bed an area of privacy, the 1972 case of *Eisenstadt v. Baird* invalidated a Massachusetts law forbidding the dissemination of contraception information to the unmarried. In doing so, the Court stated that "if the right of privacy means anything, it is the right of the individual, married or single, to be free from unwarranted governmental intrusion into matters as fundamentally affecting a person as the decision whether to bear or beget a child" (*Eisenstadt v. Baird*, 1972, p. 453). Other decisions have established one's home as a protected sphere of privacy which the law cannot invade (Brent, 1976).

The right to privacy was also invoked by the Court in 1973 in one of its most controversial cases, *Roe v. Wade*, which permitted abortion. Suing under the assumed name of Jane Roe, a Texas resident argued that her state's law against abortion denied her a constitutional right. The Court agreed that "the right of personal privacy includes the abortion decision" (*Roe v. Wade*, 1973, p. 113). However, it held, by a seven-to-two margin, that such a right is not absolute and that the state has certain legitimate interests it may preserve through law, such as the protection of a viable fetus. Nonetheless, the Court declared that a fetus is not a person and therefore not entitled to constitutional protection. The effect of the Roe case, and of related litigation, was to invalidate most state laws against abortion. The Court did suggest that abortion procedures could be regulated during the second trimester and that all but therapeutic abortions might be outlawed during the third, but a woman's right to a first-trimester abortion was made nearly absolute.

In pinning the decision squarely on the right to privacy, articulated only eight years before in the Griswold decision, the Court apparently had given reformers a most important tool to use against repressive sex laws. However, the Court has recently moved in an apparently conservative direction, and the Roe decision may represent the farthest the Court is willing to go for some time. The outlook for the future is uncertain.

So far, the courts have declined to place all private adult consensual behavior within the right to privacy, despite opportunities to do so. This is particularly notable in cases involving tests of laws which criminalize consensual homosexual acts. Some legal scholars find that the right to privacy ought to cover that situation amply, but few courts have so ruled (Barnett, 1973; W. C. Jones, 1976). The Supreme Court

has considered one case on this issue, *Doe v. Commonwealth Attorney*, but affirmed, without comment, a lower court decision that Virginia could constitutionally prohibit homosexual acts. Apparently, the right to privacy stops here, and, for the foreseeable future, change is more likely to come about through legislative process than in the courts (W. C. Jones, 1976). Such a legislative approach can be seen in the small but growing number of counties and municipalities which have passed laws forbidding discrimination in housing, public accommodations, or employment on the basis of sexual orientation (*Sexual Law Reporter*, 1976, p. 31). However, the Anita Bryant crusade in Dade County, Florida (see Figure 21.2), points up some of the problems of this approach.

Victimless Crimes

If the arena for sex-law reform in the near future is to be legislatures rather than courts, we are likely to hear a good deal about "victimless crimes." This principle asserts that when an act does no legal harm to anyone or does not provide a demonstrable victim, it cannot be reasonably defined as a crime. Around this concept, which applies to a good deal more than sexual behavior, a great deal of legislative change is taking place and is likely to continue. The thrust of the argument is well articulated by University of Chicago Law School Dean Norval Morris:

> Most of our legislation concerning drunkeness, narcotics, gambling and sexual behavior is wholly misguided. It is based on an exaggerated conception of the capacity of the criminal law to influence men and, ironically, on a simultaneous belief in the limited capacity of men to govern themselves. We incur enormous collateral costs for that exaggeration and we overload our criminal justice system to a degree that renders it grossly defective where we really need protection—from violence and depreda-

"Be right with you, maám, soon as I've brought these lawbreakers to justice."

FIGURE 21.4
A cartoonist's view of victimless crime. [Copyright © 1976 The Chicago Sun-Times. Reproduced by courtesy of Wil-Jo Associates, Inc., and Bill Mauldin.]

tions on our property. But in attempting to remedy this situation, we should not substitute a mindless "legalization" of what we now proscribe as crime. Instead, regulatory programs, backed up by criminal sanctions, must take the place of our present unenforceable, crime-breeding and corrupting prohibitions. (1973, p. 11)

The victimless-crime argument should appeal not only to the public's sense of privacy but also to its pocketbooks. Crimes in which there is no readily identifiable victim account for over half the cases handled by American courts (Boruchowitz, 1973). If the court dockets could be cleared and law enforcement officers reassigned, protection against violent crimes would be rendered more efficient and less expensive.

The application of the principle to some of the issues discussed above should be obvious. A sexual act performed by consenting adults, whatever it might be, produces neither a victim nor legal harm. The only conceivable end served by criminalizing such an act is the protection of "public morals," which, in a society with many values, seems an end not worth the cost, if it is even possible. If sodomy laws, for example, are removed by a state legislature, the victimless-crime argument is likely to be used, by itself or in combination with an appeal to the right to privacy.

The most common reference to the decriminalization of victimless crimes is with respect to prostitution. Police efforts at curbing the "oldest profession" seem to be expensive, unsuccessful, and open to corruption and dubious practices. If prostitution were no longer defined as a crime, it is argued, all those involved—the prostitute, her patron, the police, and society at large—would benefit (Rosenbleet and Pariente, 1973). Indeed, it has been suggested that much of the demonstrable harm associated with prostitution, such as the committing of robbery and other crimes by prostitutes and pimps and its connections with organized crime, has resulted *because* the practice is illegal (Caughey, 1974). Likewise, the offensiveness of public solicitation might be avoided if prostitution were decriminalized and allowed to operate as a business rather than a clandestine affair. Indeed, prostitution could even be legalized and regulated, providing clients protection from disease, giving prostitutes freedom from victimization, and supplying the government with tax revenues! The argument that prostitution is a leading contributor to the spread of venereal disease also seems to lack basis in fact.[5] Therefore, if prostitution does not necessarily lead to crime, public offense, or the spread of VD, how does its continued criminalization benefit society?

In a society in which crimes of violence and crimes against property endanger everyone, it seems reasonable to expect increasing decriminalization of acts that do not clearly harm people in order that police and the courts may be freer to attack crimes that do. In England, the Wolfenden recommendations were adopted; prostitution is legal, while solicitation is regulated. Whether, or how soon, American legislatures will follow this example remains to be seen. Nonetheless, the movement to eliminate victimless crimes is established and seems likely to grow.

---

[5]Studies indicate that no more than 5 percent of the venereal disease in the United States is attributable to prostitution. Further, the 15- to 30-year-old age group accounts for 84 percent of reported VD, while the 30- to 60-year-old age group accounts for 70 percent of visits to prostitutes (Caughey, 1974).

The Problem of Obscenity and Pornography

In the entire area of sexual regulation, there is no subject on which there has been more heat and less light generated than that of obscenity and pornography. A substantial portion of the American populace apparently finds pornography offensive and wishes it suppressed. Many others do not share this view and find any form of censorship outrageous and unconstitutional. Antivice crusaders consider "smut" dangerous to the average citizen, and yet few social scientists have found any evidence that it is (see, for example, M. J. Goldstein and Kant, 1975). Legislators are swamped with demands that something be done, while the courts have labored unsuccessfully for years to balance the First Amendment right of freedom of speech with an apparent national desire to outlaw, or at least regulate, pornography. The enormous amount of energy and money spent on the issue suggests that pornography is a problem, but hardly anyone seems to be able to explain why it is a problem or even to define it, and it will probably be a long time before any generally satisfactory resolution can be achieved.

The discussion will begin with a problem of definition. Here it is helpful to distinguish between "pornography" as a popular term and "obscenity" as a legal concept. "Pornography" comes from the Greek word *porneia*, which means quite simply "prostitution." In general usage today, it refers to literature, art, film, speech, and so on, that are sexually arousing, or presumed to be arousing, in nature. It may be "soft-core," that is, suggestive, or "hard-core," which usually means that there is explicit depiction of some sort of sexual activity. Pornography, as such, has never been illegal, but obscenity is. The word "obscene" suggests that which is foul, disgusting, or lewd, and it is used as a legal term for that which is offensive to the authorities or to society (Wilson, 1973).

Whatever its origin, obscenity has been the

FIGURE 21.5
Can love survive in the age of porn?
[Drawing by W. Miller; © 1974,
The New Yorker Magazine, Inc.]

legal issue ever since the Supreme Court decided the Roth case in 1957. The Court explicitly
stated that obscenity was not protected by the
First Amendment—which guarantees freedom
of speech and the press and which, by long-
recognized extensions, includes film, pictures,
literature, and other forms of artistic expression.
However, it also ruled that not all sexual expression is obscene, defining obscenity as material "which deals with sex in a manner appealing to prurient interest" (*U.S. v. Roth*, 1957, p.
487). The Roth decision evoked much controversy, both from those who thought the Court
had opened the floodgates of pornography and
from civil libertarians who found the definition
too limiting of freedom. The Court continued

to try to refine the test for obscenity. In the
1966 Memoirs case, obscenity was additionally
defined as that which is "utterly without redeeming social importance." In the Ginzburg
decision the same year, the Court upheld the
obscenity conviction of a publisher for "pandering" in his advertising, that is, flagrantly ex-
ploiting the sexually arousing nature of his publication. However, none of these tests was
persuasive to more than five members of the
Court, much less to the public at large.[6]

---

[6]Perhaps the frustration of defining obscenity is best expressed by
Justice Potter Stewart in *Jacobelis v. Ohio* (1964): "I shall not further
attempt to define [hard-core pornography], and perhaps I could not
ever succeed in intelligibly doing so. But I know it when I see it"
(378 U.S. 197).

The next attempt by the Supreme Court to define obscenity came in the 1973 case of *Miller v. California*. Rejecting the "utterly without redeeming social value" test, Chief Justice Burger and the four justices concurring with him proposed the following definition:

(a) whether "the average person, applying contemporary community standards" would find that the work, taken as a whole, appeals to the prurient interest, (b) whether the work depicts or describes, in a patently offensive way, sexual conduct specifically defined by the applicable state law, and (c) whether the work, taken as a whole, lacks serious literary, artistic, political or scientific value. (*Miller v. California*, 1973, p. 24)

The goals of this decision seem to be to define as obscenity "hard-core pornography" in the popular sense, to require from state statutes precise descriptions of that which is to be outlawed, and to give governments more power to regulate it (Gruntz, 1974). The notable problem in the Miller standards, at least for civil libertarians, is the "contemporary community standards" provision. This allows the local community to determine what is obscene, rather than using national norms. This makes it impossible to predict what a given jury in a particular town might find obscene.

It seems doubtful that the Court has in fact settled the matter with the Miller decision. Many people in the United States take the view consistently held by Justices Hugo Black and William Douglas that *no* provision for the suppression of *any* such work is constitutional. In this view, censorship of any sort is intolerable and a threat to civil rights and liberties. Others will be willing to see the government regulate pornography—prevent its sale to children, confine it to certain locations, require clear warnings in advertisements and on packaging, and so on. Even if the Miller definition is widely accepted, there are other problems that go beyond that issue.

Of principal concern to social scientists, and to some legal scholars, is what harm, if any, pornography does. The number of empirical studies is rather small, but what evidence there is tends to suggest that there is no harm in it. Pornography does not appear to have adverse effects on people in the short run (Howard et al., 1973; Mann et al., 1973; Mosher, 1973). Consumers of pornography are not notably deviant (Nawy, 1973), and, over the long run, pornography does not seem to lead to pathological behavior (Davis and Braucht, 1973; M. J. Goldstein, 1973). Indeed, in Denmark there was a marked reduction in certain kinds of sexual crime, notably child molestation, following the complete decriminalization of activities connected with the distribution of sexually explicit literature (Kutchinsky, 1973). This sort of evidence led the Commission on Obscenity and Pornography to issue a report in 1970 which favored regulations preventing the distribution of sexually explicit material to children and unconsenting adults but which recommended no such prohibition to consenting adults (Kemp, 1974).

Further research needs to be done in this field, and a way will have to be found to balance the conflicting views and demands of the American public with the available data and the protections afforded by the First Amendment. If anything is clear it is that there is no agreement on what obscenity is, on whether it is harmful, and on whether any prohibitions are reasonable (Wallace, 1973; Wilson and Abelson, 1973). Perhaps we are back where we started, observing that, in an aspect of life as important and value-laden as human sexuality, legislation is difficult at best and dangerous at worst. It may be that the best thing the government can do about crime in the bedroom is to draw the drapes, close the door, and walk quietly away.

SUMMARY

It is reasonable to suggest that laws to protect adults from coercion, children from sexual exploitation, and the public from offensive behavior are justifiable. However, many laws against sexual conduct originated in a desire to promote public morality, and it is hard to justify them.

The laws governing sexual conduct are concerned with crimes of exploitation and force (such as rape, carnal knowledge of a juvenile, and child molestation), various consensual acts (such as fornication, adultery, sodomy, and other "unnatural acts"), offenses against public taste (exhibitionism, voyeurism, solicitation, disorderly conduct, lewdness, and the like), crimes against procreation (contraception and abortion), and criminal commercial sex (notably prostitution and obscenity). These laws are often capriciously enforced, and this unequal enforcement has high social costs which may require reform.

Certain trends can be discerned in the reform of such sex laws. The British Wolfenden report and the American Model Penal Code are early examples of proposals to decriminalize much sexual behavior. The legal principle which has accounted for much court action to reform laws against contraception and abortion is the "right to privacy," which has not yet been broadened to include consenting acts by adults. A factor which has influenced legislators, and will probably continue to do so, is the movement for the decriminalization of "victimless crimes." The issue of pornography and obsceni-ty, which includes such problems as definition, conflicting societal values, and actual demonstration of effects, is a confusing one.

SUGGESTIONS FOR FURTHER READING

Boggan, E. C., Haft, M. G., Lister, C., and Rupp, J. P. *The rights of gay people.* New York: Avon, 1975. Prepared by the American Civil Liberties Union, this is a comprehensive review of the legal problems faced by homosexuals and also includes a good deal about laws affecting a wide variety of sexual behaviors.

Broun, Heywood, and Leech, Margaret. *Anthony Comstock: Roundsman of the Lord.* New York: Boni, 1927. A well-written and entertaining biography of the great crusader against vice. It is useful for its background view on how many sex laws got on the books.

Great Britain Committee on Homosexual Offenses and Prostitution. *The Wolfenden report.* (American ed.). New York: Stein and Day, 1963. This classic study, with its proposal for the decriminalization of homosexual acts and prostitution, is the starting point for any study of sex-law reform.

Sexual Law Reporter. (1800 North Highland Avenue, Suite 106, Los Angeles, California 90028.) This bimonthly publication is invaluable for keeping track of court cases, changes in legislation, and other important aspects of the field.

SEX
EDUCATION

CITED

A little girl was taking a shower with her mother. She looked up at her mother, and said "Mommy, why am I so plain, and you're so fancy?"*

Children are often curious about sex. That is perfectly normal and good, and it motivates them to learn. The only problem is that adults often do not know what to do about it. This chapter will be about concepts and methods that are useful in sex education, both in a formal school curriculum and in informal sex education in the home or some other situation.

IN THE HOME, IN THE SCHOOL, OR SOMEWHERE ELSE?

When a group of concerned parents get together and urge a school system to begin a sex education curriculum, invariably some upright citizens of the community raise a protest. They may say that sex education promotes promiscuity, communism, or some other disaster, and they are sure that it should take place only in the home (or possibly the church), but certainly not in the schools.

What these upright citizens overlook is the realistic alternative to sex education in the

schools. For most children, the primary source of sex information in childhood is friends (see Table 22.1), and that is the classic case of the blind leading the blind. Mothers come in a poor third, and fathers even further down the list, as actual sources of sex information. Interestingly, young people would prefer to hear about sex from their parents (J. H. Gagnon, 1965b). But—although there are certainly exceptions—many parents handle their children's questions about sex by issuing orders rather than by having a discussion (Libby and Nass, 1971). The

TABLE 22.1
CHILDREN'S MAIN SOURCES OF
SEXUAL INFORMATION

Source	Males, %	Females, %
Friends	59	46
Reading	20	22
Mother	3	16
Father	6	1
School program	3	5
Adults outside the home	6	4
Brothers, sisters	4	6
Others and no answer	7	7

Source: Morton Hunt. *Sexual behavior in the 1970s.* Chicago: Playboy Press, 1974, p. 122. Roughly similar results have been obtained by J. H. Gagnon (1965) and Athanasiou et al. (1970).

---

* *Source*: Rosemary Zumwalt. Plain and fancy: A content analysis of children's jokes dealing with adult sexuality. *Western Folklore*, 1976, **35**, p. 258.

following comments from parents exemplify such attitudes:

"I try to keep them from knowing too much."

"My parents did not tell me about it. I don't discuss it, either."

"I just tell them to behave and keep their eyes open." (Libby and Nass, 1971, pp. 230, 233)

The fact is that many children are given no sex education in the home. Rather, they learn about sex in the street, and the result is a massive amount of misinformation. Thus, people who say that sex education should be carried out in the home, not in the school, are not making a sensible argument.

In fact, most parents favor sex education in the schools. According to a Gallup poll, 71 percent of parents are in favor of it (Breasted, 1970). Those who are opposed to sex education constitute a rather small group that makes a great deal of noise, leading one to overestimate their numbers.

EFFECTS OF SEX EDUCATION

One argument made by people opposed to sex education in the schools is that it leads to terrible consequences, particularly increases in premarital sex and promiscuity. Is there any scientific evidence backing this assertion?

In 1967 a national probability sample of 1177 college students were interviewed about their current sexual behavior and their previous sources of sex information (Spanier, 1976,

FIGURE 22.1
"A Hurry Call," by William Balfour-Ker. The stork and the doctor seem to be in more of a hurry than most parents are to give their children some sex education.
[The Bettman Archive, Inc.]

1977). The results indicated that having sex education in the schools had had little effect on the students' premarital sexual activity; current factors—such as dating patterns—seemed to be much more important influences (Spanier, 1976). Respondents who listed teachers as a major source of sex information were not more sexually active than other respondents. Indeed, there was a slight trend, among females, for those who had had sex education from teachers to be *less* sexually experienced than those who had not (Spanier, 1977). Thus, the evidence does not support the contention that sex education encourages premarital sexual experimentation.

In contrast, there is evidence that responsible sex education may have a number of desirable effects. On the basis of a study of 600 teenagers, one investigator concluded that if an adolescent "obtained his sex knowledge from parents or adults with whom a positive identification exists, there appeared to be less tendency toward involvement in promiscuity" (Deschin, 1963). Other findings suggest that an adequate sex education contributes positively to general psychological adjustment (McCary, 1973, p. 16). Finally, institution of sex education programs in schools has been reported to reduce the incidence of gonorrhea by as much as 50 percent in a year's time (M. I. Levine, 1970).

PURPOSES OF SEX EDUCATION

The Sex Information and Education Council of the United States (SIECUS), under the directorship of Dr. Mary Calderone, has been one of the most active groups promoting quality sex education. According to SIECUS, the goals of sex education should be:

1 To provide for the individual an adequate knowledge of his or her own physical, mental, and emotional maturation processes as related to sex.
2 To eliminate fears and anxieties relative to individual sexual development and adjustments.
3 To develop objective and understanding attitudes toward sex in all of its various manifestations—in the individual and in others.
4 To give the individual insight concerning her or his relationships to members of both genders and to help him or her understand their obligations and responsibilities to others.
5 To provide an appreciation of the positive satisfaction that wholesome human relations can bring in both individual and family living.
6 To build an understanding of the need for the moral values that are essential to provide rational bases for making decisions.
7 To provide enough knowledge about the misuses and aberrations of sex to enable individuals to protect themselves against exploitation and against injury to their physical or mental health.
8 To provide an incentive to work for a society in which such evils as prostitution and illegitimacy, archaic sex laws, irrational fears of sex, and sexual exploitation are nonexistent.
9 To provide the understanding and conditioning that will enable each individual to use his or her sexuality effectively and creatively in the several roles of spouse, parent, community member, and citizen (Kirkendall, 1965)

I couldn't have said it better myself, and so I won't try to.

THE TEACHER

Suppose you have decided to start a program of sex education. Whether it is to be carried out in the school, the home, or someplace else, the first thing you need is a teacher. What qualifications should this person have?[1]

First, the person should be fairly well edu-

---

[1]The American Association of Sex Educators, Counselors, and Therapists (5010 Wisconsin Avenue, N.W., Washington, D.C. 20016) is a good professional organization that can provide further information.

cated in sexual matters. Reading a text such as this one (or Broderick and Bernard, 1969, or R. S. Rogers, 1974, which are geared for sex education) or taking a university course in sexuality would be a good way to acquire the knowledge that is needed. But do not assume that a teacher has to have a Ph.D. in sex; the important qualifications are a good basic knowledge, a willingness to admit when he or she does not know the answer, and the patience to look things up (and a knowledge of where to look).

Equally important is the teacher's comfort with sexual topics. Even when parents or other adults willingly give accurate factual information to children about sex, they may still convey negative attitudes because they become anxious or blush while answering the child's ques-

tions or because they use euphemisms rather than direct sexual terms. Thus, it is important for the teacher to feel relaxed and comfortable discussing sex. Some people just are that way; others must work to learn this attitude. There are a number of ways to do this. One is for the teacher to role-play, with another adult, having sexual discussions with children. Comfort is gained with practice.

A good teacher is also a good listener who can assess what the child knows from the questions asked and who can understand what a child really wants to know when she or he asks a question. According to a joke, little Billy ran into the kitchen in his home one day after kindergarten and asked his mother where he had come from; she gritted her teeth, realized the time had come, and proceeded with a

FIGURE 22.2
A modern sex-education class in the schools. [Charles Moore/Black Star.]

15-minute discussion of intercourse, conception, and birth, blushing the whole time. Billy listened, but at the end he appeared somewhat confused and walked away shaking his head and saying, "That's funny. Jimmy says he came from Illinois."

WHAT TO TEACH
AT DIFFERENT AGES

Sex education is not something that can be carried out all at once in one week during fifth grade. Like teaching arithmetic, it is a process that must begin when children are small. They should learn simple concepts first, progressing to more difficult ones as they grow older. What one teaches at any particular age depends on the child's sexual behavior (see Chapter 10), sexual knowledge, and sexual interests at that age. This section will concentrate on theories and research that provide information on these last two points.

A Theoretical View: Piaget

The Swiss psychologist Jean Piaget believes that children are all little philosophers, constructing their own views of the universe that make sense; thus they pass through various stages of cognitive (intellectual) development during which they have different understandings of natural events.

Piaget believes that during the earliest phases of understanding about reproduction, at about ages 3 to 5, children are in a *preartificialistic* stage (Moore and Kendall, 1971). At this age, children believe that a baby, such as a little brother or sister, has always existed. They have no notion that something might have caused or created its existence. Instead, they only wonder where (geographically) the baby was before it was in their house.

In the second stage, children have *artificialistic* concepts of reproduction and believe that parents cause the creation of babies, al-

though they may have bizarre ways of explaining how parents do this, as some of the following examples will show. This stage lasts from perhaps age 6 to age 10.

Finally, in the *naturalistic* stage, children come to have a more and more scientific understanding of processes involved in reproduction.

Children's Sex Knowledge

A few researchers (though not nearly enough) have investigated what children know about sex and reproduction at various ages.

In one study, Israeli children aged 4 to $5\frac{1}{2}$ were questioned about sex and reproduction (Kreitler and Kreitler, 1966). About 60 percent of the children could describe the sex organs of the opposite gender. More than 90 percent knew that a baby came from the mother's enlarged belly. But, when asked what the mother does in order to get a baby, many of them responded that she must eat a lot or that she swallows the baby. These answers are reminiscent of Freud's notions. Only about 2 percent of the boys and one of the girls mentioned intercourse.

When the children were asked how the baby gets out, most said that the mother's belly had to be cut open. One wonders what the effects are when children hold such an alarming view of birth.

The children also were asked how the father helps in this process. Their answers typically involved things like feeding the mother, earning money, and helping the mother, once again demonstrating that they had no knowledge of intercourse.

One other interesting point emerged from this study. Some of the children were of European and American ancestry, while others were of non-Western ancestry (North African or Arab, for example). The sex knowledge of the children from these two groups differed greatly, with the Western children generally knowing considerably more. For example, 77 percent of the Western boys, but only 40 percent of the non-Western boys, could describe the sex organs of the opposite gender. This shows how much children's sex knowledge depends on their home environment.

This study was repeated in the United States with children aged 3 to 5½ (Moore and Kendall, 1971). The authors particularly noted the children's poor sexual vocabulary. For example, when children were asked, "What do you call the water that comes out of your body when you use the toilet?" only 2 of the 38 girls and 1 of the 31 boys used the word "urine." The rest used slang terms such as "tinkle" or "wee-wee," presumably because their parents had taught them these labels or had taught them no label at all.

When asked where the urine comes out, over half of the boys had a label ("penis" or some other word), compared with only 14 percent of the girls.[2] Once again, though, many children did not know the correct names of the sexual organs. One wonders what the long-term effects of this lack of vocabulary might be—whether, for example, it might hinder people from communicating about sexual matters in adulthood. Most authorities in the field recommend that children be taught accurate labels from the first; it is, after all, just as easy to teach children to say "penis" as it is to teach them to say "peter."

As was true of the Israeli children, almost none of the children in this study knew about intercourse. When asked what a mother must do in order to have a baby, many gave responses like "go to the doctor" and "go to the hospital." Only 6 percent knew that the father had a role in reproduction, and only one child used the word "intercourse."

Stages of understanding Psychologist Anne Bernstein (1976; Bernstein and Cowan, 1975)

---

[2]It occurs to me that it is probably not easy for girls to come up with such a label; probably "vulva" would be the most accurate.

has investigated children's understanding of reproduction, basing her research on Piaget's idea that children go through stages in their understanding. She found that children do proceed through the following levels (stages) of understanding about reproduction.

Level 1: Geography Most 3- to 4-year-olds believe that a baby has always existed and may believe that it was located somewhere else (geographically) before it got inside the mother. The following is an example of the responses of a Level 1 child:

> (How did the baby happen to be in your Mommy's tummy?) It just grows inside. (How did it get there?) It's there all the time. Mommy doesn't have to do anything. She waits until she feels it. (You said that the baby wasn't in there when you were there.) Yeah, then he was in the other place . . . in America. (In America?) Yeah, in somebody else's tummy. (Bernstein and Cowan, 1975, p. 86)

Level 2: Manufacturing At around age 4, children begin to understand that something causes babies to come into existence. However, they think a manufacturing process is involved, as in the production of a refrigerator or a TV. A Level 2 child described how people get babies as follows:

> Maybe they just paint the right bones. . . . Maybe they just paint the bones and paint the blood, and paint the blue blood. . . . (Bernstein and Cowan, 1975, p. 86)

Level 3: Transitional By age 7 or 8, children explain reproduction as a mixture of technology and physiology, but they stick to feasible occurrences. They no longer think that the mother opens up her tummy to let the baby out. Level 3 children may know that three things are involved in making a baby: a social relationship between two people, such as love or marriage;

QUESTIONS CHILDREN ASK ABOUT SEX

The following are typical questions that children ask at various ages:

The Primary Grades
What is being born?
Where was I before I was born?
Why can't I have a baby?
Did I come from an egg?
Why can't I marry Daddy?

The Intermediate Grades
How do babies start?
How does the sperm get into the egg?
How long does it take for a baby to get ready to be born?
How can you tell if the baby will be a boy or a girl?
Do boys menstruate?
When are we old enough to mate?
When the husband and wife mate, does menstruation occur?
Do you have to go to the bathroom to bleed?
Can you have a baby when you are 13 years old?
Does it hurt to have a baby?
Why do mothers nurse their babies?
When do boys start to change?
Can a boy have a baby?
Why do some mothers die when babies are born?
Do you menstruate the rest of your life once you start?

Seventh, Eighth, and Ninth Grades
ABOUT DATING
Is it bad or good to go steady?
Do you have to have a sense of humor to be popular? Do you have to follow the fad to be popular?
What do you do if you're chicken to ask a girl to go on a date?
What do boys look for in a girl?

ABOUT PETTING

What is petting?

On a date, is it customary to kiss the girl after the date? If so, under what conditions should you do it?

How do you French-kiss a girl?

What is necking?

What should a girl do or say if her boyfriend wants to have sexual intercourse with her and she doesn't, but she still wants to keep him as a boyfriend?

ABOUT TERMINOLOGY

What does "molested" mean?

What is nude?

What is the cherry that is inside the girl?

What causes a boner?

What is a queer?

What is the womb?

What are the testes?

What does "circumcise" mean?

ABOUT ANATOMY

Why don't girls have penises?

Why does sex appeal start at adolescence?

What are hormones?

ABOUT GROWTH AND DEVELOPMENT

Is there any limit to a boy's sperm?

Is it milk in the girl's breast? Is the vagina between the girl's legs?

What does semen look like?

Does a girl ever have a wet dream?

Why does a boy's penis get hard and stiff when he gets sexually emotional?

ABOUT MENSTRUATION

When do you start?

What is a period?

Why do some girls start menstruation later or earlier than others?

When girls start to menstruate, do they need Kotex?

Why are girls using Tampax?

Can you ride horseback when you have your period?

ABOUT MASTURBATION

Is it bad for boys to masturbate?

What is masturbation?

Do all boys masturbate, and at what age?

Are there such things as homosexual women?
What is the difference between homosexuals, lesbians, and queers?

Can boys possibly go to the bathroom during the time they make a
   woman pregnant? What position are the man and woman in
   when the man makes the woman pregnant?
Are the testes empty after sexual intercourse?
Does sexual intercourse hurt?
What does "sexual intercourse" mean?

Tenth, Eleventh, and Twelfth Grades

What is prostitution?
Is "making love" to a person the same as sexual intercourse?
What is an orgasm?
What is a virgin?

Source: Esther D. Schulz and Sally R. Williams. *Family life and sex education: Curriculum and instruction.* New York: Harcourt, Brace, & World, 1969. See also Ruth V. Byler. *Teach us what we want to know.* New York: Mental Health Materials Center, for the Connecticut State Board of Education, 1969.

---

sexual intercourse; and the union of sperm and egg.

The combination of manufacturing ideas and biology ideas is illustrated by a Level 3 child's explanation of why the male's contribution is necessary:

> Well, the father puts the shell. I forget what it's called, but he puts something in for the egg. If he didn't then a baby couldn't come. Because it needs the stuff that the father gives. It helps it grow. I think that the stuff has the food part, maybe, and maybe it helps protect it. I think he gives the shell part, and the shell part, I think, is the skin. (Bernstein, 1976, p. 34)

In Piaget's terms, these children are in a transitional phase between the preoperational and the concrete operational stages of thought.

Level 4: Concrete physiology   Level 4 and the successive levels are qualitatively different from the previous ones because children now have an understanding of the physical facts of life and of the importance of sperm and egg. At Levels 4, 5, and 6, they come increasingly closer to scientific understandings.

Though Level 4 children know about egg and sperm, they may not know why they have to unite. An 8-year-old said:

> The man and the woman get together, and then they put a speck, then the man has his seed and the woman has an egg. They have to come together or else the baby won't really get hatched very well. The seed makes the egg grow. It's just like plants. If you plant a seed, a flower will grow. (Bernstein, 1976, p. 34)

Level 5: Preformation At level 5, children (usually 11- or 12-year-olds) believe that the baby already exists (is preformed) in either the sperm or the egg. They think that the other germ cell or intercourse simply makes conditions suitable for the baby to grow. For example:

> Well, if they're the man that made love to your mother, then your father because you really originally came out of him, and then went into your mother. Well, you were a sperm inside of him, there. So that you're the, you're really his daughter or son. 'Cause he was the one that really had you first. (Why must the egg be there for the sperm to develop into a baby?) 'Cause otherwise the sperm will have, uh, nothing to nourish it, or sort of keep it warm or, you know, able to move or something. Just has, it's not, just has to have the egg to be able to do something, develop. It just dies if it doesn't have the egg. (Bernstein and Cowan, 1975, p. 89)

Level 6: Physical causality Level 6 children, who are generally 12 or older, give a good physiological explanation of reproduction that includes the idea that the embryo begins its biological existence at the moment of conception and that it is the product of genetic material from both parents. A Level 6 child said:

> The sperm encounters one ovum, and one sperm breaks into the ovum which produces, the sperm makes like a cell, and the cell separates and divides. And so it's dividing, and the ovum goes through a tube and embeds itself in the wall of the, I think it's the fetus of the woman. (Bernstein and Cowan, 1975, p. 89)

Bernstein's findings have important implications for sex education (Bernstein, 1976). Educators should be aware of the level of the child's understanding and should not inundate him or her with information appropriate for a child three or four levels higher. Instead, there should be an attempt to clarify misunderstandings inherent in the child's beliefs. For example,

a Level 1 child believes that a baby has always existed. To such a child, you might say, "To make a baby person, you need two grown-up persons, one a man and one a woman." To the Level 2 child, who believes that babies are manufactured, you might say, "That's an interesting way of looking at things. That's the way you'd make a doll. You would buy a head and some hair and put it all together. But making a real, live baby is different from making a doll or a cake or an airplane" (Bernstein, 1976, p. 35).

Children's questions about sex Children's knowledge of, and interest in, sex are reflected in the questions they ask. In a study of children's questions about sex, it was found that many questions are asked at around age 5, a time when children are generally asking questions. Boys also tended to ask a lot of questions at around age 9, and girls at ages 9 and 13 (Byler, 1969; Hattendorf, 1932). The areas of sexual curiosity were (beginning with the most common) the origin of babies, the coming of another baby, intrauterine growth, the process of birth, the organs and functions of the body, physical sex differences, the relation of the father to reproduction, and marriage.

Sex educators have found that children tend to ask typical questions at various ages. A sampling of such questions is given in the Focus.

Children's dirty jokes We can also tell something about children's sexual knowledge and interest by the dirty jokes they tell.

Anthropologist Rosemary Zumwalt collected dirty jokes from girls between the ages of 7 and 10 as part of her study of children's folklore (1976). The following is typical of the jokes they told her:

> There's this little boy, and he wanted to take a bath with his dad. And his dad said, "If you promise not to look under the curtain." And

A SAMPLE SEX EDUCATION CURRICULUM

CONCEPTS TO BE LEARNED AT THE DIFFERENT GRADE LEVELS

Kindergarten and Grade 1

1 Use of correct terminology, such as "penis" and "breast"
2 Respecting the privacy and rights of others, such as privacy in the bathroom
3 The arrival of a new baby as a happy occasion
4 Safety going to and from school; what to do if offered a ride by a stranger

Grades 2 and 3

1 Understanding human growth and development
2 Understanding feelings (emotions), both one's own and those of others; understanding feelings of love and affection
3 Understanding how families and the community help each other

Grade 4

1 Body structures and functions, such as the circulatory system and the excretory system
2 Heredity
3 Being a good family member
4 Being a good friend
5 Growing up emotionally; acceptable ways to get rid of anger

Grade 5

1 Growth patterns and rates of development; the changes of puberty
2 Changes in the male and female reproductive organs
3 The baby, including embryonic development and birth
4 Good health habits
5 Living with parents and friends while growing up

Grade 6

1 Structure and function of cells
2 Emotions, including acceptability of "gender-inappropriate" emotions, such as crying by a boy

3 Sexual anatomy and hormones

Grade 7

1 Understanding one's personality and emotions; attraction to members of the opposite gender
2 Family structures in the United States, including families in which the mother holds a job outside the home, and single parent families
3 Male and female reproductive processes

Grade 8

1 Emotions, including the development of the sex drive and the need to control it
2 Dating, including necking and petting and problems related to dating
3 Continued discussion of the family
4 Review of the female and male reproductive processes

Grade 9

1 Mental and emotional health
2 Family relationships, including the development of independence and sound judgments
3 Boy-girl relationships, including dating, going steady, necking, and petting; understanding the meaning of the terms "sexual intercourse," "sexual relations," "premarital relations," and "premarital intercourse"

Grades 10 and 11

1 Psychosocial development; personality
2 Boy-girl relationships in light of both immediate and long-range goals
3 Family planning
4 Growth and reproduction

Grade 12

1 Preparation for marriage
2 Adjustments in marriage; potential problems
3 Planning for parenthood
4 Family living
5 Attitudes toward sex and sexual behavior; different value systems

Source: Growth patterns and sex education. *The Journal of School Health,* May 1967, pp. 1–136.

then he took a shower, and he looked under the curtain. And he said, "Dad, what's that long hairy thing?" And the father says, "That's my banana."

Then he asks his mom, "Can I take a shower with you, Mom?" She says, "If you promise not to look under the curtain." And they get into the shower, and he looks under the curtain. And he says, "Mom, what's that thing?" And she says, "That's my fruit bowl." And he says, "Mom, can I sleep with you and Dad?" And she says, "Yes, if you promise not to look under the covers." And he looks under the covers and says, "Mom, Dad's banana is in your fruit bowl!" (Zumwalt, 1976, p. 261)

Children's dirty jokes reflect several themes in their attitudes toward sexuality and in their interactions with their parents on the issue. First, children seem to view their parents as always trying to keep sex—such as nudity and sexual organs—a secret from them. The parents consistently tell children not to look under the cover, for example. Second, the jokes reflect children's fascination with sex, particularly with the penis, the vagina, the breasts, and intercourse. The jokes generally revolve around these topics and children's attempts to find out about them. Third, the jokes seem to satirize adults' use of euphemisms for sexual terms. The joke above hinges on a parent's using a term such as "banana" instead of "penis." Most frequently, the fanciful names used for the sexual organs involve food (banana, hot dog), power (light bulbs, light sockets), or animals (gorilla). Commenting on the bathtub-shower form of dirty joke, an authority said, "In all forms of the . . . joke, the wonderful humor to the child is the mocking of the parents' evasions, which are somehow so foolishly phrased . . ." (Legman, 1968, p. 53).

Teenagers have outgrown this sort of joke, but they tell a parallel one:

This little boy walks into the bathroom, and he catches his mother naked. She was a little embarrassed. He said, "Mommy, what's that?" And she says, "Oh, that's where God hit me with an axe." And the little kid says, "Got you right in the cunt, eh?" (Zumwalt, 1976, p. 267)

Once again, this joke has the theme of a parent's embarrassment and use of evasions and euphemisms when dealing with sex. But now the child (teenager) reflects a sophistication about sex, perhaps even a greater sophistication than the parent has.

Sex educators should remember that children are aware of adults' attempts to "cover up" and of their embarrassment and their use of euphemisms, as these jokes indicate.

CURRICULUM

Space does not permit outlining a complete sex education curriculum here. Instead, a brief outline of major concepts to be covered in one major curriculum is given in the Focus. Further references to curriculum materials are provided at the end of this chapter in the Suggestions for Further Reading.

Note that the sample curriculum in the Focus exemplifies several principles. First, sex education must be carried out at all grade levels. It cannot be accomplished all at once in a week (or a day) during the fifth or sixth grade. Curriculum materials are therefore geared to the age of the child and build on each other from year to year. For example, by the time conception and intercourse are discussed in grade 6 or 7, the child is already familiar with parts of the anatomy and understands terms such as "penis," "vagina," and "uterus." Second, correct terminology should be taught from the beginning. Even children in kindergarten and first grade should learn terms such as "penis" and "vagina."[3] Third, the curriculum should reflect the need to teach children about the emotional and social aspects of sex—such as dealing with sexual feelings and going on dates—as well as the biological aspects. These are important principles for any sex education curriculum.

SUMMARY

Most children receive their sex education from their peers, not from their parents; as a result, those who argue for sex education in the home rather than the school are not being realistic. Most Americans actually favor sex education in the school. Further, the presumed negative effects of sex education are not substantiated by available data.

The purposes of sex education include providing children with an adequate knowledge of the physical and emotional aspects of sex and eliminating unwarranted fears and anxieties.

A good instructor in sex education must have some accurate knowledge about sex, must be comfortable discussing it, and must be good at listening to children's questions.

What one teaches in sex education at each age depends on what children are thinking about at that age. According to Piaget, children pass through various stages in their understanding of sex. First, they believe that a baby has always existed. Later they realize that the par-

---

[3]Use of euphemisms and analogies by adults can cause children to have somewhat confused understandings of sex. One 4-year-old girl, when asked how a lady would get a baby to grow in her tummy, responded, "Get a duck." As it turns out, one widely distributed sex-education book for children begins with a pencil dot (representing an ovum) and then proceeds through the sex lives of flowers, bees, rabbits, giraffes, chickens, and dogs, before getting to humans. No wonder the little girl thought that, in order to have a baby, you have to begin with a duck (Bernstein, 1976).

ents caused the baby's creation, though they have little idea of exactly how. Older children acquire a more and more scientific understanding of reproduction.

Children aged 4 to $5\frac{1}{2}$ believe that eating something has to do with pregnancy and that birth may be accomplished by cutting open the mother's belly. Children generally do not know the correct names of the sexual organs.

Children's dirty jokes reflect their parents' attempts to hide sex from them, their parents' use of euphemisms rather than accurate terms, and children's great fascination with sexual organs and with intercourse.

SUGGESTIONS FOR FURTHER READING

Fischer, H. L., Krajicek, M. J., and Borthick, W. A. *Sex education for the developmentally disabled.* Baltimore: University Park Press, 1973. Retarded children need sex education just as much as other children do, and this book provides a guide.

Gordon, Sol. *Let's make sex a household word: A guide for parents and children.* New York: John Day, 1975.

Growth patterns and sex education. *The Journal of School Health*, May 1967, 1–136. The whole issue is devoted to providing a detailed sex education curriculum for kindergarten through grade 12 (portions of which were summarized in the Focus).

Mayle, P., Robins, A., and Walter, P. *Where did I come from?* Secaucus, N.J.: Lyle Stuart, 1973. A delightful sex education book for young children. Its companion volume, *What's happening to me?* is for children approaching puberty.

23

SEXUALITY
IN THE FUTURE

CITED

We study the future the better to understand a present that will not stand still for inspection.*

There have been dramatic changes in sexuality in the last 30 years. Within our lifetimes, we will surely see more, equally dramatic changes. The changes that are occurring are in two principle areas: technologies and lifestyles.

TECHNOLOGIES

Technological advances affect our sexuality. Perhaps the best example is the birth control pill. We are now able to separate sex from reproduction and (because of the way the Pill is used) from contraception. Surely the Pill has contributed to the liberation of women and to changes in gender roles. It has probably also contributed to changes in sexual behavior and attitudes, in both premarital and marital sex.

Some recent scientific breakthroughs that may have an impact on sex in the future will be considered below.

*Source: Marshall McLuhan and George B. Leonard. The future of sex. In R. T. Francoeur and A. K. Francoeur (Eds.), The future of sexual relations. Englewood Cliffs, N.J.: Prentice-Hall, 1974, p. 15.

Artificial Insemination

Artificial insemination involves artificially placing semen in the vagina to produce a pregnancy; thus it is a means of accomplishing reproduction without having sexual intercourse. Artificial insemination in animals was first done in 1776. In 1949, when British scientists successfully froze sperm without any apparent damage to it, a new era of reproductive technology for animals began (Francoeur, 1974). Today cattle are routinely bred by artificial insemination.

In humans, two kinds of artificial insemination have been used: artificial insemination by the husband (AIH) and artificial insemination by a donor (AID). AIH can be used when the husband has a low sperm count. Several samples of his semen are collected and pooled to make one sample with a higher count. This sample is then placed in the woman's vagina at the time of ovulation. AID is used when the husband is sterile. A donor provides semen to impregnate the wife. Estimates suggest that about 1 percent of all the children born in the United States today are conceived by means of artificial insemination (Francoeur, 1974).

Sperm Banks

Since it is now possible to freeze sperm, it is possible to store it, and that is just what some people are doing, using frozen human sperm banks. In 1972, there were 18 such facilities in the United States (Francoeur, 1974). The sperm banks open up many new possibilities for various life choices. For example, suppose that a couple decide, after having had two children, that they want a permanent method of contraception. The husband then has a vasectomy. Two years after he has the vasectomy, however, one of their children dies, and they very much want to have another baby. If the man has stored samples of his semen in a sperm bank, they can have another child.

Young men are also using sperm banks to store sperm before they undergo radiation therapy for cancer. They can later father children without fearing that they will transmit damaged chromosomes (as a result of the radiation) to their offspring.

Embryo Transplants

In embryo transplantation, a fertilized, developing egg (embryo) is transferred from the uterus of one woman to the uterus of another woman. This technique may enable a woman who can conceive but who always miscarries early in the pregnancy to have a baby.

Embryo transplants have been done routinely in cattle and rabbits since the 1950s. An important milestone was reached on September 5, 1975, when a female baboon gave birth to a healthy male infant baboon, after the embryo was transplanted from another female (Kraemer et al., 1976). This represented the first successful embryo transplant in a primate. Attempts to do embryo transplants in humans began in 1970; at this writing, however, there has been no successful embryo transplant in humans—successful in the sense that it resulted in a full-term pregnancy. It seems likely, though, that this will be accomplished sometime in the next decade.

The technique would be a boon to some couples, but it would also raise some complex legal and ethical issues. For example, if the surrogate, or host, mother refused to give up the baby after it was born, what would be her rights? If she contracted German measles early in the pregnancy and the baby was deformed, who would be responsible for rearing it? New technologies often raise such ethical and legal issues, which in turn may require us to do some serious thinking about exactly what we mean by "parenthood."

Test-tube Babies

It is possible for scientists to make sperm and egg unite outside the human body (in a "test tube"); the fertilized egg can then be implanted in the uterus of a woman and carried to term. This technique will be of great benefit to couples who are infertile because the woman's fallopian tubes are blocked (a fairly common cause of infertility). The woman's egg could be taken from her body and mixed with sperm from the husband, and the fertilized ovum could then be implanted in her uterus.

A milestone was reached with the birth of Louise Brown in England on July 25, 1978. Obstetrician Patrick Steptoe and physiologist Robert Edwards had fertilized the mother's egg with her husband's sperm in a laboratory dish and implanted the embryo in the mother's uterus. The pregnancy went smoothly, and Louise was born healthy and normal, the first test-tube baby.

Cloning

Cloning is the reproduction of an individual from a single cell taken from a "donor" or "parent." The technique involves replacing the nucleus of an ovum with the nucleus from a body cell of the donor. This produces an embryo that is genetically identical to the donor. Normally, of course, a child has only half of its genes in common with the mother; the other half come from the father. Therefore, children are never genetically identical to either parent. But in cloning, no sperm is necessary, and the result is an individual who is genetically identical to the donor.

The concept of cloning raises ugly possibilities such as an army of 100,000 genetically identical individuals. At present, cloning is not feasible scientifically, but it may be in the future (see, for example, Galston, 1975).

Choosing Your Baby's Gender

Scientists are working on techniques that will allow couples to choose whether to have a boy or a girl. The techniques developed by Shettles (see Chapter 5) are a step in that direction, since they seem to improve the chances of having a baby of the chosen gender. Other techniques that will make the outcome even more certain are being investigated.

Such a technology would be good for parents who have six girls and really want a boy or for people who would like to have two children, one of each gender. Problems might arise, though. Some scientists fear that the result of being able to choose gender would be a great imbalance in our population, with many more males than females, since many couples prefer their first child to be a boy.

LIFESTYLES

Sexual behavior and sexual lifestyles have changed in the last few decades. What will the trend be between now and the year 2000?

One of two trends might be predicted: a continuation of the liberalization of sexuality or a reactionary backlash toward sexual conservatism. I think that the former will occur, at least in moderation. That is, I think that continued grad-

ual changes in sexuality will extend the trends of the past few decades. But major, unforeseeable events—such as war or famine or major technological changes—would substantially alter any predicted pattern, and we have no way of knowing whether such events will occur.

Heterosexuality

Premarital sex will probably become increasingly common, and 90 percent of both males and females are likely to engage in it (Hunt, 1974). Attitudes toward it will also become more favorable, partly because everyone is doing it. I doubt, though, whether promiscuity will become common. Affection seems likely to remain as a standard that makes intercourse acceptable, and premarital sex will still lead to marriage. With increasing openness about premarital sex, contraceptive use will also increase, thereby (one hopes) decreasing the number of unwanted pregnancies.

Marital sex will increasingly be thought of as a means of improving the emotional quality of a marriage. But with the increasing participation of women in the labor force, the incidence of extramarital sex and divorce will increase (J. H. Gagnon, 1977).

Homosexuality and Bisexuality

There is no current evidence that there has been an increase in the incidence of homosexuality during the past several decades, and so there seems to be no reason to predict such an increase in the future. On the other hand, with more openness about sexuality and sexual experimentation, there may be more bisexuality—or at least more experimental bisexuality—in the future.

Hot Sex and Cool Sex

Marshall McLuhan made the distinction between "hot media" and "cool media." This can be extended to a distinction between "hot sex" and "cool sex" (Francoeur and Francoeur, 1974; McLuhan and Leonard, 1974). Basically, something that is hot calls forth a strong emotional response, while something that is cool does not. Our culture has been characterized by hot sex, but in the future we may have cool sex.

Hot sex is jealous, possessive, and highly property-oriented. In hot sex, sex becomes equated with intercourse, and orgasm becomes a goal. Sex is highly structured, with many rules and regulations and with much game playing. Gender roles are highly stereotyped, with an accompanying male dominance. Hot sex involves genital hedonism—treating others as sex objects and chalking up conquests; thus it becomes impersonal. The irony is that Victorian sexuality and our current "liberated" sexuality are both hot. Hot sex is exemplified as much by the *Playboy* bunny as by the young man in 1900 who had his sexual initiation with a prostitute. As one observer commented, in the current generation we have merely moved the fig leaf to the face (Francoeur and Francoeur, 1974).

Cool sex, in contrast, is highly person-oriented. It is open, involved, and intimate, and sex is viewed as a means of communication, one of the ways we deeply know another person. Gender roles are flexible and not stereotyped; they are egalitarian, and the emphasis is on friendship. Cool sex is less demanding, and intercourse and orgasm are not goals.

Strangely, the more sex increases in its incidence and variety, the less significance it has. Thus, our culture's current trend toward intensifying hot sex seems likely to lead to cool sex. As sex becomes more common, it becomes

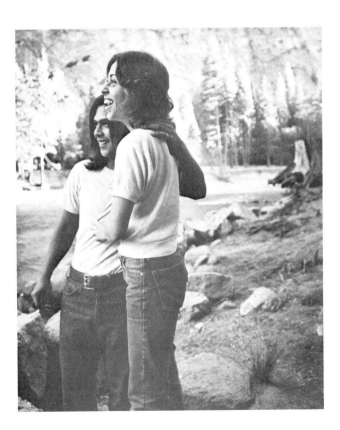

FIGURE 23.1
Are androgynous people—and relationships—the trend for the future? [*Ken Heyman.*]

more commonplace and integrated more into our lives, and that fosters a cool-sex approach.

Gender Roles

Spurred on by the feminist movement and the more recent men's liberation movement, our society is undergoing substantial changes in gender roles. The majority of women now hold jobs outside the home, and women constitute about 40 percent of the work force. More women than ever before are seeking advanced degrees, and we see many more female faces in medical school and law school classes than before. My discussions with college students indicate that most young people, at least ideally, believe that their lives should not be restricted by gender roles.

Some scholars, though, believe that the public aspects of gender roles (such as women holding jobs outside the home) change much more quickly than the subtler, private aspects (such as who drives when both a man and a woman are in the car) (see, for example, Haavio-Mannila, 1967). Thus, while some indicators suggest that we are experiencing considerable change in gender roles, the subtle aspects may persist.

Many experts on gender roles believe that androgyny—in which both men and women are free to have both masculine and feminine characteristics—is the wave of the future (e.g., Bem, 1974). It will be interesting to see whether it really is.

Some Hard Decisions

As a society, we typically await technological or lifestyle changes in sexuality passively. An alternative would be to do some social planning: to decide what we want our sexuality to be like in the future and then to shape technology to our values, rather than the reverse. Rather than wondering what the future will bring, we might take the future into our own hands and mold it.

Doing this would involve making some hard decisions about values. We would have to decide what a "good" sexual lifestyle is. What criterion would be used to decide that? That is a difficult question. As a beginning, however, I would suggest: "The question is which modification will be the most humane, most functional, most growth-promoting . . ." (Francoeur and Francoeur, 1974). We would do best to begin facing such issues.

I hope that we can move away from viewing sex as something we must absolutely *not* do (to prove our virtue) or, alternatively, as something we *must* do (to prove our status or competence) and see it as an integrated, enriching part of our lives. A character in a novel expressed it well:

> He felt sorry for young people today, under such intense pressures to fill every available moment with sex. "Damned tiring, if nothing else. Well, in my day we were damned if we did, and now you're damned if you don't. Hope it levels off someday into something healthier than either one." (Byfield and Tedeschi, 1975, p. 162)

GLOSSARY

abortion The ending of a pregnancy and the expulsion of the contents of the uterus; may be spontaneous or induced by human intervention (page 150).

abstinence (sexual) Not engaging in sexual activity (page 367).

adultery Sexual intercourse between a married person and someone other than her or his spouse (page 261).

agape A Greek word meaning selfless love of others (page 395).

amenorrhea The absence of menstruation (page 75).

amniotic fluid The watery fluid surrounding a developing fetus in the uterus (page 95).

anal intercourse Sexual behavior in which one person's penis is inserted into another's anus (page 198).

anaphrodisiac A substance that decreases sexual desire (page 200).

androgens "Male" sex hormones, produced in the testes; an example is testosterone. In females, the adrenal glands produce androgens (page 50).

androgyny Having both feminine and masculine characteristics (page 292).

anilingus Mouth-anus stimulation (page 199).

anorgasmia The inability of a woman to orgasm; a sexual dysfunction (page 415).

aphrodisiac A substance that increases sexual desire (page 199).

areola The dark area of skin surrounding the nipple of the breast (page 39).

artificial insemination Artificially putting semen into a woman's vagina or uterus for the purpose of inducing pregnancy (page 526).

autoeroticism Sexual self-stimulation; masturbation is one example (page 185).

Bartholin's glands Two tiny glands located on either side of the vaginal entrance (page 32).

bestiality Sexual contact with an animal; also called *zoophilia* (page 366).

bisexual A person who has some sexual contacts with males and some with females (page 342).

blastocyst A small mass of cells that results after several days of cell division by the fertilized egg (page 94).

breech presentation Birth of a baby with buttocks and/or feet first (page 110).

bulbourethral glands See *Cowper's glands.*

butch A very masculine lesbian; may also refer to a very masculine male homosexual (page 324).

Candida albicans A yeast or fungus in the vagina; if its growth gets out of control, it causes vaginitis, or irritation of the vagina, with an accompanying discharge (page 454).

carpopedal spasm A spastic contraction of the hands or feet which may occur during orgasm (page 169).

castration The removal (usually by means of surgery) of the gonads (the testes in men or the ovaries in women) (page 65).

celibate Unmarried; also used to refer to someone who abstains from sexual activity (page 367).

cervix The lower part of the uterus; the part next to the vagina (page 36).

cesarean section Surgical delivery of a baby through an incision in the abdominal wall (page 110).

chancre A painless open sore with a hard ridge around it; it is an early symptom of syphilis (page 447).

chancroid A venereal disease (page 451).

chastity Sexual abstinence (page 367).

circumcision The surgical removal of the foreskin of the penis (page 42).

climacteric See *menopause.*

climax An orgasm (page 168).

clitoris A small, highly sensitive sexual organ in the female, located in front of the vaginal entrance (page 30).

cloning Producing many genetically identical individuals from a single parent (page 527).

cohabitation Living together (page 250).

coitus Sexual intercourse; insertion of the penis into the vagina (page 192).

coitus interruptus See *withdrawal.*

coitus reservatus Sexual intercourse in which the man intentionally refrains from ejaculating.

colostrum A watery substance that is secreted from the breast at the end of pregnancy and during the first few days after delivery (page 103).

conceptus The product of conception; sometimes used to refer to the embryo or fetus (page 93).

condom A male contraceptive sheath that is placed over the penis (page 140).

contraceptive technique A method of preventing conception (page 126).

coprophilia A sexual variation in which arousal is associated with defecation or feces (page 374).

copulation Sexual intercourse.

corona The rim of tissue between the glans and the shaft of the penis (page 40).

corpora cavernosa Two cylindrical masses of erectile tissue running the length of the penis; also present in the clitoris (page 40).

corpus luteum The mass of cells remaining after a follicle has released an egg; it secretes progesterone (page 71).

corpus spongiosum A cylinder of erectile tissue running the length of the penis (page 40).

Cowper's glands A pair of glands that secrete substances into the male's urethra (page 47).

crabs See *Pediculosis pubis.*

cremaster muscle A muscle in the scrotum.

cryptorchidism Undescended testes (page 55).

cul-de-sac The end of the vagina, past the cervix (page 148).

cunnilingus Mouth stimulation of the female genitals (page 197).

cystitis Inflammation of the urinary bladder; the major symptom is a burning sensation while urinating (page 456).

defloration The rupture of a virgin's hymen, through intercourse or other means (page 34).

detumescence The return of an erect penis to the flaccid (unaroused) state (page 171).

diaphragm A cap-shaped rubber contraceptive device that fits inside a woman's vagina. over the cervix (page 138).

diethylstilbestrol (DES) A potent estrogen drug used in the "morning-after" pill (page 136).

dildo An artificial penis (page 188).

douche To flush out the inside of the vagina with a liquid (page 142).

dysmenorrhea Painful menstruation (page 74).

dyspareunia Painful intercourse (page 416).

ectopic pregnancy A pregnancy in which the fertilized egg implants somewhere other than the uterus (page 118).

edema An excessive accumulation of fluid in a part of the body (page 119).

ejaculation The expulsion of semen from the penis, usually during orgasm (page 168).

Electra complex In Freudian theory, the little girl's sexual desires for her father; the female analog of the Oedipus complex (page 7).

embryo In humans, the term used to refer to the unborn young from the first to the eighth weeks after conception (page 93).

endocrine gland A gland that secretes substances (hormones) directly into the bloodstream (page 50).

endometriosis A condition in which the endometrium grows in some place other than the uterus, such as the fallopian tubes (page 75).

endometrium The inner lining of the uterus (page 37).

epididymis Highly coiled tubules located on the edge of the testis; the site of sperm maturation (page 47).

episiotomy An incision that is sometimes made at the vaginal entrance during delivery (page 109).

erectile dysfunction The inability to get or maintain an erection (page 413).

erection An enlargement and hardening of the penis which occurs during sexual arousal (page 163).

erogenous zones Areas of the body that are particularly sensitive to sexual stimulation (page 6).

estrogen A group of "female" sex hormones; also produced in smaller quantities in males (page 52).

estrus The period of ovulation and sexual activity in nonhuman female mammals (page 70).

eunuch A castrated male.

exhibitionist A person who derives sexual gratification from exposing his or her genitals to others (page 362).

extramarital sex Sexual activity by a married person with someone other than her or his spouse (page 261).

fallopian tube The tube extending from the uterus to the ovary (page 37).

fellatio Mouth stimulation of the penis (page 198).

femme A feminine lesbian (page 324).

fertilization The union of sperm and egg, resulting in conception (page 92).

fetishism A sexual variation in which an inanimate object causes sexual arousal (page 350).

fetus In humans, the term used to refer to the unborn young from the third month after conception until birth (page 93).

follicle The capsule of cells surrounding an egg in the ovary (page 38).

follicle-stimulating hormone (FSH) A hormone secreted by the pituitary; it stimulates follicle development in females and sperm production in males (page 51).

foreskin The sheath of skin covering the tip of the penis or clitoris (page 41).

fornication Sexual intercourse between two unmarried people.

frigidity Lack of sexual response in a woman (page 415).

gametes Sperm or eggs.

gay Homosexual (page 316).

gender identity The psychological sense of one's own maleness or femaleness (page 57).

genitals The sexual or reproductive organs.

gerontophilia Sexual attraction to the elderly.

gestation The period of pregnancy; the time from conception until birth.

gigolo A male who sells his sexual services to women (page 372).

glans The tip of the penis or clitoris (page 40).

gonads The ovaries or testes (page 53).

gonorrhea A common venereal disease (page 442).

granuloma inguinale A rare venereal disease (page 452).

hermaphrodite A person with both male and female sex glands, that is, both ovaries and testicular tissue (see also *pseudohermaphrodite*) (page 56).

herpes genitalis A disease characterized by painful bumps on the genitals (page 452).

heterosexual A person who is sexually attracted to, or engages in sexual activity primarily with, members of the opposite gender.

homologous organs Organs in the male and female that develop from the same embryonic tissue (page 56).

homosexual A person who is sexually attracted to, or engages in sexual activity primarily with, members of her or his own gender (page 316).

human chorionic gonadotropin (HCG) A hormone produced by the placenta; HCG is what is detected in most pregnancy tests (page 99).

hymen A membrane that partially covers the vaginal opening (page 33).

hypothalamus A part of the brain which is important in regulating certain body functions (page 50).

hysterectomy Surgical removal of the uterus (page 461).

hysterotomy A method of abortion sometimes used during the second trimester (page 152).

implantation The burrowing of the fertilized egg into the lining of the uterus (page 92).

impotence See *erectile dysfunction.*

impregnate To make pregnant.

incest Sexual intercourse between close relatives, such as a brother and sister (page 364).

inguinal canal In the male, the passageway from the abdomen to the scrotum through which the testes usually descend shortly before birth (page 55).

inner lips Thin folds of skin on either side of the vaginal entrance (page 32).

intercourse (sexual) Sexual activity in which the penis is inserted into the vagina; coitus (see also *anal intercourse*) (page 192).

interfemoral intercourse Sexual activity in which the penis moves between the thighs (page 332).

interstitial cells Cells in the testes which manufacture male sex hormones; also called *Leydig cells* (page 44).

interstitial-cell-stimulating hormone (ICSH) A hormone manufactured by the pituitary that stimulates the interstitial cells of the testes to produce testosterone; identical to the hormone LH in the female (page 51).

intrauterine device (IUD) A plastic or metal device that is inserted into the uterus for contraceptive purposes (page 136).

intromission Insertion of the penis into the vagina (page 41).

labia majora See *outer lips.*

labia minora See *inner lips.*

labor The series of processes involved in giving birth (page 108).

lactation Secretion of milk from the female's breasts (page 116).

Lamaze method A method of "prepared" childbirth (page 112).

laparoscopy A method of female sterilization (page 148).

lesbian A female homosexual (page 316).

Leydig cells See *interstitial cells.*

libido The sex drive (page 6).

lochia A discharge from the uterus and vagina that occurs during the first few weeks after childbirth.

luteinizing hormone (LH) A hormone secreted by the pituitary. In females, it causes ovulation; called *ICSH* in males (page 51).

lymphogranuloma venereum (LGV) A virus-caused disease affecting the lymph glands in the genital region (page 452).

masochism A sexual variation in which the person derives sexual pleasure from experiencing physical or mental pain (page 36).

masturbation Self-stimulation of the genitals to produce sexual arousal (page 185).

menarche The first menstruation (page 63).

menopause The gradual cessation of menstruation in a woman, generally at around age 50 (page 82).

menses The menstrual flow.

menstruation A bloody discharge of the lining of the uterus, generally occurring about once a month in women (page 71).

miscarriage A pregnancy that terminates on its own; spontaneous abortion (page 121).

monilia A yeast infection of the vagina (page 454).

mons pubis The fatty pad of tissue under the pubic hair; also called the *mons* or *mons veneris* (page 32).

mucosa Mucous membrane (page 34).

Müllerian ducts In the embryo, a pair of ducts that eventually become part of the female reproductive system (page 55).

multiparous A term used to refer to a woman who has had more than one baby (page 35).

myotonia Muscle tension (page 162).

necrophilia A sexual variation in which there is attraction to a corpse (page 364).
nocturnal emission Involuntary orgasm and ejaculation while asleep (page 65).
nulliparous A term used to refer to a woman who has never given birth to a baby (page 35).
nymphomania An extraordinarily high, insatiable sex drive in a woman (page 366).

obscenity Something that is offensive according to accepted standards of decency; the legal term for pornography (page 505).
Oedipus complex In Freudian theory, the sexual attraction of a little boy to his mother (page 7).
onanism Withdrawal of the penis from the vagina before ejaculation; sometimes also used to refer to masturbation (page 142).
oral-genital sex Sexual activity in which the mouth is used to stimulate the genitals (page 197).
orgasm An intense sensation that occurs at the peak of sexual arousal and is followed by release of sexual tensions (page 168).
orgasmic platform The thickening of the walls of the outer third of the vagina that occurs during sexual arousal (page 165).
outer lips The fatty pads of tissue lying on either side of the vaginal opening and inner lips (page 32).
ovaries The paired sex glands in the female which produce ova (eggs) and sex hormones (page 38).
oviduct Fallopian tube (page 37).
ovulation Release of an egg by the ovaries (page 71).
oxytocin A hormone secreted by the pituitary which stimulates the contractions of the uterus during childbirth; also involved in breast-feeding (page 116).

pander To procure a prostitute for a client; sometimes used to mean any catering to another's sexual desires (page 371).
paraphilia A sexual variation (page 348).
parturition Childbirth (page 108).
pederasty Sexual relations between a man and a boy; sometimes also used to mean anal intercourse (page 364).
Pediculosis pubis Lice attaching themselves to the roots of the pubic hair; "crabs" (page 453).
pedophilia A sexual variation in which an adult is sexually attracted to children; child molesting (page 363).
penis A male sexual organ (page 40).
perineum The area between the vaginal opening and the anus (page 32).
perversion A sexual deviation (page 348).

phallus Penis (page 43).
pheromones Chemical substances secreted outside the body that are important in communication between animals (page 179).
phimosis A condition in which the foreskin is so tight that it cannot be retracted (page 42).
pimp A prostitute's protector; One who procures a prostitute's services for another (page 371).
pituitary gland A gland located on the lower surface of the brain; it secretes several hormones important to sexual and reproductive functioning (page 50).
placenta An organ formed on the wall of the uterus through which the fetus receives oxygen and nutrients and gets rid of waste products (page 94).
plateau phase Masters and Johnson's term for the second phase of sexual response, occurring just before orgasm (page 164).
pornography Sexually arousing art, literature, or films (page 505).
postpartum period The period of time following childbirth (page 114).
premarital intercourse Intercourse before marriage (page 242).
premature ejaculation A sexual dysfunction in which the male ejaculates too soon (page 413).
prenatal Before birth (page 50).
prepuce Foreskin (page 41).
priapism A rare condition in which erections are long-lasting and painful.
progesterone A female sex hormone produced by the corpus luteum in the ovary (page 52).
prolactin A hormone secreted by the pituitary; it is involved in lactation (page 52).
promiscuous A term used to refer to someone who engages in sexual activity with many different people (page 248).
prophylactic A drug or device used to prevent disease, often specifically venereal disease (page 453).
prostate The gland in the male, located below the bladder, that secretes most of the fluid in semen (page 47).
prostitution Indiscriminate sexual activity for payment (page 367).
pseudohermaphrodite An individual who has a mixture of male and female reproductive structures, so that it is not clear whether the individual is a male or a female (page 56).
puberty The period of time during which the body matures from that of a child to that of an adult capable of reproducing (page 59).
pubic lice See *Pediculosis pubis*.
pubococcygeal muscle A muscle around the vaginal entrance (page 35).
pudendum The external genitals of the female.

rape Forcible sexual relations with an individual without that person's consent (page 376).

refractory period The period following orgasm during which the male cannot be sexually aroused (page 171).

resolution phase Masters and Johnson's term for the last phase of sexual response, in which the body returns to the unaroused state (page 170).

retarded ejaculation A sexual dysfunction in which the male cannot have an orgasm, even though he is highly aroused (page 415).

retrograde ejaculation A condition in which orgasm in the male is not accompanied by an external ejaculation; instead, the ejaculate goes into the urinary bladder (page 175).

rhythm method A method of birth control that involves abstaining from sexual intercourse during the fertile days of the woman's menstrual cycle (page 143).

sadism A sexual variation in which the person derives sexual pleasure from inflicting pain on someone else (page 360).

satyriasis An extraordinarily high level of sex drive in a male (page 366).

scrotum The pouch of skin that contains the testes (page 44).

secondary sex characteristics The physical characteristics, other than the sex organs, that distinguish the male from the female; examples are the woman's breasts and the man's beard.

semen The fluid that is ejaculated from the penis during orgasm; it contains sperm (page 47).

seminal vesicles The two organs lying on either side of the prostate (page 47).

seminiferous tubules Highly coiled tubules in the testes that manufacture sperm (page 44).

sensate focus exercises Exercises prescribed by sex therapists to increase sexual response (page 431).

sex flush A rashlike condition on the skin that occurs during sexual arousal (page 164).

sexual dysfunction A problem with sexual responding that causes a person mental distress; examples are erectile dysfunction in men and anorgasmia in women (page 412).

sexual identity A person's sense of his or her own sexual nature, whether heterosexual, homosexual, or bisexual (page 343).

situation ethics As defined by Joseph Fletcher, a way of making ethical decisions on the basis of the concrete situation and the people involved, rather than on the basis of rules (page 468).

smegma A cheesy substance formed under the foreskin of the penis (page 42).

sodomy An ambiguous legal term which may refer to anal intercourse, sexual relations with animals, or mouth-genital sex (page 483).

sperm The mature male reproductive cell, capable of fertilizing an egg (page 45).

spermatogenesis The production of sperm (page 45).

spermicide A substance that kills sperm (page 141).

spirochete A spiral-shaped bacterium; one kind causes syphilis (page 446).

statutory rape Sexual relations with a person who is below the legal "age of consent" (page 376).

sterile Incapable of reproducing (page 145).

sterilization technique A procedure by which an individual is made incapable of reproducing (page 145).

swinging An exchange of sex partners between married couples (page 264).

syphilis A venereal disease (page 445).

testes The sex glands of the male, located in the scrotum; they manufacture sperm and sex hormones (page 44).

testosterone A hormone secreted by the testes in the male; it maintains secondary sex characteristics (page 51).

transsexual A person who feels that he or she is trapped in the body of the wrong gender; a person who undergoes a sex-change operation (page 352).

transvestism Dressing in the clothing of the opposite gender (page 359).

trichomoniasis A vaginal infection (page 455).

trimester Three months (page 94).

troilism A sexual variation in which three people engage in sexual activity together (page 373).

tubal ligation A surgical method of female sterilization (page 148).

tumescence Swelling due to congestion with body fluids (page 171).

umbilical cord The tube that connects the fetus to the placenta (page 95).

urethra The tube through which urine leaves the bladder and passes out of the body; in males, also the tube through which semen is discharged (page 40).

urophilia (or urolagnia) A sexual variation in which the person derives sexual pleasure from urine or urination (page 374).

uterus The organ in the female in which the fetus develops (page 36).

vagina The barrel-shaped organ in the female into which the penis is inserted during intercourse and through which a baby passes during birth (page 34).

vaginismus A strong, spastic contraction of the muscles around the vagina, closing off the vaginal entrance and making intercourse impossible (page 416).

vaginitis An inflammation or irritation of the vagina, usually due to infection (page 454).

varicocele Essentially, varicose veins in the testes; may be related to infertility in men.

vas deferens The ducts through which sperm pass on their way from the testes to the urethra (page 47).

vasectomy A surgical procedure for male sterilization involving severing of the vas deferens (page 146).

vasocongestion An accumulation of blood in the blood vessels of a region of the body, especially the genitals; a swelling or erection results (page 162).

venereal disease A disease transmitted primarily by sexual intercourse (page 442).

virgin A girl or woman who has never had sexual intercourse (page 34).

voyeurism A sexual variation in which the person derives sexual pleasure from watching nudes or watching others have sexual intercourse; also called *scoptophilia* and *Peeping Tomism* (page 361).

vulva The collective term for the external genitals of the female; includes the mons, clitoris, inner and outer lips, and vaginal and urethral openings (page 30).

Wassermann test A blood test for syphilis (page 447).

withdrawal A method of birth control in which the male withdraws his penis from the vagina before he ejaculates (page 142).

Wolffian ducts Embryonic ducts which form part of the male's reproductive system (page 55).

zoophilia See *bestiality.*

zygote The fertilized egg (page 92).

BIBLIOGRAPHY

Abraham, Karl. *Selected papers on psychoanalysis.* New York: Basic Books, 1953.

Adams, Clifford R. An informal preliminary report on some factors relating to sexual responsiveness of certain college wives. In M. F. DeMartino (Ed.), *Sexual behavior and personality characteristics.* New York: Grove Press, 1966.

Adams, James F. *Understanding adolescence.* Boston: Allyn and Bacon, 1973.

Aiken, D. L. Ex-sailor charges jail rape, stirs up storm. *The Advocate,* Sept. 26, 1973, 5.

Albin, Rochelle S. Psychological studies of rape. *Signs,* 1977, **3**, 423–435.

Allgeier, Elizabeth R. Heterosexuality and sex-typing. Paper presented at meetings of the Midwestern Psychological Association, Chicago, May 1976.

American Law Institute. *Model penal code: Proposed official draft.* Philadelphia: ALI, 1962.

American Psychological Association, Ad hoc Committee on Ethical Standards in Psychological Research. *Ethical principles in the conduct of research with human participants.* Washington, D.C.: APA, 1973.

Amir, Menachem. *Patterns in forcible rape.* Chicago: University of Chicago Press, 1971.

Andrews, Eva, and Cappon, Daniel. Autism and schizophrenia in a child guidance clinic. *Canadian Psychiatric Association Journal,* 1957, **2**, 1–25.

Angrist, Shirley S. The study of sex roles. *Journal of Social Issues,* 1969, **25**, 215–232.

Anonymous. When a woman is attacked. In L. G. Schultz (Ed.), *Rape victimology.* Springfield, Ill.: Charles C Thomas, 1975.

Aquinas, St. Thomas. *Summa theologica.* Vol. 43. (Translated by Thomas Gilly, O.P.) New York: McGraw-Hill, 1968.

Arafat, Ibtihaj S., and Cotton, Wayne L. Masturbation practices of males and females. *Journal of Sex Research,* 1974, **10**, 293–307.

Aristotle. *Nicomachean ethics.* (Translated by W. D. Ross.) Oxford: Clarendon Press, 1925.

Asken, Michael J. Psychoemotional aspects of mastectomy: A review of recent literature. *American Journal of Psychiatry,* 1975, **132**, 56–59.

Associated Press. German drug may reduce sex offenses. *Houston Chronicle,* Aug. 28, 1971.

Athanasiou, Robert, et al. Sex. *Psychology Today,* 1970, **4**(2), 39–52.

Augustine, St. *The city of God.* (Translated by Marcus Dods.) New York: Modern Library, 1950.

Bancroft, John. *Deviant sexual behavior: Modification and assessment.* New York: Oxford University Press, 1974.

Bandura, Albert. *Principles of behavior modification.* New York: Holt, 1969.

Bandura, Albert, and Walters, Richard H. *Social learning and personality development.* New York: Holt, 1963.

Barclay, Andrew M. Sexual fantasies in men and women. *Medical Aspects of Human Sexuality,* 1973, **7**, 209–212.

Bardwick, Judith M. *Psychology of women: A study of biocultural conflicts.* New York: Harper & Row, 1971.

Barker, William J., and Perlman, Daniel. Volunteer bias and personality traits in sexual standards research. *Archives of Sexual Behavior,* 1975, **4**, 161–171.

Barlow, David H. Increasing heterosexual responsiveness in the treatment of sexual deviation: A review of the clinical and experimental evidence. *Behavior Therapy,* 1973, **4**, 655–671.

Barlow, David H., and Agras, W. S. Fading to increase heterosexual responsiveness in homosexuals. *Journal of Applied Behavior Analysis,* 1973, **6**, 355–366.

Barnett, W. *Sexual freedom and the Constitution.* Albuquerque: University of New Mexico Press, 1973.

Bart, Pauline B. Depression in middle-aged women. In V. G. Gornick and B. K. Moran (Eds.), *Woman in sexist society.* New York: Basic Books, 1971.

Bartell, Gilbert D. Group sex among the mid-Americans. *Journal of Sex Research,* 1970, **6**, 113–130.

Beach, Frank A. Evolutionary changes in the physiological control of mating behavior in mammals. *Psychological Review,* 1947, **54**, 297–315.

Beach, Frank A. Cross-species comparisons and the human heritage. *Archives of Sexual Behavior,* 1976, **5**, 469–485.

Beach, Frank, and Merari, A. Coital behavior in dogs. V. Effects of estrogen and progesterone on mating and other forms of social behavior in the bitch. *Journal of Comparative and Physiological Psychology Monograph,* 1970, **70**(1), Part 2, 1–22.

Beatty, R. A. The genetics of the mammalian gamete. *Biological Review,* 1970, **45**, 73–119.

Behrman, Richard E., and Rosen, Tove S. HEW Publication No. 05 76-128, 1976, 12-1–12-116.

Bell, Alan P. Childhood and adolescent sexuality. Address delivered at the Institute for Sex Research, Indiana University, Summer 1974. (a)

Bell, Alan P. Homosexualities: Their range and character. In *Nebraska Symposium on Motivation 1973.* Lincoln: University of Nebraska Press, 1974. (b)

Bell, Robert R. *Premarital sex in a changing society.* Englewood Cliffs, N.J.: Prentice-Hall, 1966.

Bem, Sandra L. The measurement of psychological androgyny. *Journal of Consulting and Clinical Psychology,* 1974, **42,** 155–162.

Bem, Sandra L. Sex-role adaptability: One consequence of psychological androgyny. *Journal of Personality and Social Psychology,* 1975, **31,** 634–643.

Bem, Sandra L., and Bem, D. J. Case study of non-conscious ideology: Training the woman to know her place. In D. J. Bem (Ed.), *Beliefs, attitudes, and human affairs.* Belmont, Calif.: Brooks/Cole, 1970.

Bem, S. L., Martyna, W., and Watson, C. Sex-typing and androgyny: Further explorations of the expressive domain. *Journal of Personality and Social Psychology,* 1976, **34,** 1016–1023.

Benjamin, Harry, and Masters, R. E. L. *Prostitution and morality.* New York: Julian Press, 1964.

Benney, M., Riesman, D., and Star, S. Age and sex in the interview. *American Journal of Sociology,* 1956, **62,** 143–152.

Berg, Phyllis A., and Hyde, Janet S. Race and sex differences in causal attributions of success and failure. Paper presented at meetings of the American Psychological Association, Washington, D.C., August 1976.

Bermant, Gordon, and Davidson, Julian M. *Biological bases of sexual behavior.* New York: Harper & Row, 1974.

Bernardo, Felix. Widowhood status in the United States: Perspective on a neglected aspect of the family life-cycle. *Family Coordinator,* 1968, **17,** 191–203.

Berne, Eric. *Sex in human loving.* New York: Simon & Schuster, 1970.

Bernstein, Anne C. How children learn about sex and birth. *Psychology Today,* 1976, **9**(8), 31.

Bernstein, Anne C., and Cowan, Philip A. Children's concepts of how people get babies. *Child Development,* 1975, **46,** 77–92.

Berscheid, Ellen, and Walster, Elaine. A little bit about love. In T. L. Huston (Ed.), *Foundations of interpersonal attraction.* New York: Academic Press, 1974.

Berscheid, Ellen, et al. Physical attractiveness and dating choice: A test of the matching hypothesis. *Journal of Experimental Social Psychology,* 1971, **7,** 173–189.

Bess, Barbara E., and Janus, Samuel S. Prostitution. In B. J. Sadock et al. (Eds.), *The sexual experience.* Baltimore: Williams & Wilkins, 1976.

Bibring, Grete, et al. A study of the psychological processes in pregnancy and of the earliest mother-child relationship. *The psychoanalytic study of the child.* Vol. XVI. New York: International Universities Press, 1961. Pp. 9–72.

Bieber, Irving. A discussion of "Homosexuality: The ethical challenge." *Journal of Consulting and Clinical Psychology,* 1976, **44,** 163–166.

Bieber, Irving, et al. *Homosexuality: A psychoanalytic study of male homosexuals.* New York: Basic Books, 1962.

Billings, E. L., Billings, J. J., and Catarinch, M. *Atlas of the ovulation method.* Collegeville, Minn.: Liturgical Press, 1974.

Bingham, H. C. Sex development in apes. *Comparative Psychology Monographs,* 1928, **5,** 1–165.

Birnbaum, Judith A. Life patterns and self-esteem in gifted family-oriented and career-committed women. In M. Mednick, L. W. Hoffman, and S. Tangri (Eds.), *Women: Social psychological perspectives on achievement.* New York: Psychological Dimensions, 1976.

Biskind, Morton S. The relation of nutritional deficiency to impaired libido and potency in the male. *Journal of Gerontology,* 1947, **2,** 303–314.

Blanchard, W. H. The group process in gang rape. *Journal of Social Psychology,* 1959, **49,** 259–266.

Block, Jeanne H. Issues, problems, and pitfalls in assessing sex differences. *Merrill-Palmer Quarterly,* 1976, **22,** 283–308.

Blumstein, Philip W., and Schwartz, Pepper. Lesbianism and bisexuality. In E. Goode (Ed.), *Sexual deviance and sexual deviants.* New York: Morrow Press, 1974.

Blumstein, Philip W., and Schwartz, Pepper. Bisexual women. In J. P. Wiseman (Ed.), *The social psychology of sex.* New York: Harper and Row, 1976.

Boggan, E. C., Haft, M. G., Lister, C., and Rupp, J. P. *The civil rights of gay people.* New York: Discus Books, 1975.

Bohmer, Carol. Judicial attitudes toward rape victims. *Judicature,* 1974, **57,** 303–307.

Bolles, Robert C. *Theory of motivation.* New York: Harper & Row, 1967.

Bonaparte, Marie. *Female sexuality.* New York: Grove Press, 1965. (First published by International Universities Press, 1953.)

Boruchowitz, Robert C. Victimless crimes: A proposal to free the courts. *Judicature,* 1973, **57,** 69–78.

Boston Women's Health Book Collective. *Our bodies, ourselves.* New York: Simon & Schuster, 1976.

Breast cancer: Second thoughts about routine mammography. *Science,* 1976, **193,** 555.

Breasted, Mary. *Oh, sex education.* New York: Praeger, 1970.

Brecher, Edward M. Marijuana. *Consumer Reports,* March–April, 1975, **40,** 3–4.

Brecher, Ruth, and Brecher, Edward.

(Eds.) *An analysis of human sexual response.* New York: Signet Books, New American Library, 1966.

Brent, Jonathan. A general introduction to privacy. *Massachusetts Law Quarterly*, 1976, **61**, 10–18.

Brinton, Crane. *A history of Western morals.* New York: Harcourt, Brace, 1959.

Broderick, Carlfred B. Sexual behavior among preadolescents. *Journal of Social Issues*, 1966, **22**(2), 6–21. (a)

Broderick, Carlfred B. Socio-sexual development in a suburban community. *Journal of Sex Research*, 1966, **2**, 1–24. (b)

Broderick, Carlfred B., and Bernard, Jessie. *The individual, sex, and society.* Baltimore: Johns Hopkins Press, 1969.

Brodsky, Carroll M. Rape at work. In M. J. Walker and S. L. Brodsky (Eds.), *Sexual assault: The victim and the rapist.* Lexington, Mass.: Lexington Books, 1976.

Bronson, F. Pheromonal influences on mammalian reproduction. In M. Diamond (Ed.), *Perspectives in reproduction and sexual behavior.* Bloomington: Indiana University Press, 1968. Pp. 341–362.

Broun, Heywood, and Leech, Margaret. *Anthony Comstock: Roundsman of the Lord.* New York: Boni, 1927.

Broverman, Inge K., et al. Sex-role stereotypes: A current appraisal. *Journal of Social Issues*, 1972, **28**(2), 59–78.

Brown, Daniel G. Female orgasm and sexual inadequacy. In Ruth Brecher and Edward Brecher (Eds.), *An analysis of human sexual response.* New York: Signet Books, New American Library, 1966.

Brownmiller, Susan. *Against our will: Men, women, and rape.* New York: Simon and Schuster, 1975.

Bruce, H. M. Pheromones and behavior in mice. *Acta Neurologica Belgica*, 1969, **69**, 529–538.

Bruser, M. Sporting activities during pregnancy. Cited in Sports and pregnancy. *Briefs: Footnotes on Maternity Care*, 1969, **33**(4), 51–53.

Brussel, J. A. Comment following Menachem Amir, Forcible rape. *Sexual Behavior*, 1971, **1**, 8.

Bryan, James H. Apprenticeships in prostitution. *Social Problems*, 1965, **12**, 278–297.

Bullough, Vern L. *Sexual variance in society and history.* New York: Wiley, 1976.

Burgess, Ann W., and Holmstrom, Lynda L. Rape trauma syndrome. *American Journal of Psychiatry*, 1974, **131**, 981–986. (a)

Burgess, Ann W., and Holmstrom, Lynda L. *Rape: Victims of crisis.* Bowie, Md.: Robert J. Brady, 1974 (b)

Burton, Frances D. Sexual climax in *Macaca Mulatta. Proceedings of the Third International Congress on Primatology*, 1970, **3**, 180–191.

Buss, Arnold. *Psychopathology.* New York: Wiley, 1966.

Butler, Julius C., and Wagner, Nathaniel N. Sexuality during pregnancy and postpartum. In R. Green (Ed.), *Human sexuality: A health practitioner's text.* Baltimore: Williams & Wilkins, 1975.

Byfield, Barbara N., and Tedeschi, Frank L. *Solemn high murder.* Garden City, N.Y.: Doubleday, 1975.

Byler, Ruth V. *Teach us what we want to know.* New York: Mental Health Materials Center, for the Connecticut State Board of Education, 1969.

Byrne, Donn. *The attraction paradigm.* New York: Academic Press, 1971.

Byrne, Donn. A pregnant pause in the sexual revolution. *Psychology Today*, 1977, **11**(2), 67–68.

Byrne, D., Ervin, C. E., and Lamberth, J. Continuity between the experimental study of attraction and real-life computer dating. *Journal of Personality and Social Psychology*, 1970, **16**, 157–165.

Callahan, Daniel. *Abortion, law, and morality.* New York: Macmillan, 1970.

Carpenter, C. R. Sexual behavior of free ranging rhesus monkeys (*Macaca mulatta*). *Journal of Comparative and Physiological Psychology*, 1942, **33**, 113–162.

Catterall, R. D. *A short textbook of venereology.* Philadelphia: Lippincott, 1974.

Caughey, Madeline S. The principle of harm and its application to laws criminalizing prostitution. *Denver Law Journal*, 1974, **51**, 235–262.

Chafetz, Janet S. *Masculine/feminine or human? An overview of the sociology of sex roles.* Itasca, Ill.: F. E. Peacock, 1974.

Chappell, D., Geis, G., and Fogarty, F. Forcible rape: Bibliography. *Journal of Criminal Law and Criminology*, 1974, **65**, 248–263.

Chein, Isidor, Gerard, D., Lee, R., and Rosenfeld, E. *Narcotics, delinquency, and social policy.* London: Tavistock, 1964.

Chesler, Phyllis. *Women and madness.* Garden City, N.Y.: Doubleday, 1972.

Chiazze, L., Jr., et al. The length and variability of the human menstrual cycle. *Journal of the American Medical Association*, 1968, **203**, 6.

Clanton, Gordon. The contemporary experience of adultery: Bob and Carol and Updike and Rimmer. In R. W. Libby and R. N. Whitehurst (Eds.), *Renovating marriage.* Danville, Calif.: Consensus Publishers, 1973.

Clark, Alexander L., and Wallin, Paul. The accuracy of husbands' and wives' reports of the frequency of marital coitus. *Population Studies*, 1964, **18**, 165–173.

Cochran, W. G., Mosteller, F., and Tukey, J. W. Statistical problems of the Kinsey report. *Journal of the American Statistical Association*, 1953, **48**, 673–716.

Cofer, Charles N. *Motivation and emotion.* Glenview, Ill.: Scott, Foresman, 1972.

Cohen, Michael W., and Friedman, Stanford B. Nonsexual motivation of adolescent sexual behavior. *Medical Aspects of Human Sexuality*, 1975, **9**(9), 9–31.

Cohen, M. L., Garofalo, R., Boucher, R., and Seghorn, T. The psychology of rapists. *Seminars in Psychiatry*, 1971, **3**, 307–327.

Cohn, Frederick. *Understanding human sexuality*. Englewood Cliffs, N. J.: Prentice-Hall, 1974.

Cole, Theodore M. Sexuality and the spinal cord injured. In R. Green (Ed.), *Human sexuality: A health practitioner's text*. Baltimore: Williams & Wilkins, 1975.

Comfort, Alex. Likelihood of human pheromones. *Nature*, 1971, **230**, 432–433.

Comfort, Alex. *The joy of sex*. New York: Crown, 1972.

Conn, Jacob H. Children's awareness of the origin of babies. *Journal of Child Psychiatry*, 1948, **1**, 140–176.

Conn, Jacob H., and Hanner, Leo. Children's awareness of sex differences. *Journal of Child Psychiatry*, 1947, **1**, 3–57.

Cox, Harvey (Ed.) *The situation ethics debate*. Philadelphia: Westminster Press, 1968.

Cozby, P. C. Self-disclosure: A literature review. *Psychological Bulletin*, 1973, **79**, 73–91.

Craven, J., and Polak, A. Cantharidin poisoning. *British Medical Journal*, 1954, **2**, 1386–1388.

Croft-Cooke, Rupert. *The unrecorded life of Oscar Wilde*. New York: McKay, 1972.

Cushman, P. Sexual behavior in heroin addiction and methadone maintenance. *New York State Medical Journal*, 1972, **27**, 1961.

Dalton, Katharina. *The premenstrual syndrome*. Springfield, Ill.: Charles C Thomas, 1964.

Dalton, Katharina. The influence of mother's menstruation on her child. *Proceedings of the Royal Society for Medicine*, 1966, **59**, 1014.

Dalton, Katharina. *The menstrual cycle*. New York: Pantheon Books, 1969.

Davis, Keith E., and Braucht, G. Nicholas. Exposure to pornography, character and sexual deviance: A retrospective study. *Journal of Social Issues*, 1973, **29**, 183–196.

Davison, G. C. Homosexuality: The ethical challenge. *Journal of Consulting and Clinical Psychology*, 1976, **44**, 157–162.

Davison, G. C., and Neale, J. M. *Abnormal psychology: An experimental clinical approach*. New York: Wiley, 1974.

Deaux, Kay. *The behavior of women and men*. Belmont, Calif.: Brooks/Cole, 1976.

Delaney, J., Lupton, M. J., and Toth, E. *The curse: A cultural history of menstruation*. New York: Dutton, 1976.

DeLora, Joann S., and Warren, Carol A. B. *Understanding sexual interaction*. Boston: Houghton Mifflin, 1977.

Deschin, C. S. Teen-agers and venereal disease: A sociological study of 600 teen-agers in NYC social hygiene clinics. *American Journal of Nursing*, 1963, **63**, 63–67.

Dickinson, Robert L. *Atlas of human sex anatomy*. Baltimore: Williams & Wilkins, 1949.

Dishotsky, N., Loughman, W., Mogar, R., and Lipscomb, W. LSD and genetic damage. *Science*, 1971, **172**, 431–440.

Ditman, Keith. Inhibition of ejaculation by chlorprothixens. *American Journal of Psychiatry*, 1964, **120**, 1004–1005.

Dörner, G. Prophylaxie und therapie angeborener sexual deviationen. *Deutsche Medizinische Wochenschrift-Sonderdruck*, Feb. 2, 1969.

Dotti, A., and Reda, M. Major tranquilizers and sexual function. In M. Sandler and G. L. Gessa (Eds.), *Sexual behavior: Pharmacology and biochemistry*. New York: Raven Press, 1975.

Douglas, Mary. *Purity and danger: An analysis of concepts of pollution and taboo*. Baltimore: Penguin, 1970.

Dreger, Ralph M., et al. Behavioral classification project. *Journal of Consulting Psychology*, 1964, **28**, 1–13.

Driscoll, James P. Transsexuals. *Transaction*, March-April 1971, 28–31.

Driscoll, R., Davis, K. E., and Lipetz, M. E. Parental interference and romantic love: The Romeo and Juliet effect. *Journal of Personality and Social Psychology*, 1972, **24**, 1–10.

Dutton, Donald G., and Aron, Arthur P. Some evidence for heightened sexual attraction under conditions of high anxiety. *Journal of Personality and Social Psychology*, 1974, **30**, 470–517.

Eastman, N. J. The geographic distribution of pregnancy in the United States. National Research Council, Working Group on Relation of Nutrition to the Toxemias of Pregnancy. November, 1968. (Cited in L. M. Hellman and J. A. Pritchard, *Williams obstetrics*. (14th ed.) New York: Appleton-Century-Crofts, 1971.)

Ehrlich, June, and Riesman, David. Age and authority in the interview. *Public Opinion Quarterly*, 1961, **23**, 39–56.

Ehrlich, Paul A., and Ehrlich, Anne H. *Population, resources, environment*. (2nd ed.) San Francisco: Freeman, 1972.

Elder, Glen. Appearance and education in marriage mobility. *American Sociological Review*, 1969, **34**, 519–533.

Elias, James, and Gebhard, Paul. Sexuality and sexual learning in childhood. *Phi Delta Kappan*, 1969, **50**, 401–405.

Ellis, Albert. *The American sexual tragedy*. New York: Grove Press, 1962.

Ellis, Albert, and Brancale, Ralph. *Psychology of sex offenders*. Springfield, Ill.: Charles C Thomas, 1956.

Erikson, Erik H. *Childhood and society*. New York: Norton, 1950.

Erikson, Erik H. *Identity: Youth and crisis*. New York: Norton, 1968.

Ervin, Clinton V. Psychologic adjustment to mastectomy. *Medical Aspects of Human Sexuality*, 1973, **7**(2), 42–65.

Erwin, J., and Maple, Terry. Ambisexual behavior with male-male anal penetration in male rhesus monkeys. *Archives of Sexual Behavior*, 1976, **5**, 9–14.

Evans, R. B. Sixteen personality factor questionnaire scores of homosexual men. *Journal of Consulting and Clinical Psychology*, 1970, **34**, 212–215.

Everett, Guy M. Amyl nitrate ("poppers") as an aphrodisiac. In M. Sandler and G. L. Gessa (Eds.), *Sexual behavior: Pharmacology and biochemistry*. New York: Raven Press, 1975.

Fasteau, Marc F. *The male machine*. New York: McGraw-Hill, 1974.

Federal Bureau of Investigation. *Uniform Crime Reports*, 1973, 1975.

Ferber, Andrew S., et al. Men with vasectomies: A study of medical, sexual, and psychosocial changes. *Psychosomatic Medicine*, 1967, **29**, 354–366.

Fisher, J. D., et al. Hands touching hands: Affective and evaluative effects of an interpersonal touch. Paper presented at meetings of the American Psychological Association, Chicago, September 1975.

Fisher, Seymour. *Understanding the female orgasm*. New York: Basic Books, 1973.

Fletcher, Joseph. *Situation ethics*. Philadelphia: Westminster Press, 1966.

Fletcher, Joseph. *Moral responsibility: Situation ethics at work*. Philadelphia: Westminster Press, 1967.

Ford, Clellan S., and Beach, Frank A. *Patterns of sexual behavior*. New York: Harper & Row, 1951.

Forer, Bertram R. Use of physical contact. In L. N. Soloman and B. Berzon (Eds.), *New perspectives on encounter groups*. San Francisco: Jossey-Bass, 1972.

Forssman, H., and Thuwe, I. One hundred and twenty children born after application for therapeutic abortion refused. *Acta Psychiatrica Scandinavica*, 1966, **42**, 71–88.

Fox, C. A., et al. Studies on the relationship between plasma testosterone levels and human sexual activity. *Journal of Endocrinology*, 1972, **52**, 51–58.

Francoeur, Anna K., and Francoeur, Robert T. Hot and cool sex: Closed and open marriage. In R. T. Francoeur and A. K. Francoeur (Eds.), *The future of sexual relations*. Englewood Cliffs, N.J.: Prentice-Hall, 1974.

Francoeur, Robert T. The technologies of man-made sex. In R. T. Francoeur and A. K. Francoeur (Eds.), *The future of sexual relations*. Englewood Cliffs, N.J.: Prentice-Hall, 1974.

Frank, Lawrence K. *The conduct of sex*. New York: Morrow, 1961.

Frank, R. T. The hormonal causes of premenstrual tension. *Archives of Neurological Psychiatry*, 1931, **26**, 1053.

Freedman, A. M. Drugs and sexual behavior. In B. J. Sadock et al. (Eds.), *The sexual experience*. Baltimore: Williams & Wilkins, 1976.

Freedman, Mark. Homosexuals may be healthier than straights. *Psychology Today*, 1975, **8**(10), 28–32.

Freud, S. The psychogenesis of a case of homosexuality in a woman (1920). In *The Collected Papers*. Vol. II. London: Hogarth, 1948. Pp. 202–231.

Friday, N. *My secret garden: Women's sexual fantasies*. New York: Simon & Schuster, 1973.

Friday, N. *Forbidden flowers: More women's sexual fantasies*. New York: Simon & Schuster, 1975.

Frodi, A., Macaulay, J., and Thome, P. R. Are women always less aggressive than men? A review of the experimental literature. *Psychological Bulletin*, 1977, **84**, 634–660.

Fromm, Erich. *The art of loving*. New York: Harper & Row, 1956.

Fry, William F. Psychodynamics of sexual humor: Sex and the elderly. *Medical Aspects of Human Sexuality*, 1976, **10**(2), 140.

Fulton, Gere. *Sexual awareness*. Boston: Holbrook Press, 1974.

Fulton, Gere B. Bioethics and health education: Some issues of the biological revolution. *Journal of School Health*, 1977, **47**, 205–211.

Gagnon, F. Contribution to study of etiology and prevention of cancer of cervix of uterus. *American Journal of Obstetrics and Gynecology*, 1950, **60**, 516.

Gagnon, John H. Female child victims of sex offenses. *Social Problems*, 1965, **13**, 176–192. (a)

Gagnon, John H. Sexuality and sexual learning in the child. *Psychiatry*, 1965, **28**, 212–228. (b)

Gagnon, John H. *Human sexualities*. Glenview, Ill.: Scott, Foresman, 1977.

Gagnon, John H., and Simon, William (Eds.) *Sexual deviance*. New York: Harper & Row, 1967.

Gagnon, John H., and Simon, William. *Sexual conduct: The social origins of human sexuality*. Chicago: Aldine, 1973.

Gallo, Maria Teresa de, and Alzate, Heli. Brothel prostitution in Colombia. *Archives of Sexual Behavior*, 1976, **5**, 1–7.

Galston, A. W. Here come the clones. *Natural History*, 1975, **84**, 72–75.

Garner, Brian, and Smith, Richard W. Are there really any gay male athletes? An empirical survey. *Journal of Sex Research*, 1977, **13**, 22–34.

Garrett, Thomas, and Wright, Richard. Wives of rapists and incest offenders. *Journal of Sex Research*, 1975, **11**, 149–157.

Gebhard, Paul H. Postmarital coitus among widows and divorcées. In P. Bohannan (Ed.), *Divorce and after*. Garden City, N.Y.: Doubleday, 1968.

Gebhard, Paul H. Misconceptions about female prostitutes. *Medical As-*

pects of Human Sexuality, March 1969, **3**, 24–30.

Gebhard, Paul H. Human sexual behavior: A summary statement. In D. S. Marshall and R. C. Suggs (Eds.), *Human sexual behavior.* New York: Basic Books, 1971.

Gebhard, Paul H., Gagnon, J. H., Pomeroy, W. B., and Christenson, Cornelia V. *Sex offenders: An analysis of types.* New York: Harper & Row, 1965.

Gillette, Paul J. *Vasectomy: The male sterilization operation.* New York: Paperback Library, 1972.

Gilmartin, Brian G. That swinging couple down the block. *Psychology Today*, 1975, **8**(9), 54.

Ginsberg, G. L., Frosch, W. A., and Shapiro, T. The new impotence. *Archives of General Psychiatry*, 1972, **26**(3), 218–220.

Glass, S. J., Deuel, H. J., and Wright, C. A. Sex hormone studies in male homosexuality. *Endocrinology*, 1940, **26**, 590–594.

Glassberg, B. Y. The quandary of a virginal male. *Family Coordinator*, 1970, **19**, 82–85.

Goergen, Donald. *The sexual celibate.* New York: Seabury Press, 1974.

Golde, Peggy, and Kogan, Nathan. A sentence completion procedure for assessing attitudes toward old people. *Journal of Gerontology*, 1959, **14**, 355–363.

Goldstein, Bernard. *Human sexuality.* New York: McGraw-Hill, 1976.

Goldstein, Michael J. Exposure to erotic stimuli and sexual deviance. *Journal of Social Issues*, 1973, **29**, 197–219.

Goldstein, Michael J., and Kant, Harold. *Pornography and sexual deviance.* Berkeley: University of California Press, 1973.

Goode, Erich. *The marijuana smokers.* New York: Basic Books, 1970.

Gordon, E. M. Acceptance of pregnancy before and since oral contraception. *Obstetrics and Gynecology*, 1967, **29**, 144–146.

Gordon, R. E., and Gordon, K. K. Factors in postpartum emotional adjustment. *American Journal of Orthopsychiatry*, 1967, **37**, 359–360.

Gordon, R. E., Kapostons, E. F., and Gordon, K. K. Factors in postpartum emotional adjustment. *Obstetrics and Gynecology*, 1965, **25**, 158–166.

Gould, R. Vasectomy complications (a 1110 patient study). Paper presented at the twelfth annual meeting of the American Association of Planned Parenthood Physicians, Memphis, April 1974.

Gove, W. R., and Tudor, Jeannette F. Adult sex roles and mental illness. *American Journal of Sociology*, 1973, **78**, 812–835.

Gray, A. H. *Men, women, and God.* New York: Association Press, 1922.

Great Britain Committee on Homosexual Offenses and Prostitution. *The Wolfenden report.* (American ed.) New York: Stein and Day, 1963.

Green, Richard M. Mythological, historical, and cross-cultural aspects of transsexualism. In H. Benjamin (Ed.), *The transsexual phenomenon.* New York: Julian Press, 1966.

Green, Richard. Homosexuality as mental illness. *International Journal of Psychiatry*, 1972, **10**, 77–98.

Green, Richard. Adults who want to change sex; adolescents who crossdress; and children called "sissy" and "tomboy." In R. Green (Ed.), *Human sexuality: A health practitioner's text.* Baltimore: Williams & Wilkins, 1975.

Greene, F., Kirk, R. M., and Thompson, I. M. Retrograde ejaculation. *Medical Aspects of Human Sexuality*, 1970, **4**(12), 59–65.

Griffin, Bernard Cardinal. Report of the Roman Catholic Advisory Commission on Prostitution and Homosexual Offenses and the Present Law. *Dublin Review*, 1956, **471**, 60–65.

Groat, H. Theodore, and Neal, A. G. A social psychological approach to family formation. In K. C. W. Kammeyer (Ed.), *Population studies: Se-*

lected essays and research. (2nd ed.) Chicago: Rand McNally, 1975.

Gruntz, Louis G. Jr. Obscenity 1973: Remodeling the house that *Roth* built. *Loyola Law Review*, 1974, **20**, 159–174.

Guttmacher, Allan F. The attitudes of 3,381 physicians towards contraception and the contraceptives they prescribe. *Human Biology*, 1947, **12**, 1–12.

Haavio-Mannila, Elina. Sex differentiation in role expectations and performance. *Journal of Marriage and the Family*, 1967, **29**, 568–578.

Hackett, C. J. On the origin of the human treponematoses. *Bulletin of the World Health Organization*, 1963, **29**, 7–41.

Haider, I. Thioridazine and sexual dysfunctions. *International Journal of Neuropsychiatry*, 1966, 255–257.

Hair, Paul. *Before the bawdy court.* London: Eleck, 1972.

Halikas, J. A., Goodwin, P. H., and Guze, S. B. Marijuana effects: A survey of regular users. *Journal of the American Medical Association*, 1971, **217**, 692.

Halleck, S. Sex and mental health on the campus. *Journal of the American Medical Association*, 1967, **200**, 684.

Halverson, H. M. Genital and sphincter behavior of the male infant. *Journal of Genetic Psychology*, 1940, **43**, 95–136.

Hamilton, G. V. A study of sexual tendencies in monkeys and baboons. *Journal of Animal Behavior*, 1914, **4**, 295–318.

Hand, J. R. Surgery of the penis and urethra. In M. F. Campbell and J. H. Harrison (Eds.), *Urology.* vol. 3. Philadelphia: Saunders, 1970.

Hansfield, H. A., Lipman, T. O., Harnisch, J. P., Tronca, E., and Holmes, K. K. Asymptomatic gonorrhea in men: Diagnosis, natural course, prevalence, and significance. *New England Journal of Medicine*, 1975, **290**(3), 117–123.

Harbison, R. D., and Mantilla-Plata, B. Prenatal toxicity, maternal distribution and placental transfer of tetrahydrocannabinol. *Journal of Pharmacology and Experimental Therapeutics*, 1972, **180**, 446–453.

Hariton, E. Barbara. The sexual fantasies of women. *Psychology Today*, 1973, **6**(10), 39–44.

Harlow, H. F., Harlow, M. K., and Hause, F. W. The maternal affectional system of rhesus monkeys. In H. L. Rheingold (Ed.), *Maternal behavior in mammals*. New York: Wiley, 1963.

Harris, G. W., and Levine, S. Sexual differentiation of the brain and its experimental control. *Journal of Physiology*, 1965, **181**, 379–400.

Hartley, Ruth E. Sex-role pressures in the socialization of the male child. *Psychological Reports*, 1959, **5**, 457–468.

Hartman, William E., and Fithian, Marilyn A. *Treatment of sexual dysfunction*. New York: Jason Aronson, 1974.

Hatcher, Robert A., et al. *Contraceptive technology 1976–1977*. (8th ed.) New York: Irvington, 1976.

Hattendorf, K. W. A study of the questions of young children. *Journal of Social Psychology*, 1932, **3**, 37–65.

Hayes, A. *Sexual physiology of woman*. Boston: Peabody Medical Institute, 1869.

Heath, Robert C. Pleasure and brain activity in man. *Journal of Nervous and Mental Disease*, 1972, **154**, 3–18.

Heilbrun, Carolyn G. *Toward a recognition of androgyny*. New York: Knopf, 1973.

Heiman, Julia R. The physiology of erotica: Women's sexual arousal. *Psychology Today*, 1975, **8**(11), 90–94.

Hellerstein, Herman K., and Friedman, Ernest H. Sexual activity and the post coronary patient. *Medical Aspects of Human Sexuality*, March 1969, **3**, 70–74.

Hellman, L. M., and Pritchard, J. A. *Williams obstetrics*. (14th ed.) New York: Appleton-Century-Crofts, 1971.

Hembree, W. C., et al. Marihuana effects upon human gonadal function. In G. G. Nahas et al. (Eds.), *Marihuana: Chemistry, biochemistry, and cellular effects*. New York: Springer-Verlag, 1976.

Henley, Nancy M. The politics of touch. In P. Brown (Ed.), *Radical psychology*. New York: Harper & Row, 1973. (a)

Henley, Nancy M. Status and sex: Some touching observations. *Bulletin of the Psychonomic Society*, 1973, **2**, 91–93. (b)

Herbert, J. The effect of estrogen applied directly to the genitalia upon the sexual attractiveness of the female rhesus monkey. *Excerpta Medica International Congress Series*, 1966, **3**, 212.

Herbst, A. Clear cell adenocarcinoma of the genital tract in young females. *New England Journal of Medicine*, 1972, **287**(25), 1259–1264.

Heron, Alastair (Ed.) *Toward a Quaker view of sex*. (Rev. ed.) London: Friends Service Committee, 1964.

Hersey, R. B. Emotional cycles in man. *Journal of Mental Science*, 1931, **77**, 151–169.

Heston, Leonard, and Shields, J. Homosexuality in twins: A family study and a registry study. *Archives of General Psychiatry*, 1968, **18**, 149–160.

Hite, Shere. *The Hite report*. New York: Macmillan, 1976.

Hoffman, Lois W. Effects of maternal employment on the child: A review of the research. *Developmental Psychology*, 1974, **10**, 204–228.

Hollister, Leo E. The mystique of social drugs and sex. In M. Sandler and G. L. Gessa (Eds.), *Sexual behavior: Pharmacology and biochemistry*. New York: Raven Press, 1975.

Holmberg, A. R. The Siriono. Unpublished doctoral dissertation, Yale University, 1946. (Cited in Clellan S. Ford and Frank A. Beach, *Patterns of sexual behavior*. New York: Harper & Row, 1951.)

Hooker, Evelyn. The adjustment of the male overt homosexual. *Journal of Projective Techniques*, 1957, **21**, 18–31.

Hooker, Evelyn. An empirical study of some relations between sexual patterns and gender identity in male homosexuals. In J. Money (Ed.), *Sex research: New developments*. New York: Holt, 1965.

Hopkins, June H. The lesbian personality. *British Journal of Psychiatry*, 1969, **115**, 1433–1436.

Horner, Matina S. Fail: Bright women. *Psychology Today*, 1969, **3**(6), 36.

Horner, Matina S. Femininity and achievement: A basic inconsistency. In J. Bardwick et al. (Eds.), *Feminine personality and conflict*. Belmont, Calif.: Brooks/Cole, 1970.

Horner, Matina S. Toward an understanding of achievement-related conflicts in women. *Journal of Social Issues*, 1972, **28**(2), 157–175.

Horstman, W. Homosexuality and psychopathology. Unpublished doctoral dissertation, University of Oregon, 1972.

Howard, J. L., Liptzin, M. B., and Reifler, C. B. Is pornography a problem? *Journal of Social Issues*, 1973, **29**, 133–145.

Hughes, J. Failure to ejaculate with chlordiazepoxide. *American Journal of Psychiatry*, 1964, **121**, 610–611.

Hunt, Morton. *The world of the formerly married*. New York: McGraw-Hill, 1966.

Hunt, Morton, *Sexual behavior in the 1970s*. Chicago: Playboy Press, 1974.

Hyde, H. Montgomery. *Oscar Wilde*. New York: Farrar, Straus & Giroux, 1975.

Hyde, Janet S., and Rosenberg, B. G. *Half the human experience: The psychology of women*. Lexington, Mass.: Heath, 1976.

Idänpään-Heikkila, J., et al. Placental transfer of tritiated-1-Δ^9-tetrahydrocannabinol. *New England Journal of Medicine*, 1969, **281**, 330.

Intelligence report. *Parade*, July 25, 1971.

Isbell, H. Prospectus in research on opiate addiction. In D. M. Wilner and G. G. Kasserbaum (Eds.), *Narcotics*. New York: McGraw-Hill, 1965.

Israel, Spencer L. *Diagnosis and treatment of menstrual disorders and sterility*. (5th ed.) New York: Harper & Row, 1967.

Ivey, M. E., and Bardwick, Judith M. Patterns of affective fluctuation in the menstrual cycle. *Psychosomatic Medicine*, 1968, **30**, 336–345.

"J." *The sensuous woman*. New York: Lyle Stuart, 1969.

Jackman, N. R., O'Toole, R., and Geis, G. The self-image of the prostitute. *Sociological Quarterly*, 1963, **4**, 150–161.

Jensen, Gordon D. Adolescent sexuality. In B. J. Sadock et al. (Eds.), *The sexual experience*. Baltimore: Williams & Wilkins, 1976. (a)

Jensen, Gordon D. Cross-cultural studies and animal studies of sex. In B. J. Sadock et al. (Eds.), *The sexual experience*. Baltimore: Williams & Wilkins, 1976. (b)

Jones, Hardin, and Jones, Helen. *Sensual drugs*. New York: Cambridge University Press, 1977.

Jones, J. R. Plasma testosterone concentrations in female transsexuals. *Archives of Sexual Behavior*, 1972, **2**.

Jones, W. C. *Doe v. commonwealth attorney*: Closing the door to a fundamental right to sexual privacy. *Denver Law Journal*, 1976, **53**, 553–576.

Jost, A. Hormonal factors in the sex differentiation of the mammalian foetus. *Philosophical Transactions of the Society of London*, Ser. B, 1970, **259**, 119–131.

Jourard, Sidney M. Some lethal aspects of the male role. In Sidney M. Jourard, *The transparent self*. Princeton, N.J.: Van Nostrand, 1971.

Jourard, Sidney M., and Lasakow, P. Some factors in self-disclosure. *Journal of Abnormal and Social Psychology*, 1958, **56**, 91–98.

Kaats, Gilbert, and Davis, Keith. Effects of volunteer biases in studies of sexual behavior and attitudes. *Journal of Sex Research*, 1971, **7**, 26–34.

Kallman, Franz J. Comparative twin study on the genetic aspects of male homosexuality. *Journal of Nervous and Mental Disease*, 1952, **115**, 283–298. (a)

Kallman, Franz J. Twin and sibship study of overt male homosexuality. *American Journal of Human Genetics*, 1952, **4**, 136–146. (b)

Kando, Thomas. *Sex change: The achievement of gender identity among feminized transsexuals*. Springfield, Ill.: Charles C Thomas, 1973.

Kanin, Eugene J. Selected dyadic aspects of male sex aggression. *Journal of Sex Research*, 1969, **5**, 12–28.

Kantner, John F., and Zelnik, Melvin. Sexual experience of young unmarried women in the United States. *Family Planning Perspectives*, 1972, **4**(4), 9–18.

Kantner, John F., and Zelnik, Melvin. Contraception and pregnancy: Experience of young unmarried women in the United States. *Family Planning Perspectives*, 1973, **5**(1), 21–35.

Kaplan, Helen S. *The new sex therapy*. New York: Brunner/Mazel, 1974.

Kaplan, Helen S., and Sager, C. J. Sexual patterns at different ages. *Medical Aspects of Human Sexuality*, June 1971, 10–23.

Karpman, Benjamin. *The sexual offender and his offenses*. New York: Julian Press, 1954.

Kassel, Victor. Sex in nursing homes. *Medical Aspects of Human Sexuality*, 1976, **10**(3), 126.

Katchadourian, Herant L., and Lunde, D. T. *Fundamentals of human sexuality*. New York: Holt, 1975.

Kegel, A. H. Sexual functions of the pubbococcygeus muscle. *Western Journal of Surgery*, 1952, **60**, 521–524.

Kemp, Karl H. Comment: Recent obscenity cases. *Arkansas Law Review*, 1974, **28**, 335–356.

Kempf, E. J. The social and sexual behavior of infrahuman primates with some comparable facts in human behavior. *Psychoanalytic Review*, 1917, **4**, 127–154.

Key, Mary R. *Male/female language*. Metuchen, N.J.: Scarecrow Press, 1975.

Kinsey, A. C., Pomeroy, W. B., and Martin, C. E. *Sexual behavior in the human male*. Philadelphia: Saunders, 1948.

Kinsey, A. C., Pomeroy, W. B., Martin, C. E., and Gebhard, P. H. *Sexual behavior in the human female*. Philadelphia: Saunders, 1953.

Kirby, Douglas. The methods and methodological problems of sex research. In J. S. DeLora and C. A. B. Warren, *Understanding sexual interaction*. Boston: Houghton Mifflin, 1977.

Kirkendall, Lester A. *Sex education*. SIECUS Study Guide No. 1. New York: Sex Information and Education Council of the United States, 1965.

Kirkendall, Lester A. A humanistic view of sexual relationship. In J. C. Wynn (Ed.), *Sexual ethics and Christian responsibility*. New York: Association Press, 1970.

Klaus, Marshall A., et al. Maternal attachment: Importance of the first postpartum days. *New England Journal of Medicine*, 1972, **286**, 460–463.

Kohlberg, Lawrence. A cognitive-developmental analysis of children's sex-role concepts and attitudes. In E. E. Maccoby (Ed.), *The development of sex differences*. Stanford, Calif.: Stanford University Press, 1966.

Kohli, K. L., and Sobrero, A. J. Vasectomy: A study of psychosexual and general reactions. *Social Biology*, 1973, **20**, 298–302.

Kolodny, R. C., Masters, W. H., Kolodner, R. M., and Toro, G. Depression of plasma testosterone levels after chronic intensive marihuana use. *New England Journal of Medicine*, 1974, **290**, 872–874.

Kraemer, D., Moore, G., and Kramen, M. Baboon infant produced by embryo transfer. *Science*, 1976, **192**, 1246–1247.

Kreitler, Hans, and Kreitler, Shulamith. Children's concepts of sex and birth. *Child Development*, 1966, **37**, 363–378.

Kronhausen, Phyllis, and Kronhausen, Eberhard. *The sexually responsive woman*. New York: Grove Press, 1964.

Kutchinsky, Berl. The effect of easy availability of pornography on the incidence of sex crimes: The Danish experience. *Journal of Social Issues*, 1973, **29**, 163–181.

Ladner, Joyce A. *Tomorrow's tomorrow: The black woman*. Garden City, N.Y.: Doubleday, 1971.

Lakoff, Robin. Language and woman's place. *Language in Society*, 1973, **2**, 45–79.

Lanson, Lucienne. *From woman to woman*. New York: Knopf, 1975.

Laumann, Edward O. Friends of urban men: An assessment of accuracy in reporting their socioeconomic attributes, mutual choice, and attitude agreement. *Sociometry*, 1969, **32**, 54–69.

Leavitt, Fred. *Drugs and behavior*. Philadelphia: Saunders, 1974.

Lee, John Alan. Styles of loving. *Psychology Today*, 1974, **8**(5), 43–51.

Lee, John Alan. A typology of styles of loving. *Personality and Social Psychology Bulletin*, 1977, **3**, 173–182.

Legman, Gershon. *Rationale of the dirty joke*. New York: Grove Press, 1968.

Leiblum, S. R., Rosen, R. C., and Pierce, D. Group treatment format: Mixed sexual dysfunctions. *Archives of Sexual Behavior*, 1976, **5**, 313–322.

LeMagnen, J. Les pheromones olfacto-sexuals chez le rat blanc. *Archives des Sciences Physiologiques*, 1952, **6**, 295–332.

Lemere, Frederick, and Smith, James W. Alcohol-induced sexual impotence. *American Journal of Psychiatry*, 1973, **130**, 212.

Lester, David. Incest. *Journal of Sex Research*, 1972, **8**, 268–285.

Levin, Robert J., and Levin, Amy. Sexual pleasure: The surprising preferences of 100,000 women. *Redbook*, September 1975, 51.

Levin, Robert J., and Levin, Amy. The *Redbook* Report on premarital and extramarital sex. *Redbook*, October, 1975, 38.

Levine, E. M., Gruenewald, D., and Shaiova, C. H. Behavioral differences and emotional conflict among male-to-female transsexuals. *Archives of Sexual Behavior*, 1976, **5**, 81–86.

Levine, M. I. Sex education in the public elementary and high school curriculum. In D. L. Taylor (Ed.), *Human sexual development*. Philadelphia: Davis, 1970.

Lewis, C. S. *The four loves*. New York: Harcourt, Brace & World, 1960.

LeWitter, Maximillian, and Abarbanel, Albert. Aging and sex. In A. Ellis and A. Abarbanel (Eds.), *The encyclopedia of sexual behavior*. New York: Jason Aronson, 1973.

Libby, Roger W., and Nass, Gilbert D. Parental views on teenage sexual behavior. *Journal of Sex Research*, 1971, **7**, 226–236.

Licklider, S. Jewish penile carcinoma. *Journal of Urology*, 1961, **86**, 98.

Lobitz, W. Charles, and LoPiccolo, Joseph. New methods in the behavioral treatment of sexual dysfunction. *Journal of Therapy and Experimental Psychiatry*, 1972, **3**, 265–271.

Lobsenz, Norman. Sex and the senior citizen. *The New York Times Magazine*, Jan. 20, 1974, 87–91.

LoPiccolo, Joseph, and Lobitz, Charles. The role of masturbation in the treatment of sexual dysfunction. *Archives of Sexual Behavior*, 1972, **2**, 163–171.

Loraine, J. A., Adampopoulos, D. A., Kirkhan, K. E., Ismail, A. A., and Dove, G. A. Patterns of hormone excretion in male and female homosexuals. *Nature*, 1971, **234**, 552–554.

Lorenz, Konrad. *On aggression*. New York: Harcourt, Brace & World, 1966.

Louria, Donald B. Sexual use of amyl nitrate. *Medical Aspects of Human Sexuality*, January 1970, 89.

Luce, Gay. *Biological rhythms in psychiatry and medicine*. New York: Dover, 1970.

Maccoby, Eleanor E., and Jacklin, Carol N. *The psychology of sex differences*. Stanford, Calif.: Stanford University Press, 1974.

MacDougald, D. Aphrodisiacs and anaphrodisiacs. In A. Ellis and A. Abarbanel (Eds.), *The encyclopedia of sexual behavior*. Vol. 1. New York: Hawthorn, 1961.

Mack, Thomas M., et al. Estrogens and endometrial cancer in a retirement community. *New England Journal of Medicine*, 1976, **294**, 1262–1267.

MacLean, Paul. New finding relevant to the evolution of psychosexual functions of the brain. *Journal of Nervous and Mental Disease*, 1962, **135**, 289–301.

Maisch, Herbert. *Incest*. New York: Stein and Day, 1972.

Malinowski, Bronislaw. *The sexual life of savages*. New York: Harcourt, Brace & World, 1929.

Manabe, Y. Artificial abortion at midtrimester by mechanical stimulation of the uterus. *American Journal of Obstetrics and Gynecology*, 1969, **105**, 132–146.

Mann, J., Sidman, J., and Starr, S. Evaluating social consequences of erotic films: An experimental approach. *Journal of Social Issues*, 1973, **29**, 113–131.

Marks, Isaac, and Gelder, Michael. Transvestism and fetishism: Clinical and psychological changes during faradic aversion. *British Journal of Psychiatry*, 1967, **113**, 711–729.

Marmor, Judd (Ed.) *Sexual inversion: The multiple roots of homosexuality.* New York: Basic Books, 1965.

Marmor, Judd. Sex for non-sexual reasons. *Medical Aspects of Human Sexuality,* 1969, **3**(6), 8–21.

Marmor, Judd. "Normal" and "deviant" sexual behavior. *Journal of the American Medical Association,* 1971, **217**, 165–170.

Marmor, Judd. Frigidity, dyspareunia, and vaginismus. In B. J. Sadock et al. (Eds.), *The sexual experience.* Baltimore: Williams & Wilkins, 1976. (a)

Marmor, Judd. Impotence and ejaculatory disturbances. In B. Sadock et al. (Eds.), *The sexual experience.* Baltimore: Williams & Wilkins, 1976. (b)

Martin, Del, and Lyon, Phyllis. *Lesbian/woman.* San Francisco: Glide Publications, 1972.

Martinson, Floyd M. *Infant and child sexuality: A sociological perspective.* St. Peter, Minn.: Book Mark, 1973.

Marx, Jean L. Estrogen drugs: Do they increase the risk of cancer? *Science,* 1976, **191**, 838.

Maslow, Abraham H. *Toward a psychology of being.* (2nd ed.) Princeton, N.J.: Van Nostrand, 1968.

Maslow, Abraham H. *Motivation and personality.* (2nd ed.) New York: Harper & Row, 1970.

Maslow, Abraham, and Sakoda, J. Volunteer-error in the Kinsey study. *Journal of Abnormal and Social Psychology,* 1952, **47**, 259–267.

Masters, William H., and Johnson, Virginia. `Human sexual response.* Boston: Little, Brown, 1966.

Masters, William H., and Johnson, Virginia E. *Human sexual inadequacy.* Boston: Little, Brown, 1970.

Masters, William H., and Johnson, Virginia. What men stand to gain from women's liberation. In William H. Masters and Virginia Johnson, *The pleasure bond.* Boston: Little, Brown, 1974.

May, Rollo. *Love and will.* New York: Dell Books, 1974.

McArthur, Leslie Z., and Resko, Beth G. The portrayal of men and women in American television commercials. *Journal of Social Psychology,* 1975, **97**, 209–220.

McBride, Arthur F., and Hebb, D. O. Behavior of the captive bottle-nose dolphin, *Tursiops truncatus. Journal of Comparative and Physiological Psychology,* 1948, **41**, 111–123.

McCaghy, Charles H. Child molesting. *Sexual Behavior,* 1971, **1**, 16–24.

McCary, James L. Nymphomania: A case history. *Medical Aspects of Human Sexuality,* November 1972, **6**, 192–202.

McCary, James L. *Human sexuality.* Princeton, N.J.: Van Nostrand, 1973.

McGlothlin, W., Sparkes, R., and Arnold, D. Effect of LSD on human pregnancy. *Journal of the American Medical Association,* 1970, **212**, 1483–1487.

McGuire, R. J., Carlisle, J. M., and Young, B. G. Sexual deviations as conditioned behavior: A hypothesis. *Behavioral Research and Therapy,* 1965, **2**, 185–190.

McIntosh, Mary. The homosexual role. *Social Problems,* 1968, **16**(2), 182–192.

McKinlay, Sonja M., and Jeffreys, Margot. The menopausal syndrome. *British Journal of Preventive and Social Medicine,* 1974, **28**(2), 108.

McLuhan, Marshall, and Leonard, George B. The future of sex. In R. T. Francoeur and A. K. Francoeur (Eds.), *The future of sexual relations.* Englewood Cliffs, N.J.: Prentice-Hall, 1974.

McNeill, John J. *The Church and the homosexual.* Kansas City: Sheed, Andrews, & McMeel, 1976.

Mead, Margaret. *Sex and temperament in three primitive societies.* New York: Morrow, 1935.

Mead, Margaret, and Newton, Niles. Fatherhood. In S. A. Richardson and A. F. Guttmacher (Eds.), *Childbearing: Its social and psychological aspects.* Baltimore: Williams & Wilkins, 1967.

Mendelsohn, Jack H., et al. Plasma testosterone levels before, during, and after chronic marihuana smoking. *New England Journal of Medicine,* 1974, **291**, 1051–1055.

Michael, Richard P., and Keverne, E. B. Pheromones in the communication of sexual status in primates. *Nature,* 1968, **218**, 746–749.

Michael, R. P., Bonsall, R. W., and Warner, Patricia. Human vaginal secretions: Volatile fatty acid content. *Science,* 1974, **186**, 1217–1219.

Middleton, R. Brother-sister and father-daughter marriage in ancient Egypt. *American Sociological Review,* 1962, **27**, 603–611.

Migeon, C. J., Rivarola, M. A., and Forest, M. G. Studies of androgens in transsexual subjects: Effects of estrogen therapy. *Johns Hopkins Medical Journal,* 1968, **123**, 128–133.

Millar, J. D. The national venereal disease problem. *Epidemic venereal disease: Proceedings of the Second International Symposium on Venereal Disease.* St. Louis: American Social Health Association and Pfizer Laboratories, 1972.

Mischel, Walter. Continuity and change in personality. *American Psychologist,* 1969, **24**, 1012–1018.

Money, John, and Ehrhardt, Anke. *Man and woman, boy and girl.* Baltimore: Johns Hopkins Press, 1972.

Money, John, and Yankowitz, R. The sympathetic-inhibiting effects of the drug Ismelin on human male eroticism with a note on Mellaril. *Journal of Sex Research,* 1967, **3**, 69–82.

Montreal Health Press. *VD handbook.* Montreal: MHP, 1972.

Montreal Health Press. *Birth control handbook.* (12th ed.) Montreal: MHP, 1975.

Moore, James E., and Kendall, Diane G. Children's concepts of reproduction. *Journal of Sex Research,* 1971, **7**, 42–61.

Morris, Norval J. The law is a busybody. *The New York Times Magazine,* Apr. 18, 1973, 58–64.

Mosher, Donald L. Sex differences, sex experience, sex guilt and explicitly sexual films. *Journal of Social Issues,* 1973, **29**, 95–112.

Mulvihill, D. J., et al. *Crimes of violence: A staff report to the National Commission on the Causes and Prevention of Violence.* Washington, D.C.: GPO, 1969.

Murdock, George P. *Social structure.* New York: Macmillan, 1949.

Nawy, Harold. In the pursuit of happiness? Consumers of erotica in San Francisco. *Journal of Social Issues,* 1973, **29**, 147–161.

Neiger, S. Sex potions. *Sexology,* 1968, 730–733.

Neugarten, Bernice L., and Kraines, Ruth J. "Menopausal symptoms" in women of various ages. *Psychosomatic Medicine,* 1965, **27**, 266.

Newton, Niles. Trebly sensuous woman. *Psychology Today,* 1971, **5**(2), 18.

Newton, Niles A. Childbearing in broad perspective. In Boston Children's Medical Center, *Pregnancy, birth and the newborn baby.* New York: Delacorte Press, 1972.

Nickolls, L., and Teare, D. Poisoning by cantharidin. *British Medical Journal,* 1954, Part 2, 1384–1386.

Noss, John B. *Man's religions.* (3rd ed.) New York: Macmillan, 1963.

Novak, E. R., Jones, G. S., and Jones, H. W. *Novak's textbook of gynecology.* (9th ed.) Baltimore: Williams & Wilkins, 1975.

Novell, H. A. Psychological factors in premenstrual tension and dysmenorrhea. *Clinical Obstetrics and Gynecology,* 1965, **8**, 222–232.

Offer, Daniel, and Simon, William. Stages of sexual development. In B. J. Sadock et al. (Eds.), *The sexual experience.* Baltimore: Williams & Wilkins, 1976.

Olds, James. Pleasure centers in the brain. *Scientific American,* 1956, **193**, 105–116.

Olds, James, and Milner, Peter. Positive reinforcement produced by electrical stimulation of the septal area and other regions of the rat brain. *Journal of Comparative and Physiological Psychology,* 1954, **47**, 419–427.

Olds, Sally, and Eiger, M. S. *The complete book of breastfeeding.* New York: Bantam, 1973.

O'Neill, Nena, and O'Neill, George. Marriage: A contemporary model. In B. J. Sadock et al. (Eds.), *The sexual experience.* Baltimore: Williams & Wilkins, 1976.

O'Neill, George, and O'Neill, Nena. *Open marriage: A new life style for couples.* New York: M. Evans, 1972.

Osofsky, Joy D., and Osofsky, Howard J. The psychological reactions of patients to legalized abortions. *American Journal of Orthopsychiatry,* 1972, **42**, 48–60.

Packer, H. L. *The limits of the criminal sanction.* Stanford, Calif.: Stanford University Press, 1968.

Paige, Karen E. Effects of oral contraceptives on affective fluctuations associated with the menstrual cycle. *Psychosomatic Medicine,* 1971, **33**, 515–537.

Paige, Karen E. Women learn to sing the menstrual blues. *Psychology Today,* 1973, **7**(4), 41.

Papalia, Diane E., and Olds, Sally W. *A child's world: Infancy through adolescence.* New York: McGraw-Hill, 1975.

Parlee, Mary Brown. The premenstrual syndrome. *Psychological Bulletin,* 1973, **80**, 454–465.

Perloff, W. H. Hormones and homosexuality. In J. Marmor (Ed.), *Sexual inversion: The multiple roots of homosexuality.* New York: Basic Books, 1965.

Peterson, W., Morese, K., and Kaltreider, D. Smoking and prematurity: A preliminary report based on a study of 7740 Caucasians. *Obstetrics and Gynecology,* 1965, **26**, 775–779.

Pfeiffer, Eric. Sex and aging. In L. Gross (Ed.), *Sexual issues in marriage,* New York: Spectrum, 1975.

Pfeiffer, E., Verwoerdt, A., and Wang, H.-S. Sexual behavior in aged men and women. *Archives of General Psychiatry,* 1968, **19**, 753–758.

Phoenix, C. H., Goy, R. W., Gerall, A. A., and Young, W. C. Organizing action of prenatally administered testosterone propionate on the tissues mediating mating behavior in the female guinea pig. *Endocrinology,* 1959, **65**, 369–382.

Pittenger, W. Norman. *Making sexuality human.* Philadelphia: Pilgrim Press, 1970.

Pittenger, W. Norman. *Love and control in sexuality.* Philadelphia: United Church Press, 1974.

Pittenger, W. Norman. A theological approach to understanding homosexuality. In Ruth T. Barnhouse and Urban T. Holmes III (Eds.), *Male and female.* New York: Seabury Press, 1976.

Plato. *Symposium.* In Irwin Edman (Ed.), *The works of Plato.* New York: Modern Library, 1956.

Pleck, Joseph H., and Sawyer, Jack. *Men and masculinity.* Englewood Cliffs, N.J.: Prentice-Hall, 1974.

Pomeroy, Wardell B. Normal vs. abnormal sex. *Sexology,* 1966, **32**, 436–439.

Pomeroy, Wardell B. *Dr. Kinsey and the Institute for Sex Research.* New York: Harper & Row, 1972.

Pomeroy, Wardell B. The diagnosis and treatment of transvestites and transsexuals. *Journal of Sex and Marital Therapy,* 1975, **1**, 215–224.

Pope Paul VI. *Humanae vitae.* (English text in *The New York Times,* July 30, 1968, 20.)

Powdermaker, Hortense. *Life in Lesu.* New York: Norton, 1933.

Presser, H. B., and Bumpass, L. L. The acceptability of contraceptive sterilization among U.S. couples: 1970. *Family Planning Perspectives,* 1972, **4**(4), 18.

Prince, Virginia, and Butler, P. M. Survey of 504 cases of transvestism. *Psychological Reports,* 1972, **31**, 903–917.

Rada, R. T. Alcoholism and forcible rape. *American Journal of Psychiatry,* 1975, **132**, 444–446.

Rainwater, Lee. *Family design.* Chicago: Aldine, 1965.

Rainwater, Lee. Marital sexuality in four "cultures of poverty." In D. S. Marshall and R. C. Suggs (Eds.), *Human sexual behavior*. New York: Basic Books, 1971.

Rainwater, Lee, and Weinstein, K. K. *And the poor get children*. Chicago: Quadrangle, 1960.

Ramey, Estelle, Men's cycles. *Ms.*, Spring 1972, 8–14.

Ramsey, Glenn V. The sex information of younger boys. *American Journal of Orthopsychiatry*, 1943, **13**, 347–352. (a)

Ramsey, Glenn V. The sexual development of boys. *American Journal of Psychology*, 1943, **56**, 217–233. (b)

Raphael, Bette-Jane. The myth of the male orgasm. *Village Voice*, Oct. 25, 1973. (Reprinted in *Psychology Today*, **7**(8), 1974.)

Ravenholt, R., and Levinski, M. Smoking during pregnancy. *Lancet*, 1965, **1**, 961.

Reevy, William R. Child sexuality. In A. Ellis and A. Abarbanel (Eds.), *The encyclopedia of sexual behavior*. New York: Hawthorn, 1967.

Reiss, Ira L. *Premarital sexual standards in America*. New York: Free Press, 1960.

Reiss, Ira L. Sexual codes in teen-age culture. *The Annals*, November 1961, 53–62.

Reiss, Ira L. *The social context of premarital sexual permissiveness*. New York: Holt, 1967.

Reuben, David. *Everything you always wanted to know about sex but were afraid to ask*. New York: Bantam, 1969.

Rhodes, Richard. Sex and sin in Sheboygan. *Playboy*, August 1972, 186–190.

Ribble, Margaret A. *The personality of the young child*. New York: Columbia University Press, 1955.

Rice, Berkeley. Rx: Sex for senior citizens. *Psychology Today*, 1974, **8**(1), 18–20.

Richardson, Stephen A. People with cerebral palsy talk for themselves. *Developmental Medicine and Child Neurology*, 1972, **14**, 524–535.

Robinson, D., and Rock, J. Intrascrotal hyperthermia induced by scrotal insulation: Effect on spermatogenesis. *Obstetrics and Gynecology*, 1967, **29**, 217.

Rogers, Carl R. *Client-centered therapy: Its current practice, implications, and theory*. Boston: Houghton Mifflin, 1951.

Rogers, Rex S. *Sex education: Rationale and reaction*. New York: Cambridge University Press, 1974.

Rosaldo, Michelle Z. Woman, culture, and society: A theoretical overview. In M. Z. Rosaldo and L. Lamphere (Eds.), *Woman, culture, and society*. Stanford, Calif.: Stanford University Press, 1974.

Rose, R. M. Testosterone, aggression, and homosexuality: A review of the literature and implications for future research. In E. J. Sachar (Ed.), *Topics in psychoendocrinology*. New York: Grune & Stratton, 1975.

Rosebury, Theodor. *Microbes and morals: The strange story of venereal disease*. New York: Viking Press, 1971.

Rosen, David H. *Lesbianism: A study of female homosexuality*. Springfield, Ill.: Charles C Thomas, 1974.

Rosenbleet, C., and Pariente, B. J. The prostitution of the criminal law. *American Criminal Law Review*, 1973, **11**, 373–427.

Rosenkrantz, P. S., et al. Sex-role stereotypes and self-concepts in college students. *Journal of Consulting and Clinical Psychology*, 1968, **32**, 287–295.

Rothchild, Ellen. Answering young children's sex questions. *Medical Aspects of Human Sexuality*, December 1975, 23.

Rotkin, I. D. Relation of adolescent coitus to cervical cancer risk. *Journal of the American Medical Association*, 1962, **179**, 110.

Rotkin, I. D. A comparison review of key epidemiological studies in cervical cancer related to current searches for transmissible agents. *Cancer Research*, 1973, **33**, 1353.

Rubin, Isadore. *Sexual life after sixty*. New York: Basic Books, 1965.

Rubin, Isadore. Sex after forty—and after seventy. In Ruth Brecher and Edward Brecher (Eds.), *An analysis of human sexual response*. New York: Signet Books, New American Library, 1966.

Rubin, Zick. Measurement of romantic love. *Journal of Personality and Social Psychology*, 1970, **16**, 265–273.

Rubin, Zick. *Liking and loving: An invitation to social psychology*. New York: Holt, 1973.

Russell, Diana. *The politics of rape: The victim's perspective*. New York: Stein and Day, 1975.

Rylander, Gösta. Clinical and medico-criminological aspects of addiction to central stimulating drugs. In Folke Sjoqvist and Malcolm Tottie (Eds.), *Abuse of central stimulants*. New York: Raven Press, 1969.

Sacred Congregation for the Doctrine of the Faith. Declaration on certain questions concerning sexual ethics. (English text in *The New York Times*, Jan. 16, 1976, p. 2.)

Sadock, Benjamin J., and Sadock, Virginia A. Techniques of coitus. In B. J. Sadock et al. (Eds.), *The sexual experience*. Baltimore: Williams & Wilkins, 1976.

Saegert, S., Swap, W., and Zajonc, R. B. Exposure, context, and interpersonal attraction. *Journal of Personality and Social Psychology*, 1973, **25**, 234–242.

Sagarin, Edward. Power to the peephole. *Sexual Behavior*, 1973, **3**, 2–7.

Sagarin, Edward. Incest: Problems of definition and frequency. *Journal of Sex Research*, 1977, **13**, 126–135.

Salhanick, H. A., and Margulis, R. H. Hormonal physiology of the ovary. In J. J. Gold (Ed.), *Textbook of gynecologic endocrinology*. New York: Harper & Row, 1968.

Sandberg, E. C., and Jacobs, R. I. Psychology of the misuse and rejection of contraception. *American Journal of Obstetrics and Gynecology*, 1971, **110**, 227–242.

Sayers, Dorothy. *Unpopular opinions.* London: Gollancz, 1946.

Schachter, Stanley. The interaction of cognitive and physiological determinants of emotional state. In L. Berkowitz (Ed.); *Advances in experimental social psychology.* Vol. 1. New York: Academic Press, 1964.

Schachter, Stanley, and Singer, J. F. Cognitive, social, and physiological determinants of emotional state. *Psychological Review,* 1962, **69**, 379–399.

Schaffer, H. R., and Emerson, Peggy E. Patterns of response to physical contact in early human development. *Journal of Child Psychology and Psychiatry,* 1964, **5**, 1–13.

Schmidt, Gunter. Personal communication, 1977.

Schmidt, Gunter, and Sigusch, Volkmar. Sex differences in response to psychosexual stimulation by films and slides. *Journal of Sex Research,* 1970, **6**, 268–283.

Schmidt, G., Sigusch, V., and Schäfer, S. Responses to reading erotic stories: Male-female differences. *Archives of Sexual Behavior,* 1973, **2**, 181–199.

Schmitt, Madeline H. Superiority of breast-feeding: Fact or fancy? *American Journal of Nursing,* 1970, **70**, 1488–1493.

Schneidman, Barbara, and McGuire, Linda. Group therapy for nonorgasmic women: Two age levels. *Archives of Sexual Behavior,* 1976, **5**, 239–248.

Schofield, Alfred T., and Vaughan-Jackson, Percy. *What a boy should know.* New York: Cassell, 1913.

Schoof-Tams, K., Schlaegel, J., and Walczak, L. Differentiation of sexual morality between 11 and 16 years. *Archives of Sexual Behavior,* 1976, **5**, 353–370.

Schull, William J., and Neel, James V. *The effects of inbreeding on Japanese children.* New York: Harper & Row, 1965.

Sciarra, J. J., Markland, C., and Speidel, J. J. *Control of male fertility.* New York: Harper & Row, 1975.

Scott, John Paul. The effects of early experience on social behavior and organization. In W. Etkin (Ed.), *Social behavior and organization among vertebrates.* Chicago: University of Chicago Press, 1964.

Selkin, J. Rape. *Psychology Today,* 1975, **8**(8), 70.

Semans, J. Premature ejaculation: A new approach. *Southern Medical Journal,* 1956, **49**, 353–358.

Shaffer, Leigh S. The golden fleece: Anti-intellectualism and social science. *American Psychologist,* 1977, **32**, 814–823.

Shaver, Phillip. Questions concerning fear of success and its conceptual relatives. *Sex Roles,* 1976, **2**, 305–320.

Sheehy, Gail. *Hustling: Prostitution in our wide open society.* New York: Delacorte Press, 1973.

Sherfey, Mary Jane. The evolution and nature of female sexuality in relation to psychoanalytic theory. *Journal of the American Psychoanalytic Association,* 1966, **14**, 28–128.

Sherman, Julia. *On the psychology of women: A survey of empirical studies.* Springfield, Ill.: Charles C Thomas, 1971.

Shettles, Landrum B. Predetermining children's sex. *Medical Aspects of Human Sexuality,* June 1972, 172.

Shope, David F. *Interpersonal sexuality.* Philadelphia: Saunders, 1975.

Shore, M. F. Drugs can be dangerous during pregnancy and lactation. *Canadian Pharmaceutical Journal,* December 1970.

Simon Population Trust. Vasectomy: Follow-up of a thousand cases. Cambridge, England, 1969, **12**, 1–17. (Cited in Wiest, W. M., and Janke, L. D. Methodological critique of research on psychological effects of vasectomy. *Psychosomatic Medicine,* 1974, **36**, 438–449.)

Slotkin, J. S. On a possible lack of incest regulations in Old Iran. *American Anthropologist,* 1947, **49**, 612–617.

Slovenko, Ralph. *Sexual behavior and the law.* Springfield, Ill.: Charles C Thomas, 1965.

Smith, R. Spencer. Voyeurism: A review of literature. *Archives of Sexual Behavior,* 1976, **5**, 585–608.

Smith, Stuart L. Mood and the menstrual cycle. In E. J. Sachar (Ed.), *Topics in psychoendocrinology.* New York: Grune & Stratton, 1975.

Snelling, H. A. What is rape? In L. G. Schultz (Ed.), *Rape victimology.* Springfield, Ill.: Charles C Thomas, 1975.

Sommer, Barbara. The effect of menstruation on cognitive and perceptual-motor behavior: A review. *Psychosomatic Medicine,* 1973, **35**, 515–534.

Sorensen, Robert C. *Adolescent sexuality in contemporary America.* New York: World, 1973.

Sotile, Wayne M., and Kilmann, Peter R. Treatments of psychogenic female sexual dysfunctions. *Psychological Bulletin,* 1977, **84**, 619–633.

Southam, A. L., and Gonzaga, F. P. Systemic changes during the menstrual cycle. *American Journal of Obstetrics and Gynecology,* 1965, **91**, 142–165.

Spanier, Graham B. Formal and informal sex education as determinants of premarital sexual behavior. *Archives of Sexual Behavior,* 1976, **5**, 39–67.

Spanier, Graham B. Sources of sex information and premarital sexual behavior. *Journal of Sex Research,* 1977, **13**, 73–88.

Speroff, L., Glass, R. H., and Kase, N. G. *Clinical gynecologic endocrinology and infertility.* Baltimore: Williams & Wilkins, 1973.

Spitz, René A. Autoeroticism: Some empirical findings and hypotheses on three of its manifestations in the first year of life. *The Psychoanalytic Study of the Child.* Vol. III–IV. New York: International Universities Press, 1949. Pp. 85–120.

Spivack, G., and Spotts, J. The Devereux Child Behavior Scale: Symptom behaviors in latency age children.

American Journal of Mental Retardation, 1965, **69**, 839–853.

Staples, Robert. Research on black sexuality: Its implication for family life, education, and public policy. *The Family Coordinator*, 1972, **21**, 183–188.

Stephan, W., Berscheid, E., and Walster, E. Sexual arousal and heterosexual perception. *Journal of Personality and Social Psychology*, 1971, **20**, 93–101.

Stephens, W. N. A cross-cultural study of menstrual taboos. *Genetic Psychology Monographs*, 1961, **64**, 385–416.

Stone, Abraham. *The practice of contraception*. Baltimore: Williams & Wilkins, 1931.

Stout, J. Quaker tells of rape in D.C. jail. *Washington Star-News*, Aug. 25, 1973.

Sullivan, W. Boys and girls are now maturing earlier. *The New York Times*, Jan. 24, 1971.

Szasz, Thomas S. Legal and moral aspects of homosexuality. In J. Marmor (Ed.), *Sexual inversion: The multiple roots of homosexuality*. New York: Basic Books, 1965.

Tanner, James M. Puberty. In A. McLaren (Ed.), *Advances in reproductive physiology*. Vol. II. New York: Academic Press, 1967.

Tart, Charles. Marijuana intoxication: Common experiences. *Nature*, 1970, **226**, 701–704.

Tart, Charles. *On being stoned*. Palo Alto, Calif.: Science and Behavior Books, 1971.

Tavris, Carol. Masculinity. *Psychology Today*, 1977, **10**(8), 34.

Teen-age sex: Letting the pendulum swing. *Time*, Aug. 21, 1972, 34–38.

Terman, Lewis M. Kinsey's *Sexual behavior in the human male*: Some comments and criticisms. *Psychological Bulletin*, 1948, **45**, 443–459.

Terman, Lewis M. Correlates of orgasm adequacy in a group of 556 wives. *Journal of Psychology*, 1951, **32**, 115–172.

Terman, Lewis M., et al. *Psychological factors in marital happiness*. New York: McGraw-Hill, 1938.

Thielicke, Helmut. *The ethics of sex*. New York: Harper & Row, 1964.

Thorpe, L. P., Katz, B., and Lewis, R. T. *The psychology of abnormal behavior*. New York: Ronald Press, 1961.

Towne, J. E. Carcinoma of cervix in nulliparous and celibate women. *American Journal of Obstetrics and Gynecology*, 1955, **69**, 606.

Tsuji, I., et al. The sexual function in patients with spinal cord injury. *Urology International*, 1961, **12**, 270–280.

Udry, J. Richard, and Morris, N. M. Distribution of coitus in the menstrual cycle. *Nature*, 1968, **220**, 593–596.

U.S. Bureau of the Census. *U.S. Fact Book: The American Almanac*. New York: Grosset and Dunlap, 1976.

U.S. Department of Commerce. *Some demographic aspects of aging in the U.S.: Growth of the population 65 years and over*. Washington, D.C.: GPO, 1973.

U.S. Public Health Service, Center for Disease Control. Comparative risks of three methods of midtrimester abortion. *Morbidity and Mortality Weekly Report*, Nov. 26, 1976, 370. (a)

U.S. Public Health Service, Center for Disease Control. *VD fact sheet 1976*. HEW Publication No. (CDC) 77-8195, 1976. (b)

U.S. Public Health Service, Center for Disease Control. *Abortion surveillance 1975*. Atlanta: CDC, 1977.

Vance, Ellen B., and Wagner, Nathaniel N. Written descriptions of orgasm A study of sex differences. *Archives of Sexual Behavior*, 1976, **5**, 87–98.

Vandenberg, Steven G. Assortative mating, or who marries whom? *Behavior Genetics*, 1972, **2**, 127–158.

Velarde, Albert J., and Warlick, Mark. Massage parlors: The sensuality business. *Society*, 1973, **11**(1), 63–74.

Wabrek, Alan J., and Wabrek, Carolyn J. Dyspareunia. *Journal of Sex and Marital Therapy*, 1975, **1**, 234–241.

Wagner, Nathaniel, and Solberg, Don. Pregnancy and sexuality. *Medical Aspects of Human Sexuality*, 1974, **8**(3), 44–79.

Wallace, Douglas H. Obscenity and contemporary standards: A survey. *Journal of Social Issues*, 1973, **29**, 53–68.

Wallin, Paul. An appraisal of some methodological aspects of the Kinsey report. *American Sociological Review*, 1949, **14**, 197–210.

Walster, Elaine, et al. "Playing hard-to-get": Understanding an elusive phenomenon. *Journal of Personality and Social Psychology*, 1973, **26**, 113–121.

Walters, C., Shurley, J. T., and Parsons, O. A. Differences in male and female responses to underwater sensory deprivation: An exploratory study. *Journal of Nervous and Mental Disease*, 1962, **135**, 302–310.

Warren, Carol A. B. *Identity and community in the gay world*. New York: Wiley, 1974.

Weideger, Paula. *Menstruation and menopause*. New York: Knopf, 1976.

Weinberg, Martin S., and Williams, Colin. *Male homosexuals: Their problems and adaptations*. New York: Oxford University Press, 1974.

Weinberg, Samuel K. *Incest behavior*. New York: Citadel Press, 1955.

Weiner, L., et al. Carcinoma of the cervix in Jewish women. *American Journal of Obstetrics and Gynecology*, 1951, **61**, 418.

Weis, Kurt, and Borges, Sandra S. Victimology and rape: The case of the legitimate victim. *Issues in Criminology*, 1973, **8**(2), 71–115.

Weiss, Howard D. Mechanism of erection. *Medical Aspects of Human Sexuality*, 1973, **7**(2), 21–40.

Weiss, Noel S., et al. Increasing incidence of endometrial cancer in the United States. *New England Journal* of *Medicine*, 1976, **294**, 1259–1261.

Weitzman, L. J., Eifles D., Hokada, E., and Ross, C. Sex role socialization in picture books for pre-school children. *American Journal of Sociology*, 1972, **72**, 1125–1150.

Werry, J. S., and Quay, H. C. The prevalence of behavior symptoms in younger elementary school children. *American Journal of Orthopsychiatry*, 1971, **41**, 136–143.

Wessman, Alden E., and Ricks, David F. *Mood and personality*. New York: Holt, 1966.

Westoff, Charles. Coital frequency and contraception. *Family Planning Perspectives*, 1974, **6**(3), 136–141.

Westoff, Charles, and Bumpass, Larry. The revolution in birth control practices of U.S. Roman Catholics. *Science*, 1973, **179**, 41–44.

Wheeler, Robert G. The intrauterine membrane. In R. G. Wheeler, G. W. Duncan, and J. J. Speidel (Eds.), *Intrauterine devices*. New York: Academic Press, 1975.

Wickler, Wolfgang. *The sexual code*. New York: Anchor Books, 1973. (Original in German, 1969.)

Wiest, William M., and Janke, L. D. Methodological critique of research on psychological effects of vasectomy. *Psychosomatic Medicine*, 1974, **36**, 438–449.

Williams, Colin J., and Weinberg, Martin S. *Homosexuals and the military: A study of less than honorable discharge*. New York: Harper & Row, 1971.

Wilson, W. Cody. Pornography: The emergence of a social issue and the beginning of psychological study. *Journal of Social Issues*, 1973, **29**, 7–17.

Wilson, W. Cody. The distribution of selected sexual attitudes and behaviors among the adult population of the United States. *Journal of Sex Research*, 1975, **11**, 46–64.

Wilson, W. Cody, and Abelson, Herbert I. Experience with and attitudes toward explicit sexual materials. *Journal of Social Issues*, 1973, **29**, 19–39.

Winick, Charles, and Kinsie, Paul M. *The lively commerce*. New York: Quadrangle, 1971.

Winick, Charles, and Kinsie, Paul M. Prostitutes. *Psychology Today*, 1972, **5**(9), 57.

Wolff, Charlotte. *Love between women*. New York: Harper & Row, 1971.

Women on Words and Images. *Dick and Jane as victims: Sex stereotyping in children's readers*. Princeton, N.J.: WWI, 1972.

Woods, James S. Drug effects on human sexual behavior. In N. F. Woods (Ed.), *Human sexuality in health and illness*. St. Louis: Mosby, 1975.

Wysor, Bettie. *The lesbian myth*. New York: Random House, 1974.

Yalom, Irvin D. Aggression and forbiddenness in voyeurism. *Archives of General Psychiatry*, 1960, **3**, 317.

Yerushalmy, J. Mother's cigarette smoking and survival of infant. *American Journal of Obstetrics and Gynecology*, 1964, **88**, 505–518.

Yorburg, Betty. *Sexual identity: Sex roles and social change*. New York: Wiley, 1974.

Young, Wayland. Prostitution. In J. D. Douglas (Ed.), *Observations of deviance*. New York: Random House, 1970.

Zeiss, A. M., Rosen, G. M., and Zeiss, R. A. Orgasm during intercourse: A treatment strategy for women. *Journal of Consulting and Clinical Psychology*, 1977, **45**, 891–895.

Zelnik, Melvin, and Kantner, John F. Sexual and contraceptive experience of young unmarried women in the United States, 1976 and 1971. *Family Planning Perspectives*, 1977, **9**(2), 55–71.

Zilbergeld, B. Group treatment of sexual dysfunction in men without partners. *Journal of Sex and Marital Therapy*, 1975, **1**, 204–214.

Zimbardo, Phillip G., and Meadow, Wendy. Sexism springs eternal—in *The Reader's Digest*. Paper presented at meetings of the Western Psychological Association, San Francisco, April 1974.

Zuckerman, M., and Wheeler, L. To dispel fantasies about the fantasy-based measure of fear of success. *Psychological Bulletin*, 1975, **82**, 932–946.

Zumpe, Doris, and Michael, R. P. The clutching reaction and orgasm in the female rhesus monkey (*Macaca mulatta*). *Journal of Endocrinology*, 1968, **40**, 117–123.

Zumwalt, Rosemary. Plain and fancy: A content analysis of children's jokes dealing with adult sexuality. *Western Folklore*, 1976, **35**, 258–267.

INDEX

INDEX

Shafer, P., 374
Shaffer, L. S., 408
Shankweiler, P., 302–303
Shaver, P., 282
Sheehy, G., 371, 374
Sherfey, M. J., 304, 313–314
Sherman, J., 102–104, 115
Shettles, L. B., 46–48
Shields, J., 338
Shope, D. F., 187–188, 298
Sigusch, V., 227, 299
Silent rape reaction, 380
Simenauer, J., 308–311
Simon, W., 253, 350
Simon Population Trust, 148
Simonson, A., 494
Singer, J. F., 401–403
Singles, 266–267
Situation ethics, 467, 468, 484–486
Situational homosexuality, 324
Sixty-nining, 198
Skene's glands, 32
Skinner, B. F., 10
Slater, P. E., 202–203
Slotkin, J. S., 366
Slovenko, R., 491, 493–497
Smegma, 42
Smith, J. W., 421
Smith, L. G., 406–407
Smith, R. S., 362
Smith, R. W., 318
Smith, S. L., 78–79
Snelling, H. A., 376
Sobrero, A. J., 148
Social class, 20–21
Social learning theory, 11
Socialization, 13, 277, 381, 386
Sociological theory, 13, 341–342
Sodomy, 199, 366, 483, 495–497
Solberg, D., 105
Solicitation, sexual, 497
Sommer, B., 77–78
Sorensen, R. C., 221, 233, 241–242, 246–249, 320
Sotile, W. M., 438

Southam, A. L., 75
Spanier, G. B., 511–512
Spectatoring, 423–424
Speculum, 39
Sperm, 45–47, 90–94
Sperm banks, 527
Spermatogenesis, 44–45
Spermatogonium, 45
Spermicides, 141–142
Speroff, L., 122
Spinal cord, 173–176
  injury to, 426–427
Spirochete, 446
Spivack, G., 285
Spotts, J., 285
Squeeze technique, 433
Staples, R., 22
Statistics, 227–229
Statutory rape, 492–495
Stephan, W., 403
Stephens, W. N., 80
Stereotypes:
  gender role, 276, 279, 284
  about homosexuals, 317–321
Sterile, 122, 413
Sterilization techniques, 145–149
  female, 148–149
  male, 146–148
Stone, A., 47
Stop-start technique, 434
Stout, J., 387
Subincision, 42
Sublimation, 6
Sullivan, W., 66
Superego, 6
Supreme Court, U.S., 495, 497, 502–503, 506–507
Surrogates, 430
Survey research, 211–221
Swinging, 226, 264–266
Sympathetic pregnancy, 102
Syphilis, 445–451
Szasz, T. S., 241, 335

Tanner. J. M., 64, 68
Tart, C., 421

Tavris, C., 285–286, 291
Teare, D., 200
Tearoom trade, 225–226, 329–331
Techniques, sexual, 18, 246, 257–258
Tedeschi, F. L., 530
Teenage pregnancy, 149–150
Teenage sex, 305
Teratogenic, 119
Terman, L. M., 172, 296
Testes, 44–47
Test-tube babies, 527
Testicular feminizing syndrome, 58
Testosterone, 44, 179, 270
Thanatos, 6
Thermography, 457
Thielicke, H., 481, 482, 484
Thorpe, L. P., 364
Thrush, 454
Thuwe, I., 153
Towne, J. E., 461
Toxemia, 119
Transactional analysis, 12–13
Transsexual, 352–358
Transvestism, 358–360
Treponema pallidum, 446
Trichomoniasis, 455–456
Trimester, 94–104
Troilism, 373
Tsuji, I., 427
Tubal ligation, 148–149
Tudor, J. F., 284
Tumescence, 40
Tunica albuginea, 45
Turner, C. D., 68
Two-career family, 261

Udry, J. R., 78
Umbilical cord, 95
Undescended testes, 55
U.S. Bureau of the Census, 283
U.S. Department of Commerce, 283